CALIFORNIA BEACHES

CALIFORNIA BEACHES

The Best Places to Swim, Play, Eat, and Stay on the Coast

THIRD EDITION

Parke Puterbaugh & Alan Bisbort

AVALON
TRAVEL

**FOGHORN OUTDOORS
CALIFORNIA BEACHES
The Best Places to Swim,
Stay, Eat, and Play on the Coast**

Third Edition

Parke Puterbaugh & Alan Bisbort

Please send all feedback about this book to:

**ⒻOGHORN OUTDOORS®
California Beaches**
Avalon Travel Publishing
1400 65th Street, Suite 250
Emeryville, CA 94608, USA
email: atpfeedback@avalonpub.com
website: www.foghorn.com

Printing History
1st edition—1996
3rd edition—April 2003
5 4 3 2 1

ISBN: 1-56691-424-8
ISSN: 1542-6076

Editor: Marisa Solís
Series Manager: Marisa Solís
Copy Editor: Deana Shields
Graphics Coordinator: Melissa Sherowski
Production Coordinator: Darren Alessi
Cover Designer: Jacob Goolkasian
Interior Designer: Darren Alessi
Map Editor: Olivia Solís
Cartographers: Kat Kalamaras, Jacob Goolkasian, Mike Morgenfeld
Indexer: Rachel Kuhn

Front cover photo: © Nik Wheeler

Printed in the United States of America by Arvato Services Inc.

Distributed by Publishers Group West

Foghorn Outdoors and the Foghorn Outdoors logo are the property of Avalon Travel Publishing, a division of Avalon Publishing Group. All other marks and logos depicted are the property of the original owners.

Contents

Southern California

Special Topics

Special Topics

Getting to and from Catalina Island 166; Paradise Found: Catalina Island's Little Harbor Beach 170; Queen Mary Facts 'n' Figgers 173; Shooting Hoops with the Toast of the Coast 178; Crosstown Traffic: Driving in Los Angeles 182; Zen in Redondo 186; Eavesdropping in Hermosa Beach: "I'm Very There" 190; Looking for Signs of Life in Hermosa Beach 192; The Art of Surfing 196; "Catch a Wave": A Brief History of Surf Music 198; Want to Be an L.A. County Lifeguard? 201; The Dandelion under the Pillow 206; Beach Flicks 212; Pollution Report Card: L.A. County Beaches 220; Art and History in Old Malibu 224; The Original Metal Heads 227

Central California

Special Topics

Ventura's Most Wanted 242; Adventuring on the Channel Islands 248; Thar She Blows! 250; "Don't Do Anything Rational" 254; Surf Kayaking: The Latest Outrage 256; Talking Trash at the Beach 260; Nollan v. California Coastal Commission 264; Where's the Beach? 267

Special Topics

You Stay, You Pay: The Incredible Inflated Hotel Resort Surcharge Scam 282; The Other Side of Paradise 286; Post-Party Animals: Nightlife on the Sober Side 293; The Battle over Haskell's Beach 296; Guadalupe Dunes Disaster 303

Special Topics

Dune Struck 313; Dune Buggers 314; Clamming for Pismos 316; Avila Beach: Oil's Well That Ends Well 321; There Otter Be a Law 327; Touring Hearst Castle 336

Special Topics

Living with Big Sur 350; Margaret W. Owings: An Environmental Legacy 353; Big Sur Land Trust 356; The Henry Miller Library 359; Mayor Clint 365; The 17-Mile Drive: A Must to Avoid 372; Paella Fandango 380; Monterey National Marine Sanctuary 382; Monterey Bay Aquarium 384; Canning Cannery Row 389; Full Moon over Monterey 392; Waiting for Fort Ord 394; Salinas: A Side Trip to Steinbeck Country 396

Special Topics

Scenes from Santa Cruz 418; Best of Santa Cruz 422; Young and in the Way 424; Room Rate Roulette in Santa Cruz 426

Special Topics

Northern California

Special Topic

Special Topics

*Bolinas Lagoon Needs Restoring **489**; A Horse Is a Horse—Unless It's from Marin County **497***

Special Topics

*Sonoma Coast Safety Check **514**; Navigating the North Coast **518**; We Brake for Cows **520**; Bobbing for Abalone **522***

Special Topics

Rubes with a View **534;** *Canoeing the Big* **544;** *Cafe Beaujolais* **547;** *Let's Get Lost: A Side Trip to Sinkyone Wilderness State Park* **554**

Special Topics

"Lamb Lips of Oblivion": Hibernating among the Humboldt Hippies **568;** *Riding with the King: A Drive through the King Range National Conservation Area* **572;** *Litter Longevity* **576;** *Top Universities for Beach Lovers in California* **582**

Special Topics

Trees of Mystery 602; The Regal Redwoods 606

Maps

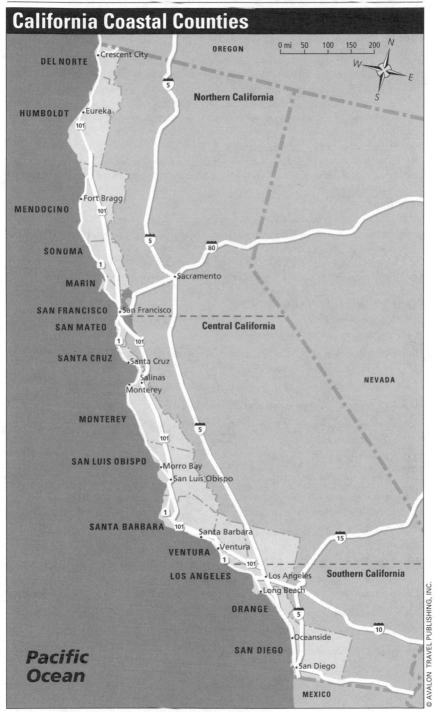

California Coastal Counties

OREGON

0 mi   50   100   150   200   N
W — E
S

DEL NORTE   • Crescent City

Northern California

HUMBOLDT   • Eureka

101

• Fort Bragg

MENDOCINO   101

SONOMA

MARIN   1

• Sacramento

SAN FRANCISCO   • San Francisco

SAN MATEO   Central California

1   101

SANTA CRUZ   • Santa Cruz

Salinas

• Monterey

NEVADA

MONTEREY

101

SAN LUIS OBISPO   • Morro Bay

• San Luis Obispo

1

SANTA BARBARA   101   • Santa Barbara

VENTURA   • Ventura

1   101

LOS ANGELES   • Los Angeles   Southern California

• Long Beach

ORANGE   5

10

• Oceanside

SAN DIEGO

Pacific Ocean

• San Diego

MEXICO

© AVALON TRAVEL PUBLISHING, INC.

How to Use This Book

Foghorn Outdoors California Beaches is divided into three regions: Southern, Central, and Northern California. The book reads from south to north, meticulously combing the state's 15 coastal counties, which are given individual chapters. Each chapter opens with a map that identifies a given county's beaches. Numbers on the map are keyed to informational beach profiles, which follow the map. Next come writeups of individual communities and their beaches. For each location, an introductory essay orients the reader to the area's history, culture, attractions, personality, and appeal (or lack thereof). Additional information follows under these headings: Beaches, Bunking Down (accommodations), Coastal Cuisine (restaurants), and Night Moves (nightlife).

Beaches

We offer the lowdown on what you can expect to see and do at every publicly accessible beach in a given area. This includes a description of its natural features, as well as relevant and interesting observations that will help fix an image of a given beach in the reader's mind. Each beach also has its own "beach profile": a list of practical information, including how to get there, activities, parking and day-use fees, hours, facilities, and a contact number.

What the Symbols Mean

In the heading of each beach profile symbols indicate what activities can be done at this locale or in its immediate vicinity. They are as follows:

- **Biking/jogging:** paved, multiuse, beachside recreational path for bicyclists, joggers, walkers, and in-line skaters
- **Camping:** developed campground(s) on site
- **Diving/snorkeling:** good diving and/or snorkeling spot
- **Hiking:** marked trail(s) for nature observation or exceptional beach hiking opportunities
- **Nude beach:** clothing optional
- **Pier:** wooden or concrete structure from which people fish or stroll
- **Surfing:** waves sufficiently sizable and well-formed to draw more than the occasional surfer
- **Volleyball:** volleyball nets and standards on beach

What the Rating Symbol Means

Following the symbols, we've rated each beach on a 1–5 scale according to its overall appeal. It is our attempt to answer "How desirable a beach is this to visit?" The scale is as follows:

- **5** — **extraordinary;** beach heaven
- **4** — **excellent;** an above-average beach
- **3** — **good;** a decent beach that's well worth a visit

— **fair;** a below-average beach

 — **abysmal;** keep driving

These ratings represent the informed opinions of two well-traveled beach bums. If you disagree or want to pass along suggestions or information, please contact us in care of Avalon Travel Publishing. It will help with future editions.

We've also included information on facilities available at each beach. They are as follows:

- **concession** (food and drink available on or near beach)
- **lifeguards**
- **picnic area**
- **restrooms** (anything from portable toilets on up)
- **showers**
- **visitor center** (staffed facility with information and exhibits)

Shore Things

We've introduced this section, a listing of up to 13 goods and services, as a kind of quick-and-dirty Yellow Pages in selected communities. At least one business or organization is listed with address and phone number.

- **Bike/skate rentals:** bicycles, in-line skates, and other fun stuff
- **Boat cruise:** sightseeing trips on the water
- **Dive shop:** rent/buy scuba equipment or book a dive trip
- **Ecotourism:** canoe/kayak outfitter or guide, or a park where ecotourist outings can be taken
- **Fishing charters:** guided fishing trips
- **Lighthouse**
- **Marina:** boat dockage
- **Pier**
- **Rainy day attraction:** something to do when the weather is inclement
- **Shopping/browsing:** interesting shopping district, area, or mall
- **Surf report:** for up-to-date surf information over the phone
- **Surf shop:** surfboards, surf gear, swimwear
- **Vacation rentals:** realtors who rent beach houses, cottages, and/or condos

Bunking Down

We write about the better lodging choices you will find in a given locale. We have endeavored to provide a helpful sampling of beachside B&Bs, resorts, and hotels worth considering when planning a California coast vacation. If you have a favorite lodging place that isn't mentioned, drop us a line and we'll check it out for the next edition.

Room rates fluctuate according to day of week, time of year, special events, and the economy—in short, all of the factors that determine what price the market will bear at a given time.

Our $ to $$$$ price range is a general indication of the nightly cost of a standard room with two beds in season.

$ = under $80 per night

$$ = $80–129

$$$ = $130–179

$$$$ = $180 and up

Coastal Cuisine

We offer a sampling of better restaurants specializing in seafood and/or regional California cuisine located on or near the beach. We cast a favorable eye upon places that have been around for a while and have maintained a consistent reputation and level of quality. We welcome your comments, particularly if a favorite eatery has been overlooked. Our $ to $$$$ price range reflects the cost of an average à la carte dinner entrée.

$ = $8 and under

$$ = $9–15

$$$ = $16–22

$$$$ = $23 and over

Night Moves

Night Moves means nightlife, and to us nightlife means people congregating to relax or blow off steam after the sun sets. Our listings run the gamut from surf bars to coffeehouses to rock clubs with live music to dance clubs with deejays—anywhere you can kick back and have fun after the sun has set.

For More Information

We've provided contact information for local chambers of commerce and convention and visitors bureaus.

Our Commitment

We are committed to making *Foghorn Outdoors California Beaches* the most accurate, comprehensive, and fun-to-read guide to the Golden State's beaches and beach communities. We have set foot on every California beach that's accessible by car, foot, or boat. Moreover, we have visited every establishment mentioned herein. Our information is up-to-date as of the time of publication. Despite our best efforts, however, we cannot control price fluctuations or the fact that seemingly solid establishments may go out of business, change owners, or change names from time to time. Therefore, if you're planning a beach vacation based on our writings, it is always a good idea to call ahead to verify prices and policies.

Our opinions—and they are plentiful—are entirely our own. If you want to provide feedback or share information, please feel contact us in care of the publisher.

Correspondence may be addressed to:
Foghorn Outdoors California Beaches 3rd Edition
Avalon Travel Publishing
1400 65th Street, Suite 250
Emeryville, CA 94608
email: atpfeedback@avalonpub.com (please put "California Beaches" in the subject line)

Introduction

Preface to the Third Edition

We have spent a fair portion of our adult lives dodging gainful employment in order to visit and write about beaches. We have written four books on beaches, and this is the third edition of our *Foghorn Outdoors California Beaches* tome, first published in 1996. Why do we do it? We love California—the beaches, the outdoors, the cool people, the cool coastal climate. It never fails to put a smile on our faces.

Foghorn Outdoors California Beaches is aimed at all who are curious about the greatest coastline in America. One simple statistic says it all: California lays claim to 1,264 miles of beautiful and changeable coastline. Beaches have insinuated themselves into the psyche of Californians like nowhere else. Much of the state's population is pressed against the coast, and they live or play at the beach with great frequency. Others cross mountains and valleys to get to them on a more occasional basis. Many cross state lines and even international borders to spend time on the Golden State's beaches.

Whether you're planning a trip to the coast or simply want to do some armchair beachcombing, you can vicariously visit every publicly accessible beach in the state—more than 400 of them—via *Foghorn Outdoors California Beaches*. It is a travelogue in the sense that you can wander up the coast with us and find continuity in the journey and a spirit of close cultural observation in the writing. It is a travel guide in that we've provided plenty of useful information, such as directions, phone numbers, entrance fees, hours of operation, and beach ratings. We've also spiked the book with sidebars—some offering practical information, others anecdotal accounts of various and sundry encounters—to break up a very long trip with the reader's equivalent of rest stops.

Foghorn Outdoors California Beaches should be viewed as both a useful tool and an entertaining read. Our methodology is simple: we travel around, work hard and play hard, do a lot of research, mull over our experiences, and then tell the truth as we see it. We make no bones about being opinionated. People spend a lot of money on trips and vacations, so they deserve to hear the truth—or at least a candid and informed opinion—before ransoming their time and money.

We could not have had a better time putting together this new edition, which meant eagerly embarking on yet another border-to-border, beach-by-beach pilgrimage. We came looking not just for beaches, but striking scenery, coastal geology, local color, and beach activities, plus great places to sleep, eat, and have fun after the sun goes down.

Foghorn Outdoors California Beaches covers a lot of ground. We've written about every coastal community, from San Diego to Smith River, including each beach that can be reached by foot, car, or ferry.

Come on and make the trip with us!

—Parke Puterbaugh and Alan Bisbort
April 2003

The Best of the Best along the California Coast

Can't decide where to swim, play, eat, or stay this weekend? Here are our picks for the best locations in 11 categories:

BEST BEACHES

Top 10 Beaches in Southern California*
Black's Beach, San Diego, page 67
Crystal Cove State Park, Corona del Mar, page 104
Doheny State Beach, Dana Point, page 99
Hermosa Beach, Hermosa Beach, page 189
Huntington City Beach, Huntington Beach, page 106
Leo Carrillo State Beach, Malibu, page 228
Newport Beach Municipal Beach, Newport Beach, page 137
Pacific Beach, Pacific Beach, page 51
Victoria Beach, Laguna Beach, page 126
Zuma County Beach, Malibu, page 226

Top 10 Beaches in Central California*
Año Nuevo State Reserve, San Mateo County, page 441
Asilomar State Beach, Pacific Grove, page 377
Bonny Doon Beach, Santa Cruz County, page 430
Cowell Beach, Santa Cruz, page 416
East Beach, Santa Barbara, page 289
McGrath State Beach, Oxnard, page 246
Moonstone Beach, Cambria, page 333
New Brighton State Beach, Capitola, page 412
Pfeiffer Beach, Big Sur, page 358
Pismo State Beach, Pismo Beach, page 317

Top 10 Beaches in Northern California*
Agate Beach, Trinidad, page 590
Black Sands Beach, Shelter Cove, page 570
Dead Man's Beach, Shelter Cove, page 570
Enderts Beach, Crescent City, page 605
Gold Bluffs Beach, Orick, page 593
High Bluff Beach, Klamath, page 601
Kehoe Beach, Point Reyes, page 494
Limantour Beach, Point Reyes, page 492
MacKerricher State Park, Fort Bragg, page 553
Stinson Beach, Stinson Beach, page 486

BEST LODGING

Top 10 Beachside Hotels*

Top 10 Coastal Lodgings*

Top 5 Coastal Bed-and-Breakfasts*

BEST DINING

Top 10 Coastal Restaurants*

River's End, Jenner, page 519
Ventana, Big Sur, page 362

BEST OUTDOOR RECREATION

Top 5 Coastal Running/Biking Paths
1. **South Bay Bicycle Trail, Torrance to Malibu,** Los Angeles County, page 187
2. **West Cliff Drive,** Santa Cruz, page 416
3. **Hunington Beach Path/Bolsa Chica Bike Path,** Huntington Beach, page 145
4. **Coast Path,** Santa Barbara, page 289
5. **Ocean Front Promenade,** Newport Beach and Balboa, page 137

Top 5 Coastal Hiking Trails
1. **Lost Coast Trail, Shelter Cove to Mattole River,** Humboldt County, page 573
2. **Coastal Trail, Redwoods National Park,** Humboldt and Del Norte counties, page 592
3. **Coast Trail, Point Reyes National Seashore,** Marin County, page 492
4. **Little Harbor Trail, Catalina Island,** Los Angeles County, page 167
5. **Point Conception Trail, Jalama Beach to Point Conception,** Santa Barbara County, page 300

Top 5 Coastal Campgrounds
1. **Leo Carrillo State Park,** Malibu, page 228
2. **New Brighton State Beach,** Capitola, page 412
3. **Andrew Molera State Park,** Big Sur, page 358
4. **MacKerricher State Park,** Fort Bragg, page 553
5. **Carpinteria State Beach,** Carpinteria, page 279

Top 5 Piers
1. **Huntington Pier,** Huntington Beach, page 145
2. **San Clemente Municipal Pier,** San Clemente, page 114
3. **Santa Monica Pier,** Santa Monica, page 214
4. **Ocean Beach Pier,** Ocean Beach, page 42
5. **Ventura Pier,** Ventura, page 258

* in alphabetical order

Southern California

Chapter 1
San Diego County

Southern California

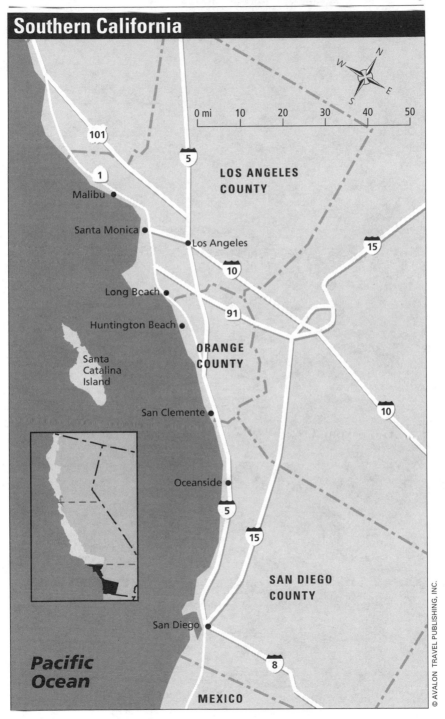

Pacific Ocean

San Diego County

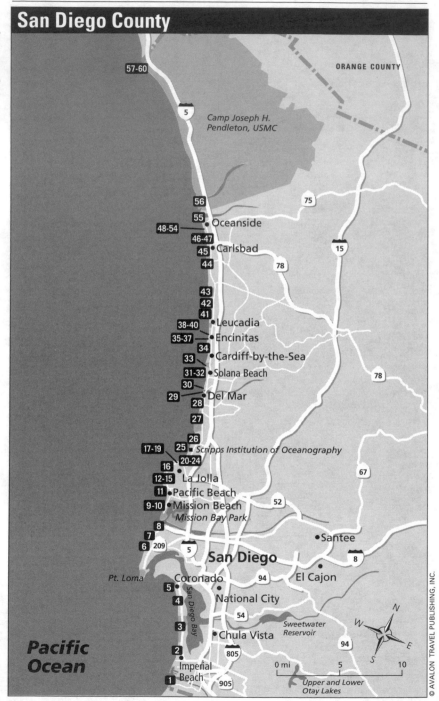

San Diego County

ORANGE COUNTY

57-60

5

Camp Joseph H.
Pendleton, USMC

56

75

55 ● Oceanside

48-54

15

46-47

● Carlsbad

45

44

78

43

42

41

38-40 ● Leucadia

35-37 ● Encinitas

34

33 ● Cardiff-by-the-Sea

78

31-32 ● Solana Beach

30

29 28 ● Del Mar

27

26

17-19 25 ■ Scripps Institution of Oceanography

20-24

16

12-15 ● La Jolla

67

11 ● Pacific Beach

52

9-10 ● Mission Beach

Mission Bay Park

8

7

6 209

● Santee

5 ● **San Diego**

Pt. Loma Coronado

94 ● El Cajon

8

5 ● National City

4

54

San Diego Bay

● Chula Vista

Sweetwater
Reservoir

3

94

**Pacific
Ocean**

2

805

Imperial
Beach

905

0 mi   5   10

Upper and Lower
Otay Lakes

N
W   E
S

© AVALON TRAVEL PUBLISHING, INC.

San Diego County Beaches

1 Border Field State Park, page 24

Location: From I-5 near the Mexican border, take Dairy Mart Road exit. Turn right onto Dairy Mart Road. Follow for 1.5 miles, then turn right on Monument Road and follow into park.
Parking/fees: $3 entrance fee per vehicle if kiosk is attended; free otherwise
Hours: 9:30 A.M.–5 P.M.
Facilities: restrooms, picnic tables, and fire pits
Contact: Tijuana Estuary Visitor Center, 858/575-3613

2 Imperial Beach, page 30

Location: Seacoast Drive between Palm and Encanto Avenues in Imperial Beach
Parking/fees: metered lot and street parking
Hours: 24 hours
Facilities: lifeguards, restrooms, and showers
Contact: Imperial Beach Lifeguard Station, 619/423-8328; surf report, 619/595-3954

3 Silver Strand State Beach, page 37

Location: between Imperial Beach and Coronado, at 5000 Silver Strand Boulevard/Highway 75
Parking/fees: $3 entrance fee per vehicle. Camping fees are $8 per night, plus $7.50 reservation fee.
Hours: 8 A.M.–8 P.M. PDT (8 A.M.–7 P.M. PST)
Facilities: lifeguards, restrooms, showers, picnic area, and fire pits
Contact: Silver Strand State Beach, 619/435-5184

4 Coronado Shores Beach, page 37

Location: At the south end of Coronado, at the Coronado Shores condo complex, on Silver Strand Boulevard/Highway 75
Parking/fees: free parking lot
Hours: 5 A.M.–11 P.M.
Facilities: none
Contact: Coronado Recreation Services, 619/522-7342

5 Coronado City Beach (a.k.a. Central Beach), page 37

Location: in Coronado at Ocean Boulevard and F Avenue
Parking/fees: metered street parking
Hours: 5 A.M.–11 P.M.
Facilities: lifeguards, restrooms, picnic area, and fire rings
Contact: Coronado Recreation Services, 619/522-7342

Map of San Diego County—Page 10

6 Sunset Cliffs Park, page 42

Location: along Sunset Cliffs Boulevard between Ladera Street and Point Loma Avenue in Ocean Beach
Parking/fees: free parking lot at Cornish Drive and Ladera Street
Hours: 24 hours
Facilities: restrooms
Contact: San Diego Coastline Parks, 619/221-8901; surf report, 619/221-8884

7 Ocean Beach City Beach, page 41

Location: in Ocean Beach between the west ends of Niagara and Pescadero Avenues
Parking/fees: metered lot and street parking
Hours: 4 A.M.–2 A.M.
Facilities: restrooms and lifeguards
Contact: San Diego Coastline Parks, 619/221-8901; surf report, 619/221-8884

8 Ocean Beach Park, page 41

Location: in Ocean Beach at the end of Voltaire Street
Parking/fees: metered parking lot
Hours: 4 A.M.–2 A.M.
Facilities: lifeguards, restrooms, showers, and picnic area
Contact: San Diego Coastline Parks, 619/221-8901; surf report, 619/221-8884

9 South Mission Beach, page 45

Location: south end of Mission Boulevard, from Avalon Place down to Mission Bay Channel in Mission Beach
Parking/fees: free parking lot
Hours: 4 A.M.–2 A.M.
Facilities: lifeguards, restrooms, and showers
Contact: San Diego Coastline Parks, 619/221-8901; surf report, 619/221-8884

10 Mission Beach, page 45

Location: Ventura Place at Mission Boulevard in Mission Beach
Parking/fees: free parking lots
Hours: 4 A.M.–2 A.M.
Facilities: lifeguards and restrooms
Contact: San Diego Coastline Parks, 619/221-8901; surf report, 619/221-8884

Map of Southern California—Page 9

11 Pacific Beach, page 51

Location: from Crystal Pier (Garnet Avenue and Mission Boulevard in Pacific Beach) south to Mission Beach
Parking/fees: metered street parking
Hours: 4 A.M.–2 A.M.
Facilities: concessions, lifeguards, restrooms, showers
Contact: San Diego Coastline Parks, 619/221-8901; surf report, 619/221-8884

12 North Pacific Beach, page 51

Location: from Crystal Pier (Garnet Avenue and Mission Boulevard) in Pacific Beach) north to Tourmaline Street in La Jolla
Parking/fees: limited street parking
Hours: 4 A.M.–2 A.M.
Facilities: concessions, lifeguards, restrooms, showers
Contact: San Diego Coastline Parks, 619/221-8901; surf report, 619/221-8884

13 Tourmaline Surfing Park, pages 51 and 58

Location: west end of Tourmaline Street, at Chelsea Street and Crystal Drive, in La Jolla
Parking/fees: free parking lot
Hours: 4 A.M.–2 A.M.
Facilities: lifeguards, restrooms, showers, and picnic area
Contact: San Diego Coastline Parks, 619/221-8901; surf report, 619/221-8884

14 Bird Rock Beach, page 59

Location: in La Jolla at the end of Bird Rock Avenue
Parking/fees: free street parking
Hours: 4 A.M.–2 A.M.
Facilities: none
Contact: San Diego Coastline Parks, 619/221-8901; surf report, 619/221-8884

15 La Jolla Strand Park, page 59

Location: in La Jolla at Neptune Place and Palomar Avenue
Parking/fees: free street parking
Hours: 4 A.M.–2 A.M.
Facilities: none
Contact: San Diego Coastline Parks, 619/221-8901; surf report, 619/221-8884

16 Windansea Beach, page 59

Location: in La Jolla at Neptune Place and Bonair Street

Map of San Diego County—Page 10

Parking/fees: free street parking
Hours: 4 A.M.–2 A.M.
Facilities: none
Contact: San Diego Coastline Parks, 619/221-8901; surf report, 619/221-8884

17 Marine Street Beach, page 59

Location: in La Jolla at the end of Marine Street
Parking/fees: free street parking
Hours: 4 A.M.–2 A.M.
Facilities: none
Contact: San Diego Coastline Parks, 619/221-8901; surf report, 619/221-8884

18 Whispering Sands Beach, page 61

Location: in La Jolla at the end of Bishop's Lane
Parking/fees: free street parking
Hours: 4 A.M.–2 A.M.
Facilities: none
Contact: San Diego Coastline Parks, 619/221-8901; surf report, 619/221-8884

19 Wipeout Beach, page 61

Location: in La Jolla on Coast Boulevard
Parking/fees: free street parking
Hours: 4 A.M.–2 A.M.
Facilities: none
Contact: San Diego Coastline Parks, 619/221-8901; surf report, 619/221-8884

20 Children's Pool Beach, page 61

Location: in La Jolla at Coast Boulevard and Jenner Street
Parking/fees: free and metered street parking
Hours: 4 A.M.–2 A.M.
Facilities: lifeguards
Contact: San Diego Coastline Parks, 619/221-8901; surf report, 619/221-8884

21 Shell Beach, page 61

Location: base of stairwell at south end of Ellen Scripps Park (Coast Boulevard at Girard Avenue) in La Jolla
Parking/fees: free and metered street parking
Hours: 4 A.M.–2 A.M.
Facilities: lifeguards and restrooms
Contact: San Diego Coastline Parks, 619/221-8901; surf report, 619/221-8884

Map of Southern California—Page 9

22 Boomer Beach, page 61

Location: south end of La Jolla Cove, reachable from Ellen Scripps Park (Coast Boulevard at Girard Avenue) in La Jolla
Parking/fees: free and metered street parking
Hours: 4 A.M.–2 A.M.
Facilities: lifeguards and restrooms
Contact: San Diego Coastline Parks, 619/221-8901; surf report, 619/221-8884

23 La Jolla Cove, page 61

Location: in La Jolla at Coast Boulevard and Girard Avenue
Parking/fees: free and metered street parking
Hours: 4 A.M.–2 A.M.
Facilities: lifeguards and restrooms
Contact: San Diego Coastline Parks, 619/221-8901; surf report, 619/221-8884

24 La Jolla Shores Beach–Kellogg Park, page 63

Location: in La Jolla Shores at Camino Del Oro and Calle Frescota
Parking/fees: metered parking lots
Hours: 4 A.M.–2 A.M.
Facilities: lifeguards, restrooms, showers, picnic tables, and fire pits
Contact: San Diego Coastline Parks, 619/221-8901; surf report, 619/221-8884

25 Scripps Beach, page 67

Location: 0.6 miles north of Scripps Institution of Oceanography. From La Jolla Shores, proceed north on La Jolla Shores Drive for one mile. Turn left on El Paseo Grande and right on Discovery Way.
Parking/fees: metered parking lots after 5 p.m. on weekdays and on holidays and weekends; very limited street parking before 5 p.m. on weekdays
Hours: 4 A.M.–2 A.M.
Facilities: none
Contact: Scripps Institution of Oceanography, 858/534-3624

26 Black's Beach (a.k.a. Torrey Pines City Beach), page 68

Location: Hike down to the beach via the steep, gated, paved path that begins at the junction of La Jolla Farms Road and Blackgold Road in La Jolla. Or walk north along the beach from Scripps Pier or south from Torrey Pines State Beach.
Parking/fees: limited free street parking on La Jolla Farms Road; $2 entrance fee at Torrey Pines State Beach
Hours: 4 A.M.–2 A.M.

Map of San Diego County—Page 10

Facilities: none
Contact: San Diego Coastline Parks, 619/221-8901; surf report, 619/221-8884

27 Torrey Pines State Beach, pages 67 and 68

Location: in Torrey Pines. Take the Carmel Valley Road exit off I-5, five miles north of La Jolla. Turn onto McGonigle Road and follow it to the beach.
Parking/fees: $3 entrance fee per vehicle, or free along U.S. 101, 6 A.M.–11 P.M.
Hours: 8 A.M.–10 P.M.
Facilities: lifeguards, restrooms, and picnic tables
Contact: Torrey Pines State Beach, 619/755-2063

28 Del Mar City Beach, page 71

Location: in Del Mar at the west end of Camino Del Mar and 15th Street
Parking/fees: metered parking lot
Hours: 24 hours
Facilities: lifeguards, restrooms, and showers
Contact: Del Mar Community Services, 858/755-1524

29 Del Mar Shores, page 71

Location: Del Mar Shores Terrace at South Sierra Avenue in Solana Beach
Parking/fees: free street parking and free parking lots
Hours: 6 A.M.–10 P.M.
Facilities: lifeguards (seasonal)
Contact: Solana Beach Department of Marine Safety, 858/755-1569

30 Seascape Surf, page 73

Location: stairwell at 500 block of South Sierra Avenue in Solana Beach
Parking/fees: free parking lot and street parking
Hours: 6 A.M.–10 P.M.
Facilities: lifeguards (seasonal) and showers
Contact: Solana Beach Department of Marine Safety, 858/755-1569

31 Fletcher Cove Park, page 73

Location: 111 South Sierra Avenue in Solana Beach
Parking/fees: free parking lot
Hours: 6 A.M.–10 P.M.
Facilities: lifeguards, restrooms, showers and picnic tables
Contact: Solana Beach Department of Marine Safety, 858/755-1569

Map of Southern California—Page 9

San Diego County

32 Tide Beach Park, page 73

Location: Pacific Avenue and Solana Vista Drive
Parking/fees: free street parking
Hours: 6 A.M.–10 P.M.
Facilities: lifeguards (seasonal) and showers
Contact: Solana Beach Department of Marine Safety, 858/755-1569

33 Cardiff State Beach, page 76

Location: one mile south of Cardiff-by-the-Sea along Old U.S. 101 at San Elijo Lagoon
Parking/fees: $3 fee if kiosk is attended; free otherwise
Hours: dawn to dusk
Facilities: none
Contact: San Elijo State Beach, 760/753-5091

34 San Elijo State Beach, page 77

Location: Cardiff-by-the-Sea along Old U.S. 101 at Chesterfield Drive
Parking/fees: $3 entrance fee per vehicle. Camping fees are $13–22 per night, plus $7.50 reservation fee.
Hours: 7 A.M.–10 P.M.
Facilities: lifeguards, restrooms, showers, and picnic tables
Contact: San Elijo State Beach, 760/753-5091

35 Swami's Surf Beach, page 83

Location: 1298 First Street, below Seacliff Roadside Park in Encinitas
Parking/fees: free parking lot
Hours: 5 A.M.–10 P.M.
Facilities: lifeguards, restrooms, and picnic area
Contact: Encinitas Community Services, 760/633-2880

36 Boneyard Beach, page 83

Location: in Encinitas north of Swami's, between E and J Streets
Parking/fees: free street parking
Hours: 5 A.M.–10 P.M.
Facilities: none
Contact: Encinitas Community Services, 760/633-2880

37 D Street Viewpoint, page 83

Location: in Encinitas at 450 D Street
Parking/fees: free parking lot

Map of San Diego County—Page 10

Hours: 5 A.M.–10 P.M.
Facilities: lifeguards
Contact: Encinitas Community Services, 760/633-2880

38 Moonlight Beach, page 83

Location: in Encinitas at Fourth and B Streets
Parking/fees: free parking lot
Hours: 5 A.M.–10 P.M.
Facilities: lifeguards, restrooms, showers, picnic tables, and fire rings
Contact: Encinitas Community Services, 760/633-2880

39 Stone Steps Beach, page 83

Location: in Encinitas at Neptune Avenue and El Portal Street
Parking/fees: free street parking
Hours: 5 A.M.–10 P.M.
Facilities: lifeguards
Contact: Encinitas Community Services, 760/633-2880

40 Encinitas Beach, page 83

Location: in Encinitas north of Stone Steps Beach
Parking/fees: free street parking at Stone Steps Beach
Hours: 5 A.M.–10 P.M.
Facilities: none
Contact: Encinitas Community Services, 760/633-2880

41 Beacon's Beach, page 83

Location: in Leucadia at 948 Neptune Avenue
Parking/fees: free street parking
Hours: 5 A.M.–10 P.M.
Facilities: lifeguards
Contact: Encinitas Community Services, 760/633-2880

42 Grandview, page 84

Location: in Leucadia at the north end of Neptune Avenue
Parking/fees: free parking lot
Hours: 5 A.M.–10 P.M.
Facilities: none
Contact: Encinitas Community Services, 760/633-2880

Map of Southern California—Page 9

43 Ponto Beach (South Carlsbad State Beach), page 87

Location: between Leucadia and Carlsbad on Old U.S. 101. Take the La Costa Drive exit off I-5 and follow it until it ends at Old U.S. 101 (Carlsbad Avenue) at Batiquitos Lagoon.
Parking/fees: free roadside parking
Hours: 6 A.M.–10 P.M.
Facilities: restrooms, showers, picnic tables, and barbecue grills
Contact: South Carlsbad State Beach, 760/438-3143

44 South Carlsbad State Beach, page 88

Location: three miles south of Carlsbad, along Carlsbad Boulevard
Parking/fees: $3 entrance fee per vehicle. Camping fees are $13–22 per night, plus a $7.50 reservation fee.
Hours: 6 A.M.–10 P.M.
Facilities: lifeguards, restrooms, showers, and picnic tables.
Contact: South Carlsbad State Beach, 760/438-3143

45 Carlsbad State Beach (a.k.a. Tamarack Surf Beach), page 88

Location: Carlsbad Boulevard at Tamarack Avenue in Carlsbad
Parking/fees: $3 entrance fee per vehicle
Hours: 6 A.M.–10 P.M.
Facilities: lifeguards, restrooms, and picnic tables
Contact: South Carlsbad State Beach, 760/438-3143

46 Carlsbad State Beach (a.k.a. Robert C. Frazee State Beach), page 88

Location: in Carlsbad along Carlsbad Boulevard at Ocean Street
Parking/fees: free street parking
Hours: 6 A.M.–11 P.M.
Facilities: none
Contact: South Carlsbad State Beach, 760/438-3143

47 South Oceanside Beach, page 93

Location: Cassidy and Pacific Streets in Oceanside
Parking/fees: free street parking
Hours: Open 24 hours
Facilities: none
Contact: Oceanside Department of Harbors and Beaches, 760/966-4535

48 Buccaneer Beach, page 93

Location: 1506 South Pacific Street in Oceanside

Map of San Diego County—Page 10

Parking/fees: free parking lot
Hours: 24 hours
Facilities: concession, lifeguards, picnic area, restrooms, and showers
Contact: Oceanside Department of Harbors and Beaches, 760/966-4535

49 Oceanside Boulevard Beach, page 93

Location: Oceanside Boulevard at Pacific Street in Oceanside
Parking/fees: free street parking
Hours: 24 hours
Facilities: concession, lifeguards, picnic area, restrooms, and showers
Contact: Oceanside Department of Harbors and Beaches, 760/966-4535

50 Wisconsin Street Beach, page 93

Location: Wisconsin Street at The Strand in Oceanside
Parking/fees: pay parking lot and metered street parking
Hours: 24 hours
Facilities: lifeguards, restrooms, and showers
Contact: Oceanside Department of Harbors and Beaches, 760/966-4535

51 Tyson Street Beach, page 93

Location: Tyson Street at The Strand in Oceanside
Parking/fees: metered street parking
Hours: 24 hours
Facilities: concession, lifeguards, picnic area, restrooms, and showers
Contact: Oceanside Department of Harbors and Beaches, 760/966-4535

52 Pier View South (a.k.a. Oceanside Pier Beach), page 93

Location: in Oceanside along Pacific Street, between Witherby Street and the San Luis River
Parking/fees: metered lot and street parking
Hours: 24 hours
Facilities: concession, lifeguards, restrooms, showers, and picnic tables
Contact: Oceanside Department of Harbors and Beaches, 760/966-4535

53 Pier View North (a.k.a. Oceanside Pier Beach), page 93

Location: in Oceanside along Pacific Street, between Witherby Street and the San Luis River
Parking/fees: metered lot and street parking
Hours: 24 hours
Facilities: concession, lifeguards, restrooms, showers, and picnic tables
Contact: Oceanside Department of Harbors and Beaches, 760/966-4535

Map of Southern California—Page 9

54 Breakwater Way, page 93

Location: in Oceanside at the end of Harbor Drive, off Pacific Street
Parking/fees: $5 entrance fee per vehicle.
Hours: 24 hours
Facilities: lifeguards, restrooms, and picnic areas
Contact: Oceanside Department of Harbors and Beaches, 760/966-4535

55 Harbor Beach, page 93

Location: in Oceanside at the end of Harbor Drive, off Pacific Street
Parking/fees: $5 entrance fee per vehicle. RV camping fee is $15 per night.
Hours: 24 hours
Facilities: lifeguards, restrooms, and picnic areas
Contact: Oceanside Department of Harbors and Beaches, 760/966-4535

56 Del Mar Beach (Camp Pendleton), page 95

Location: north of Oceanside Harbor, inside Camp Pendleton Military Base
Parking/fees: free parking lot; the lot and beach are accessible only to military personnel and their guests
Hours: 8 A.M.–7 P.M. (4 P.M. in winter)
Facilities: concession, lifeguards, restrooms, showers, and picnic areas
Contact: Del Mar Lifeguard Station, 760/725-2134 (2078)

57 Bluffs Beach (San Onofre State Beach), page 95

Location: three miles south of San Clemente via Basilone Road exit off I-5; six blufftop trails lead to beach from San Onofre Bluffs Campground
Parking/fees: $5 entrance fee per vehicle. Camping fees are $13–16 per night, plus a $7.50 reservation fee.
Hours: 6 A.M.–10 P.M.
Facilities: lifeguards, restrooms, showers, and picnic tables
Contact: San Onofre State Beach, 949/492-4872

58 Old Man's Beach (San Onofre State Beach), page 95

Location: three miles south of San Clemente via Basilone Road exit off I-5; between the bluffs
Parking/fees: $5 entrance fee per vehicle. Camping fees are $13–16 per night, plus a $7.50 reservation fee.
Hours: 6 A.M.–10 P.M.
Facilities: lifeguards, restrooms, showers, picnic tables
Contact: San Onofre State Beach, 949/492-4872

Map of San Diego County—Page 10

San Diego County

59 San Onofre Recreational Beach (a.k.a. Churches Beach; Camp Pendleton), page 95

Location: north end of Camp Pendleton, at San Onofre State Beach
Parking/fees: free parking lot; the lot and beach are accessible only to military personnel and their guests
Hours: 8 A.M.–7 P.M. (4 P.M. in winter)
Facilities: concession, lifeguards, restrooms, showers, and picnic areas
Contact: San Onofre Lifeguard Station, 760/725-7979

60 Trestles Beach (San Onofre State Beach), page 96

Location: accessible only by a one-mile hike along path accessed at Christianos Road near I-5 in San Clemente
Parking/fees: free parking lot at Christianos Road and El Camino Real
Hours: 6 A.M.–10 P.M.
Facilities: none
Contact: San Onofre State Beach, 949/492-4872

Map of Southern California—Page 9

San Diego County

The United States could not have rolled out a more inviting welcome mat on its southwest border than San Diego County's beaches. They extend for 76 miles, from the wide-open party towns of Ocean Beach, Mission Beach, and Pacific Beach to the upscale, uphill village of La Jolla, and from the rugged setting of Torrey Pines State Beach to the discreet charms of north county communities like Del Mar and Carlsbad. Admittedly, it all ends with a thud at the military city of Oceanside and the nuclear reactors at San Onofre. But the many miles of this state-sized county cover a broad range of settings: lengthy stretches of soft sand; thin, silvery strands of hard-packed sand; cobble-covered beaches that have lost their sand; and rocky coves, sea caves, and sandstone cliffs. There are also bays, lagoons, estuaries, and underwater reserves. And there is beach erosion as well—an endemic problem that has necessitated large-scale "beach renourishment" projects along various thinning parts of the cost. In 2001, for instance, 12 beaches, mostly in northern San Diego County, received a sand transfusion.

San Diego's varied coastal locales play host to every manner of activity that beach lovers live to indulge in: surfing, swimming, sailing, sunbathing, biking, fishing, camping, volleyball, and ogling one another. Then there are the post-sundown activities in these mostly revved-up beach towns: beer drinking, taco scarfing, partying, flirting, hanging out . . . you get the idea. In short, San Diego County is the apotheosis of the beach life. No other county in California—or in the country, for that matter—compares to it. In our eyes its communities offer the quintessential Southern California beach experience.

This was brought home to us on a recent Fourth of July. At midnight, on some inexplicable impulse, we found ourselves wandering out to Windansea Beach in La Jolla. The surfers were off partying at their favorite dive bars and overcrowded apartments, but the waves continued to roar. We sat on a stony ledge, inhaling huge drafts of salt-sprayed air while staring at the dark, endlessly churning sea. It could have been the setting for everything from *Endless Summer* to more '60s flicks than you could shake a beach blanket at. Whoosh, splash, boom, roar. This short detour to Windansea Beach invigorated us for days thereafter, like a contact high with a vast oceanic fountain of youth.

Map of San Diego County—Page 10

San Diego County

Border Field State Park

We tend to spill more words on Border Field than this godforsaken place merits because it's where California begins and is therefore where our coastal treks begin as well. It is a fascinating place for a variety of reasons, none of which have much to do with beaches. So if you want to skip this epistle about a crumbling park in the middle of nowhere, you won't hurt our feelings. If you are into the symbolism of starting points, however, then Border Field must be visited.

Border Field is on the California-Mexico border. Depending on how you look at it, **Border Field State Park** is either the beginning or the end of California. Some folks might say Border Field is the end of the world, and not because it's hard to find. In fact, Border Field is incredibly easy to find, which is part of the problem. The people who find it most frequently are illegal aliens—that is, immigrants who either scale the 10-foot fence that separates the United States from Mexico or brazenly wade out beyond the restraining wall at low tide and walk into the United States, as if they were beachcombing.

For those fun-seekers who visit Border Field legally, this makes for an intriguing sociological study but a bummer of a beach trip. Whereas some might argue that only sadists would go out of their way to visit Border Field State Park, we make it a perverse ritual of sorts to begin every trip to California here. On our most recent visit, in May 2002, torrential rains had nearly washed out the final leg of the rutted dirt road that leads to Border Field's parking area, on the bluff above the beach. We could see the cement monument that marks the international boundary and the bullfight ring of Tijuana just beyond the chain-link fence that separates the two nations, but we could not get up to them. We were more than willing to give it a try but did not think our rental car could ford the muddy impasse. So, we

stopped, waded into the mud on foot, took some photographs, made note of the metaphorical separation (so near yet so far), and saluted our friends south of the border before turning back. Still, even in what some might term a hellhole we had to pause to admire the hard blue sky and small, puffy white clouds, rimmed with silver linings, and the extensive marsh grasses of the estuary—among the last significant coastal wetlands in California.

The effect is one of stark dichotomies: the lulling sound of crashing waves suddenly interrupted by the screech of an Immigration Service paddy wagon lurching from behind a clump of dried grass to snag another undocumented alien. Another contrast: a gorgeous stretch of wild, windswept sand surrounded by wildflowers, marshlands, and jagged geological formations—dotted with signs warning that swimming is prohibited indefinitely due to raw sewage spills washing northward from Tijuana. Even when the water is sewage free, the rip currents and in-shore holes can be nasty, and there's no lifeguard on duty. As a sign at the park entrance starkly puts it, "Swimming and Wading Unsafe."

Yes, Border Field State Park can be a party pooper. The area, however, is not without historic and environmental interest, or beach-basking potential. The border, which runs from Border Field east for 1,952 miles, was established on October 10, 1849, the date California was officially whisked away from Mexico to become a part of the United States. A cement monument to this event stands nearby, and informative placards strewn about the park recount both nations' histories and prehistories (one rather curiously refers to Native Americans as "the first emigrants"). Other signs contain tidbits about the ancient geological uplift that created this ruggedly beautiful beach and the wildlife that presumably still roams it. Unfortunately, the words on most of the

Map of Southern California—Page 9

markers have been worn away by sun, sand, and surf. The spray-painted Spanish graffiti on the walls is more legible. More overwhelming than anything nature might devise is the sprawl of Tijuana, which is separated from the park by only a fence. Tijuana is a city twice the size of San Diego that is growing at an alarming rate. It is the land of last hope for rural Mexicans who come looking for work or wait until dark to make the illegal stroll north. A sobering statistic: 400 people a year die while trying to cross illegally from Mexico to the United States. That number is greater than were ever killed trying to scale the Berlin Wall.

A flying saucer–shaped bullring looms less than 100 yards away and cries of "Olé" are heard on weekends as another beast bites the dust for the sadistic pleasure of man. Across from the bullring, less than 50 feet from where we stood on a prior visit, a group of sun-baked men passed a bagged bottle among themselves, staring back at, or perhaps through, us.

One of the few pleasant pastimes that can be enjoyed at Border Field is riding horses. Horses can be ridden on designated trails in the adjoining Tijuana River National Estuarine Reserve.

For More Information

Border Field State Park, 619/575-3613, www.cal-parks.ca.gov

Imperial Beach

Border Field may abut our border with Mexico, but America really begins at Imperial Beach (population 27,000), the southernmost beach town in California. Here you'll find the southernmost strip malls, condos, homes, lawns, burger stands, pool halls, trailer parks, libraries, baseball fields, and skateboard ramps. You'll also find a modestly sized community of mostly middle-class citizens trying hard as heck to ignore the looming presence of Tijuana, so close by that on smog-free days the bullring is visible from the beach.

It is perhaps more accurate to say that Southern California begins at Imperial Beach, because everything here seems tailor-made for summer fun: a beautiful beach that runs for 2.5 miles; the sturdy, 1,500-foot Imperial Beach Pier; healthy surf and an army of surfers; a lifeguard crew of 17; nearly year-round sun; and pleasant natural backdrops to both the east (distant hills and mesas) and south (Tijuana Slough National Wildlife Refuge). On top of that, folks here make a concerted effort to sell the town as a placid resort, billing it as the "South Coast Hideaway."

Yes, Imperial Beach has it all. So why the hangdog expressions? Well, this is the resort beach most impacted by the sins of Tijuana. In 1993, for instance, the beach was closed for 193 days due to sewage contaminants in the ocean. The issue of raw sewage and ocean contamination became a hot one in the mid-'90s. Another issue came to a head in 1996 and 1997, as local community governments, led by the mayor of Imperial Beach, implemented an aggressive sand-replenishment program on the thinning beaches of southern San Diego County. They needed not only cleaner sand but more of it. The winter of 1997–1998 brought some vicious El Niño–fueled storms that ate away at the town's sandy treasure, though natural accretion brought some of the sand back in summer 1999—just in time for the unveiling of Imperial Beach's renovated Pier Plaza. This pierside park complex includes picnic pavilions, shops, a play area, and a sculptural tribute to the sport of wave-riding called *Surfhenge* (it looks like multicolored McDonald's arches). Cleverly enough, Pier Plaza even includes surfboard benches to sit on and snippets of Imperial Beach's early history as a wave-rider's mecca.

Map of San Diego County—Page 10

On the Border

All the issues that plague California have been compressed onto the beaches near the Mexican border. You name it, they got it: illegal immigration, sewage disposal, farm runoff, ocean contamination, shoddy development, erosion, vandalism, overpopulation, litter.

We learned this on our first visit to Border Field State Park and the Tijuana River Estuary back in 1994. The trip started out promisingly, with green, irrigated sod fields bordering Dairy Mart and Monument Roads and rugged, dry hills in the distance suggesting a raw, lunarlike landscape. It did not take long for things to turn nasty.

Hand-lettered signs sprang up on the side of Monument Road as we headed toward the ocean. One announced: "Environmentalists Destroy Human Lives." Another trumpeted: "Welcome to No Man's Land. Environmentalists. Illegal Aliens. Smuggling. Flooding. Sewage. Garbage." A series of signs, arrayed Burma Shave–style, blamed environmentalists for hurting the economy, for "desperate animals caught in the mud," and for the drownings of 24 illegals. At the bottom of one such sign were spray-painted the ominous words: "Remember Waco, Texas."

On the Mexican side, shoddily built villas could be seen dotting the dry brown hillsides, some clinging treacherously to their high perches, which are now illuminated at night by powerful mobile floodlights. Border Patrol minivans could also be seen, secreted behind clumps of dry weeds and dirt. Like enormous metal insects, the feds' paddy wagons lie in wait for fence-hoppers who might try their luck inland from the more popular Border Field State Park. This entire end of the U.S.–Mexico boundary is the most sievelike in the country, accounting for nearly one-third of all illegal alien arrests. As many as 80,000 arrests have been made in the peak months of April and May, when seasonal employment lures migrant workers.

Things did not improve at the beach. The state park ranger who took our fare was as beat as the scene around him. "Do you ever get busy at the park?" we asked, cheerful naïfs that we are.

"We used to," he said, ever so slowly, "but not no more."

Then he sighed and, as if cutting off further questions, said, "It's a long story. . . . It has nothing to do with the park."

Indeed, the parkland seemed a splendid setting. Then we pulled into a parking lot filled with vehicles sporting Mexican license plates or no plates at all. One group of Mexicans in cowboy hats had disassembled a car, leaving the engine's parts strewn about the asphalt. They were in no hurry to reassemble it.

Map of Southern California—Page 9

Mexican radio stations blared from every direction like a musical EKG. Families ate food from plastic bags, bickered and laughed, and fell asleep on the grass and walls. Screaming kids were running everywhere. None, curiously, ventured down to the ocean, where the waves seemed much more enticing than the hot asphalt. Pregnant women fanned themselves with the lids of takeout fried-chicken buckets. One young couple groped passionately in the grass while an infant lay napping beside their intertwined bodies. At this point we realized we weren't at the beach. We were in a documentary film.

We asked one of the friendly tykes why he wasn't playing in the ocean.

"I used to but not no more."

"Why? Too cold?" No answer. "Smell bad?"

Big smile and a nod. Then holding his nose, he spewed, "Pee-yoo!"

The ocean waters for several miles north of the border smell bad most of the time. The Mexican sewage treatment plants can't keep up with the load from the burgeoning population and when the system breaks down, raw sewage flows into the surrounding Tijuana River Estuary and, ultimately, into the ocean. This creates what the Mexicans call *aguas negras* (black waters)— as much as 20 million gallons of it in a single day, which necessitates the closing of beaches within 50 miles by San Diego health officials.

The sewage issue is one for which the United States has been no less culpable than Mexico. On the American side, a gleaming new complex— the South Bay Water Reclamation Project—was up and running in May 2002. When fully on line, it will treat up to 15 million gallons of sewage a day from the communities of San Ysidro, Chula Vista, and Imperial Beach. As if pushing the fecal finger of fate further, new "planned communities" are being built ass up against the Mexican border. Along Dairy Mart Road, in fact, some hubristic homeowners let the international boundary's fence and barb wire serve double duty as their backyard property line. On the Mexican side, a "bi-national" border sewage treatment plant—the Bajagua project, to be built in Tijuana—has been batted around for years and, as of this writing, is still being debated. Furthermore, in 1999, another much-needed treatment facility—the International Wastewater Treament Plant—began pumping partially treated sewage from Tijuana into the ocean via an outfall off Imperial Beach.

On a less gloomy note, we noticed that the ominous hand-painted signs along Monument Road were gone, and a Border Patrol guard informed us that illegal border crossings were at an 18-year low. He also cogently observed, "We don't have any room to talk about Mexico when you look at the way we treat our own beaches and oceans."

Map of San Diego County—Page 10

Tough Times on the Tijuana River Estuary

As you watch any of the 340 bird species that have been spotted in the Tijuana River Valley, you'd never know that a raging controversy runs through the beautiful estuary. The Tijuana River Estuary is an integral part of California's remaining coastal wetlands, 90 percent of which have been lost to dredging, development, and pollution. More pertinent to this densely populated area, the **Tijuana River National Estuarine Research Reserve** (which also encompasses the Tijuana Slough National Wildlife Refuge to the north) is a vital natural buffer between the urban behemoths of Tijuana and San Diego. Located between Border Field State Park and Imperial Beach, it is among the last wetlands in San Diego County. First, let's define a few terms:

• An **estuary** is a semi-enclosed body of water that usually forms at the mouth of a river. It is brackish as a result of the mixing of fresh water (through rain and river flow) and salt water (from the ocean's incoming tides pushing upriver).

• **Wetlands** refer to land surfaces inundated with water all or part of the time. They are a rich haven for wildlife of all kinds. As a placard at the nearby Border Field State Park says: "Two-thirds of all fish and shellfish found in coastal waters spend part of their lives in estuaries like this one."

• An **estuarine reserve** is a designation by the federal government that permanently protects an estuary. It is not a park, per se, but a tract of land set aside and protected in perpetuity.

Most of the Tijuana River runs through Mexico, draining 1,700 square miles. The five-mile tail end of the river cuts across the U.S. border and snakes through San Diego County, where it meets the ocean. Those five miles and the 3,000 acres of federal and private land drained by it have been battled over as intensely as any five miles of the western front in World War I.

The 3,000 acres are owned by private parties, the city of San Diego, the county of San Diego, the state of California, and the federal government, which administers the majority of it (2,531 acres). Each has an idea about how best

---

If you catch Imperial Beach at the right time, you are in for some pleasant surprises. The surf is among the most challenging in San Diego County. In fact, it was the first real big-wave surfing spot on the Southern California surfing scene, dating back to the '40s. (Before Imperial Beach's incorporation in 1956, surfers called this sacred area "Tijuana Sloughs.") Today, surfers of all ages vie for space near the pier, which provides an excellent vantage point from which spectators can view their prodigious skills.

After one particularly nice run by a blond surfer—during which he executed several 360-degree spin moves to keep abreast of his chosen wave—the grandfatherly chap next to us shouted down to him, "Good show!" The surfer shrugged and said, "No, I blew it!" But he was obviously pleased someone had noticed his skill.

The downside to this churning surf is the danger it poses to the uninitiated. In 2001 the vigilant lifeguards in Imperial Beach made more than 600 rescues (there were no drown-

Map of Southern California—Page 9

to save the estuary from the many slings and arrows constantly hurled at it, including raw sewage, agricultural runoff, flood from winter rains, drought, vandalism, and poaching.

In the grand laissez-faire manner that defines Southern California's real estate cartel, the private landowners blame the bureaucrats for the ills that have befallen the area. This attitude is usually couched in terms of "all those much-needed jobs that are lost because of the evil environmentalists who are playing God." The environmentalists, in turn, blame the Mexican bureaucrats. The tourists don't blame anyone because they stopped coming here years ago.

Regardless of who did what to whom and why, everyone agrees that some sort of intervention is needed to protect the reserve. Unclear on what sort of intervention is best? So are the experts. Meanwhile, each night the cat-and-mouse game between cops and illegals goes on in the grasslands, as does the dumping of chemicals and sewage. Somehow the birds and the bees and the fish make the best of it.

All this is a crying shame because the best way to see the estuary is on foot, without the extra political baggage of the ongoing dispute. To help with this, a free walker's guide to the Tijuana River National Estuarine Research Reserve is available from the **Southwest Wetlands Interpretive Association** (P.O. Box 575, Imperial Beach, CA 92032, 619/435-5184). This useful tool reveals the lay of the land—from footpaths and horse trails to hitching posts and overlooks. We recommend a look-see at this wonderful, threatened spot to anyone concerned about coastal ecology. There is no better learning lab than the Tijuana River Estuary. Here you discover the difference between mudflats, tidal sloughs, uplands, riverbeds, and low, middle, and high marshes. Then there are the hundreds of species of plants and animals that live here. One of the tips in the walker's guide should be mandatory etiquette at every beach in the world: "Feel free to pick up as much litter as you like!" The reserve itself has a visitor center (301 Caspian Way, Imperial Beach, 619/575-3613), from which one can access the trails. The visitor center is open Wednesday to Sunday, 10 A.M.–6 P.M. in summer and to 5 P.M. in winter.

ings). In addition to powerful waves, rip currents—some extending out as far as three-quarters of a mile—are capable of pulling even the strongest swimmer under. This only adds to the appeal for surfers and lifeguards, who are often one and the same. As one lifeguard said, "We are one of the last truly open beaches. You can surf anywhere."

Beaches

Two main drags, Palm and Coronado Avenues, lead to the ocean. These parallel routes are the commercial corridors for vacationers and day-tripping inlanders, a hodgepodge of liquor stores, taco huts, shacklike bars, pool halls, car dealers, car repair shops, car washes, tire outlets, and mobile homes. Also in the mix are new condos and apartments trying to gentrify the flotsam out of existence, but they must resort to outrageous enticements ("first three months rent free") to sell their upscale wares.

Seacoast Drive parallels the ocean, and it is

here you'll want to be. The beach at **Imperial Beach** has been extended on several occasions by massive infusions of sand from nearby San Diego Bay. Dredgings are deposited in front of what was once a seawall, periodically leaving the town with a sandy, brownish gold facelift. At the residential south end of Seacoast Drive, however, the beach is essentially gone, the raging Pacific held back by riprap and prayers.

Swimming can be exciting but treacherous. To add to the thrill, the ocean floor drops off dramatically where the dredged sand ends. Advisories are issued daily and, on particularly rough days, lifeguards will temporarily suspend swimming. Every summer Imperial Beach celebrates Sandcastle Days, which culminates with the **U.S. Open Sandcastle Competition**—the world's longest-running sand-sculpting contest. The 23rd annual Sandcastle Competition will be held July 25–27, 2003.

Bunking Down

The best and beachiest motel is the **Seacoast Inn** (800 Seacoast Drive, 619/424-7556, $$), just north of the pier. It is the very essence of what we conceive a beach motel to be. It faces a wide beach, and if the ocean's too rough, cold, or polluted, there's a lima bean–shaped pool ringed with palm trees out back. Beyond this, a string of budget motels lines the I-5 off-ramps, with rooms going for bottom-dollar prices, often as low as $30. But who wants to hear the drone of cars all night when, for a few dollars more, you can hear the ocean roar?

Coastal Cuisine

The most scenic dining spot in Imperial Beach is the **Tin Fish,** at the end of the Imperial Beach Pier. Fried platters are the favorite, but you can opt for something healthier like grilled halibut or grilled calamari. And you can take in all the surfing and angling going on all around you. A good bet for seafood and breakfast is **IB Seafood and Breakfast** (809 Seacoast Drive, 619/429-8029, $$). Ask about fresh-fish specials at dinnertime. As for breakfast, what else but an IB High Surf Omelette (bacon, sausage, cheese, and onion)? Not that you'll have the wherewithal to surf after downing that leviathan. Also near the ocean is the **Beach Club Grille** (710 Seacoast Drive, 619/628-0777, $). Adjacent to Dunes Park playground, it's a good place to hit for deli fare or a gyro.

You won't have to wander far in this border town to find tolerable taco huts. Here are three of them: **Mi Ranchito Taco Shop** (805 Seacoast Drive, 619/424-8260, $), **Tacos Corita** (757 Seacoast Drive, 619/429-6565, $) and **El Tapatio's** (260 Palm Avenue, 619/423-3443, $). Over the years we've scarfed Mexican grub at all three establishments, leaving happily with full stomachs and the knowledge that we ate well for next to nothing.

Night Moves

Beer joints and pool halls line Palm and Coronado Avenues. **Ye Olde Plank Inn** (24 Palm Avenue, 619/423-5976) is the most inviting and friendly of this lot. The most appealing beachfront tavern is the **IB Forum** (1079 Seacoast Drive, 619/429-7507), which accurately bills itself as "the most southwesterly bar and grill in the U.S." You can grill your own steaks here. The IB Forum celebrated its tenth anniversary in the summer of 2002.

For More Information

Imperial Beach Chamber of Commerce, 600 Palm Avenue, Suite 115, Imperial Beach, CA 91932, 619/424-3151, website: www.ci. imperial-beach.ca.us

Map of Southern California—Page 9

San Diego

A thousand years ago, the land on which San Diego now stands was a paradise inhabited by the Kumeyaay. They thrived along the bountiful waters of this big bay, one of the largest natural harbors in the world. With Point Loma to the west, fish- and wildlife-rich marshlands to the south, and protective mountains to the east, they no doubt thanked the gods profusely for their good fortune.

Of course, fortunes like this don't remain secret for long. In the 16th century, Portuguese explorer Juan Rodríguez Cabrillo stumbled upon the Kumeyaays' bay. The last of the conquistadors, Cabrillo came in search of gold. Instead

---

 ## Dropping the Population Bomb on California

Along the southern coast, on restroom walls and in other public spaces, we noticed a lot of graffiti. Among the ivylike tagging we kept seeing the message "Stop Breeding." Though somewhat overstated, we couldn't help but understand the frustration that would drive someone to such extremes. Indeed, in California, the population bomb has hit with a resounding and furious fallout. And it is in your face if you look for it at the beaches of Southern California. The numbers say it all:

- California's population has more than tripled since 1950. Given current trends, it will double in 25 years. It has increased by 10 percent in the 1990s alone.
- Even without illegal immigration, California is the chosen home of 35 percent of the nation's legal immigrants. Between 1980 and 1990, Los Angeles alone had two million legal immigrants, one million of whom were from Mexico and El Salvador. Los Angeles County is now 40 percent Hispanic and 10 percent Asian.
- Southern California is home to almost half of the state's 32.7 million residents, and 90 percent live within 100 miles of the beach.
- Due to population growth and ever-expanding private development, the state's wetlands have almost vanished. The state animal, the grizzly bear, is gone. The state ranks first in the United States in the number of endangered and threatened species.
- Air pollution from urban areas costs state farmers $100 million in lost crops annually.
- Between 1971 and 1996, the number of motor vehicles in California more than doubled, from 12 million to 25 million, as did gasoline usage.
- The *Los Angeles Times* reported in May 2002 that Orange County's population increased by 44,000 in just the previous 18 months—that's 44,000 new residents they know about, that is.

Map of San Diego County—Page 10

Skeptics in Paradise

Despite the rosy prose of San Diego's tourist brochures, "America's Finest City" is beginning to show some wear and tear. Part of this is due to circumstances beyond San Diego's control—illegal immigration, for example, saps the local tax base to pay for things like the 4,100 babies delivered each year to Mexican women who sneak over the border in their ninth month. The crush of humanity on both sides of this border also contributes to the sprawl that never ends. The land boom in San Diego, in fact, has spawned a religion of growth, with 30 pages in the Yellow Pages devoted to real estate. The result: new condos, new faux adobes, new fast-food franchises, new resorts as far as the eye can see (which isn't far on smoggy days). And still there's a purported housing shortage.

Yet despite its reputation for pro-growth, head-in-the-sand conservatism, San Diego is an enlightened city in many ways. The rumblings of healthy skepticism and honest discourse about urban issues can be found everywhere. In its "manifesto," a local arts publication writes, "We reject the dehumanization of art. . . . We are committed to the handmade object. . . . We are not interested in what is fashionable, popular, or politically correct." And so on, for half a page. Perhaps the oddest place we found such rumblings was in the *Golden Triangle Metropolitan,* a local publication devoted to "a business lifestyle," wherein developers and CEOs are regularly profiled as "visionaries," and their high-rise buildings and planned communities are depicted as acts of the gods. In a column called "Golden Triangle Dreamer,"

he sailed into this perfect harbor on September 28, 1542. He named it San Miguel and claimed it for his royal patrons. Then he sailed away. This one quick visit earned Cabrillo the distinction of having "discovered" the West Coast. Cabrillo brought his knowledge of the Kumeyaays' paradise back to Europe with him. Sixty years later, explorer Sebastian Vizcaino sailed into San Miguel and renamed it San Diego de Alcala.

On July 2, 1769, the Catholic mystic-priest Father Junipero Serra established the first Spanish mission in California on Presidio Hill in San Diego de Alcala. More a visionary than a humble padre, the charismatic Serra inaugurated an ambitious plan for his town, blending a military battalion and Catholic parish into a philosophy of conquest that would be-

come known as the "mission system." His mission was clear enough (to convert the heathen natives), and his system eventually spanned 21 settlements, a network that subjugated the native populations of California.

Serra's recruitment method was known as "the cross or the sword." By the time the Spanish overlords were finished, the Kumeyaay had been left either dead by the sword or dependent on the mercy of the cross. Serra's legacy, known as Old Town San Diego, stands in testament to his achievement. Today it's mostly a shopping mall set among period buildings. Yet Old Town is home to Serra's original mission and chapel, where mass is still held every Sunday.

California remained loyal to Spain and then

Map of Southern California—Page 9

several average citizens were asked: "If you could have one wish for the city, what would it be?" Here are some random responses:
- "I wish we had more of a village feeling."
- "I wish I didn't have to drive everywhere."
- "I wish the city was hipper."
- "I wish the city had more soul."
- "I wish we had more public art."
- "Everything is part of a development or a mall. . . . It's sterile."

These answers fly directly in the face of what the editors perhaps intended. It's the "business lifestyle" they suck up to that worships the gleaming chrome, mirrored-glass, and exhaust-plumed asphalt that defines the "new" San Diego, as created by its urban "visionaries."

But the unanimous response from those who are forced to reside in the communities built by such visionaries is one of frustration and a desire to see cities and beach resorts become more livable and human-scaled. We couldn't agree more. And the best part is that San Diego, unlike Los Angeles, still has time to make more corrections. The regional land conservation plan mandated by the Clinton administration in 1998 has helped. And we have to say that, with each visit, San Diego seems more appealing to us.

San Diego has, in fact, grown on us over the past 15 years, which is strange given how it has grown on the map during the same time period. Normally, we run in horror of such sprawl, but San Diego is not Los Angeles (something the city has proudly proclaimed for decades). Los Angeles is something we reluctantly endure in order to get at its beaches, whereas we've found San Diego an inviting city to explore in and of itself.

Mexico, after the latter won independence in 1821. California was admitted to the United States and San Diego was incorporated in September 1850. San Diego County became the first county in California. In 1867, a fast-talking Easterner named Alonzo Horton purchased San Diego's entire waterfront and laid out a grid of streets upon which the business district was built. Even today, Horton's "new town" looks new, dominated by nondescript skyscrapers. A plaza stands in tribute to Horton—another upscale shopping and hotel area.

In 1884, the transcontinental railroad reached San Diego. In 1917, the U.S. Navy landed here, building shipyards and installations on every available scrap of land and creating a gray military presence that dominated San Diego until recent times. Because of the harbor, San Diego soon became the permanent base for the nation's largest West Coast fleet, numbering well over 100,000 personnel. This, of course, attracted military contractors, which subsisted on the government tab for years. However, the military downsizing of the early '90s hit San Diego particularly hard. When we were researching our first edition in 1994, 1,900 employees had just been let go by General Dynamics, and Convair had released a few hundred more, bringing its total down to 1,922 from a one-time peak of 46,859. Not to worry, pledged the city boosters. Indeed, the city rebounded with the nation's tech-driven economic upturn during the Clinton years. And now the war on terrorism may keep San

Map of San Diego County—Page 10

Diego and defense contractors booming for years to come.

In some ways, San Diego is still a navy town, but it's been looking elsewhere for its identity. As the seventh-largest metropolitan area in the country, with a bayfront that is the envy of the world, it certainly has ample resources to draw upon. In fact, the area has swelled like a dry sponge dropped in a tidepool. Many people are retiring here, while others sail in as part of the leisure-boat crowd. Its population is 1,277,000. That figure, it should be noted, includes not just the city of San Diego proper but surrounding communities that fall under its municipal umbrella, including Ocean Beach, Mission Beach, Pacific Beach, and La Jolla. The city receives 30,000 new residents annually and boasted almost 14.8 million overnight visitors in 2001.

There is a reason for this prodigious immigration. The weather in San Diego is ideal for anyone who doesn't crave variety. Temperatures year-round rarely stray from the 70s. It seldom rains in the summer, and when it does, according to a local resident, people stare at the heavens as if witnessing a solar eclipse. Within easy reach are beautiful mountains and unique desert communities (including one with the intriguing name of Plaster City). There are zoos, museums, and theaters galore. And, of course, there are 70 miles of ocean beaches in the county.

San Diegans love their city. Almost everyone we've met in San Diego over the years has been so upbeat and friendly that we took them to be hirelings of the chamber of commerce. The self-smitten San Diegans have adopted all of the following nicknames for their town: Sports Town USA, Golf Land USA, America's Finest City, California's Oldest City, The Place Where California Began, California's Plymouth Rock.

Even areas of dubious history or merit are trumped up into Disneyesque attractions, carrying touristy names such as Seaport Village and Gaslamp Quarter. Then there are the genuinely worthwhile attractions like Balboa Park and about 90 museums. All of the happy interfacing that takes place here requires a maze of superhighways. These interstates intertwine across the scorched brown terrain like seaweed, giving a novice driver headaches, twinges of anxiety, and watery eyes. You may be told otherwise by the locals, but there is smog in San Diego.

The pace of life here is deceptive. Though leisurely on the surface, the city throbs with an undercurrent of manic activity. Cars are in constant motion, glittering like metallic bugs in the dry heat as they roll along the freeways. Bicycles, in-line skates, skateboards, unicycles, and even pogo sticks hound the heels of sedate pedestrians. Joggers blip past the harborfront. Sailboats and yachts cut through the bay like stilettos. The race is on among the new blood of San Diego, even if you can't figure out where the finish line is or what you get if you win. Perhaps an eternal round of golf.

Once a novice driver gets acclimated to the pace, the lure of San Diego is obvious. It starts at the water, with its appealing and ever-expanding harborfront. Because our yacht was repossessed in a previous lifetime, we spent less time on the bay—except for a meal, a stroll along the Embarcadero's Marina Park, and a visit to Balboa Park—and drove straight to the beaches of San Diego. This is where we encourage our readers to start and finish their experiences of this remarkable city. Each of the beach communities within reach of downtown San Diego—Coronado, Point Loma, Ocean Beach, Mission Beach, Pacific Beach—has been written up in the following pages. Each has its own unique flavor. Each is worth a separate summer vacation. We only wish we had additional lifetimes to devote to that pursuit.

Shore Things

• **Bike/skate rentals:** Aquarius, 747 Pacific Beach Drive, Pacific Beach, 619/488-9733; Hamel's, 704 Ventura Place, Mission Beach, 619/488-5050

Map of Southern California—Page 9

- **Boat cruise:** San Diego Harbor Excursion, 1050 North Harbor Drive, San Diego, 619/234-4111
- **Dive shop:** Blue Escape Dive, 1617 Quivara Road #B, San Diego, 619/223-3483
- **Ecotourism:** H&M Landing, 2803 Emerson Street, San Diego, 619/222-1144 (whale-watching); Seal Tours, Seaport Village, 619/298-8687; La Jolla Kayak & Company, 2199 Avenida de la Playa, La Jolla, 619/459-1114
- **Fishing charters:** Islandia Sportfishing, 1551 West Mission Bay Drive, San Diego, 619/222-1164
- **Marina:** Commercial Basin, Shelter Island, 619/291-3900; Sheraton, Harbor Island, San Diego, 619/291-2900
- **Piers:** Crystal Pier, Mission Boulevard at Garnet Avenue, Pacific Beach; Imperial Beach Pier, Seacoast Drive, Imperial Beach
- **Rainy day attraction:** Birch Aquarium, Scripps Institute, 2300 Expedition Way, La Jolla (I-5 at La Jolla Village Drive exit), 619/534-3474

- **Shopping/browsing:** Gaslamp Quarter Downtown Historical District, Third and Fourth Avenues, San Diego
- **Surf report:** 619/221-8884
- **Surf shop:** South Coast Surf Shop, 5023 Newport Avenue, San Diego, 619/223-7017; Bob's Mission Surf, 4320 Mission Boulevard, Mission Beach, 619/483-8837
- **Vacation rentals:** Penny Realty, 4444 Mission Boulevard, San Diego, 619/272-3900 or 800/748-6704

For More Information

San Diego Convention and Visitors Bureau, 11 Horton Plaza, San Diego, CA 92101, 619/236-1212, website: www.sandicgo.org; Greater San Diego Chamber of Commerce, 402 West Broadway, San Diego, CA 92101, 619/232-0124, website: www.sdchamber.org; San Diego Visitor Information Center, 2688 East Mission Bay Drive, San Diego, CA 92109, 619/276-8200 or 800/422-4749, website: www.infosandiego.com

Coronado

Coronado gleams with a gilded, moneyed loveliness that stands in stark contrast to the border-town blues of nearby Imperial Beach. Driving north from Imperial Beach along Silver Strand Boulevard, you pass from a land of no money to a land of new money. First you notice the yachts that fill the Glorietta Bay Marina, their long masts standing as tall and straight as a fistful of pencils jammed in a cup. Then you realize that the price of gas has jumped 25 cents a gallon in the space of 10 miles. Finally, turning onto Orange Avenue, which leads into downtown Coronado, you roll by a historic old resort hotel and rows of opulent private homes fronted by lawns that are better tended than country-club putting greens.

The rich have perched alongside the naval air base on this spit of land enfolding San Diego Bay. They have erected high-rise condos, private estates, and tropical gardens where flow-

ers of flaming crimson, deep purple, and passion pink add a splash of color to what would be, in its natural state, an arid landscape. Coronado (population 24,100) is a verdant garden by the sea, an oasis made possible by sprinkler systems, cheap immigrant labor, and big money. The story of Coronado's founding is emblematic of how it went in the glory days of California's birth: some wealthy guy would get an idea, and all of a sudden a desert would magically become a Technicolor resort in year-round bloom. Coronado's past is linked with some of the wealthiest figures in California's history, and their presence sets a standard of luxurious living that endures to this day.

The founding fathers of Coronado are railroad tycoon Elisha Babcock Jr. and piano magnate H. L. Story. The two spent time hunting on the wild, majestic Coronado peninsula, enjoying the place so much that they eventually

Map of San Diego County—Page 10

switched their quarry from rabbits and quail to tourist dollars. The pair formed a syndicate, the Coronado Beach Company, and bought the entire peninsula for $110,000 in 1885. On January 12, 1887, ground was broken on the Hotel del Coronado, which they envisioned as a wondrous resort that would become the "talk of the Western world." Barely a year later, "the Del," as it is informally known, was open for business.

Babcock and Story were later joined in their venture by John D. Spreckels, a wealthy San Francisco-reared heir to a sugar fortune who sailed his yacht down to San Diego in 1887, dropped anchor, and essentially brought the city to life. He built the first wharves in San Diego's natural harbor and linked the city to the outside world with the construction of the San Diego, Arizona, and Eastern Railway. He also bought newspapers, installed streetcars, and founded a bank. To his eternal credit, he ensured that the development of San Diego proceeded along pleasingly aesthetic lines, seeing to it that the city was generously laid out with parks and that the parks were planted with his favorite flowers: geraniums. His financial stake in the Del grew to the point that he bought out the other partners by the turn of the century. There have been only four owners since Spreckels, and in the new millennium the Hotel del Coronado projects a casually lavish splendor, much as it did a century ago.

The centerpiece of Coronado, the Del is a vast, rambling, capacious resort that's far more inviting than your typically stuffy corporate high-rise hotel. The grounds are impeccably well maintained, with walkways that meander among tropical greenery and such exotica as the rare "dragon tree" (imported from China in the 1920s). The Del lives up to its reputation by sweating the details so that pampered guests can take their ease. Most of them seem to realize that lying out on a breezy deck in a chaise lounge, with an icy drink and a gaggle of musicians tooting jazz on a small bandstand, is what a vacation is all about.

If you can afford it, Coronado is the ideal vacation town, as tourism is the only industry in what is otherwise an upscale bedroom and retirement community. There's evidence of money everywhere. Even the sand on Coronado's beaches is speckled with what looks like gold dust, glittering every time it's overwashed by a wandering wave. The feel-good feeling radiates outward from the Hotel del Coronado to the downtown area, where a graceful S curve carries motorists through a squeaky-clean shopping district of modestly upscale shops and restaurants along Orange Avenue. Coronado's cafés and stores service the needs of locals and tourists alike. Everyone casually strolls, bikes, or in-line skates along the sun-dappled streets in search of swimwear, surfboards, frozen yogurt, and real estate.

Continue away from the beach along Fourth Avenue and soon you'll be headed out of town via the narrow San Diego–Coronado Bridge, a breathtaking engineering marvel that arches like a roller coaster and makes a 90-degree turn at mid-span. It's high enough that navy destroyers can pass beneath it. It also attracts would-be jumpers, judging from signs lining the bridge that offer a phone number for suicide counseling. Incidentally, they stopped charging a toll to cross the San Diego–Coronado Bridge as of June 27, 2002.

The naval presence is everywhere. The North Island Naval Air Station claims to be the birthplace of naval aviation (in 1911). From its airstrip, Charles Lindbergh took off for New York, where he embarked upon his famous transatlantic flight in 1927. Today, it occupies 2,500 acres and employs over 30,000 personnel. A few miles south, recruits are trained at the U.S. Naval Amphibious Base, along San Diego Bay.

Beaches

Heading north from Imperial Beach along Silver Strand Boulevard, you begin to see the pipe rooftops of Coronado Cays, clustered togeth-

Map of Southern California—Page 9

er so tightly that the development looks like one continuous orange roof. Along the south side of the bay is the South Bay Marine Biological Study Area, a wildlife refuge that affords visitors a close look at a wetland environment. A nature trail leads into the study area, where bird-watching is excellent. On the ocean side of the highway, **Silver Strand State Beach**, a long beach occupying a skinny splinter of land no more than two football fields wide, connects Imperial Beach with Coronado. In season, RVs are jammed together as close as possible while still allowing their occupants to open the doors. The 2.5-mile beach can take on all comers, with parking for more than 1,000 vehicles.

Being so far south, the waters here are as swimmable as any in California from the standpoint of temperature, topping off at around 70 degrees by late summer. However, it's less swimmable than many from a pollution standpoint. The beach has recovered from El Niño-inflicted erosion in the late '90s and is again wide, clean, and expansive. On smog-free days, the views in all directions are stunning.

Coronado Shores Beach fills the breach between Silver Strand State Beach and Coronado City Beach. It's accessible via the Coronado Shores condo development—a ghastly, humongous array of seaside towers—and is widely used by surfers, swimmers, shell collectors, and anglers.

Coronado City Beach (a.k.a. Central Beach) runs for 1.5 miles, from the Hotel del Coronado up to the airstrip at the North Island Naval Air Station. The beach is wide and flat, dimpled with half-formed dunes. The north end of the beach is locally known as Dog Beach, for obvious reasons. To our inquiring eyes on a recent visit, the early-summer waves were tame, and the beachgoers were similarly benign. A wall of boulders stands where the beach meets Ocean Boulevard, which has plentiful on-street parking. In Coronado parking doesn't seem to be as horrific a problem as it does elsewhere in Southern California beach towns. On a gorgeous Saturday over a Fourth of July weekend, we found metered, on-street parking both available and reasonably priced at a quarter an hour. A good omen. Away from the beachfront, between Sixth and Ninth Streets along Orange Avenue, free street parking borders a lovely green park.

Beaches, in fact, abound on both the bay and the ocean—28 miles of them in all. Renting a bike is a good way to check them out, as 15 miles of bike paths wind their way around Coronado and down toward Silver Strand State Beach. Bikes and 'blades can be rented at **Bikes and Beyond** (1201 First Avenue, 619/435-7180) and **Little Sam's Island and Beach Fun** (1343 Orange Avenue, 619/435-4068).

Bunking Down

On the outdoor deck of the **Hotel del Coronado** (1500 Orange Avenue, 619/435-6611, $$$$), we heard a quintet playing a mix of blues and jazz. An elderly black man was singing, "I got the blues." He must have been the only one within earshot who did, as the crowd—a well-heeled lot who were either reclining on chaise lounges amid a sea of red-and-white umbrellas, playing tennis, or swimming in the Olympic pool—were having the time of their lives. A food kiosk offered "super burgers," "yummy hot dogs," and "healthy chicken breasts." It was quite a sight: a herd of happy people renting a small piece of paradise, basking in the midday sun. On another deck Frank Sinatra could be heard belting out the words "I'm king of the hill, top of the heap, A Number One. . . ." His lyrics were reaching the right audience, bathing the upscale resort crowd in positive reinforcement.

The Del claims to be the largest full-service beachfront resort on the Pacific Coast. We've certainly seen nothing in our travels to dispute that. The resort encompasses 689 rooms, and every one is different. Built in 11 months according to plans that were improvised day by day, the hotel is one of the architectural wonders of the Western world. At the time of its construction, it was the largest electrically lighted structure outside New York City. Four hundred rooms are originals, dating from 1888; the rest are in a wing constructed in the 1960s. Try to stay in the main part of the hotel. This four-story marvel rambles around in a rectangle that surrounds a green courtyard filled with palm trees and brightly colored flowers. The on-premises amenities include two giant outdoor pools, six tennis courts, volleyball nets, and a croquet green. Just be advised that you will pay dearly for all this privileged access, as oceanfront rooms start at around $480 per night.

More impressive than the statistics is the feeling of informal elegance that fills the place. Rambling around the Del is like exploring a rich old relative's mansion. If you come here, you may be living above your station (as we most definitely were), but you'll be made to feel right at home. "You've stayed with us before?" asks a bellhop as you arrive, as if assuming you've returned to renew an old friendship. The hotel's brick-red turrets and gleaming white Victorian exterior make it look less like a hotel than a castle. Indeed, it is a national landmark that has played host to 11 U.S. presidents. Hollywood seems to like the place, too. *Some Like It Hot,* starring Marilyn Monroe, was filmed here, and the Emerald City in *The Wizard of Oz* was patterned after the Hotel del Coronado's castle-like design.

Across the street is the mission-style **El Cordova** (1351 Orange Avenue, 619/435-4131, $$$), whose 40 rooms are like small apartments, tucked into stairwells around a brick courtyard of ground-level shops and restaurants. Originally a private mansion built in 1902, when the area was still relatively rural, El Cordova opened as a hotel in 1930 and is currently maintained as one of the most homey and nicely appointed suite-style hotels we've encountered in our coastal travels.

Over on the bay, the former mansion of sugar baron John D. Spreckels is the centerpiece of the **Glorietta Bay Inn** (1630 Glorietta Boulevard, 619/435-3101, $$$), a relaxed but regal inn. Many rooms overlook the bay, while others face out on gardens. The setting is quiet, yet downtown Coronado is just a few walkable blocks away. The staff here is unusually friendly and attentive. We're forever in their debt for finding and forwarding to us a computer memory card we left behind on one visit.

Coastal Cuisine

The best and most neighborly place to start the day is **Coronado Bakery** (1206 Ocean Avenue, 619/435-9272, $), which is a locals' favorite, and one of ours, too. You've got to try the "glazed rings" (doughnuts) or muffins (e.g., pumpkin raisin walnut bran) and watch the world jog by as you ingest delicious calories from a streetside table.

We had our first encounter with healthy, low-fat Mexican cuisine (no, that's not necessarily an oxymoron) in Coronado, courtesy of a fast-food chain called **La Salsa!** (1360 Orange Avenue, 619/435-7778, $). The legend printed on the beverage cups relates the chain's culinary philosophy: "No can openers. No microwaves. No freezers. No lard. Skinless chicken. Lean steak." We ordered vegetable tacos and watched the cook carefully slice onions and tomatoes, grill and place them on a soft taco, slather on black beans and top it all off with shredded cheese, lettuce, avocado wedges, and fresh cilantro. Customers can ladle on salsa from a salsa bar, choosing from four grades of heat. Although the California Burrito has 18 grams of fat (it's the avocado's fault), by Mexican food standards even this is lean cuisine. La Salsa! has franchises all over Southern California, including locations in La Jolla, Pacific Beach, and Newport Beach. Coastal travelers craving a Mexican meal that won't send them down the road to a coronary bypass should keep this name handy.

Map of Southern California—Page 9

Good-quality Mexican food in a sit-down environment is served at **Miguel's Cocina** (1351 Orange Avenue, 619/437-5237, $$), in the courtyard of El Cordova Hotel. It's known for fish tacos, which we can unhesitatingly recommend. Also very good are calamari torta (sautéed squid steak) and chicken torta (charbroiled free-range chicken), served on a torta roll with avocado, tomato, lettuce, and sauces.

Another reasonably priced and down-to-earth Coronado eatery is the **Fish Company** (1007 C Avenue, 619/435-3945, $$), a fresh-fish market and outdoor café with catch-of-the-day specials and a sushi bar.

On the bayside is the locally popular **Bay Beach Cafe** (1201 First Street, 619/435-4900, $$). Set among a dockside bazaar called Ferry Landing Marketplace, it looks out on the San Diego skyline. It's especially good at dinner, when seafood specials turn up on the menu. Incidentally, the San Diego Bay Ferry shuttles commuters between San Diego's B Street Pier, Coronado's Ferry Landing Marketplace, and the Naval Air Station North Island.

At the upper end of the scale is **Azzura Point** at Loews Coronado Bay Resort (4000 Coronado Bay Road, 619/424-4477, $$$$), which is posh and expensive. You'll pay $25–60 per person for its culinary innovation and world-class views. Though Azzura Point lost an executive chef to the newly opened Nine-Ten in La Jolla, it remains one of the choicest "big occasion" restaurants in the San Diego area. Try the salmon in black truffle sauce or 10-spice ahi tuna. **Chez Loma French Bistro** (1132 Loma Avenue, 619/435-0661, $$$) puts a French twist on fresh California ingredients in a romantic setting. It has the added advantage of history, occupying a landmark building dating from 1889.

Over at the Hotel del Coronado, the **Crown-Coronet Room** (1500 Orange Avenue, 619/435-6611, $$$) has served kings, presidents, movie stars, sheiks, and tycoons from all over the world. It is the largest of six restaurants on the premises. The room is as long as a football field, and

the ceiling is 33 feet high, making it one of the largest freestanding wood structures in North America. At ground level, the menu tends toward "progressive continental" preparations, and the panoramic view is as delectable as the food. The most formal dining room at the Del is the **Prince of Wales Room** (1500 Orange Avenue, 619/435-6611, $$$$). We were advised of the dress code by our bellhop: "California formal—which means coat and tie and shoes."

Finally, a popular afternoon or after-dinner stop is **MooTime Creamery** (1025 Orange Avenue, 619/435-2422, $), a retro dessert diner with a life-size Elvis Presley sculpture out front. It also has a smaller unit inside the Hotel del Coronado.

Night Moves

Don't come to Coronado expecting nightlife. In fact, you can expect to be largely free of it. (Sometimes this is a blessing.) Your choices on the Coronado side of the San Diego–Coronado Bridge are pretty much limited to a handful of Irish pubs along Orange Avenue. The busiest of these is **McP's Irish Pub & Grill** (1107 Orange Avenue, 619/435-5280), which has been around since 1982 (it was founded by a former Navy SEAL) and bills itself as "Coronado's hottest night spot." By the standards of low-key Coronado, McP's does get fairly raucous.

For some serious whoopee head to San Diego over the bridge, which deposits you on Harbor Drive. Then proceed north to Fifth Avenue, which leads into downtown San Diego and its bustling Gaslamp Quarter district. There you'll find an abundance of restaurants and nightclubs.

For More Information

Coronado Visitors Bureau, 1047 B Avenue, Coronado, CA 92118-3418, 619/437-8788 or 800/622-8300, website: www.coronado.ca.us; Coronado Chamber of Commerce, 1224 10th Street, Coronado, CA 92118, 619/435-9260

Map of San Diego County—Page 10

San Diego County

Point Loma

Heading out to Point Loma from Ocean Beach, the land rises—first gently, then steeply—until you're high above the beaches and the bay. From this promontory the ocean glitters like a diamond choker and the cliffs take on a deep red hue at dusk. The area of Point Loma that enjoys these views, roughly between Ocean Beach and the Naval Ocean System Center, looks to be one of the choicest places to live in San Diego.

For a free glimpse of some of the most dramatic scenery on the peninsula, drive along Sunset Cliffs Boulevard from Point Loma Avenue to Ladera Street. This area is known as Sunset Cliffs Park; rather than an actual picnic-and-Frisbee green space, it is a series of parking areas and dirt trails that run along cliffs, allowing you to scuttle down like a crab to the edge of a heart-stopping drop-off. Some determined surfers and divers make their way down the steep paths to the sandy and rocky coves below. Be cautious, however; cliffs here are succumbing to wave-driven erosion at an alarming rate. Several parking turnouts have been closed, and signs at other turnouts warn visitors to keep a safe distance.

To continue out Point Loma, turn off Sunset Cliffs Boulevard onto Hill Street—an aptly named vertical grade—and then hang a right onto Catalina Boulevard/Highway 209. This becomes Cabrillo Memorial Drive and leads out to **Cabrillo National Monument** at the tip of the peninsula. The landform narrows as you pass through the gates of the Naval Ocean System Center and past a large military cemetery filled with small white crosses. This is **Fort Rosecrans National Cemetery,** and it spreads along the rolling contours of the peninsula— as tranquil a resting place as Arlington National Cemetery.

At **Cabrillo National Monument,** a fee of $5 per car will gain access to a stone statue of the Spanish conquistador and explorer Juan Rodríguez Cabrillo; views over San Diego Bay and Coronado; and the **Old Point Loma Lighthouse,** a harbor light and coastal beacon that illuminated the coast from 1855 to 1891. A skylighted visitor center houses exhibits on Cabrillo's voyage and a well-stocked bookstore and gift shop.

For hiking and nature study, there's a one-mile (one-way) trail on the bay side and tidepools on the ocean side. Also on the bay side, inside the crook formed where Point Loma bends south, are two islands created in the '60s from dredge spoil. ("Dredge spoil" is the stuff hauled off a bay or ocean floor to deepen a channel for boat traffic.) The resulting sandbanks were christened **Shelter Island** and **Harbor Island,** and developers poured millions into building high-rise resorts, restaurants, and yacht basins. Familiar hotel and motel chains (Sheraton, Best Western, Holiday Inn) have perched upon these artificial paradises. Both are slanted to boaters and convention crowds, though Shelter Island has the decided advantage of a sandy beach.

For More Information

Peninsula Chamber of Commerce, P.O. Box 7018, San Diego, CA 92107, 619/223-9767

Map of Southern California—Page 9

San Diego County

Ocean Beach

In the medical profession it's a maxim that a patient's condition either improves or worsens over time, which is another way of saying that nothing remains the same for very long. The same bit of wisdom holds true for beach towns. Having taken the pulse of the California coast at regular intervals over the past quarter century, we've discovered that it's possible to come back to a community after several years' absence and sense immediately whether it's gone up or down. Ocean Beach, happily, has gone up. During our earliest visits we found it to be a low-rent slum by the sea. In an earlier book, we bluntly described it as "a sub-Coney Island maze of dirty streets, litter-strewn parking lots, sun-faded storefronts, and rough-looking bars." That no longer is true. Ocean Beach—or "O.B." for short—has gotten a much-needed makeover. And while no one will mistake it for La Jolla just yet, it's a comfortably funky beach town with just enough upscale refurbishing to inspire visitors to stick around rather than hurry away.

That is to say, Ocean Beach (population 28,000) has improved in much-needed ways, but not to the point that it has become unrecognizable. The community is a mix of the raunchy, the respectable and the alternative. On one side of a street you'll see a decrepit bungalow occupied by ragtag post-hippies drinking and grunting at one another in the yard. On the other side will sit a well-tended house with a neatly clipped lawn and a new coat of paint. The two opposing sensibilities—upscale and downtrodden—are literally staring each other down, though apparently coexisting.

The heart of Ocean Beach is along Newport Avenue from Sunset Cliffs Boulevard till it ends at the beach. What used to be an ugly array of failing liquor stores and five-and-dimes now runs the gamut from decent, lively burger joints for the surfer crowd to trendy restaurants with neon-scripted names. The sidewalks are clean and litter-free. Where was once a liquor store is now a fitness center. Even the local tattoo parlor seems vaguely respectable, offering custom tattooing "in the San Diego tradition." Aqua-colored tiles have been glued in a line along the curb with the names of local businesses inscribed on them.

Cute. Likable. Two words we never thought we'd associate with Ocean Beach.

Beaches

Ocean Beach has gone to the dogs. We mean that literally and, oddly enough, positively. Where Voltaire Street runs out at the beach is **Ocean Beach Park.** At the north end is Dog Beach, a stretch of sand given over to the frolics of our canine friends. The sign reads: "Welcome to Dog Beach. This is a dog 'free' beach. Leashes are not required." (Even for Rottweilers and pit bulls?) Dogs do indeed have the run of the place. Their owners stand off to the side like helpless chaperones at a party gone haywire. The canine revelers scamper and yap; dig holes as if tunneling to China; sniff one another, fore and aft; relieve themselves indiscriminately; and run in and out of the water with tails wagging. In other words, they generally behave no differently than humans at the beach. We saw no fights, no snarling territorial disputes—just a happy pack of mutts and purebreds alike set free by their owners to romp to their heart's content. We should all get along so well. A P.S. on water quality, however; it's awful off Dog Beach, so leave the scampering in the surf to the dogs.

Just up from Ocean Beach Park is **Ocean Beach City Beach,** a mile-long strand of municipal beach with the pier as its heart and soul. The ocean itself is unquestionably dangerous, due to both rough surf and polluted water. According to the head of lifeguard operations for San Diego County, "My impression is that Imperial Beach and Ocean Beach

O.B. Rules

Ocean Beach (O.B. for short) has long been the red-headed stepchild of San Diego's beach brood, left to its own devices along with the transients, bikers, punks, leather-skinned old-timers, starving students, and unemployed roustabouts who call it home. In recent years, as upscale coastal development opportunities have dwindled elsewhere, O.B. has found itself going toe-to-toe with the gentrifiers in order to keep its funky, bohemian identity intact. We are happy to report that this scrimmage has reached a sort of Mexican standoff, with the seedier aspects of O.B. having been made only slightly less visible.

Indeed, the let-it-all-hang-out spirit of O.B. still remains proudly intact. We witnessed evidence of this at sunset one night on a recent trip. Grabbing a free parking spot in a municipal lot at the end of Newport Avenue (free parking in Southern California?!), we briskly walked out to the end of the longest pier on the West Coast just in time to see the golden orb of the sun melt into the mouth of the Pacific Ocean. All around us on this chilly May evening were town residents, sitting in groups, chatting and laughing amiably or casting lines into the briny deep in hopes of snagging one last quivering fish before dark. At the precise moment the sun fell into the oceanic soup, the groups all became reverently silent. They hooted and applauded appreciatively and then reentered their conversations and activities.

It dawned on us, walking back to the car, that O.B. is the sort of place that, were we wizards or deities, we'd like to distribute every 100 miles along Amer-

and the south end of Black's Beach are the most treacherous in San Diego. They have the strongest rip currents that are consistently pulling." Don't say we didn't warn you. Ocean Beach really took it on the chin from El Niño. Happily, the dredged sand deposited on it has restored Ocean Beach to an acceptable width and has stayed in place (for now, anyway).

Surfers congregate around the sturdy, T-shaped concrete pier. At 1,971 feet, it's the longest on the West Coast. Midway out is a café serving hot coffee and good, hearty food. We walked out on the pier and watched a group of surfers waiting for the right wave. To us, watching surfers in action is nearly as much fun as surfing itself. They bob up and down on the swells in their wet suits, making small talk until . . . here comes a monster. Just be-

fore it starts to curl, they steer into it, emerging astride their boards in a shower of flying foam while negotiating the sloping face of the spilling wave with perfect body English. Before it breaks on the beach, the surfers U-turn out of it and resume a belly-down position on the board, paddling back out to wait on another ride.

For the adventurous, the south end of Ocean Beach, along treacherous Sunset Cliffs Boulevard, offers numerous breathtaking views of the rocky coastline. A dirt parking lot at the end of Cornish Drive and a stairwell at the end of Ladera Street lead to a small rocky beach. The area is known as **Sunset Cliffs Park.** Various esoteric and locally known surfing spots, bearing such colorful names as "North Garbage" and "Bird Shit," can be found along

Map of Southern California—Page 9

ica's coastline. Places like Coronado and La Jolla, though congenial and nurturing to our spirit in different ways, do not quite give us the sociocultural jolt of reality (in the best sense of the word) that O.B. does.

For example, halfway out to the end of the pier is the **Pier Cafe**, a ramshackle little room filled with locals joking with the waitress and the cook. Beers and fish platters were on every table. Next door, the pier's fishing concession offered this seemingly unbeatable deal: for $10.95, you can fish all day. This price includes the use of a fishing pole, plus tackle and bait. To put this full day's worth of simple, honest pleasure into perspective, consider that the same amount spent at the Hotel del Coronado would net you little more than a croissant and a pat of butter.

As we walked the pier, a few yards ahead of us strolled one of O.B.'s many unmoneyed and, likely, vagrant souls. He was sporting a jacket that looked like it had been stapled together from tarpaper, spent shingles, and carpet remnants. Yet he was not slinking, looking sheepish or ashamed. This dude had a very determined, bouncy stride. Like one of Robert Crumb's cartoon figures, he was truckin' along as if he had places to go, people to meet, and dumpsters to root around in.

From here, we wandered into **South Beach Bar and Grill,** which is always packed at sundown—especially on weekends. Wait your turn and you'll get inside quickly enough. We ended our evening with an hour's pleasurable browsing at a used record store, where we purchased discs by Green Day and Phish that entertained us for the remainder of our trip. Thus, we carried a little bit of O.B. around with us on our journey up the California coast.

---

the length of Sunset Cliffs Boulevard between Point Loma Avenue and Ladera Street.

Bunking Down

The choices are limited and, cool as Ocean Beach may be for a day trip, you probably are better off staying elsewhere in San Diego. Still, the **Ocean Beach Motel** (5080 Newport Avenue, 619/223-7191, $) is a surfer's dream: plain, utilitarian, and cheap. The **Ocean Villa Motel** (5142 West Point Loma Boulevard, 619/224-3481, $) is a bit nicer and takes pains to enforce a "no pets/no parties" policy.

Coastal Cuisine

Set in a typical bungalow that is the architectural trademark of Ocean Beach, **The Bungalow** (4996 West Point Loma Boulevard,

619/224-2884, $$) offers French/Continental cuisine at moderate prices. The house specialty is duck, but fish and chicken dishes are good as well.

At the other end of the scale, **Hodad's** (5010 Newport Avenue, 619/224-4623, $) claims to serve the world's best burgers, proudly hanging a McDonald's-dissing sign that reads: "Under 99 billion sold." Another sign conveys the hang-loose atmosphere of the place: "No shirt, no shoes, no problem." The burgers are great messy slabs of beef stuck between a big bun and served in a basket. One table was fashioned from the sawed-off front of a VW bus. A buzzing hive of surfers chomps away at all hours, making a racket while gnawing on burgers the size of boogie boards.

Map of San Diego County—Page 10

Night Moves

Across the street from Hodad's, the **South Beach Bar and Grill** (5059 Newport Avenue, 619/523-6400) is a great place to eat and/or down a few. We downed a few, eyeing the action on the pier from barstools pulled up to the picture window. The brew of choice is Hale's Pale Ale (say that three times fast), poured frosty cold from the tap. The restaurant serves fresh grilled thresher shark tacos, Baja fish tacos, and ceviche cocktail, among a full menu of other tasty seafood appetizers and entrées. While we were there, Bob Marley was playing on the sound system, while the San Diego Padres were on the boob tube. At a stool adjacent to ours, a proto-typical beach girl with sun-damaged hair and reddened face reverently remarked to her male consort, "The ocean—what an amazing thing." We toasted this truism with raised mugs as the last rays of the day glinted off the distant waves.

Two spots for live music in Ocean Beach are **Winston's** (1921 Bacon Street, 619/222-3802) and **Dream Street** (2228 Bacon Street, 619/222-8131). You might hear rock, reggae, punk, or cover bands with names like Downpour and Fortress.

For More Information

Peninsula Chamber of Commerce, P.O. Box 7018, San Diego, CA 92107, 619/223-9767

Mission Beach

Mission Beach and Pacific Beach—neighboring communities welded together by paved, three-mile Ocean Front Walk—complement one another. This stretch of San Diego's shoreline epitomizes what a trip to a Southern California beach ought to be. Mission Beach, with a population of around 6,000, is the smaller of the two fraternal beach towns. Each is a "Community of San Diego," which is to say, they're not technically autonomous, though in reality they seem quite disconnected from San Diego proper.

It is not until you've made your way to the Mission Beach/Pacific Beach strand that you actually feel as if you're entering the pumping aorta of a true California beach town. You know, the kind you've always heard about: skateboards, roller skates, and in-line skates, volleyball on the beach, surfboards, surf shops, surf bars, surf bums, surf bunnies, and more bronzed flesh than you'll see on any 10 MTV Spring Break specials. Mission Beach is a great, relaxed party town where college students from UC San Diego and other nearby schools live the beach life to its fullest, majoring in sun, surf, sand, suds, and good times, in addition to whatever it is they're purportedly studying up the hill in La Jolla. Our observation is that surfers and other twenty-somethings are happily non-materialistic, living in the outdoors beside the ocean with a few pairs of cutoff jeans and a diet of cheap tacos and beer. Who needs more?

Mission Beach, though limited in area as a peninsula, is wall-to-wall real estate. In that sense, it is indistinguishable from Pacific Beach. Added to the eclectic mix of types who come here—from families and preppies to punks and the homeless—is a veneer of understated civility and good, clean fun that wasn't always evident before. This renaissance was symbolically ushered in by the 1990 reopening of **Belmont Park,** an antique amusement park and shopping area with a mountainous red, white, and blue roller coaster (the 77-year-old, 73-foot-high Giant Dipper) that defines the revived spirits of the town. More moms, pops, and kids are coming to Mission Beach, yet it still retains a tolerant attitude toward fun in the sun. This is important, as no less an authority than Sir Kenneth Clark proclaimed tolerance to be the key element of all civilizations.

Perhaps the scene around here takes its re-

Map of Southern California—Page 9

laxed cue from the beat cops. They wear shorts, ride bikes, mingle, laugh, and eat ice cream cones like everyone else. They don't needlessly provoke confrontations; in fact, they spend a good deal of time defusing them. Even the homeless have found a haven of sorts in Mission Bay Park, a nice swath of green across from Belmont Park where they loll on the grass next to their shopping carts. Tanned redder than rare roast beef, they chat, drink from bags, and pass out without fanfare. Again, tolerance is the key.

Two different waterfronts are available to visitors here: the ocean and the bay. They offering opposing but equally appealing beach styles. The oceanfront was, is, and always will be *Animal House* and *American Graffiti* rolled into one. Mission Beach is not unlike Mardi Gras, except that it goes on for months instead of days. The human parade provides endless hours of spectator sport available only in Southern California. Strolling Ocean Front Walk, the paved oceanfront promenade that runs along Mission and Pacific Beaches, on any summer day is like walking along fraternity row during Rush Week. Shirtless guys clutch tall beers and lean off balconies of their rented apartments, passing judgment on the human parade below or squirting one another with water guns, while bikini-clad beauties casually lean back in chaise lounges and toy with mixed drinks and sunscreen, lathering their lithe bodies while the guys leer and yelp and yahoo. We saw a pet pig on someone's patio, strutting and wagging its tail like a dog. Meanwhile, one sun-bronzed fellow calmly stood atop his skateboard while two leashed, panting dogs gamely pulled him down the boardwalk like miniature huskies.

The scene on Mission Bay is more middle-class than back-of-the-class. Executive types and their families play badminton on putting green–type grass along the water. Barbecue grills are on display, as are American flags. Catamarans are lashed to the dock or pulled onto the sand. Another three-mile paved track, Bay Side Walk, runs along the water, but the pace back here is more leisurely, less chaotic. It is most popular with joggers, who no doubt appreciate the safety factor. The houses and villas are a pleasant and eclectic blend of architectural styles, and they're fun to study while strolling beside the bay.

Our advice to novice visitors is to leave the car at the motel and rent bikes at one of the outfitters on Ocean Front Walk. Mission Beach has devoted only a limited amount of its precious open space to parking. If you do drive in Mission Beach, try to park on the bayfront, at Mission Bay Aquatic Center. To get there from Mission Boulevard (the main drag), turn east toward the bay on Santa Clara Place and follow it into the lot. It is within walking distance of the beach, as well as a host of great bars and restaurants.

Beaches

South Mission Beach begins at the channel that leads into San Diego Bay. The beach is especially wide and suitable for volleyball here. In fact, this is a very recreation oriented beach, with basketball courts and permissible areas to play "Over the Line." The central axis in **Mission Beach** is at the foot of Ventura Street, by Belmont Park, the main lifeguard stand, and a cluster of shops and restaurants. Mission Beach has designated areas for board surfing, bodysurfing, and swimming. Water conditions are updated on a board outside the lifeguard station (e.g., "Lots of rip currents and deep holes on the inside of the surf zone. Ask us where to swim."). Mission Beach runs up to, and into, Pacific Beach. It's neither clear nor important where one ends and the other begins, as it is all one happy boardwalked two-mile strand, from Mission Bay Channel to Crystal Pier.

On Ocean Front Walk, a human comedy that would have amused the French writer Honore de Balzac glides past on bikes, in-line

Map of San Diego County—Page 10

California Coastal Commission and Public Beach Access

The only qualification for a beach's inclusion in this book is public access—that is, the public must legally be able to reach it. Technically, that part of the beach shoreward of the mean high-tide line is classified as "public trust land," meaning that it is held in trust by the government on behalf of the public. In other words, what is commonly called the "wet sand" part of the beach is owned by and open to all. This concept dates back to English common law. The hitch is getting onto the beach, which often involves crossing private property.

Making beaches accessible is the official business of the California Coastal Commission (CCC), established after the passage of Proposition 20 (the Coastal Initiative) in 1972. The enactment of the California Coastal Act in 1976 accorded the CCC permanent status as a state agency. In terms of mission, the legislature declared that the CCC's "basic goals" are to "maximize public access to and along the coast, and maximize public recreational opportunities in the coastal zone consistent with sound resources conservation principles and constitutionally protected rights of private property owners."

During the past three decades, the CCC has managed to open beach access points all along the California coast. One strategy they routinely employed in the past required public easements as a virtual precondition for granting building or remodeling permits to landowners in the coastal zone. This was challenged in a well-publicized court case (*Nollan v. California Coastal Commission;* see sidebar in the Ventura County chapter) and struck down by the U.S. Supreme Court in 1987. In its wake, the CCC has had to proceed more cautiously, and the number of new access points has shrunk to a trickle.

Fortunately, the state owns 283 miles of the California coastline (roughly one-quarter of its length), and those are maintained as state parks and beaches. Add to that the miles of coast owned by federal, county and municipal governments, and approximately half of California's 1,100-mile coastline is public. That's the good news. The bad news is that much more of this marvelous coastline should be open to all. In our view, no one should "own" a beach.

We tracked down Linda Locklin, Coastal Access Program Manager for the California Coastal Commission, to talk about the state of public-access efforts on California's beaches in the new millennium.

Are new public beach access points being added often or occasionally?
Occasionally. Unfortunately, it's pretty slow. Probably no more than one a year. It's not something that's constantly happening.

For a period of time, it did seem to be happening with more regularity.
Yes and no. The big changes come when the state has money and we go out

Map of Southern California—Page 9

and buy or acquire property through various programs. That is really cyclical, relating to funding that the state has. The state has not been in good shape for a while, so we haven't been buying a whole lot. Beyond that, you might also read or hear about the commission conditioning individual landowners through our regulatory program to record public access easements on their property. Over 1,300 of those have been recorded over the years. But taking them from a legal document to opening them up is a very slow process.

So a lot of recorded easements haven't yet been formally identified as public beach access points yet?
Well, it depends on the type of easement. They are called "offers to dedicate"— OTDs is the acronym we use—and generally they fall into two kinds. There's the lateral kind, which is parallel to the shoreline. Many of those are part of a sandy beach and are already being used by the general public. Ninety percent of our easements are laterals, and at least half of those are segments of sandy beach that people already recreate on, picnic on, or whatever. The other kind— the 10 percent that get the most press and are the most important—are called verticals. They are pathways between houses or across property that lead from the road to the beach. Those are the ones we work really hard to open up.

What about the case Nollan v. California Coastal Commission? It's a landmark case in the property-rights movement.
That case, of course, was very significant to the commission. What it really did was raise the bar very high as to the kinds of findings we have to make before we can impose a public-access requirement. It's made it a lot more difficult, meaning that the percentage of OTDs we can require as part of a project are significantly less than they were before Nollan. So we don't get the OTDs in nearly the numbers we used to.

What parts of the state are in greatest need of more and better public access to beaches?
The two areas we're most concerned with increasing public access are Malibu and Mendocino County. Statewide, Malibu has the greatest number of people that go to the beach, and there are simply not enough access points for them to utilize. Mendocino is a very large county with somewhat limited public access points. Those are the two we focus on.

How many miles of beach in California are publicly owned?
We say half is public and half is private. Beyond that, while a beach might be private in the sense that the upland homeowner owns down to the mean high-tide line, the sandy beach is in many cases used by the public. So while the sandy beach is privately owned, technically and legally, the public is using it.

Have there been any substantive changes to the California Coastal Act since its passage?
No. There's always some horrific bill pending to punch big holes in it, but there haven't been any significant changes.

skates, shopping carts, and anything else to which wheels can be affixed. Somehow they don't collide, even though all are traveling at different speeds. In the midst of all this sauntered an old crone with a Hefty sack full of returnable cans and bottles, riffling through the trash cans for more. A gang of sun- and booze-battered longhairs of late-'60s vintage came riding around the corner on low-to-the-ground banana bikes that looked like something our sisters played on when they were six. It is all in the spirit of Mission Beach, a town where the laugh track runs continuously.

One summer day, we waded along the ocean's edge for a good distance. The water, at first cold to our feet, felt good and warmed quickly. Mission Beach, incidentally, appears friendly to surfers of all skill levels. The surf is more forgiving to beginners than La Jolla's storied beaches, but under the right swell conditions, Mission Beach also presents challenges for experts.

Bunking Down

The rents on the bayfront are higher than those on the oceanfront, but the noise factor has to be considered. You do want to go to sleep eventually, right? We saw a cozy little cottage on the bay side that rented for $750 a month, but next door was a chic *Architectural Digest* centerfold that was going for closer to $750 a week. The scuttlebutt is that all the good, affordable ones are booked months, if not years, in advance, usually by people who faithfully return each summer. We can't blame them. For rentals in the area, contact **Discover Pacific Beach** (910 Grand Avenue, Suite 113, Pacific Beach, 858/273-3303).

This leaves motels, of which there aren't many in Mission Beach. The largest and best option is the **Catamaran Resort Hotel** (3999 Mission Boulevard, 858/488-1081, $$$), with 313 units, many with bay views. There's a safe bay beach at the back, where you can rent sailboats and get windsurfing lessons, and there's a tropical pool on the premises. Things occasionally get hopping at the on-premises lounge,

tastefully named the Cannibal Bar, if you're looking for a little après du sail.

Coastal Cuisine

As if to reinforce the twin themes of fun and nourishment, the best places to eat in Mission Beach are often the best places to drink, too. Our favorites are **Guava Beach Bar and Grill** (3714 Mission Boulevard, 858/488-6688, $$) and **Santa Clara Grill** (3704 Mission Boulevard, 858/488-9484, $$), side by side one block back from the beach. With doelike innocence, the friendly waitresses at both places hustle about, making small talk and refilling drinks within seconds of last sips. Their menus are also similar, with a Mexican flavor to most of the staples and all items reasonably priced and perfectly unfancy. Guava Beach offers "Baja Bargains" every day, happy-hour specials like the Cabo quesadilla with sour cream, spicy Rosarito fish taco, and brie and calypso salsa quesadilla.

Santa Clara is equally good-humored, with the added dimension of a patio from which you can easily eavesdrop on the packs of baying revelers on the sidewalk behind the palm trees. Here are excerpts from the menu: "If you want something that is not on the menu, ask for it. The waiter will discuss it with the dishwasher. If you must sing, please refer to the *Anderson Book of Etiquette* as to the type of music best suited for an establishment specializing in great beach food. Pink Floyd and Devo are not acceptable. Whistling is permitted."

Night Moves

There are two camps in Mission Beach's nightlife: those who are preparing to party and those who are already partying heartily. The prelude to a party animal's evening in Mission Beach is to watch the sunset from one of several Ocean Front Walk bars. The hottest one during our expedition was **'Canes** (3105 Ocean Front Walk, 858/488-1780). If you can find the roller coaster, you can find 'Canes, which practically sits in its shadow. Formerly one of the legendary

Map of Southern California—Page 9

Red Onion clubs and then a popular place called Chillers (we've imbibed at both incarnations), 'Canes carries on the tradition with live rock and roll. The club regularly brings in great national acts, too. We kicked ourselves for missing, by one day, an appearance by NOFX and Rancid, two of the more intelligent punk bands rattling the cage.

The **Open Bar** (4302 Mission Boulevard, 858/270-3221) is one block off the beach, but equally popular with locals for preludes to serious partying. Ditto for the **Pennant** (2893 Mission Boulevard, 858/488-1671), at the south end of the peninsula. It is a sloppy hut with a wooden bar and booths, plastic cups of draft beer, boisterous and sometimes slurred conversations.

Acapulco Joe's Cantina (3840 Mission Boulevard, 858/488-2340) is yet another friendly tavern that also serves full meals. Next door is one of our new favorites, the **Liars' Club** (3844 Mission Boulevard, 858/488-2340). Its jukebox and draft beer selections have attracted a loyal local following. Most Mission Beachers who don't hunker down for the duration at one of these spots end up heading to the even more boisterous bars in Pacific Beach.

For More Information

San Diego Visitor Information Center, 2688 East Mission Bay Drive, San Diego, CA 92109, 858/276-8200 or 800/422-4749, website: www.info san diego.com

Mission Bay

Tucked behind the peninsula of Mission Beach, Mission Bay is a world unto itself and a beach haven that, though popular, remains nicely out of the way. The beaches here are on the bay, of course, and many visitors come to sail out on the water, not splash about the calm shoreline. This 4,600-acre aquatic park—the largest on the West Coast—can be accessed via numerous ramps, landings, and marinas to the north and west and on Fiesta Isle, the largest of the two man-made islands in the bay itself. Watery activities pursued here include fishing, sailing, windsurfing, water-skiing, and swimming, and the sight of people doing all of these things at once gives the scenic and unpolluted bay a sort of relaxed elegance, not unlike a Seurat painting of a scene along the Seine.

Mission Bay is also a living lesson in democracy. Everyone comes here, from wealthy bon vivants, relaxing on deck in a sailor suit and cap, to camping anglers, bunking in tents and RVs at the two campgrounds on the north shore. The bay is, in fact, appealing in so many ways that it's almost a shame it has to "compete" with the ocean beaches just a Frisbee toss to the west. But that only means there's plenty for everyone in San Diego.

From a tourist's standpoint, the centerpiece of Mission Bay Park is **Sea World** (500 Sea World Drive, 619/226-3901). This 150-acre marine zoo stars Shamu (a two-ton killer whale), dolphins, otters, walruses, sharks, eels, and stingrays. There are also shark and penguin encounters, Dolphin Discovery, and Cirque de la Mer (Circus of the Sea). Sea World isn't cheap ($32.95 for kids 3–9, $39.95 for seniors 55 and over, and $42.95 for everyone else), but it's open 9 A.M.–11 P.M. in the summer (9 A.M.–dusk the rest of the year). If you hang out long enough you might get your money's worth.

Beaches

They're not ocean beaches, but there's a bevy of sandy bay beaches to be found on **Vacation** and **Fiesta Islands,** as well as Mission Bay's mainland shoreline. Probably the best among half a dozen of them is to be found at **De Anza Cove**, on the bay's northeast flank. Here you'll find a well-equipped public park, as well as private campgrounds for tents and trailers.

Bunking Down

The best seat in the house at Mission Bay is a sleeping bag. Two excellent and affiliated RV campgrounds are available. **De Anza Harbor Resort** (2727 De Anza Road, 858/273-3211, $), off North Mission Bay Drive, has 250 spaces for RVs ($39–45 per night, 858/273-3211). The much larger and more scenic **Campland on the Bay** (2211 Pacific Beach Drive, 858/581-4200, $) is a "premium RV resort" boasting 750 spaces for both tents and RVs ($40–65 per night). Sea World is right across the bay.

If you want more in the way of creature comforts, try the **San Diego Paradise Point Resort** (1404 West Vacation Road, 858/274-4630, $$$) on Vacation Island in Mission Bay. It's stocked to the gills with everything you could possibly desire, including five pools, a golf course, and a bayside beach. Formerly the San Diego Princess Resort, the property has undergone several phases of renovation in recent years. The goal is to recapture its original charm, back when it was a "vacation village" conceived by a Hollywood producer turned resort developer back in 1962. Rates run $185 and up for a standard guest room.

Coastal Cuisine

For dinner we ventured over to the San Diego Paradise Point Resort, on the smaller of two man-made isles in the heart of Mission Bay. In a setting of tropical gardens, **Baleen** (1404 West Vacation Road, 619/274-4630, $$$$) serves superb seafood-oriented cuisine, offering a dining experience that's tough to top in San Diego. Every table in the spacious and casually elegant dining room has a postcard-perfect view of the bay. Wood-roasted fish such as mahimahi and salmon are highly recommended. Just be forewarned that everything is à la carte, and you'll pay $23–30 per entrée, plus $6.50 for vegetable side dishes and $7 for desserts, accruing a very pricey tab on your culinary pleasure cruise.

For More Information

San Diego Visitor Information Center, 2688 East Mission Bay Drive, San Diego, CA 92109, 619/276-8200 or 800/422-4749, website: www.info san diego.com

Pacific Beach

Any beach town that names itself after the world's largest ocean better have the waves to back it up. Happily, Pacific Beach (or "P.B." as it is known to locals) has waves upon waves of great surf, great beaches, great weather, great bars, and great cheap eateries. In short, Pacific Beach (population 40,000) is the quintessential Southern California beach town and is among our favorites on either coast. Despite the occasional encounter with a shirtless drunk sporting a bad attitude, P.B. is still the place to go if you want to have serious fun in San Diego.

There is an unstated rivalry between Pacific Beach and La Jolla, the jewel on the hill four miles north. Natives have bemoaned the gentrification that has trickled down from their wealthier neighbor. They've mockingly dubbed themselves "Baja La Jolla" for all the rich preppies who come here to party. And, indeed, some overly trendy boutiques have muscled onto the scene in Pacific Beach. Still, it seems unlikely that any business that charges $32 for designer T-shirts is going to last long.

The irony about this give-and-take between the two towns is that P.B. itself, beyond the commercial corridors of Garnet Avenue and Mission Boulevard, is a well-tended, suburban, and relatively pricey place in which to live. That left us wondering where all the wasted Marky Mark lookalikes go at the end of the night. There must be a whole lotta house sharin' goin' on. We know for a fact there's a whole lotta shakin' goin' on in those shared houses,

Map of Southern California—Page 9

as a stroll down any Pacific Beach side street after dark will reveal. One night, while setting out for a round of Garnet Avenue pub-crawling, we parked in front of a house where beer, music, and conversation were flowing loudly from a second-story balcony. A coed, oblivious to the fact she was broadcasting her monologue to an entire city block, shamelessly recounted the previous night's drunken revelry to her male consorts: "I woke up with my head on his ass and his head in my crotch," she chortled. "At least we still had our clothes on," she added demurely. What a tease.

You've gotta love the carefree mindset of the P.B. surfer dude. Late one afternoon, we popped into a drugstore for notebooks and drinks. The tanned surfer clerk at the front register didn't just point us to the proper aisle. Hell, this genial, sunny dude gave us a guided tour of the entire store! We learned more about his life in five minutes than a team of therapists would have gotten out of either of us in a week. He even complimented us on our choice of thirst-slaking beverages, proudly informing us that he had risen at 7 A.M. to stock that very drink refrigerator himself. As he was ringing us up, he sincerely offered us his best wishes. And we sincerely bade him the same.

On the way out, we passed a man entering the store. He was dressed in a toga, with a band of ivy tied around his head. He was not in a costume drama, as far as we could tell. Out in the parking lot, we came upon a classic Mutt-and-Jeff duo, P.B.-style: a short, shirtless, tattooed construction worker and a tall, gangly, long-haired dude on crutches. The guy with crutches was toting a 12-pack of Budweiser, lightened by the brewskis the pair had already knocked back. They spied a woman coming out of the drugstore and stopped to admire her pulchritude. (There's nothing subtle about P.B. dudes with beer in them.) The woman, blond and surgically improved but no more attractive than 90 percent of the gals in P.B., climbed into her shiny black, vanity-plated SUV. Hobbling

toward her, the dude on crutches urgently shouted, "Miss! Miss!" The woman rolled her window partway down, perhaps thinking there was something wrong with one of her tires. "You're sexy!" the guy on crutches blurted with a crooked grin. "There, I said it!" Then he hobbled away, giggling with his drinking buddy.

Two blocks away, on the boardwalk near Crystal Pier, two athletic California beauties were jogging side by side. After they passed a gaggle of guys, one gasped to the other, "Did you check out those dudes, dude?"

So it goes in P.B., dude, a party town without equal.

Beaches

The main beach at P.B. is part of a two-mile strand that extends south from Crystal Pier down to Mission Bay Channel. It is, quite simply, the most popular beach in San Diego and is jam-packed all summer long. Surfers in particular like **Pacific Beach,** rising with the sun to catch the early-morning waves. Areas for swimmers and surfers are marked off, to avoid confusion and collision. A cement walkway for strollers, runners, bladers, skateboarders, pets and owners, plus those who simply like to ogle the passing parade, links Pacific Beach and Mission Beach. A crew of San Diego city lifeguards surveys the scene at both beaches.

On the north side of Crystal Pier is **North Pacific Beach,** which runs for a mile up to **Tourmaline Surfing Park** in La Jolla. North Pacific Beach is a little narrower and rawer than the main beach strand—the cliffs begin to rise en route to La Jolla's curvaceous coves—and a bit less crowded as a result.

Bunking Down

The **Pacific Terrace Hotel** (610 Diamond Street, 858/581-3500, $$$$) is the best place to stay in the area. The three-story pink and brown hotel blends as unobtrusively with the sand as a 73-room inn possibly can, and the location, just north of the Crystal Pier on the beach, is unsurpassable.

Map of San Diego County—Page 10

Bad Vibes after Dark

Southern Californians are unabashedly sensual. They are children of the sun, as Jim Morrison dubbed them, physically fit and mentally uncomplicated. The state of profligate fun that colors their every waking activity is played to an unending soundtrack of laughter and rock and roll, and they never seem to tire of each other's presence. This is never more evident than at night when they come out to play after a hard day of hanging out in the ever-present sun.

On the surface the nocturnal rites of Southern California unfold in a relaxed and thoroughly appealing state of anarchy that somehow manages to stay within the bounds of civilization most of the time. Perhaps this is simply due to the fact that every day is perfect here. (This is no myth.) Since tomorrow is a clean slate, it's no big deal if things don't work out today. Southern Californians owe this sunny outlook to the fact that they are always engaged in some physical activity and therefore don't have time to develop the pathologies that haunt sedentary sorts in other places. Of course, all this fun in the sun also leaves little time to develop the mind, beyond periodic dabbling in the latest New Age manifesto. Hey, if there's an awesome happy hour going on somewhere, who's got time to get serious? And, more important, who needs to?

If it all seems too good to be true, it is. The pressure of paradise produces its own pathologies. We saw this dark side rear its head one night in Pacific Beach. Actually, it was the Fourth of July, of all symbolic days, and the festivities had come to a begrudging end around 2 A.M., at which point a hungry contingent of beach bums descended on one of several Mexican fast-food outlets that stay open all night in P.B. We did likewise.

At the first taco hut we visited, a sad-comic scene ensued. While we studied the hand-lettered menu, a grocery cart entered from stage right, listing like a rusty galleon with a tall load of empty cans and Hefty bags. The cart was pushed by a sun-pulverized woman of indeterminate age, perhaps 35, perhaps 70. (Who can tell, really, about people who live in public parks?) She was wearing a grease-stained miniskirt, a fluorescent orange fanny pack, dirty knee socks, and torn, untied sneakers too small for her swollen feet. From out of the shadows staggered her consort: a shirtless, shoeless man with tattoos covering his bare, distended belly. He answered to the name of "Bear," a sobriquet the woman hurled at him to get his attention as he stumbled across the street.

Map of Southern California—Page 9

The woman loudly begged Bear for a dollar, the modest sum needed to buy an order of rolled tacos. Bear growled and extended his paw, proffering a moist, wadded bill extracted from the unfathomable folds of his soiled jeans. While she approached the window to order, he proceeded to gruffly panhandle the other people in line. We left at that point, figuring the all-too-familiar scene would deteriorate into more pathos than we could stomach after a night of prowling among the Barbies and Kens of San Diego.

As it happened, the second Mexican fast-food joint we visited provided the actual violence that had only been hinted at by the first. After ordering quesadillas, we retreated to a corner booth, feeling bad for the Chicano behind the counter. Before taking our order he had been verbally abused by a Surfer Joe–type who accused him, in mock Mexican dialect, of withholding the sour cream from his burrito. The place was as loud as the bar we'd just left; the revelry just never seems to die down in Pacific Beach.

We set about trying to enjoy our food, though the helpings were so large that they seemed to multiply like protoplasm with each bite. As we were finishing, an odd series of events took place. Like a row of dominos stood back to back, it only took one jolt to send them all tumbling down. The "jolt" was provided by a skateboarding local and his companion, a blond woman whose expanding girth was covered by a pair of overalls. Her mate took offense at something he heard in line. This ignited a bizarre scene that ended with an athletic African-American who was not even involved in the original dispute punching the woman in overalls so hard that her head hit the front window of the restaurant with a sickening thud. A college kid ran outside to break up the fight, during which a heavy wooden trash can got overturned. He ended up being pummeled, as was the original wastrel who'd set things off. After leaving the parking lot strewn with four prone, moaning bodies, the assailant took off down Garnet Avenue. The cops arrived at that point, trying to sort out something that had no rationale. The final grace note was provided by one of the original disputants, the oblivious guy in line whose chance remark had touched off the fracas. Exiting the restaurant with his takeout order, he surveyed the parking lot and exclaimed, "I started all this, and I didn't even get punched!"

The quesadillas weighed heavy on our stomachs as we rehashed this turn of events. In a way, we felt like we'd lost some of our innocence about Southern California. For all its paradisiacal trappings—and the day at the beach that was now ending had been one of the most perfect we've encountered in our many years of coastal combing—we detected an underlying dissatisfaction, the ennui of the pampered American psyche that wants more of everything: sex, money, power, sun, surf, and good times.

Map of San Diego County—Page 10

Built on the site of what used to be a transient flophouse, the Pacific Terrace is a modern luxury hotel, comfortable and clean without being stuffy. Many of the rooms have balconies overlooking the ocean and the large heated pool. Purchased in 1989 by a large property management corporation, the Pacific Terrace has embraced some La Jollan affectations in recent years (valets in safari outfits), but no other place on the beach in San Diego can match it. However, with rooms starting at $260 a night in the summer, it is not for beach bums on a budget.

In contrast to the Pacific Terrace, the **Crystal Pier Motel** (4500 Ocean Boulevard, 858/483-6983, $) is more affordably priced. The name does not lie. It sits directly on the short, historic Crystal Pier (dating from 1927). The rooms are actually separate cottages affixed to both sides of the weather-beaten pier. Each cottage has a different sea creature carved into the cute blue shutters (in case you forget your room number, just remember "Sea Horse"), as well as an enviable pierside private patio. The Crystal Pier Motel is popular with fishing families, members of which drop their lines into the water from their patios. It's not luxurious, but it is clean and unique.

Coastal Cuisine

Restaurant-wise, P.B. is a battle royal between burgers, burritos, and fish 'n' chips, with no clear winner. Too many franchises have muscled their way onto the scene in recent years, but there is an alternative: buy the same fare from the locals. For example, the best burgers in town are served at **Cass Street Bar and Grill** (4612 Cass Street, 858/270-1320, $), which is also a great watering hole for locals, many of whom eat here so often it might as well be an extension of their refrigerators.

Close by, for seafood, try **The Fishery** (5040 Cass Street, 858/272-9985, $$$), where you can sit down beneath mounted fish and dig into California swordfish piccata or cast iron-blackened ahi. Mosey over to Thomas Avenue,

where you'll find the **Green Flash** (701 Thomas Avenue, 858/270-7715, $$) and **Nick's at the Beach** (809 Thomas Avenue, 858/270-1730, $$). Beyond that, we've never seen a town so thick with taco shops, burger stands, bars, and other spots to duck into for quick, cheap bites.

Night Moves

In the immortal words of a local P.B. party animal, "For me there's living at the beach. Then there's middle age. And then there's death." Perhaps this deep philosophical musing best captures the transcendent wildness of the nightlife here. On our numerous visits to P.B., we've hung out at enough places to fill a scorecard and once even managed to get pulled over by the cops. We looked at it as a rite of passage.

The old reliables—**Cass Street Bar and Grill** (4612 Cass Street, 858/270-1320) and **Kahuna's Surf Bar** (873 Turquoise Street, 858/488-6201)—are still around. The latter is perhaps the ultimate unrefined surf bar on the Southern California coast. As with the pipeline of a wave, only dauntless surfers venture inside. Surf music plays on the jukebox, longboards hang from the ceiling, surfing footage plays continuously on video monitors, and the place is packed with rowdies, especially on the "rage nights" of Friday and Saturday. When we last visited, the place was run by a scary-looking guy with a gray beard and baggy, soiled shorts. Throughout the evening he taunted and regaled the crowd over a microphone, offering free shots of tequila to any woman who'd bare her breasts for him, leaping over the bar to referee a fistfight that he helped instigate, and leading cheers of "Kahuna! Kahuna! Kahuna!" as he paced behind the bar like a trapped panther.

Moondoggies (832 Garnet Avenue, 858/483-6550) is a tamer, trendier chain sports/surf bar that caters more to surfer wannabes. It's got comedy nights, deejay nights (one devoted to "industrial" music—yecch), and drink specials (like "Surfers on Acid"), and we could care less if it went under tomorrow.

Map of Southern California—Page 9

San Diego County

Two other old reliables on the P.B. scene are **Hennessey's Tavern** (4650 Mission Boulevard, 858/483-8847) and **Pacific Beach Bar and Grill** (860 Garnet Avenue, 858/272-4745). The former, though part of a chain, has been adopted by locals mainly because it occupies the site of a late, lamented Mexican cantina. The latter has an excellent jukebox, an outdoor patio, and a line out the door all night long. Year after year, it remains the most popular spot in town. There are generally more people waiting outside to get in here than there are partying inside at most other bars, so come early and grab a meal from the surprisingly voluminous and tasty menu. Try a Longboarder: corn tortillas stuffed with mahimahi, salsa fresca, and white sauce. The main dining room has long wooden tables with cheap plastic deck chairs at which you sit unabashedly with others, as if on a big indoor picnic, which makes for good and downright unavoidable mingling. On a recent visit, we were joined by six garrulous UCSD students who might've been even louder had they not been stuffing their faces so frantically.

The place with the longest lines and loudest crowds on our last cakewalk up Garnet Avenue was the **Typhoon Saloon** (1165 Garnet Avenue, 858/373-3474). Security personnel in yellow slickers self-importantly communicate with one another via walkie-talkie, and this "bad-ass" joint teems with noise and bodies on the move and on the make.

If dance music is your thing, try **Club Tremors** (860 Garnet Avenue, 858/272-7278), which shares an address and is associated with the infinitely more preferable Pacific Beach Bar and Grill. Like luscious lemmings who come to honor a monument to their own narcissism, guys and dolls crowd into Tremors on hot summer nights, primped and preened and mirror-conscious. Formerly the trendy Club Diego's, it's a massive multimedia complex. You must pay a cover to hear taped hip-hop music played at a volume that could scare off the gulls circling nearby. It certainly sent us fleeing. Similar deejay fare is offered at the tony new **Plan B** (945 Garnet Avenue, 858/483-9921).

If you're as averse to electronic dance music as we are, there are plenty of alternatives in Pacific Beach. Two of our favorites are **Plum Crazy Saloon** (1060 Garnet Avenue, 858/270-1212) and **Cafe Crema** (1001 Garnet Avenue, 858/273-3558). The former is an extremely friendly place, with good music, countless drink specials (68 beers on tap!), pool tables, and delirious locals, typified by a blond woman who pantomimed every song played, replete with pelvis and lip twitches and tabletop leg kicks. Cafe Crema is part of the coffeehouse craze, which has overtaken even beery P.B. Open 22 hours a day, Cafe Crema bakes its own pastries and offers an excellent array of rich coffees, plus treats like "Latte of the Month" and "Creme de la Crema" (44 ounces of espresso, ice cream, whipped cream, chocolate, and banana), as well as healthy soups and salads, and alcoholic beverages. Books and magazines are strewn about, card and chess games are in progress, and folk music is earnestly strummed. Last time we dropped in, a professorial duo delivered an earnest, academic seminar on acoustic blues. Most of the inattentive clientele was absorbed in novels, textbooks, and alternative newspapers. It was a Friday night, and all hell was breaking loose on the streets and in the darkened saloons of P.B. The well-lit Cafe Crema, by contrast, offered a civilized, if woozy, alternative to the alcohol-fueled festivities outside the picture windows.

Speaking of which, **Blind Melons** (710 Garnet Avenue, 858/483-7844) rocks P.B. with live music at the foot of Crystal Pier. Blues-rock seems to be the genre of choice at this corner bar, where we heard a Janis Joplin sound-alike going for broke one balmy weekend afternoon.

For More Information

Discover Pacific Beach, 910 Grand Avenue #113, Pacific Beach, CA 92109, 858/273-3303, website: www.pacificbeach.org

Map of San Diego County—Page 10

San Diego County

La Jolla

On May 3, 1987, the town of La Jolla celebrated its centennial. In its coverage of the event, the *La Jolla Light* recounted the glorious spring afternoon in 1887 when La Jolla came into being. The first line of the story said it all: "It could not have been a better day for selling real estate." It was boom time in California, and settlers scurried westward to join in the land grab. One historical account claims they were sold a false bill of goods: "The plots were touted as having water mains and convenient telephone and rail service, none of which was true." It didn't matter. The setting was so much like paradise, perched high above the ocean on tawny, pine-covered bluffs, that no one was about to quibble over phone lines.

La Jolla (pronounced la-HOY-a) means "the jewel" in Spanish. Indeed, La Jolla does look like a jewel—maybe the prize bauble on the marble-topped vanity of coastal California. Wealth is palpable, both in the natural bounty of a marvelous setting and the material prosperity evident in the cars residents drive, clothes they wear, houses they live in, and the shops that cater to their every caviar-like whim. They make their money hawking real estate and trading stocks, occupations that allow them to bask in a perfect environment, squired away in upscale, uphill semi-exclusivity. The tone is set by signs that welcome visitors with the warning, "No shouting within city limits."

Technically, La Jolla (population 42,600) is a "Community of San Diego," but in every imaginable way it is a world removed. The freeway cacophony of downtown San Diego is miles away. La Jolla is distanced by attitude and altitude from rabble-rousing Pacific Beach and Mission Beach. Every attempt is made to cultivate a village atmosphere. La Jollans boast of having a "significantly high standard of living." It is a community whose residents lead a life of sensory indulgence. They are impeccably attired. They appreciate good food, wine, and art. They are masters at landscaping. Their hair is perfect. And, like all busy people pursuing wealth and privilege in the new millennium, they often appear to be harried as they bustle around their little seaside sanctuary.

The corporate heart of La Jolla is the intersection of Prospect and Fay Streets, which

---

 ## Top 10 Things to Do on the Fourth of July

On our nation's birthday, this was listed on the blackboard by the lifeguard shack at La Jolla Cove:

10. Watch fireworks.
9. Drink a beer.
8. Look for a parking space.
7. Eat veggie burgers and tofu dogs.
6. Drink another beer.
5. Yell at the guy who "stole" your parking space.
4. Swim at the Cove.
3. Drink another beer.
2. Ask the lifeguard a question.
1. Feel very patriotic.

Map of Southern California—Page 9

looks like a bonsai version of Wall Street. Outside the offices of Paine Webber and Merrill Lynch are arrayed gleaming rows of Mercedes and BMWs—foreign-made cars for patriotic free-enterprise capitalists. The working women, who tend toward the real-estate professions, likewise fix their steely gazes on the pot of gold at the end of the corporate rainbow. We actually overheard a couple of them at a seaside café discussing, over lunch, the origin and meaning of the company name "Re/Max."

The men all look to be some indeterminate, forever-young age, resembling those perfectly coifed leading men on daytime-TV melodramas. They include gray-haired bon vivants driving racy red convertibles, consorting with blonde gold-diggers half their ages. We spied one younger, upwardly mobile professional, whose dirty-blond long hair was heavily moussed and neatly swept back, pecking furiously at a calculator while nursing a grande latte at the local Starbucks. We could imagine him, like a surfing Superman, changing out of his Clark Kent office attire into baggies and sandals, grabbing his board and making for the waves at Windansea when 5 P.M. rolled around.

The ocean exerts a near-mystical pull upon all who live in La Jolla. At day's end they gravitate to the ocean's edge, gazing over the broad expanse at the setting sun like Bedouins engaged in prayer rituals. They watch from porches and balconies. They pull up to curbs in cars and vans with surfboards jammed in back or tethered on top. They jog along Coast Boulevard. Some bring picnic baskets, crawling onto sandstone shelves to toast the rosy sun as it slides into the crystal goblet of the Pacific.

The scene at sundown is emblematic of the Southern California experience. On one especially lovely late afternoon in midsummer, we set up camp at Windansea to watch the unfolding parade. Vans lined the street, their doors slid open to reveal fur-covered seats, carpeted floors, and knee-high card tables at which guys in cutoffs sat cross-legged, cracking jokes and

sipping beer. A trio of divers with yellow tanks strapped to their backs waded into the water, caucusing briefly before disappearing beneath the surface. An apple-cheeked beauty with shiny blond hair jogged by wearing a turquoise sweatshirt and coral sweatpants. A surfer in a wet suit came sprinting down a side street, board tucked under one arm, anxiously scanning the waves. People assumed the lotus position on rock ledges, hands shielding eyes from the harsh glare of the dimming sun as they gazed seaward. A girl in a bulky sweater, guitar slung over a shoulder, sang, strummed and strolled out onto the rocks as if serenading the sea. On the water a surfer caught an amazing ride, tunneling through the foam and down a sloping wave until he was shooting the curl. Moment by moment, the setting sun slowly turned the buff colored sandstone to honey.

Despite its lofty perch, cracks in La Jolla's facade have periodically emerged, depending on the temper of the rocky markets. Prospect Street has seen a gradual incursion of less tony shops. In the midst of all the jewelers, perfumeries, and art galleries displaying Miró lithographs have come low-rent T-shirt stores and bargain rug merchants. Even McDonald's—designated a "McSnack" and mercifully lacking in golden arches—has stiff-armed its way onto a prime block of Prospect Street. We've seen panhandlers wandering the streets, a further blight to La Jolla's formerly unalloyed brilliance. One evening we followed the incongruous sound of banjo-picking to a downtown street corner, where a faux hillbilly whose hat lay upturned at his feet played bluegrass for the well-to-do Californians who strolled around him. On the street, a woman offered Tarot readings and on-the-spot counseling to those wandering by. She gazed deeply into the eyes of a customer, holding her hand while consulting the cards. We tried to read her lips; it looked like she was saying, "I can feel your pain."

Despite occasional signs of slippage along the fault line dividing haves and have-nots, La

Surfer Girls

Don't tell our wives, but among the sexiest sights we've seen in our nearly two decades of beach wandering took place in Martin County, Florida, at one of that county's many numbered (and splendored) public beach accesses. After a day of snarled driving through the condo canyons of the Gold Coast, we parked the rental car in the shell-covered lot and made our way through the sea-grape canopy over the boardwalk-covered dunes, and then stopped as we came to the edge of the beach. There, before us, was a lithe young woman in a cherry red, buttock-clinging one-piece bathing suit (no wet suit for this tough gal) heading into the roiling surf, with a surfboard under one arm and her long tresses caressing the tops of her shoulders and then spilling down her backside. Godiva meets surf diva.

Whatever or whoever she was, she provided a sight for sore eyes. This is the sort of thing—a glimpse of spontaneous purely American surf culture—that makes the years of road weariness all worthwhile, and partly explains why we continue to do what we do into middle age. No, we are not voyeurs. We observe all proper protocol for sensitive males. Nonetheless, we could not take our eyes off this young woman surfer. We ended up watching her, and her companions, for the next hour. They were no hobbyists, no weekend water warriors. They were serious about surfing and damn good at it, taking long rides on waves that we could barely see from the shore. We say this with no condescension (or even lust, in the exploitative sense) in our hearts. The truth of the matter is that we are in awe of women who can surf.

Cut to the Left Coast, 2002, where we came across **Surf Diva Surf School,** in La Jolla Shores. The school was founded in 1996 by Isabelle ("Izzy") Tihanyi, a legendary surfer who has competed in professional tournaments but now serves as a mentor to future Lisa Andersens (speaking of Florida-based

Jolla remains Southern California's premier ocean-resort community, possessing a setting as splendid as any on the coast.

Beaches

The ruddy sandstone cliffs and caves of La Jolla are a perpetual work-in-progress. The humans who scamper along the sandy, erodable rocks overlooking the sea are unwittingly contributing as much to its sculpted form as the force of the waves that batter it from below. The beaches of La Jolla are among the most varied and striking on the Southern Califor-

nia coast. A new discovery waits around every turn in La Jolla, be it a blufftop vista, a stairwell leading to a small, sandy cove beach, or a rocky tidepooling zone. In their geological undulations and scenic variety, La Jolla's beaches are comparable with upcoast Laguna Beach. Both are among our favorite stretches of coastline in all of California.

La Jolla's sandy procession starts from the south with **Tourmaline Surfing Park,** at the west end of Tourmaline Street along the border between Pacific Beach and La Jolla. Tourmaline Surfing Park is off-limits to swimmers

Map of Southern California—Page 9

blonde goddesses). Among the things that Tihanyi and her instructors teach are how to read waves; how to "pop up" (go from a horizontal to a vertical position, like a human jack-in-the-box); how to maintain proper knees-bent, arms-out standing position; how to paddle against the prodigious West Coast waves; how to maintain balance on the board; and, of course, how to safely take a spill.

Surf Diva is not for wimpettes. Surfing is fairly strenuous exercise at times. As Tihanyi told one magazine, "An hour of surfing is equivalent to 200 push-ups, and if you catch fifty waves, it's like doing sprints all day long." Tihanyi also suggests that students be competent swimmers (able to swim 200 yards) and "be comfortable in the ocean."

While this may seem like a cute faddish thing—sort of like eating grubs on *Survivor*—the presence of women on surfboards is a big deal in California surf culture. Prior to the last decade, women were to be neither seen nor heard anywhere near the water. In some of the more hard-core surfing zones, testosterone pumped furiously and male surfers guarded their territory as ferociously as pit bulls. Part of that urge to fight came from the sheer crush of humanity in California and the limited number of world-class surfing areas. Part of it came from the lack of the mediating influence of the fairer gender. Thus, in our humble opinion, the presence of women on surfboards can only be a good thing.

Surf Diva charges $98 for a two-day weekend surfing clinic. The school provides equipment (boards, wet suits, lines, etc.), but women should bring all other items they'd normally bring to the beach (sunscreen, swimsuit, towels, sunglasses, hat, bottled water, food). Preregistration is required. The closest lodging is the Sea Lodge at La Jolla Shores (8110 Camino del Oro, 858/459-8271), right on the beach.

For more information contact Surf Diva, 2160 Avenida de la Playa, La Jolla, CA 92037, 858/454-8273, www.surfdiva.com.

but is nirvana to surfers. Waves here are notoriously large and break a good distance from shore. There are no sand beaches to speak of between Tourmaline Surfing Park and Windansea Park, but there is public access to the shoreline—and excellent opportunities for tidepooling—at **Bird Rock Beach.** This residential area features some of the most palatial homes and desirable real estate in La Jolla. Stairs leading to the rocky beach can be found at the foot of Bird Rock Avenue and at North Bird Rock Vista Point (on Camino de la Costa between Cresta and Corta Avenues).

La Jolla's beach bounty—and the more public parts of its coast—begin at Winamar Avenue and continue up to La Jolla Cove. A paved path at the end of Winamar Avenue leads to a small, sandy beach. This is the start of an impressive trio of beaches—**La Jolla Strand Park, Windansea Beach,** and **Marine Street Beach**—that collectively occupy about a mile of prime La Jolla coastline. The beaches are flatter, sandier, more expansive, and less dramatic than the ones up along Coast Boulevard. These in-town favorites draw sizable numbers of surfers, anglers, swimmers, and divers.

"Did You Giggle Together?"

The high-pressure lifestyle of making and spending money in volatile economic times is bound to take a toll that no amount of tennis or scuba diving can adequately soothe. This perhaps explains why La Jolla, a town of 40,000, lists 200 psychologists and psychiatrists in its Yellow Pages, not to mention the usual array of psychic problem-solvers (mediums, astrologers, fortune-tellers). Stress remains a hot topic of conversation. Signs of trouble in paradise are evident and even audible, as we discovered one afternoon. While strolling past a gorgeous estate in La Jolla, we suddenly heard its occupants scream so loudly at each other we thought the stucco was going to crack.

Relationships are casually psychoanalyzed down to the most intimate details. At dinner one night, we were seated near a medical professional and his date (whose occupation went undivulged). Both were in their early 40s, recently divorced, and talkative to the point of indiscretion. We certainly heard every word.

The male interrogated his partner with highly personal questions whose premises were either profound or silly, depending on which side of the New Age fence you sit. "Did you ever get to the point where you dug each other on a soul level, or was it all fantasy?" he earnestly queried. "Did you giggle together?" he asked with deep concern. By this time we were giggling together, heads buried in our plates so as not to draw attention. The conversation proceeded to a lengthy recounting of a humiliating tongue-lashing he'd received from a psychic nutritionist with whom he'd consulted. Despite his wounded ego, he generously interpreted her insults as "a loving gesture."

This recalls another true story, related to us by a transplanted Easterner now living in suburban San Diego. The new arrival attempted to organize a reading circle. He explained the concept to his well-tanned but apparently poorly read neighbors, one of whom looked perplexed. "You mean we read books and then sit around and talk about them?" he asked. That's the idea, he was told. "Indoors?" he asked incredulously.

As the fabled locale of Tom Wolfe's Pump House Gang, Windansea is legendary among Southern California's surf elite. The famous "pump house" itself is located at Gravilla Street and Neptune Place. The waves are equally impressive at La Jolla Strand Park and Marine Street Beach, offshore of which lie Big Rock and Horseshoe Reefs.

Along Coast Boulevard, from its southern intersection with Prospect Street up to Ellen Scripps Park and La Jolla Cove, are arrayed small beaches and inviting green spaces for swimming, sunning, surfing, and picnicking. The linear park along Coast Boulevard is equipped with benches and huts that people use for barbecues or as places to erect an easel and paint the coastal scenery. The seaside path along this stretch of coast is pure delight; we can scarcely imagine a better way to greet the morning or end the day. Our strategy is to park on Coast Boulevard (free street parking) and walk its length, resting on benches or lolling on grassy knolls every few hundred feet.

The coast vistas are among the finest in the world. Beach accesses along this enchanted strip commence with Nicholson Point Park, between the 100 and 200 blocks of Coast Boulevard, where a hard-to-find stairwell leads to a small, sandy cove. Next up are two small beaches known mainly to locals—**Whispering Sands Beach,** at the end of Bishop's Lane, and **Wipeout Beach,** south of Ellen Scripps Park on Coast Boulevard.

The crème de la crème of La Jolla's beaches is **Children's Pool Beach,** where Coast Boulevard meets Jenner Street. A breakwater curves out and around, protecting the beach's inner flank from waves and creating an ideal place to swim or sun. At least that's what the local harbor seals and sea lions think. They've appropriated Children's Pool Beach, while humans discreetly watch them doing nothing from the breakwater or blufftop. Waves slam the base of the breakwater, which has a walkway with a handrail from which one can survey the seals' and sea lions' laid-back version of beach blanket bingo. Sea spray from crashing waves sometimes soaks those standing on the breakwater, which can be refreshing on a hot day or a shivery nuisance on a cool one.

One summer afternoon we counted 44 sea mammals sunning themselves on Children's Pool Beach. Arrayed in the sand like fat sausages, they bark, cuddle, roll over, and occasionally shuffle and flop into the water for a cooling lap. Typically, they "haul out" of the water to relax and sun themselves for seven hours a day. They seem perfectly content to be around humans and their point-and-shoot cameras. Don't let your kids get too close, though. They are marine animals, capable of inflicting injury, no matter how "cute" they may appear. Nonetheless, it's a strikingly pleasant scene here all the way around.

Just north of Children's Pool Beach is **Ellen Scripps Park,** a blufftop green that's perfect for picnicking, Frisbee tossing, or simply lying on your back and looking up at the sky. One Fourth of July, we saw people doing all those things and more. Vendors sell inexpensive, often environmentally themed T-shirts. Windswept trees form a canopy over the sidewalk, sculpted so that their limbs grow horizontally. A broad, brown band of kelp floats offshore. Those who are so inclined can stroll out onto a staircase of sandstone ledges and watch the sunset.

At the south end of Ellen Scripps Park, stairs lead to **Shell Beach,** a steep, sloping beach tucked into a small cove, whose coarse brown sand is evidence of a rough, high-energy surf zone. Shell Beach gets packed with sunbathers, but few venture beyond the point where the waves break. Just below Point La Jolla, at the west end of La Jolla Cove, is **Boomer Beach,** a popular spot for bodysurfing. Surfboards are forbidden because of dangerous rip currents.

The beach at **La Jolla Cove** is the most popular in the vicinity, and it's invariably choked with a thick tide of beach blankets and bodies at the height of summer. It is staffed by lifeguards who post jargon-filled daily swimming and diving conditions on a blackboard; e.g., "Surf: Picking up slightly 1–2' west with a southern component that is spuratically *(sic)* trying." During one of our visits in early July, the water temperature hit 69.2 degrees and the locals were exultant. To them this was bathwater, very close to the yearly high of 71 degrees, reached in August and September. Further cause for celebration was this note, posted on an information board near the lifeguard stand: "Ocean water testing at the cove and shore will be suspended until October. Results have shown that water off the cove is generally excellent during the summer and early fall months." In other words, you don't have to worry about swimming in a soup of fecal coliform bacteria, as you might elsewhere in Southern California.

La Jolla Cove and Underwater Marine Reserve stretches in a broad, tongue-shaped curve

San Diego County

The World According to Surfer Jeff

We had just finished swimming laps and lifting weights at our hotel's pool and exercise area, thereby maintaining the Olympic stamina that allows us to keep pace with the tireless surfing, partying, and scene-making triathletes of Southern California after the sun goes down. Heading for the hot tub, we spotted a tow-headed lad. From a distance he looked to be eight or nine years old. He turned out to be a surf bum in his mid-20s named Jeffrey. He hailed us as we approached, offering a congratulatory pep talk about keeping in shape while handing us each a beer—lukewarm Bud Lights plucked from a 12-pack that was already more than half demolished. He was not a registered guest at the hotel, just a local who'd wandered onto the property to dangle his feet in the hot tub and knock back some brews.

His worldview was a mixture of hedonism and pathos, an outlook common to those who outwardly "have it all" and yet feel a spiritual void inside themselves. It is the animus behind just about every song the Eagles ever wrote, including "Hotel California," the ultimate anthem to the have-everything, feel-nothing, paradise-sucks outpouring of spiritual hand-wringing that most hedonists eventually wind up espousing, if only to make themselves feel less guilty for having so much fun. We refer to it as "sunny angst."

Surfer Jeff was the peroxide-blond embodiment of sunny angst. After handing us our beers, he struck up a friendly conversation, quickly informing us total strangers that "it's time for me to get my life together." He paused, then confessed, "I'm getting old. I'm almost 25." He'd like to get out of La Jolla, he said. It's a town where "your life is everyone else's business," where tongues wag and people stab you in the back to get ahead. He admitted to having family problems; his folks were less than thrilled that their high-school dropout son was still perfecting his form on the waves but had no career prospects. In addition, he intimated that among the townsfolk he was widely regarded as a wastrel who'd worn out his welcome. "I've got a bad reputation around here," he confessed. "I don't know why, but I do."

Outwardly, he was an exemplary specimen of young California manhood,

from Ellen Scripps Park up to Scripps Pier, at which point the coast resumes its northwesterly course. The area has been designated an ecological reserve in which boats, spears, floats, dogs (between 9 A.M. and 6 P.M.), and glass are prohibited. The public beach at the west end of La Jolla Cove (by Ellen Scripps Park) is protected and calm, and therefore gets quite crowded. The cove itself fills with scuba divers, snorkel- ers, and long-distance swimmers, some of whom are well over 60. They make the chilly swim across the cove, emerging like amphibians at La Jolla Shores. Then they shake themselves off until presentably drip-dried and hitchhike back to La Jolla, wearing only their Speedos. The locals know them on sight, so rides come easily.

Incidentally, another local attraction is the **Coast Walk,** a cliff-hugging and footbridge-

Map of Southern California—Page 9

neatly massaged by sun, wind, and waves to a lean, statuesque ideal of perfection. His skin had been burnished to a ruddy brown, while his windblown hair bore the color of Midwestern hay. He positively glowed with the boisterous virility of a life lived outdoors. But now he found himself an unwilling adult with no career and no life beyond that of hanging 10 and then guzzling at least that number once he'd climbed out of the water. "I've got no tools," he lamented, holding up his hands as if to display his lack of real-world skills.

He possesses nothing beyond an ability to ride the waves and to party all night long. That may be all you need to get by while in the throes of a reckless California youth, but it won't pay the bills or feed a family. Not that he's got (or wants) a family or that he will ever succumb to the rat race of working to acquire consumer goods, however forcefully they're urged on him by a culture that won't take no for an answer. In Surfer Jeff's world, who really needs anything more than a warm day, a nice southern swell, and a tall, cool brew?

Beneath the veneer of gotta-get-my-life-together beats the heart of a guy who's basically content, periodically offering displays of regretful sensitivity to convince himself and others that he's "serious" about the future. In reality, his philosophy is like that of Henry Miller, who opened the novel *Tropic of Cancer* with these lines: "I have no money, no resources, no hopes. I am the happiest man alive." Surfer Jeff cast that sentiment in his own words: "I've tried to get away, but the beach keeps calling me back. There's just something about it. It's so much fun that there's no real incentive to think of doing anything else. Just when you get bored with the whole scene, there's always somebody new who will wander down the beach with a cooler full of beer. It's like, 'Where's the next pool? Where's the next party? Where are we going now?'"

At this point a friend who waited tables in the hotel restaurant wandered into the pool area for a smoke. Surfer Jeff instantly switched out of his introspective mode and loudly greeted his buddy with a series of birdlike squawking noises that recalled one of Jerry Lewis's more sophomoric film roles. They slapped a mighty high five, and the new arrival accepted the beer reflexively shoved at him, even though he was still on duty in a tuxedo. They talked about plans for later that evening. "If you come up with something to do," pleaded Surfer Jeff, "please drag my sorry ass along with you, man."

crossing dirt path for the hale and hardy that begins above **La Jolla Caves** and proceeds about halfway toward La Jolla Shores. The caves lie 144 steps below the Coast Walk; both sights are worth the trouble.

The focal point of La Jolla Shores, a suburb northeast of La Jolla, is **La Jolla Shores Beach–Kellogg Park**. The mile-long beach is flat and the summer waves often gentle enough to make this a good family beach. Kellogg Park is a grassy picnic and play area behind the beach. Our first impression of La Jolla Shores Beach–Kellogg Park, on one slamming summer day, was that it looked like a refugee camp. The sand was as thick as a bamboo jungle with people. Packs of children threw black-sand mudballs at one another and screamed as they braved the surf on the broad beach. La Jolla

Map of San Diego County—Page 10

Shores Beach–Kellogg Park belongs to the people, and the people do indeed turn out to frolic on it. We've rarely seen a beach as crowded as this one, though it's calmer on weekdays and at other times of the year, as we've verified on subsequent visits.

One memorable year we ended a daylong Fourth of July ramble around town at Windansea. We wound up wandering out to the beach after demurring on a party to which some surfers had invited us. It had sounded promising: the waiter/surfer/college student who told us to come described life at his apartment complex, a few short strides from Windansea, as a nonstop episode of *Melrose Place*. Apparently, we came too late. By the time we arrived, it looked more like an episode of *Sanford and Son*. Trash cans full of empty beer cans and pizza boxes were already being dragged to the curb, and except for a rap record blaring in the apartment and a girl skating in the driveway, the party was over. We kept walking down Bonair Street till it ended at Windansea. Then we perched on a sandstone ledge, listening to the soothing sounds of the sea in the aftermath of the holiday fireworks. We've said it before and we'll say it again: California can be a paradise to rival any on earth.

Bunking Down

The inns and hotels of La Jolla tend to be on the sumptuous (read: expensive) side, so don't come here looking for budget Best Westerns. The nicest are the European-style hotels downtown and overlooking the cove. Our pick of the litter is the **Grande Colonial Hotel** (910 Prospect Street, 858/454-2181, $$$$), a well-appointed hostelry that dates from 1913. Rooms are plush, and amenities include a heated pool in a gorgeous courtyard and free valet parking. You'll pay anywhere from $179 for a standard village view room to $339 for a deluxe ocean view. Then there's the lavishly appointed **La Valencia** (1132 Prospect Street, 858/454-0771, $$$$), a salmon-colored stucco wonder that looks and feels like "old California," if

not the Old World. They charge some mad money here: $300–550 per night. You could buy a decent surfboard for one night's stay here! In any case, the beaches of La Jolla are just steps away out the back doors of the Colonial Inn and La Valencia.

Even closer is **La Jolla Cove Suites** (1155 Coast Boulevard, 858/459-2621, $$$), a four-story modern structure that trades what it lacks in architectural distinction for a prime location directly overlooking La Jolla Cove and a few steps away from Ellen Scripps Park. Oceanfront balconies, heated pool, and proximity to La Jolla's downtown shopping district are added pluses. Rooms run $139–226; suites are more expensive.

Another of the fancy in-town hotels, the **Empress Hotel of La Jolla** (7766 Fay Avenue, 858/454-3001, $$$), swaddles its guests with Old World elegance and contemporary luxury. Large, comfortable rooms are appointed with marble-tiled baths, well-stocked minibars, and terrycloth robes that hang inside mirrored closet doors. Mauve cloth napkins are placed next to a gilt-edged ice bucket. (You get the idea.) On the lobby level is a gourmet Italian restaurant called **Manhattan**; in the basement, an exercise room, spa, sauna, and showers. Rooms are surprisingly affordable; in the summer of 2002, a room for two was going for $139–179—a bargain by La Jolla standards.

Being partial to beachside locations, we've found the **Sea Lodge** (8110 Camino Del Oro, 858/459-8271, $$$$) to be the best combination of location and comfort in the area. Its 128 rooms surround a tropical plant–filled terra-cotta courtyard. All rooms have balconies or lanais, and La Jolla Shores Beach–Kellogg Park is literally steps away. The feeling out here is more outdoorsy, rustic, and recreational than it is in La Jolla's business district. With its arched, wood-plank ceilings, it feels more like a ski lodge than a sea lodge—until you sniff the salt air blowing off the ocean. Recreational facilities include a heated outdoor pool and

Map of Southern California—Page 9

tennis courts; the hotel also will provide guests with beach equipment, such as chairs, umbrellas, and volleyball equipment. It's highly recommended—and very expensive ($320 and up, in season).

The **Hotel La Jolla at the Shores** (7955 La Jolla Shores Drive, 858/459-0261, $$$) is a modern, 11-story high-rise four blocks from La Jolla Shores Beach–Kellogg Park. In addition to panoramic ocean views from the recently renovated rooms, the Hotel La Jolla boasts a world-class restaurant, **Crescent Shores Grill** (858/459-0541, $$$), on its top floor. The menu is oriented toward California/American cuisine: steak, seafood, pasta, and good wines. In-season rates at the hotel run $169 on up.

Finally, for corporate chain partisans, the 400-room **Sheraton Grande Torrey Pines** (10950 North Torrey Pines Road, 858/558-1500, $$$$) overlooks the ocean and sits next to a golf course. A perfectly adequate and reasonably priced **Radisson Hotel** (3299 Holiday Court, 858/453-5500, $$) reposes in the hills west of town center, where I-5 meets La Jolla Village Drive.

Coastal Cuisine

La Jolla's restaurant scene is dominated by **George's at the Cove** (1250 Prospect Street, 858/454-4244, $$$), a three-story restaurant that offers diners the option of semiformal indoor dining downstairs or a more casual setting on an outdoor deck that overlooks La Jolla Cove. On a midsummer evening, we took the latter option, enjoying the extensive view out to sea and up the coast. We dined on grilled marinated swordfish and a mixed grill of three fish, both of which were absolutely delicious. The third-level deck looks out on the ocean as if from the bow of a ship. Plexiglas panes keep the wind at bay, and heat lamps provide a note of warmth to counter the chill. Yes, we were dining on the beach in Southern California in July, and heat lamps were needed. There's a pronounced fall-like tang in the air even in midsummer along the

California coast, thanks to the ocean's giant cooling engine.

Downstairs, the more formal dining room at George's specializes in creative seafood preparations done with a California flair—e.g., apple-smoked salmon served with fennel, miso, and Hawaiian pesto, and halibut in chicken fumet with poached leeks, garlic, and shallots. George himself can be seen bustling around the premises, impeccably attired and super-competent, yet possessing a dry, seen-it-all wit reminiscent of John Cleese. George's at the Cove is a La Jolla landmark and a must-try for visitors.

On the Mexican side you'll find decent sit-down Spanish and Mexican restaurants along Prospect Street, such as **Jose's Court Room** (see "Night Moves").

Overlooking the water near La Jolla Cove is **Brockton Villa** (1235 Coast Boulevard, 858/454-7393, $$$). This historic, restored "red rooster" beach cottage gained a second lease on life as a popular breakfast and lunch spot. (It also serves dinner now.) A favorite dish is chicken curry with jasmine rice. We dug into a delicious Moroccan halibut salad and pulled pork quesadilla after a long hike around La Jolla's curvy, majestic shoreline on as perfect a day as you could ever hope to find.

La Jolla's dining scene is rich and varied enough to reward serendipitous browsing. We had an excellent late lunch at **Bollicina** (8008 Girard Avenue, 858/454-2222, $$$). It's a great multilevel Italian restaurant and martini bar just up the hill from La Jolla Cove. Bubbling water tanks are shaped like martini glasses. The restaurant's main emphasis is salmon, prepared in all sorts of ways. Try the riso salmon entrée (chunks of fish in riso pasta with a side of penne—simple but good) or a salmon sandwich on focaccia. Have a salmon lunch or dinner with a martini to wash it down and you'll be thanking us for the tip.

Tapenade (7612 Fay Avenue, 858/552-7500, $$$) is a relatively recent arrival (1998). A nice but not too fancy place, Tapenade has an excellent, unpretentious menu inspired by the Provence region of France. Be sure to try the wild mushroom ravioli. **Pannikin Coffee** (7458 Girard Avenue, 858/454-6365, $) has been around since 1968. It's great to sip coffee or Mexican hot chocolate on the patio.

Night Moves

La Jolla has steadily been losing some of its stuffy air, which has helped liven up its formerly stultifying nightlife. Today the multilevel minimalls of Prospect Street contain the likes of a **Hard Rock Café** (909 Prospect Street, 858/454-5101) and **Moondoggies** (909 Prospect Street, 858/454-9664), one of a small but growing chain of spacious, upscale surf bars (find the oxymoron). However, in our judgment **Jose's Court Room** (1037 Prospect Street, 858/454-7655) is the place to go. A combination Mexican restaurant and bar, it was by far the liveliest joint we encountered in La Jolla. A loud CD jukebox sprayed its decibels upon a throbbing, three-deep crowd of beautiful people surrounding the oval island of the bar. The Mexican grub is good, but folks (especially singles) really crowd in for the company. So call out for an ice-cold Pacifico and join in the brew-ha-ha.

It's always a good idea to check what's on at the **La Jolla Playhouse** (2910 Village Drive, 858/550-1070), which was founded over 50 years ago by Gregory Peck, Dorothy McGuire, and Mel Ferrer.

For More Information

La Jolla Chamber of Commerce, 7734 Hershel Avenue, La Jolla, CA 92037, 858/454-1444, website: www.lajolla.com

---

 # The Scripps Institution of Oceanography

Founded as an independent research lab in 1903 by a University of California, Berkeley, biology professor, the **Scripps Institution of Oceanography** is one of the oldest centers for marine research in the world. It was named the Scripps Institution for Biological Research in 1912, owing to the munificence of its benefactors, Ellen Browning Scripps and E. W. Scripps. As time passed it came to focus its research efforts on the sea—an evolution that was recognized in 1925 when it was re-christened the Scripps Institution of Oceanography. The institution's assets include a fleet of four oceanographic vessels and two research platforms; classrooms and laboratories; shoreline and underwater reserves; seismological observatory and satellite oceanography facility; pier and aquarium/bookstore; major marine sciences library; and faculty and staff numbering more than 1,000. At any given time there may be 250 research programs underway, ranging from beach erosion to the physiology of invertebrates. If study in the fields of oceanography, marine biology, and earth sciences interests you, Scripps is the place to go for graduate training.

Even if doctoral studies in the geomorphology of ocean basins or manganese-nodule formation is not in your future, Scripps still has something to offer: the **Stephen Birch Aquarium Museum,** which is open to the public 9 A.M.–5 P.M. daily. Admission is $7.50 for adults, $5 for students, and $4 for children (ages 3 to 17). The **Birch Aquarium and Ellen Browning Scripps Memo-**

Map of Southern California—Page 9

Scripps Beach

A few miles north of La Jolla lies **Scripps Beach.** It belongs to the University of California at San Diego Scripps Institution of Oceanography (SIO, for short), which maintains research facilities here. At Scripps you'll find a sandy beach and research pier. Offshore is a rocky reef and submarine canyon. People generally come to Scripps to tour the Birch Aquarium, which is the most public of its facilities. If you're looking for a beach to frolic on, you're better off heading down to La Jolla Shores or up to Black's Beach/Torrey Pines State Beach.

For More Information

Scripps Institution of Oceanography, 9500 Gilman Drive, La Jolla, CA 92093, 858/534-3624, website: http://scripps.ucsd.edu

Black's Beach (a.k.a. Torrey Pines City Beach) and Torrey Pines State Beach

Before we hit the beach, let's spend a moment looking down on it from **Torrey Pines State Reserve.** One of the gems of the state park system, the reserve occupies a setting so peaceful you'll easily forget it brushes against a city of over a million. Trails lead into stands of the

rial Pier are in La Jolla Shores, just up from La Jolla Shores Beach–Kellogg Park. The glass tanks of the aquarium contain everything from a 12-foot spiny lobster to an old gray grouper who cowers grumpily in a corner. Highlights include rainbow-colored exotics from Micronesia and the frozen-in-glass coelacanth, a nearly extinct relic from an ancient biological regime that looks like a battered piece of luggage.

As a museum attached to a university-funded research facility, it's not nearly as vast and "oh, wow" as, say, the Monterey Bay Aquarium up the coast. But Scripps does offer a squid's-eye view of everything from kelp beds to coral reefs, plus a taste of the important research being conducted at the institution. On that last note we'd like to lob this bit of wisdom at our readers, copied years ago from one of the exhibits, as we've seen evidence of its truth on every coast we've traveled: "Man has interfered with nature's supply of sand to our beaches, thus compounding the erosion problem, and we are now seeing the results of this intervention. Putting it bluntly, we are losing our beaches." Scripps, however, is not losing its beach. In fact, Scripps Beach and the surrounding tidepools offer a wonderful way to learn about coastal ecosystems. Look but don't touch. It's all part of the Scripps Shoreline Underwater Reserve.

For more information contact the Scripps Institute of Oceanography, 8602 La Jolla Shores Drive, La Jolla, CA 92037, 858/534-3624. Or contact the Stephen Birch Aquarium Museum, 2300 Expedition Way, La Jolla, CA 92037, 858/534-3474, website: www.aqua.ucsd.edu.

Map of San Diego County—Page 10

rare, long-needled Torrey pine, which grow only in this park and on Santa Rosa Island, 175 miles to the northwest. A 1.6-mile hike leads out to **Razor Point,** a breathtaking overlook from atop a 300-foot bluff. On a clear day, you can view the swell-dappled surface of the Pacific Ocean to the distant horizon. An old lodge, dating from 1902, serves as a visitor center. Some 436 plant and animal species are native to the park, including 144 birds, 110 invertebrates, 85 plants, 39 mammals, 28 reptiles, 23 fish, and seven amphibians.

In addition to its flora, fauna, and spectacular geology, the reserve is rich in fossils, and is close to where archeologists discovered the bones of Del Mar Man, believed to be the oldest human remains yet discovered in North America. The tranquillity of the park is interrupted only by rustling breezes and the occasional sight of a gopher breaking open a Hottentot fig. The park offers a truly all-natural remedy for urban stress: an oasis of calm set beneath an awesome canopy of *Pinus torreyana.* On weekends, ranger-led walks are conducted at 10:30 A.M. and 2 P.M. It's a very peaceful place to commune with nature and one of the better spots for coastal hiking in Southern California.

The shore below Torrey Pines is **Black's Beach,** probably the most infamous nude beach in the country, and **Torrey Pines State Beach.** This lengthy strand lies at the base of the tall bluffs between Scripps Pier and Los Penasquitos Lagoon, and is as controversial as it is hard to reach. It is so out of the way we wonder why anyone would bother to get uptight about people enjoying the sun, surf, and sand in the buff. Yet the dimensions of the feud have occasionally plunged Black's Beach into the national news. Nudity was banned on Black's Beach in 1977, when a voter referendum revoked the "clothing optional" status. However, nudity has been the unofficial norm since then at Black's Beach. It is now official to the extent that an area of the beach—roughly be-

tween the Glider Part to the south and Mussel Rocks to the north—has been parceled off for nudists and marked with signs to that effect. Since July 7, 1999, the city's anti-nudity municipal code has been enforced on the southernmost section of Black's Beach, from Scripps Pier north for about seven-tenths of a mile. The fine for nudity outside of the marked area is $135, and for lewd conduct it's much worse. In other words, no lewd conduct. Got that?

From our perspective, the concern over nudity is grossly overstated. On a sparkling June afternoon some years back—Mother's Day, as fate would have it—all we saw were half a dozen men wandering the beach wearing only white socks and tennis shoes. On a warm afternoon in mid-July several years ago the sum total of bathers in the buff consisted of an overweight couple of AARP age and several bearded male loners. We saw scant public nudity on Black's Beach on a balmy weekend in May 2002. Though we hiked till our feet hurt, we saw nothing but the occasional solitary bare-assed male. We did see lots of families, some picnicking on blankets. This gave the lie to the general impression of Black's Beach as America's premier nude beach.

If you're curious, we were finally able to decode the putative partitioning of who disrobes where along Black Beach's two-mile stretch, thanks to a gatekeeper at Torrey Pines. Here's the lowdown: the north end is for men, the middle part is coed, and the south end is for surfers. "It's our Hawaii," said the gatekeeper, whose attention had to be pried away from a pod of dolphins whose offshore movements he was monitoring with a pair of binoculars. A surfer himself, he added: "The waves are good all over the coast, but for some reason they're particularly big down there." That is because a nearshore submarine canyon amplifies the swell, creating waves twice the height of others in the area.

The walk down to and along Black's Beach from Torrey Pines State Beach is one of the great environmental beach hikes in America.

Map of Southern California—Page 9

It includes a perilous scuttle around a point of land, called Flatrock, into which the merest sliver of a foothold has been carved into the rock. It is impassable at high tide. The geology of Torrey Pines and Black's Beach is an awesome spectacle. The sandstone cliffs are fascinatingly textured and colored with bands of red, yellow, and orange. Boulders and mounds of talus occasionally lie at the base of the cliffs. You might see an environmental artist creating human figures from rocks. We watched one tireless soul, who had created several dozen such sculptures for passersby to enjoy. Obviously, he could not sell or take them home. He was simply motivated by a compulsion to create something from the formless mounds of rock. The little figures did seem to have lifelike qualities, as if he'd created a village of hobbits from the variously shaped stones he stacked and arrayed.

Getting to Black's Beach is actually easier from above. A stairway descends from the Glider Port (off Scenic Torrey Pines Road). Steeply etched into the cliffs, this point of entry comes with a warning: "Stairway and cliffs unsafe and unstable." The warning goes unheeded, and the foot of the staircase roughly demarcates the surfer's zone from the coed nudists' encampment. The safest way down, however, is via the service road that begins where Blackgold and La Jolla Farms Roads meet. You can't drive a car down to it, but your own two feet will deposit you on the beach in 10 minutes or so. Free on-street parking is available, and there is a sufficient number of spaces (with two-hour limits) to handle demand most of the

time, summer weekends and holidays excepted. The road to the beach drops steeply in a series of switchbacks, passing warning signs ("Danger: Hazardous Cliffs Subject to Landslide") and irreverent graffiti ("Do Not Eat or Feed Nudists") before depositing walkers onto the south end of Black's Beach, with Scripps Pier in plain view.

For our money, though, we prefer the longer, ground-level hike south from Torrey Pines State Beach, which offers a Kodak carousel's worth of dramatic slide-worthy scenery: enormous toppled boulders, giant talus piles at the base of the towering cliffs, and huge sheets of blackboard-smooth rock. The whole landscape has a wild, otherworldly appearance, which no painter can capture and no photograph does justice. You simply must see it for yourself. Hikers should keep a watchful eye on incoming tides, which could potentially strand the unwary in a cove.

The less adventurous or ambulatory may prefer to stay put near the parking lots at Torrey Pines State Beach, a day-use beach. An ample parking area abuts Los Penasquitos Lagoon. Arrive early if you want a parking spot on a good beach day. Just be aware that the cobble-filled beach is inferior to the sandy, scenic, and less crowded expanses of Black's Beach. Our advice: take a hike!

For More Information

Torrey Pines State Reserve and Torrey Pines State Beach, 858/755-2063, website: www.calparks.ca.gov

Map of San Diego County—Page 10

Del Mar

The boutiquing of Southern California reaches a modest crescendo in Del Mar (population 4,400). Del Mar is a trendy, buzzing little hive in town and a jazzed-up mall-o-drama out by its famous racetrack. The pace of traffic has picked up, giving Camino Del Mar a taste of the fumy, bumper-to-bumper backup that congests Laguna Beach. That's not to say the place has lost its charm, just that it's experiencing growing pains. But this is par for the coast; there's scarcely an available acre within sight of water in Southern California that hasn't been built up or targeted for development.

All the same, Del Mar is the closest you will come to finding a true village atmosphere in coastal San Diego County. Thanks to the vigilant attempts of the populace to keep development under control, coupled with the relaxed atmosphere of the beach and racetrack, Del Mar has the air of a less harried time in California's past. To a great extent, it has geography to thank. Del Mar is on a hill between two lagoons, with a canyon to the east and ocean to the west. If you're entering town from the east, a heart-stopping plunge down Del Mar Heights Road lets you know you're nearing the water. During our travels for this third edition, Del Mar is where we began our coastal trek. When we came over the crest of the hill and saw the Pacific Ocean laid out before us, ahhhs of contentment at this auspicious sight simultaneously issued from our lips.

The land thins to precipitous strips at the lagoons: Los Penasquitos to the south (at Torrey Pines State Reserve) and San Dieguito behind and around the river mouth at the north end of town. There's only so much you can build out here that hasn't already been constructed or attempted. In the mid-1980s environmental prerogatives saved the San Dieguito Lagoon from plans to construct a cluster of hotels, shops, and freeway access ramps.

In town the only major project that's survived the legal gauntlet has been **L'Auberge Del Mar**, a $45 million luxury hotel and spa built on the site of the old Del Mar Hotel (which was demolished in 1967). Even so, it took the developer, a Del Mar resident, more than a decade to gain approval of the plan. The heart of the village, along Camino Del Mar from about Sixth to 15th Streets, is a cavalcade of small shops catering to a consumer's every whim. Folks mosey from cafés to shops, grazing and browsing, as traffic moves in fits and starts along Camino Del Mar while drivers scour the streets for parking spaces. The modest town center is a tasteful smattering of New Age shops (Earth Song Books), classy cantinas (El Fuego), and restaurants of long standing (Bully's North). Away from the main drag, Del Mar's blocks are filled with small but smartly designed trophy homes with amazingly landscaped lots on which every square foot is maximized.

The town is best known for the thoroughbred racing season at the **Del Mar Thoroughbred Club**. The brief, 43-day season runs from late July to early September, packing the town with racing buffs. The racetrack was built in the 1930s as the brainchild of local celebrities Bing Crosby, Jimmy Durante, and Pat O'Brien. Their cosponsor in the venture was the Works Progress Administration, which pulled out midway through construction. The celebs were left holding the bag, having to borrow funds to bring the track to completion. Crosby wrote and recorded a song to commemorate the track's opening in 1937. "Where the Surf Meets the Turf" is still played before the first race with all the dewy-eyed sentimentality of "My Old Kentucky Home" at Churchill Downs. The track lies inside a triangle formed by Via de la Valle, Camino Del Mar, and Jimmy Durante Way. The grounds are also the site of the annual **Del Mar Fair**, a June/July to-do that draws three-quarters of a million San Diegans.

Map of Southern California—Page 9

The rest of the year is given over to horse shows, trade shows, and concerts.

Before the first ". . . and they're off!" echoed around the track, Del Mar was already trotting along on an initially shaky but eventually well-heeled course. In 1883 developer Jacob Taylor Shell bought the strip of coastline upon which Del Mar sits today. He built a seaside spa on his 338 acres that included the Casa Del Mar Hotel, a dance pavilion, a bathhouse and pool, and a railroad depot. It briefly thrived before succumbing to bankruptcy, flood, and fire (in that order) by 1890. The town received a facelift during the roaring '20s: a renovated hotel, rebuilt pier, and new roads into town. The fairgrounds came in 1936, the racetrack a year later. Del Mar has grown slowly but steadily ever since, trying its best to remain—as a *Newsweek* article described it nearly 30 years ago—"a sleepy little seacoast town."

Beaches

Del Mar City Beach was a sunbather's paradise, quickly filling to capacity on summer days until 1998's winter storms nearly washed it away. It has since been "renourished" as part of an ongoing and expensive beach restoration project in northern San Diego County. Short concrete seawalls offer scant protection to homes that have been built too close to the water's edge. The high tide line, marked by seaweed and scalloped wave lines, runs up to the very base of the seawalls, which does not bode well for the future.

Even so, there is much to commend the beach at Del Mar, which widens as one nears the bridge over San Dieguito Lagoon. The main beach area has been subdivided into areas for different activities, with arrows delineating "Surfing and Beach Games" from "No Surfing and Beach Games." The south end of the beach has gone to the dogs, with leashed and unleashed canines chasing tennis balls into the water and romping around the sand. Many folks come here with their animal companions,

so this might not be the best stretch of sand for sunbathing unless you're really into wet noses and sandy pawprints.

Finding a spot to lie out on the beach is less of a problem than finding a place to park close by. There's on-street metered parking along Coast Boulevard and a few pay lots. The early bird gets the parking spot while the loser cruises; parking in the summer months is pure hell. The beach itself is great for swimming and bodysurfing.

A grassy play area, **Seagrove Park,** sits on the short bluffs overlooking the beach from the south end. Del Mar's green blufftop park is reminiscent of the village greens that are a mainstay of New England towns. On a sunny weekend afternoon—and few of them aren't sunny—coeds from UCSD, picnicking families, joggers, bicyclists, and walkers pack the park and its walkways.

Del Mar Bluffs City Park is just north of Del Mar City Beach, across the mouth of the San Dieguito River, where the land begins to rise again. A small sand beach here is popular with fishers. A steep wooden staircase laden with sand leads to a spectacular overlook from the top of the bluff. The panorama encompasses the ocean, racetrack, and town. Straddling Del Mar and neighboring Solana Beach is **Del Mar Shores,** a sandy stretch reachable from a tiny municipal parking lot at Del Mar Shores Terrace. These beaches are popular with locals and tourists alike, not the least reason being that in season you might catch trainers working their horses on the beach. Skin diving and surf casting are also popular here.

Bunking Down

Some things never change. **Del Mar Motel on the Beach** (1702 Coast Boulevard, 858/755-1534, $$) is where it's always been: smack dab on the beach. A charmingly unpretentious place that's been around since 1946, it's the only place in the area that can make that claim.

Such homey motels are more the exception than the rule, as Del Mar and other North Coast communities are more typically represented these days by places like **L'Auberge Del Mar** (1540 Camino Del Mar, 858/259-1515, $$$$). You'll pay through the nose to be pampered at this resort spa. Visitors can select seaweed body packs, aromatherapy, reflexology, Shiatsu massage, and the ever-popular Balneo Therapy Revitalizing Bath from a menu of spa services more extensive than the list of ice cream flavors at Ben & Jerry's. It's a splendid resort, to be sure, with beautiful interiors, inviting pool area, multilevel decks, and walkways that meander among walled-in gardens that suggest a place far removed from the reality of a busy street corner. Large and well-landscaped grounds confer that all-important sense of splendid isolation that justifies room rates that run $200-385 in season (and around $700-800 a night for suites).

We are partial to the **Best Western Stratford Inn of Del Mar** (710 Camino Del Mar, 858/755-1501, $$), within walking distance of town but burrowed into a hillside in a real neighborhood. Constructed of gray, weathered wood, the Stratford Inn blends nicely into its environment. The grounds are invitingly quiet, featuring two heated pools.

Coastal Cuisine

Down by Del Mar City Beach, a pair of restaurants with picture-window views of the ocean do a brisk business. **Jake's Del Mar** (1660 Coast Boulevard, 858/755-2002, $$$) and the **Poseidon Restaurant** (1670 Coast Boulevard, 858/755-9345, $$$) are the places to go if you want to dine by the water. Jake's offers a more imaginative menu of seafood prepared with a creative, Pacific Rim–style orientation, such as sesame-seared ahi with dark soy honey glaze. The Pacific seafood chowder (with fish, clams, and diced veggies) is rated among the best on the coast. The Poseidon sticks more closely to baked or broiled seafood basics. Both restau-

rants are overpriced—the cheapest entrée at Jake's, for instance, is $16, and the general range is $18–23—but you're paying not only for food but location, ambience, and a bit of history. The Poseidon has an especially inviting modern interior of varnished pine walls, tile floors, and big panoramic windows facing the ocean. It is a "view" restaurant offering breakfast, lunch, and a seafood-themed dinner menu.

The toast of the waterfront these days is **Pacifica Del Mar** (1555 Camino del Mar, 858/792-0476, $$$$). It is the best restaurant in town. You can't go wrong with choices like barbecued sugar-spiced salmon, which is the signature dish on a Pacific Rim–themed menu.

The **Fish Market** (640 Via De La Valle, 858/755-2277, $$) is an unpretentious, bustling sure bet for fresh seafood. If you're in a quandary about what to order, walk up to the fresh-fish counter, decide what looks good to you, and order it back at your table. The market smokes its own fish—the salmon/albacore combo is a must-try appetizer. Fresh fish entrées range from Utah rainbow trout to local thresher shark, plus skewers of scallops, oysters, ahi, and more. The Fish Market is close to the racetrack.

A good choice in town is **Carlos & Annie's Café** (1454 Camino Del Mar, 858/755-4601, $$), a Southwestern-themed restaurant that regularly wins "best breakfast" awards on the strength of such offerings as Carlos' Omelette (chicken, salsa, avocado, cheese, and Spanish sauce). On the other side of the street, **Café Del Mar** (1247 Camino Del Mar, 858/481-1133, $$) serves brick-oven pizza and creative pasta dishes, such as sautéed salmon with dill vodka sauce over penne, all priced very reasonably.

Night Moves

Generally, the night moves made in Del Mar are the sort of stretching and yawning calisthenics performed immediately before crawling into bed. As in most professedly quiet towns, there's not much to do beyond eating well, strolling a few blocks through the village

Map of Southern California—Page 9

after dinner, or maybe downing a highball at L'Auberge Del Mar to the polite accompaniment of a tinkling piano. You might find a little action in the bar at **Bully's North** (1404 Camino Del Mar, 858/755-1660), a prime-rib palace with an outdoor patio that's open till midnight. Otherwise, if you want nightlife you'll just have to roll up to Solana Beach, which has plenty of it.

For More Information

Del Mar Regional Chamber of Commerce, 1104 Camino Del Mar, Del Mar, CA 92014, 858/755-4844, website: www.delmarchamber.org

Solana Beach

Solana Beach's claim to fame has been as party headquarters for north San Diego County. The townsfolk, whose per capita income of $65,000 per year is said to be even greater than that of Del Mar, haven't exactly been thrilled that their community has been the one to play Pied Piper to a hip-hopping party crowd. They've been working to change their image with tighter permitting and more vigilant law enforcement. As a result the nightlife has gradually become more evenly spread around this end of the county, spilling into Cardiff and up into Carlsbad. Ultimately, northern San Diego County is one big seaside overflow valve for the city of San Diego, 25 miles to the south.

Solana Beach (population 13,000) calls itself "the best spot under the sun." It's got two miles of beach, a number of decent restaurants and delis, and the Belly Up Tavern, one of the best live-music clubs in the country (see "Night Moves"). In the past decade, Solana Beach has become a trendier spot, with splashy architectural and landscaping statements being made by hip entrepreneurs who've gravitated here. The San Diego Freeway (I-5) splits the town into east and west halves. U.S. 101 is the coast road in these parts, and this is where the town lets its hair down.

On an odd note, Solana Beach was the home base of the Heaven's Gate religious cult, whose members committed group suicide in March 1997. Economically, they fit the profile of the area. Mostly young, they designed websites for a living. They wore Nike tennis shoes ("just do it") the night 39 of them made their attempted afterlife rendezvous with a comet.

Beaches

Access to Solana Beach's beaches is blocked, to a great degree, by residential housing. However, you can get through at **Seascape Surf Park,** accessible from the 500 block of South Sierra Avenue. A half mile north, Sierra Avenue meets Lomas Santa Fe Boulevard, dumping traffic into a large free parking lot at Fletcher Cove.

The main beach in Solana Beech, **Fletcher Cove Park** is the site of a run-down community center, basketball hoop, and two shuffleboard courts. It's an attractive natural setting, especially from the blufftop vista point, which looks out over the pretty but fragile cliffs to the churning ocean below. It was here that we saw an old codger, a postal employee, taking a midday siesta on a park bench. You could hardly blame him. The cove was blasted into being by early settlers, who dynamited the cliff bases. (Imagine the environmental furor that would cause today!) The sandy beach at Fletcher Cove Park is the best that's available within city limits, so it is a popular place with the locals. It was devastated by El Niño storms in the winter of 1998, so sand was trucked in from Yuma, Arizona, to raise the beach by six feet. The northern end is good for surfing.

A half mile farther north is **Tide Beach Park.** At the base of a bluff reachable by a stairway, it's good for tidepooling, spear

Map of San Diego County—Page 10

SANDAG Pumps Up the Beaches!

When the storms of El Niño or Old Man Winter strip San Diego's beaches of sand, there's only one thing to do: put it back! Of course, you can't put the same sand back, but replacement sand can be dredged and spread on the beaches. It doesn't matter to most people if it doesn't exactly match the old sand in terms of color and grain size, or that it doesn't feel the same to the feet. Any sand is better than no sand, right? So keep it coming!

That's where SANDAG comes in. SANDAG is an acronym for **San Diego Association of Governments**. Among other things, it's working like a fitness instructor to pump up the beaches of San Diego County. As SANDAG rightly points out, the main source of sand for the beaches of California—the state's rivers, which carry ground rock particles to the ocean, where longshore currents distribute them on beaches—has largely dried up thanks to damming projects. In effect, the beaches of California are trapped behind dams. Jetties and breakwaters along the coast contribute to the problem, since they interrupt the longshore (i.e., shore-parallel) transport of sand, thereby starving beaches on the down-drift side of the construction. In that sense, San Diego County itself is partly to blame for its narrowing beaches, owing to harbor projects in Oceanside and San Diego. Regardless of fault, the end result is, as SANDAG puts it, "a severe sand deficit on the region's beaches."

In 2001, SANDAG oversaw a pilot project to dredge sand from offshore ocean-floor sites and deposit it on thinning beaches. More than two million cubic yards were dredged and deposited on a dozen sand-starved San Diego beaches, most of them in northern San Diego County. The lion's share of funding—$16.5 million, or 92 percent—came from state and federal sources,

fishing, surf casting, and scuba diving. Nearly all of Tide Beach Park was lost in the winter of 1998, and subsequent renourishment projects have replaced sand with pebbles, making barefooting nearly impossible. The reef here is known as Table Tops. It makes for striking scenery but not much of a swimming beach.

Bunking Down

Solana Beach really isn't geared toward the tourist trade. The best choices are franchises: the **Courtyard by Marriott Solana Beach** (717 South U.S. 101, 858/792-8200, $$) and **Holiday Inn Express** (621 South U.S. 101, 858/350-

0111, $$). Both are clean, attractive hotels within walking distance of the beach.

Coastal Cuisine

A hip hangout and relatively recent arrival on the otherwise starved Solana Beach dining scene is **Pacific Coast Grill** (437 South U.S. 101, 858/794-4632, $$$). Diners can bring their dogs and sit on the garden patio (thereby obviating the need for a doggie bag). A good spread of Mexican food can be had at **Fidel's** (607 Valley Avenue, 858/755-5292, $$), a crowded cantina with an unpretentious atmosphere.

Map of Southern California—Page 9

while the affected cities kicked in $1.5 million. The project was approved and funded before the economy began heading south (like the sand is supposed to do). It goes without saying that funding for these wishful sand-replacement therapies will be harder to come by as governments grapple with more pressing problems.

The real long-term solutions to eroding beaches will involve doses of medicine that communities might not want to swallow. They include beach retreat (moving structures back from vulnerable, eroding beach margins); forbidding hardened structures like jetties and seawalls (which cause and exacerbate erosion, respectively); and decommissioning some of those damned dams. In our experience of these things, common sense and logic will not prevail. Only when environmental cataclysm imposes its own solutions will the matter be addressed with any sort of authority.

Even now, SANDAG and its member cities are calling for more sand—two million more cubic yards per year for the next 15 years or every other year for the next 30 years. That is the amount, they say, that will be needed to restore the beaches to their rightful width. Total cost, in 2002 dollars, would be $262.5 million, though that figure will surely rise as materials and labor costs increase in coming decades. And just what kind of Band-Aid solution is this anyway? Beach renourishment is an artificial solution to a human-generated problem. It can't proceed indefinitely, since both sand and money sources have their limits. Meanwhile, as expensive replenished beaches inevitably get stripped of their sand by the ceaseless work of storms and currents while natural sand sources remain blocked, California's coastal communities will find themselves back to square one. The real solutions necessary to restore balance will never happen until we stop attempting to live out of balance with nature in an artificial, engineered paradise.

Night Moves

The **Belly Up Tavern** (143 South Cedros Avenue, 858/481-8140) enjoys a national reputation and is beloved by musicians and music fans alike. A roomy club, it is typical of other well-run, similarly sized nightclubs around the country that provide a living to musicians who might otherwise be applying for unemployment benefits. These include ghosts of the 1960s who have gone from stardom to cult status, as well as current up-and-comers. One night we caught a droll, low-key set by Dan Hicks, the San Francisco Scene pioneer and gypsy jazz-pop stylist whose justifiably cynical disenchantment with the music business

made for entertaining between-song patter. Roots-oriented journeymen like Dave Alvin and Jorma Kaukonen and bluesy jam bands like the Radiators, along with a hefty number of reggae and R&B acts, fill the calendar at the Belly Up. The acoustics are great throughout, and the whole operation is first-class. Note that you must be 21 or older to come here. Also, the club has added a bistro-style restaurant, the **Wild Note Cafe,** next door (143 South Cedros Avenue, 858/720-9000). The food is affordable, healthy, and hearty, while the music tends toward singer/songwriters and light jazz and funk. One duo name we'll never forget: Bongo and John.

Map of San Diego County—Page 10

For More Information

Solana Beach Chamber of Commerce, 210 West Plaza Street, Solana Beach, CA 92075, 858/755-4775, website: www.solanabeachchamber.com

Cardiff-by-the-Sea

Cardiff-by-the-Sea takes its name from the Welsh seaport city. It is the most unassuming of the north San Diego County beach towns. The only industry that Cardiff (population 11,800) ever had dates back to 1912—a kelp-processing operation that closed three years later. Its chief attractions are the quiet residential neighborhoods east of U.S. 101 and two state beaches by lagoons at opposite ends of town. Most of Cardiff lies uphill and east of the beach and railroad tracks, Given the condition of the beaches, these residents are no doubt glad they don't own beachfront property. Technically, Cardiff-by-the-Sea is part of the City of Encinitas, having participated in a four-in-one municipal conjoining back in 1986.

In reality, the town has its own identity (low-key) and crisis (ruined beaches).

Beaches

Cardiff State Beach lies west of San Elijo Lagoon, separated from it by Old U.S. 101. The beach was once great for swimming, windsurfing, board surfing, and surf casting, but nearly all of the beach and the sidewalk and fencing behind it were lost to El Niño. Cardiff is among the most severely impacted beaches in California. It is hard to describe the devastation, except to say that the scene is one of cataclysm. The parking lots are rutted and narrowed, the collection kiosks abandoned. The chain-link fences are listing, having absorbed

---

 ## California State Parks' Rollercoaster Ride

First the good news: The state of California cut entrance and camping fees to state parks and beaches by half or more, effective January 1, 2001. Now the bad news: The state of California hiked entrance and camping fees to state parks and beaches, effective January 1, 2003. Rates are not quite back to what they were prior to the 2001 cuts, but they're darn close. Though there are no rollercoasters in any of California's 266 state parks, the system itself appears to have been on a bit of a rollercoaster ride with the confusing slide down and back up again of the pricing structure in a few short years.

How can this be? Well, let's at least credit state park administrators with good intentions. Rates were rolled back in 2001 because the state, realizing the fee structure was excessive, sincerely wanted to get more people into parks. The impetus to cut fees came from Governor Gray Davis and Rusty Areias, director of California State Parks. "It was obvious that fees were too high," Vic Maris, director of visitor services, told us in a June 2002 interview. "We don't want to be restricting people from coming to parks because of their economic position."

And so instead of shelling out $2–$6 at entrance kiosks, visitors found themselves paying only $1–$3, while downwardly revised camping fees ran just $8–$18 per night. The cost of an annual pass to state parks got slashed from

---

repeated poundings from an ocean that has sent the beach into retreat—except there's no place to retreat to, because of the seaside parking lots, restaurants, and highway. It is a disaster area, pure and simple, with gouged chunks of concrete and rusted metal skeletons littering the landscape in mute testimony to the ocean's might.

San Elijo State Beach is best known for camping, being the southernmost developed campground in the state system. Set high atop a jagged cliff, San Elijo's 171 sites fill up quickly. Reserve early, especially for the summer months. The campground is nicely laid out, with scraggly hedges providing some shade and privacy. The sites closest to the cliff's edge are the best. From these spots you can hear the waves crashing at night. You're also closer to the wooden stairs that lead to the beach. It is a long, lifeguarded beach and a good place to savor a gorgeous California sunset. The ongo-

ing problem is that the narrowing campground has been pinned between a rock (U.S. 101) and a sandy place (the eroding beach). There is talk of rerouting the channel connecting the lagoon and ocean so that it doesn't run on a beach-paralleling north-south route, which wreaks havoc on the bluffs and beach at Cardiff-by-the-Sea.

To the east is the San Elijo Lagoon Ecological Reserve, a 1,000-acre wildlife haven that is one of the last wetlands of this size and purity in Southern California. Thanks to local activists, not only are the wetlands saved from developers, but the lagoon is accessible to hikers and bird-watchers.

Bunking Down

If camping in the sand at San Elijo State Beach (see "Beaches") is too rustic for your taste, try the **Countryside Inn** (1661 Villa Cardiff Drive, 760/944-0427, $$). It's a 102-room Colonial-style

---

$70 to $35. Park visitation increased by 14% after the cuts; in particular, weekday attendance shot up.

With more people visiting parks and less money coming in, we asked how the revenue shortfall would be addressed. "The legislature voted to augment the loss we took in fees with an increase in general funding," Maris explained. "So the amount of budget money we have is about the same." Moreover, in March 2001, California voters approved Proposition 12—a $2.1 billion bond act for state parks that's the largest of its kind in U.S. history.

Despite all the sunny news, we privately wondered whether the California legislature would remain so generous toward parks if the economy kept tanking. To our thinking, that's all the more reason to appropriate funds, since affordable recreation becomes an even greater necessity for a financially strapped populace. However, the impact of the Bush recession proved too much to absorb, and prices went up again.

The first hit came in October 2002, when it was announced campers would henceforth be assessed a $7.50 per-reservation processing charge. In late December, the revised fee structure for 2003 was released. State-park entrance fees rose from $1–$3 to $2–$5, while camping fees jumped from $8–$18 to $13–$21. The silver lining to all this is that fees are still slightly lower than they were in 2000. As for the bargain bonanza of 2001–2002, it was fun while it lasted.

Map of San Diego County—Page 10

hotel with bed-and-breakfast amenities. One of the more striking constructions along this stretch of coast is **Cardiff by the Sea Lodge** (142 Chesterfield Drive, 760/944-6474, $$$). With its themed rooms, circular architecture, and rooftop fire pit for sunset savoring, this 17-room lodge makes a cozy romantic hideaway for couples.

Coastal Cuisine

Cardiff has its own beachside "restaurant row" along Old U.S. 101. The place to dine in Cardiff is the **Beach House** (2530 South U.S. 101, 760/753-1321, $$$), a pricey, glitzy seafood restaurant so close to the beach the fish could practically swim from the ocean to the broiler. A rock revetment is all that stands between restaurant and waves. The parking lot attests to its popularity, as an army of young valets in tennis shorts and monogrammed pullovers take turns running the 40-yard dash, car keys jangling, to park or retrieve vehicles. The ocean views are fantastic, so try to come at sunset.

Next door, **Charlie's by the Sea** (2526 South U.S. 101, 760/942-1300, $$$) forthrightly advertises "any closer and you'd be wet." In truth, any closer and it'll be closed, as Charlie's by the Sea looks more like Charlie's *in* the Sea. The stylistically varied menu offers such entrées as macadamia-dusted scallops, sesame-seared salmon, and sea bass stuffed with smoked lobster and crab. Again, the picture windows look out on the vast churning ocean and the boulders that protect the restaurant from its fury.

Another neighbor on Cardiff's restaurant row is the **Chart House** (2588 South U.S. 101, 760/436-4044, $$$). It's part of a national chain that serves excellent and inventive seafood dishes (sesame-crusted salmon, grilled tuna with mango relish). If you miss it here, there are Chart Houses in Coronado, La Jolla, Oceanside, and Malibu, all of which have unsurpassable ocean views. Try to wrangle a window table, because the sights are as good as the edibles. Avoid the valet fee at the Chart House and Beach House by parking by the side of U.S. 101 for free.

Night Moves

The **Kraken Bar & Restaurant** (2531 South U.S. 101, 760/436-6483) bills itself as "the bar by the beach . . . where the locals still and probably always will party." It has pool tables, pinball machines, six color TVs, and two (count 'em!) satellite dishes. Summer happy hour runs 4 P.M.–7 P.M.

For More Information

Cardiff-by-the-Sea Chamber of Commerce, 2051 San Elijo Avenue, Cardiff-by-the-Sea, CA 92007, 760/436-0431, website: www.cardiff bythesea.org

Encinitas and Leucadia

As of 1986, Encinitas became a four-way community comprising four formerly autonomous towns: Encinitas, Leucadia, Cardiff-by-the-Sea, and Olivenhain. The conjoining is mainly a governmental matter. Olivenhain is rural and inland, while Cardiff stands apart from the others by virtue of geography and character. Encinitas and Leucadia, however, do seem joined at the hip—with the emphasis on hip, for these are two of San Diego County's swingingest coast communities.

Encinitas is bounded at the south and north by the San Elijo and Batiquitos lagoons. The town is subdivided into "Historic Encinitas"—the area along U.S. 101, near the beaches—and "New Encinitas," along El Camino Real. The town's main problem is beach erosion. For years it's been fighting to save its beaches and oceanfront real estate. At one time there were Sixth and Fifth Streets in Encinitas. Maps clearly show they existed. They do not exist now, having been annexed by the Pacific Ocean. A local geologist, using old surveys and maps, has determined that 800 feet of Encinitas's

Map of Southern California—Page 9

shoreline has disappeared in the last hundred years. The cliffs are made of sandstone, shale, and siltstone. Constant assault by waves opens cracks and fissures that eventually cause the cliff tops to pitch forward. Some coastal access points have washed out, and their precipitous stairwells are off-limits. This is not to say Encinitas's beachfront does not have appeal. Despite the obstacles, the beaches are popular, primarily with teenagers (many from inland communities). Occasionally they exhibit threatening behavior and upset residents who have been coming here for years. The biggest story in town during one visit concerned "drunken abuse" taking place along the stairwell to Stone Steps Beach, where beer-drinking slackers were trying to intimidate families into leaving "their" beach, forcing them to join the crowds down at Moonlight Beach.

One of our favorite places in historic downtown Encinitas is **La Paloma Theater** (471 South U.S. 101, 760/436-5774). A slice of SoCal's sociocultural past, this funky old single-screen movie palace dates from 1927. Today, it hosts everything from rock bands to first-run films to independent flicks. Spirit, one of California's greatest rock groups—fronted by the late, lamented guitarist Randy California—recorded a live album here. When we came through in 1994, the premiere of the surfing documentary *Endless Summer II* was being accorded the same fanfare at La Paloma as the latest Austin Powers sequel receives in Los Angeles. If you can believe it, they still show *The Rocky Horror Picture Show* on Fridays at midnight.

Another must-see attraction in Encinitas is **Quail Botanical Gardens** (230 Quail Gardens Drive, 619/436-3036). It's a 30-acre collection of plants and trees native to California, as well as exotic tropicals, palms, and bamboos. Visitors can take a self-guided tour of the premises, which include a chaparral grove, a bird sanctuary, and more than 5,000 species of botanical life. Several of the many exotic environments include Africa, New Zealand, and the Canary

Islands. Admission is $5 for adults and $2 for children 5–12, and it's open 9 A.M.–5 P.M. daily year-round. Interestingly, in the hills surrounding Encinitas, a thriving nursery and greenhouse industry grows most of the carnations dyed and sold on city streets around the world.

Leucadia is welded to Encinitas at a point where the latter's strip malls give way to un-moored (that is, un-malled) businesses, some of which look one season away from bankruptcy. Founded by English spiritualists in 1888, Leucadia lies along a congenial, tree-lined, and slightly run-down stretch of U.S. 101 that parallels the crumbling sea cliffs. Leucadia retains a bit more of an alternative flavor than Encinitas. It's the kind of place where vegetarians and old VW bugs go to roost. The town that time forgot, Leucadia seems happily stuck in a tie-dyed mindset that feels more like the 1960s than the new millennium.

We like it here, as they've managed to keep heavy-handed developmental imperatives at bay. Instead you'll find small nonfranchised businesses from taco shops to smoothie stands, from psychics to espresso bars, from greenhouses to New Agey places with names like The Energy Within. Eucalyptus trees line the road, and a homey, naturalistic ambience is exuded. Railroad tracks run beside the road. A huge hill separates the road and town from the beach. Turn west off the highway onto any side street and you'll climb way up and then descend way down toward the lately replenished beaches.

Leucadia means "Isle of Paradise" in Greek, and the streets here are named for Greek deities (Daphne, Diana, Phoebe, Glaucus). But as in the Elysian Fields, not much goes on here. The number-one industry appears to be the selling of used merchandise, with a disproportionate number of businesses along U.S. 101 involved in the secondhand trade (thrift shops, consignments, used clothing, etc.). Our favorite was a yellow U-Haul on whose sides was inscribed an offer to buy used blue jeans 10 A.M.–3 P.M. on Sundays. A roadside motel

Surf Writers

Because of their good surf, hidden coves, and relative affordability, Encinitas and Leucadia are popular with surfers, especially older ones with the means to live on the coast. Among the best known is Chris Ahrens, the publisher of *Longboarder* magazine and author of a book of true surf stories called *Good Things Love Water*. It's a sympathetic, if somewhat sentimental, collection of tall tales and profiles. One surfer described it as "someone standing around a fire ring talking with other surfers." *Longboarder* magazine still lives, too, and it shares the magazine rack with *Surfers' Journal, Longboard Quarterly, Surfer,* and others.

In an interview for a local paper, Ahrens nailed down the surfer's raison d'être: "Once you're out in the water, the rules of the land are left behind. A whole new government takes place. It's a kind of peaceful anarchy."

Other surf writers of distinction include Greg Noll, whose *Da Bull: Life Over the Edge* is an oral history of this big-wave cat. Mike Doyle, a surfing legend in his own right, has published a memoir called *Morning Glass,* which captures the halcyon days of surfing. The diary-like entries are written chronologically and make a good historical reference tool.

We can't resist commenting on the notorious *Pump House Gang* by Tom Wolfe, his 1966 attempt to capture the manners and mores of a group of surf bums who made their home on the beaches of La Jolla. His sneering portrait is universally reviled by all surfers. Here is an excerpt: "Their backs look like some kind of salmon-colored porcelain shells. They were staring out to sea like Phrygian sacristans looking for a sign. . . . I foresaw the day when the California coastline would be littered with the bodies of aged and abandoned Surferkinder, like so many beached whales."

Here is an eclectic selection of books on the subject of surfers and surfing:
- *Book of Waves,* by Drew Kampion.
- *California Coastal Access Guide* (Berkeley: University of California Press, fifth edition, 1997). Theoretically, this resource guide provides definitive information, in written and tabular form, on every publicly accessible beach. Unfortunately, it has not been updated in many years. Even the latest 1997 "revision" appeared to be little more than the previous 1991 edition with a new cover slapped on it.
- *California Surfriders,* by John Heath "Doc" Ball. First published in 1946 and now reprinted, this pictorial record of "thrills, spills, personalities, and places of California surfing" was lovingly put together by Doc Ball, the first professional surf photographer.
- *Caught Inside: A Surfer's Year on the California Coast,* by Daniel Duane. An episodic, readable account of a guy who spent a year chasing waves. He doesn't sugarcoat the surfing life—some of the characters he befriends are despicable scourges—which makes the book all the more authentic.

Map of Southern California—Page 9

- *Complete Guide to Surfing,* by Peter L. Dixon. Part history but mostly how-to, it's a good, contemporary (published in 2001) overview.
- *Cowabunga: A History of Surfing,* by Lee Wardlaw. Although not as definitive as *Surfing: The Ultimate Pleasure* (see below), it has its charms.
- *Fiberglass Ding Repair,* by Franklin Pierce. The best guide to repairing your surfboard. For nonsurfers, a "ding" is a divot, scratch, cut, smash, shark bite, or blemish on the surface of your best friend, the board.
- *Girl in the Curl: A Century of Women in Surfing,* by Andrea Gabbard. The fairer sex gets its turn in the lineup.
- *Hawaiian Surfriders 1935,* by Tom Blake. This is the first book ever written on the history of the sport. The author is the inventor of the paddle board and a surfing legend in his own right.
- *Learning Hawaiian Surfing: A Royal Sport at Waikiki Beach, Honolulu, 1907,* by Jack London. Yes, this is *the* Jack London, who learned the sport in the summer of 1907 from the great George Freeth.
- *Let's Go, Let's Go!—The Biography of Lorrin "Whitey" Harrison: California's Legendary Surf Pioneer,* by Rosie Harrison Clark.
- *Mr. Sunset: The Jeff Hakman Story,* by Phil Jarratt.
- *Stoked: A History of Surf Culture,* by Drew Kampion.
- *Surfer's Start-up: A Beginner's Guide to Surfing,* by Doug Werner. An easy-to-read and best-selling how-to guide. Warner also wrote *Longboarder's Start-up: A Guide to Longboard Surfing.*
- *Surfing California,* by Bank Wright. A guide to the best surfing beaches, written in inimitable surf speak by one of the legends.
- *Surfing San Onofre to Point Dume 1936–1942,* by Don James.
- *Surfing: The Sport of Hawaiian Kings,* by Ben R. Finney and James D. Houston.
- *Surfing: The Ultimate Pleasure,* by Leonard Lucernos. By general consensus, this is the best book on the history of the sport.
- *The Big Drop! Classic Big Wave Surfing Stories,* by John Long and Hai Van Sponholz (eds.).
- *The Surfin'ary,* by Trevor Cralle. There are 3,000 entries in this surfer's dictionary.
- *Waikiki Beach Boys,* by Grady Timmons. A chronicle of the original Hawaiians who gave the world the sport of surfing.
- Finally, a timely title: *Surf Rage: A Surfer's Guide to Turning Negatives into Positives.* The author, Nat Young, wrote this book after being assaulted while trying to surf his home break. He is to be commended for bringing the darker side of surfing to light. We hope it does some good.

If you're ever in the area, the **California Surf Museum** (223 North Coast Highway, Oceanside, 760/721-6876) is a good place to begin your hunt for many of these titles. Some titles are out of print. If you can't find them at used bookstores, there's always eBay!

Map of San Diego County—Page 10

Self-Realization Fellowship Hermitage and Meditation Gardens

The most intriguing spot in Encinitas is a place of worship. The 17-acre grounds of the **Self-Realization Fellowship Hermitage and Meditation Gardens** (215 K Street, Encinitas, 760/753-2888) cling to the cliffs at the southern end of town. The nearby **Self-Realization Fellowship Temple** (939 Second Street, Encinitas, 760/436-7220) is visually dominated by three towers that loom above U.S. 101 like an exotic hallucination. The lotus towers were designed by Paramahansa Yogananda (1893–1952), the spiritual leader who founded the center in 1937 and built the temple in 1938. At the time, it was the largest building on the Southern California coast.

Yogananda dedicated his life to uniting East and West through the ancient art of meditation. He lived in the hermitage for several years and helped design the cliffside meditation gardens and planted the ancient ming tree on the site of his favorite pond, which was drained when the cliffs collapsed in 1941. Yogananda made a name for himself internationally with his *Autobiography of a Yogi*, which he completed here in 1946. It is now considered a spiritual literature classic. The lively, detailed text traces the spiritual awakening of this gentle man, whose teachings had a profound effect on the lives of many Westerners, including Greta Garbo, Leopold Stokowski, and Christopher Isherwood.

The best indication of Yogananda's spiritual openness is that his retreat and gardens have always been open to visitors. You are free to stroll and meditate to your heart's content, with no attempts at proselytizing. The meditation gardens are open for visitation Tuesday to Saturday 9 A.M.–5 P.M. and Sunday 11 A.M.–5 P.M. The nearby temple is open daily (except Monday) for meditation and prayer from noon to 4 P.M. Incidentally, the gardens are just steps away from a great beach (Swami's) and an eatery called Swami's Cafe.

called the Ocean Inn is not on the ocean at all, being situated at the foot of a hill blocks from the Pacific. A generic trailer bears the misleadingly pastoral name Mobile Village—Valley of Dreams.

Still, folks in Leucadia live and let live, work construction jobs when available, eat tacos and brown rice, use environmentally safe products, and stare unconcerned as cars pass through town. They simply don't need vacationers in Leucadia, which is just as well, because the beaches aren't big enough to attract them and

the cliffs are eroding away. The sign at one washed-out beach access had this spray-painted addendum: "No tourists. Go home." It might as well have read "No beach. Go home." In a funny way, being so removed from the breakneck world of the 21st century, it's the sort of place we don't just like visiting but could easily see ourselves calling home.

Beaches

The beaches of Encinitas look a lot healthier than they did in the last decade, thanks to a

Map of Southern California—Page 9

major sand renourishment project. Still, you can renourish the beaches—that is, as long as the funding and sand supply hold out—but you're only delaying the inevitable. A wise investor would not want to own oceanfront property in Encinitas, no matter how splendid the view. Signs warn of "Unstable Cliffs" and "Frequent Bluff Failure," and the sandstone along this stretch of coast seems particularly erodable. At least in the short term, however, the beaches of Encinitas are more fun to play on than they've been in a while.

Starting from the south, **Swami's Surf Beach** is below Seacliff Roadside Park (free parking, day-use only), a blufftop city park at the south end of the Self-Realization Fellowship Retreat, Gardens, and Hermitage. During the winter, this is surfer heaven, and in the summer it's still plenty of rough fun for surfriders. A long stairwell topped by white wooden crests leads along the cliff face to a fabled small beach. Surfers bob a good distance from shore while lifeguards look on. The cliff face has been reinforced with plantings, and the stretch of bluff from here north to D Street has been designated a Marine Life Refuge. Swami's Cafe is across from the Moonie temple and the beach.

Just above Swami's, and accessible only on foot from it, is **Boneyard Beach.** At low tide, small, protective coves afford romantics, nudists, and surfers privacy for their various activities. Just don't get caught by a rising tide with your drawers down.

D Street Viewpoint is accessible at the end of D Street in Encinitas. Steps lead down to a rock-backed city-run beach not unlike Swami's, with a lifeguard. Speaking of views, we caught a dandy one at the D Street beach overlook. Stairs descend along the cliff face, with gorgeous plantings on either side. At the top of the stairs, we admired both the beach vista and a nearly perfect specimen of teenage California pulchritude hanging out with her degenerate surfer pals. She had on the shortest pair of cutoff jeans imaginable, plus a midriff-

baring top, and straight Michelle Phillips-style blonde hair. This is, we decided, what they mean by California dreaming.

At the foot of Encinitas Boulevard is **Moonlight Beach,** the centerpiece of the coast in these parts. There's a free municipal parking lot, plenty of facilities, volleyball nets, recently pumped-in sand, and a pack of happy sunbathers. If you're not partaking of the party on the sand—and Moonlight Beach is one of the most accessible and popular beaches in north San Diego County—then you should at least drop by to gaze down on the action from the blufftop parking lot. What a view! Just one troubling thing: water quality can be a cloudy issue at Moonlight Beach, which earned a D grade in 2001 and 2002 from Heal the Bay, a Santa Monica-based nonprofit organization that monitors water quality along the California coast. This stuck out in our minds because we recall actually seeing fecal matter on Moonlight Beach—the result of a sewage-treatment plant overflow, we were told—back in the mid-1980s.

The access to **Stone Steps Beach** is on Neptune Avenue. Park for free in the quiet neighborhood along Neptune's curbs and climb down the steep and plentiful (97 by our count) stone steps, paying homage to the mural of a mermaid on the half-shell. A lifeguard stand, marked with surf and tide advisories, is at the bottom of the stairwell. The beach attracts scores of surfers. If you walk north from Stone Steps Beach, you'll reach the **Encinitas Beach.** There is no other direct access to it from shore, which makes it secluded enough to please space-seeking swimmers, surfers, and solitary sorts.

Formerly Leucadia State Beach but now a city-managed area, **Beacon's Beach** lies at the foot of a yellow sandstone cliff and can be reached by hiking down a treacherous trail of sandbags, stairs, and switchbacks. You can park for free at the Beacon's Beach access and scuttle down to the beach, where the copious kelp that washes ashore gets entangled with the equally abundant litter. You can look up and down the coast from the base of the cliffs at Beacon's Beach and see the same things: steep, eroding cliffs and packs of surfers competing for waves. From "Kenzie of Leucadia," a Beacon's booster: "Locals love to boast that the only place more crowded than our line-up is I-5 at rush hour after a heavy rainstorm."

Above the beach in the lot, a roving surfing instructor (his van read "Kahuna Bob's Surf School") was giving preliminary lessons to a group of youngsters who looked so eager to hit the water that they were positively shivering with excitement. (Call **Kahuna Bob's Surf School,** 760/721-7700.) Beyond them, another Leucadia resident, also a surfer, stared wistfully at Beacon's rugged waves. He'd suffered a shoulder injury in a nasty spill some weeks earlier and found himself beached until it healed. In the meantime he pedaled a bike to stay in shape, but it just wasn't the same. Leucadia was his alternative to Pacific Beach, where he'd been living until he was squeezed out by mounting crowds and rents. Pacific Beach had, in turn, been his alternative to Ocean Beach, which had been his alternative to Imperial Beach. Gradually, he said, he will make his way north to the magic land of Santa Barbara. "I want to live at the beach forever," he announced with no solicitation. For now Leucadia is home; relaxed, uncrowded, and nontrendy, it is his isle of paradise. Besides, he knows someone with private access to the beach.

At the north end of Neptune Avenue is the newest of the area's beach accesses, **Grandview,** run by the city of Encinitas. It's nicely landscaped, with palm trees running down the hill beside the stairwell. It's a grand spot from which to wistfully gaze at the horizon, especially (of course) at sunset.

Shore Things

• **Bike/skate rentals:** The Board Source, 1650 North Coast Highway, Leucadia, 760/653-0146;

Dan's Coast Cyclery, 533 South Coast U.S. 101, Encinitas, 760/753-5867

• **Ecotourism:** San Elijo Lagoon Ecological Reserve, Cardiff-by-the-Sea, 760/753-5091

• **Rainy day attraction:** Self-Realization Fellowship Retreat, Gardens, and Hermitage (215 K Street, Encinitas, 760/753-1811)

• **Shopping/browsing:** Carlsbad Company Stores, Paseo del Norte, Carlsbad, 760/804-9000

• **Surf shop:** Mitch's, 363 U.S. 101, Solana Beach, 760/481-1354; Salty Sister, 2796 Carlsbad Boulevard, Carlsbad, 760/434-1122

• **Vacation rentals:** A&N, 6986 El Camino Real, Suite H, Carlsbad, 760/438-6811

Bunking Down

Beware of motels with "Ocean" or "Beach" in their names that are located on a highway bypass nowhere near a beach. In particular they must be avoided in Encinitas and Leucadia, where flyblown motels tout "sea breezes" and "views" when the only views they offer are of a gun shop on one side and a consignment shop on the other. The only place that's actually on the beach in either town is the **Moonlight Beach Motel** (233 Second Street, 760/753-0623, $), a functional and affordable three-story place with balcony views of the town's biggest beach.

The **Pacific Surf Inn** (1076 North U.S. 101, 760/436-8763, $) in Leucadia looks clean and well-tended. An offbeat alternative is **Leucadia Inn-by-the-Sea** (960 North Coast Highway, Leucadia, 760/942-1668, $$). Though it's not "by" the sea but three blocks away on a busy highway, its six "whimsical theme rooms" will amuse lovers of roadside oddities. They range from African Safari to Hollywood Nostalgia and from Nantucket to Mexico, which is quite a spread.

Other viable bunking options are the campground at San Elijo State Beach, straddling Cardiff-by-the-Sea and Encinitas, and a **Holiday Inn Express** (607 Leucadia Boulevard, 760/944-3800, $) in Leucadia.

Map of Southern California—Page 9

Coastal Cuisine

Along U.S. 101 to the south, Encinitas is top-heavy with Italian and Mexican cafés. Their shopping-plaza backdrops are good indicators of the predictable fare they offer. Keep driving until you get to the town center. There you'll find several more-than-serviceable dining spots. The best seafood is at **Shrimply Delicious** (559 Old U.S. 101, 760/944-9172, $$), which serves, to quote from a menu, "live fresh fish steamed in spices from the Deep South. If you are looking for a quick bite, this is definitely not for you." The restaurant takes cash only, and the names of entrées, including Sons of the Beaches and Love at First Bite, reflect the friendly ambience. It's open for lunch and dinner.

Just up the road, **DB Hackers** (101 Old U.S. 101, 760/436-3162, $) serves the "quick bite" of seafood Shrimply Delicious eschews. The entrées are mostly fried and the outdoor patio treats you to car noise and construction, but the staff is friendly and the food is relatively cheap. We were more than sufficiently rejuvenated by the fish tacos and the Jimmy Cliff tape that was playing.

For breakfast go to **George's Restaurant** (641 South U.S. 101, 760/942-9549, $), a legendary place that was the original home of the Cali-fornia Surf Museum (now in Oceanside). The specialty is Surf's Up, a no-nonsense feed with scrambled eggs, ham, and American cheese on an English muffin, served with hash browns.

Night Moves

The friendliest bar in town is the **Full Moon Saloon** (485 First Street, 760/436-7397), which offers live music and a game room. Our "best band name" award goes to Semisi and the Fula Bula Band, a reggae contingent playing at the Full Moon during one of our layovers in the area. More live music can be found at **First Street Bar** (656 First Street, 760/944-0233), which is popular with locals and is regularly voted best neighborhood bar by its regulars.

Encinitas and Leucadia have, over the years, attracted a sizable contingent of New Age groupies and ex-hippies, some of whom can be found knocking back a house decaf at the **Naked Bean Coffee Co.** (1126 First Street, 760/634-1347), which also features live music on weekends.

For More Information

Encinitas Chamber of Commerce, 138 Encinitas Boulevard, Encinitas, CA 92024, 760/753-6041, website: www.encinitaschamber.com

Carlsbad

Carlsbad is an anomaly. Of all the towns that cling to the Southern California coast, it is the only one not founded by a Spaniard or profoundly shaped by Latin influences. Instead, Carlsbad was the brainstorm of Gerhard Schutte, a German who came west from Nebraska to found a town of "small farms and gracious homes." His dream was made possible in 1883, when the Arizona Eastern Railway was completed, linking Southern California with the rest of civilization. This line also opened the land between Los Angeles and San Diego to homesteaders. Schutte headed up the list and moved on out.

Spanish and Native American influences are not entirely absent from the historical record. For centuries prior to Schutte's arrival, the Luseino tribe lived on the land between the two lagoons that form the boundaries of Carlsbad. However, they were quickly run off or subjugated by the missions when, in 1769, conquistador Gaspar de Portola arrived with his faith-filled sidekick, Father Juan Crespi. Even though the entire area was under Spanish rule, the only lingering trace of their influence today is Agua Hedionda, the name given to one of the local lagoons. It means "Stinking Waters."

Next Stop Beaches: All Aboard the Coaster

One of the nicer developments in North San Diego has been the Coaster, a "beach train" that offers regular rail service among the coastal cities of Solana Beach, Encinitas, Carlsbad, and Oceanside. The Coaster also serves Old Town San Diego, Downtown San Diego, and Sorrento Valley. It is a truly viable alternative, environmentally and mentally, to the agony of freeway and coast highway car travel. The Coaster is scenic, too, running on tracks that parallel the ocean for most of its route. Regularly scheduled service throughout the day, from early morning to early evening, Monday through Saturday, is offered to the above destinations. At each station, you are dropped off, quite literally, a few paces from the beach.

For more information contact **North County Transit District,** 810 Mission Avenue, Oceanside, CA 92054, 760/966-6500, website: www.sdcommute.com/service/coasterpage.htm.

By the time Schutte arrived, the mission system was destroyed and the land grab was on. Schutte and his followers purchased a chunk of real estate and began planting eucalyptus trees and squaring off lots for a town. In the process they discovered that the mineral water from their wells was identical to that found at the renowned Ninth Spa in Karlsbad, Bohemia (now Karlovy Vary, in the Czech Republic). The town took its name and identity from that happenstance, becoming a bastion of Old Europe in the New World. When word got out about the water, settlers began arriving. Humble, hardworking, and mostly English, these folks built their town to reflect their no-nonsense values.

Surprisingly little of the town has changed to this day. Original buildings are restored, and the subsequent growth of the town adheres to an established code, allowing Carlsbad to justifiably call itself a "village by the sea." With its Victorian, Dutch, and Bohemian architecture, Carlsbad has retained an appealingly antiquarian personality. This is remarkable when you consider that it sits between the military metropolis of Oceanside to the north and the asphalt sprawl of metropolitan San Diego to the south.

Some of the local buildings—such as Magee House, Twin Inns, and the Santa Fe Railway Station—have been designated National Historic Landmarks. The best place to orient yourself to town history is the Visitor Information Center, inside the **Santa Fe Railway Station** on Carlsbad Village Drive. Built in 1887, it's the oldest commercial structure in town.

Another must-see is the **Alt Karlsbad Haus,** on Carlsbad Boulevard. Built in 1964 on the site of the first mineral well, it's an exact replica of Antonín Dvořák's house in Prague. The great composer, whose patriotic *New World Symphony* had achieved national notoriety when the town was founded, is honored by a plaque on one wall. On another wall is a plaque that reads, "The formation of the Hanseatic League in the 13th Century gave birth to modern civilization, and through commerce and trade lifted Europe out of the Dark Ages." This is not the sort of plaque one is accustomed to reading in Southern California. Incidentally, Dvořák was a Bohemian who, out of love for his adopted home, offered to write a new national anthem for America. His spirit is a fitting one to symbolize the village of Carlsbad, which has lifted itself above the Dark Ages of the early 21st century by holding fast to civilized values.

Today, Carlsbad (population 83,000) seems to have everything going for it. Its public school system is one of the best in the country. The unemployment rate is the lowest in San Diego County. The public library is larger than some college libraries. The average daily temperature ranges from 58 degrees in January to 73 degrees in July. The young people look healthy, happy, and well groomed. ("Hey, John," one Beaver Cleaver lookalike yells out a car window to a pal. "Your new haircut looks great!") The old folks who choose to live out their years here look contented, too. After a few hours, you begin to wonder if this isn't the town Norman Rockwell was painting all those years.

Yes, Carlsbad is not just a place to vacation. It's a place to settle down and attend the church of your choice. This is a town of churches: Lutheran rest homes stand hard by humble Hispanic Pentecostal churches. We passed one of the latter, a sort of Quonset hut with a steeple, on the way to dinner. The door was open to the street and we heard the congregation singing and banging drums and tambourines. Two hours later, on our return stroll, they were still at it, exhorted by a shouting minister.

Of the 37 square miles that fall within the city limits, less than one-half have been developed, and the residents are vigilant against creeping mall sprawl. According to a resident, "We're putting the screws on too much more growth." Of course there's always something nipping at those Utopian heels. Most recently, it's a children's theme park called **Legoland** ("your destination for real family fun!"), which was built on Carlsbad Ranch, east of town. California's first new theme park in 25 years, the 128-acre **Legoland** (760/918-5346) opened March

20, 1999, to much fanfare. Legoland has nine play areas inside the park. They have bucolic names like "The Garden," "The Ridge," "The Lake," "The Village Green." (Hey, you can find all these things in Carlsbad without having to pay admission!) There are more than 50 rides on property. World landmarks, animals, and what-have-you have been rendered in plastic Lego bricks by the millions. We don't know what it all signifies, but this much we can tell you: adults pay $39.95 to enter, while kids 16 and under and seniors 61 and over are charged $33.95 apiece. In addition, you're hit with a $7 parking fee. A family of four will spend $154.80 at Legoland even before the kids whine for their first soda pop or souvenir trinket.

We're more inclined to head to **Carlsbad Mineral Water Spa** (2802 Carlsbad Boulevard, 760/434-1887) for a rejuvenating soak. It's been around since 1882 and is a California Historic Site. More to the point, the pure water that comes from a 1,700-foot aquifer is 9,500 years old and full of rejuvenating minerals. The spa offers body wraps, massages, mud facials, mineral baths, and more.

Beaches

A good deal of the beach in the Carlsbad area eroded since the construction of Oceanside Harbor to the north, and El Niño storms claimed more of the sand in the late 1990s. We came in the summer of 2002 expecting the worst on the beaches of Carlsbad—a sandless, eroded plain of cobbles, such as we'd seen in years past—but a beach renourishment project has brought a new look and width to this formerly ravaged shoreline. That's not to say that this sand transfusion has addressed every problem, but it has restored a viable swimming beach to Carlsbad State Beach in the short term.

Coming from the south, **Ponto Beach**—a unit of **South Carlsbad State Beach**—is up first. It's by Batiquitos Lagoon, between Carlsbad and Leucadia. These days, the location is a bit distressed, with an ad hoc string of parking spaces along the west side of Carlsbad Boulevard (U.S. 101). A rusty chain-link fence keeps people away from the crumbling cliff edges. There's an abandoned parking lot and fences everywhere. The future is not promising, and the present at Ponto is fairly dismal. Though surfers still get their kicks here, it's not the kind of place others would go out of their way to visit.

The main unit of **South Carlsbad State Beach** is in some disarray, too. At one time, this was a highly desirable 226-site state-park campground occupying an inspirational blufftop setting overlooking the beach. Now campers are shoehorned into a narrow strip between the eroding cliffs and the four-lane boulevard. South Carlsbad appears to be fighting a losing battle against the elements. In some forthcoming year, the campground will succumb and the road will be next. Already, you can see stretches of U.S. 101 hereabouts ("Old Coast Road") that have been abandoned and relocated east.

South Carlsbad State Beach runs into **Carlsbad State Beach,** which runs for four miles. A portion of Carlsbad State Beach has been designated **Tamarack Surf Beach** (where Tamarack Avenue meets Carlsbad Boulevard). This is a busy place; we found the sizable parking lot at Tamarack full on a Monday afternoon around sunset. Carlsbad State Beach is popular with all sorts of recreating types: bodysurfers, boogie boarders, swimmers, divers, and surf casters. Incidentally, another in-town stretch of sand has been designated **Robert C. Frazee State Beach,** but it (like Tamarack Surf Beach) is part of Carlsbad State Beach.

Carlsbad is a great town for walking, especially along its beaches. Two jogging/biking paths—one that runs beside Carlsbad Boulevard and one below it by the seawall that protects the beach—draw a tireless troupe of California aerobicizers. They jog, they bike, they racewalk, they skateboard, they huff and puff . . . anything to maintain those hourglass figures. We watched a pair of toned-up girls sprinting up and down the stairs that link Carlsbad's pathways while conversing breathlessly about clothes, dates, and office politics. Many bring along their dogs, who run with their owners or pull them on skateboards.

The north part of town has been generously seeded with street-end accesses, each of which has stairs that lead to the beach (but no facilities). As in south Oceanside, north Carlsbad is a largely middle-class residential neighborhood, and the main point of these accesses appears to be to allow local residents to get to the beach.

Believe it or not, the "stinking waters" at **Agua Hedionda Lagoon** (east of Carlsbad City Beach) are popular with swimmers and waterskiers. Boats and water-skis can be rented at **Snug Harbor Marina** (4215 Harrison Street, 760/434-3089). A nice hiking/biking trail runs along the shore of the lagoon.

Bunking Down

It's not cheap to stay in the "village by the sea." The village mentality can be a little tough on the wallet. **La Costa Resort & Spa** (2100 Costa del Mar Road, 760/438-9111, $$$$), a 500-room golf and tennis resort, attracts celebrities by the Lear-jet load and hosts golf and tennis tournaments. It's got two PGA courses and 21 tennis courts, plus a spa and "Chopra Center" (as in Deepak, the spirituality guru), where you can "harness your creative genius, create perfect health, and access blissful, peaceful states of existence." With room rates that range $340–520 nightly (more for suites), you'll need all the bliss you can manage.

A few steps down in price ($194–275) and many steps closer to the beach is the **Carlsbad Inn Beach Resort** (3075 Carlsbad Boulevard, 760/434-7020, $$$), an appealing beach and tennis complex built in the center of town under the community's watchful Old World architectural guidelines. A swimming pool, workout room, and kids' spa make this a winner. Another worthy beachfront choice is the **Tama-**

Map of Southern California—Page 9

rack Beach Resort (3200 Carlsbad Boulevard, 760/729-3500, $$$), which is more like a timeshare condominium than a motel. Each suite has a washer and dryer, full kitchen, and stereo. For a front and center location on the beach, you can't better the **Best Western Beach Terrace Inn** (2775 Ocean Street, 760/729-5951, $$$). Located in a quiet residential neighborhood, the Beach Terrace Inn has as sunny a disposition as you'll find at the beach. Plus, you can practically jump off the balcony into the ocean (though we'd advise against it). Nearly as appealing is the **Best Western Beach View Lodge** (3180 Carlsbad Boulevard, 760/729-1151, $$), which lies close to but not quite on the ocean and will earn you a significant break on rates relative to the other resorts and inns mentioned herein.

Coastal Cuisine

If you like fried seafood, it can be ordered by the basket at **Harbor Fish South** (3179 Carlsbad Boulevard, 760/729-4161, $), an outdoor-patio joint beside the ocean and next to a surf shop. The clientele is young and less discriminating than the folks at La Costa. The Surfer's Special, for instance, is a cheeseburger and fries. But the view and ambience are perfectly beachy. Somewhat disappointingly, the fish in the fish 'n' chips basket is not local but comes from Alaskan waters.

The best local seafood we found was at **Fish House Vera Cruz** (417 Carlsbad Village Drive, 760/434-6777, $$), a pleasant stroll over the railroad tracks just east of the town center. The name derives from a fishing boat that scours the Pacific coast from Baja to Alaska to nab the goodies they serve here. Everything is mesquite-grilled to perfection, and prices are moderate. The place even looks like the hold of a fishing vessel, with lots of nautical knickknacks.

Niemans (300 Carlsbad Village Drive, 760/729-4131, $$$) is worth visiting because it's housed in the oldest Victorian structure in town. If you're not inclined toward "proper attire," you can at least stroll the grounds and pretend to be studying the menu, which tends toward hearty fare (prime rib, filet mignon, leg of lamb) with a smattering of seafood items.

Night Moves

In a Norman Rockwell kind of town, you're lucky to find a place that serves even something as harmless as frozen yogurt after dark. Carlsbad, fortunately, does have a semblance of nightlife. The primary source of activity is **Sandbar Café** (3878 Carlsbad Boulevard, 760/729-3170), which sits across the street from the roaring ocean surf and is home to live rock and blues on most nights. It draws from miles around those who dig a spacious dance floor. Another hopping haunt is the local **Hennessey's Tavern** (2777 Roosevelt Street, 760/729-6951), which has live music on weekends. For more low-key good times the **Kafana Coffee Shop** (3076 Carlsbad Boulevard, 760/720-0074) offers warbling folkies and good, stiff belts of caffeine.

For More Information

Carlsbad Convention and Visitors Bureau, 400 Carlsbad Village Drive, Carlsbad, CA 92008, 760/434-6093 or 800/227-5722, website: www.visit carlsbad.com; Carlsbad Chamber of Commerce, Paseo del Norte #128, Carlsbad, CA 92008, 760/931-8400, website: www.carlsbad.org

Map of San Diego County—Page 10

Oceanside

For decades Oceanside has been a sprawling military/urban wasteland. Though the reputation hasn't changed much over the years, the city lately appears to be on the upswing. Yes, the past is behind Oceanside and the future's so bright you gotta wear shades. At least it's been sprucing itself up and putting its best foot forward. We're pleased to report that Oceanside has been steadily improving since we first began visiting in the mid-1980s. Back then, it wore the sad-sack look of a military town that existed largely to serve the practical and prurient needs of thousands of U.S. Marines stationed at Camp Pendleton. Although we certainly wouldn't describe it as a destination mecca for those traveling the California coast, there's no reason to actively avoid it these days, either.

To fully understand Oceanside (population 161,000), it's necessary to do like the Marines and hit the beaches. You would expect a town with a name like Oceanside to be blessed in that department. From Buccaneer Beach to Oceanside Pier to Harbor Beach, this unpretentious place has been adopted by beachgoers from as far afield as Encinitas. They come to Oceanside because their own beaches are either crowded or disappearing, and because parking is easier, prices are cheaper, and attitudes are conducive to casual enjoyment.

Even given these enviable conditions, Oceanside has a tale of woe regarding the beach that sits on either side of the formidable Oceanside Pier (which, at 1,942 feet, is the second longest on the West Coast). According to the still-angry locals, the main culprit is the U.S. Army Corps of Engineers. In the 1960s, having conducted only minimal study of the impact on the surrounding coastline, the Corps created a harbor at Oceanside. This one is big, slick, and modern, with 950 slips for pleasure craft and yachts, a marina, restaurants, condominiums, and a shopping plaza designed to resemble a Cape Cod seaport village.

Before the architectural surgery, Oceanside had one of the widest, longest, and best-loved beaches on the southern coast. It was a Sahara of sand that was especially attractive to surfers. Imagine, if you will, a sea monster coming ashore and taking a five-acre bite out of the center of this beach, then spitting the sand back into the water several miles offshore. This, essentially, is what has happened in Oceanside. According to a local historian who was in high school at the time, he and his classmates, as a science project, conducted a study of the proposed harbor project. They foresaw the damage that would be done to their beloved beach. They presented their study to the Corps and were basically told, "Beat it, kids, you don't know what you're talking about."

Alas, they did know. Photographs of Oceanside City Beach taken in 1946 show an uninterrupted swath of sand as wide and straight as any we've seen on either coast. The same beach today is certainly lovely to behold, but it's nowhere near the size of the beach back in the 1940s. The jetty that was meant to ward off rough waters from luxury vessels in the harbor was built at the wrong angle. The sand that normally flowed south with the longshore currents in years past now winds up at the bottom of an offshore canyon, lost forever. To make this tale even more shameful, the Army Corps of Engineers must dredge the harbor two or three times a year to keep it navigable. "It's amazing that Carlsbad doesn't sue the Corps," opined our local historian, referring to the devastating effects of the disrupted sand flow south of Oceanside. "It's a pretty big thing to lose your beach."

Thankfully, a sand-bypassing operation has been developed that has begun to replenish the shoreline. It involves shooting sand through six-inch tubes located around the harbor, where it can resume its natural southerly drift with the currents. In a sense, Oceanside has lost

Map of Southern California—Page 9

California Surf Museum

As everyone knows, surfing is more than a sport. In Southern California, perhaps more than anywhere else except Hawaii, it is a religion. Around these parts, the church of choice is the **California Surf Museum** (223 North Coast Highway, 760/721-6876), near the Oceanside Pier.

The museum's history is not unlike that of a wandering religious mystic. Founded in 1985 by Jane Schmauss and Stuart Resor, the museum was originally housed at George's Restaurant in Encinitas. It was moved to Pacific Beach, then back to Encinitas's Moonlight Plaza. Finally it arrived at its Canaan—a former VFW hall and beach bar that sits in the heart of surfer country.

The California Surf Museum is a delight for both devotees of the sport and the merely curious. Here the history and lore of surfing are lovingly told with original relics, informative placards, vintage photographs, clothing, clippings, books, and shrines to dead surfers. Exhibits are changed regularly, and various events celebrate the sport's history, which is particularly rich in this locale. In 1994 they celebrated the 80th birthday of Lorrin "Whitey" Harrison, a lifelong surfer who still surfed daily at San Onofre. Another event featured the work of LeRoy "Granny" Grannis, a 76-year-old whose surfing pictures are the pinnacle of action photography. The current exhibit when we passed through in 2002 was a "Tribute to Doc Ball and the Early California Surfriders."

The most sacred moments and mementos are devoted to the pantheon of greats who've taken that one last ride to surfer heaven. Their stories read like the lives of saints. They include:

• Duke Kahanamoku, the Polynesian who popularized surfing worldwide. He also re-introduced surfing to Hawaii after missionaries forbade it. He took his nickname from the Duke of Edinburgh and won three gold medals in swimming at the 1912 Olympics. One of the Duke's long redwood boards is on display at the museum.

• George Freeth, the Hawaiian who introduced surfing to California and then became a lifeguard in Oceanside. Freeth died of pneumonia in 1910 after rescuing several people in the rough waters off Oceanside Pier.

• Bob Simmons, whose only possessions were a 1937 Ford sedan and a longboard. This daredevil developed the "spoon nose" (a lift at the front of the board that helps avoid nose-dives) and was the first surfer to use rope hand grips. He was inexhaustible, surfing from sunup to sundown. On September 27, 1954, while surfing off Windansea in La Jolla, Simmons caught a wave bigger than even he could handle. His board made it to shore, but he never did.

Anecdotes like these and the countless items for perusal and sale bring surfing alive, even for the uninitiated. The museum is open from Thursday through Monday 10 A.M.–4 P.M. Admission is free! Hang ten here, and tell 'em we sent you.

Map of San Diego County—Page 10

and found its beach. Happily, the city is gearing up for another boom. The 100 acres behind the pier—except for the California Surf Museum (see sidebar, "California Surf Museum")—have been slated for development. The Marriott hotel chain has already signed on, and four 10-story buildings are on the drawing board. But unlike the residents of most coastal towns, the natives aren't opposed to a massive facelift in Oceanside. And, so far, all change has been for the better.

"It won't be Cement City, like they did to Huntington Beach," a longtime local told us. "It will be more like a seaport village, made of wood, with an educational Sea Center. We want it." No, after all it's been through, the dauntless, rough-and-tumble city of Oceanside deserves it.

The main reason for Oceanside's size and almost the sole reason for its existence is **Camp Pendleton.** Occupying 250,000 acres (200 square miles), it is the world's largest U.S. Marine base. Camp Pendleton is literally next door to Oceanside, its back gate opening onto Oceanside Harbor. Sixty thousand marine and civilian personnel work and train at the camp. Those who don't live on base reside in Oceanside with their families.

At first glimpse Oceanside doesn't look like the stereotypical military town. Great pains have been made to disguise this fact, especially on the water. Still, Oceanside is at its core a military town, and this makes for such incongruous sightings as a champagne brunch at the **Taste of Europe** restaurant two blocks from the **Paradise-by-the-Sea RV Park.** It may not be a bona fide war zone, as many landlocked military towns are. But as you pull away from the upscale harbor you begin to notice that Oceanside boasts more liquor stores than you can shake an empty fifth of Old Granddad at. So it goes in a military town—even one that's trying hard to play up its beachier assets. Broken-bulb saloons, low-rent food stands, thrift shops full of Persian Gulf war relics, discount

clothiers, and chockablock flat-roofed duplexes—all are signs of a military lifestyle that has remained virtually unchanged since World War II. No slight intended, as one of us was an army brat who spent the happiest years of his childhood on and around military bases.

Incidentally, the **Buena Vista Lagoon Ecological Reserve** is south of town, between Oceanside and Carlsbad. This large natural wetland—one of the few remaining in Southern California—is a habitat for birds and vegetation (including rare species of both). A trail along the shoreline makes for pleasant sightings. The **Buena Vista Audubon Nature Center** (2202 South Coast Highway, 760/439-2473) provides exhibits, lectures, and group tours; it's open 10 A.M.–2 P.M. Tuesday–Saturday.

Oh yes, extra credit is available for those willing to drive four miles inland on Highway 76 to see **Mission San Luis Rey de Francia** (4050 Mission Avenue, 760/757-3651). Founded in 1798 by Father Fermin de Lasuen, the "King of the Missions" was named for King Louis XI of France. The largest of the Franciscan-run missions, it was lavishly decorated to be something of a showpiece. Today, it houses an active order of Franciscan monks and a museum, which is open to the public for viewing and souvenir buying. A fiesta is held here every year during the third week of July. Of particular interest are the paintings by local Native Americans.

Beaches

Palm-lined Pacific Street runs along Oceanside's beach from the south end of town up to Oceanside Pier. Hereabouts is a pleasant residential neighborhood of newish homes that betray a fondness for the New England architectural style rather than the Spanish vernacular of stucco and pipe roofs one generally finds in Southern California. Beach accesses are plentiful at street ends and parking on side streets is abundant. At the south end, however, a wall of riprap boulders remains in place, protecting home-

Map of Southern California—Page 9

owners from the ocean's incursions along an unrenourished section of shoreline.

Oceanside's sandy bounty begins inauspiciously with **South Oceanside Beach** (on South Pacific Street). You park in the neighborhood along an enormous cement embankment and pass between condos onto hard-packed sand; not worth the trouble, as much better beaches lie ahead.

More easily accessed is **Buccaneer Beach,** which is in the same residential neighborhood. The beach here is a tiny pocket of sand free of rocks and debris. It's nice, but nicer still is pondering what the beach would be like if it weren't hogged by all the houses built right on top of it. Across the street is **Buccaneer Park,** an inviting green space with play area, picnic tables, snack bar, restrooms, and showers. Also quite nice is **Loma Alta Marsh,** a small lagoon east of the beach. A trail passes beneath a railroad trestle, and birds can be heard chirping happily.

Several more beach accesses with lifeguard towers are strewn between Buccaneer Park and Oceanside Pier. Named for the streets that meet Pacific Street in their vicinity, they are (from south to north) **Oceanside Boulevard Beach, Wisconsin Street Beach** and **Tyson Street Beach.** The last of these has a park with picnic tables and playground, much as at Buccaneer Park. It's hard not to like Oceanside from the perspective of these grassy seaside parks and broad, sandy beaches.

A one-way oceanfront street with benches and green space called The Strand flares off of Pacific Street south of the pier and rejoins it just north of the pier. It's great for family strolls or lonely naps in the grass. Down by Oceanside Pier, you'll find a wide, pleasant beach extending in both directions. A sand renourishment project undertaken in 2001 has for the most part remained in place along this popular stretch. (Of course, all that could change in a single stormy winter.) The area south of the pier is called **Pier View South.** It is a narrower strand than the beach between

the pier and breakwater, which is designated **Pier View North.**

The beach just south of Oceanside Harbor is called **Breakwater Way,** and it is a quiet, safe, and relatively out-of-the-way family beach. The jetties up at this end of Oceanside protect the mouth of the San Luis Rey River. North of the river is Oceanside Harbor and **Harbor Beach.** Because it abuts the north jetty, which intercepts the ocean's attempted transport of sand across the river mouth, Harbor Beach is among the widest beaches in San Diego County. The beach and harbor area are filled with amenities, from picnic tables and volleyball nets to deep-sea fishing trips and kayak rentals. Motels, shops, and restaurants, too! Oceanside Harbor even has its own fishing pier, making this a two-pier town.

The beaches in the vicinity of the pier can get crowded on summer weekends, but owing to the fact that Oceanside is a military town and not a tourist destination—or even a huge favorite with day-tripping inlanders—it is not as jammed as other in-town beaches in northern San Diego County (which is one more reason to come here). The Oceanside town planners have done their best to make the pier an inviting area, with stands of palm trees, green and cleanly kept park space, a pierside amphitheater and concessions (including, unfortunately, a McDonald's, which says volumes about the typical beach visitor). The sand is soft, light brown, and well patrolled by lifeguards; there are a dozen lifeguard stands along Oceanside's beaches. You can park near the pier along Pacific Street for 50 cents an hour—a bargain, by beach standards. (Not to digress, but just to give an idea of the flavor of life in Oceanside, here's a newsy tidbit from January 2002: "No leads have been developed in the theft of 10 parking meters last week from the downtown area, police said.")

The massive Oceanside Pier is a broad, dark-planked old affair with a devoted fishing clientele. No license is needed to fish off the pier,

Map of San Diego County—Page 10

and a trolley runs to and from it. A community center is attached to the pier in the complex at its base; its gym is open to the public. Just behind the pier sits the **California Surf Museum** (see sidebar), a required stop for people who like people who like beaches.

Shore Things

• **Bike/skate rentals:** El Camino Bike Shop, 121 North El Camino Real, Encinitas, 760/436-2340; Millennial Motors, 505 Mission Avenue, Oceanside, 760/722-2225
• **Boat cruise:** Helgren's Oceanside Sportfishing, 315 Harbor Drive South, Oceanside, 760/722-2133
• **Dive shop:** Pyramid Divers, 282 Harbor Drive South, Oceanside, 760/433-6842
• **Ecotourism:** Buena Vista Audubon Society Nature Center, 2202 South Coast Highway, Oceanside, 760/439-2473
• **Fishing charters:** Helgren's Oceanside Sportfishing, 315 Harbor Drive South, 760/722-2133
• **Marina:** Oceanside Harbor & Marina, 1540 Harbor Drive, 760/966-4580
• **Pier:** Oceanside Pier, Pacific Street and the Strand, Oceanside, 760/966-4535
• **Rainy day attraction:** Mission San Luis Rey, 4050 Mission Avenue, 760/757-3651
• **Shopping/browsing:** Carlsbad Company Stores, Paseo del Norte, Carlsbad, 760/804-9000
• **Surf shop:** Action Beach Board Shop, 310 Mission Avenue, Oceanside, 760/722-7101

Bunking Down

Oceanside is sorely lacking in motels as accommodating as its beaches. **Oceanside Marina Inn** (2008 Harbor Drive North, 760/722-1561, $$$) has kitchens and fireplaces to go with its location at Oceanside Harbor. They've been talking for years about plans for hotels behind the Oceanside Pier, but nothing's materialized yet. If you're not staying on the harbor, then you're probably best off staying at the **Best Western Oceanside Inn** (1680 Oceanside Boulevard, 760/722-1821, $$). A

well-appointed chain motel adjacent to I-5, it offers pools, saunas, and large, clean rooms.

Coastal Cuisine

Meals in Oceanside are grabbed on the run or casually eaten at picnic tables or beach blankets. The surfer theme is mined at the **Longboarder Cafe** (228 North Coast Highway, 760/721-6776, $) and the **Beach Break Cafe** (1902 South Coast Highway, 760/439-6355, $), which serve hearty staples (pancakes, omelettes, salads, burgers, burritos) in bright, ocean-themed surroundings.

A good, cheap quick south of the border–style bite can be had at **Johnny Mañana's** (308 Mission Avenue, 760/721-9999, $). Heaping helpings of fresh, guilt-free Mexican fare are served at low prices in a pleasant, beachy atmosphere. The house special is a BLT burrito, served with guacamole and salsa. It's hard to spend more than five or six bucks here. You can make off with a plain cheese quesadilla and a cold Pacifico beer, served with complimentary salsa and chips, for under $4. The breakfast burrito has jump-started many a surfer's morning. *¡Arriba!*

The oldest restaurant in Oceanside is **101 Cafe** (631 South Coast Highway, 760/722-5220, $), a '50s-themed flashback to the world of *Happy Days* on Old U.S. 101. The restaurant's origins, in fact, go all the way back to 1928. Stick-to-the-ribs sandwiches, salads, and burgers rule the menu, and time seemingly stands still.

Night Moves

Oceanside's nightlife can be a bit raw. After a week of sweating in the hills of Camp Pendleton, a marine can work up a profound thirst. To quench it he or she heads into Oceanside, where bar signs offer greetings like "Welcoming Those Who Have Served and Those Serving." Here's a sampling of the cocktail lounges in Oceanside: **Bub's Whiskey Dive** (301 Pier View Way, 760/757-2827), **The Rusty**

Spur (406 Pier View Way, 760/722-2216), and One More That's It Pub (431 Airport Road, 760/433-3781). Bottom's up, and better you than us.

For More Information

Oceanside Chamber of Commerce, 928 North Coast Highway, Oceanside, CA 92054, 760/722-1534, website: www.oceansidechamber.com

San Onofre State Beach

The last stop in San Diego County, **San Onofre State Beach** butts up against the Orange County line. Several things about San Onofre might make some visitors uneasy. First, it sits in the shadow of the San Onofre Nuclear Generating Station, whose twin peaks are visible from the park. Second, San Onofre is surrounded by **Camp Pendleton,** the largest U.S. Marine base in the nation. In fact, the park lies on Marine Corps land that has been leased to the state. Camp Pendleton occupies a staggering 250,000 acres, and you never know what might whiz by this deceptively empty landscape. We were enjoying the view from a freeway vista point when an amphibious tank came roaring across the terrain, kicking up dust. We also heard a few jets break the sound barrier. Third, the area is full of rattlesnakes. This is the only venomous snake species found in California, but they sink their fangs into roughly 200 unlucky Southlanders a year. Other snakes native to San Onofre include red racer, gopher, and king. Even so, the most common animal-related injury is the bite of the stingray, which settles in the sand close to shore.

On the positive side, because it lies on a military reservation, San Onofre is gloriously undeveloped. This is what the California coast used to look like way back when—except, of course, for the nuclear power plant. The lengthy stretch of beach at the south end of San Onofre—often referred to as **Bluffs Beach** or simply **San Onofre State Beach**—can be accessed via six numbered trails that descend steeply to it. It is a lengthy beach, with three miles of campsites running along the abandoned stretch of coastal highway (San Onofre Beach Road) above it. At the north end of the campground

is a day-use area with parking. There's nothing fancy about **San Onofre Bluffs Campground,** whose 176 sites offer little in the way of shade and can get noisy (thanks to their proximity to I-5). **San Mateo Campground,** a more recent addition, has 161 sites (157 with electrical and water hookups) and lies a mile east of I-5. A mile-long trail leads from this campground to the famed Trestles surfing beach.

San Onofre State Beach is ideal for beginners—the Waikiki of California, we've seen it called—and surf camps are held along its shores. Wanna learn how to surf while camping at San Onofre to boot? Contact Jason Senn at **Endless Summer Surf Camp** (949/498-7862). This San Clemente–based surf expert offers five- and seven-day overnight surf camp packages for $475 and $575, respectively.

Okay, things get a little confusing at this point, so follow closely. Proceeding north from the campground, you encounter San Onofre Nuclear Generating Station (SONGS, of all unlikely acronyms); Old Man's Beach (part of San Onofre State Beach); San Onofre Recreational Beach (which belongs to Camp Pendleton); and Trestles Beach (part of San Onofre State Beach).

Old Man's Beach is a popular spot for older surfers on longboards ("geezers," in surfing lingo). The vibe is mellower than at beaches where adrenalized young surf punks on shortboards carry out their version of *The Fight Club* for wave-riding rights. Mexican-style thatched cabanas and volleyball nets add to the festive air. Next up is **San Onofre Recreational Beach** (a.k.a. Churches Beach), one of two lifeguarded beaches for Camp Pendleton military personnel only. (The other is **Del Mar**

Map of San Diego County—Page 10

San Diego County

Beach, just above Oceanside.) Rounding out the lineup at San Onofre is **Trestles Beach.** At San Mateo Point, Trestles offers the best break in San Diego County and one of the best in the continental United States. Trestles is a big reason why so many world-class surfers make their home in nearby San Clemente—and why so many surfers go to the trouble of trotting a mile down a pathway with a surfboard on their head to get there.

For More Information

San Onofre State Park, 949/492-4872, website: www.cal-parks.ca.gov

Map of Southern California—Page 9

© ROBERT HOLMES/CALTOUR

Chapter 2
Orange County

Orange County

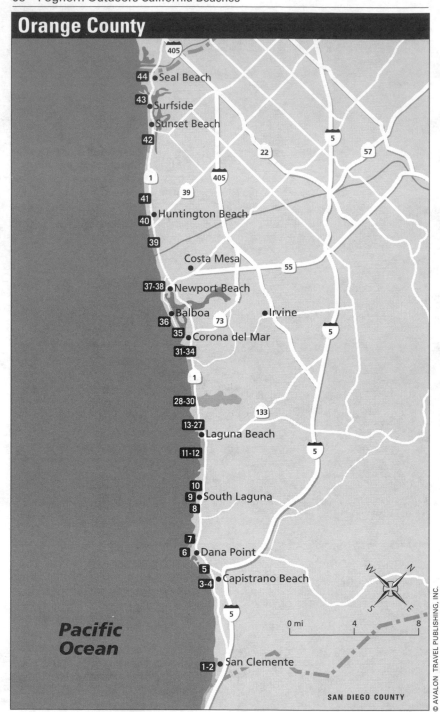

Orange County Beaches

1 San Clemente State Beach, page 111

Location: Take the Avenida Calafia exit from I-5 in San Clemente and follow it west to park.
Parking/fees: $5 entrance fee per vehicle. Camping fees are $13–22 per night, plus a $7.50 reservation fee.
Hours: 6 A.M.–10 P.M. (to 8 P.M. December–February)
Facilities: lifeguards, restrooms, showers, and picnic areas
Contact: San Clemente State Beach, 949/492-3156

2 San Clemente City Beach, page 111

Location: Avenida del Mar at Avenida Victoria in San Clemente
Parking/fees: metered street parking
Hours: 4 A.M.–midnight.
Facilities: concession, lifeguards, restrooms, showers, and picnic area
Contact: San Clemente Department of Marine Safety, 949/361-8219

3 Poche Beach, page 116

Location: Camino Capistrano at Pacific Coast Highway in Capistrano Beach
Parking/fees: free street parking
Hours: 6 A.M.–10 P.M.
Facilities: none
Contact: South Beaches Operation Office of Orange County Harbors, Beaches, and Parks, 949/661-7013

4 Capistrano Beach, page 115

Location: El Camino Real at Palisade Drive in Capistrano Beach
Parking/fees: metered parking lots
Hours: 6 A.M.–10 P.M.
Facilities: concession, lifeguards, restrooms, showers, and picnic tables
Contact: South Beaches Operation Office of Orange County Harbors, Beaches, and Parks, 949/661-7013

5 Doheny State Beach, page 115

Location: Dana Point Harbor Drive off Pacific Coast Highway in Dana Point
Parking/fees: $5 entrance fee per vehicle. Camping fees are $13–16 per night, plus a $7.50 reservation fee.

Map of Orange County—Page 98

Hours: 6 A.M.–10 P.M. (to 8 P.M. October–March)
Facilities: concession, lifeguards, restrooms, showers, and picnic areas
Contact: Doheny State Beach, 949/496-6171

6 Dana Point Harbor, page 120

Location: Ensenada Place at Dana Point Harbor in Dana Point
Parking/fees: free parking lot
Hours: 6 a.m.–midnight
Facilities: concession, restrooms, showers, and picnic areas
Contact: South Beaches Operation Office of Orange County Harbors, Beaches, and Parks, 949/661-7013

7 Salt Creek County Beach, page 120

Location: Pacific Coast Highway at Ritz-Carlton Drive between Dana Point and South Laguna
Parking/fees: metered parking lot
Hours: 5 A.M.–midnight
Facilities: concession, lifeguards, restrooms, showers, and picnic tables
Contact: South Beaches Operation Office of Orange County Harbors, Beaches, and Parks, 949/661-7013

8 1,000 Steps Beach, page 125

Location: Ninth Avenue at Pacific Coast Highway in South Laguna
Parking/fees: metered street parking
Hours: 6 A.M.–9 P.M.
Facilities: lifeguards
Contact: South Beaches Operation Office of Orange County Harbors, Beaches, and Parks, 949/661-7013

9 West Street Beach, page 125

Location: West Street at Pacific Coast Highway in South Laguna
Parking/fees: metered street parking
Hours: 6 A.M.–10 P.M.
Facilities: none
Contact: South Beaches Operation Office of Orange County Harbors, Beaches, and Parks, 949/661-7013

10 Aliso Creek County Beach, page 125

Location: 31,000 block of Pacific Coast Highway in South Laguna
Parking/fees: metered parking lot

Map of Southern California—Page 9

Hours: 6 A.M.–10 P.M.

Facilities: concessions, lifeguards, restrooms, showers, and picnic tables

Contact: South Beaches Operation Office of Orange County Harbors, Beaches, and Parks, 949/661-7013

11 Victoria Beach, page 126

Location: Victoria Drive off Pacific Coast Highway in Laguna Beach

Parking/fees: metered street parking

Hours: 6 A.M.–midnight

Facilities: none

Contact: Laguna Beach Department of Marine Safety, 949/494-6572

12 Woods Cove, page 126

Location: Diamond Street off Pacific Coast Highway in Laguna Beach.

Parking/fees: metered street parking

Hours: 6 A.M.–midnight

Facilities: none

Contact: Laguna Beach Department of Marine Safety, 949/494-6572

13 Pearl Street Beach, page 126

Location: Pearl Street off Pacific Coast Highway in Laguna Beach.

Parking/fees: metered street parking

Hours: 6 A.M.–midnight

Facilities: none

Contact: Laguna Beach Department of Marine Safety, 949/494-6572

14 Bluebird Beach, page 126

Location: Bluebird Canyon Road off Pacific Coast Highway in Laguna Beach

Parking/fees: metered street parking

Hours: 6 A.M.–midnight

Facilities: none

Contact: Laguna Beach Department of Marine Safety, 949/494-6572

15 Mountain Road Beach, page 126

Location: Mountain Road off Pacific Coast Highway in Laguna Beach

Parking/fees: metered street parking

Hours: 6 A.M.–midnight

Facilities: none

Contact: Laguna Beach Department of Marine Safety, 949/494-6572

Orange County

Map of Orange County—Page 98

16 Brooks Beach, page 126

Location: Brooks Street off Pacific Coast Highway in Laguna Beach
Parking/fees: metered street parking
Hours: 6 A.M.–midnight
Facilities: none
Contact: Laguna Beach Department of Marine Safety, 949/494-6572

17 Oak Street Beach, page 126

Location: Oak Street off Pacific Coast Highway in Laguna Beach
Parking/fees: metered street parking
Hours: 6 A.M.–midnight
Facilities: none
Contact: Laguna Beach Department of Marine Safety, 949/494-6572

18 Thalia Street Beach, page 126

Location: Thalia Street off Pacific Coast Highway in Laguna Beach
Parking/fees: metered street parking
Hours: 6 A.M.–midnight
Facilities: none
Contact: Laguna Beach Department of Marine Safety, 949/494-6572

19 St. Ann's Beach, page 126

Location: St. Ann's Drive off Pacific Coast Highway in Laguna Beach
Parking/fees: metered street parking
Hours: 6 A.M.–midnight
Facilities: none
Contact: Laguna Beach Department of Marine Safety, 949/494-6572

20 Sleepy Hollow Beach, page 126

Location: Sleepy Hollow Lane off Pacific Coast Highway in Laguna Beach
Parking/fees: metered street parking
Hours: 6 A.M.–midnight
Facilities: none
Contact: Laguna Beach Department of Marine Safety, 949/494-6572

21 Main Beach (a.k.a. Laguna Beach Municipal Park), page 125

Location: between Broadway and Ocean Avenues at Pacific Coast Highway in Laguna Beach
Parking/fees: metered street parking
Hours: 6 A.M.–midnight

Map of Southern California—Page 9

Facilities: lifeguards, restrooms, showers, and picnic tables
Contact: Laguna Beach Department of Marine Safety, 949/494-6572

22 Rockpile Beach, page 127

Location: Cliff Drive at Jasmine Street, below Heisler Park, in Laguna Beach
Parking/fees: metered street parking
Hours: 6 A.M.–midnight
Facilities: none
Contact: Laguna Beach Department of Marine Safety, 949/494-6572

23 Picnic Beach, page 127

Location: Cliff Drive at Myrtle Street, below Heisler Park, in Laguna Beach
Parking/fees: metered street parking
Hours: 6 A.M.–midnight
Facilities: lifeguards and picnic tables
Contact: Laguna Beach Department of Marine Safety, 949/494-6572

24 Diver's Cove, page 127

Location: 600 block of Cliff Drive in Laguna Beach
Parking/fees: metered street parking
Hours: 6 A.M.–midnight
Facilities: none
Contact: Laguna Beach Department of Marine Safety, 949/494-6572

25 Boat Canyon Beach, page 127

Location: off Cliff Drive, west of Boat Canyon Park, via stairwell beside Diver's Cove Condominiums in Laguna Beach
Parking/fees: metered street parking
Hours: 6 A.M.–midnight
Facilities: none
Contact: Laguna Beach Department of Marine Safety, 949/494-6572

26 Shaw's Cove, page 127

Location: Cliff Drive at Fairview Street in Laguna Beach
Parking/fees: metered street parking
Hours: 6 A.M.–midnight
Facilities: none
Contact: Laguna Beach Department of Marine Safety, 949/494-6572

Map of Orange County—Page 98

27 Crescent Bay Point Park, page 127

Location: Crescent Bay Drive at Pacific Coast Highway in Laguna Beach
Parking/fees: free street parking
Hours: 6 A.M.–midnight
Facilities: lifeguards and restrooms
Contact: Laguna Beach Department of Marine Safety, 949/494-6572

28 Reef Point (Crystal Cove State Park), page 132

Location: Pacific Coast Highway between Laguna Beach and Corona del Mar
Parking/fees: $5 entrance fee per vehicle. Camping fee at hike-in campground three miles inland is $7 per night.
Hours: 6 A.M.–10 P.M. (6 A.M.–8 P.M. in winter months)
Facilities: lifeguards, picnic tables, showers, restrooms, and visitor center (at El Moro Canyon)
Contact: Crystal Cove State Park, 949/494-3539

29 Los Trancos (Crystal Cove State Park), page 132

Location: Pacific Coast Highway between Laguna Beach and Corona del Mar
Parking/fees: $5 entrance fee per vehicle
Hours: 6 A.M.–10 P.M. (6 A.M.–8 P.M. in winter months)
Facilities: lifeguards, picnic tables, showers, and restrooms.
Contact: Crystal Cove State Park, 949/494-3539

30 Pelican Point (Crystal Cove State Park), page 132

Location: Pacific Coast Highway between Laguna Beach and Corona del Mar
Parking/fees: $5 entrance fee per vehicle
Hours: 6 A.M.–10 P.M. (6 A.M.–8 P.M. in winter months)
Facilities: lifeguards, picnic tables, showers, and restrooms.
Contact: Crystal Cove State Park, 949/494-3539

31 Little Corona del Mar Beach, page 133

Location: Ocean Boulevard at Poppy Avenue in Corona del Mar
Parking/fees: free street parking
Hours: 6 A.M.–10 P.M.
Facilities: None.
Contact: Newport Beach Marine Department, 949/673-3047

32 Corona del Mar Beach (a.k.a. Main Beach), page 133

Location: Ocean Boulevard at Iris Avenue in Corona del Mar

Map of Southern California—Page 9

Orange County

Parking/fees: $6 entrance fee per vehicle.
Hours: 8 A.M.–10 P.M. PDT (8 A.M.–8 P.M. PST).
Facilities: concession, lifeguards, restrooms, showers, and picnic tables
Contact: Newport Beach Marine Department, 949/673-3047

33 Rocky Point (a.k.a. Pirates Cove), page 133

Location: Ocean Boulevard at Harbor Channel in Corona del Mar
Parking/fees: free street parking
Hours: 6 A.M.–10 P.M.
Facilities: none
Contact: Newport Beach Marine Department, 949/673-3047

34 China Cove Beach, page 133

Location: Ocean Boulevard at Fernleaf Avenue in Corona del Mar
Parking/fees: free street parking
Hours: 6 A.M.–10 P.M.
Facilities: none
Contact: Newport Beach Marine Department, 949/673-3047

35 West Jetty View Park (a.k.a. The Wedge), page 137

Location: end of Channel Road at tip of Balboa Peninsula, in Balboa
Parking/fees: free parking lot
Hours: 6 A.M.–10 P.M.
Facilities: none
Contact: Newport Beach Marine Department, 949/673-3047

36 Balboa Beach, page 137

Location: Balboa Boulevard at Balboa Pier in Balboa
Parking/fees: metered street parking
Hours: 6 A.M.–10 P.M.
Facilities: lifeguards, restrooms, showers, and picnic tables
Contact: Newport Beach Marine Department, 949/673-3047

37 Newport Beach Municipal Beach, page 137

Location: Ocean Front at Newport Pier in Newport Beach
Parking/fees: metered lot and street parking.
Hours: 6 A.M.–10 P.M.
Facilities: lifeguards, restrooms, showers, and picnic tables
Contact: Newport Beach Marine Department, 949/673-3047

Map of Orange County—Page 98

38 Santa Ana River County Beach, page 138

Location: Seashore Drive between Summit and 61st Streets in Newport Beach
Parking/fees: metered street parking
Hours: 6 A.M.–10 P.M.
Facilities: lifeguards
Contact: North Beaches Operation Office of Orange County Harbors, Beaches, and Parks, 949/723-4511

39 Huntington State Beach, page 145

Location: Pacific Coast Highway from Santa Ana River to Beach Boulevard in Huntington Beach
Parking/fees: $5 entrance fee per vehicle
Hours: 6 A.M.–10 P.M. PDT (6 A.M.–8 P.M. PST).
Facilities: lifeguards, restrooms, showers, and picnic tables
Contact: Huntington State Beach, 714/536-1454

40 Huntington City Beach, page 145

Location: Pacific Coast Highway from Beach Boulevard to Goldenwest Street in Huntington Beach
Parking/fees: $7 entrance fee per vehicle. RV camping fee (October–February only) is $15 per night.
Hours: 6 A.M.–10 P.M.
Facilities: lifeguards, restrooms, showers, and picnic tables
Contact: Huntington City Beach, 714/536-5280

41 Bolsa Chica State Beach, page 145

Location: Pacific Coast Highway at Warner Avenue in Huntington Beach
Parking/fees: $5 entrance fee per vehicle. RV camping fee is $19 per night, plus a $7.50 reservation fee.
Hours: 6 A.M.–10 P.M.
Facilities: lifeguards, restrooms, showers, and picnic tables
Contact: Bolsa Chica State Beach, 714/846-3460

42 Sunset Beach, page 150

Location: Warner Street off Pacific Coast Highway in Sunset Beach
Parking/fees: free parking lot
Hours: 6 A.M.–10 P.M.
Facilities: lifeguards, picnic tables, restrooms, and showers
Contact: North Beaches Operation Office of Orange County Harbors, Beaches, and Parks, 714/723-4511

Map of Southern California—Page 9

43 Surfside Beach, page 150

Location: Anderson Avenue at Pacific Coast Highway in Surfside
Parking/fees: no parking; accessible only via pedestrian gate
Hours: 6 A.M.–10 P.M.
Facilities: none
Contact: North Beaches Operation Office of Orange County Harbors, Beaches, and Parks, 714/723-4511

44 Seal Beach, page 151

Location: Main Street at Seal Beach Pier in Seal Beach
Parking/fees: metered street parking
Hours: 4:30 A.M.–10 P.M.
Facilities: lifeguards, restrooms, and showers
Contact: Seal Beach Lifeguard Station, 562/430-2613

Orange County

Orange County

Although the oranges are mostly gone and the county embodies the worst aspects of America's addiction to cars, shopping malls, suburban sprawl, right-wing politics, environmental despoliation, and corporate wheeling-dealing, the glorious beaches of Orange County are here (we hope and pray) forever. They start with pleasant understatement at San Clemente, an almost quaint community that's lifted into the present tense mainly by its world-class surfing scene. And they work their way up to Seal Beach, which is altogether more charming than its proximity to Huntington Beach and Long Beach might otherwise suggest.

Most of Orange County's oceanfront was similarly low-key only decades ago. Many beaches singled out by name in the Beach Boys' 1963 classic "Surfin' USA" are in Orange County. But in the years since they celebrated Southern California in song, a major real-estate land rush has effectively walled off much of the prime beachfront in Orange County for the private enjoyment of . . . God knows who. Nobody we consort with, that's for sure! The worst sins were committed at Dana Point and Huntington Beach—great surfing spots where those who most love the shore (and who have the least impact upon it) are now persona non grata. They're the ones with living memories of how these places used to be.

Orange County's mid-'90s fiscal meltdown, California's turn-of-the-millennium dot-com collapse, and the nation's stock market slide and corporate accounting scandals of 2002 revealed the viciously destructive end results of the greedhead agenda. Perhaps these revelations will pave the way for a more environmentally and socially responsible mind-set that will spare Orange County's lovely shoreline from additional developmental desecration. Granted, it's a far-fetched theory, but we're not above grasping at straws. In reality, we know full well that in a place where money and its materialistic flaunting function as a surrogate religion, a change in the status quo will be slow in coming and staunchly resisted.

The legendary reputation of Orange County as a bastion of starchy conservatism is well deserved. The county's conservative bent has also given rise to its attitudinal opposite: a culture of punk-rock and hard-core bands who loathe their parents and, by extension, all forms of authority. This at least portends a healthy—or unhealthy, but who cares—counterbalance to all the stuffed-shirt bottom-liners. Regardless of Orange County's intractable politics, many of the beaches here are treasures that compare with oranges fresh off the tree. And two of its beach towns—Laguna Beach and Newport Beach—are among our all-time favorites.

Map of Southern California—Page 9

The Orange County Theme

(sung to the tune of "The Green Acres Theme")
   (male voice):
"Orange County is the place for me
Golf course living is the life I lead
Fairways spreading out so far and wide
Suburban sprawl
To hell with the countryside"
   (female voice):
"Newport is where I'd rather be
Golfing just makes no sense to me
Shopping binges are what I adore
Darling, I love you
But give me Fashion Island's stores"
   (he):
"Golf balls!"
   (she):
"Mega malls!"
   (he):
"Cell phones!"
   (she):
"Bank loans!"
   (both):
"We are alike
We love our silly life!
Orange County
We are there!"

Orange County

Map of Orange County—Page 98

San Clemente

Nestled in the hilly contours of the California coast halfway between San Diego and Los Angeles, San Clemente is fully removed from the sprawl that slithers toward it from all directions. It has little in common with the harried metropolitan world that bears down upon it. Rather, San Clemente (population 50,000) is an entity unto itself, rather like a small-scale Santa Barbara.

Promoting this sense of cozy self-containment is the layout of city streets, which take their cue from the area's geography. San Clemente's roads meander in awkward semicircles, following topographical contours. This confuses one's sense of direction and forces visitors to pay closer attention to their surroundings than they would if driving some boring old grid. And pay attention you do: to beautiful houses, verdant shrubs and gorgeous flowers, and surrounding hills that plunge dramatically to the sea.

The town is built above some striking beaches, with weathered bluffs and scantily vegetated hills rising behind it. Avenida del Mar links El Camino Real (the main drag, which parallels I-5) with the municipal pier and beach. It passes through the heart of town, a shopping and business district that could pass for Anytown, USA. For every cutesy boutique there's a plain old mom-and-pop store serving some basic community need for things like prescription drugs, camera equipment, stationery, and "notions." (When was the last time you heard that word used?) You can sip a civilized cup of coffee at an outdoor café and watch folks amble by, evincing none of the stressful hysteria that sends the rest of us to shrinks, doctors, and an early grave.

Perhaps it is this restful calm that inspired a sitting U.S. president to acquire a second home in San Clemente. The late Richard Nixon put this small town on the map in 1969 by turning Casa Pacifica—a Spanish-style, red-roofed estate at the south end of town—into the Western White House. Built in 1927 by one Hamilton Cotton, Casa Pacifica served as Nixon's home away from the White House during the tumultuous era of Vietnam and Watergate. Coincidentally, the estate faced one of the best surfing spots in all of California (Cotton Point, informally known as "Cotton's"), and surfer lore is filled with tales of trying to outfox the Secret Service in an effort to get to it. Though the way to the waves is more easily negotiated these days, it's still no picnic. Surfers face a half-mile hike down paths of scalding sand and asphalt with boards atop their heads. There's nothing to suggest the Prez attempted the feat himself, but maybe he was actually hipper than anyone knew. During a tape-recorded tour of the Nixon Library (40 miles from San Clemente, in Yorba Linda), the late president allows that "if there had been a good rap group around in those days, I might have chosen a career in music instead of politics." Would he have called the act Tricky Dick and DJ Watergate?

The return to pre-presidential calm after Nixon left office suited San Clemente just fine. It's a lovely, unassuming town that looks much as it did when it was advertised to prospective buyers in 1925 as "a village done in the fashion of Old Spain." Named in 1602 by the explorer Sebastian Vizcaino in honor of Saint Clement—whose feast day coincided with the date of discovery—San Clemente was one of California's first planned communities. The founder was Ole Hanson, a former mayor of Seattle. In 1925 Hanson and three partners purchased and designed a 2,000-acre parcel in the classic Spanish style, hoping to attract folks who'd grown tired of big-city living to "San Clemente by the Sea." More of an aesthetic visionary than today's barf-it-up developers, Hanson rhapsodized, "San Clemente is just a painting five miles long and over a mile wide . . . its foreground the sea, its background the hills. We use for our pigments flowers and shrubs and trees and red tile and white plaster." Some 75 years later, the painting remains sufficiently impressive to make an art lover out of any visitor.

Beaches

San Clemente is a town so full of civic pride that it has its own city song, "On the Beach of San Clemente." We can't warble that little ditty, but we'll happily sing the praises of San Clemente's beaches. Avenida del Mar slams to an end at **San Clemente City Beach,** where a historic 1,200-foot pier dates from the 1920s. There's a municipal parking lot, restrooms and showers, and all the usual amenities of a well-tended city beach. The beach is accessible from the west end of Avenida del Mar and numerous street ends and paths along the two-mile stretch from San Clemente State Beach to Ole Hanson Beach Club (a public pool and playground), with the city beach at the center.

A small, hut-like Amtrak station sits next to railroad tracks so close to the ocean they practically get licked by the waves at high tide. The surf is strong all along the coast around here, drawing an enthusiastic knot of surfing devotees. At high tide large breakers slam into the pier pilings, turning the frothing water a milky green. The soft, brown-sand beach draws a vibrant young crowd, with surfers congregating around the pier.

Seaside bed-and-breakfasts and outdoor cafés face the beach along Avenida Victoria, which runs beside the ocean for a short distance before looping up, up, and away. On a nice summer day—and all the ones we've ever spent in San Clemente have been ideal—the area in the vicinity of San Clemente City Beach has the charmingly upscale aura of a Mediterranean village, with climate to match. You couldn't ask for better weather: average highs of 68 degrees in June, 73 degrees in September (the hottest month), and 66 degrees in December. There

are less than 10 inches of rain and 342 days of sunshine per year. In a word, it's perfect.

San Clemente State Beach offers some of the best coastal camping (153 sites, of which 72 have RV hookups) in the state. Whereas the municipal beach is wide and hospitable to swimmers and surfers, the state beach is narrow, prone to rip currents, and almost primevally wild. A campground overlooks the mile-long beach from atop 50-foot bluffs. Trees afford some protection from the summer sun, and the place vaguely recalls national parks of the Southwest—Bryce or Zion Canyon, for instance—in miniature. An asphalt trail leads down a steep, dramatically eroded ravine to the beach. Railroad tracks run extremely close to the water, protected by riprap. Near the water's edge, the sand slopes sharply. Breakers scurry up the beach face, and an occasional tongue of foam licks the dry sand above it. It's great for beach hiking; the solitude and the scenic backdrop are stunning. Diving is popular but swimming is discouraged, and surfers choose to hotfoot down to better waves at Cotton's and Trestle's, which straddle the San Diego County line from opposite sides of San Mateo Point. If you happen to see a surfer or two studying the distant waves from a freeway off-ramp south of town, they're weighing whether it's worth the long walk to the water. And a long, sandy scramble it is, from the south end of El Camino Real near Carl's Jr. (which is where most people park) down to Trestle's, which is part of San Onofre State Beach.

San Clemente is home to the **Surfrider Foundation** (122 South El Camino Real #67, San Clemente, CA 92672, 949/492-8170, website: www.surfrider.org), the advocacy group that acts on behalf of coastal environmental matters and other issues of interest to surfers.

Shore Things

• **Bike/skate rentals:** San Clemente Cyclery and Sport, 400 South El Camino Real, San Clemente, 949/492-8690

Orange County

Map of Orange County—Page 98

Getting around the Big Orange

As a "humor columnist" for a local real-estate publication put it, "Orange County is car culture. . . . You can be sleepless in Seattle, but don't get caught being carless in Orange County. Other cities have mass transit; here it's auto transit en masse."

As his column unfolded, the darker reality of all this exhaust fume-sucking, maniacal stop-start driving and stroke-inducing gridlock reared its ugly head. For example, this dimwit admitted that "some of us spend more time driving than we do with our families. Cell phones keep us connected, but it's a poor substitute for actually being there." Hear, hear! What a sensitive observation! Oops, is that a call coming in?

As for his tips about getting around Orange County, he offered these knee-slappers: "Avoid the El Toro Y at all times. . . . There is never a good time to drive the 22. . . . Avoid the 55 north during daylight hours. . . . And evenings, avoid every road to the beach in the summer." And so on.

We know from personal experience that driving in Orange County is not the least bit amusing or something to be made light of. It is a waking nightmare. This reality was brought home to us when we attempted to attend a Angels (the 2002 world champions) vs. Baltimore Orioles baseball game in Anaheim one summer evening. The city of Anaheim was only 18 miles east of our motel in Newport Beach. No problem! Or so we thought.

This is the same route that leads to Disneyland, the same route driven from the coast by every other beachgoer who merrily imagines a pleasant day trip to that Mickey Mouse trap during their summer vacation. Personally, we can't imagine anything more pleasant than the beaches of Newport Beach. Still, some visitors feel duty-bound to patronize Disneyland Resort, which comprises the old warhorse Disneyland Park and Disney CEO Michael Eisner's latest boondoggle, Disney's California Adventure. Just for the record, it costs $45 for adults and $35 for children 3–9 for a single-day pass to one or the other (but not both) of the Disneyland Resort theme parks in Anaheim. (For more information, call 714/781-7290.)

Our baseball adventure mired us in an unmoving traffic jam both before and after the game. Although we allowed plenty of time to get to the stadium, we missed the first inning. Afterward, at 11 P.M. on a weeknight, traffic was backed up even worse than before the game. We found ourselves sitting on the freeway for what seemed like an eternity. The delay wasn't due to wrecks or a departing game crowd (hell, only 15,000 people attended). It was due partly to road construction—the freeway widening and repairing never ends in Southern California—and partly to the traffic that never abates at any hour. As midnight approached, the delay became absurd. An hour and a half to go 18 miles?

Map of Southern California—Page 9

Orange County continues subsidizing freeway building and widening projects with revenue from "Measure M," a half-cent sales tax approved by voters in 1990. The proceeds from Measure M fund countywide transportation improvements, with 43 percent earmarked for freeways. The question is, do more and wider freeways truly represent any sort of sound, sane "improvement"? Road building has reached such an unutterable state of lunacy in Orange County that at the El Toro Y—the infamous bottleneck where the San Diego Freeway (I-405) and Santa Ana Freeway (I-5) meet—has been expanded to 26 lanes at its widest point. Moreover, they're proud of this "modern interchange," which is blithely referred to as "Orange County's Main Street."

Despite the terrible waste inherent in Orange County's driving addiction—the reckless consumption of fossil fuel (especially in the SUV era), business cost ($20.7 billion is lost annually due to traffic delays in California), and lost hours with the family or for personal pleasure—Orange County has been slow to implement long-term transportation solutions. On a positive note, plans are underway to construct a light rail system, the **CenterLine,** that will connect some of the most densely populated and highly traveled population centers. The first phase in this long-overdue project will be an 18-mile, 22-station line between Santa Ana and Irvine. Yet according to the Orange County Transportation Authority's own timetable, the CenterLine won't be up and running until "late 2011." Don't hold your breath.

The CenterLine is a promising start, though it won't even begin to solve the profound disconnect from reality that is at the heart of Orange County's transportation woes. Part of the problem is that head-in-the-sand hubs like Anaheim have refused to take part in the system. If the big players won't show some leadership, then the Orange crush on the freeways will only get worse, if such a thing is possible. Future generations will curse those leaders who are dragging their feet now.

For now, the most beach-friendly mode of conveyance is the excellent bus system run by the Orange County Transportation Authority. Many routes operate from inland cities to such coastal locales as Huntington Beach, Seal Beach, Newport Beach, Laguna Beach, Dana Point, and San Clemente. The coast-hugging Bus Route 1 runs along Pacific Coast Highway from San Clemente to Long Beach. Yes, you can travel Orange County's entire coastline for a mere $1 fare! Moreover, any and all routes in the county can be ridden for $2.50 per day (about the price of a gallon of gas) or $37.50 per month. We call that a bargain and a bright note amid all of Orange County's freeway madness.

For information, schedules, and fares, contact the **Orange County Transportation Authority,** 550 South Main Street, P.O. Box 14184, Orange, CA 92868, 714/636-7433, website: www.octa.net.

Orange County

Map of Orange County—Page 98

• **Ecotourism:** Orange County Marine Institute, 24200 Dana Point Harbor Drive, Dana Point, 949/496-2274

• **Marina:** Dana Point Marina, 24701 Dana Drive, Dana Point, 949/496-6137

• **Pier:** San Clemente Pier, 611 South Avenida Victoria, San Clemente, 949/492-8335

• **Rainy day attraction:** Mission San Juan Capistrano, 31522 Camino Capistrano, San Juan Capistrano, 949/248-2048

• **Shopping/browsing:** Laguna Village, 577 South Coast Highway, Laguna Beach, 949/494-1956

• **Sportfishing:** Dana Point Sportfishing, 34675 Golden Lantern, Dana Point, 949/496-5794

• **Surf report:** 949/492-1011

• **Surf shops:** Rip Curl Surf Center, 3801 South El Camino Real, San Clemente, 949/498-4920; Costa Azul, 689 South Coast Highway, Laguna Beach, 949/4971423

• **Vacation rentals:** Laguna Beach Oceanfront Rental, 900 Glenneyre Street, Laguna Beach, 949/494-8110

Bunking Down

Across the street from San Clemente Municipal Pier is a charming block where a smattering of bed-and-breakfasts offer wonderful beach views at top-end prices. One is **Casa Tropicana** (610 Avenida Victoria, 949/492-1234, $$$), whose theme rooms (e.g., Out of Africa, Emerald Forest, and South Pacific) overlook the pier at prices that will quickly bring you down to earth (up to $350 a night). Another is the **Villa del Mar Inn** (612 Avenida Victoria, 949/498-5080, $$$), whose condo-style suites offer beach-facing sundecks, big living rooms, and fully equipped kitchens. Rooms run $150–199 in the high season and drop by $70 a night in the rest of the year. Since the weather barely changes from month to month, the off-season rates are a real bargain.

The **San Clemente Inn** (2600 Avenida del Presidente, 949/492-6103, $$), which abuts San Clemente State Park, operates as a hotel condominium, offering apartment-style suites on grounds that include a pool and spa, shuffleboard courts, and gargantuan pineapple trees. In this largely unfancy town, the **Holiday Inn San Clemente Resort** (111 South Avenida del Estrella, 949/361-3000, $$), a white-stucco wonder convenient to the beach, has the chain-motel competition beat when it comes to amenities: heated pool, spa, fitness center, sundeck with a view, decent on-site restaurant.

Coastal Cuisine

Look no farther than the San Clemente Municipal Pier for dinner. You have two choices: the **Fisherman's Restaurant** (611 Avenida Victoria, 949/498-6390, $$$), on the left side of the pier, and **Fisherman's Bar** (611 Avenida Victoria, 949/498-6390, $$) on the right. They serve good, fresh Pacific seafood at both places. The restaurant's dinner menu ranges from fish 'n' chips to whole Dungeness crab. If you're toting a huge appetite, ante up for an all-you-can-eat feast of clams, halibut, salmon, swordfish, or crab, served with salad, rice pilaf, sourdough bread, and Fisherman's chowder. The bar tends more toward heavy appetizers.

Across the street, the **Beach Garden Cafe** (685 1/2 Avenida Victoria, 949/498-8145, $) is a cute, modern eatery serving omelettes, sandwiches, pizzas, and entrées such as fish 'n' chips. On a more gustatorily substantial note, the **Rib Trader** (911 South El Camino Real, 949/492-6665, $$$) serves ribs, steaks, and other hearty surf-and-turf fare. It's also got a bar area set off from the main dining room that's a favorite place for the surfing cult to congregate and quaff a few after the sun's gone down.

Finally, in deference to the surfing community, we feel obliged to mention **Surfin' Donuts Coffee House** (1822 South El Camino Real, 949/492-1249 and 1110 South El Camino Real, 949/361-2120, $). After all, some of the best surfing spots, surfboard makers, and surfing magazines are headquartered here in unassuming San Clemente. In a town geared to surfers, it stands to reason that you can get some of the best "surfin' donuts" in all creation, too.

Night Moves

After sunset, best watched from the pier, San Clemente gets quieter than an orange grove. Laguna Beach and San Juan Capistrano are the nearest outposts of serious nightlife. A cocktail waitress at the San Clemente Pier tipped us off to a particularly lively club up the coast where it was reggae night. "Have you ever heard of reggae music?" she asked, as if she were an elementary school teacher introducing a new vowel sound. We didn't feel like letting our dreadlocks down that night and remained happily glued to our perches at **Fisherman's Bar** (611 Avenida Victoria, 949/498-6390), enjoying the pier's relative tranquillity.

For More Information

San Clemente Chamber of Commerce, 1100 North El Camino Real, San Clemente, CA 92672, 949/492-1131, website: www.sc chamber.com

Capistrano Beach

Enfolding the coastline between Dana Point and San Clemente, the Capistrano Beach area has been rather overoptimistically marketed as "California's Riviera." In actuality, Capistrano Beach is a small and relatively uncrowded seaside sanctuary. That quality, a virtual novelty in overbuilt Southern California, sets Capistrano Beach apart from its neighbors. For instance, San Juan Capistrano—a larger town that has scared away its famous swallows by razing orange groves and constructing shopping malls and boxy stucco homes on every available square inch—offers what more cliché-minded travel writers would refer to as "fabulous shopping opportunities." To us it's just another infernal gash in the landscape drawn to bleed the unconscious consumer. Much of Orange County, particularly its interior sprawl, has come to resemble a Hieronymous Bosch vision of hell, with groaning condominiums and howling land speculators for harpies.

Stick to the beach; it's pleasant out here, and there's plenty to go around. Capistrano Beach has got a nice, unhurried way about it. Whether you're looking out to sea from the beach or the palisades above, it's a pianissimo passage in the Wagnerian symphony of overdevelopment that characterizes much of the coast from San Diego to Los Angeles.

Beaches

Doheny State Beach and **Capistrano Beach Park** are the main access points in an unbroken stretch that runs along Capistrano Bight up to Dana Point. On a nice day the beaches here almost look too good to be true: a mirage of white sand and emerald water gleaming beneath a bright blue sky. Down on the shoreline, Capistrano Beach boasts a wide, unblemished public beach. A road called the Palisades drops down from steep residential hills to meet Pacific Coast Highway near the entrance to Capistrano Beach. A large parking lot with inexpensive metered parking faces the ocean, and pedestrian overpasses cross the highway at several points. The beach is popular but seldom overrun. At 7 A.M. one drizzly May morning, a group of teenage girls enthusiastically engaged in a little pre-school volleyball practice. Meanwhile, cars parked along the lip of the lot, their drivers lost in meditative contemplation before heading off to a hard day of hammering nails or making deals.

The parking lot runs beside the beach for a good distance, and people aerobicize along it in jogging shoes and in-line skates. By mid-morning a furious full-court basketball game was in progress. In the distance surfers congregated off Doheny Point. Just another day

Where Have All the Swallows Gone?

The story of the swallows of San Juan Capistrano is a major chapter in California's legend and lore. Each year the swallows, ever-reliable in the constancy of their reappearance, make the 6,000-mile trip from Goya, Argentina, to **Mission San Juan Capistrano.** They arrive on March 19, build nests and hatch their chicks, then depart for the winter on October 23. You can set your calendar by them. The date of their spring arrival is known as **St. Joseph's Day** (a.k.a. Swallow Day). Large numbers of tourists turn out to greet the swallows, a ritual highlighted for years by the 8 A.M. ringing of the mission bells. Everybody oohs and ahs over the return of the little five-inch gliding birds. It's a great day for birds and bird-watchers alike.

However, the truth of the matter may be a little harder to, uh, swallow. In 1993, for instance, an estimated 25,000 tourists doubled the town's population over the weekend. Thousands turned out in the early morning to witness the flapping of four startled birds who were roused from the mission eaves by the aged bell-ringer. The swallows of Capistrano were outnumbered, according to published accounts, by pigeons. Nonetheless, a celebratory parade of 4,000 people, many on horseback, took place in the afternoon. That's a human-to-bird ratio of 1,000 to 1. Does something seem cuckoo about all this? Still, the feeder roads get clogged and the hotels and restaurants are booked solid over the St. Joseph's Day weekend. The irony is that the swallows, driven away by renovations at Mission San Juan Capistrano, among other things, have gone elsewhere. In 1998, they set up camp at the Tillman Water Reclamation Plant, in the San Fernando Valley.

in the life of a prime Southern California beach. At the south end of Capistrano Beach, where Camino Capistrano runs out at Pacific Coast Highway, a pedestrian underpass leads to **Poche Beach,** a sandy surfing beach just above the landslide that closed a stretch of PCH in 1993. Incidentally, *Surfer* magazine is published in Capistrano Beach, and surfboards are manufactured here.

Bunking Down

On the landward side of Pacific Coast Highway is **Capistrano Surfside Inn** (34680 Pacific Coast Highway, 949/240-7681, $$$), a time-share condo complex that also operates like a hotel. Commodious one- and two-bedroom suites come

with full kitchens and outdoor balconies stocked with furniture and gas grills. A schedule of optional activities for guests includes day trips to beaches on Mexico's Baja Peninsula. Close by is **Holiday Inn Express** (34744 Pacific Coast Highway, 949/240-0150, $$$). Formerly the Capistrano Edgewater Inn, it offers comparable prices, views, and amenities.

Coastal Cuisine

A famous Mexican restaurant called **Olamendi's** (34660 Pacific Coast Highway, 949/661-1005, $$) does a big business in burritos across from the beach. Its popularity is easy to gauge from the frequently full parking lot. Inside, moderately priced Mexican food of good qual-

Map of Southern California—Page 9

ity is served at padded, semicircular booths. Tacos, burritos, and enchiladas are presented every conceivable way (stuffed with shredded beef, steak, chicken, fish, pork, and cheese). The menu carries a one-word endorsement from the late Richard Nixon: "Excellent." Up by the cash register hangs a picture of El Presidente, nervously posed with the kitchen staff. If you're hankering for something more high-end, head to nearby Dana Point or San Juan Capistrano.

Night Moves

The after-hours options in Capistrano Beach are as weak as the glow from a child's night-light, but you stand a good chance of catching some great music at the **Coach House** (33157 Camino Capistrano, 949/496-8930) in nearby San Juan Capistrano. This 480-seat hall books folkie singer/songwriters, alternative rockers, and roots-oriented musicians. You might see anyone from Shawn Colvin to Norah Jones,

Marc Cohn, or Dave Alvin on the marquee when you're passing through, as we did in July 2002. Coach House serves an appetizer-heavy dinner menu, too.

Incidentally, "San Juan Cap" (as it's known to locals) is a formerly quaint, mission-style community now beset with endless malls whose acreage rivals that of a cattle ranch. The train station is the hub of weekend nightlife. Everyone from wandering minstrels on down performs for the assembled masses, some of whom ride the rails down from Los Angeles just to be part of the crowd.

For More Information

Dana Point Chamber of Commerce, 24681 La Plaza, Suite 115, Dana Point, CA 92524, 949/496-1555, website: www.danapoint-chamber.com; San Juan Capistrano Chamber of Commerce, 31781 Camino Capistrano, San Juan Capistrano, CA 92675, 949/493-4700, website: www.sanjuancapistrano.com

Dana Point

A nine-foot bronze statue of seaman and writer Richard Henry Dana Jr. looks out over the harbor that's named after him. Dana came here in the 1830s aboard the square rigger *Pilgrim*. He recorded his experiences as a naïf on the high seas in the autobiographical narrative *Two Years Before the Mast*, a California literary classic. He also described the cliff-backed cove at Dana Point as "the only romantic spot in California." We beg to differ with the estimable writer on this point. Number one, there are plenty of romantic spots in California. Number two, Dana Point is no longer one of them.

Of course Dana himself had nothing to do with the artificial facelift that turned the rugged environment he knew and loved into a sanitized playground for the wealthy, so we won't hold him accountable on this last point. Instead, we'll direct our venom toward those dis-

semblers of public-relations jive who use his words to promote the arid development that calmed the waves and transformed the landscape. The refashioning of Dana Point (population 35,000) into a 2,500-slip yacht harbor—which began in 1969, when the Orange County Board of Supervisors approved construction of a jetty, harbor, and harborside community—is the sort of tale that would have inspired a salty young sailor like Dana to mutiny. Indeed, were Dana around to see the area today, he would scarcely comprehend the changes that have taken place since his time. The man-made Dana Harbor has stilled the waves for yuppie yachts, while Mariner's Village developers have erected a faux New England fishing village that is a mockery of the real thing.

The brotherhood of surfers is still steamed about what the 1.5-mile jetty did to the surf at Doheny State Beach. "The mellow lines of

Map of Orange County—Page 98

Orange County

Golf Course Living—or Selling Orange County by the Hook and Slice

Orange County is California's cradle of Republican values. Beyond its beautiful beaches, the county has all the lingering appeal of a bank waiting area. Every man-made structure is replete with fake fountains and forests of weeping figs.

Orange County's local cultural heroes are Mickey Mouse and John Wayne. The local political icon is Richard Nixon, whose library and grave are in Yorba Linda.

The irony of all this staunch conservatism is that 30 years ago Orange County was a sleepy rural retreat from Los Angeles. Cities such as Anaheim were where little old ladies dreamed of going to get away from Los Angeles. Most of the land was either covered by livestock or orange groves.

But the little old ladies passed away. In their place came a glad-handing battalion of mall designers, entrepreneurs, interstate makers, and commercial developers. All put pressure on pliable government officials to do their bidding. It's the American way, right?

No, it was the will of the Irvine Company, who orchestrated the whole onslaught. The Irvine Company is the mysterious realty octopus that owns most of the undeveloped land in Orange County. It has built its empire on an equally mysterious real-estate plan. Instead of selling land, it is leased in 99-year increments, thereby ensuring that no one but the company actually owns it. What the company doesn't lease, it sits on, waiting as market forces drive up land values.

Originally, most of Orange County was a land grant called Irvine Ranch, a huge slab of what was then Mexico wrested by Spaniards from the Native Americans. Irvine Ranch is five times the size of Manhattan, the largest private real-estate holding in a major U.S. metropolitan area. Just the name "Irvine Ranch" evokes the Father Knows Best patriarchy that governs every square foot of Orange County. Instead of cows, Irvine Ranch is grazed by golfers. Instead of orange trees, palm trees have been geometrically arranged around climate-controlled corporate campuses. To the east, the faceless, interchangeable towns that orbit them have been erected. For example, 130,000

Map of Southern California—Page 9

people live in a city called Orange. Ever heard of Orange? Does it evoke any tangible associations—natural, historical, cultural? Orange's claim to fame, so far as we could tell, is that it's home to "Southern California's largest entertainment and retail center" (read: nightmarishly sprawling mall). In fact, you can choose from three of them in Orange: The Block at Orange, The Mall of Orange, and Stadium Promenade. The Block at Orange is the newest arrival, and it features a 30-screen cinema!

Another 143,000 people live in Irvine, a "planned community" that is livable and safe but antiseptic as Listerine. Ditto Costa Mesa, clocking in with 110,000. Another 338,000 live in Santa Ana, 328,000 in Anaheim, and 134,000 in Pasadena. It is a sprawl that is best summed up by this headline from a local newspaper: "Coto de Caza set to open five new neighborhoods." In Orange County the old catchphrase "There goes the neighborhood" has been replaced with a new one: "Here comes the neighborhood."

It goes without saying that the money in Orange County is made primarily through real-estate transactions. In fact, land development is still the most lucrative industry, with annual profit margins of as much as 50 percent. You cannot go far without seeing a sign boasting "Phase 4 Now Selling" or "Starting at $395,000" (for a condo!) or some variation on this theme. Indeed, if Northern California and the Western states are wondering where all their water is going, just come to Orange County. Every swath of green that doesn't have a hacienda plopped onto it (with requisite backyard pool) is devoted to the preternaturally lush contours of a golf course. They've even devised a euphemism for their lifestyle: "golf course living."

Okay, enough of this bashing. To us the beaches are the only areas of Orange County that retain any vestiges of or links with the historical and geological past. Despite the fact that the moneyed minions have succeeded in snuffing out the Old California feel of former beach haunts such as Dana Point and Huntington Beach, the towns of San Clemente, Laguna Beach, Newport Beach, and Seal Beach have retained much of their original charm.

Huntington Beach and Dana Point lost their battles because they were meccas for surfers—nonspenders who are run off the land whenever big money bullies its way into town. Still, some very important lessons about coastal development have been learned in Orange County. As we see it, Orange County represents an endpoint of greed and despoliation against which the rest of America's coastal communities ought to be on guard.

Orange County

Map of Orange County—Page 98

Doheny are all but gone, replaced by the calm water of Dana Point Harbor," lamented surfing historian and chronicler Allan "Bank" Wright. In an essay entitled "The Boutiquing of the California Coast," lifelong surfer, beach aficionado, and journalist John McKinney writes how he nearly aborted a planned hike on the California coast because he grew so disgusted with the barricading of Dana Point. Stranded outside a gated residential community, McKinney wrote, "As I stand with Dana's memorial . . . the sun, which I cannot see, drops toward the ocean, which I cannot see, showering golden light on sandstone cliffs, where I cannot legally walk." Of the yacht basin, he wrote, " I walk across the acres of hot asphalt comprising the Dana Harbor parking lot. The sight of the huge plasticky and antiseptic marina takes the wind out of my sails. A favorite surfing spot of my adolescence has been totally destroyed."

It's not only the squeaky clean fake seaport experience that rankles. Pacific Coast Highway has become clogged on both sides through the Dana Point/South Laguna corridor with strip malls. The buildup along the traffic-choked highway has been torrential since the mid-1980s, with very little unviolated "outdoors" visible anymore. Despite efforts to promote and trade on that very quality, it has all but vanished. Nonetheless, gaily colored ceremonial nylon flags fly from shops and subdevelopments alike. Those flags have lately taken on a patriotic air, being splashed with the red, white, and blue. But this seems as fraudulent as a flag decal on a gas-guzzling SUV. What is so all-American about tampering with what once was one of America's finest chain of beaches? It is, in fact, tantamount to treason.

Beaches

Two great Orange County beaches flank Dana Point. **Doheny State Beach** is enfolded by the long arm of the south jetty that protects Dana Harbor. Although the surf has been tamed, it's

a great beginner's beach for surfers and still gets some decent peelers on a south swell. Swimmers, meanwhile, enjoy the relative calm of Doheny's wide, white beach, which runs for three-quarters of a mile. An early-morning arrival on summer days is recommended. An interpretive center offers a touch tank and five aquariums. A wooded 120-site campground, grassy picnic area, and bike path make this 62-acre park an exceptional unit in the state-park system.

North of Dana Point, **Salt Creek County Beach** preserves a mile-long stretch of beach, extending from the point up toward South Laguna. It's a historic spot, since it represents one of the earliest volleys fired in the battle for public beach access—especially in Orange County, where Salt Creek became a cause célèbre from the mid-'70s to the mid-'90s. As usual, it pitted public beach advocates against privatization schemers. For the most part, the public won. Situated on the bluffs above and behind the beach is **Bluff Park,** a section of county beach that has everything you could ask for: trails, picnic tables, restrooms, outdoor showers, grills and fire rings, basketball courts, and views of Catalina Island. It is also a good spot for whale-watching during the peak months of February and early March.

Mentioned only for the sake of completeness, there is a small calm-water beach at **Dana Point Harbor** among the shops and boat slips.

Bunking Down

Posh and pricey are the bywords in Dana Point. The **Ritz-Carlton Laguna Niguel** (1 Ritz-Carlton Drive, 949/240-2000, $$$$) swaddles guests in five-star luxury. It is probably the premier resort on the Southern California coast. We are hard-pressed to think of one more imposing in its roll call of amenities: four tennis courts, three restaurants, two heated pools, and an 18-hole golf course—everything but the proverbial partridge in a pear tree. And the view, from a bluff 150 feet above the ocean, is

Map of Southern California—Page 9

exceptional. As they put it, "We overlook nothing but the Pacific."

Marriott's **Laguna Cliffs Resort** (25135 Park Lantern Drive, 949/661-5000, $$$$) is another opulent, sprawling pleasure dome whose 12 acres include biking and jogging trails. All 350 rooms are ocean-view. In addition to health clubs, tennis courts, a basketball court (where one of us trounced the other in a game of horse), and spas, it's got one of the finest gourmet restaurants in the state, **Watercolors**.

The latest entry in the froufrou market is **St. Regis Monarch Beach Resort and Spa** (One Monarch Beach Drive, 949/234-3400, $$$$). Room rates on summer weekends start at $415. The 400-room, Tuscan-style resort sits east side of Highway 1, peering down at the far Pacific. Yes, it is not oceanside but ocean *view*. It's a beach resort without a beach and a fitting symbol for all that's gone wrong at Dana Point.

For budget accommodations, drive a few miles up the coast to South Laguna, where unfancy beachside motels are strewn along Pacific Coast Highway.

Coastal Cuisine

We've stated our biases against the exclusivity and landscape-shattering development at Dana Point. That doesn't mean we don't find things to admire about a few properties, particularly the Ritz-Carlton Laguna Niguel and the Marriott's Laguna Cliffs. Both are first-class resorts that live up to every expectation.

Watercolors, the restaurant at **Marriott's Laguna Cliffs Resort** (25135 Park Lantern Drive, 949/661-5000, $$$), went way beyond our expectations. The meal commenced with a pair of appetizers—tuna tartare and spring rolls filled with slices of grilled duck—so artistically rendered that we almost didn't dare disturb them. They proved as delicious to eat as they were to look at. Entrée preparations were similarly sumptuous. The room is light and airy, done in peach tones and brass accents, and the prevailing style is contemporary American cuisine: healthy, creative, and appealing to the eye and palate.

Night Moves

The lounges at the hotel resorts—particularly the Ritz-Carlton, which has an on-premises nightclub—are your primary options. After a day of tennis, golf, or sailing and a good meal, you might not feel like much more than a civilized nightcap in any case. If you do, however, there's an old reliable **Hennessey's Tavern** (34111 La Plaza, 949/488-0121) in Dana Point.

For More Information

Dana Point Chamber of Commerce, 24681 La Plaza, Suite 115, Dana Point, CA 92629, 949/496-1555, website: www.danapoint-chamber.com

Laguna Beach and South Laguna

When people hear the name Laguna Beach, they tend to think of faraway places: the French Riviera, the Greek Isles, the coast of Italy. They think of anywhere but Orange County, California, where the town is an anomaly: a seaside village that attracts free spirits. It is a cultural anomaly, serving as a kind of Arts and Entertainment channel to the rest of Orange County's *Jackass*-style MTV. And compared to its soulless suburban sprawl and fiercely unforgiving arch-conservatism, Laguna Beach is an island, set apart from the rest of Orange County by geography—hills and canyons on three sides, ocean to the west—and the disposition of its inhabitants, which is more creative than mercenary. The argument was stated in a local publication by a resident who may have revealed more than she intended when she wrote: "Whatever you do, the waves will take your troubles far out to sea, leaving you mindless."

Above all else, Laguna Beach is an artist's

Map of Orange County—Page 98

Laguna Beach's Art Affairs

If you come to Laguna Beach in the summer, chances are you'll spend as much time looking at paintings of the ocean as you will at the actual thing. These three art festivals keep things hopping all summer long in Laguna Beach:

Art-A-Fair (777 Laguna Canyon Road, 949/494-4514) and the **Sawdust Festival** (935 Laguna Canyon Road, 949/494-3030) run from July 1 through August 29. Art-A-Fair is a juried art show that also features demonstrations and workshops. The Sawdust Festival is more of the same, plus food and entertainment, such as a juggler of fiery batons who wouldn't be out of place on Venice Beach.

The venerable **Festival of Arts** (650 Laguna Canyon Road, 949/494-1145) and its highlight, the Pageant of the Masters, runs from July 7 through August 28. It has been an annual feature of Laguna Beach life for more than 60 years. The **Pageant of the Masters** brings to life approximately 40 pieces of classic art using live, human subjects. Actors and locals three-dimensionally re-create paintings by the likes of Matisse, Van Gogh, Magritte, and Seurat for staged, 90-second sittings that take several hours (if not months) to prepare. The evening culminates in a grand tableaux vivant setting of Da Vinci's Last Supper. The effect is both lifelike and eerily two-dimensional, thanks to creative lighting techniques.

The art scene is strong all year-round, as well. The first Thursday of every month is devoted to the **Artwalk,** in which tours are led through the local galleries and the artists leave their studio doors open to all comers and goers. The quality of the art varies widely. We saw eye-catching expressionist paintings and inventive takes on what would normally be clichéd coastal landscape paintings, as well as exceptional nature photography. But we also saw some paintings, in high-end galleries no less, that were little better than paint-by-numbers in quality and others that would not be out of place on the front of a sappy greeting card (e.g., portraits of waifish girls licking ice cream cones, sailboats in the harbor at sunset), not to mention oh-too-cute-to-be-tolerated sculptures of playing children and frisky dolphins. All in all, though, the diversity of the galleries and their distribution among all the nooks and crannies of this rare jewel of a town—a work of art in itself—is well worth your time discovering for yourself.

colony. There are more than 90 art galleries in Laguna Beach, the lion's share arrayed along Pacific Coast Highway. Whereas other beach towns in Southern California host surfing competitions, lifeguard races, and volleyball tournaments, Laguna Beach (population 25,000) sponsors three art festivals every summer, among them the nationally renowned event Pageant of the Masters (see sidebar, "Laguna Beach's Summer–Long Art Affairs"). Easels are as abundant as surfboards, especially around sunset, when artists strive to capture the gold fire that illuminates the town's myriad coves and beaches.

Map of Southern California—Page 9

South Laguna begins around Salt Creek County Beach and runs north to about Ocean Vista Drive (just below Victoria Beach). The differences between South Laguna and Laguna Beach are strictly jurisdictional and nomenclatural. In the words of a longtime resident, "It's all Laguna Beach to me." Indeed, they blend so thoroughly that only a mapmaker can tell them apart.

People who call Laguna Beach home love everything about it except for one thing: traffic. They revere the intellectual camaraderie that encourages self-expression and tolerates eccentricity; the cool, even climate; the striking beauty of cliffs that plunge to a dramatic shoreline (sometimes taking homes with them); and the quasi-European orientation of the community, with its emphasis on high culture and old money. There's even room for surfers, skateboarders, and all the less intellectual flotsam that washes ashore. Their presence helps keep the community from becoming swamped by its own pretensions.

That's not to say that there's never been trouble in paradise. An October 1993 fire in Laguna Beach destroyed hundreds of millions of dollars' worth of homes, with most of the damage confined to the canyons and houses ill-advisedly built in them. The AIDS plague has claimed a lot of local residents in this gay-friendly community.

Laguna Beach has always marched to the beat of a different drummer. Unlike much of California, which was parceled out in the form of land grants by the rulers of Spain and Mexico to friends of the throne, Laguna was homesteaded by tree-planting pioneers following the region's annexation by the United States. It was initially called Lagonas, from the Shoshone word for lakes, because of the freshwater lagoons situated behind the beaches where creeks pour into the ocean. The first arrivals were Mormons, who were followed by Methodists. Laguna's first hostelry opened in 1886 and has been operating ever since as Hotel Laguna.

Artists began forming an enclave here in the early 1900s, around which time the name was changed to Laguna Beach. Gradually, a style known as California impressionism began to evolve after an artist named Lewis Botts painted his famous *Girl of the Golden West* in 1914. Much in the style of Monet's French impressionist school, they painted the natural surroundings with rapid brush strokes and an eye for how sunlight bathed the landscape. The Laguna Beach Art Association was founded in 1918, and thereafter art galleries began popping up all over. Today, small galleries hang signs in their front windows that read: "We buy Old Laguna and Old European paintings."

The artistic imperative meanders all the way down Laguna Canyon Road to the water. At Main Beach, an art deco chess table fashioned in a colorful mosaic of ceramic tiles sits in the grassy picnic area for all to admire or use. Don't be surprised to see eye-catching professional models posing and preening on the beach. A lot of fashion models and film-industry types live in Laguna Beach. The former estate of Bette Davis is a local landmark. From its earliest days, the town has been a gathering place for the jet set. Celebrity residents have included Charlie Chaplin, Judy Garland, Rudolph Valentino, and Gregory Peck.

The main artery through Laguna Beach is Pacific Coast Highway, which unfortunately snakes right through the center of town. The steady stream of traffic mars the town's otherwise genteel village atmosphere. There is simply no other way to get from Dana Point to Newport Beach. A proposed freeway bypass a few miles inland was nixed years ago. All the whizzing traffic makes hazardous sport of getting in and out of a parked car. If traffic were rerouted away from town, Laguna Beach would be a far more pleasant place. As it is, the constant thunder of traffic, much of it aggressively hurrying through town on the only coastal artery, seriously blemishes the Laguna Beach experience.

Orange County

Map of Orange County—Page 98

 **Gay Laguna**

Laguna Beach is California's answer to Provincetown, Massachusetts. Both are venerable destinations for the gay community set in heavenly, protective coastal locales where eccentricity and self-expression are not just accepted, but are practically mandatory. Because these communities have always had a tolerant, artistic, and stylish bent, gay visitors or residents have never had to hide their lifestyles here, never had to apologize, never been denied a safe haven. Thus, they really let it all hang out.

In short, gay pride rules in Laguna. And, after the devastation wrought by AIDS in the 1980s and 1990s tempered some of the excess, gay flamboyance seems to be on the rebound. For one thing, disco—the flamboyant, thumping dance music that dominated the Reagan era—seems to be pumping up Laguna Beach during the reign of George W. Bush, too. Everywhere we went in 2002, we heard the unmistakable sound of drum machines and the breathless warbling of disco divas panting about and pining over a heart that breaks 10 times a night, every night, without fail. The doors were shaking with it at the windowless gay clubs. It poured from speakers at the Koffee Klatch first thing in the morning. It throbbed in the background at many a Laguna restaurant, martini or champagne bar.

Most of the wait staff, hotel desk clerks, bartenders, baristas, and visitors we encountered on our most recent swing through Laguna were friendly, health club–buffed, handsome gay males. As we searched for a place to eat late one Sunday night, a gay man asked, "Do you guys like alternative restaurants?" Without pondering what exactly was implied by "alternative"—we thought he meant "adventuresome" and "ethnic" in culinary orientation—we perhaps too enthusiastically crowed, "Yeah!" The man looked us over and said, "Well, then you'll like Woody's." When we asked him to repeat the name, he said, "It's Woody's . . . as in woody" (as in slang for erection). He laughed knowingly and only when we arrived at Woody's did we realize it was a popular gay hangout. Happily, it is also an excellent restaurant, with a friendly, attentive staff and a live-and-let-live philosophy.

The gay high holiday in Laguna is the **Hunks in Trunks Festival,** which was creating a town-wide buzz during our last visit. This was not some one-night gimmick sponsored by a gay disco but a community-wide effort culminating in five days of frivolity and fun on the sand, in the surf, and on the dance floor. This Memorial Day bacchanal was hosted by numerous restaurants (including Woody's) and venues throughout Laguna Beach, and tunes were spun by a ledger sheet of different deejays, plus a performance by "pop/dance diva" Lisa Frazier. Ultimately, the goal was to conduct a "male model calendar search," with proceeds going to AIDS research.

For more information on the gay scene in Laguna Beach, go to **www.gay lagunabeach.org.**

Map of Southern California—Page 9

Orange County

Beyond the vehicular onslaught, Laguna has atmosphere, culture, scenic beauty, and fantastic beaches. The town at one time even had an unofficial greeter, Eiler Larson by name. This friendly, shaggy mountain man from Denmark would stand at the city limits, hollering "How are you?" to those coming and "Leaving so soon?" to those going for eight hours a day. After he died, numerous tributary wood likenesses began appearing on the town's sidewalks.

The community has its own activist beautification council, which successfully battled outside business interests that wanted to refashion Laguna Beach into a convention center during the 1970s. The would-be developers were sent packing and the threatened town center instead became the landscaped, open-air Main Beach Park. Along the coastline such happy endings are all too rare. This one deserves a standing ovation.

Laguna Beach still holds fast to its "walking village atmosphere." Though some grumble about the "mansionization of Laguna" that's taken place on the hillsides, the town has by and large maintained its architectural charm—largely because Laguna Beach has retained its activist edge. "There is a vocal design and review process in the community," an involved local told us. "People have a say here in what goes on."

Beaches

Laguna Beach comes stocked with beaches—more than 20 named ones tucked into coves along a hilly, undulating coastline. To give you an idea of its ruggedness, this small town's elevation ranges from sea level to 1,039 feet. **Main Beach** (a.k.a. Laguna Beach Municipal Park) is just that: the main place to congregate and recreate in Laguna. In a town of tiny coves and pocket beaches, this is the big enchilada. Balls are bounced and batted during daylight hours. With its volleyball and basketball courts, picnicking green, and long, sandy beach bordered by a winding boardwalk, Main Beach is a buzzing hive of activity and a great spot for sitting on a bench and surveying the very eclectic scene.

Beyond Main Beach, smaller beaches can be found in both directions along Pacific Coast Highway. It seems that every side street ends at the cliffs, with a stairway leading to a fan-shaped cove. We'll survey the more noteworthy ones, starting from the south with **1,000 Steps Beach**. It's where Ninth Avenue meets Pacific Coast Highway in South Laguna. You'll have to park a few blocks away on the highway's asphalt shoulder, since all the curbs are red in the immediate vicinity, but the walk from your car to the top of the stairs will warm up your calf muscles for the trek down the lengthy cement staircase to the beach. At the bottom of the stairs is a small beach pinned against steep cliffs. Gibraltar-sized rocks frame the cove, and huge waves run up on the beach with great force. Houses cling precariously to the eroding cliffs, each with its own set of ladder-like stairs. Climbing out of this grotto is the real acid test—and that's an apt choice of words, since Timothy Leary and his LSD-imbibing gang frequented this beach in the 1960s. The ascent actually numbers 219 steps, and you can amuse yourself on the return trip by reading the graffiti scrawled onto the vertical face of each step.

West Street Beach is one of the better bodysurfing spots in a town renowned for its waves. Shoehorned into a small cove at the base of a stairwell at the end of West Street, about 10 blocks north of 1,000 Steps Beach, it has a volleyball court and is seasonally popular with locals.

Aliso Creek County Beach lies along the heart of the motel/taco stand/gas station corridor of South Laguna. Ample metered parking draws the summertime masses, as does the fine board and bodysurfing. The beach slopes steeply down to the breaking waves, which makes for hazardous swimming. All the same, it's packed with families. You'll also find a playground, fire rings, benches, restrooms, and a short pier with snack bar. When pushed along by the powerful south swell, the waves appear taller than the people playing in them. They break with a mighty crack, sending foam cascading up the brown, sandy beach. We saw happy packs of kids building communal sand castles and getting knocked over by the waves.

The lagoon formed where Aliso Creek empties into the ocean is a popular birdbath, which contributes to its poor water quality. The creek becomes steep-sided on its southern bank as it approaches the ocean. Don't climb into the creek, as its near-constant contamination is an issue that plagues Laguna Beach. Nonpoint source pollution from developments up the canyon fouls the creek, necessitating warning signs. But what to do? Officials haven't figured that out yet, despite much head-scratching, finger-pointing, and public debate. Parents, keep an eye on your young ones here. If the creek is contaminated, it stands to reason that the ocean into which it empties is polluted, too, in the immediate vicinity. The twin threats of water quality and water safety make this a less than ideal family beach, when all is said and done.

The prettiest beach in Laguna, **Victoria Beach** (a.k.a. Vic Beach), is one of the hardest to find. Given the lack of signs, it would appear the locals want to keep it that way. The beach can be entered at several points along Victoria Drive, a street off Pacific Coast Highway that's lined with homes pressed together as close as any block of Victorians in San Francisco. Residents have traded space for easy access to a common, sandy front yard along the ocean. Hiking down from the walkway and stairs at the north end of Victoria Beach, you pass private homes behind a yellow cinder-block wall. A final curve deposits you on one of the nicest beaches in Southern California—one that's especially popular with bodysurfers. It is broad and uncrowded, known mostly by locals, and an inviting spot to drop a beach towel.

Moving north from Vic Beach, **Woods Cove** is a small beach bounded by rocks (there's an especially large one at the north end) popular with locals and largely unknown to others. Diving and tidepooling are the big draws here, but watch out for hazardous surf. Nearby **Pearl Street Beach** is another small, locally popular cove beach bounded by rocky reefs. **Bluebird Beach** is right in front of the Surf & Sand Resort (see "Bunking Down"), and it's a smooth, sandy beach that's good for bodysurfing, boogie boarding, or just soaking up rays on a beach chair.

As you move more into central Laguna Beach, the distances between the rocky points that bound the cove beaches increase. **Mountain Road Beach** has a wide sand beach, but the surf is strewn with hazards: rip currents, submerged rocks, and offshore reefs, so proceed with caution. At the end of Brooks Street, facing Halfway Rock, is **Brooks Beach,** a rocky beach that surfing authority Bank Wright says serves up "the cleanest, best-shaped big wave in Laguna Beach." Have it your way. . . . Would you like some southern swell on that wave? Maybe a garland of kelp? A shark-fin appetizer? Brooks Beach is strictly for surfers. Everyone has his or her own favorite hidden cove in Laguna Beach, so there are potentially as many beaches as there are street ends. Don't expect locals to divulge their secrets to a stranger, but feel free to poke around—you might stumble on an unpeopled cove if you're lucky.

Bring the Frisbee to **Oak Street Beach,** which runs for a block or so on either side of Oak Street. A series of offshore reefs makes this a hot surfing spot, as are adjoining **Thalia Street Beach** and **St. Ann's Beach,** though neither is recommended for swimming because of their rocky reef bottoms. Moreover, St. Ann's has the worst rip current in Laguna Beach. All that changes in the matter of a block or so at **Sleepy Hollow Beach,** whose sandy-bottomed beach makes it fine for swimming and bodysurfing (not so hot for surfing). Sleepy Hollow Beach is popular with guests of Vacation Village Hotel, which overlooks it. You are at this point just south of Main Beach, about which we've already commented.

Jumping north of Main Beach, lovely **Heisler Park** serves as a point of entry to **Rockpile Beach** and **Picnic Beach**. Up at this north end of Laguna Beach, the erodable sandstone coast gives way to sturdier volcanic rocks that form points, with bays cut into the softer shales. The foremost feature at Heisler Park is the walkway that lines the coastal bluffs for about a mile. At dusk it's a magical sight. As fog settles in, the town's twinkling lights come on, rendering a real-life canvas as fanciful as any impressionist's pointillistic study. Rockpile and Picnic Beaches are accessible from Heisler Park via a stairway and ramp, respectively. Rockpile is a rocky, surfer's-only spot in front of the Laguna Art Museum, where Jasmine Street meets Cliff Drive. At high tide, the beach disappears altogether. Picnic tables are nestled among the trees of Heisler Park, giving Picnic Beach its name. Down below, the beach is a diver's paradise but no picnic for swimmers.

Along the 600 block of Cliff Drive, at the north end of Heisler Park, is **Diver's Cove**, a family-friendly, football-field sized beach that draws scuba divers and wading kiddies. Adjoining it to the north is **Boat Canyon Beach,** another rocky-bottomed diver's special that's a no-go for swimmers. A few blocks up, picturesque **Shaw's Cove**—yet another diver's dream (anglers, too)—has the bonus of tidepools at its south end.

The procession of public beaches ends at **Crescent Bay Point Park,** a blufftop green with views of Seal Rock and Laguna Beach and a beach, whose big, tubular waves make for great—and sometimes scary—bodysurfing. Anglers cast from the surf or the rocks, and ocean frolickers brave the somewhat risky (beware rip currents) surf. Because it is one of the longer beaches, running for a quarter mile, it is also one of the more popular in the area, so expect to find weekend crowds.

There are two pieces of good news on Laguna's beachfront. The first is the arrival of a new public beach access adjacent to Laguna Beach Colony, a luxury enclave completed in fall 2002. To get the permits to build this project, the developers were required to deed a third of the land back to the town of Laguna Beach. The "colony" is an eyesore, but the 10-acre beach park—set between Aliso Creek County Beach and Victoria Beach (named **Treasure Island** but not yet open for public use)—will be a delight.

The second bit of good news is the **Beach Tram**—a town-run free shuttle bus that services the whole of Laguna Beach, from Aliso Creek to Crescent Bay Point Park. The shuttle also services two parking lots in the canyons. This has not only cut down on traffic and parking woes, but it's a sensible way to curb emissions from vehicles that would normally be stuck in never-ending, nerve-jangling Highway 1 gridlock.

Bunking Down

You can expect to pay $300 and up a night for the finer European inn-type lodgings in Laguna Beach. The **Surf & Sand Resort** (1555 South Pacific Coast Highway, 949/497-4477, $$$$) is the hostelry of first choice. For starters, it is right on Bluebird Beach (named for Bluebird Canyon Road), one of the more pleasant beaches in town. Rooms are pleasantly and airily appointed, and the oceanfront ones are so close to the water that the crashing, splashing symphony of waves lulls visitors into a blissful California state of mind (and a good night's sleep). The rooms are done in light brown earth tones, and the beds are exceptionally comfortable. The pool deck is on the far side of the Surf & Sand's excellent restaurant, Splashes. You literally might wind up making a splash of another sort if you walk through the restaurant in a bathing suit at lunch hour. Seaview rooms at the Surf & Sand run about $395 nightly in summer.

Orange County

Nearby, **Cap'n Laguna Inn on the Beach** (1441 South Pacific Coast Highway, 949/494-6533, $$$) offers the same paradisiacal setting without the gourmet trimmings and mandatory valet parking.

The **Inn at Laguna Beach** (211 North Pacific Coast Highway, 949/497-9722, $$$$) also has an unbeatable location—just above Main Beach on a bluff next to the best restaurant in town, Las Brisas. Your biggest problem will be deciding how to allocate time: hanging out on Main Beach, sitting on a private ocean-facing balcony, sunbathing on the rooftop sundeck, or strolling Cliff Drive. Moreover, the Inn at Laguna Beach has an amenity worth its weight in gold: an on-site underground garage. Alternatively, if you're feeling sentimental for Old California, you can always stay at the **Hotel Laguna** (425 South Pacific Coast Highway, 949/494-1151, $$$$), a midtown treasure whose beginnings date back to the very founding of Laguna Beach. It's popular with European visitors and is oh-so-civilized.

South Laguna is the site of **Aliso Creek Inn** (31106 South Pacific Coast Highway, 949/499-2271, $$$). Aliso Creek runs through the property, and you can follow it to the beach of the same name, which is only a thousand feet away via a pedestrian underpass. Despite its proximity to the ocean, the inn feels like another world. With views up a canyon and out on mountains, its grounds are woodsy and secluded—a rare find in the midst of a beach town. All rooms are spacious one- and two-bedroom townhouses. The grounds encompass a nine-hole golf course, a large heated pool, and Ben Brown's Restaurant, which serves continental fare. Deer and raccoons, even bobcats and mountain lions, have been spotted on rare occasions.

A string of park-at-your-door motels cut from plainer cloth can be found in South Laguna. The **Best Western Laguna Reef Inn** (30806 South Pacific Coast Highway, 949/499-2227, $$) is the nicest of these, offering clean rooms

and a heated pool for half the tariff in Laguna Beach proper. Note: The Laguna Beach Visitor Information Center will assist with hotel and restaurant reservations; call 800/877-1115.

Coastal Cuisine

The food scene in Laguna Beach is a sensual indulgence bordering on the obscene. After one magnificent meal after another over the years, we've come to understand why the Romans invented vomitoriums.

Stalwart favorites from Laguna Beach's prodigious list of top-flight eateries include **Five Feet** (328 Glenneyre, 949/497-4955, $$$$) and **230 Forest Avenue** (230 Forest Avenue, 949/494-2545, $$$$). At Five Feet, chef Michael Kang oversees the preparation of "contemporary Chinese cuisine," an atypically creative East-meets-West hybrid that results in such signature dishes as catfish with tomato ginger citrus sauce and wok-fried veal medallions and scallops in Thai basil garlic chili sauce. Kang calls his entrées "whimsical creations"; you'll call them heaven on a plate. With its sleek, urbane atmosphere, 230 Forest Avenue is Laguna's most popular spot for people-watching and martini-downing. Menu choices range from affordable pasta bowls to boldly simple preparations like seared peppercorn ahi, hazelnut-crusted halibut, and macadamia-crusted mahimahi.

Head to **Splashes** (1555 South Coast Highway, 949/497-4477, $$$$) for a refined, cosmopolitan meal in the unparalleled setting of a small, square dining room overlooking the ocean. Located in the Surf & Sand Resort, 25 feet above breaking waves, Splashes occupies a casually elegant setting with an indoor dining room and an outdoor deck a mere wave's splash from the churning Pacific. Chef Christopher Blobaum favors organic ingredients and Mediterranean cuisine. Signature seafood dishes include Pacific swordfish with herb risotto and lemon sauce and sautéed halibut with clams, capers, and black olives. Expect to spend about $80–100 for two, and don't pass up such desserts as chocolate *fondant* with banana ice cream. A postprandial stroll around hilly Laguna Beach will help assuage any guilt pangs. For fine and fun dining with a view, nothing in Laguna can top **Las Brisas** (361 Cliff Drive, 949/497-5434, $$$). The indoor dining room and outdoor patio overlook Main Beach and the ocean from the blufftop at the south end of Heisler Park. The house specialty is seafood with a south-of-the-border flair—everything from fresh sea-bass ceviche to Mexican lobster. The lunch ensaladas are too good to be true. Save room for dessert. The restaurant serves a breakfast buffet, lunch, and dinner, with a popular five-course weekend brunch.

The **Beach House Inn** (619 Sleepy Hollow Lane, 949/494-9707, $$$) is another fine dining option. The glass-walled dining room faces the ocean, so book your reservation at sunset. The menu selections tend toward creative, California nouvelle-style preparations of seafood. The broiled filet of sole, for example, is accompanied by bananas sautéed in butter and brown sugar, plus chutney and grated coconut. In an old house that used to belong to actor Slim Summerville (one of the original Keystone Cops), the Beach House Inn has retained its original architecture, and a relaxed air pervades the dining room.

The **White House Restaurant** (340 South Pacific Coast Highway, 949/494-8088, $$) is a local institution with a schizophrenic personality. It's a romantic room at the dinner hour that turns into a popular nightspot afterward. The interior of this 1918-vintage restaurant, once patronized by the likes of Bing Crosby, is filled with Tiffany lamps and varnished wood tables. Specialties include fresh pastas and halibut Maison. Later on, the house shakes to everything from reggae bands to local rockers.

After a late arrival in Laguna Beach one Sunday night, we were famished and therefore prepared to take whatever we could find open.

Fortunately, we were directed to **Woody's at the Beach** (1305 South Coast Highway, 949/376-8809, $$$), which would be a pleasant surprise at any hour. The tangy Dungeness crab and corn bisque made a soup-erb starter. The miso-crusted mahimahi was masterfully presented, with the filet served atop brown rice with wedges of grilled eggplant arrayed around it and the entire plate swimming in a satay-style peanut sauce. The changeable menu might also include such items as tamarind glazed rare ahi and roasted striped bass with artichoke ratatouille, saffron cream, and roasted pepper coulis. This is not the sort of inventive fare one would expect from a restaurant whose sign out front is fashioned from a surfboard, or where the background music tends toward softly throbbing disco.

Down in South Laguna, your best bets are Mexican. At least ours were. A surfer/rocker who grew up here turned us on to **Papa's Tacos** (31622 Pacific Coast Highway, 949/499-9822, $), and after feeding on the plate-filling fish tacos and blackened shrimp quesadillas, all we can do is add a hearty "come to Papa's." Another local favorite is the **Coyote Grill** (31621 Pacific Coast Highway, 949/499-4033, $$$), whose motto is "A Taste of Baja at the Beach." A message on the menu says, "When we open our doors, we open our hearts." When we opened their doors, we opened our mouths for things like lobster Puerto Nuevo (whole lobster grilled with all the fixings) and *pescados frescos.* That's "fresh fish" to all of you who don't *habla español,* and it changes daily according to what's available. Coyote Grill is a three-meal-a-day restaurant whose outdoor deck makes a pleasant spot to enjoy a late-afternoon drink.

More and better restaurants arrive with every season in Laguna Beach—certainly more than we can possibly chart. Among the newest, a trusted Laguna native recommended **Picayo** (610 North Coast Highway, 949/497-5051, $$$) and **Vertical** (234 Forest Avenue, 949/494-0990, $$$). We window-shopped at the latter,

Orange County

Hanging Out with the Surf Addicts

Orange County

Some years ago, we arrived in Laguna Beach exhausted from our nighttime rambles around the coastal party towns of San Diego County. After a big meal and an after-dinner walk, we were ready to call it a night when the sounds of live music came wafting across the street. Seduced by the siren call of electric guitars, we followed the noise to its origins: a blurry cacophony created by three bands playing simultaneously at open-doored bars in close proximity. The nightlife of Laguna Beach is compacted into the midtown area near Main Beach. One can walk from club to club without having to get into a car. That seems a logical enough arrangement, but rarely are beach bars laid out so conveniently.

The contenders in this Thursday-night battle of the bands were Low Tolerance, a serviceable rock-and-roll bar band, playing at the White House Restaurant; the Missiles of October, a popular local band with a U2-ish bent who packed the house and sidewalks outside the Marine Room Tavern; and the Surf Addicts, a surf-punk trio who were blasting away at Hennessey's Tavern. We opted for the Surf Addicts, as their music sounded the most fun to our ears.

The story and sound of this now-defunct band are fairly typical of the Southern California experience. They wrote witty songs about the archetypal SoCal surfer/party-dude lifestyle. They sang about living hard, having fun, and taking chances but getting out alive. "I want to live on the edge without falling over," explained the group's singer/guitarist in a post-show confab over a

a stylish, open-aired, sleekly appointed space. The chef-owner calls his cuisine "casual, bold, exciting, playful, visionary." You are invited to "design" your own meal and pair it with wine by the taste, glass, flight (hence the name "Vertical"), or bottle. Vertical offers "boutique wine" samplings on the second and fourth Thursdays of every month.

Incidentally, a good place to start the day in Laguna Beach is **The Koffee Klatch** (1440 South Coast Highway, 949/376-6867, $), a locals' hangout nestled among the art galleries.

Night Moves

As the dinner hour wanes, several of Laguna's more popular restaurants morph into nightspots. The **White House Restaurant** (340 South Pacific Coast Highway, 949/494-8088) is popular with locals. Bar bands on weekends and reggae during the week seem to be the rule. **Las Brisas** (361 Cliff Drive, 949/497-5434) also attracts a sizable crowd of folks who hang out at the bar to meet and mingle. The **Marine Room Tavern** (214 Ocean Avenue, 949/494-3027) draws a mixed bag of bands, anything from country-rock to alternative. Across the street, **Hennessey's Tavern** (213 Ocean Avenue, 949/494-2743) is the kind of place that does a good business no matter what. On one of our visits, the band that was playing finished a poor second, in terms of patron interest, to the daredevil boating video on the big-screen TV. It all depends on the band, the night, and the mood as to which club is packing 'em in. Closely

Map of Southern California—Page 9

table full of beer mugs. For him surfing was an activity as reflexive as breathing. He'd found his own private slice of wavy heaven, a cove beach in South Laguna that few others know about.

His idea of a perfect day in Laguna began with a hard bout of surfing, followed by a lunchtime chowdown at Papa's Tacos (a Mexican food joint beloved by locals) and a gig with the Surf Addicts that evening. Early in his career he wanted to join a reggae band. Then one day it occurred to him to write, sing, and play what he knows. In his case he knew best about surfing and partying in Laguna Beach. "We always partied with tourist girls," he told us, "so I wrote a song called 'Tourist Girls.' I grew up partying in Laguna, so I wrote a song called 'Party in Laguna.' I've always imagined what it would be like to surf Hawaii. I thought it would be kind of scary facing waves of that size, so I wrote a song around the line 'Don't hair out'—meaning don't chicken out—'in Wainea.'"

The Surf Addicts musically encapsulated a lifestyle in a fun, infectious way. Their songs were about real, recognizable things. Their tunes took interesting and unexpected turns, and they were solid instrumentalists. To us they sounded like the Police, the Beach Boys, and the Clash all riding the same surfboard. Their tapes were sold in surf shops and local record stores, but they rarely played outside the area and now there's nary a trace of them. But having witnessed their bracing, breakneck live show, we still find them hard to forget. They took the feeling of riding a wave or chugging a beer and turned it into music that made you want to do both. One thing's for sure: they made two road-weary beach bums glad to be wide awake and rocking at the beach at two in the morning.

Orange County

quartered down by Main Beach, the Marine Room, Hennessey's, and the White House are the Big Three in Laguna Beach.

For More Information

Laguna Beach Visitor Information Center, 252 Broadway, Laguna Beach, CA 92651, 949/497-9229 or 800/877-1115; Laguna Beach Chamber of Commerce, 357 Glenneyre Street, Laguna Beach, CA 92651, 949/494-1018, website: www.lagunabeachinfo.org

Map of Orange County—Page 98

Crystal Cove State Park

This state park, between Laguna Beach and Corona del Mar, is a happy surprise on the Orange County coast. Stretching from the ocean into the wooded San Joaquin Hills, its 2,791 acres provide excellent hiking opportunities, three separate coastal accesses (Pelican Point, Los Trancos, and Reef Point), 3.5 miles of beautiful golden-sand beach, an "underwater park" (Irvine Coast Marine Life Refuge), and a 32-site walk-in environmental campground three miles inland. With this bounty, **Crystal Cove State Park** is known to swimmers, surfers, sunbathers, and divers.

As if that weren't enough, a county-run upland parcel of 2,000 acres known as **Laguna Coast Wilderness Park** and the 11,500-acre **Irvine Ranch Land Reserve** combine with Crystal Cove State Park to provide a huge mountain-to-ocean tract of natural habitat within otherwise densely populated Orange County. The Irvine reserve is a permanent conservation easement deeded by the Irvine Company to the Nature Conservancy in 2001. On the environmental front, it is not all bad news in Orange County after all.

Reef Point is the southernmost access to Crystal Cove, with a stairway to a beach, hiking trail, bike path, and restrooms. **Los Trancos** has the largest parking lot, located on the east side of Pacific Coast Highway, with a tunnel leading under the highway to the beach. **Pelican Point** is the northernmost access, with a blufftop trail leading to a steep beach access ramp. The beach itself is covered with silvery drift logs, rounded cobbles, and coarse, golden-brown sand. From it you gaze up onto ochre-colored bluffs and grassy, rolling hills beyond. People run, hike, or repose on the beach, whose quietude is a balm from all the automotive mania of the coast cities to the north and south. Modest day-use fees are charged.

One sour note to this pristine coastal glory is the Newport Coast development just north of Pelican Point. Bought by the obsessively acquisitive Disney Corporation, this private community is devoted to luxury time-share condominiums for the loophole-loving rich, who will write off the cost of these multimillion-dollar second homes on their taxes. Just across the street from this newly sprung monolith is the Shake Shake, a 75-year-old smoothie stand that's much more in keeping with the true spirit of the beach life. Buy one of the healthy $3 smoothies—orange date and raspberry peach sound good—and thumb your nose at Newport Coast while you're at it.

The long-range plan is to create a Historic District within the state park to preserve and protect a cummunity of 46 small cottages that date from the 1930s. Meanwhile, down at Reef Point, the El Toro mobile home park, which is a bit of an eyesore, is being "converted" to a public campground, picnic area, and lifeguarded beach. Although no one likes to see people displaced, this is ultimately a good thing for the public and the long-term health of the natural habitat.

For More Information

Crystal Cove State Beach, 8471 Pacific Coast Highway, Laguna Beach, CA, 949/494-3539, website: www.parks.ca.gov

Map of Southern California—Page 9

Corona del Mar

Corona del Mar literally translates as "Crown of the Sea," but to us it simply means "the good life." When this book hits the best-seller lists (hope springs eternal!) or we win the lottery, Corona del Mar would be high on our list of places where we'd happily relocate. For one thing, this small (population 15,000), mostly residential, and fabulously wealthy neighbor of Newport Beach is blessed with a sweeping vista of the ocean. The town's financial standing is evident in the Lamborghini car dealership and chic boutiques that do a buzzing business along the main drag. It's a shame there's nowhere viable to stay in Corona del Mar, because the beaches and the blufftop parks overlooking them are as gorgeous as any in Orange County. For the most part, people tear through town on the grievously overburdened Pacific Coast Highway. It's well worth exploring the beaches off the beaten path along Ocean Boulevard. In fact, a whole other world lies off to the side of the highway clamor.

We took time to get to know Corona del Mar better on our latest trip; henceforth, it will become a required annual visit. The primarily residential oceanfront here is a visual feast, both seaward and landward. A fascinating mix of architectural styles gives the ritzy neighborhood a distinctively civilized air. We came upon a group of *plein air* landscape painters, mostly elderly women in sun bonnets, who gather regularly for seaside painting sessions. Although they may be deemed amateurs by critics, some of their work is at least as good as the stuff that gets peddled for inflated sums in the galleries of Laguna Beach.

Beaches

A linear park runs above Corona del Mar's beaches along Ocean Boulevard. At the south end, a steep road leads down to a wonderfully secluded cove, known as **Little Corona del Mar Beach.** As you're walking, be sure to ogle the estates that line the creekside canyon above the cove. Also notice the rock formations, including a perfect arch, in the water. Little Corona del Mar Beach is a miniature paradise for snorkeling, scuba diving, and tidepooling.

Corona del Mar Beach (a.k.a. Main Beach)—which is reachable from the other end of Ocean Boulevard via a drive that drops down to it—is gorgeous, as are the people who go there. It is a gigantic triangular drape of sand studded with volleyball nets and beach blankets. More than once, we've been content just to sit and drink in this real-life version of *Baywatch* for a while.

Corona del Mar lies on the south side of Newport Harbor. Climbing the rocks at the north end of Corona del Mar Beach, in defiance of the "Don't Climb the Rocks" sign, will net you a nifty vantage point from which to view the harbor. If you scramble down from Ocean Boulevard to the sandy cove known as **Rocky Point** or Pirates Cove, you can watch boats come and go in relative solitude. Just up from Rocky Point is **China Cove Beach,** accessible via a stairwell at Ocean Boulevard and Fernleaf Avenue. You can also hike up to Rocky Point and China Cove from Corona del Mar Beach.

Back up on Ocean Boulevard, overlooking China Cove, is **Lookout Point.** It's a wonderful spot from which to gaze out on the harbor jetties, Balboa Peninsula, and the setting sun. Concrete benches provide perches for savoring the magnificent view. The grass is greener here, and we mean that literally. Any of the houses in the vicinity could be featured on the Home and Garden Channel. Especially in the dimming light of day, these contemporary and Spanish-style marvels personify the upscale California lifestyle—an aesthete's dream, with the ocean as heavenly backdrop.

Orange County

By the way, in the unlikely event that anyone who lives along Ocean Boulevard or Poppy Avenue in Corona del Mar wants to invite us to a party, consider this an automatic RSVP. We're there!

Coastal Cuisine

While it lacks lodging options, Corona del Mar has some of the glitziest restaurants in Orange County. Among the more notable ones are the posh, contemporary **Trees** (44 Heliotrope Avenue, 949/673-0910, $$$) and the British-themed, jackets-required **Five Crowns** (3801 East Pacific Coast Highway, 949/760-0331, $$$$). The latter is an elegant re-creation of England's oldest inn, Ye Old Bell, that's faithful in every detail, right down to the Elizabethan garb worn by the wait staff.

Our personal favorite is **Oysters** (2515 E. Coast Highway, 949/675-7411, $$$), an informal but elegant (read: no dress code or valet parking) place that has been working magic with Pacific Rim–style seafood preparations since 1989. A recent meal here was one of the finest, from start to finish, we've ever had in our beach travels. The oyster sampler contained four distinctive types: Fanny Bays, from British Columbia (firm, salted cucumber flavor); Hama Hamas, from Washington State (mild fruity flavor); Hog Islands, from Tomales Bay (plump, smoky flavored, indescribably delicious); and Sunset Beaches, from Puget Sound (crisp and fruity). The kung pao calamari, a popular appetizer, was sheer perfection, a peerless combination of texture and flavors, and the helping was large enough for a meal.

For entrées, the flat-iron seared Hawaiian ahi—a thick, moist slab of crimson as tender as filet mignon—was brilliantly complemented by jasmine-nori rice, spinach, and a soy-chile glaze. The misoyaki northern halibut was another masterpiece of blended flavors and textures, served with fresh soybeans, oyster mushrooms, and a potato-daiken puree. Oysters is commendably participating in a restaurant industry campaign to "Take a Pass on Chilean Sea Bass" by replacing that popular fish with halibut. Without restrictions on the fishing of this species, the Chilean sea bass may be extinct by 2005. Let's all take a pass! For dessert, the vanilla bean crème brûlée was transformed by a topping of fresh raspberries and a "blowtorch fired" sugar glaze. Our genial waiter, previously a veteran of 10 years in French restaurants, was sold on Oysters, telling us the chef stands so firmly for consistency that restaurant regulars claim to wake up fantasizing about what they will order here, knowing it will be as good as the last time. We will remember Oysters for our next visit. Until then, visions of kung pao squid dance in our heads.

For More Information

Corona del Mar Chamber of Commerce, 2843 East Pacific Coast Highway, Corona del Mar, CA 92625, 949/673-4050, website: www.cd chamber.com

Map of Southern California—Page 9

Newport Beach and Balboa

Newport Beach has been mislabeled. The goods are in order, but the writing on the can is all wrong. Before our initial visit 15 years ago, we'd been led to believe that it was "Nouveau Beach," a land of conspicuous consumption that looked down on anyone in flip-flops and cutoffs. We came expecting manic wheeler-dealer men and bored women dripping with jewelry. After all, Newport Beach was modeled on and named after Newport, Rhode Island, an exclusive community for the old-money yachting set. Indeed, Newport Beach has a few of its eastern kin's amenities, most notably the second largest pleasure-craft harbor in the country (with 10,000 berths). But Newport Beach also has an unpretentious, accommodating side

Lights, Camera, Action: From Beach Bums to TV Stars

Due to its relaxed atmosphere and gorgeous natural setting, Newport Beach has become a favorite place for film crews from Los Angeles to use as a backdrop. Getting permits to film on Santa Monica and Venice beaches has become such a hassle that many L.A. film crews don't even bother trying. We learned this firsthand one beautiful May afternoon when an L.A. film crew met us in Newport Beach for a three-hour shoot. That's right; thy humble beach bums were interviewed for the Travel Channel.

Strange as it may seem, we were interviewed on California's golden sands for a documentary about the beaches of Florida. This was done largely for convenience's sake—i.e., we were there, they were there. (Shameless plug: We have another book, *Foghorn Outdoors Florida Beaches,* that follows the same format as this one.) With Newport Pier as a backdrop, we sat on elevated director's chairs like real celebrities while a crew conducted lengthy interviews with us. (Another shameless plug: We were told afterward that we were the best-informed subjects they'd interviewed in the travel realm.) Curious onlookers would occasionally stop and stare as we pontificated about Florida beaches while California seabreezes ruffled our hair.

While we were shooting, Newport Beach's hip, athletic film commissioner pedaled up to the set on a mountain bike. An eager chap, he just wanted to make sure the shoot was proceeding satisfactorily. While he exchanged shop talk with the Travel Channel crew, we learned that a feature film was being shot farther down the beach.

"Low budget?" he was asked.

"Medium budget," he explained; "23-day shoot for $500,000, for TNT. Lots of soap stars. Light comedy. Looks good."

The title, which eludes us, was a cliché—as, no doubt, was the finished product.

Map of Orange County—Page 98

Orange County

that just doesn't jibe with its designer reputation. After numerous happy visits here, we've come to realize that Newport Beach is, at heart, a fun and funky beach town.

First of all, with a population of 70,000, Newport Beach is not a small town, nor is most of it truly on the beach. Many Newport Beach residents drive expensive imported cars with vanity plates, but they tend to live in gated subdivisions on the mainland or on the exclusive islands in Balboa Bay. The heart and soul of the city is out on Balboa Peninsula, a thin finger of land that reaches into the Pacific, then bends inward to protect the beautiful harbor. Back bays and waterways have been sculpted into the peninsula, and two small inhabited islands, Balboa and Lido, sit close by. Newport Beach is almost always sunny, relaxed, and dominated by watery pastimes. Boats dock right up against the back doors of houses.

The fun begins when you turn off Pacific Coast Highway onto Newport Boulevard or West Balboa Boulevard. The latter runs the length of Newport Beach's peninsula. It's a six-mile stretch ending at the Wedge, by the north jetty at the harbor mouth. To oversimplify, the big money is on the harbor side and all the fun is on the ocean side. Most beachgoers assemble in the general vicinity of the peninsula's ocean piers, Newport Pier and Balboa Pier.

The most boisterous activity can be found at and around Newport Pier. The first pier on this site was built in 1888 by the McFadden brothers, who founded the town and for whom the pier was originally named. Local history lingers here in the form of the beloved Dory Fleet, a fishing contingent that has launched wooden dories from this spot since 1891. Each day, the Dory Fleet leaves before dawn and returns by 7:30 A.M. to sell their fresh catch at Newport Pier. Their motto: "Our fish is the freshest fish on earth." A wooden sculpture pays tribute to these stouthearted laborers, and their method of selling

fish right on the beach creates an authentic California atmosphere. Nearby, you might see street performers addressing the crowd. We observed a balloon sculptor singing spirituals in an operatic tenor while a long-haired sea dog took Polaroids of passersby posing with his beautifully plumed parrots.

In the 1980s Newport's nouveau-riche elite—exhibiting the shortsightedness that brought them wealth but wound up bankrupting Orange County in 1994—wanted to do away with the Dory Fleet and give the Newport Pier area a sprucing up. They were quickly shot down, offering further proof that Newport Beach's ordinary townsfolk possess the sense and spirit that the more moneyed mullet-brains lack.

Balboa Pier lies two miles farther out along the peninsula. Here, things are a little less crazy. On the harbor side behind Balboa Pier is Balboa Pavilion, a Victorian landmark that dates from 1906. A renowned hot spot during the Big Band era, the pavilion still hosts events. You can catch a harbor-cruise boat (see the former homes of John Wayne, King Gillette, and Ron Popeil, inventor of the "Pocket Fisherman"!), take a whale-watching trip or board a passenger ferry to Catalina Island. A cute quarter-a-ride ferry runs continuously to Balboa Island. It is mostly residential, tightly packed with the homes of wealthy people whose cars chirp like crickets as they approach and exit with remote-controlled keys. The island has a sprinkling of upscale boutiques and tourist shops, but its most appealing feature is the walkway around it, which offers views of the bay and harbor.

Newport Beach is a quintessential California beach town by day and a rock-and-roll party zone at night. Despite the nonstop crunch of humanity, the peninsula is a friendly place. The most violent blows result from the affectionate pounding of backs, and the loudest shouts are those of approval for some minuscule sashaying bikini. One local restaurant goes so far as to offer "free salad for girls in biki-

Map of Southern California—Page 9

nis." The pedestrian's best friend in Newport Beach is Ocean Front promenade, an asphalt trail that runs along the ocean for nearly the full length of the peninsula. It is the primary route for bicyclists, joggers, and in-line skaters, and the human parade along this walkway is an intoxicating sight in and of itself.

Beaches

There are more than six miles of ocean beach and two massive piers on Balboa Peninsula. Starting at the south end, in Balboa, **West Jetty View Park** (a.k.a. The Wedge) is El Dorado for bodysurfers. Extremely rough surf, with waves as high as 20 feet, make the Wedge unsafe for board surfing and suitable only for highly experienced bodysurfers. Just across the harbor from the Wedge is Corona del Mar State Beach. Do not try to swim across. It may look like a short distance, but the water is treacherous. Just watch the boats sailing in and out of the harbor.

The stretch of sand from the Wedge to Balboa Pier is **Balboa Beach.** The dune structure along here is exceptionally healthy. This is what the Orange County coast must've looked like in the predevelopment 1950s, when it was primarily an escape for L.A. day-trippers. Families congregate on Balboa Beach for relaxed sunbathing and swimming.

The main beach on the peninsula is **Newport Beach Municipal Beach,** which runs for

 # Doin' Wheelies in Newport Beach

People of all ages and persuasions flock to the area around the Newport Beach piers and jam the Balboa Peninsula with traffic. During peak season it's not unusual to find traffic slowed to a standstill on Balboa Boulevard all the way out to Pacific Coast Highway. Traffic is a continuous thorn in Newport Beach's side, partly the result of a decision made years ago not to have I-5 built closer to the coast here. (Ironically, the decision was made in order to preserve the peace and quiet of the community.) The strategy worked for a while but backfired when Newport Beach exploded with development in the 1980s.

It goes without saying that driving here can be as gnarly as swimming through a kelp bed. Parking tickets come with stiff fines, and parking at most meters costs 25 cents for 15 minutes, with a six-hour limit. Six hours costs six bucks, and who carries 24 quarters around with them?

Thus, the best way to see the beach at Newport Beach is on bicycle, coasting to and fro on the Ocean Front promenade. The peninsula is flat and the city is bicycle-friendly. Local bike-rental outfits carry an excellent map of trails in the vicinity, with detailed tips and rules of the road that are useful anywhere, as well as local points of interest, license information and fees, hazards, and bike lanes along highways. Bike trails run as far east as Irvine, traversing the Upper Newport Bay, a state-managed ecological reserve.

Here are three places to rent bikes near Newport Pier, right in the heart of the action: **Let It Roll Bike Shop,** 126 22nd Street, 949/675-3026; **Newport Beach Bike and Skate Rental,** 2200 West Oceanfront, 949/675-1065; **Boardwalk Sports,** 100 McFadden Place, 949/673-1767.

Map of Orange County—Page 98

Orange County

two and a quarter miles from Newport Pier to the Santa Ana River Jetty. Along this golden strand surfers prefer the beaches at 52nd Street, North Jetty, and from 61st Street Beach to **Santa Ana River County Beach,** which flanks both sides of the river mouth, just south of Huntington Beach. All beaches on the Newport Beach peninsula are subject to a 10 P.M. curfew.

We're certainly not telling you anything you don't know when we say that traffic on Balboa Peninsula can get hellish on weekends and busy on summer weekdays. The only advice we can give is to bring lots of quarters for the meters—a roll or two if you want to stay all day.

Shore Things

• **Bike/skate rentals:** Newport Beach Bike Skate Rental, 2200 West Ocean Front, Newport Beach, 949/675-1065

• **Ecotourism:** Upper Newport Bay Ecological Reserve, Newport Beach, 949/640-6746

• **Marina:** Newport Dunes Resort and Marina, 1131 Back Bay Drive, Newport Beach, 949/729-3863

• **Piers:** Newport Pier, McFadden Square, 22nd Street at Newport Boulevard, Newport Beach; Balboa Pier, foot of Main Street, Balboa

• **Rainy day attraction:** Newport Harbor Nautical Museum, 151 East Coast Highway, Newport Beach, 949/673-7863

• **Shopping/browsing:** Fashion Island, Newport Center Drive, Newport Beach, 949/721-2000

• **Sportfishing:** Bongos Sportfishing Charters, 2130 Newport Boulevard, Newport Beach, 949/673-2810; Davey's Locker, Balboa Pavilion, 949/673-1434

• **Surf report:** 949/673-3371

• **Surf shop:** Green Room, 6480 Pacific Coast Highway, Newport Beach, 949/548-9944

• **Vacation rentals:** Beach 'n Bay Rental Company, 1501 West Balboa Boulevard, Balboa, 949/673-9368

Bunking Down

Nightly lodgings directly on the beach are scarcer than gulls' teeth. A particularly nice and fairly pricey one that's only a few bare feet from the surf is the **Portofino Beach Hotel** (2306 West Ocean Front, 949/673-7030, $$$). Formerly a surf shop, it's 20 elegant rooms will put you in mind of the Italian Riviera. Only a block from the beach and three blocks from the pier, **Best Western Bay Shores Inn** (1800 West Balboa Boulevard, 949/675-3463, $$$) is a salmon-colored, 21-room inn with homey, comfortable rooms. The inn provides a decent continental breakfast, not to mention everything from beach towels to boogie boards just for the asking. Plus you get a parking space—no small perk in Newport Beach.

Just off Balboa Peninsula, the most reasonably priced ($65 in season) and beach-accessible of the motels that line Pacific Coast Highway is the **Newport Channel Inn** (6030 West Pacific Coast Highway, 949/642-3030, $). It isn't fancy but it is clean and serviceable. The motel is across the street—the "street" being Pacific Coast Highway—from the wide, sandy beach at the north end of Newport Beach.

The friendly tone of the town and easy proximity to the sand makes a weekly or monthly apartment rental an appealing prospect here. Two agencies that specialize in beachfront rentals are **Villa Rentals** (427 31st Street, 949/675-4912) and **Balboa Newport Realty** (428 Third Street, 949/723-4494). The rental units on Balboa Beach are more family oriented, with a casual, kid-friendly ambience. Rates range from $750 for a week to $2,500 for a month. People recline in chaise lounges on back patios, reading newspapers and drinking highballs or coffee, oblivious to the parade passing just feet away on the Ocean Front promenade. The wildest characters you'll run across are adolescents trying to act raunchy. One 12-year-old sported a T-shirt that read "Will Work For Sex." Very funny, junior.

On either side of Newport Pier and con-

Orange County

tinuing to the north end of the peninsula, rentals are snapped up by college kids or groups of party-minded guys whose spartan pads are open to the scrutiny of passersby. Shirtless, tanned, smiling, and perpetually holding beers, they hang loose on every balcony and porch. We peered into one unkempt bungalow where a surfboard lay on a bed and a skateboard hung on the wall. Only in California. . . .

Coastal Cuisine

The **Crab Cooker** (2200 Newport Boulevard, 949/673-0100, $$), one of our favorite eateries in the universe, has been serving its patented smoked and grilled fish for almost 50 years in a building that was once a bank. "We're the only seafood joint that keeps its fish in a vault," jokes owner Bob Roubian, who is an expert on the subject of fish. He is, in fact, obsessed with them. He thinks about fish all day and dreams about fish at night. He sculpts, poeticizes, and writes songs about fish. A recording of a song he penned, "Who Hears the Fishes When They Cry," is sold at the restaurant. (He sounds like Tom Waits.) Music and fish have a lot in common, he says; both have scales. He encourages everyone to "Eat Lots A Fish." This is his motto, and it is emblazoned on the front of the building, along with such nuggets of wisdom as "Slam Some Salmon" and "The main thing is to keep the main thing the main thing."

Near Newport Pier, the Crab Cooker is a local institution for several reasons, not the least of which is that Roubian enforces strict standards on the fish he serves. He buys only fish that have been caught by the hook-and-line method and are eviscerated (bled and cleaned) within five minutes of being pulled from the water, thus assuring their freshness. Fresh fish never smells fishy, he insists; if anything, it smells a little sweet, like watermelon. His fish, shrimp, crab, and scallops are cooked on wooden skewers over a charcoal grill, because that's the way his mother did it. All din-

ners come with homemade bread, coleslaw, and Romano potatoes. You can actually make a filling meal from the Crab Cooker's incomparably good smoked albacore and smoked salmon appetizers. (Get the large versions, which are $4.25 and $6, respectively.) The food is served on paper plates, like a picnic, and it is beyond compare in quality and price.

This wonderfully ramshackle place is always packed, but don't try to call for reservations or pay with plastic. Just show up and wait your turn in line. To Roubian this is democracy at work, and he'll make no exceptions—not for a U.S. president, not for his grandmother, not even for himself. John Wayne, a longtime regular, always had to wait his turn, as did Richard Nixon. Sometimes the wait can be long, but just settle back on the wooden benches outside, have a cup of the Crab Cooker's famous seafood chowder, and write someone a postcard. (Roubian provides cards and postage, if mailed from the restaurant.) But by all means "eat lots a fish" here as often as possible.

The **Cannery** (3010 Lafayette Avenue, 949/675-5777, $$$) also serves some fine fare. The calamari appetizer is as tender a take on this staple as we've ever had, and the grilled swordfish tomatillo is a winning catch. The restaurant is in a converted cannery, with implements of the trade hung on the wall: wheels, pulleys, conveyer lines, boilers, and processing machines. You can eat inside or on a deck overlooking the water. After dinner, the Cannery morphs into one of the livelier nightspots in Newport Beach.

Even if you're not casting a line you can still land a fish on Newport Pier. At pier's end, **Newport Grill and Sushi Bar** (1 Newport Pier, 949/675-9771, $$$) serves grilled fish, sushi, and steaks from its second-floor dining room. It's easily the best view in town.

For a quick bite with a nice view, hit **Ruby's Diner** (1 Balboa Pier, 949/675-7829, $) at the end of Balboa Pier. The fare is mostly burgers and the atmosphere is faux '50s diner, rimmed

Orange County

Map of Orange County—Page 98

with neon. But the view is the second best in town and the grub is fine, as far as burgers and dogs go. Another local institution is the **Shore House Cafe** (801 East Balboa Boulevard, 949/673-7726, $$), on the main drag. At the other extreme is **21 Oceanfront** (2100 West Ocean Front, 949/673-2100, $$$$) an elegant fine-dining restaurant that serves fish flown in from all over the world. Abalone is a specialty, and entrées run $25–55. In other words, 21 Oceanfront is high-priced and high-end.

Night Moves

Most of the action after dark takes place on and around the piers. At **Balboa Pier,** set the wayback machine to the 1950s and step into a world of flirtatious adolescents on parade. Around and around the Balboa Pavilion circles an army of Annettes and Frankies too young to drink but too blitzed out on raging hormones to sit still. Dressed to thrill, they wander about, creating human logjams broken up by friendly beat cops on patrol. They walk around the pavilion again and return to the same logjam—cruising without cars, as it were.

The crowd is older, noisier, and more unpredictable at **Newport Pier.** Motorcycles and muscle T-shirts replace high fashion, and voices get raised a bit louder. The same cops survey the scene, but in a somewhat less amicable manner. Mostly, though, the chaos has a certain California etiquette to it, with lots of backslaps, handshakes, and high-fives.

Blackie's (21st Street and Ocean Front) is the beer-bar equivalent of the Crab Cooker. It is a timeless, changeless throwback, directly on Ocean Front promenade. On the door is a sign that reads "Sorry, We're Open" and on the walls are mounted hammerhead sharks, team pennants, three TVs (each tuned to a different station), pool tables, and a jukebox. It is a classic beer-drinker's oasis at any time of the day or night. We'd give you the phone number, but it's unlisted—part of its homey charm. Just to the north is **Mutt Lynch's** (23rd Street

and Ocean Front, 949/675-1556), a raucous corner joint serving passable pizza, sandwiches, and sports-bar munchies, plus geysers of beer.

Around the corner, off Ocean Front, is **Stag Bar** (121 McFadden Place, 949/673-4470). It is not, however, a stag bar. That is to say, women are welcome here. Reflecting a cutting-edge collegiate atmosphere, the Stag Bar is a raucous, beer-guzzling, hell-yessing kind of place, with a great jukebox, pool tables, and no pretensions. Draft beer is served in schooners the size of bazookas. On an otherwise slow Monday night in early spring when the rest of Newport Beach was dead, we watched the Stag Bar slowly but surely fill to capacity from our barside perches. By midnight the place was thumping to the beat of pool cues, jukebox jive, and erupting laughter. It occurred to us that, for a so-called stag bar, there were sure a lot of women. In fact, they outnumbered the men, at least on this particular evening. Because you cannot legally smoke in any bar or restaurant in California, the sidewalk outside the Stag Bar gets crowded with barflies taking frequent cigarette breaks. The smoke drifts into the bar, virtually negating the anti-smoking law's directive. We watched three comely college coeds celebrate the rites of spring by playing pool and drinking beer. The noise level grew and the shots became less accurate with each swig, but no one seemed to notice—ah, the delightful incoherence of youth. Meanwhile, a discombobulated woman who had just panhandled us for a buck wandered outside, where she collapsed in a heap on the sidewalk. We reminisced with the bartender about various punk bands we'd seen over the years, while the jukebox pumped out tunes by Sublime, X, and Social Distortion. We programmed a few selections of our own, including, appropriately, "L.A. Woman," by the Doors. We also played "Whole Lotta Rosie," by AC/DC (the live version).

Speaking of rosie, you can do a beer-fueled version of ring-around-the-rosie in the Newport Pier area without having to drive a car.

Map of Southern California—Page 9

Perambulate Ocean Front, McFadden Place, and Balboa Boulevard, angling into the Stag Bar, Mutt Lynch's, Blackie's, **Baja Sharkeez** (114 McFadden Place, 949/673-0292), **Hooters** (2406 Newport Boulevard, 949/723-5800), and **Woody's Wharf** (2318 Newport Boulevard, 949/675-0474). The last of these is another wild hangout with live music (mostly blues and boogie) that gets mobbed on weekends. The clientele seems a bit wanton. It has an outdoor patio and a harborfront dining area, but the main part of the club is configured all wrong and we wound up being wedged against the bar like sardines. Still, it's a hopping place if you want to frolic with the locals, who have been doing so here for 30 years.

For More Information

Newport Beach Conference and Visitor Bureau, 3300 West Coast Highway, Newport Beach, CA 92663, 949/722-1611 or 800/942-6278, website: www.newportbeachcvb.com

Huntington Beach

Huntington Beach is an essentially faceless city whose future is being plotted to best serve the interests of the Orange County business community. Everywhere, it looks and sounds and smells like a city under construction (or reconstruction). This is not necessarily all bad news, but it does mean that Huntington Beach lacks any sort of defining personality. Newport Beach is a funky, low-to-the-ground beach town, and Laguna Beach is cultured and rarefied. By comparison, Huntington Beach feels like a completely sterile asphalt-and-concrete sprawl zone. As if its utter lack of personality weren't bad enough, its beachfront is hemmed between the fuming stacks of a power plant and an active oil field. Inland, the numbing concrete corridor of Beach Boulevard is lined for miles with strip malls and franchises all the way out to I-405.

There's a brief but welcome eruption of bright, squeaky clean commerce by the Huntington Beach Pier along Pacific Coast Highway at Beach Boulevard. The pier and the surfing scene are easily the best things about Huntington Beach. To be sure, the development landward of the beach seems endless (e.g., "4 New Home Neighborhoods Open Soon!), as Huntington Beach—with a population of 200,000, the county's third and the state's 13th largest city—is completely at the mercy of the real-estate industry. It looks like utter madness to us.

Once upon a time Huntington Beach was just another cow town close to Los Angeles with a beautiful beach that was much beloved by the surfing cult. They knew it then as "Surf City," and it still gets called that now, though more by businessmen looking for a marketing handle than by loyal surfers. In Huntington Beach, as Jan and Dean sang in their number-one hit from 1963, the surf was always up and there was the added incentive of "two girls for every boy." During the golden era of surfing in the 1950s and '60s, the surfers pretty much had the place to themselves. As recently as the mid-'80s, Huntington Beach was a pretty sleepy-looking place along Pacific Coast Highway, lined with unpretentious food shacks (usually Mexican), surf shops, and one-story motor courts. The town would awaken only for the annual Labor Day surfing tournament and the de rigueur riot that often accompanied it.

All that began to change with the arrival of the Waterfront Hilton Beach Resort, a 12-story, 290-room hotel. It has been joined by the Pierside Pavilion and Promenade—clusters of retail stores, restaurants, theaters, and office space that chased a lot of funky old joints off the beach. Hyatt Ocean Grand, a $142 million resort colossus, is set to open in 2003. Also in the cards is a gargantuan "mixed use" complex, including a high-end terraced retail mall, that will occupy 34 ocean-facing acres owned

Map of Orange County—Page 98

by Capital Pacific Holdings. After having remained sleepy for so many years, this flat, foursquare cow town is now all too wide awake.

With a bit of imagination, the eye can trace its way across the landscape and imagine what Huntington Beach must have looked like at some remote point in the pre-settlement past: fields of large, fully vegetated dunes extending to the east, backed by lagoons and wetlands. In the early years of this century, the town was actually named "Pacific City" by a developer who wanted to see it become the West Coast's answer to Atlantic City. Pacific City was sold to a group who renamed it Huntington Beach, hoping that by paying nominal tribute to railroad magnate H. E. Huntington he would extend his Pacific Electric Railroad to the young city. (He fell for the ploy.) In 1919 Standard Oil leased 500 acres from the Huntington Beach Company; a year later, a well came in with a roar heard for miles. Nine million gallons a year are pumped out of Huntington Beach. Oil derricks are everywhere (except tourist brochures): by the highway, in backyards, on the beach, atop offshore platforms. A gigantic active field runs for miles from Goldenwest Street north to Sunset Beach. The pumping drills extend as far as the eye can see, like an aerobics class of metallic black magpies doing toe-touching exercises.

Despite all the changes, Huntington Beach remains a people's beach. Families, surfers, and everyday folks still crowd the city and state beaches that run for a great distance in either direction from the pier. But the retail scenery around these beaches has been drastically altered. At one extreme, there's the Waterfront Hilton, a towering monolith. At the other extreme, fast-food chains now rule the waterfront where once humble but lovable nonfranchised burger and taco huts used to stand. The heart of the action is where Main Street meets Pacific Coast Highway at Huntington Beach Pier. This intersection is home of the Pierside Pavilion and Promenade, a two-story boutique mall

aimed at those whose idea of a day at the beach is shopping close to it. Lest we sound too harsh, experience has shown that shops in these glitzy new malls generally have limited life spans, while they displace less trendy stores and restaurants that might have been around for decades. In the process, we've lost—and continue to lose—many of the beachside stands that stood sentry throughout the years when *American Graffiti* was being lived in reality instead of marketed as nostalgia.

The old Huntington Beach—a motley but likable cluster of surf shops, dive bars, and food stands—has fallen to the wrecking ball. City officials referred to the forced uprooting and relocation of mobile home park–dwelling oceanside residents, in 1984-style doublespeak, as a "conversion procedure." We have no delusions: we are not lamenting the passing of great architectural landmarks or businesses that can compete in the latter-day marketplace. It's just sad to witness the end of an era. A generation from now, will anyone remember what the beach life was really like?

Consider the squabbling that ensued when Dean Torrance, of Jan and Dean fame, suggested to the Huntington Beach City Council in 1991 that they consider copyrighting the name "Surf City" for promotional purposes. "People from Iowa want to come here to the beach," noted Torrance. "All the city has to do is grab onto the coattails of this idea." A great and legitimate hook for reeling in the tourists, no? Not in the eyes of one councilman, who whined, "We want people who will spend several hundred dollars a day in our hotels and restaurants. With inland California surfers, we're lucky if they spend $10 or $15 a day." This is how minds in Orange County work: with myopic eyes fixed on the bottom line at all times.

If you want to indulge in some black humor as regards the subject of life in these parts, a revealing column called "A Clockwork Orange: Diary of a Mad County" appears in the ex-

Map of Southern California—Page 9

cellent, free alternative newspaper *OC Weekly.* (View it online at www.ocweekly.com.) The column contains items like this one, from a recent issue: "A fellow named Bo reports a 'holocaust' at Huntington State Beach, where thousands of dead grunion have washed up onto the sand, most heavily around the lifeguard station No. 8 near PCH and Magnolia Street."

Whether you're spending $10 or $300 a day, the only part of Huntington Beach that matters is its coastal frontage. The town that sprawls behind it, arrayed along broad, strip mall–lined arteries that link Pacific Coast Highway with I-405, offers the visitor little that can't be found on or close to the beach. Beach Boulevard is the Big Kahuna of commerce in the area, offering a lengthy corridor of gas stations, franchise food stands, ATM machines, and strip malls. You can venture down this sun-beaten ribbon of concrete in search of drive-through grub, suntan lotion, film, flip-flops, or a more affordable motel, if you like, but there's not much to distinguish the interior of Huntington Beach from Fresno or Des Moines.

Incidentally, we tried to get a balky laptop PC repaired in Huntington Beach. We hauled it to a computer shop way out Goldenwest Street, farther inland than we care to venture on our beach-research trips. The dude behind the counter informed us of the inflated cost of working on a PC (minimum charge: $75). We lug nearly worthless old laptops on our beach junkets for obvious reasons (i.e., they might get stolen), but they do a perfectly fine job of word processing. When we seemed disinclined to leave the malfunctioning PC for servicing, the clerk suggested something we might try to get it to work. Lo and behold, we were able to revive it back in our hotel room. What sticks in our mind about this episode was the youthful clerk's disengagement and his glassy-eyed expression, which was straight out of *Children of the Damned.* It was like communicating with a robot. His brain-dead demeanor is not, we hope, what becomes of people who live in a community where shopping-mall sterility reigns supreme.

Here's the best indication we've yet run across of the Orange County mind-set. It was reported in 1999 that Huntington Beach struck a sponsorship deal with Coca-Cola, making Coke the city's "official beverage" and forbidding the sale of Pepsi everywhere but private businesses. It's bad enough that fast-food chains, sports arenas, schools, teams, and rock bands sign exclusivity contracts with the corporations that make these sweet, fizzy beverages. But a sponsorship deal with a city? Is there no bottom they won't plumb for money out here?

This Beaver Cleaver paradise of concrete and stucco has periodically been wracked with divisive issues. From battles over construction of the Waterfront to a debate over what to do with the Bolsa Chica wetlands (develop or preserve was the choice, and of course they developed), Huntington Beach found itself in the hot seat a lot in the 1990s. Even the old reliable surfers, source of the "Surf City" drawing card, have been a scourge on occasion. Back in 1987, the same year in which Huntington Beach was declared the safest city in the United States, a major riot erupted during the Labor Day surfing tournament, making national headlines. They subsequently moved the tournament to August (when crowds would be smaller), beefed up the police presence, and worked to keep alcohol off the beach. We attended the U.S. Open of Surfing in August 1996 and had a blast. The world's best surfers in the water, live rock bands on the beach, a sea of tanned and gorgeous bodies—what's not to like?

Another positive: Huntington Beach remains among the safest of America's 100 largest cities. In Orange County, Huntington Beach was one of two with populations over 100,000 to show a decrease in crime. There were no murders in Huntington Beach in 2002 and 2001. They must be doing something right.

Map of Orange County—Page 98

Beaches

Santa Cruz and Huntington Beach have been squabbling for years over which community has earned the right to the title "Surf City," but based on all available evidence, it's not even worth debating. Huntington Beach rules! Summer surfing championships have been held here since 1928, and it is widely known as the International Surf Capital of the World. In July and August, Huntington Beach hosts the U.S. Open of Surfing, and in June the OP Pro of Surfing Championships takes place. There's always something going on here, surf-wise.

People flock to Huntington Beach from the surrounding valley towns, as well as from surf-deprived Long Beach, with boards strapped

Legend of the Duke

There's another "Duke" besides John Wayne who left his mark on Orange County. He is **Duke Kahanamoku,** a Waikiki wave-rider who became a California legend. More than anyone else, he spread the word about Huntington Beach, turning a withering, would-be resort into a bustling beach mecca. Duke was a Hawaiian native, Olympic swimmer, and a world-class surfer—one of the first, in fact, to make a living at these things. Way back at the turn of the 20th century, this Pied Piper of the waves publicly promoted the sport, gracefully skiing the sloping surf on his favorite plank. His salary was paid by railroad mogul H. E. Huntington, who wanted to give the public new incentives to travel his freshly laid stretch of track from Los Angeles to Huntington Beach. He wowed the locals in the 1920s by surfing under the pier—a dangerous but impressive feat.

Following Duke's lead, a small but growing surfing cult began pointing their longboards toward Huntington Beach. In the early 1960s surfing seized the national imagination. When the Beach Boys, Jan and Dean, and the Surfaris took the sport into the Top 40 with a string of catchy surfing anthems, the entire nation suddenly craved coastal access. Surfers trekked the entire West Coast in search of the perfect wave, but it was Huntington Beach that became known as "Surf City," after Jan and Dean's chart-topping hit. The first major surfing competition, the Pacific Coast Surfboard Championships, was held here. Since the early 1970s, the U.S. Surfboard Championships have drawn hundreds of thousands to the brown-sugar beach at Huntington.

For many years, a small bust of Duke Kahanamoku gazing seaward stood at the foot of the Huntington Beach Pier. It has since been moved inside the **Huntington Beach International Surfing Museum.** Today, the late Duke—he died in 1968 at the age of 78—is recognized, along with fellow Hawaiian native George Freeth, as the father of surfing. Remnants and relics of surfing's golden age fill the museum, including everything from wildly adorned Hawaiian shirts to a 13-foot, 135-pound wooden longboard. There's also memorabilia from the Huntington Beach Surf Theater, a bygone 1960s-era film house that showed only surf movies. Ah, yes, those were the days.

Map of Southern California—Page 9

to the roofs of everything from boat-sized woodies to old VW bugs. The beach is so extensive, sandy, and clean, and the tumbling waves that roll ashore so well formed for surfing, that Huntington was voted the sixth best beach in the world in a poll conducted by (of all things) *Lifestyles of the Rich and Famous.* Surfers tend to get a far-off look in their eyes when they ponder the unobstructed south swells that spill forward in perfect curls of wave and foam (known as "rooster tails"), which can reach up to 12 feet in height.

The beaches of Huntington Beach offer an archetypal Southern California experience. They run for 8.5 miles, encompassing **Huntington State Beach, Huntington City Beach,** and **Bolsa Chica State Beach.** The offshore breezes are refreshing, and the strand is among the widest in Southern California—at least along the adjoining state and city beaches. It only costs $5 to park at Huntington State Beach vs. $9 for Huntington City Beach. Incredible as it may seem, there is otherwise no difference between the two.

Bring your running shoes or bicycle, because you can jog or pedal for five ocean-hugging miles (10 miles round-trip) along the **Huntington Beach Path** and **Bolsa Chica Bike Path.** We've taken many rejuvenating morning runs here. Up around Bolsa Chica, the beach starts narrowing. Fences have been put up to keep people back from unstable, crumbling cliffs. In places, the beach has narrowed so severely that it is usable only at low tide. RV camping is available at Bolsa Chica in an "en route" parking lot.

When you've had enough fun on the beach, make your way to the **Huntington Beach International Surfing Museum** (411 Olive Street, 714/960-3483) and the **Surfing Walk of Fame** (Main Street at Pacific Coast Highway). At the museum—opened in 1988, and the largest of a growing number of them—you learn that surfing was first documented in 1778, when Captain James Cook of the British Navy watched Hawaiian natives ride waves on crude long-

boards. The Walk of Fame starts at Jack's Surfboards and runs up Main Street. Stone monuments salute surfers inducted in such categories as Surf Pioneer, Surf Champion, and Woman of the Year.

Shore Things

• **Bike/skate rentals:** Dwight's Beach Concession, 201 Pacific Coast Highway, 714/536-8083

• **Ecotourism:** Bolsa Chica Ecological Reserve, Amigos de Bolsa Chica, 714/897-7003

• **Marina:** Huntington Harbor Marina, 4281 Warner Avenue, 714/840-5545

• **Pier:** Huntington Beach Pier, Main Street and Pacific Coast Highway, Huntington Beach, 714/536-5281

• **Rainy day attraction:** International Surfing Museum, 411 Olive Avenue, 714/960-3483

• **Shopping/browsing:** Ocean Promenade, 101 Main Street

• **Surf report:** 714/536-9303

• **Surf shop:** Huntington Surf & Sport, 300 Pacific Coast Highway, 714/841-4000; 5th Street Surf Shop, 217 Fifth Street, 714/969-8930

• **Vacation rentals:** Western Resorts Vacations, 8907 Warner Avenue, Suite 260, Huntington Beach, CA 92657, 714/596-2015

Bunking Down

The posh, 12-story **Waterfront Hilton Beach Resort** (21100 Pacific Coast Highway, 714/960-7873, $$$) claims to be the only oceanfront hotel between Laguna Beach and Redondo Beach. On Pacific Coast Highway between Main Street and Beach Boulevard, it's an attractive tower with rooms whose balconies look out onto Huntington Pier. No creature comfort is unmet. A large, shallow pool and hot tub occupy a landscaped courtyard teeming with greenery. The marble-filled lobby, with its enormous, arching walkways, is unusually opulent for a seaside hotel. The comforters are thick and heavy, making for blissful, mummified sleep. Every aspect of the Waterfront's

Orange County

design and landscaping envelops the visitor in an illusion of tropical delight.

The only sour note is the "Legend of the Surf Hero," a promotional motif. In this "legend," Huntington Beach's legitimate past as a surfer's mecca is turned into cheesy fiction. We quote: "The Surf Hero lived more than 200 years ago in a Native American village on what is now called Huntington Beach. His name was Mankota, and he was the greatest surfer of all time, in a region where surfing was a way of life. During one summer, the spirits became angry and threatened to make the oceans' waves cease forever unless the people offered a human sacrifice. To the surprise of the people, it was Mankota who volunteered. Later that night, Mankota paddled out to the waves for the last time. He caught a massive, churning wave, dropped into the curl and was never seen again. . . . Today, on the beach where the Surf Hero took his final ride, the legend has been carefully preserved by the Waterfront Hilton Beach Resort."

C'mon now, give the surfers a break, not to mention some respect. The real legend of the local surfing scene is far more intriguing than this corporate tall tale. Duke Kahanamoku is no doubt rolling over in his grave. Moreover, the Waterfront can stand on its own without it.

By the time this book reaches print, the brand-new **Hyatt Spa Resort** will have opened next door to the Hilton. Run by the same owner as the Hyatt, it is the latest dramatic surgery done on Huntington Beach's oceanfront since we began coming in the early 1980s. On the other side of the Hilton is yet another gigantic, fenced-off lot. Behind it, earth movers are already erecting a new commercial/real estate complex. It never ends in Huntington Beach.

If you're after something a little more down to earth, try the modestly likable, single-story **Huntington Shores Motel** (21002 Pacific Coast Highway, 714/536-8861, $$). Likewise, the **Quality Inn** (800 Pacific Coast Highway, 714/536-7500, $$) has location (three blocks north of the

Huntington Beach Pier, across from the beach), price (significantly less than the Waterfront), and condition (contemporary, clean) going for it. There's a string of small motels close to the beach between Beach Boulevard and Goldenwest Street on Pacific Coast Highway.

Coastal Cuisine

The Huntington Beach dining scene is, like the town itself, rather undistinguished. One piece of good news is that down by the Huntington Beach Pier you have two upscale franchise options: **Duke's** (317 Pacific Coast Highway, 714/374-6446, $$$) and **Chimayo** (315 Pacific Coast Highway, 714/374-7273, $$$). "Duke's" refers to Duke Kahanamoku, the Hawaiian legend considered the father of surfing. The restaurant specializes in Hawaiian-style cuisine, such as huli huli chicken (grilled with soy, garlic, and ginger) and hibachi-style teriyaki ahi (grilled with lime salsa, papaya, ginger, and soy). Chimayo speaks with a Mexican accent, serving Baja lobster and mesquite-grilled fish, both of which beg to be washed down with one of the house-specialty margaritas.

Main Street, from the beach up to Olive Avenue, has some shops and restaurants that are fun to duck into. Not all of them are yuppiefied and/or nationally franchised, either. We hit **Wahoo's Fish Tacos** (120 Main Avenue, 714/536-2050, $) for a quick bite. We were first attracted by all the decals on the door and then by the casual, let-it-all-hang-out ambience of the place. For under $4 you can get a combo plate with a tasty grilled fish taco (plain or Cajun-spiced) accompanied by black or white beans and rice. You could spend an entire afternoon watching surf videos or browsing the bric-a-brac on the walls at Wahoo's, which has a few other franchises in Southern California.

You can grab a decent breakfast or lunch at the **Sugar Shack** (213 Main Street, 714/536-0355, $). Surfers and local characters hang here, too, probably because it's one of the few old haunts that hasn't been given the bum's

Map of Southern California—Page 9

Orange County

rush by developers with a myopic "vision" of Huntington Beach's future.

Out on PCH, **Tsunami Sushi Bar** (17218 Pacific Coast Highway, 562/592-5806, $$) draws twenty-something locals who jam the small place for drinks and raw fish. If there's a line, hang in there—it's worth the wait.

At the other extreme, you can always "run for the border." The local **Taco Bell** (818 Pacific Coast Highway, 714/536-1951, $) is crawling with surfers. They stand on the tiled floor, topless, shoeless, shirtless, and dripping wet, waiting for their orders to be called. This particular one, while outwardly no different than the 4,151 other Taco Bell franchises in the United States, is something of a landmark with the surfer crowd, and it was the first in the chain to serve Baja fish tacos. However, this fast-food rendition of the venerable fish taco is a pale imitation of more substantial fare to be found at countless authentic Mexican restaurants between Mission Beach and Malibu.

Night Moves

Surfers and party dudes with long memories still lament the passing of the Golden Bear, a great hangout that got nuked by the redevelopment prerogative. Most of the old bars in the vicinity of the beach, which we remember as being a little rough, have met a similar fate. In many cases, it was no great loss, but it doesn't appear that much of worth has come along to replace it beyond studied plastic re-creations of the 1950s' surf-diner motif. And so party-minded people in Huntington Beach head to **Hurricane Bar and Grill** (200 Main Street, 714/374-0500), which has live music seven days a week. Across the street is the **Huntington Beach Beer Co.** (201 Main Street, 714/960-5343), an excellent brew pub with live music on Saturdays.

For More Information

Huntington Beach Conference and Visitor Bureau, 417 Main Street, Huntington Beach, CA 92648, 714/969-3492 or 800/SAY-OCEAN, website: www.hbvisit.com; Huntington Beach Chamber of Commerce, 2100 Main Street, Huntington Beach, CA 92648, 714/536-8888, website: www.hbchamber.org

Huntington Harbor, Sunset Beach, and Surfside

Huntington Harbor is a ritzy marina and residential development that split a significant wetland in two. Some of the remains of that wetland have been preserved as **Bolsa Chica Ecological Reserve,** southeast of Huntington Harbor, and as the **Seal Beach National Wildlife Refuge,** just inland from Sunset Beach and Seal Beach.

The saga of the Bolsa Chica wetlands reads like some sort of environmental soap opera. The story dates back to 1970—more than 30 years ago—when Signal Landmark Inc. purchased 1,600 acres of coastal wetlands from the Bolsa Chica Gun Club with the intention of building homes on them. This was just about the time that the environmental movement began gaining steam and people came to appreciate the ecological significance of wetlands. Thus began a three-decade tug of war over the Bolsa Chica wetlands. Part of the fun of tracking this story has been keeping up with all the name changes on the real estate side: Signal Landmark became Koll Real Estate Group, which became California Coastal Communities, which is now attempting to do business at Bolsa Chica as, rather absurdly, Hearthside Homes.

Seemingly every month, there's some new twist, lawsuit, filing, proposal, or decision, and yet everything and nothing changes. The initial

A Surfer Looks at 50

One afternoon during lunch we overheard a fellow named Brian Goodman talking to a waitress at Woody's Diner in Sunset Beach. She was having a bad day, and he urged her to "fluff up her aura" and "receive some of our positive vibes, 'cause we're full of happiness." He was sitting with his 15-year-old son, plotting the future (surfing adventures on the Baja Peninsula) while leisurely downing a plateful of Super Spuds: hash browns fried in a skillet with mushrooms, onions, green peppers, and cheese. This stick-to-your-ribs concoction has been warming surfers' tummies at this location since the 1950s. We engaged him in conversation, and he openly shared his life story and opinions on what's been happening along the California coast in recent decades.

Of Huntington Beach, on whose sands he learned to surf, he said: "We're disgusted with it. We don't go to Main Street anymore." As thick as the development of Huntington Beach's shoreline has grown since the arrival of the colossus known as the Waterfront, Goodman revealed that plans are in the works to make it much, much worse—plans that he, as an active member of the Surfrider Foundation and a concerned resident, has been diligently battling at the grassroots level. Goodman is quick to point out that rules can be bent when influential Orange County business people want their bidding done. The "build first, ask questions later" mentality extends right down to the water. How, Goodman asks rhetorically, did the Hilton Waterfront resort get around Proposition 13, which clearly forbids the further construction of high-rise fortresses along the ocean?

Goodman has been doggedly leading the good life while fighting the good fight, but for him the "Old California" of the 1950s and 1960s is a waning mem-

plan, approved by the California Coastal Commission in 1985, was to build 5,700 homes and a 1,300-slip marina with luxury hotels on a 2,000-acre wetland tract. It was met with opposition from grassroots environmental groups like Bolsa Chica Land Trust and Amigos de Bolsa Chica. In August 1994, the Orange County Planning Commission readied a proposal to rezone the Bolsa Chica wetlands from agricultural to residential use. However, the county's environmental impact statement was challenged by the city of Huntington Beach, which threatened to sue. By November the California State Coastal Conservancy, the cities of Huntington Beach and Seal Beach, the Sierra Club, and the League of Women Voters had all weighed in with preservation opinions. In addition to its inherent value as a wetland, it was pointed out that Bolsa Chica is a valuable archeological site. More "cogged stones"—used in Native American rituals between 6,000 and 3,500 B.C.—have been found here than anywhere else. "It is the mother of cogged-stone sites," said Pat Ware, president of the Pacific Coast Archeological Society.

Gradually, it dawned on people that, having destroyed 95 percent of its coastal wetlands, the state of California could ill afford to lose another acre. As regards Bolsa Chica, the state acquired 300 acres of its wetlands from what

Map of Southern California—Page 9

ory. He speaks fondly of nights spent sleeping sitting up in a Jeep at Bolsa Chica (known to locals as Tin Can Beach) in order to rise with the sun and go surfing. A wearying day on the waves would be followed by a hearty plate of Super Spuds at a bait and donut shop on the site of what is now Woody's Diner. Today, here he is, decades later, still surfing waves and scarfing spuds on the same spot, but disenchanted with the corporate makeover of his beloved California coast. He mourns the loss of Dana Point as a surfer's mecca since the man-made harbor eliminated one of the most challenging point breaks on the West Coast. And so he's got his eyes pointed south, beyond California, where he'll stake his claim in "some Third World nation." There he'll scan the horizon for the perfect wave that will carry him to a beach where he won't have to look at some moneyed bigwig's vacation home.

Goodman is like a surfing Fred MacMurray: he's middle-aged, and he speaks fondly of "my three sons," whom he has looked after responsibly and well. Goodman feels he has fulfilled his responsibility as a parent and can turn his attention to his own further adventures. Already, he shares a year-round lease on a shack at a beach on the Baja, well south of anything that could be described as Americanized. A paltry $900 gets it for the whole year. Divide that by six tenants, and you're talking next to nothing in living expenses. It's a sweet life. The locals like the gringos, and vice versa. Goodman has his sights set on a full-time move in that direction.

His smile is genuine and constant, the sense of pleasure he derives from his largely nonmaterialistic life an inspiration as he stares at age 50. Unlike those who are fretting over adjustable rate mortgages on their Huntington Beach condos, Goodman is living free and easy, able to pull up anchor and move on at a whim. "I've still got places to go and things to see and waves to ride," he concludes with a gleam.

Orange County

was then Signal in 1978. But the tide really turned in 1997 with the purchase by the state's Lands Commission of 880 acres of Bolsa Chica wetlands. Meanwhile, both before and after that sale, plans to develop Bolsa Chica kept shrinking in size. The dimensions of the proposals have gone down from 5,700 homes (1985) to 4,884 homes (1989) to 3,300 homes (1994) to 2,400 homes (1997) to 1,235 homes (1997) to 388 homes (2001). That is where it stands right now, as Hearthside Homes' proposal to build 388 homes on 100 acres of the upper mesa at Bolsa Chica is under review by various agencies. The good news is that, despite 30-plus years of wrangling, the Bolsa Chica wetlands are under preservation and not a single home has been built to date.

Shoreward of Bolsa Chica are the small communities of Sunset Beach and Surfside. The latter is a private beach colony accessible only to pedestrians and bicyclists through a gate. Sunset Beach is more in line with the old ways of Huntington Beach back when surfers had the run of this stretch of the coast. Remnants of that time are still evident in some of the funky restaurants and bars lining Pacific Coast Highway. Still, Sunset Beach is a confusing hodgepodge of upscale and downscale, old and new, fancy and decrepit. There seems to be no rhyme or reason to the retail landscape along

Map of Orange County—Page 98

Pacific Coast Highway, which grows more incoherent with each passing year.

Beaches

Sunset Beach is the principal beach in this area of wetlands, man-made harbors, and private residential communities. While the developers make their move on Bolsa Chica, life goes on at Huntington Harbor and Sunset Beach. The first of these is a private marina that has some public docks and overnight slips for rental. The community of Sunset Beach, arrayed like a centipede along Pacific Coast Highway, has a linear park with restrooms, playground, and volleyball nets that runs between Warner Avenue and Anderson Street. This county park was acquired and constructed in the early 1970s to provide a public beach for those who couldn't gain access through the privatized beachfront of the Sunset Beach colony.

Surfside Beach is a small beach accessible at Anderson Avenue through the gates of the private Surfside community, just north of Sunset Beach. The beach at Surfside, though, is not worth the trouble it takes to get to it, as parking is virtually nonexistent. Most visitors to the area would do better to head down to the massive city and state beaches of Huntington Beach.

Coastal Cuisine

Vestiges of the area's comfortably unglamorous past can be seen in places like **Harbor House Cafe** (16341 Pacific Coast Highway, 714/592-5404, $) and **Woody's Diner** (16731 Pacific Coast Highway, 714/592-2134, $). Harbor House has been around since 1939, and the site occupied by Woody's has a long and storied history as well. Both have menus heavy on omelette, seafood, and burger variations, offering something for everyone in pleasant surroundings.

For More Information

Huntington Beach Conference and Visitor Bureau, 417 Main Street, Huntington Beach, CA 92648, 714/969-3492 or 800/SAY-OCEAN, website: www.hbvisit.com; Huntington Beach Chamber of Commerce, 2100 Main Street, Huntington Beach, CA 92648, 714/536-8888, website: www.hbchamber.org

Seal Beach

Seal Beach was named for the flappy sea mammal that was once so popular with the garment trade. By Orange County standards it's a modest town in the best sense of the word. It could have just as easily been named for its good fortune at having been "sealed" off from its neighbors. At the north end of Orange County and just across the San Gabriel River from Los Angeles County, Seal Beach is a seal among sprawling sea monsters.

Pacific Coast Highway swings wide of Seal Beach, sparing the town center the nonstop wall of traffic between Long Beach and Huntington Beach. One must vigilantly search for the turnoff at Seal Beach Boulevard or miss the town completely. Seal Beach (population 24,000) is a world unto itself, existing primarily for those who live here. It has a Main Street that looks like a Main Street should—shaded with trees, cobbled with bricks, and as civilized as one of Grandma's bedtime stories. It has a grassy park named for an American president, Dwight D. Eisenhower, whose memory is synonymous with a more reassuring past. There's a tiny historical museum housed in an antique railroad car, an art deco movie house with a Wurlitzer organ, an Irish pub, a couple of seafood restaurants, a municipal pier, and a city beach.

The main drag along the beach impresses with its lack of gratuitous commerce and its goshdarn normalcy. The hottest ticket in town when we last visited was a Lion's Club fish fry. The community bulletin board was filled with

Swindlin' USA

(sung to the tune of "Surfin' USA")
"If every realtor had an ocean
There would be hell to pay
They'd be sellin' off the coastline
Like California
You'll see 'em building marinas
Time-sharing condos, too
Goofy goofy golf courses
Swindlin' USA

"You'll catch 'em boutiquing Del Mar
Up to Orange County Line
Installing spas and Jacuzzis
And pouring vintage wine
All over the Southland
Like down Doheny way
Developmental frenzy
Swindlin' USA

"They'll all be planning out a ruse
They'll pay some bribes real soon
They're shaking down their bankers
Condos and cash will bloom
They'll be bulldozing all summer
Phase One by fall, hooray!
Tell the surfers they're comin'
Swindlin' USA

"At Huntington and Newport
They always get their way
They're draining Bolsa Chica
Big homes and green fairways
All over the coastline
They're wrecking beach and bay
Developers gone crazy
Swindlin' USA"

Orange County

solicitations for recipe-swapping and pen pals. Of course, we quickly signed up for the latter.

Beaches

For all its small-town charm, **Seal Beach** is not completely undiscovered, as the surf here is middling popular. Many of the surfers who make the trek are too young to drive, so they ride the bus from Long Beach, boards tucked under their arms like briefcases. At 9:30 on a Monday morning, we counted 78 surfers on the north side of Seal Beach Pier. Looking like tropical fish in their fluorescent wet suits, they sat passively on their boards and stared west, bobbing up and down, not speaking to one another, just waiting for the perfect wave.

The wait can be a long one. The surf here approaches the beaches that run for half a mile on each side of the pier at a southerly angle. Sometimes this produces ideal waves, some-

times not. The surf's erratic quality keeps the town from becoming another Huntington Beach. Even when the waves aren't cooperating, though, the currents and crosswinds are swift and potentially treacherous. Signs warn: "Beware of Beach Hazards, Long Shore Currents, Rip Currents, Inshore Holes, Sand Bars, Underwater Objects, Pier Seawall, and Rock Structures."

The El Niño winter of 1997–1998 devastated Seal Beach. It's taken a lot of work to get the beach in working order. Nearby jetties and the cement base of the Seal Beach Pier, which acts as a kind of groin, conspire to impact natural sand-transporting mechanisms, to Seal Beach's detriment. The beach is 50 yards narrower on the north side than on the south. Planners who constructed the jetty did not intend this to happen—instead, the jetty was meant to hold the sand equally on both sides.

Surfing is allowed on the shorter stretch of

Map of Orange County—Page 98

Beach Games

The play's the thing in Southern California, at least at the beach. Most career choices, in fact, revolve in some way around outdoor activities. If one is not involved in real estate—selling or developing chunks of oceanfront that are the leisure set's most precious commodity—one is connected to the service fields that minister to the whims or needs of a populace that worships the sun.

Although nonacquisitive surfers would appear to be immune to this buy-and-sell world, even they get sucked into it, as do construction workers, waitpersons, motel maintenance staff, barkeeps, and salespeople. We figured that if we lived in Southern California we might make pretty good yardmen, sculpting yucca plants into likenesses of the legendary surfer Duke Kahanamoku.

That said, let the beach games begin, and may they never end! The following are some of the most popular games we've witnessed on our beach journeys:

• **Frisbee:** What can we say? The equipment is cheap, and the only rule is not to throw it out to sea. Any game in which a dog can participate is one we feel well qualified to play. Moreover, there's always a chance that the little plastic saucer will get away from you and land near a babe.

• **Hacky-sack:** You generally see circles of shirtless guys (often Deadheads or jam-band fans) kicking the hacky-sack around. Basically, the object is to keep a leather bean bag in the air with the use of your feet. It requires dexterity, concentration, endurance, and a lack of anything better to do.

• **Over the Line (OTL):** This exciting combination of softball, volleyball, and cricket is played on the hot, golden sand in bare feet. The only equipment needed is a bat, a softball, and gloves (optional for real OTL studs). The OTL field is paced off, 60 feet in width (or 22 paces), with no limit on length. Two teams of three players each compete. As in softball, teams alternate batting and fielding, with three outs per inning, but the game lasts only five innings. Two foul balls or one strike constitutes an out, as does a caught fly ball. Another switch: the pitcher throws to his or her own teammates, kneeling three feet away in the sand and lobbing the ball into an optimum swinging zone (not unlike setting up a spike in volleyball). A "hit" is required to land "over the line" (about 55 feet, or 20 paces, from the batter) and between foul lines.

beach north of the pier and on Surfside Beach, below the south jetty (and belonging, in fact, to the small community of Surfside). The longest and widest stretch of beach, between the pier and the south jetty, is reserved for swimmers and sunbathers. The 1,885-foot pier was destroyed in January 1983 by the same storm that leveled Huntington Pier. The Seal Beach Pier was rebuilt the next year, with a placard to commemorate the town's industriousness and a cute bronze sculpture of a seal.

Oh, so you noticed the oil platforms offshore? Well, that's part of the scenery over which the town has no control. Occasionally, in fact, Seal Beach is the unwilling recipient of an oil spill that closes the beach until it's

Map of Southern California—Page 9

Orange County

Three hits in an inning scores one run; every subsequent hit in the same inning counts as a run as well. For more on rules and tournaments, see the Old Mission Bay Athletic Club's website at www.ombac.org.

• **Paddleball:** A combination of tennis, handball, and ping-pong, this game is played as singles or doubles on a miniature tennis court. The rules are the same as tennis, with the exception of the racket, which is a wobbly-centered thing that looks like an oversized ping-pong paddle. The paddle cuts down on the range of a struck ball and presumably its velocity (although it looked plenty fast to us). When the sport is played well—as it is on the courts in Venice Beach and Santa Monica—it can be as exciting as Centre Court at Wimbledon (well, close). In the limited space of a paddleball court, doubles requires a series of movements as intricate as kabuki dance. Check it out.

• **Skee-ball:** Okay, it's not a beach game per se. But it is the only beach arcade game on either coast at which we excel. The best part of skee-ball is the choice of prizes you can win by scoring big: plastic spider rings, harmonicas shaped like crabs, and pirate eye patches. Where else can you land such booty?

• **Volleyball:** If you don't already know the rules of volleyball, move to the back of the bus. What makes this game so "California" are the two-person teams that play on the beach. How, you find yourself wondering in awe, do two people in bare feet cover that much ground? Will that bikini top stay on? And most important, how can anyone ever hope to return one of those spikes, routinely clocked at over 100 miles per hour? (Answer: They rarely do, which is why these games move so swiftly.) On some beaches—Manhattan Beach and Santa Cruz, for instance—volleyball is not just a game but an obsession. It's also a professional sport, one that has been embraced by advertisers, fashion designers, and ESPN.

• **Whiffleball:** You can make any batter look foolish if you're tossing one of these plastic balls with the wacky waffle holes. The game is played like baseball, though no gloves are needed. The best setup we observed was at Mission Beach, where some guys had put their beer-laden cooler near home plate and used the ocean as the outfield. If the batted ball went beyond where the waves broke, it was a home run. If it landed in the waves, it was a double. The object was to bat and drink from the cooler as much as possible.

cleaned up. During one of our visits, Seal Beach was hit by a small but nasty spill from a leaky pipe on an offshore platform. While the oil-company execs ducked culpability, the town mobilized with bulldozers and volunteers to clean up the mess. As we were leaving, the beach had been reopened. Meanwhile, angry letters to the editor began to appear.

"The rigs not only besmirch the coastline," wrote one citizen, "they pose a constant threat to our beaches and sea life." Let's guess: next came the press release from the oil company publicists reassuring the townsfolk how environmentally conscious they are. Then local officials reminded the citizens about the money and jobs the oil companies bring the local

Map of Orange County—Page 98

economy. Everyone forgets for a while, then another small but nasty spill occurs, and the cycle beings anew.

Anyway, here's to the good folks of Seal Beach. May your sand remain clean and may your beach stay in place for another year.

Bunking Down

In this homey town, there's really only one large motel, the **Pacific Inn of Seal Beach** (600 Marina Drive, 562/493-7501, $$). This former Radisson Inn is an easy walk from the beach, pier, and Main Street. Two small pools are on the premises.

You may opt for the 24-room **Seal Beach Inn and Gardens** (212 Fifth Street, 562/493-2416, $$$), a restored 60-year-old inn with splendid gardens. It combines the best of bed-and-breakfast and hotel amenities under one roof.

Coastal Cuisine

Walt's Wharf (201 Main Street, 562/598-4433,

$$$) attracts the most devoted following. It's more upscale than most other restaurants in town, drawing a gregarious crowd in the late afternoon. There are nearly as many fish to choose from as there are imported beers on tap, and the seafood is as fresh as it comes.

Night Moves

Don't leave **Walt's Wharf** (201 Main Street, 562/598-4433) if you're looking for something to do after dinner. It's got a great bar with a kick-back-and-relax ambience and excellent appetizers to go with the brew. There's also a **Hennessey's Tavern** (140 Main Street, 562/598-4419) across the street. Hennessey's, a Southern California chain mining an Irish pub theme, is an old reliable watering hole no matter where the location.

For More Information

Seal Beach Chamber of Commerce, 311 Main Street, Seal Beach, CA 90740, 562/799-0179, website: www.sealbeachchamber.com

Map of Southern California—Page 9

© ROBERT HOLMES/CALTOUR

Chapter 3
Los Angeles County

Los Angeles County

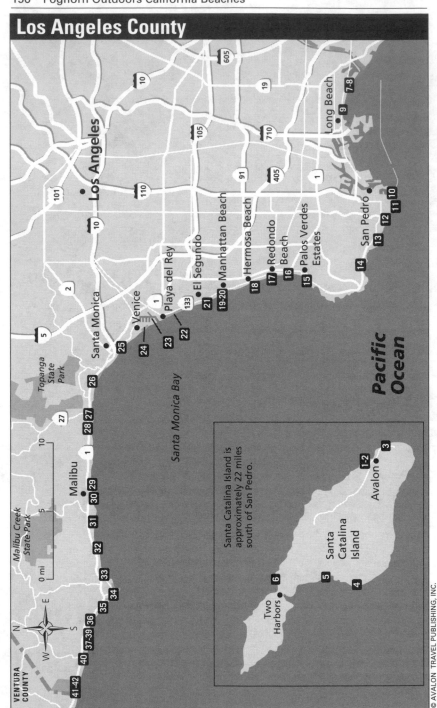

© AVALON TRAVEL PUBLISHING, INC.

Los Angeles County Beaches

1 Descanso Beach, page 169

Location: at Descanso Beach Club, beside the Casino on Avalon Harbor
Parking/fees: $1.50 per person entrance fee
Hours: 9 A.M.–sunset
Facilities: concession, restrooms, and showers
Contact: Descanso Beach Club, 310/510-7408

2 Crescent Beach, page 169

Location: Crescent Avenue at Green Pleasure Pier in Avalon
Parking/fees: no cars allowed
Hours: 24 hours
Facilities: concession, lifeguards, and restrooms
Contact: Santa Catalina Island Conservancy, 310/510-1421

3 Pebbly Beach, page 169

Location: on Santa Catalina Island along Pebbly Beach Road, one mile southeast of Avalon Harbor
Parking/fees: no cars allowed
Hours: 24 hours
Facilities: none
Contact: Santa Catalina Island Conservancy, 310/510-1421

4 Ben Weston Beach, page 169

Location: on Santa Catalina Island at the end of Middle Canyon Trail, 11.5 miles south of Two Harbors
Parking/fees: no cars allowed
Hours: sunrise to sunset
Facilities: picnic area
Contact: Santa Catalina Island Conservancy, 310/510-1421

5 Little Harbor Beach, page 169

Location: seven miles south of Two Harbors on the western side of Santa Catalina Island
Parking/fees: no cars allowed. Camping fees are $12 per adult and $6 per child per night.
Hours: sunrise–sunset

Los Angeles County

Facilities: restrooms, showers, and picnic tables
Contact: Santa Catalina Island Conservancy, 310/510-1421

6 Little Fisherman's Cove, page 169

Location: Two Harbors, 12 miles northwest of Avalon, on Catalina Island
Parking/fees: no cars allowed. Camping fees are $12 per adult and $6 per child.
Hours: sunrise–sunset
Facilities: restrooms, showers, and picnic tables
Contact: Santa Catalina Island Conservancy, 310/510-1421

7 Alamitos Bay Beach (a.k.a. Horny Corners), page 176

Location: Bayshore Drive at Second Street in Belmont Shore area of Long Beach
Parking/fees: free street parking
Hours: 5 A.M.–10 P.M.
Facilities: lifeguards and restrooms
Contact: Long Beach Marine Services, 562/594-0951

8 Belmont Shore, page 176

Location: in the Belmont Shore area of Long Beach, along Ocean Boulevard between 39th and 54th Places
Parking/fees: metered street parking
Hours: 5 A.M.–10 P.M.
Facilities: lifeguards and restrooms
Contact: Long Beach Marine Services, 562/594-0951

9 Long Beach City Beach, page 175

Location: in Long Beach along Ocean Boulevard, from Belmont Pier to Alamitos Avenue
Parking/fees: metered lot and street parking
Hours: 5 A.M.–10 P.M.
Facilities: concession, lifeguards, restrooms, and showers
Contact: Long Beach Department of Marine Services, 562/594-0951

10 Cabrillo City Beach, page 180

Location: Stephen M. White Drive at 40th Street in San Pedro
Parking/fees: $5 entrance fee per vehicle
Hours: 5 A.M.–10:30 P.M.
Facilities: concession, lifeguards, restrooms, showers, and picnic tables
Contact: Los Angeles County Lifeguard Service, Southern Section, 310/832-1179

Map of Southern California—Page 9

11 Point Fermin Park, page 181

Location: Gaffey Street at Paseo del Mar, near Point Fermin Lighthouse in San Pedro
Parking/fees: free parking lot
Hours: 6 A.M.–sunset
Facilities: restrooms and picnic tables
Contact: Los Angeles County Lifeguard Service, Southern Section, 310/832-1179

12 White Point County Park, page 181

Location: From Pasco del Mar in San Pedro, turn right on Kay Fiorentino Drive and follow it to the park. On the left side of the parking lot is White Point County Park, on the right side is Royal Palms County Beach.
Parking/fees: $2 entrance fee per vehicle on weekdays, $5–6 on weekends
Hours: 6 A.M.–sunset
Facilities: restrooms
Contact: Los Angeles County Lifeguard Service, Southern Section, 310/832-1179

13 Royal Palms County Beach, page 181

Location: From Paseo del Mar in San Pedro, turn right on Kay Fiorentino Drive and follow it to the park. On the left side of the parking lot is White Point County Park, on the right side is Royal Palms County Beach.
Parking/fees: $5 entrance fee per vehicle
Hours: 6 A.M.–sunset
Facilities: lifeguards and restrooms
Contact: Los Angeles County Lifeguard Service, Southern Section, 310/832-1179

14 Abalone Cove Beach, page 184

Location: Palos Verdes Drive at Narcissa Drive on the southwest corner of Palos Verdes Peninsula
Parking/fees: $4 entrance fee per vehicle
Hours: 6 A.M.–sunset
Facilities: lifeguards, restrooms, and picnic area
Contact: Los Angeles County Lifeguard Service, Southern Section, 310/832-1179

15 Malaga Cove, page 184

Location: Paseo del Mar at Via Arroyo on northwest corner of Palos Verdes Peninsula
Parking/fees: free parking lot
Hours: 6 A.M.–sunset
Facilities: lifeguards, restrooms, and showers
Contact: Los Angeles County Lifeguard Service, Southern Section, 310/832-1179

Los Angeles County

Map of Los Angeles County—Page 156

16 Torrance City Beach, page 187

Location: along Paseo de la Playa in Torrance
Parking/fees: $4 entrance fee per vehicle
Hours: 6 A.M.–sunset
Facilities: lifeguards, restrooms, and showers
Contact: Los Angeles County Lifeguard Service, Southern Section, 310/832-1179

17 Redondo State Beach, page 187

Location: Torrance Boulevard at Esplanade in Redondo Beach
Parking/fees: metered street and lot parking
Hours: 6 A.M.–sunset
Facilities: concessions, lifeguards, restrooms, and showers
Contact: Los Angeles County Lifeguard Service, Southern Section, 310/832-1179

18 Hermosa City Beach, page 189

Location: Pier Avenue at Hermosa Avenue in Hermosa Beach
Parking/fees: metered street parking
Hours: 6 A.M.–sunset
Facilities: concessions, lifeguards, restrooms, and showers
Contact: Los Angeles County Lifeguard Service, Southern Section, 310/832-1179

19 Manhattan County Beach, page 197

Location: the Strand at Manhattan Pier in Manhattan Beach
Parking/fees: metered street and lot parking
Hours: 6 A.M.–sunset
Facilities: concession, lifeguards, restrooms, and showers
Contact: Los Angeles County Lifeguard Service, Southern Section, 310/832-1179

20 El Porto Beach (Manhattan County Beach), page 197

Location: end of 45th Street in Manhattan Beach
Parking/fees: metered street parking
Hours: 6 A.M.–sunset
Facilities: lifeguards, restrooms, and showers
Contact: Los Angeles County Lifeguard Service, Southern Section, 310/832-1179

21 El Segundo Beach (Dockweiler State Beach), page 200

Location: Grand Avenue at Vista del Mar Boulevard in El Segundo
Parking/fees: $6 entrance fee per vehicle
Hours: 6 A.M.–10 P.M.

Map of Southern California—Page 9

Facilities: lifeguards and restrooms
Contact: Los Angeles County Lifeguard Service, Southern Section, 310/832-1179

22 Dockweiler State Beach, page 200

Location: Vista del Mar Boulevard at Imperial Highway in Playa del Rey
Parking/fees: $5 entrance fee per vehicle. Camping fees are $16.35–26.35 per night.
Hours: 6 A.M.–10 P.M.
Facilities: concession, lifeguards, restrooms, showers, and picnic tables
Contact: Los Angeles County Lifeguard Service, Southern Section, 310/832-1179

23 Mother's Beach, page 203

Location: Basin D on Panay Way in Marina del Rey
Parking/fees: metered parking lot
Hours: sunrise to 10 P.M.
Facilities: lifeguards, restrooms, showers, and picnic tables
Contact: Marina del Rey Parks, Beaches, and Harbors, 310/305-9503

24 Venice City Beach, page 209

Location: Washington Boulevard at Ocean Front Walk in Venice
Parking/fees: metered street parking
Hours: 5 A.M.–10:30 P.M.
Facilities: concession, lifeguards, restrooms, showers, and picnic areas
Contact: Los Angeles County Lifeguard Service, Central Section, 310/394-3264

25 Santa Monica State Beach, page 214

Location: Ocean Avenue at Colorado Avenue in Santa Monica
Parking/fees: $6 entrance fee per vehicle or metered street parking
Hours: 6 A.M.–sunset
Facilities: concession, lifeguards, restrooms, showers, and picnic tables
Contact: Los Angeles County Lifeguard Service, Central Section, 310/394-3264

26 Will Rogers State Beach, page 219

Location: 16000 block of Highway 1 in Pacific Palisades
Parking/fees: $6 entrance fee per vehicle
Hours: 8 A.M.–7 P.M.
Facilities: concession, lifeguards, restrooms, and showers
Contact: Los Angeles County Department of Beaches and Harbors, 310/305-9503

Map of Los Angeles County—Page 156

27 Topanga County Beach, page 226

Location: 18500 Pacific Coast Highway in Malibu
Parking/fees: $5 entrance fee per vehicle
Hours: 6 A.M.–sunset
Facilities: concession, lifeguards, restrooms, showers, and picnic tables
Contact: Los Angeles County Lifeguard Service, Northern Section, 310/394-3264

28 Las Tunas County Beach, page 226

Location: 19400 Pacific Coast Highway in Malibu
Parking/fees: free parking lot
Hours: 6 A.M.–sunset
Facilities: lifeguards and picnic tables
Contact: Los Angeles County Lifeguard Service, Northern Section, 310/394-3264

29 Surfrider Beach (Malibu Lagoon County Beach), page 226

Location: Pacific Coast Highway at Malibu Pier
Parking/fees: $5 entrance fee per vehicle
Hours: 6 A.M.–sunset
Facilities: concession, lifeguards, showers, and restrooms
Contact: Los Angeles County Lifeguard Service, Northern Section, 310/394-3264

30 Malibu Lagoon County Beach, page 226

Location: Pacific Coast Highway at Malibu Creek
Parking/fees: $5 entrance fee per vehicle
Hours: 6 A.M.–sunset
Facilities: lifeguards, restrooms, showers, and picnic tables
Contact: Los Angeles County Lifeguard Service, Northern Section, 310/394-3264

31 Dan Blocker County Beach, page 226

Location: 26000 Pacific Coast Highway in Malibu
Parking/fees: limited free roadside parking
Hours: 6 A.M.–sunset
Facilities: lifeguards and restrooms
Contact: Los Angeles County Lifeguard Service, Northern Section, 310/394-3264

32 Escondido Beach, page 226

Location: path at Escondido Creek near Malibu Cove Colony Drive in Malibu
Parking/fees: limited free roadside parking
Hours: sunrise–sunset

Los Angeles County

Facilities: none
Contact: Malibu Division of the Angeles District of the California Department of Parks and Recreation, 310/457-8140

33 Paradise Cove, page 226

Location: 28128 Pacific Coast Highway in Malibu
Parking/fees: $25 entrance fee per car
Hours: sunrise–sunset
Facilities: concession, lifeguards, and restrooms
Contact: Paradise Cove, 310/457-2511

34 Point Dume County Beach (a.k.a. Westward Beach), page 226

Location: end of Westward Beach Road, on the north side of Point Dume, in Malibu
Parking/fees: $6 entrance fee per car
Hours: 6 A.M.–sunset
Facilities: lifeguards, restrooms, and showers
Contact: Los Angeles County Lifeguard Service, Northern Section, 310/394-3264

35 Zuma County Beach, page 226

Location: four miles north of Malibu at 30000 Pacific Coast Highway
Parking/fees: $6 entrance fee per vehicle
Hours: 6 A.M.–sunset
Facilities: concession, lifeguards, restrooms, and showers
Contact: Los Angeles County Lifeguard Service, Northern Section, 310/394-3264

36 Broad Beach, page 227

Location: stairways lead to the beach from Broad Beach Road at Highway 1 in Malibu
Parking/fees: limited free street parking
Hours: 6 A.M.–sunset
Facilities: none
Contact: Los Angeles County Department of Beaches and Harbors, 310/305-9503

37 El Matador State Beach, page 227

Location: six miles north of Malibu at 32350 Pacific Coast Highway
Parking/fees: $2 entrance fee per vehicle
Hours: 6 A.M.–sunset
Facilities: restrooms
Contact: Malibu Sector, Angeles District, California State Parks, 310/457-8143

38 La Piedra State Beach, page 227

Location: seven miles north of Malibu at 32700 Pacific Coast Highway
Parking/fees: $2 entrance fee per vehicle
Hours: 6 A.M.–sunset
Facilities: restrooms
Contact: Malibu Sector, Angeles District, California State Parks, 310/457-8143

39 El Pescador State Beach, page 227

Location: 7.5 miles north of Malibu at 32900 Pacific Coast Highway
Parking/fees: $2 entrance fee per vehicle
Hours: 6 A.M.–sunset
Facilities: restrooms
Contact: Malibu Sector, Angeles District, California State Parks, 310/457-8143

40 Nicholas Canyon County Beach, page 228

Location: nine miles north of Malibu at Nicholas Canyon Road and Highway 1
Parking/fees: $6 entrance fee per vehicle
Hours: 6 A.M.–sunset
Facilities: lifeguards, restrooms, and picnic tables
Contact: Los Angeles County Lifeguard Service, Northern Section, 310/394-3264

41 Leo Carrillo State Park, page 228

Location: one mile south of the Ventura County line at 36000 Pacific Coast Highway
Parking/fees: $5 entrance fee per vehicle. Camping fees are $13–16 per night, plus a $7.50 reservation fee.
Hours: 8 A.M.–sunset
Facilities: concession, lifeguards, restrooms, showers, and picnic tables
Contact: Leo Carrillo State Beach, 818/880-0350

42 County Line Beach (Leo Carrillo State Park), page 228

Location: Pacific Coast Highway at Ventura County line
Parking/fees: limited free roadside parking
Hours: 8 A.M.–sunset
Facilities: none
Contact: Leo Carrillo State Beach, 818/880-0350

Los Angeles County

Los Angeles County

We could have written a separate book about Los Angeles County's coastline, home to everything from the *Queen Mary* ocean liner in Long Beach to chainsaw jugglers in Venice Beach to the rich and famous who live in the secluded Malibu Colony. Just the familiar ring of the names of its beaches is enough to evoke images of endless summers, bottomless margaritas, and incomparable bathing beauties. Who can resist the lure of Santa Catalina Island; Redondo, Hermosa, and Manhattan Beaches, down along the South Bay; Venice, Santa Monica, and Marina del Rey, all part of the pulse of daily life in Los Angeles? Even Malibu's 27-mile stretch, most of it blessedly celebrity-free, is like a preview of the wilds one finds farther up the coast at Big Sur. As beleaguered as this county is, Los Angeles gets an "A" for making its beaches safe and accessible to nine million residents and 65 million tourists a year. It's just the rest of Los Angeles that drives us batty (but we won't obsess). So pick a beach, stick to it, and let the world that lies east of your chosen Eden go about its clamorous business while you fine-tune your tan.

Los Angeles County

Map of Los Angeles County—Page 156

Santa Catalina Island

To visit Santa Catalina Island is to step back into the past. The prehistoric past, that is. Most of the island—86 percent of its 76 square miles, to be exact—is owned and protected by the Santa Catalina Island Conservancy, a nonprofit outfit that has maintained it as a wilderness preserve since 1972. Consequently, Catalina looks the way it did when sun-worshipping Native Americans inhabited it 4,000 years ago. Even the Spaniards, who arrived with Juan Rodríguez Cabrillo in 1542 and again with Sebastian Vizcaino in 1602, didn't leave any scuff marks behind. Today, only 3,500 or so live on the island—and most of them, by far, are concentrated in the town of Avalon.

Catalina is a rugged, rocky island 21 miles long and eight miles wide. Its jagged green hills rise out of the Pacific Ocean. Mount Oriaba,

at 2,069 feet, is the highest peak. On days when the Santa Ana winds blow Southern California's smog away, Los Angelenos can clearly see the island.

Because the natural order has been allowed to prevail, Catalina Island is a different world from mainland California. The ecosystem is unique, with several species of plants and animals endemic to the island. The most celebrated flora is the Catalina ironwood, a tree that teeters on the brink of extinction; only two wild groves are left. A total of 395 species of plant life are native to Catalina, and a fascinating variety of animals make their home here. The island has its own subspecies of ground squirrel and fox, the latter a beautiful but elusive creature. Buffalo freely roam the island's interior. An original herd of 14 buffa-

 Getting to and from Catalina Island

Although passenger ferries to Santa Catalina Island leave from four mainland points (Long Beach, San Pedro, Huntington Harbor, and Newport Beach), the logistics are about the same. Parking on the mainland is not included and generally costs $7.50 a day at the terminal. The extremely relaxing passage over to Catalina takes about two hours one-way. It costs an additional $3–5 to bring a bike or a surfboard.

- **Catalina Cruises:** Boats depart daily from Long Beach to Avalon and Two Harbors. Call 310/510-0325 or 800/CATALINA for reservations. Round-trip fare is $25 for adults and $20 for kids.
- **Catalina Express Commuter:** Boats run year-round from San Pedro, Long Beach, and Dana Point terminals to Avalon and Two Harbors. Call 310/519-1212, 800/464-4228, or 800/833-6685 for reservations. Round-trip fare is $36.
- **Catalina Flyer:** This catamaran departs Balboa Pavilion in Newport Beach daily. For reservations call 949/673-5245. Round-trip fare is $33.
- **Catalina-Vegas Airlines:** A 40-minute flight from San Diego to Airport in the Sky at mid-island is available. Call 619/292-7311 for reservations.
- **Helitrans Air Service:** Regular helicopter transport is available from Long Beach, San Pedro, and Costa Mesa. For reservations contact Island Express, 1175 Queens Highway South, Long Beach, 800/2AVALON.

Map of Southern California—Page 9

Los Angeles County

lo was brought here in 1924 for the filming of *The Vanishing American;* now it numbers 400. Attempts to remove introduced herds of goats, sheep, and cattle have helped to restore indigenous vegetation. Wild pigs, goats, and deer also have the run of the place, though attempts to wipe out these feral intruders have met with less success. Some of the world's finest purebred Arabian horses are raised at El Rancho Escondido, a private ranch that is separate from the conservancy.

Unfortunately for humans (but fortunately for plants and wildlife), visitors can't easily reach many of the island's natural wonders, because exploration is fairly restricted. A permit is needed to travel anywhere more than a mile beyond the city limits of Avalon. Hiking and biking permits can be obtained by dropping by the **Santa Catalina Island Conservancy's** headquarters in Avalon (125 Claressa Avenue, 310/510-1421), where you'll also find trail maps, rules and regulations, and other information about the island. These permits can also be obtained at Two Harbors Visitor Services and Airport in the Sky. Hiking permits are free. Biking permits cost $50 per person and $75 per family and are good for a year (from May 1 through April 30). Hikers and bikers must return by dusk—unless, of course, they're camping and have the necessary permits for that.

Camping is a whole other matter. There are five campgrounds on the island: Two Harbors, Hermit Gulch, Little Harbor, Black Jack, and Parson's Landing. Camping reservations can be made at any of them by calling 310/510-8368. Alternatively, camping reservations can be made through the Santa Catalina Island Company by mail, fax, or online at www.catalina.com/camping. You can call the Santa Catalina Island Company at 310/510-2800 and ask that a camping brochure and request form be mailed to you. Finally, if you're on the island, you can book a campsite at three places in Avalon (Hotel Atwater, 125 Sumner Street,

310/510-1788; Pavilion Lodge, 150 Metropole Avenue, 310/510-2500; Discovery Tours, Crescent Avenue, across from Green Pleasure Pier, 310/510-2000) or at one place in Two Harbors (Two Harbors Visitor Services, at the foot of the main pier). Camping fees are $12 per adult and $6 per child ages 2-11. The season runs late March through the end of October; fees drop somewhat the rest of the year.

Here's a quick lowdown on the campgrounds. **Hermit Gulch Campground** is only 1.5 miles from Avalon, nestled in Avalon Canyon near the Wrigley Memorial and Botanical Garden. It's stocked with restrooms, showers, picnic tables, vending machines, grills, microwave, ice, and on-site ranger. **Two Harbors** is at a narrow isthmus about 20 miles up-island from Avalon, and there are primitive tent sites, less primitive tent cabins, and downright comfy "Catalina Cabins" with beds, refrigerator, heater, closet, and outdoor community kitchen. **Black Jack** is in the island's interior at the highest elevation. **Little Harbor** faces west onto two sandy beaches and is seven miles from Two Harbors; sites have picnic tables, fire rings, and barbecue grills, and the campground has chemical toilets, cold showers, and potable water. **Parson's Landing** is the most remote campground, lying up at the north end of the island. You'll find chemical toilets but no fresh water and no showers. You're on your own, but you're on the beach. It's a shadeless beach, however.

All of these permits and prohibitions are sensible and laudable. They keep the island free of Jeep-driving bozos waving shotguns at the wild buffalo. The flip side to this, though, is that most visitors are off-loaded into the harborfront encampment of Avalon and see little more of the island. Avalon lies on the eastern side of Catalina, facing the mainland. Passenger ferries from San Pedro, Long Beach, and Newport Beach dock here, making the town something of a tourist side-pocket on the otherwise empty green billiard table of Catalina Island.

Los Angeles County

Map of Los Angeles County—Page 156

The first person we encountered at the end of the ferry gangplank at the Green Pleasure Pier in Avalon was a bearded son of a gun with a sailor's cap scrunched atop his gnarled web of red hair. With no encouragement from us—we were perfectly content to lug our bags—he pronounced himself "our man." This meant that for a modest fee he'd tote our bags to the hotel, which he warned was "all the way over on the other side of town." Avalon is all of one square mile, and many of its hotels are within easy walking distance of the harbor. Our man no doubt serves some useful purpose here. Just decide before being browbeaten by him or his like whether you can manage for yourself.

There are excellent ways to see other parts of the island without having to trek like sherpas. Several different bus tours depart the Avalon Harbor area regularly, and taxis can be hired for private trips. The most reasonable of the bus tours is the Skyline Drive ($10.50 for adults, $7 for kids), a two-hour trip that ventures 10 miles into the heart of the conservancy. The Inland Motor Tour ($19.50 for adults, $12.50 for kids) is a four-hour version of the trip. Glass-bottomed boat tours ($5 for adults, $3.25 for kids) operate out of Avalon Harbor, offering eyewitness proof of the prodigious underwater life teeming in the blue-green waters. Other boat tours sail around the southern tip of Catalina to the western side of the island, where the only other "town," Two Harbors, is located. Two Harbors is a jumping-off point for some of the best hiking trails on Catalina. There are snorkeling tours, too, and buffet cruises. For information on tours call or drop by the **Catalina Island Visitor Bureau,** on the Green Pleasure Pier (310/510-1520), or **Two Harbors Visitor Services** (211 Catalina Avenue in Avalon and at the foot of the main pier in Two Harbors, 310/510-2800).

Many people travel to the island from the mainland on their own boats, at times turning the channel into a watery version of the Santa Ana Freeway. Some even swim over from Los Angeles. Each year an Ocean Marathon is held; the record time is 7.5 hours.

The salvation of our visit was a golf cart. Everyone on Catalina uses them, and they can be rented for $15–20 an hour, or around $50 for an entire day. After two hours of exhilarating travel into the arrow-marked hills above Avalon, we had seen everything we wanted to see. We also got a sufficiently uplifting feel for the natural riches of the island's interior to make us fantasize about a backpacking expedition at some later date.

Steer your golf cart south out of Avalon on Pebbly Beach Road. This state route hugs the shoreline, revealing placid waters with a rocky bottom—perfect for snorkeling and scuba diving, not so hot for swimming (brrr). After two miles the road moves inland, up a steep and winding grade that peaks at Mount Ada and the Wrigley Mansion. Incredible as it may seem, Catalina Island used to belong to William Wrigley Jr., the chewing-gum magnate and owner of the Chicago Cubs. Upon his death he deeded the island to the organization that now maintains it as a nature conservancy. Along this route you'll pass the second oldest golf course in the country. It's a nine-holer that was wedged into a rugged canyon in 1892. The road also skirts the now-overgrown field where the Cubs held their spring training from 1921 to 1951 (with four years off for World War II).

The nicest Wrigley legacy is **William Wrigley Jr. Botanical Gardens.** The Wrigley Memorial, set at the top of the gardens, is an imposing structure (232 feet by 130 feet) that dwarfs the surrounding Avalon Canyon like a misplaced Lincoln Memorial. The memorial took a year to build, and plaques attest to its tonnage, craftsmanship, and sturdiness. The plaque at the courtyard entrance reads, "The building is dedicated to William Wrigley Jr., who in 1919 recognized the potential of Santa Catalina as a nature preserve."

The gardens next to the memorial are a pleasure to stroll. Laid out in sections, they feature

Map of Southern California—Page 9

Catalina's indigenous plants, as well as oddities from around the world, like South Africa's red-hot poker. The most intriguing part of the garden is the separate wing devoted to cacti, some of which are the strangest and most Freudian we've ever seen.

One other noteworthy attraction is the **Casino,** a Mediterranean-style structure built by Wrigley on Avalon Harbor in 1929. It dominates the waterfront the way Wrigley's memorial overwhelms Avalon Canyon. At one time big bands blew hot and cool in the ballroom of this casino, which has also been used as a backdrop in many Hollywood films. Today, the Catalina Island Museum, featuring historic artifacts of human habitation on the island, is housed in its basement, and first-run movies play on the first floor.

Beaches

Crescent Beach (in Avalon) and **Pebbly Beach** (just south of Avalon) provide access to chilly, waveless harbor water. Crescent Beach has a bathhouse at 228 Crescent Avenue with lockers and a laundry. The beach itself is a tiny line of sand upon which you might place towels. A private beach, **Descanso Beach,** can be accessed via the beach club near the casino. Nonmembers must pay for access to this safe, sandy beach and its cabanas. Kayaks can be rented at Descanso Beach Ocean Sports (310/510-1226) or Wet Spot Rentals (310/510-2229).

Cove beaches can also be found farther up the north side of the island, above Avalon. (Gallagher Beach, Lava Wall Beach, and Starlight Beach are among the ones that have names.) This area is pocked with pebbly or sandy coves, offering environmental camping on a first-come, first-served basis. **Little Fisherman's Cove** is the site of a campground right on the water close to Two Harbors, where you'll find a restaurant, bar, and dive shop.

The best pure ocean beaches are on the western side of the island, necessitating a long walk or a bus or boat ride from Two Harbors. Little Harbor Beach (see sidebar, "Paradise Found: Catalina Island's Little Harbor Beach") is a wide, sandy protected beach—a real jewel for swimmers, snorkelers, divers, and campers. Four miles south is **Ben Weston Beach,** a nice sandy cove. Again, this beach requires some advance planning to gain access to it—not to mention an 11.5-mile trek from Two Harbors. For divers, the **Casino Point Underwater Park** sits just off Descanso Beach. Home to a sunken 70-foot schooner and all the squiggly marine life it attracts, the park can be explored via **Catalina Scuba Luv** (126 Catalina Avenue, Avalon, 310/510-2350) or **Catalina Divers Supply** (310/510-0330).

Bunking Down

First, for bicyclists and hikers, the campgrounds on Catalina are among the most secluded in California. Permits are required for bicycles and hiking, and separate permits are required for camping. The best conduit to campground reservations and hiking trails is **Two Harbors Visitor Services** (310/510-2800). For bike permits contact **Catalina Island Conservancy** (125 Claressa Avenue, Avalon, 310/510-1421). The **Hermit Gulch Campground** (310/510-8368), a mile outside Avalon, is privately run. Two county-run campgrounds within a reasonable hike of town—**Bird Park Campground** (75 sites) and **Black Jack Campground** (75 sites)—can be reserved through the County Parks and Recreation Department, but neither is anywhere near a beach.

Almost all of the lodgings on the island are in Avalon. In fact, Avalon seems like one large hotel. Our first night in town some years back reminded us of "Duncan," the Paul Simon song: "Couple in the next room bound to win a prize/They've been going at it all night long." We holed up in a Mediterranean-style "villa" that shall remain nameless, the brochure for which promised "a touch of Old World elegance and luxury." By "Old World," they apparently meant a windowless room

Map of Los Angeles County—Page 156

Paradise Found: Catalina Island's Little Harbor Beach

Though most of Santa Catalina Island's visitors confine their explorations to Avalon, there is an up-island sanctuary well worth checking out. Little Harbor Beach is a palm-fringed, crescent-shaped semitropical paradise midway down the windward, southwest-facing side of the island. Mountains rising to heights of more than 2,000 feet form a stunning backdrop for the wide, sandy cove. Little Harbor is actually three beaches in one: there's Little Harbor proper, which has a beachside campground; a small, unnamed cove that's a Gauguin-in-Tahiti paradise; and then Shark's Cove. The three adjacent coves, separated by rocky protrusions, amount to about one-third of a mile of wild, gorgeous beach out of range of civilization.

Getting to this end of the island is half the fun, particularly if you enjoy a long hike. The cross-island hike to Little Harbor can be undertaken from Avalon or Two Harbors, the island's two population centers. The trek from Avalon is longer and more arduous, following a calf-bruising 17-mile trail that ascends spiny ridges and drops into canyons. The 6.8-mile walk from Two Harbors can be made either along the main road, which passes by Little Harbor en route to Avalon, or via the Banning House Road Trail. The latter is more interesting and invigorating, hugging the coastline and making significant elevation changes.

The 17-site campground at Little Harbor comes equipped with outdoor showers, chemical toilets, and running water. Some visitors arrive via private boat, anchoring offshore and camping at Little Harbor. Anglers catch halibut and sun worshippers catch rays on the beach. Little Harbor is protected from the ocean by a small peninsula and offshore reef, making it excellent for snorkeling and scuba diving. Shark Harbor, which adjoins Little Harbor, gets the wave action and is good for bodysurfing and boogie boarding. Have no fear of the name, however. Shark Harbor is named for a rock that looks like the dorsal fin of a great white.

Kayaks, diving gear, backpacking equipment, and more can be rented at Two Harbors. The Santa Catalina Island Company runs buses out to Little Harbor, arranges interisland and cross-channel transportation, assists in travel planning, and issues camping and hiking permits. Call 310/510-2800 for information and reservations.

with cots, tiny shower stall, a sliding glass door for an entrance, and the thinnest walls this side of an eggshell. For this you pay over $100 a night. Moral of the story: Book carefully on Catalina Island.

The next night we found sane and commodious sanctuary at the **Pavilion Lodge** (513 Crescent Avenue, 310/510-2500 or 800/851-0216, $$). The lodge spreads back from the harborfront street into a landscaped courtyard, replete with a two-ton piece of redwood that drifted from the mainland and was placed here

Map of Southern California—Page 9

with the aid of several trucks, tractors, and herniated laborers. The rooms are quiet and comfortable, too. Ah, golden slumbers.

The most venerable hotel in town is the **Glenmore Plaza Hotel** (120 Sumner Avenue, 310/510-0017, $$$). This pastel-tinted beauty is over a century old and has hosted such eminences as Teddy Roosevelt (who hunted on the island) and Clark Gable. The wicker-filled rooms are airy and large, and the room rate includes wine and cheese in the courtyard each afternoon and a continental breakfast. However, Avalon's poshest hotel is the **Hotel Metropole** (205 Crescent Avenue, 310/510-1884, $$$), a three-story beauty set in the Metropole Marketplace, overlooking Avalon Harbor.

Over at Two Harbors, lodging can be found at **Banning House Lodge** (Two Harbors, 310/510-2800, $$$), an 11-room bed-and-breakfast built in 1910 as a summer home for the Bannings, two island-owner siblings. This homey, unpretentious inn looks out over Two Harbors' Isthmus Cove from its hillside perch.

Crowds throng to Catalina Island in the summer, but the island is no less charming during its "undiscovered season," September–April, when the room rates run considerably lower. Oh, and there's nary a chain hotel or motel to be found.

Coastal Cuisine

Around dinnertime one evening an elderly gentleman with hearing aids and a cane stood wheezing in front of a seafood restaurant on Crescent Avenue, Avalon's waterfront thoroughfare. Winded from his search for a suitable meal—a stroll that had covered three blocks and several posted menus—he turned on his wife when she sweetly suggested they eat at a place with a "pot roast and potato pancake" special. "I'm not going to put that junk in my mouth!" he cried in frustration. Propped up by his cane, he turned and shuffled farther down the street, bound and determined to find something more to his liking.

Most visitors to Catalina Island find themselves in the same, ahem, boat. A hungry army, they wander the quaint Mediterranean streets of Avalon at sundown, studying one menu after another for some clue as to the cuisine. Much of the seafood here is brought over from the mainland. Even the little pierside food hut serves a pretty bland paper boatload of fish 'n' chips. It also offers abalone burgers and buffalo burgers, which were described to us by a buffalo-booster as being "leaner than beef." Even the restaurant touted as the best seafood place in Avalon seemed suspect. Upon close inspection the posted review upon which the place built its reputation turned out to be a thinly veiled pan.

Solomon's Landing (101 Marilla Street, 310/510-1474, $$) at least offers a nice indoor/outdoor patio and a few fresh seafood entrées mingled among the Mexican specialties. The best bet for seafood—and the only seafood restaurant on Avalon Bay—is **Armstrong's Fish Market & Seafood Restaurant** (306 Crescent Avenue, 310/510-0113, $$).

One night years ago during our first visit to the island, we settled on **Antonio's Pizzeria & Cabaret** (230 Crescent Avenue, 310/510-0008, $) because of the intriguing sign in the window: "This restaurant has been declared a genuine Catalina bomb shelter—come on in and bask in the ambience of the decaying '50s while the world passes on." The place has moved from its original Sumner Street haunt to Crescent Avenue, into a building that is not bomb-proof, but where the spirit of the original lives on.

Night Moves

Unless you know someone at the members-only **Catalina Yacht Club** or the **Tuna Club**—the latter of which was founded in 1898 and has boasted Winston Churchill, Richard Nixon, King Olaf, and Hal Roach as members—your night moves will be as humble as the lonely buffalo. The best places are the lounge inside **Solomon's Landing** (101 Marilla Street, 310/510-1474) and

Los Angeles County

J. L.'s Locker Room (126 Sumner Street, 310/510-0258), a sports bar. Rams, Angels, and Dodgers photos adorn the walls, some inscribed to J. L. himself by players who have come all the way to Catalina to quaff a cold one at his pub.

For More Information

Catalina Island Chamber of Commerce and Visitors Bureau, 1 Green Pleasure Pier, P.O. Box 217, Avalon, CA 90704, 310/510-1520, website: www.catalina.com

Long Beach

This is a city whose fortunes tend to rise and fall with those of a famous British cruise ship. The *Queen Mary* is to Long Beach what London Bridge is to Lake Havasu City, Arizona: a grand relic of the crumbling British empire purchased and brought to America to confer a borrowed identity upon a place that has little of its own. In 1967, the ailing city of Long Beach welcomed the arrival of the *Queen Mary*. The world's largest ocean liner had itself fallen on hard times, as people had come to prefer the convenience of flying to making the time-consuming passage by water. The old boat was docked in the Port of Long Beach and refurbished into a combination hotel and tourist attraction. More important, perhaps, was the symbolism of the luxury liner. Laid to rest in Long Beach after 1,001 transatlantic crossings, the grande dame of the high seas became the city's beacon for a hopeful future.

It hasn't quite worked out that way. In terms of tourist revenue, the *Queen Mary* has had good years and bad years, and it's been as much of an albatross as a savior. The *Queen Mary*'s one-time companion in tourism—the *Spruce Goose*, a gargantuan wooden airplane that never flew, built by Howard Hughes before he began growing his fingernails—was sold off in 1992 and hauled off to Oregon. A 1993 editorial in the *Long Beach Press-Telegram* wondered, "Who will save the Queen?" Citing maintenance problems, declining attendance, and the need for massive capital improvements at a time when no funding could be found, the editorial concluded: "The signal coming from the *Queen Mary* isn't all that clear, but it's beginning to sound like an S.O.S." The boat was re-christened on September 26, 1994, exactly 60 years after being launched on its maiden voyage in Clydebank, Scotland. The grandson of the vessel's namesake broke a bottle of champagne on its hull, but only a few hundred people showed up for the occasion.

Nearly ten years later, little has changed. In 2001, the *Queen Mary* laid off 175 employees. Four auctions of original *Queen Mary* furniture, fixtures, art, and tableware were conducted in 1996 and 1997. In 1997, Joe Prevratil—the *Queen Mary*'s president and CEO—was revealed to be hatching a secret plan to have the ship towed to Tokyo. Many complain of the exorbitant cost of touring the ship ($19 for general admission and $8 for parking) or bunking down in one of the 365 staterooms ($109–169 per night).

During an overnight stay aboard the *Queen Mary,* we found the old ocean liner to be eerily deserted. Our fellow passengers included two elderly couples dancing to a jazz trio playing for an otherwise empty house at the Observation Bar; a smattering of foreigners as confused as we were about the layout of the boat; and a housekeeping staff who could not tell us how to get from one point to another. Admittedly, the *Queen Mary*—like the Long Beach Convention and Entertainment Center and all the surrounding hotels and restaurants that serve business travelers—does most of its business during the August-to-November "convention season." Even so, the historic vessel—a living museum that served both as a luxury liner "where the rich and famous took their ease" and as a World War II troop carrier—should be hauling aboard at least a

Map of Southern California—Page 9

Los Angeles County

Queen Mary Facts 'n' Figgers

Number of workers involved in construction: 300,000
Date work began: December 1, 1930
Date launched: September 26, 1934
Maiden voyage: May 27, 1936
Date retired: September 19, 1967
Number of transatlantic crossings: 1,001
Period of wartime service: 6.5 years (March 1940 to September 1946)
Number of troops transported in World War II: 765,429
Number of miles sailed in World War II: 569,429
Bounty placed on ship by Adolf Hitler: $250,000
World War II nickname: "The Gray Ghost"
Passenger capacity: 1,957
Officers and crew: 1,174
Number of decks: 12
Number of lifeboats: 24
Number of portholes: 2,000
Number of rivets: 10 million
Length of ship: 1,020 feet
Weight of ship: 90,985 tons
Height of ship (keel to top deck): 92 feet
Cruising speed: 34 mph
Fuel consumption: 0.0025 miles per gallon (13 feet per gallon)
Fuel consumed per crossing (from Southampton, England, to New York City):
    1,267,600 gallons
Fresh meat consumed per crossing: 77,000 pounds (38.5 tons)
Capacity of wine cellar: 15,000 bottles
Record number of passengers carried at one time: 16,683 (during World War II)
Record time, Atlantic crossing: 4 days, 10 hours, 6 minutes (August 24–29, 1966)

The *Queen Mary* is open year-round 10 A.M.–6 P.M. It is at the south end of I-710 (Long Beach Freeway). Self-guided tours cost about $13 for adults, $11 for seniors 55 and up, and $8 for children ages 4–11. For more information contact the Queen Mary Seaport, 1126 Queens Highway, Long Beach, CA 90802, 562/435-3511.

Los Angeles County

moderate catch of tourist business during summer months.

The truth hurts, but Long Beach is simply not a prime vacation destination. Beyond the *Queen Mary*, this is a town ruled by its harbor, which primarily exists to serve naval and shipping interests. Away from its harbor, Long Beach has big-city problems but lacks sufficient big-city compensations to make it very tolerable or interesting. Thus, local boosters and PR people are reduced to touting entertainment and recreational

Map of Los Angeles County—Page 156

options that surround Long Beach—such as Disneyland, Catalina Island, and Knott's Berry Farm—rather than the city itself.

After the *Queen Mary*—which celebrated its 35th anniversary in Long Beach in December 2002—has been talked up and talked out, antsy visitors may find themselves in figurative dry dock, their remaining options running to things like driving past the world's largest whale mural, which covers the Long Beach Arena. A local columnist, attempting a feel-good broadside on behalf of downtown Long Beach, wrote the following, which unintentionally confirmed our worst suspicions: "Anything can happen downtown. If it rains, you get wet. If it's hot out, you sweat. Panhandlers may ask you for money. A few people get mugged. Downtown is life."

Well, at least Long Beach—a city of 462,000 that is California's fifth largest—never stops trying to improve itself. The downtown intersection of Broadway and Pine Avenue has become the center of a gentrified urban island. The concentration of music clubs, restaurants, movie theaters, and coffeehouses is a strategy we saw repeated elsewhere in metropolitan Southern California (such as in Santa Monica). There's safety and strength in numbers, it seems, though sleazy sorts can still violate the permeable borders. The entire neighborhood throbs in hot pink and purple neon, implicitly buzzing the message "class and cool" but instead saying "trendy urban cliché." At least there is good food and music to be had in downtown Long Beach, and it feels reasonably secure.

Also well worth a visit is the **Museum of Latin American Art** (628 Alamitos Avenue, 562/437-1689). Having opened in 1996 in the burgeoning East Village Arts District, this beautiful facility features contemporary works by Latin American artists. It is affiliated with **Viva** (644 Alamitos Street, 562/435-4048, $), a nearby restaurant that serves lunch only. The many dishes on the menu come from Cuba, Chile,

Peru, Colombia, et alia. It's a great way to travel abroad without leaving the table.

Hundreds of millions of dollars have been pumped into redeveloping Long Beach's shoreline and downtown. The **Long Beach Convention and Entertainment Center** (300 East Ocean Boulevard, 562/436-3636) boasts 224,000 square feet of meeting and exhibit space. The complex also includes the 13,500-seat Long Beach Arena (home of the Long Beach Ice Dogs professional hockey team) and the 3,050-seat **Terrace Theater,** a performing arts center. Since 1992, a major waterfront project—first called Disney SeaPark, then Queensway Bay, next The Pike at Rainbow Harbor, and now simply The Pike Project—has been planned, presented, and battled over (and over). Ten years after Disney was sent packing, the bickering continues. Nevertheless, the $100 million **Pike Project**—waterfront dining, entertainment, and retail complex—is slated to celebrate its official opening in October 2003. It has been hailed as the largest waterfront development in California history.

Already, the area has seen the arrival of the **Aquarium of the Pacific** (100 Aquarium Way, 562/590-3100), which opened in 1998. With more than 12,000 maritime creatures and 550 species, it is one of the nation's largest aquariums. Exhibits highlight underwater life in the three regions of the Pacific Ocean: Southern California/Baja Peninsula, the Tropical Pacific, and the Northern Pacific. (Be sure to check out the Shark Lagoon.) Admission is $18.75 for adults, $9.95 for children 3–11. The Aquarium of the Pacific adjoins Rainbow Harbor, a landscaped park with a 2,000-foot public esplanade, a fleet of commercial vessels, and the tall ships *California* and *American Pride.* Still, in typical Long Beach fashion, all is not well with the Aquarium of the Pacific. Attendance has been healthy but not sufficient to allow the aquarium to pay its own way, so Long Beach has had to help out with bond payments, inciting the usual rounds of editorials and citizen grousing in this financially strapped city.

Long Beach has been trying to rebound since taking a direct hit on June 23, 1995—a day referred to as "Black Friday"—when the Defense Base Closure and Realignment Commission announced the 1997 closing of the Long Beach Naval Shipyard. The city lost an estimated 3,000 military jobs and about $757 million a year in lost wages and spending. The announcement came a year after the Long Beach Naval Station and the Long Beach Naval Hospital closed their doors, taking a staggering 17,500 military and civilian jobs from the community.

Though most visitors never see it, there's more to Long Beach than the downtown waterfront. Miles and miles of poor, ethnic neighborhoods roll inland, interspersed with block-long car washes, hangar-sized topless bars, huge rail yards, and horrific industrial plants that make you understand why British poet/visionary William Blake coined the term "dark satanic mills." One blighted ghetto bears the nickname "Dogtown." A hip-hop hotbed, Long Beach has produced such dogged gangsta rappers as Snoop Dogg and Nate Dogg.

Sometimes statistics say a lot. Long Beach—a troubled big city that wrestles to stay afloat like the *Queen Mary*—saw its murder rate jump 52.3 percent in the first half of 2002, compared with the same period a year earlier.

On a brighter note, Belmont Shore, a self-contained neighborhood along the water in south Long Beach, has excellent ocean- and bay-beach access and lively shopping and nightlife along Second Street. If you find yourself priced out of the high-rise hotels near the Long Beach Convention and Entertainment Center, Belmont Shore is a viable place to stay. We prefer it, in fact.

Long Beach, when all is said and done, is really more oriented to convention business than pleasure travelers. Though its future looks promising, it is for now better described as a jumping-off point for attractions in the surrounding area than a bona fide destination in and of itself.

Beaches

Away from the downtown waterfront redevelopment zone, there are some fine neighborhoods along the water in Long Beach. Heading south along Ocean Boulevard from the Long Beach Freeway to its end at Alamitos Bay in Belmont Shore, you pass miles of beautifully landscaped, architecturally varied homes facing the green, linear Bluff Park that runs along the oceanfront. Long Beach has its own sandy, extensive city beach, but water quality can be poor and the offshore breakwater keeps the waves at bay, so to speak. Yes, the same breakwater that makes Long Beach's man-made harbor the busiest port on the West Coast cuts off the surf completely. The ocean is calmer than a farm pond. No waves roll ashore here, forcing natives to head to points north and south to surf and swim. Over a Memorial Day weekend, the beach was all but empty. Those who could afford to had high-tailed it out of Long Beach for Santa Catalina Island or the Baja Peninsula. The rest simply threw surfboards and wet suits in the back and pointed their wheels to Huntington Beach.

Long Beach City Beach runs for four miles, between First Place and 72nd Place seaward of Ocean Avenue. It's a nice expanse of sand, but there are much better ocean beaches in the vicinity—for instance Seal Beach (see the Orange County chapter) or the beaches of the South Bay Peninsula. The city beach is bisected by Belmont Pier, a 1,620-foot pier used by locals who appear not to be fishing for recreation but out of necessity, angling for their dinner. Looking across the rippled waters of Long Beach Harbor, one spies what appears to be a series of small resort islands with 10-story hotels built on them. They are, in fact, oil derricks, dressed up to be more appealing from the vantage point of the shoreline. These

Map of Los Angeles County—Page 156

Los Angeles County

artificial islands received their designer look from the Disney organization. Named after dead astronauts (e.g., Island Grissom, Island Chaffee), the derricks are hidden behind high-rise camouflage and bathed in peach and green lighting; Long Beach's offshore oil industry is innovative—at least in its exterior design.

The best beach in Long Beach turns out to be on the bay—specifically, the inner flank of **Alamitos Bay Beach** in Belmont Shore. It's a calm-water strip of sand that runs along Bay Shore Drive between Ocean Avenue and Second Street. Locals refer to this bayside beach by the nickname Horny Corners. Old folks, young kids, hot babes from Cal State Long Beach, scarlet-skinned dudes with yellow hair—all are content to lie prone on a beach towel. Some fling Frisbees, others read or gawk at the flesh parade, and a few rent kayaks. Some even swim in the bay's glass-smooth waters. Bay Shore Drive is blocked off all summer, in deference to walkers, in-line skaters, parents with strollers, and so on.

Belmont Shore also has 15 blocks of ocean frontage along Ocean Boulevard.

Bunking Down

There are too many high-rise hotels and not enough bodies to fill them in Long Beach. The $80 million, 398-room, 15-story **Long Beach Hilton World Trade Center** (2 World Trade Center, 562/983-1200, $$$), which opened in 1991, contributed further to what was already a soft, saturated hotel market. Already, plans for further new hotel construction have fallen through. Take your pick of the brand names, all of them towering above the action in the area of the convention center, downtown, and waterfront. Other impressive contenders for your lodging dollar include the **Westin Long Beach** (333 East Ocean Boulevard, 562/436-3000, $$$) and the **Hyatt Regency Long Beach** (200 South Pine Avenue, 562/491-1234, $$$). If you've got a yen to stay on the beach at a budget price, the **Edgewater Beach Motel** (1724

East Ocean Boulevard, 562/437-3090, $) fits the bill, offering views of Catalina from its deck and five-minute proximity to the downtown hubbub.

Then there's the **Hotel Queen Mary** (1126 Queens Highway, 562/499-3511, $$$). Her 365 staterooms are the largest ever built aboard a ship. Whereas they might have been a blast to stay in on a high-seas voyage four decades ago, today they are substantially less commodious than the rooms you'll find at one of the downtown high-rises (or even at a generic Travelodge). There's but a single porthole in each standard room that faces the water, providing a small, circular shaft of light onto the harbor. The rooms are dark and mildly claustrophobic, the bathrooms are small (and the plastic shower stalls scandalously cheap), yet the beds are comfortable and the unique experience of bunking down aboard a grand old ocean liner compensates for some of the drawbacks. To be perfectly honest, however, we'd recommend taking a daytime tour of the *Queen Mary* and laying your head elsewhere in Long Beach.

Coastal Cuisine

The restaurant scene here has labored to keep pace with the city's fast-breaking redevelopment program, but these things take time. How do you convince a three-star chef to move to Long Beach—tell him that the offshore oil platforms look like the Eiffel Tower? Nonetheless, it is possible to ante up for more than fish 'n' chips and saloon burgers, thanks to places like **Dominick's East Village** (555 East Ocean Boulevard, 562/437-0626, $$$), a New York-style Italian eatery—modeled, in fact, after Carmine's—that is housed in a downtown bank building. It's a great place to eat, with lots of atmosphere and hearty food. We defy you to go home hungry after a lunch or dinner here. Many entrées are available in half or full orders. No lightweights in the appetite department, neither of us could entirely finish even a half order (on top of soup and appetizers, granted), delicious though they were. We recommend putanesca with fresh tuna, spaghetti with mixed seafood, and sautéed calamari with tomato sauce and garlic. Baked fish are served whole in a sauce of lemon, olives, and olive oil. What more can we add but *"mangia, mangia."*

The oldest seafood restaurant in town, **Fish Tale** (5506 East Britton Drive, 562/594-8771, $$) got larger new digs, but the old ambience (fish tales, antique artifacts) is still intact, as are the heaping helpings of fresh fish. There's also an oyster bar on the premises. Downtown, the **Pine Avenue Fish House** (100 West Broadway, 562/432-7463, $$$) is a terrific choice for grilled or broiled fish served with light, creative, and tasty sauces, such as Chilean sea bass with dill chardonnay sauce (a house favorite) or blackened halibut with corn relish and red pepper coulis. The award-winning cioppino—a tomato-based fisherman's stew with clams, mussels, shrimp, crab, squid, and fish— is another excellent choice.

All manner of varied ethnic cuisine is available in Long Beach, but we were most surprised to find a place that served real Southern-style barbecue. The down-home fare at **Johnny Reb's Southern Smokehouse** (4663 Long Beach Boulevard, 562/423-7327, $$)—pit-cooked barbecue, crackling fried chicken, coleslaw, and hush puppies—sent this pair of erstwhile rebels home happier than hot hogs in cool mud.

We can't quit without mentioning **Joe Jost's** (2803 East Anaheim Avenue, 562/439-5446, $). It's the oldest continuously operating bar in California, and it has been run by three generations of Josts. Papa Joe, God rest his soul, invented a deli sandwich that has become a local institution. Called Joe's Special, it consists of a hunk of Polish sausage surrounded by a slice of Swiss cheese with a pickle spear stuck into a V-shaped slit, all stuffed between mustard-slathered pieces of rye bread and wrapped in a waxed-paper handle. Joe Jost's serves hundreds of them every day, and just as many of the other house specialty, a basket of

pretzels, peppers, and pickled eggs. As for what's on tap at Joe Jost's, they pump ice-cold Blitz beer, brewed in Oregon, in 20-ounce schooners.

Night Moves

The centerpiece of the Broadway/Pine Avenue downtown renaissance is a 16-screen AMC cineplex at **Pine Square** (245 Pine Avenue, 562/435-1355). Surrounding it is a neon galaxy of munchie parlors, coffeehouses, restaurants, and clubs. The **System M Caffe Gallery** (213-A Pine Avenue, 562/435-2525) is the gathering place for Long Beach's new bohemians, with gentlemen on the outdoor patio affecting pince-nez, goatees, and Kramer-like explosions of hair while sucking contemplatively on cigarettes and watching the smoke curl against the fuchsia glow of the restaurant's neon. Food, drinks, coffee, and art are served within.

In the same vicinity the **Blue Cafe** (210 Promenade, 562/983-7111) pays homage to the electric guitar along a largely undeveloped pedestrian promenade. Regionally popular blues, rock, and alternative musicians perform here for a modest cover charge. We paid $4 apiece on a Monday night to see a local band called Standard Fruit and had a fine time. Bathed in ubiquitous neon, it is, like every other business on this embryonic scene, an outpost of civility trying to stay afloat in a sea of economic uncertainty.

From there we felt like getting rowdy, so we proceeded down to Belmont Shore, a livelier and more organic community in south Long Beach. We've always had a good time rambling around the bars and taverns of Second Street. They are jam-packed with friendly and fun-loving college kids, neighborhood residents, and navy guys out for a brew. Take your pick and pull up a bar stool. There's **Legends** (5236 East Second Street, 562/433-5743), a sports bar that's always abuzz with folks ogling the action on the big screen; **Panama Joe's** (5100 East Second Street, 562/434-7417), an upscale "meet market" that gets good bands

Los Angeles County

Shooting Hoops with the Toast of the Coast

We came to the **Acapulco Inn** looking for a Pop-a-Shot machine, a game found in many bars that allows you to fire little basketballs at a miniature net six feet away. For two guys who'd spent their college years in North Carolina, where basketball is king, an opportunity to shoot hoops, even in as scaled-down a fashion as this, was a welcome diversion. Fortunately, these stand-up shooting galleries are found in bars and pool halls all over Southern California.

With a mound of quarters in our pockets and frosty mugs in hand, we prepared to fritter away another five bucks or so feeding our basketball jones in the corner of the Acapulco Inn, a way-cool beer bar in Belmont Shore.

We were beaten by a millisecond to the hoops game by a pair of dudes named Kevin and Greg. The latter was a construction foreman, the former a construction worker and one-time marine. They'd just gotten their paychecks and were spending them as quickly as possible on draft beer and miniature basketball. They asked us to join them, so we had a nightlong round-robin, four-man basketball shootout that grew so noisy we would have been thrown out of any other bar but this one. Kevin wore a baseball cap, smoked fat cigars, made pitchers of beer disappear like magic, and had a wicked set shot. When he found his rhythm, he racked up the points.

A nonstop talker and self-promoter, he would lapse into a deadly accurate Dick Vitale impersonation after scoring a particularly high game. "Oh, baybee!" he hollered, audible from inside a locked bathroom. "He's shooting out the lights tonight! Rock and roll!" He scored an evening-high 46, leaving the rest of us in the dust, and gloated to all within earshot that his score was unbeatable. That is, until one of us entered what sports commentator Vitale would have referred to as "a zone," swishing one after another and mounting up a final score of 54. It silenced Kevin for a little while. He gnawed on his cigar, looking annoyed. Then he tried to top it, feverishly popping quarters, game after game, until he bounced a ball so hard in frustration that it hit the ceiling. Then he declared he had finally had enough.

At this point he took a seat at the bar and shared with us his wisdom on any subject we cared to name. He knew everything about everything, challenging us to stump him and offering to fill in the holes in our impoverished fund of knowledge. Elvis Presley, surfing, world geography, sports, the fairer sex, bar

Map of Southern California—Page 9

brawling—he was a walking Jeopardy game who knew all the answers. An affable guy, likable almost in spite of himself, he embodied a good-natured self-centeredness that we'd seen across Southern California. This expressed itself in boundless braggadocio and a glaring lack of curiosity about anything outside his sphere of experience. He was the Sun King; the world revolved around him. He also made a blanket offer to drop whatever he was doing at any time to share with us his firsthand knowledge of the coast on behalf of our book. He'd be glad to take us around. In fact we'd better call him, he said, jabbing a finger at us for emphasis.

Would he remember any of this in the morning? Probably not. He was a decorated marine who'd served honorably in the Persian Gulf. He also claimed to be the world's biggest Elvis Presley expert, challenging us to stump him with trivia. On one of his many trips to Graceland, he claimed, he loudly broke wind on the premises, thereby cementing some sort of spiritual bond with the King. He was very proud of this accomplishment.

He matter-of-factly gave us the lowdown on sexual mores in Southern California during the age of AIDS: "You can't just pick up women and have one-nighters anymore. They won't let you have sex for one, two, three months. You'll have to go out with them awhile and prove you're serious before they'll let you into bed with them. While you're waiting, you just have to look at your videos or skin mags or whatever gets you off."

As the beer flowed so did his rhetoric.

• "You want to know about surfing? I've surfed up and down the coast since I was a kid. You name it: County Line. Oil Piers. Rincon. I finished sixth out of 12 in my first amateur competition. I'll take you anywhere you want to go. I can get you onto places you won't believe. I've got three boards. Used to have four. Sold one of them. Son-of-a-bitch still hasn't paid me for it."

• "I don't like fighting, I'm a Christian person, but I won't walk away from a fight. I've been in 14 bar fights and never lost once. You want to try me? *[flexes biceps]* See that bartender? *[motions to a strapping guy with a brawny physique]* I've taken down guys bigger than him. No problem."

• "What do you want to know about Elvis Presley? You wanna know Elvis? I know Elvis. I'm the biggest Elvis fan there is. I'm only 24 and I've got records, actual vinyl records, by Elvis. The Beatles? The Beach Boys? What do you want to know? I know it all." *[puffs chest]*

We concluded that he must be the wisest man in the world, or at least in the Acapulco Inn. After all, any person who claims to have farted in the hallowed halls of Graceland can only be one more miracle away from sainthood.

Map of Los Angeles County—Page 156

on weekends; and our personal favorite, the **Acapulco Inn** (5283 East Second Street, 562/439-3517). The latter is a collegiate dive bar that's wilder than any toga party John Belushi ever attended. At the "AI," students from nearby Cal State Long Beach cut loose in a party environment so out of control on big nights that it's almost a caricature of hell-raising. The jukebox leans heavily on 1960s party favorites, while an assortment of games—including a Pop-a-Shot concession that nearly cleaned out our wallets—gives you something to do besides clutch a beer. If you can keep up with this crowd, you deserve whatever you wake up with the next morning: a hangover, a fellow party animal, or both.

For More Information

Long Beach Area Convention and Visitor Bureau, One World Trade Center, Suite 300, Long Beach, CA 90831, 562/436-3645 or 800/452-7829, website: www.golongbeach.org

San Pedro

Tucked behind the protective, ever-changing Palos Verdes Peninsula is San Pedro (population 86,000), the port town for the city of Los Angeles. In 1889, after heavy competition with other bay towns like Redondo Beach, it was chosen to house Los Angeles Harbor, thanks to the good offices of Senator Stephen M. White (after whom a main drag in town is named). Before it was enlarged to its present size, the harbor was so shallow that oceangoing vessels had to be anchored offshore and loaded and unloaded from there. Today it is known as "Worldport L.A." The harbor covers 7,000 acres and 28 miles of waterfront, making it one of the largest artificial ports in the world.

Overlooking San Pedro Harbor is formidable Fort MacArthur, once an integral part of our West Coast defense posture. San Pedro is home to 86,000 people, many of whom make their living on the docks. It was also the home of one of our favorite writers, the late Charles Bukowski. He came to live in San Pedro in 1978, leaving Los Angeles after 58 years of a squalid hand-to-mouth existence. According to biographer Neeli Cherkovski, Bukowski chose San Pedro because "unlike some of the other beach towns, the spirit of the '60s hadn't settled on it." That much is true. The real lure of San Pedro for Bukowski was its proximity to the freeways, which afforded a quick escape from anonymous middle-class respectability to the racetracks at Hollywood Park and Santa Anita. Bukowski died here in 1993.

Despite the relative lack of beaches, elbowed out by the harbor, there's plenty of waterfront activity in San Pedro. The **Cabrillo Marine Museum** (3720 Stephen M. White Drive, 310/548-7562) has 38 aquariums with marine life native to Southern California, as well as a multimedia show for kids, seasonal grunion tours, and whale-watching expeditions. It's only $2 per adult and $1 for children and seniors, but parking costs $6.50. Down on the docks is **Los Angeles Maritime Museum** (Berth 84, Sixth Street, 310/548-7618), which presents an assortment of maritime equipment, memorabilia, and historical photographs detailing the construction of the harbor and the old ferry days. A $1 donation per person is requested. In addition, you can take several tours out of San Pedro Harbor, including ferries to Santa Catalina Island and dinner and harbor cruises.

Beaches

There are a few beaches in San Pedro worth seeking out if you're in the area. The main one—and the only sandy beach in San Pedro—is **Cabrillo City Beach,** east of Point Fermin on either side of the San Pedro Breakwater. The "harbor" side of the beach is protected and calm, with a boat-launching ramp. The

Los Angeles County

Map of Southern California—Page 9

"ocean" side, on the other side of the harbor fortification, receives the full force of the ocean—real waves for board surfing and windsurfing. The tidepools are rich in marine life, and in the summer the grunion hold some epic runs here. The Cabrillo Marine Museum elaborates on the local ecology. Attached to the breakwater at Cabrillo City Beach is a 1,000-foot municipal fishing pier. **Point Fermin Park** and lighthouse are on a bluff overlooking the ocean; steep trails lead to the rocky shore below.

West of Point Fermin, the parking lot below the cliffs at White Point is divided into **White Point County Park** (left) and **Royal Palms County Beach** (right). The former is a blufftop park with playgrounds and overlooks, while the latter is a rugged, rocky shoreline popular with shell collectors and surf casters. Surfers like it, too, in winter. The most remarkable feature of White Point/Royal Palms, though, is the presence of mineral springs that lie offshore, which divers explore. When you tire of the beach, you can always wander the grounds of the old Royal Palms Hotel, which was washed away in a storm seven decades ago, though the royal palm trees remain. Tidepoolers and divers go to White Point, at the east end, while picnickers and sunbathers congregate at Royal Palms. The latter, incidentally, has received a $2.2 million sprucing up of its facilities and is really looking sharp.

Bunking Down

The **Best Western Sunrise Hotel** (525 South Harbor Boulevard, 310/548-1080, $$) happens to be the closest hotel in town to the harbor. Rooms look out on the harbor; amenities include deluxe continental breakfast, pool, and a hot tub.

Coastal Cuisine

The **22nd Street Landing Seafood Grill & Bar** (141 West 22nd Street, 310/548-4400, $$$) serves more than a dozen types of fresh fish daily in a dining room that looks out on the harbor. For seafood it's the best choice for miles around. There are also a number of excellent Italian restaurants in the area. Tops among them is **Madeo Ristorante** (295 Whaler's Walk, 310/831-1199, $$$), adjacent to the Doubletree Hotel at Cabrillo Marina.

Night Moves

Most of the restaurants on the harbor have cocktail lounges. For a nonalcoholic alternative duck into the **Sacred Grounds Coffee House & Art Gallery** (399 West Sixth Street, 310/514-0800), where art, live entertainment, and cappuccino are the house blend. Incidentally, if you really want to understand San Pedro, check out native Mike Watt's excellent 1997 CD, *Contemplating the Engine Room.*

For More Information

San Pedro Peninsula Chamber of Commerce, 360 West Seventh Street, San Pedro, CA 90731, 310/832-7272, website: www.sanpedrochamber.org

Los Angeles County

Crosstown Traffic: Driving in Los Angeles

It is nearly impossible to visit Los Angeles without spending a lot of time inside a car. If you wish to view the dubious baubles of ancient or current celebrity—Aaron Spelling's mansion, Grauman's Chinese Theatre, the condo where Nicole Brown Simpson was brutally murdered—you will have to drive and drive . . . and drive some more.

Despite the amount of lip service people pay to it, public transportation is piecemeal, almost discouraged. The **MetroRail** system operates three lines. The **Blue Line** light rail makes regular 22-mile runs from Los Angeles to Long Beach. The **Metro Red Line,** the city's first subway, opened in January 1993, running from Union Station/Gateway Center (in downtown L.A.) to Wilshire Boulevard and Western Avenue (in the Wilshire district, below Hollywood). By the year 2010 they hope to have 400 miles of track in place, carrying half a million passengers a day. The **Green Line** runs a 20-mile east-west route across southern Los Angeles County. **Metrolink** is a regional commuter rail system that serves 44 stations from its hub at Union Station/Gateway Center. For city bus and MetroRail information, contact the **Los Angeles County Metropolitan Transit Authority,** 425 South Main Street, Los Angeles, CA 90013, 213/626-4455. For information on Metrolink fares and schedules, call 213/808-5465.

Los Angeles is too spread out over its 462 square miles to make riding the bus anything but a poverty-induced exercise in masochism. And forget walking the city's streets. Pedestrians are a low priority in Southern Californian city planning. As one advocate put it, "The automobile reigns supreme in Los Angeles, and pedestrians are at the very bottom of the food chain." Walking across any street is an adventure. Crossing a busy multilane boulevard is a dare. Few drivers will voluntarily stop for anyone in a crosswalk, though new laws require they do.

So drive you must. Interstates loop into each other like asphalt pretzels. The surrounding development looks much the same, a blight of ill-planned growth that beggars the imagination. Our first rule of thumb for beach travel in California is to stay on the Pacific Coast Highway. Nothing of interest lies more than five miles inland or is worth the trouble it takes to get there. Through this simple rule we have already spared you Disneyland, not to mention the Reagan and Nixon presidential libraries.

The corollary to this is to avoid I-5 and I-405 unless you have to make a long north-south haul. Built to ease car traffic, both roads are always backed up.

Perversely, the carpool lanes on both interstates through Los Angeles and Orange Counties are nearly always clear. The number of passengers constituting a High Occupancy Vehicle (HOV) has been dropped. Now you need only two passengers per car. And still the carpool lanes are empty. That is because

Map of Southern California—Page 9

nearly everyone in Southern California is a "Lindbergh"—a solo driver. So the roads stay jammed.

Here are two indispensable driving tips (abridged) culled from *Los Angeles* magazine:

• Plan ahead. Know your destination in terms of points south and north, east, and west. Directional signs on I-405 read "Sacramento" to indicate north and "Long Beach" to indicate south. Learn the names and numbers of the freeways you'll be traveling:

Highway 2	=	Glendale Freeway
Highway 10	=	Santa Monica or San Bernardino Freeway
Highway 60	=	Pomona Freeway
Highway 90	=	Marina Freeway
Highway 91	=	Artesia Freeway
Highway 110	=	Pasadena Freeway
Highway 170	=	Hollywood Freeway
U.S. 101	=	Ventura, Hollywood, or Santa Ana Freeway
I-5	=	Golden State or Santa Ana Freeway
I-110	=	Harbor Freeway
I-405	=	San Diego Freeway
I-605	=	San Gabriel River Freeway
I-710	=	Long Beach Freeway

• Keep track of traffic over the airwaves. Many radio stations offer traffic reports. The stations with the best coverage are KNX (1070 AM) and KFWB (980 AM).

KNX, an all-news radio station, gives traffic reports every six minutes, 24 hours a day! A typical traffic update sounds like this (imagine a fast-talking, mellifluous deejay voice): "It's stop-and-go all the way from Santa Monica to Pasadena, but the good news is there are no accidents blocking the road." (This is good news?)

When an explanation for a traffic tie-up is warranted (what is called a "sigalert"), the tone of the deejay's voice doesn't modulate, and his update sounds like this: "There's a bus on top of a car near the Avalon exit on I-405. Ouch, that must smart!"

Further coloring the experience of driving in Los Angeles is the haze of smog, plus vast wastelands of junkyards and metal salvage lots, oil refineries, and Smog Check stations where you don't have to pay if your car doesn't pass— which isn't exactly a great incentive for identifying auto-emissions problems.

But Los Angeles keeps on growing and, after each earthquake, the roads are rebuilt before the homes are, inviting more cars and rubes to drive them. What's the answer? In the big picture, reconfigure society and the economy to encourage sustainable growth and to lower the birth rate. For the smaller purposes of a beach visit, our advice is to get down to the beach and stay there. Rent a bicycle or a pair of skates. Jog. Walk. But before crossing the street, look both ways. . . twice.

Los Angeles County

Map of Los Angeles County—Page 156

Palos Verdes Peninsula

The enormous landmass known as the Palos Verdes Peninsula, in the southwest corner of Los Angeles County, is one that will (as Muhammad Ali used to say) "shock and amaze ya." As is the case in the northern part of the county—with the Santa Monica Mountains, the Malibu Peninsula, and the Hollywood Hills—the Palos Verdes Peninsula is an example of the incredible diversity of landforms found in and around the City of Angels.

This craggy, lunarlike peninsula is no party to the smog dish of the Los Angeles Basin. Even though its jagged, cliff-lined shore embraces 15 miles of Pacific coastline—from San Pedro to Torrance—the Pacific Coast Highway doesn't come near it. Instead, it moves inland, leaving the tough, shifting terrain of the peninsula to the hermitic wishes of the folks who live out here on the edge of the planet.

Driving around this wondrous peninsula entails following a series of small, winding back roads that pass through a quaking, unsettled landscape. Along this Jell-O-like terrain, a road sign warns of "Constant Land Movement Next 8 Miles." What could this mean? we wondered. It means that sections of the road, particularly in the vicinity of Portuguese Bend, look like they've just been removed from a waffle iron and have more dips in them than an amusement-park roller coaster. The land here actually moves at a rate of one to six inches a month and has been doing so since the mid-1950s, when highway blasting caused the top layer of rock to separate from and slip over the lower layer (a phenomenon known as "block-glide"). A prodigious chunk of the peninsula fell into the ocean in May 1999, taking with it a portion of a new golf-course development. (Talk about poetic justice!)

You will find yourself holding your breath for reasons other than fear, however, as one seductive panorama of sky, sea, and headlands follows another until you work your way off the peninsula at Torrance. Depending on how you approach it, the drive is either an unexpectedly nice side trip or the most unusual way to enter the back door of Los Angeles. At one time the entire peninsula was the rancho of the Sepulveda family, until they sold it in 1914 to a company with plans to develop it as a "millionaire's colony." To that end they called in the landscape firm of Olmstead and Olmstead (sons of Frederick Law Olmstead, designer of New York's Central Park). The Olmstead brothers planted trees on the barren lands and built houses among them, and the millionaires dug in for the long haul. They're still dug in out here, although the nerve-jangling land movement has driven many to abandon the sloping Portuguese Bend area. The houses that didn't slip into the drink have been sold off for a song to intrepid souls unafraid to live in them. Yet the neighborhoods behind the falling ridge remain some of the most exclusive properties in Los Angeles.

Beaches

The small, sandy coves on the Palos Verdes Peninsula are difficult to get to, but they are among the most prized in the county, due partly to their very inaccessibility. The most visited are Malaga Cove and Abalone Cove Beach. **Malaga Cove**—also known as RAT (for "Right After Torrance")—is the only true sand beach on the peninsula. It's popular with surfers and swimmers who climb down with their boards and towels from the paved access point at Via Arroyo, off Palos Verdes Drive West. There's a small, free parking lot. **Abalone Cove Beach,** which straddles the legendary Portuguese Bend off Palos Verdes Drive South, can be reached via a pay parking lot. Surfers' localism is at its worst on the peninsula, however, where the best surf spots are zealously (and sometimes violently) defended by local gangs.

Map of Southern California—Page 9

Even if you don't take the plunge to the beaches, the cliff-hugging route along the outer rim of Palos Verdes makes for an exciting afternoon drive. Particularly appealing is Paseo del Mar, a loop road that leaves Palos Verdes Drive and cuts through **Palos Verdes Estates Shoreline Preserve,** which runs for 4.5 miles and comprises 130 city-owned acres above a blufftop. Several precipitous paths leave the blufftop and zigzag down to cove beaches at Lunada Bay, Bluff Cove, and Malaga Cove. On the southwestern corner of the peninsula, the small **Point Vicente Park** offers free parking, restrooms, a whale-watching deck, and displays that interpret local history and ecology. At the park's pullout a dirt trail leads to **Point Vicente Fishing Access.** This magical fishing hole draws skin- and scuba divers as well as anglers. South of Point Vicente Park is the Point Vicente Lighthouse, which was built in 1926 and is now closed to the public.

The splendid architecture on the peninsula is worth checking out from a car window. It is something every developer should witness and learn from. Hidden among the trees and hills, the human habitations don't try to compete with the grandeur of the landscape. This philosophy of architectural noninterfer-ence reaches a zenith with the **Wayfarers Chapel** (5755 Palos Verdes Drive South, 310/377-1650), on the mainland side of the road just beyond Portuguese Bend. Built in 1946 by Lloyd Wright (son of Frank), the predominantly glass edifice allows worshippers (devotees of the theologian Emanuel Swedenborg) to feel as if they're outdoors among the redwoods and gardens that surround the chapel. It is open to the public daily 11 A.M.–4 P.M. A small museum on the grounds has exhibits about "Swedenborgianism" and Helen Keller, a practitioner thereof.

One final note: It was on Palos Verdes that Marineland of the Pacific was built in 1954. Once the home and playpen for a small navy of Flippers, Orcas, and Jaws, the three-ring aquatic circus is long gone. The park's inaccessibility is the reason for its financial demise. The property was sold off, presumably to an eccentric millionaire with a penchant for large swimming pools.

For More Information

Palos Verdes Peninsula Chamber of Commerce, 4040 Palos Verdes Drive North, Rolling Hills Estates, CA 90274, 310/377-8111, website: www.palosverdes.com

Redondo Beach

Redondo Beach has fancied itself a vacation destination since the 1890s, when a trio of Spanish sisters sold the sand dunes they inherited to developers. Shipping was an important early industry, but after Redondo Beach unsuccessfully vied to have the Port of Los Angeles located here (San Pedro won), the town turned to tourism. A huge luxury hotel, along with tent cities for the fiscally challenged, drew vacationers to the pristine beach. The Hotel Redondo—which opened in 1890 and was stupidly torn down in 1926—actually was the sister establishment of the splendid Hotel del Coronado down the coast. During Redondo's heyday, folks would ride the fabled Pacific Electric "red cars" from downtown Los Angeles to the beach.

At one time Redondo Beach (population 63,600) had it all: big-band ballrooms, offshore gambling ships reached by water taxis, and a huge, heated indoor saltwater pool called "the Plunge." A Hawaiian native named George Freeth demonstrated the strange new sport of surfing to curious onlookers behind the Hotel Redondo. (Freeth was described biblically by developer Henry Huntington as "the man who could walk on water.") Redondo's glory days are documented in the **Redondo**

Los Angeles County

Zen in Redondo

While waiting for coffee in line at a Redondo Beach Starbucks, we pondered a Zen koan that manifested itself to us: "What is the sound of two jaws flapping?" Here is a verbatim exchange between two chirpy, sunny-faced Angelenos ahead of us. The undercurrent of existential dread was as palpable as the odor of roasted coffee beans.

He: Hey, I heard you got married.

She: Well, you know what they say. I'm not getting any younger!

He: I hear you.

She: He was just a friend but we kept in touch. He finally said, "Blink or get off the pot," but I wanted to have my cake and eat it too, you know?

He: I hear you.

She: There were just too many pretty boys to play with, but, you know, it felt empty. So, what about you?

He: Oh, you know how it is. Marriage has been a pretty good ride. Up and down and all around. Now I'm doing the family thing.

She: Me too . . . five months preggy!

He: Go on! I couldn't even tell.

She: Thanks. We're moving next month and . . . well, I don't know. I can't decide whether to stay at home the next five years or study for my LSAT. But I said to myself, you know, "What better time to do either!" Right?

He: Right! You look great.

She: Thanks. You too. We should keep in touch.

He: Okay. Here's my business card.

She: Well, my latte's ready. I'm so happy we had this time to talk.

He: Me too.

She: Ciao.

He: Ciao.

Beach Historical Museum (320 Knob Hill Avenue, 310/543-3108), operated by the Redondo Beach Historical Commission.

Residents would no doubt like to see those golden days return, but that will take a long reprieve from the forces of nature and economics, and that is one tall order. Of the triumvirate of beach towns that are conjoined in the South Bay area of Los Angeles, Redondo Beach was spiked the hardest by economic recession and natural disaster. Whereas its sisters in sand and sun, Hermosa Beach and Manhattan Beach, are primarily residential communities and only secondarily tourist-oriented, Redondo Beach—at least that part of town seaward of the Pacific Coast Highway—seeks and depends on visitor dollars. The lineup of waterfront attractions in Redondo Beach includes the marinas at King Harbor (there are four of them), the International Boardwalk, the town's famous "horseshoe pier," and several resort hotels. You can gauge Redondo's dependence on visitors by the size of the parking decks. Whether you're berthing a yacht in

Map of Southern California—Page 9

one of the basins or wheeling a rented Escort into one of the garages, Redondo Beach is glad to have you and your pesos jingling around town. For this reason it is the most outsider-friendly of the South Bay communities.

Happily, Redondo appears to be pulling out of the hard times that have befallen it and rekindling some of the spirit that made it a beach-lover's mecca. Having persevered through repeated bouts of storm damage, plus a catastrophic pier fire, the collapse of a parking deck, and the impact of a prolonged economic downturn in the early- to mid-1990s (known as the "California recession"), Redondo Beach has a survivor's mentality.

Today, Redondo's waterfront complex is a catacomb of parking decks, food stalls along the concrete boardwalk, and a handful of pier-based restaurants. Still, we can't help but wonder what will happen the next time the Arctic or El Niño sends another unforgiving squall Redondo's way. How long this cycle of destruction and rebuilding can continue is anyone's guess.

On a cheerier note, one of the best-loved features of the waterfront, the **South Bay Bicycle Trail**, endures. A 26-mile paved path that extends from Torrance City Beach (just south of Redondo) to Will Rogers State Beach (in Malibu), it is a two-way concrete freeway for cyclists, in-line skaters, skateboarders, and joggers. Even the odd walker can be spotted, although mere strolling is a little too undemanding for this high-speed crowd. If you're not in shape, this isn't the place to reveal your unseemly bulges. The bike path is part aerobic runway, part fashion runway, and always crowded—the place to see and be seen.

Traveling south from Hermosa Beach, the trail swings onto the streets of Redondo for a few blocks before entering the innards of the King Harbor-Pier Complex. Once past this maze, through which you're asked to walk your bike, the path resumes a straight and steady course south along Redondo State Beach, giving cyclists a superb view of the rugged bluffs of the Palos Verdes Peninsula. Cruising the South Bay is a popular pastime, and bikes can be rented at local shops, the best of which are in Hermosa Beach. The local climate almost mandates outdoor activity. The mercury rarely falls below 45 degrees in January or rises above 75 degrees in July. Los Angeles's chronic halo of smog doesn't choke the beaches of the South Bay. Cooling offshore breezes ensure that the air is generally clean and the skies blue.

And so Redondo Beach sits at the edge of the Pacific like a tarnished jewel in a splendid setting. It has been knocked around by Mother Nature and is still somewhat punch-drunk, yet its residents doggedly regroup, rebuild, and persevere.

Beaches

The beach at Redondo Beach maintains a respectable width south of the pier, but it is narrow and eroded north of it. Erosion is the result of harborfront construction, including a breakwater that diverts sand into a submarine canyon just offshore. The same canyon causes wave crests to refract in a way that concentrates their energy onto the beaches north of the canyon, occasionally wrecking beaches and the houses built along them. In severe storms, the breakwater has been overtopped and damaged. Signs warn people away from what's left of the beach in the vicinity of the harbor, where the ocean angrily slaps walls of riprap that have been erected to protect the construction behind it.

The beach scene improves markedly on the south side of the pier along the strand encompassing **Redondo State Beach** and **Torrance City Beach**. Redondo State Beach runs for about 1.5 miles from the pier south to some restrooms, on the other side of which it becomes Torrance City Beach, continuing down to the Palos Verdes Peninsula for three-quarters of a mile. It's the same beach—a flat swath of sand that widens between pier and peninsula, a nice place to come for a little more nature and a little less in the

Los Angeles County

way of crowds than you'll find at Hermosa or Manhattan Beaches. To the delight of surfers, this stretch is serviced by the west swells of winter. Incidentally, though it's now called Redondo State Beach, this beach is lifeguarded and maintained by Los Angeles County. Similar city/county arrangements and nomenclature apply throughout the county.

Bunking Down

To oversimplify, Redondo Beach has the hotels, Manhattan Beach has the restaurants, and Hermosa Beach has the nightlife. Numerous chain motels are located along and west of the Pacific Coast Highway, only one-third mile from the beach. Down along the harbor are the two top choices: the **Portofino Hotel and Yacht Club** (260 Portofino Way, 310/379-8481, $$$) and the **Holiday Inn Crowne Plaza** (300 North Harbor Drive, 310/318-8888, $$$). The latter is an especially attractive property, an airy and spacious five-story resort hotel overlooking King Harbor from the dry side of Harbor Drive. Room rates are $165 a night and up in season. Private balconies, outdoor heated pool and sundeck, exercise facilities, sports bar, piano bar, on-premises restaurant, and more make this a prime place to lie in when visiting Redondo Beach.

Another option is the **Palos Verdes Inn** (1700 South Pacific Coast Highway, 310/316-4211, $$$), only three blocks from the beach along a curve on the coastal highway, where it begins to skirt the uplands of the Palos Verdes Peninsula. The hotel is a self-contained city, with an excellent Continental restaurant (**Chez Melange,** 310/542-1222, $$$), gourmet deli (**Chez Allez,** $), live-music venue (**Club Caprice,** 310/316-1700), and half-acre pool, spa, and gardens on the premises. Rooms are comfortably furnished, and many come with ocean-view balconies.

Coastal Cuisine

In Redondo Beach, restaurants don't always go out of business due to bad reviews or word

of mouth. Big waves wreck them. Several pier restaurants have been washed into the big drink over the years. Still, the harborside restaurant scene survives, particularly the **Blue Moon Saloon** (207 North Harbor Drive, 310/373-3411, $$$), a casual seafood eatery in the Redondo Beach Marina that has endured wind and wave to emerge as a long-lived institution on the waterfront. The International Boardwalk is home to **Quality Seafood** (130 South International Boardwalk, 310/374-2382, $$), a seafood market and snack bar that displays and prepares all manner of fresh, colorful seafood: local crab and fish, plus Louisiana crawdads and New Zealand eel. Cooks will steam a crab for you on the spot, which you can take to a table and crack to your heart's content. Then there's **Sitar by the Sea** (125 West Torrance Boulevard, 310/376-9447, $$), which isn't the name of a Ravi Shankar album—though it ought to be—but an excellent Indian restaurant in the pier complex.

Night Moves

There's a **Hennessey's Tavern** (1710 South Catalina Avenue, 310/316-6658) in Riviera Village, a shopping area set back from the beach. Come to think of it, there's a Hennessey's in each of the three South Bay beach towns: Redondo, Hermosa, and Manhattan. You can also find a decent cocktail lounge at one of the seafood restaurants in King Harbor: the old reliable **Chart House** (231 Yacht Club Way, 310/372-3464) or the **Blue Moon Saloon** (207 North Harbor Drive, 310/373-3411). You might wander into a decent jam at **Papa Garo's** (1810 South Catalina Boulevard, 310/540-7272), a Mediterranean restaurant and music club where you'll find live blues music in a smoke-free environment, as incongruous as that might seem. What was formerly the Strand Supper Club is now **Club Caprice** (1700 South Pacific Coast Highway, 310/316-1700), the best music venue in town. Finally, we must mention **Moose**

McGillycuddy's (179 Harbor Drive, 310/372-9944), the only dance club in the South Bay and the heir apparent to the meet market tradition forged by the late Red Onion.

For More Information

Redondo Beach Visitors Bureau, 200 North Pacific Coast Highway, Redondo Beach, CA 90277, 310/374-2171, website: www.redondochamber.org

Hermosa Beach

In Spanish *hermosa* means "beautiful," and it's an apt description of this unpretentious community, which seems light-years removed from the smoggy hubbub of Los Angeles, against which it brushes. The more things change around it, the more Hermosa Beach (population 18,600) remains the same. It is the most relaxed and laid-back of the South Bay communities, a town full of coffee bars and shops catering to the healthful prerogatives of a physically fit populace. Living beside the ocean in an almost perfect climate tends to make people look after themselves. Even a place like the Rocky Cola Cafe, a 1950s-style burger-jukebox joint, offers a healthy menu, analyzing its food items in terms of fat grams and calories; the café leaves things like egg yolks out of its omelettes and serves black beans and brown rice as side dishes.

Hermosa Beach has a solid sense of itself and has plotted its destiny well. In 1901 the beach was surveyed for a boardwalk, in 1904 the first pier was built, and in 1907 the town of Hermosa Beach was incorporated. At that time the city gained ownership over its two-mile oceanfront in a deed mandating that it be held in perpetuity as "beach playground, free from commerce, and for the benefit of not only residents of Hermosa, but also for the sea lovers of Southern California." Those ideals remain in force today. It is an aesthetically attractive town with a gleaming, well-maintained beach.

What's most magical about Hermosa Beach is the descent down Pier Avenue toward the ocean. Rounding a curve, the road yields a spectacular view of the ocean. The light sea breeze is constant, the air feels clean and continuously refreshed, and you just can't help but stroll around Hermosa Beach in a state of grateful rejuvenation. If you want to get out of the sun, you can always duck into Nations Travel Bookstore, a shop specializing in travel guides, maps, and videos.

While you're here rent a bike or a pair of in-line skates at one of the shops down on the Strand, then take off for a spin along the bike path up to Malibu, down to Redondo—anything's possible. And the unfolding beach scenery is worth the legwork.

Parking remains the one big bugaboo in Hermosa Beach. There's barely enough of it for those who live here, much less for visitors. Street parking is hard to find and expensive, and parking-meter charges are enforced 24 hours a day. Hotel guests are covered, but daytrippers be advised: come via rapid transit, on foot, or via bicycle, if possible. Otherwise you might find yourself incurring some degree of expense and/or hassle. In the words of a letter to the editor of the *Easy Reader,* a free local paper: "The nemesis of Hermosa Beach that there's just no getting around is parking." We can second that emotion. Still, we like everything else about Hermosa Beach and recommend it highly.

Beaches

Hermosa City Beach stretches for two unblemished miles, part of the continuous strip of sand that runs along the Santa Monica Bay before slamming to a halt at the Palos Verdes Peninsula. The 1,328-foot-long Hermosa Pier is its centerpiece, offering year-round angling in the waters of Santa Monica Bay. At the foot of the pier is a statue of a surfer poised in mid-ride. Beneath the frozen surfrider's impassive gaze,

Eavesdropping in Hermosa Beach: "I'm Very There"

The following is a real-life play in one act. All conversation is reported verbatim. Scene: The bright stucco interior of the Hermosa Beach Post Office on a summer afternoon.

He: A slouching, unshaven male who looks like he's just rolled out of bed. His face is stubbly, his hair short but unkempt. He is wearing soiled cutoffs, sandals, and a T-shirt that has grayed from one too many unsorted washings.

She: A former California beach queen now gone to seed as she enters middle age. Her skin has been worn to alligator hide by the sun, her face is creased with age and worry lines, and her thighs sag with cellulite. Her hair is dirty blonde, and she wears Spandex bike shorts and a loose-fitting T-shirt. Her eyes are concealed by designer sunglasses.

[They meet at a counter in the front room of the post office, where he is addressing a package.]

He: You look great!

She: Thanks. I feel great. *[Pauses]* But it just ain't enough. *[Emits a jaded cackle, then continues]* People are so goddamned superficial out here. Everybody is chasing that big white cloud, and I don't know what it is.

He: Yeah, I know. I'm so busy, I'm just running around all the time. This is what my day looks like: I get up, go to work, look for a place to park, and work

---

swarms of people whiz by on the South Bay Bicycle Trail. Although everyone moves at different speeds and in different directions, this complex symphony of motion somehow plays through without a lot of serious spills or collisions.

In addition to all the hell-on-wheels aerobicizing along the South Bay Bicycle Trail, sand rats play volleyball and paddleball out here on the ample beach, which we have yet to see in a condition that could be described as overcrowded. One pastime that's not too big, oddly enough, is surfing. Apparently the breakwater that protects Redondo Beach's harbor knocks the waves here down to a size for which only novices and locals have much use.

Bunking Down

The best place to stay in Hermosa Beach is the **Beach House** (1300 Strand, 310/374-3001). It's perched right on the beach, with 96 "loft suites" overlooking the ocean in the vicinity of the pier. It doesn't get any better (or better situated) than the Beach House. We're also fond of a funky, down-to-earth place called the **Sea Sprite Ocean Front Motel** (1016 Strand, 310/376-6933, $$) that's perfect for a true beach lover. The Sea Sprite is an informal yet well-tended motel that rents rooms and apartment-style cottages. From the second-floor pool deck you can watch the world skate by on the bike path below or just enjoy the misty breezes rolling off the ocean. The hotel has even managed to shoehorn in a parking space for every room, a perk that's worth its weight in parking tickets. There's nothing fancy about the Sea Sprite, but when you're right on the ocean—

Map of Southern California—Page 9

for eight hours. I don't even have time to eat. I'll call to have some food delivered then shove it down when I can grab a moment. Then it's off to classes. Then I get home, and call for more takeout food while I'm doing my homework and whatever *work* work I've had to take home. I'm beat all the time. The harder I work, the more I fall behind. I just don't know what's wrong.

She: I know what you mean. I spent six years in therapy, and all I wanted to know was how to find peace. Now I've found it, but I'm in the minority.

He: I'm very there.

She: I just don't need it anymore.

He: Good for you! I've been there, done that.

She: I'm going to Costa Rica to look for work. I've had it with L.A. It's just too crowded for me. Everyone running around, getting in each other's way. You know what I mean? No one wants to admit it, but it's over. L.A. is over. I've had it.

He: Are you going to Costa Rica with your mate?

She: No. *[Thoughtful pause]* We're taking a second look at where we're at right now. If it happens, it happens. We'll see.

He: I was talking to my mate about this. A relationship starts out with a certain amount of mass, and once that mass begins falling away, you're forced to interface with one another. *[Pauses to reflect]* You know, I like that phrase.

She: That's so true. Well, gotta go. Gotta get back to work. We'll hook up sometime.

He: Bye.

She: Bye-bye.

[Both walk away.]

Los Angeles County

and you couldn't be any closer except on a surfboard—who needs marble bathrooms and turn-down service?

Hotel Hermosa (2515 Pacific Coast Highway, 310/318-6000, $$), an attractively landscaped property five blocks away from the beach, has a more upscale feel. A recent arrival, it's a Spanish-style three-story hotel with a heated pool, Japanese garden, workout facilities, and comfortable rooms, many with ocean-facing balconies. We also got a nice room for a fair price at the **Quality Inn** (901 Aviation Boulevard, 310/374-2666, $$). A large room with two beds that was spacious, well appointed, and clean for only $55 at the height of summer qualifies as a deal in our book—and you're only a bracing, 10-minute walk from the beach.

Coastal Cuisine

Restaurants are abundant in Hermosa Beach. Boasting the highest per capita income in the South Bay, the town is sufficiently cosmopolitan to support a high-quality, ethnically diverse restaurant scene. You can take your pick of Thai, Italian, Mexican, French, Peruvian, Greek, Japanese, Indian, Cajun, Middle Eastern, macrobiotic, and more in this village. The crowds really seem to gravitate to the Italian eateries like **Buena Vita** (439 Pier Avenue, 310/379-7626, $$), a popular restaurant serving a broad variety of creative pasta dishes befitting a restaurant whose name translates as "good life." Prices are very reasonable.

Sushi just might be the favorite food of all. There are more sushi bars in Hermosa Beach than you can shake a chopstick at. **Sushi Sei**

Map of Los Angeles County—Page 156

Looking for Signs of Life in Hermosa Beach

When it comes to pondering the state of humankind, we may not be the most cheerful chaps in the world, but neither are we knee-jerk pessimists. We instead like to think of ourselves as realists who refuse to avert our eyes from the cold, hard truth. On our most recent combing through Southern California, we were amply dosed with further evidence of America's slide into the cultural dumpster. This trend reaches its nadir in the Los Angeles metroplex—even down by the ocean, where at least the sea breezes used to offer an oasis of head-clearing sanity and respite from the madness of the mainland. That is no longer the case. The South Bay beach towns—Redondo Beach, Hermosa Beach, and Manhattan Beach—feel as walled-in, congested, and dominated by asinine entertainment options as any of the wretched inland cities.

Hermosa Beach is a case in point. We were utterly depressed by what has happened here since our last visit, which occurred just prior to the turning of the new millennium. The first bum note that rang loudly in our ears was the discovery that one of our favorite bookstores, Either/Or, no longer existed. A visionary, well-stocked, nonfranchised shop with an abiding reverence for the written word, Either/Or was one of the literary treasures of Los Angeles and a destination bookstore that drew enlightened minds to Hermosa Beach. Charles Bukowski used to read his poetry here, for heaven's sake. Well, the new subliteracy—a will to stupidity that trickles down through every strata of society—has made such things as independent bookstores nearly obsolete in the land of the free.

Taking Either/Or's place are a few shoddy shops aimed at the tragically hip young L.A. urbanite. In the display windows of an anti-style clothing store called Re: Style, sneering mannequins frozen in jaded poses sported black urban-badboy wool caps made by "Sinister Clothing." Hundred-dollar bills and martini glasses were imprinted on the headgear. How brutally hip! Rows of ridiculous shoes—thick-soled footwear with ludicrous patterns for the mindless urban poseur—also filled the same windows. Next door is Splash!, which dispenses bath and body products, including such essentials as "after-workout shower gel" and "Pinky Tuscadero's Bath Bomb." Adjacent to that is a store with an overturned kitchen chair in its window and a mannequin wearing a designer shirt with a tray of sushi silk-screened on it.

Do you think for a second anyone cares that a cultural landmark has been lost with the closing of Either/Or? Not in Los Angeles!

Moving on, we went to check out the nightlife on Pier Avenue, where any number of bars and clubs haunt the west end. These last few blocks have been turned into a pedestrian mall closed to vehicular traffic, where the palm trees

Map of Southern California—Page 9

have been wrapped with Christmas lights, conferring a certain "je ne sais quoi" upon the revelry. For sure, the party rages on in Hermosa Beach. There are even more places to get wasted on Pier Avenue than we remembered. By far the most popular of the bunch is Aloha Sharkeez. It is a mock surf bar with a "Hawaiian Mex" approach to food and drink, if you can imagine that improbable collision. It was jammed sardine-tight with a cross-section of hip L.A. types, all of whom seemed to be babbling on cell phones and/or smoking cigarettes with studied nonchalance. Though Aloha Sharkeez is ostensibly a surf bar, they were playing electronic dance music. No one among this culturally rootless, disfranchised set apparently noticed the irony. For the record, Wednesdays are "Big Pimpin' Blowout Night."

Next door was Patrick Molloy's, a large Irish bar that was doing no business whatsoever on this particular night. This did not stop the bar from stationing bouncers wearing "SECURITY" shirts at the door. There were more thick-necked guys providing security than there were paying customers. Admittedly, it was a chilly spring night at midweek, but that didn't stop Aloha Sharkeez from packing them in. A few more nearby bars, including an empty place optimistically called the Beach Club, were doing scant business. No doubt they all pick up on weekends and in summer. Just for the record, Hennessey's Tavern, at the end of the street closest to the pier, looks to have expanded. There is more of everything in Hermosa Beach these days except for signs of intelligence.

We bottomed out at the Lighthouse Cafe, a Hermosa Beach perennial that used to be a favorite hangout for jazz musicians and aficionados. This is where Charlie Parker discovered Chet Baker and took him under his wing. In short, the Lighthouse Cafe is a place of legend, à la Sun Studios in Memphis or CBGB's in New York City. It is not a place that should be allowed to play taped rap, hip-hop, and industrial rave music, as we witnessed. These days, they traffic in reggae bands (e.g., The Mighty Angels) and deejayed dance music. We went in hoping to catch some live music but were driven out by a deafening hail of electronic decibels. The crowd comprised brain-dead cruisers whose facial expressions would turn as stupid as barnyard animals as they circulated around the club while grooving ostentatiously to the beat. Their faces betrayed little expression beyond a self-negating affectation of cool. One limber Whoopi Goldberg look-alike circled the premises while getting her freak on with conspicuous abandon. When an egregious contemporary R&B song came on, the dance-floor filled with bumptious marionettes, including a middle-aged white guy in need of a whole-body rhythm transplant. He reminded us of Dancing Bear from the *Captain Kangaroo* show.

Our laughter rang hollow, though, as this electronic maelstrom and the new rituals of urban nightlife incited us to throw in the towel much earlier than we would have liked to. We overheard a guy on a park bench outside the club complain, "None of this makes sense." He took the words right out of our mouths.

Map of Los Angeles County—Page 156

(1040 Hermosa Avenue, 310/379-6900, $$) is the consensus choice of raw-fish fans in the South Bay, offering sushi and comedic sushi chefs. **California Beach Rock 'n Sushi** (934 Hermosa Avenue, 310/374-7758, $$) is another good place to eat it raw. But just exactly what is the connection between rock and roll and sushi here? Beats us.

We had a hearty, healthy lunch at **Rocky Cola Cafe** (1025 Pacific Coast Highway, 310/798-3111, $), a combination '50s-style diner and health-food restaurant. Amid the standard fare of burgers, floats, and onion rings is a "bodybuilder fitness menu," including such things as ahi tuna tacos (dolphin-safe, of course) and egg-white veggie omelettes. Close by, we dropped into **El Pollo Inka** (1100 Pacific Coast Highway, 310/372-1433, $$) to sample the Peruvian-style grilled chicken. It's a good, inexpensive, rotisserie-style plate of chicken, served with salad and rice or French fries. If you're feeling a bit more adventurous, you can ante up for one of the seafood dishes, such as *saltado de camarones* (sautéed shrimp, onions, tomatoes, and red pepper). Excellent!

Coffeehouses are big in the South Bay (as they are all over California). At a place called **Java Man** (157 Pier Avenue, 310/379-7209, $), we sipped on big mugs of the coffee of the day (macadamia nut) and munched pastries with the other clientele, who were similarly absorbed in the *Los Angeles Times*. One serious and sensitive fellow, though, was drawing psychedelic swirls onto paper with colored pencils, attentively rendering paisley blobs in an abstract, Romper Room-on-acid style. He accompanied these with poetic thoughts and lyric fragments. When he made a trip to the bathroom, we sauntered over to inspect his drawing pad. Sample verse: "I am looking for my vision/A sight to set me free." We returned to our java, muffins, and newspapers, burying our beaks in the latest revelations about Republican politicians' pasts.

Night Moves

We've rarely seen a row of bars and clubs as entrenched as one in Hermosa Beach. It can be found on the south side of Pier Avenue before it ends at the Strand. Such constancy is almost unheard of at the beach. Like a stack of dominoes, four clubs are arrayed in a row. It might be you, however, that's falling over by the end of the evening. Your choices are **Hennessey's Tavern** (8 Pier Avenue, 310/374-9203), a franchised Irish-themed bar/restaurant; the **Lighthouse Cafe** (30 Pier Avenue, 310/372-6911), a club that traffics in reggae and dance music; **Patrick Molloy's** (50 Pier Avenue, 310/798-9762), yet another would-be Irish bar; and **Aloha Sharkeez** (52 Pier Avenue, 310/374-7823), a faux surf bar that is the most popular spot in town. For more on what has become a somewhat tired and trendy scene, see the accompanying sidebar "Looking for Signs of Life on Hermosa Beach."

Around the corner from Pier Avenue's string of watering holes, facing the beach itself on the Strand, is the old reliable **Poop Deck** (1272 Strand, 310/372-1300), a well-worn and unfancy place where well-worn and unfancy types come to slake their thirsts on a daily basis. It's a good hangout for a celebratory brew at sundown.

Then there's the back-alley institution known as **Bestie's** (1332 Hermosa Avenue, 310/318-3818). Once owned by British soccer legend George Best, a player second only to Pele in the annals of the sport, Bestie's faithfully recreates a friendly British pub atmosphere. The menu is filled with staples of British cuisine like lamb stew and bangers and mash. Bartenders will pull you a long, cool mug of inky Guinness draft, and you can play pool, toss darts, or watch sports on one of a dozen or so TVs strung up around the premises. On weekends a back room miraculously metamorphoses into BBC, a hip dance club. Though the address is on Hermosa Avenue, Bestie's is entered from an alley behind it. Because you must know what you're looking for, Bestie's/BBC is popular with locals and all but unknown to outsiders.

For More Information

Hermosa Beach Chamber of Commerce, 323 Pier Avenue, Hermosa Beach, CA 90254, 310/376-0951, website: www.beach-web.com

Manhattan Beach

The view of the sand in either direction from Manhattan Beach Pier is enough to convince anyone that living in Los Angeles is worth every hassle—meteorological, seismic, automotive—just to have access to such splendor. Volleyball nets are strung out to the south as far as the eye can see. Surfers bob in the water, waiting for the wave that will carry them shoreward. Hot, hard-bodied babes oil down and catch rays on the beach. Weather-beaten anglers stand poised against the pier railings, their poles and lines an excuse for sitting all day in the golden sun. One old bird in an electric wheelchair had forgone the pretense of fishing. Between satisfying slugs from his thermos, he trained his binoculars on the nubile bodies lying on the sands below. Succumbing to temptation—and too ashamed to ask the old dude for a look-see—we dropped quarters into the pay telescopes mounted on the wooden railings of the pier and conducted our own onsite inspection. Why else are these telescopes here—so you can check out the oil refineries of El Segundo?

You could almost flip a coin when choosing among the three beach towns—Redondo, Hermosa, and Manhattan—strung out along the southern edge of Santa Monica Bay. The three have more similarities than differences. For starters, they're linked by the South Bay Bicycle Trail, which also serves as a boardwalk, and they all strive to cultivate as low-key a personality as possible, given their proximity to Los Angeles.

If there is any difference between Manhattan Beach and the others, it is evident away from the water. Manhattan Beach is the most moneyed, family-oriented, and residential of the three. Its 2,300 acres are as developed as a suburban community can be, crowded with smallish homes and yards that typically consist of a square foot of bleached pebbles and a dark green bush. The line of natural dunes hasn't been bulldozed away, and building heights have been held down to a bearable level. These facts, coupled with the town's sudden rollercoaster plunge toward the ocean, allow nearly all who live here an invigorating view of the Pacific Ocean. You feel the ocean in Manhattan Beach. It's like a permanent drive-in movie to help relieve the stress of the gridlock to the east.

Inside the snug city limits of Manhattan Beach (population 34,000) are 13 churches, five parks, and two libraries; one of the parks provides the setting for Sunday afternoon concerts during the summer. Most of the commerce is concentrated around the intersection of the two main drags, Manhattan Beach Boulevard and Highland Avenue. The local businesses squeezed in here are the sort of nonfranchised shops that obsessive consumers love to believe they've discovered for themselves, bearing such names as Pour Moi! La Boutique, Foote Fetish, and Le Chat. Parking isn't necessarily a problem, but it isn't cheap and it isn't easy. Street meters run 24 hours and cost 25 cents for 15 minutes, with a five-hour limit. They take quarters only. Where is somebody supposed to come by that many quarters?

There are some nagging signs that Manhattan Beach may be losing its grip on growth. A 187-acre business park has been relegated to the eastern edge of town in the flight path of Los Angeles International Airport and next to a smoke-belching power plant. With it has

Los Angeles County

Map of Los Angeles County—Page 156

The Art of Surfing

Chick Bragg is obsessed with surfing. Ever since he walked away from the baseball diamond—where his Little League teammates included Robin Yount, Pete LaCock, and Rick Dempsey—he has fallen head over curls for surfing. He is 50 and has, with remarkably few exceptions, surfed every day of his life since he was 18. When he is not in Fiji, Java, or Hawaii searching for the perfect wave, he can be found hopping over the wall in front of his tiny Manhattan Beach studio and dashing toward the water.

Chick Bragg is no shirker of worldly responsibility; he simply loves surfing. The surfing deities must have been smiling on the day he was born, because Chick Bragg was blessed with extraordinary artistic talent. In fact, as Charles Lynn Bragg he has carved out a singular artistic vision that's on display all over the planet. You've seen his work without realizing it, as it has appeared on posters, prints, coffee mugs, and T-shirts in seaside gift shops from here to Timbuktu. You've even owned some of Chick Bragg's work without even knowing it. A number of his paintings of undersea life—inspired by his secondary passions, scuba diving and underwater photography—were used by the U.S. Postal Service for a series of first-class stamps that were run off in "limited editions" of 255 million. He has also achieved a rock star–like prominence in Japan. His paintings are filled with the wonders of the water, a sort of Henry Rousseau meets Jacques-Yves Cousteau. His skill runs in the family. Chick's father is Charles Bragg, the painter, etcher, and sculptor best known for his satiric takes on the legal profession and America's right-wing pomposities.

First and foremost, Chick is a Southern California surf nut.

"I'm not really a beach guy. I just surf," he says with no irony, "The beach just happens to be where the ocean is."

He surfs mostly right across from where he lives, in the El Porto section of Manhattan Beach, about a mile north of the town pier. He does not surf any farther north, toward Playa del Rey, because the water is too polluted for his liking, despite the assurances of the Hyperion Sewage Treatment Plant that their discharge into Santa Monica Bay is within the legal limits.

A truly gentle spirit, Chick is a throwback to the civilized days of surfing.

"That stereotype of the sweet-natured surfer boy is all wrong," he said, "There is nothing sweet or gentle about these younger guys. They'll fight you over a wave. I'll share a wave, but when it gets to be a hostile situation I just get depressed and can't enjoy the rides. Young surfers have less respect for everything, and they're really impatient. I still have to compete with them, as much as I dislike it."

Speaking of the art of surfing, there's a website devoted entirely to just that. It is www.surfart.com, and it is one of the more useful, handsomely designed, and fun sites to, uh, surf that we found during our latest research on California.

Map of Southern California—Page 9

arrived an army of nouveau riche who have driven up land values with their real-estate schemes. This has caused longtime residents to skirmish with developers.

A young woman who lives in Manhattan Beach told us that the town has developed an attitude that is lacking in the more laid-back Hermosa Beach. That attitude, one supposes, comes from the money it costs to live here. One local realtor—whose slogan is "I have the right energy to sell your house"—advertised this bargain: "A classic beach home on the walk streets with fabulous ocean views." Translation: a modest wooden box with an upstairs balcony located blocks off the ocean. Asking price: $699,000. Of the mega-moneyed set that has just about displaced the beach bums, one longtime resident said, "The vibe here is spoiled, arrogant, impatient . . . as if their pampered lives are so pressured. Oh yes, and greedy."

Still, as you near the beach, all pretensions disappear in a blaze of tanned, libidinous glory. Relaxed bars, taverns, and restaurants near the pier on Manhattan Boulevard help sustain the friendly cacophony that is at the heart of the Southern California beach experience.

Beaches

Manhattan Beach's two-mile oceanfront is completely residential (i.e., no motels, few affordable rentals). The clean, sandy **Manhattan County Beach** is bisected by a 900-foot pier (at the west end of Manhattan Beach Boulevard) and backed by a seawall adorned with tasteful murals and less tasteful graffiti. The water is subject to occasional rough currents but is well patrolled by a bevy of lifeguards. Beach volleyball is not just a sport but a religion here. From the pier sand volleyball courts and nets extend down toward Hermosa Beach. North of Manhattan Beach is **El Porto Beach.** You can walk to it from Manhattan Beach or park near the ramps at 41st and 44th Streets. El Porto has full facilities and volleyball nets, but the scene here tends to be loud and uninviting.

Bunking Down

Lodging isn't Manhattan Beach's strong suit. The closest you can get to the beach is three steep uphill blocks away from the action on Highland Avenue. The **Sea View Inn** (3400 Highland Avenue, 310/545-1504, $) is the most appealing of a handful of choices. It only has eight rooms, but these surround a swimming pool away from the noise of the busy thoroughfare.

Coastal Cuisine

The most celebrated restaurant in town is **H$_2$0** (401 Manhattan Beach Boulevard, 310/545-6220, $$$), as in the chemical formula for water. The food is sumptuous and meticulously prepared nouvelle cuisine on overdrive (e.g., sautéed duck breast, bacon garlic fig sauce, with sweet potato confit hash). At night H$_2$0 doubles as an upscale club. A quick bite of fried fish can be had at the **Saltwater Cafe** at the end of Manhattan Beach Pier (2 Manhattan Beach Boulevard, 310/372-6383, $). The café's menu is written on a surfboard mounted above the takeout counter. It's nothing fancy and a tad pricey by end-of-the-pier fast-food standards. Grab a magazine off the rack out front and sit down on the bench beside the railing.

Night Moves

A clear sign of the upscaling of Manhattan Beach is the fate of La Paz, once considered to be the "king of the beach bars" and "Animal House at the beach" by the usual reliable sources of surfers and local beach bums. It was a sloppy, wonderful, ramshackle place that we feel privileged to have visited on a previous trip. La Paz is gone now, replaced by a municipal parking lot beside the pier. Picking up the slack are **Sunsets** (117 Manhattan Beach Boulevard, 310/545-2523), a "virtual Hawaiian" restaurant and bar; the **Manhattan Beach Brewing Company** (124 Manhattan Beach Boulevard, 310/798-2744), with designer home brew; and the **Shellback Tavern** (116 Manhattan Beach

Los Angeles County

"Catch a Wave": A Brief History of Surf Music

In the early 1960s, the state of California infiltrated rock and roll with a sound that could have come from nowhere else: surf music. The Beach Boys, Jan and Dean, and Dick Dale launched a nationally popular music scene out of the sun-dappled wonderland of Southern California. It was a movement that was well established before the Beatles made their first stateside splash with "I Want to Hold Your Hand."

The Beach Boys are principally deemed responsible for popularizing the California myth—a harmony-rich musical outlook based on the holy trinity of sun, surf, and fun—although Jan and Dean (with "Surf City") and the Mamas and the Papas (with "California Dreamin'") certainly warbled a few anthems of their own. The promise of a beatific adolescence in the Golden State transcended the foursquare suburban reality of cow towns like Hawthorne and Torrance. As Brian Wilson, the Beach Boys' founder, explained in 1976, "It's not just surfing; it's the outdoors and cars and sunshine; it's the society of California; it's the way of California." Southern California—the Los Angeles basin in particular—was the wellspring of the California myth.

For those who made their living plowing acreage in the Plains states or who were buried up to their knees in winter snows in the Northeast, it was a potent come-on. The California myth promised everything: health and longevity beneath a bountiful sun that shone warmly year-round; prosperity in a job-filled environment catering to the burgeoning aeronautics and communications industries; and finally, a relaxed approach to life that had "fun, fun, fun" as its first commandment.

Until the Beach Boys came along, surf music was the domain of hotshot instrumentalists such as Dick Dale, the undisputed king of surf guitar. According to Dale, "Real surfing music is instrumental, characterized by heavy staccato picking on a Fender Stratocaster guitar." A surfer could listen to one of his fast-fingered solos and feel the surging power of the ocean as it hurtled him toward shore. Such numbers as "Let's Go Trippin'," "Surf Beat," and "Miserlou" promoted a sense of identity within the surfers' ranks.

Although surf music was primarily designed for dancing at beach parties, amusement parks, and surfers' clubs, the genre left its mark on the national charts with songs by the Surfaris ("Wipe Out") and the Chantays ("Pipeline"). Both were released in 1963. The Chantays, a five-man garage band from Santa Ana, rode "Pipeline" all the way to number four. The Surfaris, a quintet from Glendora, saw "Wipe Out" soar to number two. "Wipe Out," a tumbling wave of tom-tom rolls and frenzied guitar breaks, remains the premier instrumental surf hit of all time.

Map of Southern California—Page 9

But that was just the tip of the iceberg. The Routers took a song called "Let's Go," adapted it to a new dance craze—the Pony—and had a hit with "Let's Go (Pony)," whose familiar clap and chant has since become a cheerleaders' staple. The Marketts made their mark with "Surfer's Stomp," "Balboa Blue," and "Out of Limits"—the latter based on the theme from the *Outer Limits* TV show. Then there were the Ventures, who were neither a surf band nor from California, and the Pyramids, from Long Beach, who recorded the surf classic "Penetration" and stretched the outer limits as personalities, performing with shaved heads and arriving at shows in helicopters and atop elephants.

However, it was the arrival of the Beach Boys that signaled the nationwide flowering of surf and hot-rod music. The sport's foremost cultural emissaries, the Beach Boys spread the gospel of surfing "even in places where the nearest thing to surf is maybe the froth on a chocolate shake!" (to quote the liner notes of Surfin' USA, their second album). With their earliest songs, "Surfin'" and "Surfin' Safari," the Beach Boys made a magical, intuitive leap—bridging Chuck Berry and the Four Freshmen and adding their own libretto about surfing and the California way of life.

Jan (Berry) and Dean (Torrance) were the other minstrel demigods in the car-and-surf-song sweepstakes. With "Surf City," a tune cowritten by Brian Wilson and cut with his help during the summer of 1963, Jan and Dean had the first number one surfing song. The real-life surf city they had in mind was Huntington Beach, which promotes itself with that handle to this day.

The Californians' summer fever became a national contagion. Surf music began turning up in such unlikely places as Colorado, which produced the Astronauts, and Minnesota, home of the Trashmen, whose "Surfin' Bird" went to number four. Another Midwestern band, the Rivieras, delivered the West Coast tribute "California Sun." Even sooty old New York turned out the Trade Winds. Their big hit line: "New York's a lonely town when you're the only surfer boy around."

Back on the West Coast a small cadre of writers, producers, and performers kept turning out the real thing. In addition to the Beach Boys and Jan and Dean, singing surf/car groups included the Fantastic Baggys ("Tell 'Em I'm Surfing," "Summer Means Fun"), the Rip Chords ("Hey Little Cobra," "Three Window Coupe"), and the Sunrays ("I Live for the Sun"). At mid-decade a new wave of Southern California-based acts swept the Top 40. Among them were the Turtles, Gary Lewis and the Playboys, Paul Revere and the Raiders, the Mamas and the Papas, Johnny Rivers, the Byrds, and the Monkees.

In 1967 California would enter a whole different stage: acid rock, the Summer of Love, the Monterey Pop Festival, the San Francisco Sound, and a wave of bands based around the Sunset Strip of Los Angeles. The seeds of this revolution can be traced back to five Pendleton-shirted Beach Boys and the idea they got to sing about surfing. As the late Carl Wilson of the Beach Boys once told us, "People wanted to hang out at the beach. It was really an early hippie thing." In a way, it still is.

Los Angeles County

Map of Los Angeles County—Page 156

Boulevard, 310/376-7857), which is the closest in spirit to La Paz you'll find on the beach. It serves pretty good tacos and burgers, too. Just two blocks up a steep hill from the beach is **Baja Sharkeez** (3801 Highland Avenue, 310/545-6563), the most popular surf bar in town. "If I were single," one surfer confided, "this is where I'd come. At night you can't move without knocking someone with an elbow." Saw-

dust on the floor, surf videos and sports on screens, old flotsam hanging from ceilings, and the best fish taco and veggie burrito within five miles—Baja Sharkeez has it all.

For More Information

Manhattan Beach Chamber of Commerce, 425 15th Street, Manhattan Beach, CA 90266, 310/545-5313, website: www.beach-web.com

El Segundo

Like San Pedro, El Segundo (population 16,000) is an integral part of Los Angeles, but it is mostly overlooked or ignored. It is home to a sprawl of oil refineries, oil piers, the Hyperion Sewage Treatment Plant (the Grand Coulee Dam of sewage plants), and the Scattergood Steam Generating Station. Hyperion is the "largest activated sludge plant in the world," its 330 million gallons of sewage a day treated and dumped, as sludge, in off-shore canyons. El Segundo is also directly beside Los Angeles International Airport. This bathes the town in a toxic-industrial-aeronautic cacophony that blends perfectly with the boom boxes that reign along the shore.

Beaches

In spite of the surrounding environment, El Segundo has two of the broadest beaches in the Los Angeles area: **Dockweiler State Beach** and **El Segundo Beach.** Together they comprise a six-mile stretch of sand that would make any other beach town sorely envious. Although there's beach access and large pay parking lots off El Segundo Boulevard and at the end of

Grand Avenue, the best way to see El Segundo and Dockweiler State Beaches is by bicycling along the shoreline-hugging South Bay Bicycle Trail. Almost anywhere along this stretch you can pull off the bicycle trail and the beach is all yours.

It's an odd sensation to be on a beach so huge on a picture-perfect summer day, all of five miles from the center of Los Angeles, and find the place nearly deserted. As long as you don't look shoreward at the oil refineries and sewage plant, or fret too much over the gangsta rap blaring from the direction of the parking lot, you'd swear this was as perfect a beach as you could hope to find. Dockweiler State Beach has the added incentive of a 117-site campground for RVs only at its south end. Dockweiler is so long that it encompasses the oceanfront in both El Segundo and neighboring Playa del Rey.

For More Information

El Segundo Chamber of Commerce, 427 Main Street, El Segundo, CA 90245, 310/322-1220, website: www.beach-web.com

Map of Southern California—Page 9

Playa del Rey

Playa del Rey is a largely residential town built along streets that dead-end into a lagoon at sea level and run on top of towering bluffs that look out over the beach. The chief calling card is Dockweiler State Beach, a wide, white-sand beach extending from Del Rey Lagoon south to the RV campground in El Segundo. Across the lagoon lies Venice Beach; behind it, along constructed waterways, Marina del Rey. It is due west of Los Angeles International Airport.

The drive out to Playa del Rey, west from Lincoln Boulevard through the last unblemished wetlands in Los Angeles, is relatively pleasant. It might not have been, however, had Steven Spielberg and pals had their way with the proposed (and now abandoned) Dream-Works SKG project, which would have defiled 1,087 acres of this oasis for their studio. However, the Playa Vista development project will bring to the marshland 13,000 housing units and 5 million square feet of office space.

Beaches

The word "wide" does not even begin to describe the sandy expanse at **Dockweiler State Beach,** which is shared by Playa del Rey and neighboring El Segundo (see the preceding entry for more detail). Dockweiler and adjacent beaches in Los Angeles County have been extended seaward with sand dredged from the site of the Hyperion

 ## Want to Be an L.A. County Lifeguard?

If week after week of watching the flesh parade on *Baywatch* has you eager to join the ranks of Los Angeles County lifeguards, bear in mind that the reality of landing the job is a little tougher than showing up with a Screen Actors Guild card. In fact, to make it into rookie school at the Lifeguard Training Academy, you must meet the following conditions right off the bat: 1) you must have uncorrected vision of 20/30 or better; 2) you must be able to complete a 1,000-meter swim (approximately three-fifths of a mile); 3) you must be 18 years of age or older; and 4) you must have a valid California driver's license and high school diploma.

Lifeguard trials are held once yearly in September and draw roughly 250 applicants. If chosen, new recruits begin as part-timers making $18.40 per hour and then attend 100 hours of "rookie school," where they learn first aid and safety and rescue techniques. Recertification is required every year. For more information call the **Los Angeles County Lifeguard Administrative Headquarters** (310/577-5700) or the **Lifeguard Training Academy** (310/939-7200).

However seriously you may or may not take it, *Baywatch* has indirectly saved lives. Widely viewed around the world, it has raised the level of lifeguard competence in cities such as Barcelona, Spain, which actually flew Los Angeles County lifeguards over for consultations. The meetings paid off. On one weekend in 1993 (before the consultations), there were 14 drownings on the beaches of Barcelona. During the first nine *months* of 1994, however, there were none.

Map of Los Angeles County—Page 156

Sewage Treatment Plant and the Scattergood Steam Generating Station. They can handle all eager beachgoers, all summer long. Even with all of mighty Los Angeles knocking at the back door, such beaches as Dockweiler, Venice, and Santa Monica seldom reach the saturation point. Not that they're terrifically attractive but they are indisputably large. They are also prone to closure when the waters of Santa Monica Bay become polluted with storm-drain runoff.

For More Information

Westchester/Los Angeles/Marina del Rey Chamber of Commerce, 9800 South Sepulveda Boulevard, Westchester, CA 90045, 310/305-9545, website: www.wlaxmdrchamber.com

Marina del Rey

Marina del Rey can be summed up in two words: yachting and eating. It is the world's largest recreational small-craft harbor, consisting of eight basins that collectively contain 6,000 boat slips. It also claims to have the greatest concentration of restaurants in a single square-mile area this side of New York City. The place is a magnet for money.

It's hard to imagine that until the mid-1950s the area was a swampy lagoon at the mouth of Ballona Creek. Progress, you say? Well, maybe. The construction of the marina has not been without problems. Although the East Coast has an abundance of natural harbors, the California coast has few of them, necessitating the construction of harbors, involving jetties, breakwaters, and the dredging of marinas. After opening, Marina del Rey faced a series of design-related problems. First, under a certain set of wave conditions outside the marina, the original design enabled the spread of destructive standing waves inside the marina, resulting in damaged boats and lawsuits. To rectify this designers hastily added a 1,200-foot, detached offshore breakwater in 1962. The marina has also seen the recurring problem of sand shoaling up against the north jetty and forming a bar across the southern entrance channel, which has required expensive dredging on a regular basis.

All the same, the marina generates more money than it costs to maintain, so most everyone is happy, especially L.A. boat groupies. Like a hand with eight fingers, the yacht basin

at Marina del Rey reaches inland, grabbing Los Angeles by the seat of the pants. In addition to the 6,000 boats in the water, it can store another 3,000 vessels in dry dock. There are nearly as many boats in Marina del Rey as there are residents. Admiralty Way runs in a semicircle around the harbor. It connects with Via Marina (on the west side) and Fiji Way (on the south side) to form a great horseshoe around the octet of boat basins. It is in this watery world-within-a-world that the moneyed heart of Marina del Rey can be heard to beat. Condos average in the $500,000 range. Apartment rentals are $2,000 and up, depending on what floor you're on and whether you look out on the city, ocean, or yacht basin. Some people live on their boats. A few have died on them. Dennis Wilson of the Beach Boys drowned here while diving for discarded souvenirs in a boat slip where he used to live with a former wife.

Over the past three decades, Marina del Rey (population 11,000) has blossomed like a cactus flower out of its desertlike surroundings. An impressive retail industry of waterfront restaurants, luxury hotels, dance clubs, and specialty shops has grown around the harbor. In Marina del Rey you can, as a brochure proclaims, browse for everything "from socks to solid gold." Signs heralding one's arrival in Marina del Rey offer this menu of options: "Apartments, Berths, Chandlery, Hotels, Launching, Maintenance, Moorings, Motels, Restaurants, Shops, Sportfishing, Town Houses, Yacht Sales." As you spiral closer to Admiralty Way

Los Angeles County

from the outside world—passing through the buffer zones that isolate Marina del Rey from the less glamorous neighboring communities of Culver City, Playa del Rey, and Venice—an oasis of boats, buildings, and greenery emerges out of nowhere. If you look and listen closely, you might even hear ducks quacking and waddling around a large lake that's part of a nature preserve. Off-road bike paths wind around the marina. The South Bay Bicycle Trail leaves the beach at the mouth of Ballona Creek and passes through the marina, reemerging by the ocean at Venice Pier. Four small parks within the marina add a note of greenery and tranquillity. **Burton Chase Park,** at the end of Mindinao Way, is a six-acre green space from which one can watch boats enter and exit the marina. The retail area known as **Fisherman's Village** is one of the more convincing of the nautical-themed, New England–style shopping complexes we've seen, right down to its cobblestone walks. The whole of Marina del Rey has the privileged, dreamlike aura of a mirage. It's a great mirage, if you've got the monetary means to enjoy it.

Beaches

In this case the proper heading would be the singular "beach." Because it is a protected inland harbor, Marina del Rey by definition has no ocean beaches. The marina does have one beach at the end of Basin D: **Mother's Beach,** where water-lovers can swim, windsurf, and sail on a sandy, lifeguarded stretch of sand where no waves roll ashore. Maybe that's why choosy mothers choose Mother's as a place to bring their kids to frolic in relative safety. In any case, this mushroom-shaped lagoon enables both calm-water swimming and wind-free sunbathing. The drawback is water quality. Would you want to swim in a man-made lagoon routinely fouled by boat fuel, bilgewater, and storm runoff?

Del Rey Lagoon is not a beach, but it is a park overlooking the ocean by the south jetty

at Marina del Rey, and it offers access to the northern end of Dockweiler State Beach. Facilities on this grassy, 13-acre park include picnic tables, a playground, basketball courts, and baseball diamonds.

Bunking Down

The selection of hotels and restaurants in Marina del Rey makes it the Neiman-Marcus of beach communities. Starting from the top, the vaunted **Ritz-Carlton** (4375 Admiralty Way, 310/823-1700, $$$$) brings a touch of Old World elegance to the land of new money. This 14-story masterpiece affords a choice of harbor or ocean views, swaddling guests in comfort (for a price) in a veritable island of first-class amenities: lighted tennis courts, heated outdoor pool, yacht charters, and so on.

The **Marina Beach Marriott** (4100 Admiralty Way, 310/301-3000, $$$$) offers comparable upscale accommodations in a 10-story tower that looks like a giant sand dune from the street. The balcony views—of the Malibu coastline to the north, of Palos Verdes Peninsula to the south—are majestic, especially around sunset. With a ninth-floor cocktail lounge, ground-floor California-cuisine restaurant **(Stones),** outdoor garden café and pool, and sumptuous rooms decorated in muted pastels and accented with brass and marble, you won't lack for pampering here.

If money is a consideration, nearby Culver City is loaded with cheaper chains, such as the **Culver City Travelodge** (11180 Washington Place, 310/839-1111, $), where you'll save a bundle, which you can blow on dinner and nightlife in the marina.

Coastal Cuisine

A few years back one of us had Sunday dinner with rock and roll pioneer Little Richard at **Aunt Kizzy's Back Porch** (4325 Glencoe Avenue, 310/578-1005, $$), a soul-food eatery in the Villa Marina Shopping Center. Not only can Richard sing and pound the piano, the man knows how to pick a restaurant. The culinary style is Deep South and down-home: mounds of fried chicken, pork tenderloin, homemade mashed potatoes, stewed vegetables, fruit cobblers, and other fresh desserts. Aunt Kizzy's food is so good it's enough to give you religion, if you haven't got it already.

On the waterfront **Edie's Diner** (4211 Admiralty Way, 310/823-5339, $) does a big business in burgers, fries, and pie. It's done up in diner chic, from the gleaming ceramic tile to the retro rock tunes on the booth-side jukeboxes, and the burgers are everything you'd want in a slab of ground cow: big, sloppy, and good. Edie's does breakfast as well.

If burger fare or soul food isn't in the cards, the **Dining Room** at the Ritz-Carlton (4375 Admiralty Way, 310/823-1700, $$$$) offers a sublime culinary experience at the other end of the scale, in formal surroundings (jacket required) with a French accent and fresh California ingredients.

Coffee-holics will want to head over to **Joni's Coffee Roaster Cafe** (552 Washington Boulevard, 310/305-7147, $$), a favorite gathering place of Venice-Marina bohemians and wealthy mavericks. One leather-clad wannabe biker casually ordered a glass of chardonnay and an Anchor Steam before the sun was up. "What the heck," he told the nonplussed clerk, "It's Monday morning." In addition to espresso, cappuccino, and pastries, the café offers healthful breakfasts, lunches, and dinners. Hit **Noah's Bagels** (548 Washington Boulevard, 310/574-1155, $) next door, and you're good to go.

Night Moves

A night on the town in Marina del Rey begins with a fruitless search for a parking space. The way they've got it rigged, there's next to nothing in the way of legal street parking, leaving one with no choice but to hand the keys to a valet at the club or restaurant of your choice. We despise valet parking.

In this vexatious spirit we drove around Marina del Rey looking for parking. After cruising for a while, we tried the lot at a shopping center just outside the marina, but it was filled with signs warning that all cars belonging to noncustomers would be towed. We took our chances all the same and left the car, hiking to a place called—God, it hurts just to type a name this stupid—**Moose McGillycuddy's** (13535 Mindinao Way, 310/574-3932). Moose's is an indoor/outdoor pub, grub, and disco franchise that claims the same sort of crowd that used to jam the Red Onion, a now-defunct singles-bar chain that, in its own way, helped further the 1980s population boom in Southern California.

At Moose's a young crowd hopped to the fascistic beat of the latest synthetic dance hits. Some lined up to be plastered with free temporary tattoos, which was that evening's big promotion. A salty dog who looked like the Skipper on *Gilligan's Island* circulated with a wicker basket full of plastic-wrapped Moonie roses, cutting an odd figure. In the bathroom a guy removed the sweaty T-shirt in which he'd arrived and changed into a trendier leisure-wear ensemble, looking like a discofied Clark Kent who'd come to dazzle the ladies with his sartorial Kryptonite. At one table a mutually infatuated couple took turns grooming each other, like Rhesus monkeys, with combs and brushes. We stationed ourselves at the Pop-a-Shot concession, vainly trying to impress the locals with our shooting ability and finally retreating to the outdoor patio.

Heat lamps were working hard to take the chill out of the summer night's air. Apparently we hit Los Angeles at the height of an unseasonable summer cold snap, keeping the heat-seeking Angelenos at home and indoors. It felt heavenly to us, although the bars and clubs were seeing significantly reduced numbers as a result. Though it was only July, it looked like the summer had already ended at **Yankee Doodles** (300 Washington Boulevard, 310/574-6868). However, our comely cocktail

Map of Southern California—Page 9

waitress assured us that the place would be packed tighter than a tin of sardines once the mercury returned to normal levels.

Across the street the **Baja Cantina** (311 Washington Boulevard, 310/821-2252) was hopping all night long. Maybe hot chiles were warming up the patrons in this popular Mexican restaurant and watering hole. You come in, put your name on the list, belly up to the bar, grab a Mexican beer, and wait for a table in tight quarters with what seems like half of Los Angeles. The Baja Cantina is noisy and fun, with its sociocultural ambience best suggested by two of the celebrities whose framed, autographed pictures hang on the wall: actor Tony Danza and porn star Christy Canyon.

For More Information

Westchester/Los Angeles/Marina del Rey Chamber of Commerce, 9800 South Sepulveda Boulevard, Westchester, CA 90045, 310/305-9545; website: www.wlaxmdrchamber.com

Venice

In the 1993 film *Falling Down,* the Michael Douglas character—an everyman driven to psychopathy by the stress of living in Los Angeles—cuts a swath westward across the city to Venice, committing a rash of demented crimes on his way. The police track him down, forcing a final stand at the end of Venice Pier. As he dies, falling over the pier railing after absorbing a point-blank blast from Robert Duvall's service revolver, he gives Venice a last befuddled backward glance and then splashes into the beautiful blue Pacific.

In Venice, life doesn't just imitate art. It defines it. If it's cutting edge, chances are it started in Venice—and it probably will end here, too. Venice is many things: fascinating human zoo, nasty urban war zone, and just about everything in between.

Take the pier, for example. Though it was used for this Hollywood film shoot, it has been closed to public use for several years. Like the Michael Douglas character, many alienated people gravitate to Venice to make an escape. On the other hand, many who come here—us, for example—have given it a befuddled backward glance as they headed out of town.

It's easy to trash Venice. Not for nothing is it known as the home of $2 sunglasses, $3 T-shirts, $4 Tarot readings, and $5 stress massages. New Age prophets walk shoulder to shoulder with the old-age homeless. Runaway children seek shelter in group houses, and gangs bring their hideous territorial squabbles to the shore. Cops walk the beat, half amused and half afraid.

It's easy to allow preconceptions to unfairly blind a first-time visitor to Venice's peculiar appeal. The source of that appeal goes right back to the town's roots. Venice began as the dream of a man named Abbot Kinney, who made his millions on cigarettes and spent them all in 1900 purchasing 160 acres of marshland south of Santa Monica. For some reason (nicotine frenzy perhaps), he saw similarities between his new property and the site on which Venice, Italy, was built. He commissioned two architects to design a "thoroughly equipped" city with streets, hotels, houses, and canals—15 miles of cement-bottomed canals. By June 1905, the canals were filled with water. All Kinney needed for his new Venice was people to build their dream homes beside his waterways.

Like any good businessman, Kinney lured folks here with a gimmick: gondolas and gondoliers. He imported some of Italy's finest oarsmen and had them serenade prospective buyers while rowing them up and down the canals to inspect the empty lots. He persuaded merchants to build hotels, restaurants, and shops in the architectural style of the Venetian Renaissance. He also oversaw the construction of a lecture hall, pavilion, and theater. Provocative speakers

Los Angeles County

The Dandelion Under the Pillow

"Tell someone to put a dandelion under their pillow to cure dandruff and they'll elect you President . . . of anything."
—Henry Morgan, interviewed in *The Realist,* 1960.

Some years back, a local news story captured the nation's imagination. A Los Angeles woman lost her cat on a flight from New York's La Guardia Airport to LAX. A California psychic was called in for the cat hunt. The psychic picked up some feline vibes—our theory is litter-box odor—in the cargo bay. Tracking the vibes, the psychic pinpointed the cat's location. That is, the psychic pointed to the section of the cargo bay where the cat was later found. With that tail, er, tale, California's booming alternative industry racked up yet another success story.

California is the holy land for spiritual, medical, and political alternatives. This is the state that gave us the Summer of Love and the Monterey Pop Festival—but also the Altamont disaster and the Manson family. It has produced great alternative literature and groundbreaking music. It has also given rise to taxpayer revolts and Pebble Beach. It has coughed up Jim Jones and Ronald Reagan, the Black Panthers, Jerry Brown, and the SLA and Patty Hearst. It gave us former First Lady Nancy Reagan, whose reliance on a California astrologist directed the fate of the country for a spell.

A veritable smorgasbord of healers, shakers, counselors, therapists, holistic ministers, colon irrigators, Rolfers, and other assorted gurus make their home in California. This is especially the case along the coast, where the sea breezes and unchanging weather help foster a meditative bent of mind. Every single one of these alternative healers is an expert on something. Though some are quacks, others have legitimately helped people beyond the reach of mainstream medicine while also serving to loosen the fascistic grip that the medical establishment has on our nation's health care.

One way to get a handle on available alternative services is to consult the myriad free publications devoted to this subject. Reams of paper are given over to ads that are eerily similar to the personals in metropolitan "swinger" mags. How can so many people, we wondered, ply their trade in this alternative market? If indeed they do find enough customers to make a lucrative living at it, why is the state still so bedeviled? If Los Angeles, for instance, is filled to bursting with self-actualized, empowered, tanned, and transcendentally meditated people, why is the city such a smog-strangled sprawl that its saner citizens can't wait to flee when an offer to work somewhere else comes along?

Map of Southern California—Page 9

It's not our intent to knock alternatives. In fact this guide is intended to be an alternative to the fulsome brochure copy that fills most travel books. Still, as one peruses the alternative reference tools, the notion begins creeping in that many of these experts are selling false hope. At their most innocuous they provide an entertaining sideshow.

Here's a random sampling of beach bhagwans:

- "OPENING TO THE GODDESS ENERGY: Explore and heal the denied feminne *(sic)* within. . . . $80 advance, $100 at the door."
- "SINGING, MOVING THROUGH THE FEAR, FOR NON-SINGERS WHO MUST SING: reasonable rates." (Don't karaoke bars provide this service free of charge?)
- "ENHANCED SEXUALITY TRAINING: Sexual meditation. Extended orgasm. Soul union and enlightenment. No overt sexual activity." (What a tease!)
- "PAST LIFE REGRESSION. Explore past lives for: Curiosity, Removing Blocks, Soul Cleansing. Affordable sessions. Sessions led by a metaphysical minister."
- "CLEAR KARMA NOW: Commander August Stahr offers 'Karma clearings by phone.'"
- "TRAVEL AROUND THE NATIVE AMERICAN AND CELTIC MEDICINE WHEEL . . . different journeys each week . . . $20 session."
- "AN EVENING WITH XANDO, channeled by G_. Donation. XANDO is a composite of six angelic beings."
- "POWER NEGOTIATION SKILLS. You will learn to: Formulate and dovetail outcomes for Win-Win results. Preserve the relationship while achieving your outcome. Apply these skills to business, personal, and family issues . . . $250 at the door." (In other words, learn to manipulate others blind.)
- "GRANDFATHER OF THE NEW AGE REVEALS MYSTERIES: Now nearing 70 years of age, N_ is considered the leading expert on crystal skulls. . . . They are thought to be at least 10,000 to 20,000 years old. A three-day retreat will cost $149, plus transportation to and from Arizona, plus $25 a night at the Healing Center, plus $5 for breakfast and lunch, plus $7 dinner."
- "LOVESTAR INSTITUTE. Holistic Health Psychologist Thanatologist (grief) Counselor." (Good grief!)
- "I AM A CLAIRVOYANT CHANNELER OF MULTIDIMENSIONS: Sit in the presence of Ascension and Dolphin energy attunement while receiving important messages and answers to your delicate and urgent questions."

Heard enough? If not, contact Whole Life Times, P.O. Box 1187, Malibu, CA 90265, 310/317-4200. Tell them Xando sent you.

Los Angeles County

Map of Los Angeles County—Page 156

were brought in, first-rate plays were staged, and blue-ribbon orchestras performed. All the while, the gondoliers kept singing.

Kinney's noble experiment failed, culminating in a poorly attended and abbreviated run of *Camille* starring Sarah Bernhardt, the greatest stage actress of her day. Visitors to Venice, it turned out, preferred sand and sidewalks to the interior of a concert hall. To salvage his enormous investment, the dauntless Kinney did an about-face, filling in a number of his festering, plant-choked canals and bringing in sideshow freaks, street theater, and a roller coaster. A miniature railroad was built to run along with the Ocean Front Walk, turning the town into an amusement park by the sea. In 1925 the little town became part of Los Angeles. By 1939 Kinney's conversion was complete, with Venice known as "the Playland of the Pacific" and "the Coney Island of the West."

Venice has since undergone other transformations. It was covered with oil wells, low-income housing, and boarded-up slums in the 1940s. It was adopted by beatniks in the 1950s, hippies in the 1960s, artists and fitness freaks in the 1970s, and gentrified homeowners—the original audience Kinney had dreamed of for Venice—in the 1980s. In the 1990s Venice still lives in a dream, as it always has, perceiving itself as some sort of impervious Left Bank, but one beset by problems.

Granted, certain aspects of Venice's surreal sideshow are real and fascinating. There's the endless parade of oddballs who entertain for spare change along Ocean Front Walk, the cement boardwalk that runs along the backside of Venice Beach. Although this pedestrian thoroughfare is only seven-tenths of a mile long, it is light-years beyond whatever else passes for cutting edge elsewhere in America. The best place to start a walk-through is at the Windward Avenue access, the halfway point in the human parade. Here you'll find the classic Venice on the Half Shell mural, which captures the spirit of the procession. It may sound like a cliché, but you really are likely to see anything out here. The following are just some of the things we've witnessed: guy in a turban chewing glass; guy on a unicycle juggling knives; another unicyclist juggling chainsaws; legless, armless dwarf dancing on his stumps to Latin disco music; assortment of Michael Jackson impersonators, with proud mamas pocketing the donations; "post tribal artist"; cabalistic Tarot reader; a village shaman offering a spoken "love revival"; a gypsy performing "three-day dissolving marriage ceremonies"; folk performers with purple hair; ancient black woman shrieking incoherent blues while strumming an electric guitar lent her by a well-meaning college kid; body piercers; hair braiders; X-rated comedians; conceptual artists; mural artists; caricaturists; acrobats; animals performing stupid pet tricks; transvestites; leather freaks; Rastafarians; punks, drunks, and punch-drunks; and some people who are really and truly insane.

Along this same route you'll find a few passable bars, some decent takeout food stalls, a good book shop, and a museum of Native American art. Hang around long enough and you'll also absorb the prevailing Venetian outlook: a healthy and well-cultivated disregard for chicness, big money, and normal ways of doing things.

Away from the curious clamor on Ocean Front Walk, Venice reveals another side of itself—a pleasant residential community of 50,000 filled with proud homeowners who casually enjoy the placid life along the town's back canals. In the past few years, the more secluded canals have been cleaned up, and fish are even seen in the no-longer-murky waters. The Canal Walk—between Washington Boulevard and Rose Avenue—is part of the Venice Canal Historic District, which is listed on the National Register of Historic Places. Walking here is an enjoyable and quiet diversion as you observe the fascinating and eclectic architecture and the commendable lengths that the resi-

Map of Southern California—Page 9

dents have gone to turn the tiniest plots of land into gardening masterpieces.

Community leaders regularly organize cleanups, and ad hoc action, block parties, and neighborhood watches have made inroads on crime prevention. Venice is not about to let the town go to seed as it did in the past.

The best way to see the full tableau that Venice has to offer is to book a walking tour through the **Venice Historic Society** (310/392-1014). The tour costs around $7.50, and reservations must be made ahead of time.

Although the fear of crime is less intense now, and neighborhood pride and vigilance is at an all-time high, Venice still has a ways to go. There are parts of town that even the police have been hesitant to patrol. During one of our visits, a group of Los Angeles's finest staged a protest at being transferred to the Venice beat.

We were warned repeatedly about a trend in urban crime that has been particularly prevalent in Venice: bike-jacking. Meanwhile, a beachside pavilion smells of human waste and is so thick with graffiti that you have to look closely to make out this sign: "Notice—Defacing Park Property May Result in a Maximum Penalty of $500 Fine and Six Months in Jail." At the south end of Venice Beach, the gazebos along Ocean Front Walk have not been closed down but might as well be to anyone who doesn't regularly urinate outdoors. We met a Dutch fellow who had a word for the less savory side of Venice: *onguur.* Though he claimed it was untranslatable, his facial expression told us all we needed to know. Venice can be real *onguur* sometimes.

None of this stems the flow of onlookers in Venice. Perversely, the sense of forbidden danger seems to add to its appeal. And so goes Venice, into the setting sun of the California dream, once delicious and golden, and now. . . .

Well, we'll close with a quote from one of Venice's stellar residents, Orson Bean, who wrote in *Venice* magazine: "Venice of America dares you to be happy. Someone once wrote

that the most revolutionary act possible might be three straight days of continuous happiness. People walk in Venice. They roller-skate and bicycle and skateboard. They rally to save ducks. They don't mind looking like fools. They figure everyone else enjoys it when they look like fools, so why shouldn't they?"

Beaches

Venice City Beach has never looked better. It is an amazingly wide sheet of sand, running for two miles north from Venice Pier to Santa Monica Pier. People use this beautiful, wide porch of sand for all the normal activities—swimming, sunning, hanging out—but the dimensions of the beach are so large that their numbers seem deceptively small.

The beach itself is spiked by three enormous jetties and was widened by sand dredged from the site of the massive Hyperion Sewage Treatment Plant. The most intriguing area is at the north end, where a weightlifting area attracts body freaks and has earned the name "Muscle Beach." Some incredible games of basketball are played on the nearby blacktop, with occasional visits from pro stars. The paddletennis games are as intense as any matches at Wimbledon. The beach can be accessed from any of the main east-west streets in Venice (Washington Street, Venice Boulevard, Rose Avenue, Windward Avenue, Park Boulevard) or from anywhere on the Ocean Front Walk promenade. Metered parking is available along any of these thoroughfares as well.

Bunking Down

No matter how cutting edge you feel, you do not want to stay in Venice. For one thing it's unpredictable and sometimes unsafe after dark. For another there's really not much to choose from in the way of accommodations, unless you rent a beachfront villa by the week (and that is shockingly expensive). Visit for the day and buy a T-shirt, hot dog, and a slab of pizza. Watch the street performers, then quietly take your leave, preferably back to the hotels of Marina del Rey.

All things considered, we fared okay the one time we did stay in Venice. We found a room at the **Venice Beach Hotel** (25 Windward Avenue, 310/399-9914, $). Once known as "Cotel," short for "community hotel," it is primarily for international travelers on a tight budget. A hostel, if you will, only a notch nicer. The rooms are spartan but clean, with no TV or air-conditioning and shared bathrooms, and the security is reassuringly tight (you must be buzzed in). Most of the foreigners we met at the hotel claimed to be afraid to leave it. They weren't shrinking violets, by any means; we're talking hale and hardy Europeans in their 20s who had seen their share of world travel. After experiencing Venice at night, though, they preferred the hotel's hospitality room—now expanded into "the Interclub"—to the bars and clubs on the streets below. After a few night moves of our own around Venice, we saw their point and gladly joined them.

The best compromise between Venice access and a safe and quiet stay is the **Inn at Venice Beach** (327 Washington Boulevard, 310/821-2557, $$). The rooms are clean and cheerful, and continental breakfast is served in an airy courtyard. Europeans are smitten with this place. And it's just three blocks from Venice Pier.

Coastal Cuisine

In Venice you take the bad with the good. And some good old reliables are still around. During the day the **Sidewalk Cafe** (1401 Ocean Front Walk, 310/399-5547, $) is the best vantage point from which to observe the human circus. The items on the menu have been given literary names, because the café adjoins the excellent Small World Bookstore. Breakfast, for example, can consist of an omelette named after Gertrude Stein, Carlos Castaneda, or Jack Kerouac. Lunch could be a burger named for Charles Dickens, Pablo Neruda, or James

Michener. (The latter, logically enough, features pineapples and ham.) The best place for coffee and conversation is **The Cow** (34 Washington Boulevard, $), a local hangout.

Two arrivals in Venice worth considering are the **West Beach Cafe** (60 North Venice Boulevard, 310/823-5396, $$$) and **72 Market Street** (72 Market Street, 310/392-8720, $$$). The former is a crowded, casual establishment specializing in California cuisine. 72 Market Street features "good-old American classics with a twist."

Night Moves

We first read about aromatherapy, a New Age form of healing, in a Venice weekly devoted to planetary health. This therapy is based on the belief that your nose takes in "essential oils" vital to your well-being. When unhealthy, you simply need to inhale the proper mix of oils until you're good as new. Depression, for example, can be cured by inhaling the following herbs: basil, bergamot, chamomile, clary, lavender, marjoram, rosemary, and ylang-ylang.

After sampling Venice both by day and night, we have devised our own form of aromatherapy, which we'd like to share with anyone who has grown sick and tired of life back home. Go to the south end of Venice City Beach at the end of a long, hot summer day. Stand anywhere along Ocean Front Walk and breathe deeply, keeping your mouth closed so as to maximize the essential oils your nose takes in. We promise that you'll be exclaiming "there's no place like home" in short order.

If you wish to pick through the olfactory minefield of Venice after dark, the **Town House** (52 Windward Avenue, 310/392-4040) is the place to rock out. Large and loud enough for the rowdiest bike gang, the Town House features live rock and roll most nights in summer. If you're looking for a more civilized alternative, amble up Washington Street in the direction of Marina del Rey, where you'll find coffeehouses, sports bars, and cantinas galore.

Map of Southern California—Page 9

Hinano (15 Washington Boulevard, 310/822-3902) is a "brasserie de Tahiti," a fancy way of saying friendly beach bar. Pool tables in one room, booths in the other room, Hinano is what a locals' hangout ought to be. Help yourself to free popcorn out of an old machine, order a pitcher of beer, and set a spell. What a stark contrast from **Ocean Front Cafe** (10 Washington Boulevard, 310/821-8737), the other pier-hugging bar across the street, a suffocating place that cranks up the volume in a mind-less and forced manner. We saw a dreadful karaoke duo—two valley girls dressed head to toe in black—segueing from Stevie Nicks to Bad Company. On their tip bucket was this notice: "Tip or die." We did neither, and were gone faster than you can say "Hinano."

For More Information

Venice Chamber of Commerce, P.O. Box 202, Venice, CA 90291, 310/396-7016, website: www.venice.net

Santa Monica

The most "urban" of Los Angeles's beach communities, Santa Monica (population 85,000) is a showcase for much of the best, and some of the worst, that the city has to offer. The town has a temperate, even climate—perfect for those who live outdoors or play so much in it that they might as well be doing so themselves. After the "June gloom" has run its course, the weather in Santa Monica is dependably good the rest of the year.

Santa Monica's beach is where the heart and soul of Los Angeles comes to have fun in the summer. It serves as the steam-release valve for Los Angeles's vast and diverse population, a no-frills playland that attracts close to 15 million visitors a year. That's about a quarter of the total load borne by all the beaches in Los Angeles County. Santa Monica is easily accessible to all. Perhaps for this reason it suffers in comparison to its more glittery neighbors up toward Malibu and down by Manhattan Beach. At Santa Monica it's just good people having a high old time at the beach, many of whom speak English only as a second language. Without Santa Monica in the summertime, Los Angeles would be one big, smog-laced pressure cooker.

In the process of serving as the city's back door to the beach, Santa Monica somehow manages to maintain a character and charm all its own. Grandeur and squalor are mixed here in unequal proportions, creating an appealing blend of tropical rot and urban cool that Raymond Chandler captured in his detective novels. (His fictional "Bay City" was modeled after Santa Monica.) Chandler's subterranean noir universe is but a flickering image now, seen in the architectural splendor of some of the older apartment buildings and the art deco facades of the theaters. The city is in what might be called a period of transition, as it has been for several years. Many buildings are boarded up, some are being torn down, and other marginal properties await the inevitable.

An attempt has been made to revive downtown Santa Monica, adding pedestrian shopping malls and multiscreen cinemas in hopes of bringing back the healing plasma of money that fled to the hills in the 1980s. It seems to have worked. At last count we found over 70 museums and galleries, 12 book shops, and more coffee shops than Dublin has pubs in Santa Monica's 8.3 square miles. The epicenter of this downtown renewal is the Third Street Promenade. This brick pedestrian walkway courses through four blocks of storefronts, from Colorado Avenue to Wilshire Boulevard, running parallel to the beach from three blocks back. There are several good book shops along Third Street, notably **Midnight Special** (1318 Third Street Promenade, 310/393-2923), a haven for browsers who poke about for hours among the floor to ceiling titles.

Los Angeles County

Beach Flicks

Endless Summer II, released in 1994, didn't capture the imagination of young America the way the original *Endless Summer* did in 1966. Of course the Beach Boys, the Ventures, and Jan and Dean had musically paved the way for Bruce Brown's first documentary on surfing, as Jack Kerouac's *On the Road* had put the car in gear before that.

Even before Brown's watershed flick, there were several attempts to capture the burgeoning surf culture on celluloid. Most were lame, stilted, and inaccurate—as are all attempts by adults to understand "youth culture." One thing these movies did accomplish—for which we're personally grateful—was to infuse California (and, to a lesser extent, Hawaii) with a sort of mythical, sirenlike power. As a result, everyone in America at one time or another has wanted to live beside a California beach. Here are capsule summaries of some of the best and worst of the beach flicks:

• *Back to the Beach* (1987)—Frankie, Annette, and the gang, which now includes the likes of Bob Denver (a.k.a. Gilligan) and Pee Wee Herman (a.k.a. "mud"), attempt to re-create the spirit of their early-1960s beach flicks in the late-1980s. They should've heeded the words of Thomas Wolfe when he wrote, "You can't go home again."

• *Beach Ball* (1964)—A hokey ripoff of *Beach Party* with a threadbare plot having to do with a music-store owner and a band called "the Wigglers," it stars Edd "Kookie" Byrnes and features performances by the Walker Brothers, Jerry Lee Lewis, the Four Seasons, the Nashville Teens, the Righteous Brothers, and the Supremes. Decent soundtrack, rotten movie.

• *Beach Blanket Bingo* (1965)—Buster Keaton makes an appearance, rescuing this Frankie Avalon and Annette Funicello farce, based on the latter's reaction to the former's crush on a bimbo named Sugar Cane.

• *Beach Party* (1963)—The first in the Frankie and Annette beach sagas, this had the redeeming presence of Dick Dale and the Deltones performing "Surfin' and A Swingin'" and "Secret Surfin'," plus some of the world's first surf punks, led by notorious Erich Von Zipper. This movie also had an original plot idea: an anthropologist studies surf culture through a telescope. Hey, maybe this is where Tom Wolfe got his inspiration for *The Pump House Gang*!

Los Angeles County

Though this mall dispenses the usual trendy consumer flotsam, the experience of walking through it is spiced by some unique street performers. In fact, these performers lend the promenade a flavor more distinctive than the shops. The Third Street brigade is more talented, and less scatological and dangerous, than the ragtag army in Venice. A string quartet composed of conservatory students plays Vivaldi beautifully. A small ensemble cranks out a huge big-band sound. A lonely jazzman offers mournful blues on the vibes. An old man with an ashen face sings Willie Nelson's "On the Road Again" and yodels while standing

Map of Southern California—Page 9

- **Bikini Beach** (1964)—Here's another Frankie and Annette vehicle lacking a full tank of gas, although it turns on a potentially hilarious idea—spoofing the Beatles via a teen idol named the Potato Bug. Little Stevie Wonder performs "Fingertips."

- **Blue Hawaii** (1961)—Elvis Presley stars in this sandy epic, the most intriguingly perverse aspect of which is the soundtrack, boasting winners like "Slicin' Sand," "Beach Boy Blues," and "Ito Eats."

- **Catalina Caper** (1967)—Set on the island jewel off the coast of Los Angeles, this film has the all-time greatest musical concept: Little Richard singing "Scuba Party."

- **Clambake** (1967)—The King bakes some clams, makes some clams, and goes to Las Vegas afterward to make even more. He's a water-ski instructor in this one.

- **Ghost in the Invisible Bikini** (1966)—Monsters go to the beach, with Boris Karloff and Basil Rathbone trading spooky taunts amidst the beach blankets. Gnarly.

- **Girls on the Beach** (1965)—A sorority tries to raise funds with a rock concert. They want the Beatles to perform, but they have to settle for the Beach Boys, with equally happy results. It also includes songs by the Crickets and Leslie Gore.

- **How to Stuff a Wild Bikini** (1965)—Frankie, Annette, and Erich Von Zipper reprised. In this one, Frankie hires a witch doctor to keep an eye on Annette while he is in the Navy Reserves. Mickey Rooney and Buster Keaton make cameos. You figure it out.

- **It's a Bikini World** (1967)—Tommy Kirk is sort of a poor man's Frankie Avalon. The Animals perform "We Gotta Get Out of This Place" (were they talking about this film?).

- **Muscle Beach Party** (1964)—Frankie and Annette (again) meet bodybuilders and an Italian countess, and the only winners are Dick Dale and the Deltones and Little Stevie Wonder.

- **Paradise—Hawaiian Style** (1966)—Although the hula dancers were required by film code to cover their navels under their hula skirts, the movie does have Elvis singing "Queenie Wahine's Papaya." For that, the world is eternally grateful.

- **Surf Party** (1964)—Set in Malibu, with songs by the Astronauts, the Routers, Bobby Vinton, and Jackie DeShannon.

- **Wild on the Beach** (1965)—The best thing about this beach-sploitation flick is the music: songs by the Astronauts ("Little Speedy Gonzalez," "Rock the World," "Snap It") and "Drum Dance," by the great Sandy Nelson.

on his head in a chair. Awesome! An atheist and a born-again Christian rant at each other through microphones; it is hard to decide who is the more repellent. Two silver-painted characters do coordinated, robotic choreography to hip-hop blaring from their boom box. Weird! The overwhelming feeling one gets while strolling Third Street is nostalgia for the grandeur that Santa Monica once represented. Many of the promenade businesses trade on nostalgia, re-creating the 1950s and '60s. The most popular eatery is a faux '50s diner. The hippest clothier is a thrift shop manqué that sells used clothing at boutique prices. (Ragged-looking

Map of Los Angeles County—Page 156

T-shirts for $18—what a concept!) The bars are upscale pool halls filled with yuppies slumming as bikers. The nicest theater is a beautifully restored 1940s film palace. Third Street is ultimately a mirage of fake evocations: the upscale, chrome-railed pool hall serves gourmet pizza, the '50s diner gleams with an antiseptic aura, and the mock-bohemian coffeehouses collect 18 dimes (instead of one) for a cup of coffee.

Only the presence of the homeless milling about soils the mood of sentimental yearning (unless you're nostalgic for the Great Depression). The collision of Santa Monica's downward mobility with its last-ditch attempts at creating an urban island of crime-free consumerism makes for an odd melange on the streets. We saw some strange scenes indeed. An executive in a designer running outfit was spitting orders into a mobile phone while roller-skating past a haggard woman on a bench who was flicking at invisible bugs, her belongings arrayed in bulging bags at her feet. It was hard to tell which of these two characters was more insane. Then there was the wraithlike, barefoot woman who punched the air like Fred Sanford, intimidating a striding stream of Docker shorts and Polo shirts into stepping out of her way. At a yogurt café she walked in, looked around, and snatched some food right off the plate of a startled German tourist. To curb such excesses in the city once known as "People's Republic of Santa Monica," stiff new laws on vagrancy, loitering, and overnight sleeping on the beach have been instituted.

In many ways Santa Monica remains the most appealing and unique place in Los Angeles. Certainly, it is among the last bastions of kindness, egalitarianism, and liberalism. Still, it is life lived at its extremes. On the one hand homeless occupy the parks and promenades, and proletarian hordes roam the beach and pier. On the other, luxury hotels overlook the ocean, and stores cater to people with too much disposable income. As is the case in most American cities

these days, there is no longer much in the way of a middle class or a happy medium.

Beaches

Santa Monica State Beach is easily accessible from downtown Los Angeles via the Santa Monica Freeway (I-10) or one of several primary east-west arteries (Pico, Wilshire, Santa Monica). Any number of bus lines start and end here as well. The dimensions of this beach are amazing: it is 3.3 miles long and several football fields wide. Generally it attracts a close-packed crowd of Hispanic families who bring beach towels and picnic baskets. South of Santa Monica Pier the blankets and bodies thin out. Two concrete walkways run parallel some distance back from the ocean. One ferries pedestrian traffic, while the other transports those on wheels. An army of mobile twenty- and thirty-something cyclists and inline skaters can be seen leaving vapor trails on the South Bay Bicycle Trail. You can park in state-run fee lots or take your chances feeding the meters on the streets.

The center of the action is **Santa Monica Pier,** which is among the best in the Golden State. The pier, originally built in 1874, is an antiquated slice of Americana, a West Coast Coney Island stocked with gaming arcades, T-shirt vendors (four for $10, rivaling Venice for, uh, value), fast-food stalls, and incongruously chic restaurants. This incarnation of the pier was built in 1909 but underwent a full-scale $12 million renovation completed in 1997. Tiny arcades flare off from the main concourse, creating an atmosphere not unlike the midway at a state fair. All the ingredients are here for kids to have a good time and for parents to get nostalgic about their own gloriously misspent youth: Skee-ball, basketball shoots, Wedges/Hedges, bumper cars, rocking horses, an antique carousel, and a gift shop where one can purchase a plaster cast of Elvis stranger than any to be found in Memphis.

Once part of a huge playland, replete with

a glamorous ballroom and famous "Blue Streak Racing Coaster," the old outlying structures fell to the wrecking ball some years ago, and all that remains is the pier. New cafés are planned for the future. For now, the fast-food stands are guaranteed to bring back memories of indigestion. Step right up for tacos, hot dogs, cotton candy, fried dough, and fish 'n' chips. Then head home for a large, cool drink of Alka-Seltzer.

We took our Skee-ball prizes (two tiny plastic rats and a thimble-sized trophy) and headed Back On the Beach. Yes, that's the name of a wonderful piazza on the sand, an invigorating half-mile hike north of the pier. A former private beach club and now a café with a seating capacity of 200, Back On the Beach (see "Coastal Cuisine") is a quintessential L.A. beach experience. You can eat a salad as an antidote to the pier food or simply sit back with a beverage and watch the passing parade on the South Bay Bicycle Trail. President Clinton chose this spot for his morning jog when he was in the city, and Al Pacino is regularly seen here. Even more telling is the fact that several episodes of *Beverly Hills 90210* were filmed here. Volleyball nets and playground equipment are nearby, for further diversions.

As for swimming, the waves at Santa Monica State Beach are sufficient to excite the tiny tots on their Styrofoam boards but not large enough to attract serious surfing. Several hundred yards south of the pier is the original **Muscle Beach,** where, since the 1930s, Conan-like men and women have been hoisting barbells all day long while lesser mortals stand around in the sand and applaud. Jack Lalane and Steve Reeves flexed their pecs here, and Mr. America and Mr. Universe contests have been held here. Down toward Venice you'll come to a sprawl of basketball and paddle-tennis courts, with grandstands beside them. Rest a spell and marvel at the athleticism of the men and women sweating in the sun.

The physical setting of the beach is almost as muscular as the weight lifters. Backed by a long, undeveloped bluff, Santa Monica's beach somehow seems tranquil even when thousands are jammed on the sand below—a glorious sight! Atop the bluff is Palisades Park, a shaded 26-acre jewel that runs for 14 city blocks from Colorado Avenue to Adelaide Drive. This green, shady buffer between the sand and the city is filled with benches and shuffleboard courts, and it's popular with Santa Monica's large contingent of senior citizens. It is also popular with the homeless. The two groups seem to coexist peacefully, though.

Given a city the size of Los Angeles, there are bound to be problems with its most popular beach. In the late 1980s Santa Monica Bay became a colostomy bag for the city's then sick body. The Hyperion Sewage Treatment Plant, a gargantuan facility that serves four million people and was once the pride and joy of Los Angeles (earning rapturous accolades from Aldous Huxley, of all people), broke down. Millions of gallons of raw sewage poured directly into Santa Monica Bay. This set off a chain reaction that brought the county sewage system and city government to near collapse. The mayor called for voluntary water conservation, but the filthy rich in Westside and the San Fernando Valley didn't go along with it, filling pools and watering lawns in protest. Water became even scarcer, exacerbating tensions with Arizona and Northern California. But, on the bright side, the pollution of the Santa Monica Bay provided the impetus for a slow-growth and eco-minded grassroots movement that has gained strength ever since. An organization called Heal the Bay has gone a great distance toward doing just that through environmental education and direct action.

Bunking Down

It is possible to stay near the beach in Santa Monica. Many hotels and motels, large and small, line Ocean Avenue a block or two from the pier and a pedestrian bridge away from

Map of Los Angeles County—Page 156

the beach. Staying here also solves your biggest beach problem, which is parking. Leaving your wheels in a hotel garage sure beats battling experienced, have-you-hugged-my-bumper-today natives, who will beat you to any available slot. There's only one drawback. Ocean Avenue can be loud, even at night. We learned this the hard way one year when we were younger and poorer, taking a room at the least expensive motel on the strip: a $40 jobbie. The price was cheap because it was a four-walled cell with rancid bedcovers and thin, lifeless pillows. *Caveat emptor.* These fleabags litter the roadside like yesterday's papers. Of all the smaller motels on Ocean Avenue, the **Breakers** (1501 Ocean Avenue, 310/451-4811, $$$) is the best. Of course, it is a bit expensive but solid as a rock and set off a bit from the traffic noise on the street.

A money transfusion in recent years has transformed the beachfront. Along with the older, dependable **Holiday Inn at the Pier** (120 Colorado Avenue, 310/451-0676, $$$), high-rise luxury hotels now tower over the Santa Monica Beach south of the pier. The cream of the crop is the **Loews Santa Monica Beach Hotel** (1700 Ocean Avenue, 310/458-6700, $$$$). It's an attractive upscale tower that somehow exudes a casual sort of class. (The additional parking charges aren't classy or casual, though.) The lobby alone is worth a look-see. You can hear the waves roll in from your balcony and watch the human parade roll by on the bike paths. At night milk and cookies are brought to guests' doors, providing a nice bedtime touch worthy of Mom.

Another recent arrival at Santa Monica Beach is **Le Merigot** (1740 Ocean Avenue, 310/395-9700), a J.W. Marriott Beach Resort. It's an opulent resort done in neutral tones. You're a block back from the beach, which is easily accessible via the pool area. The rooms and furniture are upscale and functional. A lobby bar and terrace make a good place to hang out and eavesdrop on conversations. One afternoon, we heard a bartender carry on about

the way things are in Los Angeles "Unlike back home, it's not enough just to say that you like a movie out here," he animatedly told an attentive imbiber while cleaning wine glasses. "You have to know the director and his previous work, who the key grip was, who cut the deal, how many theaters it opened at, and on and on. That's just the nature of the business out here. Everybody knows all the smallest details." We wondered how many hundred times he had jovially imparted this memorized speech, these same pearls of wisdom, to other strangers at the bar.

The spa at Le Merigot is not to be missed. A roomful of bikes and cardio machines, another full of free weights, and locker areas with eucalyptus steam room can all be used free of charge by guests. There's also an extensive menu of spa services. For a great workout, warm up on a stationary bike, use the Cybex machines and free weights, finish with an off-property run on the South Bay Bicycle Trail (down to Venice and back is about three miles), and then sit in eucalyptus-scented steam for as long as you can stand it. We did exactly that and had a very pleasant chat with Bill Bridges, a former pro basketball player for the L.A. Lakers. Known as a tough defender who snagged a lot of rebounds, Bridges talked hoops with us for half an hour—a great guy, and this was just one of those encounters that seems to happen in Los Angeles.

The **Bayside Hotel** (2001 Ocean Avenue, 310/396-6000, $$) earns the honor of being closest to the beach, which sits just across from it on a quiet loop road in an otherwise residential neighborhood. Nearby, the **Santa Monica Travelodge** (1525 Ocean Avenue, 310/451-0761, $$) offers the usual mid-scale chain amenities.

The retro-coolest place is **Hotel Shangri La** (1301 Ocean Avenue, 310/394-2791, $$), a seven-story art deco landmark built in 1939. It's gracefully anonymous, which is probably why people like Bill Murray and Diane Keaton stay here. Straight out of Miami's Art Deco District, the

Georgian Hotel (1415 Ocean Avenue, 310/451-3374, $$$) is an architectural wonder.

Coastal Cuisine

The Lobster (1602 Ocean Avenue, 310/458-9294, $$$$) has one of the finest settings anywhere, overlooking the Santa Monica Pier, the Pacific Ocean, and the Santa Monica Mountains. It goes without saying that you want to be here at sunset. But that's far from the only reason you'd come here. The food is sensational. The namesake lobster preparations cannot be beat. One of us ordered a pan-roasted 1.5-pound lobster served atop a bed of tomato risotto. The dish was not inexpensive ($45), but the splurge was worth it. You might get Pacific spiny lobster when they're in season (usually September through February); otherwise, your crustacean will be from Maine. Another of us had seared ahi served atop lightly sautéed greens, mushrooms, artichoke slivers, and more. Aside from being an incredible blend of flavors, it makes one feel instantly healthier.

It's hard to make a rational choice from a menu that is so appealing from top to bottom. The clams and mussels, served in a tasty, briny broth that can be eaten like soup or sopped up with bread, is a top entrée. And the desserts! After eating heartily, we recommend something fruity and fresh like Ciao Bella sorbet (a homemade strawberry sorbet served with berries) or blueberry cobbler. Beyond the superb food and view, the people-watching is not to be missed. Pay attention and you'll get a sense of how Los Angeles ticks: movers and shakers on the make, either sealing deals via cell phone or charming their consorts at the table. The energy level at the Lobster is high, the experience of dining here memorable.

The best quick bite is down at Back On the Beach (445 Palisades Road, 310/393-8282, $$), and a convenient quick morning hit can be had at Starbucks (Third Street Promenade, 310/260-9947, $). At the latter Charles Bukowski wannabes nurse bottomless mugs and work on their angst. Dinner is another matter. Santa Monica is home to some of Los Angeles's finest dining. Famed chef Wolfgang Puck's Chinois On Main (2709 Main Street, 310/392-9025, $$$$) is a celebrated bastion of haute cuisine blending French, Chinese, and Japanese elements. Rocken Rolls, chef Hans Rockenwagner's fast-food kiosk at the Third Street Promenade, is as popular as the French contemporary cuisine at his Rockenwagner restaurant and bakery (2435 Main Street, 310/399-6504, $$$$).

But we wanted seafood. We found it, sort of, at Chez Jay (1657 Ocean Avenue, 310/395-1741, $$). It's a longtime popular beach hangout run by a guy who once hunted pirate treasure. His signature dish is "spuds fried with bananas"—real surfer food that, along with his steaks, chops, and seafood, has been pleasing palates for 35 years. Nearby, another oceanfront landmark, Ivy at the Shore (1541 Ocean Avenue, 310/393-3113, $$$), serves American fare in a tropical setting adjacent to the ocean. Down toward Venice, two blocks from the ocean, is Santa Monica Fish Company (174 Kinney Street, 310/392-8366, $$), housed in an impressive ivy-covered warehouse. All the entrées, especially the local catches, are nicely prepared.

We couldn't resist a drive inland for some stargazing and schmoozing, so we did as the Clampetts did, loading up our wallets and going to Beverly . . . Hills that is. The Elysian Fields of schmoozing is The Palm (9001 Santa Monica Boulevard, 310/550-8811, $$$). It's a piece of Manhattan at the end of California's rainbow, and we were told, "If you sit at the bar for a week in the Palm, you will meet anyone you care to know." We didn't have a week, but we did lunch and met Sandy Koufax. Enough said.

One of our old favorites from Malibu, the Reel Inn (1220 Third Promenade, 310/395-5538, $$), has opened what to our taste buds is the best food joint on Third Street Promenade. You order at the front, picking your fresh line-caught fish from the display case (try the

Cajun-blackened halibut or simply grilled ahi tuna), then retreat to a picnic table until your name is called. They slop some good stuff, like Cajun rice, home fries, and coleslaw, next to it, and you're in business. Entrées start at $7.95, making the Reel Inn a real bargain. Real upscale seafood is found at Shutters on the Beach Hotel, which has the stylish One Pico (1 Pico Boulevard, 310/587-1717, $$$), as well as the pleasant Pedals Cafe right on the bike path. Pedals is a great brunch spot on weekends, with indoor and outdoor dining areas and menu choices that range from creative omelettes to grilled salmon. Look both ways before crossing because the path narrows in front of Pedals, and bikers and skaters rarely slow down.

Night Moves

Santa Monica is only one boulevard (Sunset, Wilshire, or Santa Monica) away from Hollywood. Pick up the latest copy of *L.A. Weekly, L.A. Reader, Rave!* magazine, or the *Los Angeles Times* to find out what's doing in town. The detailed listings for each night of the week will give you some idea of what the term "free will" means. It's difficult to comment in much detail about a scene as extensive as the one in Los Angeles To a pair of beach bums who have been denied good music in more beach towns than we care to count, Santa Monica and Los Angeles are almost too much of a good thing. If only it could be spaced out evenly over both coasts. . . .

The biggest musical waves on the beachfront can be ridden at Rusty's Surf Ranch (256 Santa Monica Pier, 310/393-PIER), which offers "alternative funk," "masterful power pop," and other hip goodies (as well as pool tables and a full menu) nightly. When we were in town, an adult musical comedy called "Butt Pirates of the Caribbean" was also being presented, no doubt starring a bunch of very jolly Rogers.

We next direct your attention to the vicinity of upper Santa Monica Boulevard, where the old guard clubs are still rocking the City of Angels—Club Lingerie, Whiskey a Go-Go, the Roxy, McCabe's, the Palomino. We unhesitatingly recommend the House of Blues Sunset Strip (8430 Sunset Boulevard, 323/848-5100), less exuberantly the Johnny Depp-owned Viper Room (8852 Sunset Boulevard, 310/358-1881). Every night in Los Angeles is a who's who of musicians. Closer to the beach, your main alternative is to stroll the Third Street Promenade (between Colorado Avenue and Wilshire Boulevard). Nondrinkers will dig the outdoor cafés, used book shops, street musicians, cinemas, and dessert places. Imbibers flock to Yankee Doodle's (1410 Promenade, 310/394-4632), a sports bar that epitomizes all that is faux-gettable about going out in the 1990s: overpaid yuppies affecting pirate kerchiefs and $1,000 leather jackets while playing pool and scarfing gourmet pizza. The drinks are overpriced. One large draft Fosters and a cranberry juice cost almost $10! We retreated to a corner and shot at the electronic basketball concession until our quarters ran out. You would do better to walk a little farther and seek solace at Anastasia's Asylum (1028 Wilshire Boulevard, 310/394-7113), a hip coffeehouse in the best sense. There's no cover charge, the local atmosphere is genuine, and there's live entertainment and a vegetarian menu.

For More Information

Santa Monica Convention and Visitor Bureau, 1400 Ocean Avenue, Santa Monica, CA 90405, 310/393-7593, website: www.santamonica.com; Santa Monica Chamber of Commerce, 501 Colorado Avenue, Suite 150, Santa Monica, CA 90401, 310/393-9825, website: www.smchamber.com

Map of Southern California—Page 9

Pacific Palisades

This community, nestled in the foothills of the Santa Monica Mountains from Chautauqua Boulevard to Malibu, is not a beach town, but it does look down on one of the loveliest stretches of the Pacific coast. Originally populated in the 1920s by Methodists who founded it as their "new Chautauqua," Pacific Palisades (population 23,000) is now the exclusive domain of the very rich. The streets, most of which branch off Sunset Boulevard, are winding, shaded routes, many ending in cul-de-sacs. Parts of Pacific Palisades are included on Hollywood celebrity bus tours.

We had another reason for visiting Pacific Palisades—a motive not unlike our quest for the ghost of Charles Bukowski in San Pedro (see writeup earlier in this chapter). Henry Miller retired here after Big Sur became too unnavigable for his aged body. He spent his happiest golden days riding "his best friend" (a bicycle) around these lovely streets. It was while pursuing the vision of this sweet old man that we stumbled upon the **Self-Realization Fellowship Lake Shrine** (17190 Sunset Boulevard, 310/454-4114), a 10-acre "wall-less temple," bird sanctuary, sunken garden, and altar to the "five major religions of the world." Fitting, somehow, that Henry Miller spent his final days nearby.

Beaches

Pacific Palisades puts its ocean frontage to good use. It is the site of a state beach named after our most famous cowboy-philosopher. **Will Rogers State Beach** is a sandy swath three miles long that's a favorite of sun-bronzed locals who are serious about their volleyball game and their tans. Its proximity to Hollywood makes it one of the more popular beaches in Los Angeles County. Furthermore, it is the starting point for the South Bay Bicycle Trail, which ends 20 miles later down at Torrance County Beach. That said, we'd take Zuma State Beach, up in Malibu, over Will Rogers any day. The scenery is better and the distance from the highway madness makes Zuma more appealing.

Incidentally, if you want to dig further into the life of the man who never met a man he didn't like, Rogers's 187-acre ranch is open to the public as **Will Rogers State Historical Park** (1501 Will Rogers State Park Road, 310/454-8212). Tours of the main house and grounds are offered daily, and one can also hike through the vast natural area or ride on equestrian trails.

Coastal Cuisine

Pacific Palisades has got little, if anything, to offer travelers in the way of accommodations and nightlife, being a predominantly ritzy and privacy-hoarding residential community. However, it's got a dandy restaurant on the beach that ranks among the best on the coast. **Gladstone's 4 Fish Restaurant** (17300 Pacific Coast Highway, 310/454-3474, $$$$) is indeed the place to go "4 fish" in Los Angeles County. It's worth the drive, worth the wait, and worth the price. Barrels of unshucked peanuts are set out for waiting patrons to munch on, and the oceanside location makes for superb sunset-watching. The portions are huge and the menu expansive at Gladstone's. Prime seafood entrées run in the $18–23 range and include such items as mesquite-grilled sea bass and ahi rolled in Cajun spices, then seared and cooked rare. Appetizers include plump, cold Pacific oysters, as well as ceviche salad and marinated calamari. A sashimi dinner offers a filling platter of raw seafood delights. King and queen crab legs (the latter are slightly saltier and smaller, though still huge) are worth the $30 or so you'll plunk down for them. What you can't eat at Gladstone's will be wrapped by your server in gold foil and twisted to resemble a seabird or fish—a signature touch that completes a very satisfying dining experience.

Los Angeles County

Pollution Report Card: L.A. County Beaches

So you've made it to Malibu and would love to lay eyes on one of the many celebrities from the entertainment community who make their home here. But you discover that their exclusive Malibu Colony is a gated and off-limits fortress. There's just no way for an ordinary peon from Pasadena to slip past security. Not to worry! Just head on over to Surfrider Beach, one of Malibu's largest and most popular spots to surf and swim, and hop in the water. You may wind up indirectly having a close encounter with a celebrity, or a whole bunch of them, when fecal coliform bacteria from overflowing septic tanks in the private colony gets washed into the ocean and travels with the currents to the beaches that lie due south.

Gross as it sounds, this is exactly what is happening in the waters off Surfrider Beach, where a combination of sources that the government hasn't the time, money, or inclination to untangle has been fouling the water with bacteria and sickening those who swim here with a variety of ailments that range from ear and eye infections to gastrointestinal bugs. The chief culprit is outflow from Malibu Lagoon, which serves as a catch basin for all sorts of disgusting muck. In addition to the septic tanks of Malibu Colony, culprits include doo-doo from waterbirds, urban runoff from the 110-square-mile watershed that drains into Malibu Creek, runoff from soil tilling and animal waste, and refuse from homeless encampments near Malibu Civic Center. Unlike the vast majority of beaches that border Santa Monica Bay, bacterial levels at Surfrider generally remain high during both wet and dry weather.

The picture doesn't improve much as you move down the coast. Will Rogers State Beach, in Pacific Palisades, is another pollution hot spot. For many years industrial operations such as the Chevron oil refinery and Hyperion Sewage Treatment Plant were to blame. But under pressure from environmental groups like Heal the Bay, they've gone a long way toward cleaning up their act. Chevron voluntarily extended its wastewater discharge pipes from 300 to 3,000 feet offshore and also provided funding for a pilot epidemiological study to determine the causes and prevalence of illness among bay-area beachgoers.

The guiltiest contributors to the bay's bacterial stew these days are the citizens of Los Angeles themselves. Fertilizer runoff from lawns, oil and antifreeze dumped into sewers, and garbage tossed into streets and gutters all find their way into the bay via storm drains during periods of rain. Piers are another source of human-generated contaminants that stress the bay. Eight native species of fish have been found to be contaminated with DDT and PCBs, severe and persistent toxins that were dumped into the bay during the '60s. They

Los Angeles County

are very slow to break down in the cold, mucky bay bottom where they reside and are still working their way up through the food chain.

Even national organizations such as the Natural Resource Defense Council (NRDC) have joined advocacy groups like Heal the Bay, the Surfrider Foundation, and Oceana in calling for solutions to ocean pollution. As an attorney for NRDC noted, "A relaxing day at the beach may actually be a hazard to your health." If you're concerned, take a stand and get involved. By law the beaches belong to everybody and, by God, everyone should be upset about what's happening to them.

For more information, contact the following organizations:

Heal the Bay
3220 Nebraska Avenue
Santa Monica, CA 90404
310/463-0395
website: www.healthebay.org
Heal the Bay is an increasingly powerful foundation that started out in a living room and grew to an organization with 10,000 volunteers, all upset with the condition of Santa Monica Bay. Their goal is to achieve a "fishable, swimmable, surfable" bay, and they do it by lobbying, educating the public, and barraging the media with facts, figures, and photographs. They were responsible for stopping the county of Los Angeles from dumping sewage sludge into the bay. "We know that if we get the word out that our beaches are threatened, people will take action and we will see results," executive director Adi Liberman has said. Now they monitor water quality on beaches up and down the coast and "fight to find workable solutions to the problems threatening the future of our bay and all of Southern California's coastal waters. "

Surfrider Foundation
P.O. 6010
San Clemente, CA 92674
949/492-8170
website: www.surfrider.org
In 1984 this environmental action group was founded in Malibu by surfers who saw their beloved ocean growing filthier by the day. Today, their ranks have swelled to 35,000 members in 60 chapters, with headquarters in San Clemente. Their high-profile victories have included successfully suing pulp mills for polluting Humboldt Bay and halting plans to construct a mile-long breakwater off Imperial Beach. Their Blue Water Task Force collects ocean samples for water-quality testing. They'd rather be surfing (who wouldn't?), but they've responded to the mandate for action. As former executive director Jake Grubb told Rolling Stone: "When I started surfing these waters in the early 1960s, they were green and blue. Today, they're gray or brown."

Continued on next page

Los Angeles County

Map of Los Angeles County—Page 156

Continued from previous page
Oceana
6030 Wilshire Boulevard, Suite 400
Los Angeles, CA 90036
323/936-8242
website: www.oceana.org
In 1987 Ted Danson founded American Oceans Campaign, a Santa Monica-based organization that warned people about ocean and beach pollution and educated policymakers and the public about the need to preserve and restore our shorelines. "Oceans and beaches used to be visually pleasing," Danson said in a 1995 interview. "They took your breath away and made you feel good about being alive. Now they're lined with wall-to-wall condominiums. Because of the sheer number of people, water supplies are overburdened and breaking down." Danson first got involved with the beach nearest his home—Will Rogers State Beach—and after successfully fighting the oil companies on offshore drilling, started AOC, which merged with Oceana. This larger international advocacy exists for the "sole purpose of protecting the world's oceans to sustain the circle of life."

For More Information

Pacific Palisades Chamber of Commerce, 15330 Antioch Street, Pacific Palisades, CA 90272, 310/459-7963, website: www.palisadeschamber.com

Malibu

Malibu might seem to the outside world to be some ultra-chic celebrity enclave accessible only to camera crews from *Lifestyles of the Rich and Famous,* but nothing could be farther from the truth. The fact is, there are really two Malibus. The better known of these is the "inner" Malibu—the film colony, the celebrity sandbox, the glamorous private world behind locked gates about which the rest of the world likes to fantasize. The "outer" Malibu is a 27-mile stretch of rugged coastline, plunging canyons, and towering mountains, running along the Pacific Coast Highway from Coastline Drive to the Ventura County line. Local boosters refer to the PCH through Malibu as "the longest main street in America." We like to think of it as Little Big Sur. This side of Malibu—a wild, winding corridor physically bounded by the Santa Monica Mountains and

Pacific Ocean—is accessible to all and yet is generally less familiar than the minuscule world of celebrity intrigue that makes Malibu an instant buzzword with readers and viewers of tabloid media.

The reality of Malibu (population 50,000) is very different from popular conceptions of it. Much of it is unforgiving and desolate. Steep mountains plunge to the sea, which crashes angrily against the rocks. The elements hang in precarious balance here, not infrequently tilting over into destructive chaos. Malibu is particularly subject to what native Southern Californians wearily refer to as their four seasons: fire, flood, mudslide, and earthquake. One must drive through Malibu ever vigilant for fallen rocks. Some of the cliff faces along the Pacific Coast Highway are raw where mighty chunks have torn loose and crashed onto the

Los Angeles County

roadway. Narrow ridgetops zigzag northward. Houses are hidden in the canyons between them. The hills are covered with dry, brown vegetation that turns green only when the winter rains come. The threat of fire is constant. Lightning, arson, or a careless match can ignite a blaze that, propelled by hot Santa Ana winds, is capable of racing toward the seaside colony at speeds of 100 miles per hour. The other calamity is mudslides: slow, brown waves of muck, rock, and debris that swallow up everything in their path, houses included. The elements play no favorites here. No matter how much clout they may have in Hollywood, those who live in Malibu have no control over the periodic disasters that plague the seaside colony. Nature does not obey directors' cues.

Still, those who make their residence here derive a perverse sort of pleasure from the challenges of living on the edge. Writer Joan Didion captured its allure in her 1978 essay "Quiet Days in Malibu," in which she wrote: "I had come to see the spirit of the place as one of shared isolation and adversity, and I think now that I never loved the house on the Pacific Coast Highway more than on those many days when it was impossible to leave it, when fire or flood had in fact closed the highway." A dissenting opinion was rendered in a *People* magazine cover story, which averred: "The plain truth is that [Malibu residents] are getting a noisy, shabby, perilous, and polluted pseudo-paradise."

The extent of the affront includes fecal pollution of the ocean (from untreated sewage and overflowing septic tanks) and not-infrequent offshore oil spills. Damaging waves from winter storms flood homes along eroded beaches in Malibu Colony. There is no beach out back of the Malibu Beach Inn.

Beach closures along Malibu's coast are not uncommon, due to high bacterial counts from human-generated sources of pollution. Breaches of Malibu Lagoon following heavy storms often send ribbons of foul, dark-stained water streaming into the waters near Surfrider Beach, causing mini-epidemics of nausea, vomiting, and diarrhea among surfers. One 21-year-old wave-rider—Erik Villanueva, a student at Pepperdine University, on the hills above Malibu—contracted Coxsackie B virus after paddling through a "dark stain" of pollution off Surfrider Beach in 1992. He has had two heart-transplant operations and is convinced ocean pollution is to blame. Such events have led to a frenzy of heavily funded studies looking for sources of pollution in the Malibu Creek watershed, studying illness among beachgoers throughout the bay, and monitoring the genetic material of pathogens found in the lagoon. This is another way of saying that life is not always a beach in Malibu. Surfrider Beach receives failing grades when tested for bacterial contamination.

All of this is in large part a consequence of the accelerating pace of development in Malibu. The colony has changed considerably since the late 1970s, when author Joan Didion wrote (in the essay cited earlier): "In a way it seems the most idiosyncratic of beach communities, 27 miles of coastline with no hotel, no passable restaurant, nothing to attract the traveler's dollar." Now, like every other conquered corner of America, there are plenty of hotels, tons of passable restaurants, and lots of places to spend your money, including sprawling malls that would have been unthinkable a decade ago.

In 1986 the California Coastal Commission adopted a land-use plan for Malibu that permitted significant retail growth in three areas: the Malibu Civic Center, the Point Dume/Paradise Cove area, and Pepperdine University. The same plan also okayed the construction of up to 6,582 new dwellings, nearly doubling the number that existed at that time. Many Malibu natives fought the plan, and one local activist griped, "They want to allow undisciplined, unbridled growth in Malibu." That seems to be what they're getting. In 1990 Malibu officially approved its incorporation as a

Los Angeles County

Art and History in Old Malibu

In search of art and/or history? There are two Malibu-area attractions to satisfy your hunger. The first is the J. Paul Getty Museum at the **Getty Center** (1200 Getty Center Drive, 310/440-7300). The much-hyped Getty Center, a cultural mecca, opened in 1997. This 110-acre "campus" is nestled in the Santa Monica foothills, overlooking Brentwood. The museum reflects Getty's lifelong interests as a collector of Greek and Roman antiquities, Renaissance and Baroque paintings, and European decorative arts. The museum building is a re-creation of the Villa dei Papiri, an ancient Roman country house, and the gardens are filled with plants and trees that might have been found there 2,000 years ago. The museum is open Tuesday and Wednesday 11 A.M.–7 P.M., Thursday and Friday 11 A.M.–9 P.M., and Saturday and Sunday 10 A.M.–6 P.M. Admission is free, but you're asked to make a "parking reservation" at least one month in advance, and parking costs $5.

Another curious diversion worth checking out is the historic **Adamson House and Malibu Lagoon Museum** (23200 Pacific Coast Highway, 310/456-8432), located a quick left turn north of Malibu Pier. The house and grounds formerly belonged to the Adamson family, daughter and son-in-law of the last owners of the Malibu Spanish Land Grant. They are now state property, open to the public Wednesday–Saturday 11 A.M.–2 P.M. Built in 1929, the house is a classic Moorish-Spanish Colonial Revival-style residence that serves as a museum of ceramic art and design. The fantastic flower gardens on the premises were created by covering the natural dunes with a layer of humus. History buffs should note that a historical marker commemorates this establishment as the probable site of explorer Juan Rodríguez Cabrillo's New World landing in 1542. He disembarked to greet the canoe-paddling Chumash and to claim all the lands of "Alta California" in the name of the king of Spain. Large-scale real-estate transactions such as this one were apparently a simple matter back then. You just stepped up to the counter, so to speak, and ordered.

Los Angeles County

city, something that had been rejected in ballot initiatives dating back to 1950.

The Malibu of today is a collage of the upscale and low-rent, plain and fancy, old and new. In certain ways Malibu still has an Old California feel to it, a wayback-machine aura evident in the unpretentious taverns and food stands that squat by the road, refusing to bend to trends. At the same time recent arrivals on the scene, most evidently the flashy Malibu Colony Mall, have altered the landscape so that it looks more like a Los Angeles suburb than the Malibu of old.

The real appeal of the place remains the elemental collision of geological opposites: ocean basin and mountain ridge. A drive up the Pacific Coast Highway through Malibu—particularly above Point Dume, where the development subsides—is a stunning and humbling encounter with nature in the raw. The unfolding panorama of beaches yields one remarkable vista after another.

Map of Southern California—Page 9

As for the highway, it's something of a bane in Malibu. At various points, especially along a four-mile stretch north of Topanga Canyon, it is subject to mass movements (falling rocks, landslides) from the unstable cliffs that were cut to build it. Traffic tramples through town on the four-lane Pacific Coast Highway like a stampede of cattle. On weekends the road jams to a standstill with carloads of Angelenos headed to their favorite north county beaches or to play with the boats they keep in Ventura County's yacht basins. Beach parking lots fill up quickly, and the overflow lines the highway shoulders in both directions. For pedestrians, dashing across the highway is a bit like playing Russian roulette.

A beach access point we attempted to reach during one such crossing nearly rendered us road kill. All that risk to check out a cement walk between buildings—one of the narrow accesses the California Coastal Commission has waged costly battles to establish, much to the chagrin of Malibu residents. Officially it is known as the Zonker Harris Accessway, after the *Doonesbury* cartoon character. Malibu is a thorn in the side of the Coastal Commission, as it is the most privatized stretch of California's coast and one near its largest population center.

On either side of it lies private property. You're reminded not to trespass, although California law does grant citizens the right to walk along the beach shoreward of the mean high-tide line. We did just that, ambling in the direction of the Malibu Pier past all manner of sunbathers (including some seminude beauties) who paid us no mind. The pier at Malibu is an old, broad-planked affair with a restaurant on the shore end. You can buy bait and tackle, obtain a fishing license, and charter a sportfishing boat at **Malibu Sport Fishing Landing** (23000 Pacific Coast Highway, 310/456-8030). At one time the modest commercial heart of Malibu, the pier area has been overtaken by all the new commercial develop-ment several miles north, near the fabled and private Malibu Colony.

The canyons of Malibu are cut with tortu-ous roads that wind through the Santa Monica Mountains. A drive up one of the canyon roads is a great way to pass a few hours, offering a mix of ocean vistas and mountain scenery as you make the jagged ascent. We went up Topanga Canyon Road and returned via Malibu Canyon Road, passing in a short time from cool sea level to broiling higher altitudes. Lay hands on a map of Malibu and design your own up-and-back route.

Beyond these suggestions you are more or less on your own in Malibu. Sometimes, you can be made to feel as unwanted as a stray dog shuffling along the side of the road. Unless you have a ton of money or know someone who lives here say, Larry Hagman or Goldie Hawn—you'll have a hard time fashioning any sort of extended vacation on the Malibu coast-line other than a camping trip. But, we'd rather be tenting beneath a stand of sycamores at Leo Carrillo State Beach than attempting celebri-ty sightings at Paradise Cove any day. When we think of Malibu, we think of the land, not the famous landowners.

Beaches

Because the terrain is so rugged, with the Santa Monica Mountains plunging steeply into the sea, the geography of the coastline makes for some amazing beaches along Malibu's 27 miles. About half of the Malibu coast (12.5 miles) is given over to state and county beaches, while the rest is under development. Surfrider, Zuma, and County Line are all names familiar to beachgoers and surfers worth their sea salt. But there are literally two dozen or so named beaches in Malibu. We'll hit the highlights.

Malibu's beach-erosion problems along the more developed areas southeast of Point Dume continue to worsen, as the ocean chomps hungrily at some of the most expensive real estate in the country. Out behind Gladstone's 4 Fish

Los Angeles County

Restaurant, straddling the line between Pacific Palisades and Malibu, breakers tenaciously whittle away the beachfront. A rock jetty built to keep the vanishing beach from retreating is fighting a losing battle as the sea steadily advances upon the establishment.

The first real beach in Malibu is **Topanga County Beach,** at the south end of Malibu, which runs for just over a mile. Like many in the area, it is narrow and rocky, set at the base of steep, eroding bluffs. Surfing is popular at the mouth of Topanga Creek, but there are too many rocks to allow for safe swimming along most of the beach. Above it is **Las Tunas County Beach,** a narrow, unimproved beach beneath the bluffs that holds a special attraction to surf casters.

Surfrider Beach is right up from the Malibu Pier. The beach covers 35 acres, including nearly a mile of ocean frontage. Its waves are perfectly formed and, even when small, carry surfers a good distance. The waves we've seen in summer are unspectacular in size but fascinating in form. Riding them, the surfers look as if they're walking on water, almost moving in slow motion, gliding in on perfectly shaped, long-cycle waves for what seems like an eternity. The beach is at the head of a dramatic, U-shaped cove. Kiddies, bronzed Adonises, and big-bellied men, plus the usual crew of noble surfers, pack the place. Ravishing California girls watch the guys work out on the volleyball courts or in the waves, which are fought over and claimed by the most skillful surfers. The only bum note is water quality, with bacterial contamination making wave-riding here tantamount to surfing in a petri dish. Adjacent to Surfrider is the small Malibu Lagoon Museum and Adamson House. The museum, Malibu Lagoon (at the mouth of Malibu Creek), Surfrider Beach, and the 700-foot Malibu Pier all fall within the boundaries of **Malibu Lagoon County Beach.** The lagoon is subject to contamination, and though the warm, protected waters are attractive to young children, it can be pretty scum-

my. Not for nothing does the county post advisories against swimming here.

Between Malibu Lagoon and Point Dume lie several small beaches worthy of mention. **Paradise Cove** is a private-fee beach in the heart of Malibu Colony, offering the likeliest chance of celebrity sightings. Unlike whale-watching expeditions, however, a sighting is not guaranteed. The entrance fee lands you on a beach with a short pier and a wonderful view of the opposing sandstone bluffs of Point Dume and the Santa Monica Mountains. **Escondido Beach,** at the mouth of Escondido Creek, can be reached via a stairway near Malibu Cove Colony Drive; it's a good diving area but otherwise not worth the trouble. Close by is **Dan Blocker County Beach** (formerly Corral State Beach), a lifeguarded beach (in season) that draws some surfers and divers. The beach is narrow and rocky, there are few facilities, and only roadside parking. But it's a great spot for scuba enthusiasts.

Much like the coastline in Laguna Beach and La Jolla, Malibu's is intercut with coves, many of them accessible by stairways and paths if you know what you're looking for. Keep your eyes open for some of these spots between Topanga Beach and Paradise Cove (they are numerous). Also, be prepared to park on the highway and deal with hazardous crossings. Just for the record, there are public-access stairways to the beach on the following numbered blocks of the Pacific Coast Highway: 20000, 20350, 24318, 24434, 24602, 24714, 25118, 31200, and 31344.

Around the tip of Point Dume is **Point Dume County Beach** (a.k.a. Westward Beach), on Westward Beach Road. Nearby **Zuma County Beach** is the ultimate Southern California beach: wide, wild, extending for miles, and inhabiting a stupendous natural setting. It is the largest county-owned beach, with no fewer than eight parking lots and a $6 parking charge, avoided by many who use the shoulders of the Pacific Coast Highway. The beach here de-

Map of Southern California—Page 9

The Original Metal Heads

You've seen them. They're generally older people, fully clothed on hot summer days. They move slowly up the beach, sweeping metal detectors over the golden sand at their feet. Every 10 yards or so they bend down to jab a scooper into the ground. They lift the implement, sift the sand therein, and inspect the latest treasure they've exhumed.

Have you ever wondered, as we have, what it is they find? Obviously, they must uncover something more valuable than bottle caps and beer tabs, right?

We had our questions answered one summer afternoon while soaking up sun at Zuma County Beach, in Malibu. Arthur, a pleasant old chap who sells metal detectors for a living, stopped his listening, digging, and sifting ritual long enough to give us the lowdown. He claimed you can quickly and easily recoup the cost of a metal detector by combing any busy city beach in the hard wet sand near the water at low tide. That is where the most recently lost wedding bands, gold chains, earrings, and pocket change—unknowingly jettisoned during bodysurfing, a playful swim, or even a jog in the shallows— are plucked from the sand like buried treasure. On one recent day's work, this gentleman claimed to have found half a dozen gold rings (two with inlaid diamonds), collectively valued at $5,000—about 10 times the cost of the metal detector.

While speaking with us, Arthur suddenly leapt forward, bent down, and stabbed his pronged scooper into the sand a few yards from where we were sitting. He sifted it briskly and reached in to grab a tidy fistful of spare change. He thrust his palm toward us, particularly proud to demonstrate his success so close to where we were sitting.

serves its reputation for danger, as the waves form close to shore, rising out of nowhere to back-breaking height before crashing noisily and sending tongues of seawater and foam scurrying up the sloping beach face. It's the perfect recipe for rip currents, necessitating frequent heroics from the lifeguard stands. Contrary to notions that primo Malibu beaches such as this one are peopled only with perfect specimens awaiting casting calls from soap-opera producers, Zuma is chock full of families and normal-looking folks on summer weekends. With the invigorating clean air, the azure ocean's churning fury, and the breathtaking backdrop of steep-sided, brushy moun-

tains, Zuma County Beach makes it possible to understand why residents risk life, limb, and earthly possessions to live in Malibu. Zuma comes equipped with food stands at both ends of its four-mile expanse along the Pacific Coast Highway, from the western side of Point Dume to Broad Beach Road. There is also a huge area given over to volleyball courts. West of Zuma, stairways along Broad Beach Road lead to secluded **Broad Beach.**

Next up is **Robert H. Heyer Memorial State Beach.** In fact, it is a trio of small cove beaches accessible by path and stairway. Moving west, the three beaches are **El Matador, La Piedra,** and **El Pescador,** occupying 18, 9, and

Map of Los Angeles County—Page 156

10 acres, respectively. The attraction is isolation from the madding crowd. Parking is by the honor system; you're asked to stuff $2 into a collection box. Switchback paths are carved into the crumbly cliffs. No wonder Malibu has mudslides in the rainy season; the hills are nothing more than loosely consolidated dirt clods. The beaches and offshore waters are strewn with sizable, steep-sided sea stacks. Come here for a taste of the wild side of Malibu's coastal geology. Approximately two miles west of El Pescador is **Nicholas Canyon County Beach,** slightly larger (at 23 acres) than the trio preceding it. Keep your eyes out for the turnoff down to the fee parking lot, which is directly across from the Malibu Riding and Tennis Club. You can also hike down from Leo Carrillo State Beach, which adjoins it. Formerly known as Nicholas Beach—surfers referred to it as Point Zero—it is less crowded than many Malibu beaches and relatively free of wave-hogging surf punks. It is informally used as a nude beach, though authorities try to discourage it.

Malibu's marvelous procession of beaches reaches its crescendo with **Leo Carrillo State Park.** The 3,000-acre park encompasses two sections of beach, separated by Sequit Point and totaling 1.5 miles, and a 139-site campground arrayed along a loop road in a scenic, fragrant canyon on the landward side of the Pacific Coast Highway. Nestled amid eucalyptus and sycamore groves, the campsites here are absolutely enthralling. Few other parks in the country can offer access to beach and mountains in such proximity. You are on the geological cutting edge of California's tectonic assembly line here. Carrillo's 1.5 miles' worth of beaches are steeply sloped with coarse brown sand. When we visited, little kids were getting waxed on the beach by crashing breakers, while big kids who bobbed in the offshore kelp beds atop surfboards were also being slammed to the mat by the waves' decisive crashes. The surf here is not for the inexperienced or faint

of heart, but the setting is as magnificent as any you'll find on either coast, offering sea caves and tidepools to explore, acres of sand to spread out on, and a scenic mountainous backdrop to gaze upon. For surfers it gets good southerly swells, though the offshore and onshore rocks are intimidating.

Up by the Ventura County line vans and cars line the road, and surfers scamper down the steep, reddish-brown bluffs. **County Line Beach** is a favorite of Southern California surfriders, accorded a status on par with such legendary breaks as Rincon and Windansea. And this is where Malibu and Los Angeles County finally come to an end.

Bunking Down

Malibu has exactly one luxury ocean hotel along its 27 miles, the fabulous **Malibu Beach Inn** (22878 Pacific Coast Highway, 310/456-6444, $$$$). This three-story, pink-stucco wonder is perched beside—and, at high tide, directly above—the ocean. When they say oceanfront, they're not exaggerating. You can open the balcony doors of your room and let the sounds of the churning, crashing ocean lull you to sleep. The complimentary breakfast buffet includes wonderful pastries, fresh fruit, cereal, and coffee. You can carry it to an outdoor sundeck and enjoy the morning meal over a copy of the *Los Angeles Times.* The rattan furniture and contemporary California decor enhance the sense of a relaxed getaway at the ocean's edge.

If you're going to pay top dollar for a place at the beach, you will find no nicer spot to do it than the Malibu Beach Inn. We have our own homemade souvenirs of the visit, incidentally: cassettes of waves breaking on the beach below, made with our portable recorders. The inn has won Robin Leach's seal of approval (check out the handwritten note just inside the lobby), and who better knows about refined lifestyles than he? Situated a short distance down from Malibu Pier, the inn can, incidentally, arrange delivery of a meal from Alice's Restaurant, a long-standing landmark at the base of the pier.

Coastal Cuisine

Granita (23725 West Malibu Road, 310/456-0488, $$$) is the hands-down standout on the Malibu dining scene. This star attraction in celebrity chef Wolfgang Puck's arsenal of California restaurants has won over even jaded Malibu natives, who are wowed by its beachside proximity, its underwater fantasy decor (done in handmade ceramic tile and etched glass), and such dishes as Mediterranean fish soup, lobster club sandwich, spicy shrimp pizza, and seared scallops over black-pepper fettuccine. Dress is Malibu casual: informal but neat. You may need to call up to a week in advance for a reservation, especially on weekends.

Another popular hangout is **Coogie's Beach Cafe** (23755 Malibu Road, 310/317-1444, $$), a spacious, high-ceilinged restaurant in a shopping center. Coogie's serves Malibu-style cuisine (indulgent and creative but healthy) at fair prices. All the salads are good, as are items like fresh Alaskan salmon patties with dill, served with a plate of eggs any style. It's a very Malibu kind of place, and you're likely to be surrounded by any number of Hollywood notables slumming in their casual wear. No one pays them (or you) any mind; that's part of the unspoken code of civility in celebrity-thick Malibu.

You can't get anything you want at **Alice's Restaurant** (Malibu Pier, 23000 Pacific Coast Highway, 310/456-6646, $$$), but your choices range to such satisfying selections as red snapper or shrimp sautéed with garlic, shallots, and tomatoes. The **Reel Inn** (18661 Pacific Coast Highway, 310/456-8221, $$) is a favorite of locals (especially surfing locals) who step up to the counter for everything from fresh fish to tacos.

Up at the opposite end of Malibu, directly across the street from County Line Beach, is a restaurant and fresh-seafood shop with the promising name **Neptune's Net** (42505 Pacific Coast Highway, 310/457-3095, $). It's the kind of place that we tend to romanticize—off the beaten track, filled with local color, offering fresh, nonfranchised food. In reality, much more could be done with it. Still, the location is unsurpassable.

Night Moves

Nightlife has never been a big proposition up in Malibu, the whole idea being that it is an enclave for people who prefer not to be recognized. Nonetheless, a good time can be had at the **Malibu Inn** (22969 Pacific Coast Highway, 310/456-6106), a riotously fun restaurant and saloon. Its ceiling is bedecked with a bizarre collage of metal wheels, surfboards (one serrated with shark-teeth indentations), baseball mitts, and bric-a-brac. You can order food, if you wish, through a huge, red pair of plastic lips. There's a pool table, bar, some tables, and a sawdust-strewn, wood floor in the main part of the saloon. The Malibu Inn is as down to earth as it gets. Lest you think Malibu is all reclusive celebrities and pricey cafés, duck in here for a brew with the surfing clan.

For More Information

Malibu Chamber of Commerce, 23805 Stuart Ranch Road, Suite 100, Malibu, CA 90265, 310/456-9025, website: www.malibu.org

Los Angeles County

Map of Los Angeles County—Page 156

© ROBERT HOLMES/CALTOUR

Central California

Chapter 4
Ventura County

Central California

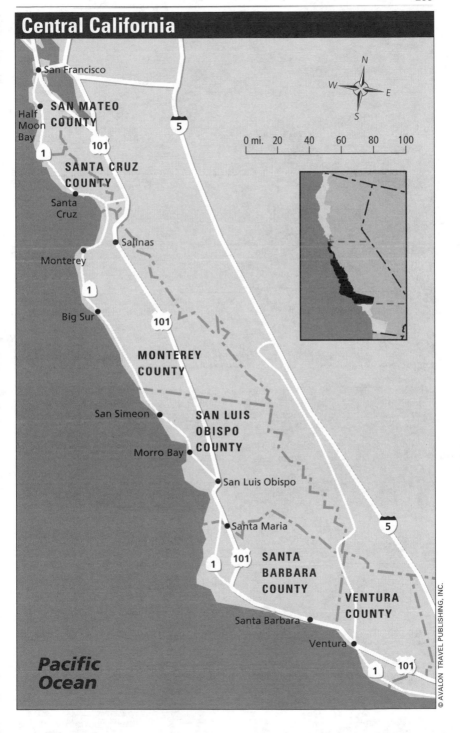

Ventura County

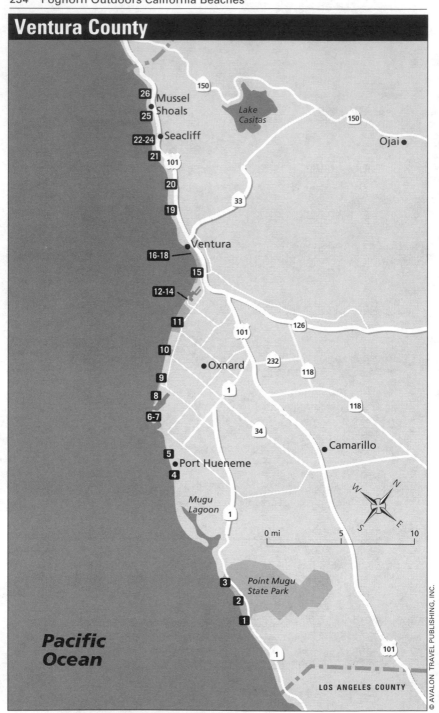

Ventura County Beaches

1 Sycamore Cove Beach (Point Mugu State Park), page 241

Location: six miles north of the Los Angeles County line on Pacific Coast Highway in southern Ventura County

Parking/fees: $5 entrance fee per vehicle. Camping fees are $13–16 per night, plus a $7.50 reservation fee.

Hours: 9 A.M.–sunset

Facilities: lifeguards, restrooms, showers, and picnic tables

Contact: Angeles District of California Department of Parks and Recreation, Malibu Sector, 310/457-8143

2 Thornhill Broome Beach (Point Mugu State Park), page 241

Location: 7.5 miles north of the Los Angeles County line on Pacific Coast Highway in southern Ventura County

Parking/fees: no day use; campers only. Camping fee is $8 per night, plus a $7.50 reservation fee.

Hours: 9 A.M.–sunset

Facilities: lifeguards, restrooms, showers, and picnic tables

Contact: Angeles District of California Department of Parks and Recreation, Malibu Sector, 310/457-8143

3 Point Mugu Beach, page 241

Location: Laguna Road and Beach Road at Point Mugu Naval Air Station, seven miles southeast of Port Hueneme

Parking/fees: Access is restricted to those with military or civilian ID cards.

Hours: 9 A.M.–sunset

Facilities: bathrooms and picnic tables

Contact: Public Affairs Office, Point Mugu Naval Air Station, 805/989-8096 (8407)

4 Ormond Beach, page 245

Location: Hueneme Road to end of Perkins Road in Port Hueneme

Parking/fees: free parking lot

Hours: 24 hours

Facilities: none

Contact: Oxnard Department of Parks and Facilities, 805/385-7950

5 Hueneme Beach Park, page 243

Location: end of Surfside Drive in Port Hueneme

Parking/fees: metered parking lot

Ventura County

Hours: sunrise–10 P.M.
Facilities: concession, lifeguards, restrooms, showers, and picnic tables
Contact: Port Hueneme Recreation and Community Services, 805/986-6542

6 Silver Strand Beach, page 245

Location: Ocean Drive at Sawtelle Avenue in Oxnard
Parking/fees: free parking lot
Hours: 24 hours
Facilities: lifeguards and restrooms
Contact: Oxnard Department of Parks and Facilities, 805/385-7950

7 Channel Islands Harbor Beach, page 246

Location: San Nicholas Street at Ocean Street in Oxnard
Parking/fees: free street parking
Hours: 24 hours
Facilities: lifeguards and restrooms
Contact: Oxnard Department of Parks and Facilities, 805/385-7950

8 Hollywood Beach, page 245

Location: 501 Ocean Drive in Oxnard
Parking/fees: free parking lot
Hours: 24 hours
Facilities: lifeguards, restrooms, and showers
Contact: Oxnard Department of Parks and Facilities, 805/385-7950

9 Oxnard Beach Park, page 246

Location: Harbor Boulevard between Beach Way and Falkirk Avenue in Oxnard
Parking/fees: 75 cents per hour or $4 per day
Hours: sunrise–sunset
Facilities: lifeguards, restrooms, and picnic tables
Contact: Oxnard Department of Parks and Facilities, 805/385-7950

10 Mandalay Beach County Park, page 246

Location: end of Mandalay Beach Road in Oxnard
Parking/fees: 75 cents per hour or $4 per day
Hours: sunrise–sunset
Facilities: none
Contact: Ventura County Department of Parks and Recreation, 805/654-3951

Ventura County

Map of Central California—Page 233

⬛ McGrath State Beach, page 246

Location: off Harbor Boulevard, five miles south of Ventura
Parking/fees: $4 entrance fee per vehicle. Camping fees are $13–16 per night, plus a $7.50 reservation fee.
Hours: 8 A.M.–8 P.M.
Facilities: lifeguards, restrooms, showers, picnic tables, and barbecue grills
Contact: McGrath State Beach, 805/654-4744

⬛ Surfers' Knoll, page 257

Location: west end of Spinnaker Drive, on the ocean side of road, in Ventura
Parking/fees: free parking lot
Hours: 24 hours
Facilities: restrooms
Contact: Ventura City Department of Parks and Recreation, 805/652-4550

⬛ Harbor Cove Beach, page 257

Location: west end of Spinnaker Drive, across the harbor from Marina Park, in Ventura
Parking/fees: free parking lot
Hours: 24 hours
Facilities: restrooms
Contact: Ventura City Department of Parks and Recreation, 805/652-4550

⬛ Marina Park, page 257

Location: south end of Pierpont Boulevard in Ventura
Parking/fees: free parking lot
Hours: 24 hours
Facilities: restrooms and picnic tables
Contact: Ventura City Department of Parks and Recreation, 805/652-4550

⬛ San Buenaventura State Beach, page 257

Location: San Pedro Street at Pierpont Boulevard in Ventura
Parking/fees: $4 entrance fee per vehicle or metered street parking
Hours: 24 hours
Facilities: concession, lifeguards, restrooms, showers, and picnic tables
Contact: Channel Coast District of the California State Parks, Gaviota Sector, 805/968-1033

⬛ Promenade Park, page 257

Location: Ventura Pier to Surfers' Point in Ventura
Parking/fees: free parking lot

Map of Ventura County—Page 234

Ventura County

Hours: 24 hours
Facilities: concession, restrooms, and picnic tables
Contact: Ventura City Department of Parks and Recreation, 805/652-4550

17 Surfers' Point, page 257

Location: Figueroa Street and Promenade at Seaside Park in Ventura
Parking/fees: free parking lot and nearby pay parking lot ($1 per hour or $5 all day)
Hours: 24 hours
Facilities: restrooms and showers
Contact: Ventura City Department of Parks and Recreation, 805/652-4550

18 Emma Wood State Beach (Group Camp), page 262

Location: Along the Pacific Coast Highway, three miles north of Ventura
Parking/fees: $4 entrance fee per vehicle. Camping fees are $15 per night in group camps 1–4 and $62 per night at RV group camp.
Hours: 8 A.M.–11 P.M.
Facilities: restrooms, showers, and picnic tables
Contact: Emma Wood State Beach, Group Camp, 805/648-4610

19 Emma Wood State Beach (North Beach), page 262

Location: Along the Pacific Coast Highway, three miles north of Ventura
Parking/fees: $4 entrance fee per vehicle. Camping fee is $8 per night, plus a $7.50 reservation fee.
Hours: 8 A.M.–11 P.M.
Facilities: lifeguards, restrooms, showers, and picnic tables
Contact: Emma Wood State Beach, North Beach, 805/648-4807

20 Solimar Beach, page 263

Location: five miles north of Ventura, along Rincon Parkway/Old Pacific Coast Highway, in Solimar
Parking/fees: free roadside parking
Hours: sunrise–sunset
Facilities: none
Contact: none

21 Faria Beach County Park, page 263

Location: Take State Beach exit from U.S. 101 north of Ventura and follow the Rincon Parkway/Old Pacific Coast Highway into Faria Beach
Parking/fees: $1–3 entrance fee per vehicle. Camping fees are $22–35 per night.
Hours: sunrise–sunset
Facilities: restrooms, showers, and picnic tables
Contact: Ventura County Department of Parks and Recreation, 805/654-3951

Map of Central California—Page 233

22 Rincon Parkway North, page 263

Location: Seacliff exit from U.S. 101 north of Ventura to Rincon Parkway/Old Pacific Coast Highway north between Faria and Hobson
Parking/fees: free roadside parking. Camping fee is $18 per night.
Hours: 24 hours
Facilities: none
Contact: Ventura County Department of Parks and Recreation, 805/654-3951

23 Hobson County Park, page 263

Location: Seacliff exit from U.S. 101 north of Ventura to Rincon Parkway/Old Pacific Coast Highway; follow north to Hobson
Parking/fees: $1–3 entrance fee per vehicle. Camping fees are $22–30 per night.
Hours: sunrise–sunset
Facilities: concession, restrooms, and showers
Contact: Ventura County Department of Parks and Recreation, 805/654-3951

24 Oil Piers Beach, page 266

Location: along Rincon Parkway/Old Pacific Coast Highway at the north end of Seacliff
Parking/fees: free roadside parking
Hours: sunrise–sunset
Facilities: none
Contact: none

25 Mussel Shoals Beach, page 266

Location: 11 miles northwest of Ventura on U.S. 101 in Mussel Shoals
Parking/fees: limited free street parking
Hours: sunrise–sunset
Facilities: none
Contact: Ventura County Department of Parks and Recreation, 805/654-3951

26 La Conchita Beach, page 266

Location: north of Mussel Shoals on U.S. 101 at La Conchita
Parking/fees: limited free roadside parking
Hours: sunrise–sunset
Facilities: none
Contact: Ventura County Department of Parks and Recreation 805/654-3951

Ventura County

Map of Ventura County—Page 234

Ventura County

It's little wonder that Ventura County has become a port of call for urban dropouts who pine for safe, sane, and smogless suburbs. Vacationers, tired of battling the Southern California throngs, have also begun pointing their rental cars toward the 42 miles of coastline in Ventura County.

Once rural and primarily agricultural—the Oxnard Plain, which dominates the eastern part of the county, is among the most fertile areas in the nation—Ventura County began growing at the point where U.S. 101/Ventura Freeway meets Highway 1/Pacific Coast Highway, near the nearly conjoined cities of Oxnard and Ventura. Despite rapid and ongoing growth, these cities retain more of a small-city feel than those on the coast of Los Angeles County. The Santa Monica Mountains, which lie between the two counties, cut them off from each other sociologically as well as geographically. To our thinking the Central Coast mentality begins here, though physically Southern California extends, by general consensus, through Santa Barbara County.

The beaches of Ventura County illustrate the yin and yang of coastline geography. Some of them, such as McGrath State Beach and San Buenaventura State Beach, are as wide and inviting as any you'll find in California. Others, especially those fronting the string of small, sea-walled communities at the north end of the county— Solimar, Seacliff, Faria, Hobson, Mussel Shoals—are seemingly down to their last grains of sand.

All are at least worth a peek, for different reasons. Even the thinnest ones, like Oil Piers, offer the heart-stopping spectacle of bronzed surfers braving the jagged shore. We also direct your attention toward the horizon, where the Channel Islands—a chain of eight pearly isles that have been called America's Galápagos—lie approximately 20 miles offshore. Five of them make up one of our most prized national parks and marine sanctuaries, beckoning intrepid beach explorers.

Ventura County

Map of Central California—Page 233

Point Mugu State Park

Point Mugu (pronounced "ma-GOO") **State Park** occupies the south end of Ventura County. The park provides the lure of excellent hiking trails and campgrounds at Sycamore Canyon and Thornhill Broome Beach. **Sycamore Cove Beach** is the park's only oceanfront day-use area, and it is stocked with everything one could want for a day at the beach, from a grassy picnic area to a sandy beach. Across the highway is Sycamore Canyon, which has a shaded, 55-site campground (no hookups). A few miles west, also along Highway 1, is **Thornhill Broome Beach**, a beachside campground that does not accommodate day-trippers.

The park's five-mile shoreline is just one facet of Point Mugu's appeal. This 15,000-acre park boasts a 70-mile network of hiking trails, most notably in Sycamore Canyon, which serves as a popular hikers' hookup to the Santa Monica Mountains. Here, majestic sycamores reach 80-foot heights. Deer and coyotes make appearances on some trails, such as the nine-mile Big Sycamore Canyon Loop, which leads to stunning ocean overlooks. The campgrounds at Sycamore Canyon and Thornhill Broome are popular with families, booking far ahead on weekends. The setting at Sycamore Cove—a sandy, crescent-shaped beach with an amazing backdrop of cool, shady sycamores running up into the folded foothills—cannot be beat.

For More Information

Point Mugu State Park, 9000 West Pacific Coast Highway, Malibu, CA 90265, 828/880-0350, website: www.cal-parks.ca.gov

Point Mugu

Point Mugu itself cannot be found in Point Mugu State Park. The jutting headland falls on land belonging to the U.S. Navy—specifically, the Point Mugu site of the Naval Base Ventura County. Home to the Pacific Seabees, this base's mission includes "troop mobilization, military training, testing and evaluation of land, sea, and air weapons systems."

Beaches

For security reasons, **Point Mugu Beach** is not accessible to the general public. It can only be accessed with military ID cards. The general public cannot use the facilities or walk on the beach, a large part of which is protected for endangered nesting least terns.

Between Point Mugu and the town of Port Hueneme lies Point Mugu Lagoon, the largest coastal estuary between San Diego and Morro Bay. Like Point Mugu Beach, however, this area is off-limits to the public.

Bunking Down

Active and retired military personal, reservists, and Department of Defense personnel can stay at the **Beach Motel** (Naval Base Ventura County, Building 774, Point Mugu, 805/989-8407, $) or the beachside RV park, where sites go for a rock-bottom $15.

For More Information

Naval Base Ventura County, Public Affairs Office, Point Mugu, CA 93042, 805/989-9234, website: www.nbvc.navy.mil

Ventura County

Map of Ventura County—Page 234

Port Hueneme

The word *hueneme* is pronounced "why-NEE-mee," as if the town is inquiring after or whining about its own identity. Lying uprange from the largest missile testing ground on the West Coast, one can't blame the locals for asking questions. Within the town limits, approaching from the south on Highway 1, farmland abounds. Scientific and uniform, row upon row and mile after mile of green stubs protrude from fields, with migrant workers bending and stooping under picked loads. A heavy industrial presence is also evident, with Kaiser Aluminum and a paper mill spewing smoke out their stacks.

Port Hueneme (population 22,250) is packed

 ## Ventura's Most Wanted

This may seem hard to believe for those of you who have followed us thus far, but one of us is a wanted man. As we write this, a bench warrant is out for the offending beach bum's arrest in Ventura County. Who knows? The other beach bum might also be wanted for harboring a fugitive or for aiding flight to avoid prosecution. The crime for which one of us is being sought in Ventura is . . . jaywalking. You read correctly. The story of how a pair of innocents like us came down on the wrong side of the law follows. As Sergeant Joe Friday used to say, "Just the facts, ma'am." Or, as native son Erle Stanley Gardner might say, "Throw the book at him."

The story starts in Marina del Rey, where we dined on raw oysters and sushi from a buffet one Friday night back in 1988. Because the raw seafood morsels had, for some reason, been incubating beneath warm lights in an unrefrigerated buffet trough, they were a perfect medium for bacterial contamination. Not being sophisticated enough at that time to know to avoid warmed raw oysters and sushi, we made pigs of ourselves from this "all you can eat" buffet. The restaurant in question no longer exists, and we came close to no longer existing ourselves in the days that followed this ill-advised repast.

The next day we both took profoundly ill, projectile vomiting as if possessed by demons. Our gastrointestinal distress reached its nadir in Ventura, where we'd grown delirious from the bacterial assault. Of course, we didn't bother to see doctors. Like fearless surfers, we decided to ride out the waves of nausea. That night in Ventura beach bum number one walked into a glass balcony door in his tenth-floor hotel room. Both of us passed sleepless and miserable nights. At six in the morning, after a horrific night of tossing and turning, beach bum number two decided to go out and buy a newspaper.

Admittedly looking a bit rough around the edges, the sick, sleep-deprived beach bum exited the lobby of the Holiday Inn Ventura Beach Resort. He crossed the deserted street in front of the hotel on this silent Sunday morn-

---

Map of Central California—Page 233

with quiet, symmetrical neighborhoods where homes and apartment complexes are laid out not unlike the rows of crops that lead up to them. This anonymous uniformity is explained by the military presence, with the Naval Base Ventura County occupying sites at Point Mugu and in Port Hueneme. The U.S. Navy's Construction Batalion Center takes up the sea lion's share of coastal access around the town center.

Beaches

At the west end of Surfside Drive is **Hueneme Beach Park,** site of a broad beach and handsome, 1,240-foot pier. Parking is self-pay, and the pier is open 24 hours a day, with cutting tables and sinks provided for filleting catches. The sand is grayish brown, wide, and dotted with volleyball nets, barbecue rings, and picnic tables. The beach ends at the south jetty of the

---

ing to purchase a newspaper from a vending box. He was accosted by an officer of the law, who appeared from nowhere, as if lying in wait. He could barely comprehend the officer's spiel about having crossed the street while the "Don't Walk" sign was flashing, and he thought he was dreaming when the cop pulled out a pad and began writing. The officer was compelled by the gravity of this pedestrian offense to issue a ticket for jaywalking. On Sunday at 6 A.M. On a quiet, carless street in Ventura.

The fine was $10. The slip of paper was chuckled over by both beach bums (providing the only levity in a week's work of death's-door illness) and quickly went missing. We were, after all, writing a book on the road while sicker than dogs. This silly ticket hardly rated as a high priority. Although forgotten by the perp, the petty offense remained in the files of the Ventura Police Department. Over the years several follow-up notices were sent to the home of the beach bum's mother in North Carolina. One tendered an offer of amnesty if the fine (which had by then been jacked up with late-payment surcharges) was paid. The next was a bench warrant, which would be rescinded only upon payment of the fine, which had ballooned to $200.

Let's get real. The "guilty" beach bum has a few words to say. Thousands of motorists speed on the Ventura Freeway as automatically as they breathe with no legal consequences, many of them with cell phones pressed to their ears, creating a very real scenario of distraction and danger. Don't you think a jaywalking ticket deserves to be forgiven? Surely the peace officers of this community have something better to do than troll for early-morning jaywalkers. This is the sort of trivial offense that would only be noticed and ticketed on the slowest day in the fictional town of Mayberry RFD. Weren't there any unsolved murders or burglaries to which they could have better devoted their time?

Despite his amusement and perplexity, the jaywalking beach bum can't help but feel a bit like Salman Rushdie on the return visits he's made to Ventura County since that fateful morn. It is no fun being wanted by the law. And so we ask, from the bottom of our GI tracts, for forgiveness of this ridiculous and now unaffordable ticket. In return, we won't ever jaywalk in your town again. Promise.

Ventura County

Map of Ventura County—Page 234

naval complex. This claims to be the only city-owned beach park in Ventura County. Every year in mid-August the city holds a weekend-long Hueneme Beach Festival featuring "plenty of fine food and beverages, tastefully served up by restaurants and food purveyors" and "rides, games, and attractions for kids of all ages" (read: a good excuse to pig out and play).

For More Information

Port Hueneme Chamber of Commerce, 220 North Market Street, Port Hueneme, CA 93041, 805/488-2023, website: www.wmplus.com/hueneme

Oxnard

While parts of town belie Oxnard's claim to being "the city that cares," much of its shoreline is a pleasant surprise. Blessed by a beautiful setting, comfortable year-round climate, large and scenic harbor, strong prevailing winds, and wide, big-duned beaches, it's a place with a lot of potential. At the same time, certain less charming areas bear the hallmarks of poverty that one associates with migrant labor and low-ranking military personnel. Nonetheless, they're working overtime to position Oxnard as a pro-business mecca, proudly heralding it as "the most business-welcoming community in Ventura County." Reading between the lines, there is a faint hint of desperation in those words.

Oxnard did not derive its name from the mighty ox. It was named for Henry Oxnard, a mogul whose sugar-beet empire was located hereabouts. With a population of 170,000, Oxnard is a medium-sized city with small-town pretensions. It lies in the middle of the fertile Oxnard Plain, with crop fields extending as far as the eye can see. This agricultural delta was created by the once-mighty Santa Clara River (whose mouth has been reduced to a thin trickle by agricultural withdrawals). The river was dammed, the delta became a plain, and the plain gave way to the multicolored fields that run to the east as far as the Santa Monica Mountains. Oxnard calls itself the Strawberry Capital of the World. California supplies 80 percent of the world's strawberries, and Oxnard celebrates with a Strawberry Festival on the third weekend in May. Other crops—such

as lemons, corn, and broccoli—are grown here, too. Trucks and trains haul off Oxnard's bounty to supermarkets the world over.

But Oxnard's "lower 40" is also filled with new middle-class housing and bank buildings—the things one associates with an up-and-comer. According to chamber of commerce–generated literature, Oxnard is "the fastest growing area in the state." It is a sentiment offered without irony, as though this were great news. Oxnard wears its recent growth as well as can be expected. Signs of it are obvious along Highway 1 on the outskirts of town, a suburbia of predictable sterility. But the beach areas, accessed via Harbor Boulevard, are low-key to the point of isolation. Oxnard's beaches are so beautiful and healthy it's surprising they haven't been exploited like those farther south. But we're not complaining.

Perhaps this is owing to the fact that Oxnard caters primarily to a boating crowd. The scenic harbor and surrounding area offer biking and hiking trails, picnic tables, tennis courts, playgrounds, and a safe, secluded harbor beach. The entire coastline is situated at the proper angle to receive wind and water currents vital to a rising water-sports capital. Channel Islands Harbor was dredged into existence in 1965 and modeled after a New England seaport, with 2,600 boat slips and a restaurant row.

It's obvious why Oxnard and neighboring Ventura are growing so quickly and how this incongruous overlap of suburbia and farmland occurred. The city is 60 miles northwest

Map of Central California—Page 233

of Los Angeles, where the Ventura Freeway meets the ocean, making it the next logical urban area for Angelenos to plunder. Actually, it is well along on its voyage of discovery, as the majority of boats docked at the harbor are owned by folks from Los Angeles. You can almost hear the old Dan Loggins song "Please Come to Boston" recast as an ode to this West Coast harbor town: "Please come to Oxnard in the springtime. . . ."

Rapid growth and low wages have generated predictable forms of socio-pathology. The symptoms: Oxford is home to 18 donut shops (Ventura has none). There are 14 pages of ads and listings for bail bond firms in the Oxnard Yellow Pages (sample lines: "Don't Guess, Call Jess," "spousal abuse specialists"). East of the city, along Highway 1, we saw a sign staked in a verdant field filled with crops and farm workers. Its curious message: "Thanks, Oxnard, for Destroying This Farmland." Are they making room for more donut shops?

Beaches

As if to reinforce the uniqueness of the coast in these parts, the 50-mile stretch from Oxnard State Beach north to Gaviota State Park (above Santa Barbara) has been given its own name—the Channel Coast, a reference to the windswept Channel Islands, which lie 20 miles offshore and are visible on clear days.

From the south, the first beach inside Oxnard's town limits is **Ormond Beach.** It's a controversial place that way off the beaten track. To get there, take Highway 1 to Hueneme Road. You'll pass acres of farmlands, eventually making a left on Perkins Road, which leads to the beach via a corridor of warehouses and industrial plants. Park at the cul-de-sac and catch a whiff of the paper mills. The beach itself is healthy, with a full dune structure and not much human visitation. It's understandable why few come here except to sit in cars on their lunch hour and drink beer from brown bags.

Ormond Beach, as the Sierra Club noted, has traditionally been used by the city of Oxnard as "the site to locate industrial development it did not want elsewhere." But Ormond Beach is a sensitive wetlands area, and with more than 90 percent of California's coastal wetlands long since destroyed, the remaining ones are hotly contested by environmental groups whenever a developer comes along with a proposal that will result in their damage or loss. That's exactly what's happened at Ormond Beach, where Occidental Petroleum wishes to site its first liquid natural gas terminal in California. So now the city of Oxnard is trying to pull a rabbit out of the hat by pleasing everybody as regards the "Ormond Beach Redevelopment Area." Here are its objectives:

• Conserve, protect and enhance the natural environment by restoring severely degraded wetlands and establish a fully functioning restored tidal connection and saltwater marsh ecosystem.

• Improve recreational and tourism opportunities.

• Strengthen market conditions and enhance economic opportunity in the city.

To this pie-in-the-sky set of competing directives, all we can say is, "You can't have your wetlands and mistreat them, too."

North of the U.S. Navy's Port Hueneme site lies **Silver Strand Beach.** To find it requires a circuitous route around the naval base: north on Ventura Road, left on Channel Islands Boulevard, left on Victoria Avenue, and left again on Ocean Drive to the Sawtelle Avenue access. Silver Strand is a free beach with lifeguards in the summer. A shipwreck, the SS *La Jenelle,* does duty as a fishing jetty at the south end of the beach. Be careful when casting, though, because it's slippery and the surf can get rough.

The best way to access Oxnard's more commendable beaches is via Harbor Boulevard. **Hollywood Beach** is a quiet city beach off Harbor Boulevard at the corner of La Brea Street and Ocean Drive; it's got volleyball nets and summer lifeguards. There's a little swimming

Ventura County

beach near the harbor, locally known as **Channel Islands Harbor Beach.** A park runs around the harbor's inner flank, offering grassy picnic sites and bike paths.

North of Hollywood Beach, also off Harbor Boulevard, is **Oxnard Beach Park,** a great day-use facility for families and large groups. The park comprises 62 acres of athletic fields, picnic tables, barbecue pits, pedestrian and bike paths, and a trail system that leads over dunes to a stretch of sand so wide it will take your breath away. The surrounding residential area, Oxnard Shores, strikes a nice balance between nature and human habitations, with low-lying architecture divided by canals, not unlike those in Venice Beach. Nonetheless, it's oddly devoid of human presence, as if a neutron bomb has gone off, leading us to wonder if these might be often-empty second homes for Los Angelenos.

Next up is **Mandalay Beach County Park,** a swath of sand whose jurisdiction and fate had been in dispute for some years; the beach is once again open and accessible. Set in an upscale subdivision that's crowned by Embassy Suites Mandalay Beach Resort, it's good to see that Mandalay's broad apron of sand isn't just being hoarded by the hoi polloi. It's a good place to go fly a kite—really!

The most precious of Oxnard's treasures is **McGrath State Beach.** This hidden jewel is one of the most appealing of the state's coastal parks. McGrath is on the north side of Oxnard at the Santa Clara River bed. McGrath State Beach offers 174 wind-protected and shaded campsites, a visitor center, nature trails, an estuary, mountainous dunes, and two miles of wide, windswept beaches. If you want to camp at McGrath, be advised that reservations fill up quickly (especially in summer), and stays are limited to one week.

Since the ocean currents are particularly strong here and the waves break on a deep, sloping shoreline, swimming is not recommended (though a lifeguard is on duty in sum-

mer). This beach is best for walking or surf casting, and the park is a living lab of natural wonders. The dune structure at McGrath is among the healthiest left in Southern California. They are nonetheless fragile and should be traversed only on designated paths. Dunes are formed when ocean currents and winds move sand around, and they are held in place when colonized by plants. These plants are easily broken or dislodged by human disturbances: feet, mountain bikes, mopeds, Jeeps, and all-terrain vehicles.

The northern 160 acres of McGrath constitute the **Santa Clara Estuary Natural Preserve,** which protects the habitat of the California least tern and the Belding's Savannah sparrow. A self-guided half-mile trail accesses a portion of the preserve, offering glimpses of the freshwater and saltwater plants and animals that intermingle in this precious ecosystem. The murky water is a rich nursery of nutrients. Shrimp feed on plankton, fish eat the shrimp, and shorebirds devour the fish. All the while the next generation spends its formative months in this protected, nurturing habitat.

Bunking Down

There are less costly places to stay in Oxnard than the **Embassy Suites Mandalay Beach Resort** (2101 Mandalay Beach Road, 805/984-2500, $$$$), but none that are so close to the beach. The Embassy Suites is directly on Mandalay Beach, and this is one good reason to stay here. It goes beyond Oxnard's wildest dreams of luxury, though at a budget-smashing price tag of $239 a night and up. It is constructed along the lines of a Spanish estate, with grottoes, fountains, gardens, and waterfalls. Buried among the manicured acreage is what is claimed to be the largest free-form swimming pool in Southern California, plus two tennis courts. Per the Embassy Suites norm, they throw in a full, cooked breakfast in the Surf Room each morning and drinks at night.

Similar comforts can be found in a less expensive harborside setting at the **Casa Sirena Hotel and Marina** (3605 Peninsula Road, 805/985-6311, $$), a three-story, 275-room resort. Tennis courts, exercise room, and patios and balconies overlooking the marina are a few of the amenities. There's also a fine restaurant, the **Lobster Trap**, on the premises.

Coastal Cuisine

The best way to check out Oxnard's showpiece, Channel Islands Harbor, is from a restaurant window, especially toward sundown when the sailboats are returning to port. The waterside **Lobster Trap** (3605 Peninsula Road, 805/985-6361, $$) is on the extensive grounds of the Casa Sirena Hotel and Marina. Established in 1969, the Lobster Trap flies in live Maine lobsters almost daily. Even more appealing are local seafood specialties, like crusted halibut.

Oxnard is otherwise largely choked with fast food franchises. Consider the following to be our fair warning as to the dimensions of this culinary dead zone. Within the borders of Ox-

nard are six McDonald's franchises, six Subways, five El Taco de Mexicos, four Taco Bells, three Burger Kings, three KFCs, three Jack in the Boxes, three Domino's Pizzas, three El Pollo Locos, two Wendy's restaurants, two Carl's Jr. burger joints, two IHOPs, two Pizza Huts, and two Little Caesar's pizza places. There is also one each of the following: Dairy Queen, Foster's Freeze, Buddy Burgers, Super Tommy's Burgers, Chili's, Wienerschnitzel, Del Taco, El Taco Loco, Super Taco, Green Burrito, Quizno's Subs, and Denny's. That is in addition to countless nonfranchised *taquerias* and Chinese takeout joints. Something is rotten in the heart (not to mention stomach) of Oxnard, and we suggest the Surgeon General send in a SWAT team before the entire city requires multiple bypass surgery.

For More Information

Oxnard Convention & Visitors Bureau, 200 West Seventh Street, Oxnard, CA 93030, 805/385-7571, website: www.oxnardtourism.com

Channel Islands

A string of eight pearl-like clusters that dot the horizon off California's Central Coast, the Channel Islands are part of a geological chain that includes Santa Catalina Island. Each of the Channel Islands has a unique ecosystem kept in changeless isolation by protective ocean boundaries. Five of the islands (Anacapa, Santa Cruz, Santa Rosa, San Miguel, and Santa Barbara) and the nautical mile that surrounds each (125,000 acres of submerged marine habitat) make up Channel Islands National Park. The other three islands are San Nicolas, San Clemente, and Santa Catalina.

The five of the islands of the National Park are not nearly as accommodating as Catalina—at least not in the conventional sense. It takes careful planning to reach them. Visitors must arrange transportation to and from the islands, and they must have a burning desire

to rough it at primitive campsites and on rugged trails. The islands do not lend themselves to quick look-sees. They require hardy souls (not to mention soles), as they can be windswept, forbidding places. On the other hand, a visit to any of them will reward you with memories to last a lifetime, and we spent a day on Santa Cruz Island that was as warm and welcoming as it could possibly be.

The Channel Islands were originally inhabited by the Chumash tribe (*chumash* means "island people"), who ventured off-island in their sturdy *tomols* (canoes) to trade with other tribes on the mainland and harvest the rich marine life in the waters of the Santa Barbara Channel.

In 1542 Europeans began to arrive. The Spanish explorer Juan Rodríguez Cabrillo came first, wintering on San Miguel. He, in fact,

Ventura County

Map of Ventura County—Page 234

Adventuring on the Channel Islands

Island Packers has been leading excursions to the Channel Islands for 35 years, and it has been the exclusive authorized vendor for this national park for as long as we've been coming to California. It's a clean, efficient operation with an informed, pleasant crew, which includes an on-board naturalist. The company offers trips of varying types—kayaking, sightseeing, whale-watching and camping—to all five of the park's Channel Islands. We opted for an all-day trip to Santa Cruz, the largest and most diverse island of the group ($48 roundtrip).

If we had more time, we would have liked to put down tent stakes near Prisoner's Harbor—a camping area at mid-island among oak trees 1,500 feet above the ocean. Instead, we got dropped off at Scorpion Ranch, on the eastern end of the island. (We saw no scorpions anywhere; that's just the name of the ranch, mate.) While there is no entrance fee for the park, overnight camping on all five islands costs $7.35 per night, plus $2.65 reservation fee per site, per night. (Call 800/365-2267 to book a reservation.)

On the trip out to Santa Cruz Island, we saw numerous sea lions, some hanging out on the buoys, and learned that there are 140,000 sea lions in the Santa Barbara Channel. We also passed oil platforms, a reminder of the car culture we were happily leaving behind. Since the boat ride gets bumpy, we recommend buying ginger snaps at the Island Packers office in Ventura before boarding. This simple morsel will tame all but the most horrendous waves of nausea (although one of us made the mistake of reading *The Perfect Storm* en route). You only have three or four hours on the island, and it would be shame to waste one of the hours recovering from seasickness.

The eight islands (five of which are officially part of the national park) are a veritable cauldron of biodiversity. They are isolated, pristine havens to more than 2,000 species of animals and plants, 145 of which are found nowhere else on earth. Just how pristine? Well, in 1970, when it was learned that DDT had been washing into the ocean and killing brown pelicans, only one chick survived on little Anacapa island. Through the banning of DDT and other stringent legal measures, the endangered pelican was given a fighting chance. Today, there are 6,000 nesting pairs of brown pelicans on West Anacapa each year—the largest rookery on the Pacific Coast. The boundary of the park extends a mile out from each island underwater.

A genial, slightly eccentric park ranger lives on the island. As our skiff rumbled toward the rocky beach at Scorpion Cove, he jitterbugged over to offer a greeting and an orientation to Santa Cruz Island. He also explained the rules, which weren't terribly hard to follow: "You can go anywhere you want on the

Map of Central California—Page 233

island. Just stay off the tops of the cliffs and be nice to my birds. They're friends of mine." The island scrub jay, a species native to the Channel Islands, is particularly friendly, which has tempted some visitors to feed them. Please resist this temptation. There are also anywhere from 5,000 to 7,000 wild pigs on the island, as well as some island foxes and wild horses. Santa Cruz Island is also home to one of the world's largest sea caves (Painted Cave), which is filled with bats. The bats, pigs, and foxes only poke their snouts out at night, so camping here will open a wholly different world than a day trip.

The first thing you notice is the quietude. Visitors discreetly sneak away from their fellow travelers to go their own ways. The second thing you notice is the outhouses, which are thankfully shrouded by the pungent smell of the eucalyptus trees among which they are situated. We took to the high trail. Either it's mismarked "moderate" or we're losing our edge, because it's pretty tough slogging part of the way. The trail goes from sea level to an elevation of 1,200 feet in half a mile, but the climb is worth every ounce of energy expended, offering an amazing view for 30 miles in every direction. Bring your own food and water, but pack light. We took sardines, crackers, fruit, and bottled water and had a perfectly fine lunch on top of Santa Cruz Island, lolling afterwards in the sun like the sea lions in Santa Barbara Channel.

If you choose to forgo a hike, you can occupy yourself for several hours by exploring the tidepools among the gigantic rocks at the south end of Scorpion Landing's beach. Each ever-changing pool is a tiny window into the teeming riches to be found among the waters of these pristine islands. Watching the starfish, anemones, snails, and crabs scuttle, crawl, and wobble is more therapeutic than any balm, lotion, granola bar, or spiritual tract to be found at California's New Age emporiums. We were even visited by an epiphany: no two tidepools look alike—which probably explains the appeal of tidepooling.

Rather than describe the experience, one of us attempted to transcribe the sounds the ocean was making as it washed over the rocks at Scorpion Landing. We used Jack Kerouac's *Big Sur* as our springboard. In a rare sober moment, Kerouac spent one night clinging to a cliff at Bixby Canyon with a plastic bag over his notebook and hand, and he jotted down what he heard the ocean saying: "Shoo—Shaw—Shirsh—Go on die salt light/You billion yeared/rock knocker/Gavroom/Seabird/Gabroobird . . . Shurning—Shurning—plop be dosh. . . ."

Here is our Kerouac-inspired "Sounds of Scorpion Cove": "Slorsh—Twikkle—sploosh boom sizzle de Gloop gloop slap duh sloop/Boink duh gloom . . . Krishlorp . . . Blurble slosh plap plap plap . . . Don't no BLOOM/And hold me clara doon . . Just dune mah moon pacific. Don't ask nothin' specific/Just take it on the chin you sit still long enough you own the whole world."

Ventura County

Map of Ventura County—Page 234

Thar She Blows!

By pure luck and amazing grace—and the kindness of Island Packers, whose crew went out of their way to track him down—we came upon an adult male blue whale *(Balaenoptera musculus)* as we were headed back to Ventura Harbor after spending the day on Santa Cruz Island. The captain had seen the male blue whale an hour earlier feeding in the waters off Santa Cruz, so—with the passengers' enthusiastic permission—he headed over to that area and cut his engines. And waited.

The blue whale is the largest animal that's ever lived on our planet. Adults average 100 feet in length and weigh 400,000 pounds. At birth they weigh 7,000 pounds! Their average life span, barring death at the hands of humans, is 70 years. Our guide informed us that a blue whale's heart is as big as a Volkswagen Bug and its tongue is bigger than the largest living land animal (the elephant). This elicited chortles from a pack of sun-dazed fishermen who were sipping beer. The blue, on a less amusing note, has been hunted to near extinction, and the only population of them that's making any sort of comeback is the 2,000 or so that summer in the waters off the central California coast. We were lucky. We hit this one right at the start of their feeding cycle in the channel waters.

Blue whales take 6–10 minutes between breaches of the ocean surface. Every person on the boat took a position along the side and anxiously scanned the water surface. Just when we were about to give up as darkness approached, the blue whale breached about 400 yards ahead of the ship. We watched as

Ventura County

died here—the result of a fall from a steep incline. (He was allegedly buried on San Miguel, but his grave has never been discovered.) By the early 1800s the Chumash were packed off to missions on the mainland, and Europeans used the islands for hunting, grazing sheep and cattle, and growing grapes for California's earliest wines. The Channel Islands have since served as defense installations, as well as living labs for scientific inquiries of the Darwinian kind. The islands were made part of the National Park System in 1980.

Because each island offers unique treasures, and the logistics for reaching them differs, the five are described individually. Some general information, however, applies to all of them. First, the headquarters for Channel Islands National Park is on the harbor in Ventura. Even

if you don't plan to visit the islands, a trip to park headquarters is worthwhile. The museum offers an excellent exhibit detailing the rich panoply of life offshore. You can also grab useful literature in the museum and shop. The best time to explore the islands is March–July, though they're open to visitation year-round.

Although you can arrange transportation to the island with any licensed pilot, most people choose to book passage at **Island Packers** (1865 Spinnaker Drive, 805/642-1393), next door to park headquarters. As the official park concessionaire, they regularly schedule departures to and from the five islands and are well-versed in the ways of the land. Fares vary for travel to each island, as do schedules and trip duration. For instance, you can book full-day (7–8 hours), half-day (3.5 hours, no landing), or in-

Map of Central California—Page 233

he blew a few toots out his blowhole and then, *whoosh,* dove headfirst into the krill patch he had discovered (the largest blues consume six tons of krill a day). We waited again. This whale, we were assured by the captain, was an unusually "friendly" blue whale, in that he was seemingly oblivious to our presence and not averse to swimming in our direction. Sure enough, when the blue whale breached the second time, he was less than 100 yards from our ship. When he dove this time, he lifted his fluke high above the surface, "sounding" in order to give himself more speed on his dive (though we'd like to think he was showboating for our benefit).

This ranks near the top of the most amazing spectacles we've ever witnessed in our decades of combing America's beaches. It rivaled the sighting of the endangered Florida panther north of the Everglades, the black bear we spotted while on the Lost Coast of Northern California, and even the virgin redwood forests of Del Norte County.

Two boat-based commercial operations serve the Channel Islands:

• **Truth Aquatics,** 301 West Cabrillo Boulevard, Santa Barbara, CA 93101, 805/962-1127, website: www.truthaquatics.com (Primarily a scuba-diving charter service, it has a varied bill of fare and three modern vessels.)

• **Island Packers,** 1867 Spinnaker Drive, Ventura, CA 93001, 805/642-1393, website: www.islandpackers.com (This is the official concessionaire for trips to Channel Islands National Park.)

One airline services Santa Rosa Island only:

• **Channel Islands Aviation,** 305 Durley Avenue, Camarillo, CA 93010, 805/987-1301, website: www.flycia.com

---

between (5–6 hours) trips to Anacapa Island, which is the closest to the mainland.

The only place to stay overnight on the islands is in a tent, and camping requires a permit from the National Park Service. A nightly fee of $10—which includes a "camping use fee" of $7.35 and a "camping reservation fee" of $2.65—is charged. Reservations can be made by calling **Biospherics, Inc.,** at 800/365-2267. (We suggest reserving six months to a year ahead.) Just so you know, there are 7 campsites on Anacapa, 40 on Santa Cruz (plus a new backcountry campground), 15 on Santa Rosa, 7 on Santa Barbara, and 9 on San Miguel. If you camp on any of the Channel Islands, you must bring fresh water, because there are no facilities (except for latrines). A park ranger is on-site in case of emergencies.

Anacapa: Actually three small islands in one, Anacapa is five miles long but covers only a single square mile of land. East Anacapa is 11 miles from Ventura, and the passage takes 75 minutes. Boats dock at Landing Cove, and the first hike a visitor takes here is straight up—154 steps to the top of the bluff, where the land levels out. From here you can visit the Anacapa Island Lighthouse, which overlooks a rocky hangout of a healthy California sea lion population. You can also take the Loop Trail, a daunting 1.5-mile hike around the island whose highlights include sea caves, sea cliffs, and incredible blufftop views. The terrain is rocky and the vegetation sparse on Anacapa—there are no trees—and the winds can be fierce. There are no sandy beaches, either, but on calm days you can swim at Land-

Ventura County

Map of Ventura County—Page 234

ing Cove and dive at Cathedral Cove along the north shore. There are seven tent sites on East Anacapa (with a total capacity of 30 people), and stays of up to 14 days are permitted. West Anacapa, the largest and westernmost of the three islets, is off-limits, being the primary nesting spot for the brown pelican. Middle Anacapa has a landing spot at East Fish Camp. The cost of a day trip to Anacapa, depending on the type and length of the trip, ranges $24–37 per adult ($48 if camping). For information and reservations, contact Island Packers at 805/642-1393.

Santa Cruz: This is the largest of the Channel Islands. Santa Cruz Island is 24 miles long and occupies 96 square miles of land. It is also the most varied in terrain and the most blessed with sandy beaches among its 77 miles of shoreline. It's home to more than 650 plant species found among 10 distinct plant communities and 140 bird species. The western 76 percent of the island is owned by the Nature Conservancy, a few scattered property owners, and the Santa Cruz Island Preserve. Structures built by French settlers in the 1890s have been preserved, including a chapel, slaughterhouse, winery (but of course!), and barns. There's a 40-site campground at Scorpion Valley and a new backcountry campsite (Del Norte) 3.5 miles inland. The fare to Santa Cruz Island, depending on dropoff point, is $42–48 per adult ($54–60 if camping), and the crossing takes two hours.

For more information on Santa Cruz Island, contact:

• Island Packers, 1867 Spinnaker Drive, Ventura, CA 93001, 805/642-1393

• Nature Conservancy, Santa Cruz Island Project, 213 Stearns Wharf, Santa Barbara, CA 93101, 805/962-9111

• Santa Cruz Island Preserve, P.O. Box 23259, Santa Barbara, CA 93121, 805/962-9111

Santa Rosa: The second largest of the Channel Islands (15 miles long, 10 miles wide, occupying 53,000 acres), Santa Rosa is the best bet for overnight stays. It's got great hiking trails, mountains, canyons, the largest marsh on the islands, and a varied shoreline with sandy beaches on which harbor seals breed. Bird-watchers, kayakers, hikers, photographers, beachcombers, and rare-animal spotters (the Channel Island fox and spotted skunk are endemic to Santa Rosa) all love this island. It's also home to a rare stand of Torrey pines. There are only 15 campsites, so reserve a site at least one year in advance. Boat trips take 3.5 hours one-way ($62 per adult, $80 if camping). Camping on Santa Rosa's beaches is allowed for "experienced kayakers and boaters on a seasonal basis." (Call 805/658-5711 for details.) For information and reservations, contact Island Packers at 805/642-1393.

San Miguel: The farthest island from the mainland, San Miguel might be the most fascinating of the bunch. It is certainly the most primitive. The middle of the five islands in terms of size (eight miles long, five miles wide), it is whipped by ferocious winds that sculpt the sand into natural monoliths, a form of mineral sandcasting known as "caliche forests." A 15-mile hiking trail cuts through a raw landscape rounded by the wind from the beach at the landing all the way to Point Bennett at the western tip. En route, you can spot seals and sea lions on the beach (upwards of 30,000 have been counted in the summer), rare birds, and ground vegetation. Historians visit the island for its 500 archeological sites and the possibility of stumbling over Cabrillo's skeleton. The fare is $90 per adult—and there is no reason to come all the way out here if you are not camping. There are nine tent sites with a total capacity of 30 people. For information and reservations, contact Island Packers at 805/642-1393.

Santa Barbara: The smallest of the Channel Islands (640 acres) lies the farthest south, necessitating another 3.5-hour boat ride ($49 per adult, $75 if camping). A visit to Santa Barbara Island almost demands an overnight stay to take advantage of the 5.5 miles of hiking trails. It's a particularly rewarding perch

Ventura County

Map of Central California—Page 233

for bird-watchers, while snorkelers are often joined by playful seals. There are no shade trees and only eight primitive campsites on the island. For information and reservations, contact Island Packers at 805/642-1393.

For More Information

Channel Islands National Park, 1901 Spinnaker Drive, Ventura, CA 93001, 805/658-5711, website: www.nps.gov/chis

Ventura

The full, legal, incorporated name of Ventura is San Buenaventura—a title officially bestowed in 1866—which is Spanish for "City of Good Fortune." Indeed, Ventura does possess the good fortune of not being anywhere near Los Angeles, from which it is separated by the Santa Monica Mountains and a one-hour freeway ride (assuming there are no traffic delays!). Ventura (population 101,000) is also lucky not to be Oxnard, a larger nearby city that absorbs more of the migratory influx from Los Angeles. Ventura is separated from Oxnard by the dry bed of the Santa Clara River, and in some ways, the two towns bear a family resemblance. Both are twin peas in the fertile pod of Ventura County and have beautiful, uncrowded beaches and breezy harbor areas. However, as far as history, charm, and personality are concerned, Ventura shines more brightly than its neighbor.

The name San Buenaventura derives from the Catholic mission established here in 1782 by Father Junipero Serra. The original mission, chapel, and grounds have all been beautifully restored and maintained, as has the downtown Old Historic District that surrounds it. The **San Buenaventura Mission** (211 East Main Street, 805/643-4318) is open daily 10 A.M.–5 P.M. for tours. The entire town has internalized the lesson that historic preservation is a key to self-preservation. Other historic buildings open for touring include a pair of adobes, the **Ortega Adobe** (215 West Main Street, 805/648-5823) and the **Olivas Adobe** (4200 Olivas Park Drive, 805/644-4346). Ortega is typical of the adobes that were found along Main Street in the 1800s, and from here

in 1897 the "Pioneer Ortega Chili" business was launched. The Olivas Adobe is a two-story hacienda built around 1849 and run today as a historical park by the city of Ventura.

Next door to the San Buenaventura Mission is the **Albinger Archaeological Museum,** which houses artifacts spanning 3,500 years and five native cultures: Native American, Spanish, Mexican, Chinese, and American. Drop by **San Buenaventura City Hall** (501 North Poli Street, 805/654-7837) or the **Ventura County Historical Museum** (100 East Main Street, 805/653-0323) to pick up a walking tour guidebook of these and other historic attractions. City Hall, built in 1914 of simulated white marble, is an impressive piece of architecture in its own right. Even Ventura's post office is worth a look. Three blocks from City Hall on Santa Clara Street, the post office houses a fascinating mural painted by Works Progress Administration artist Gordon Grant, who spent most of 1936 and 1937 working on this tribute to the heroism of the common laborer and farmer.

Certainly, Ventura offers enough in the way of history, archeology, and architecture to keep anybody busy for a few days. But there's more for the educated browser as well: bookstores—five of them in a two-block radius! Among them is the cooperative **Book Mall of Ventura** (105 South Oak Street, 805/641-2665), a 15-dealer bonanza of used, rare, and out-of-print books. Main Street Ventura is also stocked with art and antique stores, as well as a disproportionate number of thrift shops, which is bound to please that intrepid soul in search of the perfect bowling shirt. Then there's down-

"Don't Do Anything Rational"

One beautiful morning when we were out jogging up to Surfers' Point, we came upon a seventy-something character seated on the riprap alongside the dry mouth of the Ventura River. He sported a floppy tennis hat like Gilligan's, a snow-white beard, and a rueful expression. We decided to make his acquaintance and inquire about the chewed-up condition of the bike path beside the ocean.

A big winter storm took it out a decade or so ago, he said, and the only person who tried to remedy the situation, by depositing some rocks without official approval, was put in jail. The salty dog bitterly chuckled over the situation, and let loose with a series of nasty invectives in the general direction of the California Coastal Commission, local politicians, and developers.

He grew up a half-mile from where he was sitting, and he still lives in his family's house. He cut his teeth playing on the sand that once fronted—but has since washed away—what is now Emma Wood State Beach. He fondly recalled Emma when she had curvaceous dunes among which were housed World War II–era gun emplacements to fend off an anticipated Japanese land invasion. Now, he worries over other invasions that have occurred since what he described as a bucolic childhood: developers, yuppies, greedy rich people, immigrants, SUVs, and the government.

"I've seen too much change in Ventura," he said. "And all of it is horrible."

town Ventura's abundance of coffeehouses. They can be found all along California and Main Streets.

In all respects Ventura operates at a more civilized and leisurely pace than the Southern California norm. You begin to sense a real break between the Southern and Central California sensibilities. Ventura has got aspects of both: the compulsive physicality and cutting-edge cultural preoccupations of the Southland, and the less-harried and somewhat provincial outlook of the Central Coast. It was on the streets of Ventura, for instance, that we saw our first real cowboy, a strapping fellow swathed in denim and crowned with a cowboy hat who politely asked us for spare change.

Ventura admittedly faces growth issues, as ever-more escapees from Los Angeles flee their crisis-ridden city, opting to commute from or retire to Ventura County. Much of the growth has been absorbed by Oxnard, which has swelled like a goiter along the U.S. 101 corridor. This buffer has thus far tempered the impact of Los Angelization upon Ventura. Its streets are still clean. The air itself is more breathable. You don't have to keep your guard up quite so reflexively.

Ventura is trying to decide which of its identities will best attract new visitors and vacationers. Among the nifty options offered to visitors are:

• **Ventura River Trail,** a bike/hike path that follows an old railroad right of way for over six miles along a newly restored river estuary

• "Fun and Free By the Sea," an annotated list of "48 free things to do in Ventura in 48 hours"

• historic walking tours through the "old town" area that include "Murder Most Foul," "Lost Adobes of Main Street," "Victorian Ven-

Map of Central California—Page 233

At that point, one of his boyhood friends joined us.

"Yes," he gently gibed his curmudgeonly pal. "And you are talking to one of the horrible changes right here, gentlemen."

But then, they both bemoaned how developers have bought up all the farmland hereabouts. This started happening, they explained, when the state taxed the farmers at the same rate as residential subdevelopments surrounding the fields on all sides (i.e., their land was taxed on its "potential" value). "What could be more valuable than this farmland?" they mournfully asked. "It's some of the most fertile in the world." No disagreement from us.

Next they worried over the distant hills behind Ventura, an uncluttered back drop that gives the city its out-of-the-way feel. "What's going to happen when they start building up in the hills?" wondered the old guy, warming up to the subject. "All of that shit is going to just run downhill right into the ocean." We quickly agreed with them that most developers should be publicly flogged on a regular basis.

Then, they suggested that there were simply too many people in the world. Again, we agreed.

The salty dog summed it all up this way: "Too much fucking. Not enough working." Then he got up and limped back out to the walking trail and continued his wobbly morning workout.

Over his shoulder, he said, "Have a good rest of the day. Don't do anything rational."

---

tura" and "Erle Stanley Gardner's Ventura" (based on the author and native son's travels around the county)

• a diverse array of museums, everything from the **Oil Museum** to the (whoa, dude!) **Skateboarding Museum.**

This makes for a friendly, relaxed, and welcoming atmosphere—which is not to say there aren't some darker sides of the city that one might stumble onto. For example, we got out of Ventura just in time to miss a wake that was being held by the local chapter of Hell's Angels for one of their members, who was shot to death by a rival outlaw motorcycle gang the previous weekend. Talk about bad timing: this event brought hundreds of Hell's Angels from all over the state into Ventura on the same night that local merchants were launching "1st Friday: Alive After Five," an attempt to draw shoppers and diners into town on a weekend night. Though

the possibilities of yuppie-biker interaction piqued the curiosity of the sociologist in us, we peeled rubber northward to Santa Barbara.

The brightest news in these parts was the opening, in August 2002, of California State University Channel Islands, the first four-year public university in Ventura County—and the only such institution to open in the entire United States in the year 2002. This is indeed good news that ought to enliven and uplift the community. We could imagine far worse ways to pass four years than to study environmental science and resource management in these old Spanish Revival buildings a mere three miles from the Pacific Ocean. By 2025, CSU Channel Islands projects it will have 15,000 full-time students. A university is born!

If downtown Ventura is the heart of its history and culture, then Ventura Pier and Promenade are its recreational centerpieces. On

Surf Kayaking: The Latest Outrage

A new sport has emerged along the California coast, and not everyone in the water is giving it a standing ovation. The sport is called surf kayaking, and it has joined personal watercraft-riding and boogie boarding on the enemies list of the Golden State's surfers. Surf kayaking is exactly what it sounds like: one- and two-man paddlers taking waves in the same areas where surfers congregate. We first saw the dynamic at Surfers' Point in Ventura and sensed an unstated tension in the air as a group of surfers watched a kayaker take wave after wave, often cutting in front of them and never seeming to stop fussily chopping and churning about with his paddles.

It seemed comical at the time, as if some extreme sports nut had set himself an eccentric one-time challenge. As it turns out, surf kayaking is a full-fledged sport with an annual world championship. Some practitioners, like two-time world champion Dave Johnston of Santa Cruz, have been surf kayaking for 20 years. Although it looked like fun from shore, it also seemed extremely invasive. For that reason alone, our sentiments are with the surfers on this issue. After all, a kayaker can paddle in just about any body of water, whereas a surfer's sport is profoundly site-specific. Thus, the tenacity and occasional violence of surfers against encroachers like surf kayakers and Jet Skiers is an understandable matter of guarding one's sacred surf.

The rage is most pronounced at Steamer Lane in Santa Cruz. Steamer Lane is to surfing what Daytona is to stock car racing. Surf kayakers have now invaded this turf and even hold one of their most prestigious tournaments here. They are pressing the beleaguered Santa Cruz city government to establish ground rules and etiquette, for crying out loud. Etiquette?!

From the surfers' perspective, this may be the last straw. They claim that kayakers get in the way and create needless hazards to surfers, but they also take off on "the flap of the swell," chopping the top of the wave off and therefore ruining it for any surfers in the vicinity. Although we would normally steer clear of a dispute between these two camps—partly because both sports are basically great, environmentally low-impact activities—we can't help but think the surfers have the high ground here.

Come on, kayak dudes. Get out of the waves. There are plenty of other places you can yak it up.

Ventura County

weekends craftspeople and vendors peddle their wares, and in-line skaters and cyclists pedal their wheels. The wide concrete promenade extends past Surfers' Point, with benches placed at intervals for restful contemplation of the ocean. At 1,200 feet the Ventura Pier is the longest wooden pier in California. It dates back to 1872, when San Buenaventura was a busy harbor into which steamships would come and go bearing cargoes of lumber, oil, and farm products. Between the pier and the harbor lies sandy San Buenaventura State Beach. Just north of the harbor, at the end of Seaward Avenue, is a bustling little neighborhood with a "California beach town" feel to it. On the east end of Ventura's oceanfront is Ventura Harbor, which comes with the obligatory "seaside village" of shops and restaurants. Refreshingly, this one is Spanish in character, with piped-roof, mission-style architecture providing a sharp contrast to the clichéd New England fishing village motif found elsewhere on the coast.

Ventura's beachfront parks attract all kinds of folks. On a summer Sunday we saw a gaggle of surf punks cussing like troopers; a family wheezing along on a tandem bike as the kids urged their huffing and puffing head of household to pedal faster; a counterculture minstrel curled up at the base of a tree, strumming a guitar; and elderly couples serenely surveying the ocean from park benches. It was a representative cross section of humanity enjoying a day at the beach.

Beaches

The city of Ventura has some fine beaches within its borders, from Ventura Harbor up to the county fairgrounds at the north end. **San Buenaventura State Beach** is a formidable two-mile beach possessing good width and a bit of dune structure. Plenty of parking is available in lots and on the street. Crowds don't seem to be a problem. On one gorgeous summer weekend several years back, even with a hefty contingent of bikers on hand for a charity road race, plenty of spaces were available. This long beach is good for swimming and sunbathing.

North of the pier, **Promenade Park** runs along a narrow, rocky, and highly eroded oceanfront. The most inviting feature of this park is the promenade itself, which connects the pier with **Surfers' Point**. At the end of California Street ("C Street," to the locals) at Seaside Wilderness Park, Surfers' Point sits near the mouth of the Ventura River. As the name suggests, surfers take advantage of the city-run park facilities and free parking. (Pay parking is available nearby for those not lucky enough to snag a spot.)

The point gets wrapped with winter swells from the north, with a healthy helping of distant storm-generated "juice" pushing the surf up to 20 feet on the outside break. In conditions like these, Surfers' Point is not for neophytes or the faint of heart. And don't come here to swim, as there is no beach, just moss-covered rocks. About 10 years ago, a storm took out most of Ventura's oceanside biking/jogging path, and it has yet to be repaired or replaced. The California Coastal Commission has been hoping that the severely narrowed beach will regenerate naturally, and its inaction has rankled some locals.

There are also small beaches on the peninsulas that flank Ventura Harbor. **Marina Park,** on the north side of the harbor, is a playland of boat docks, volleyball and basketball courts, a fishing pier, and picnic area. Protected by jetties, **Harbor Cove Beach** is considered the safest in the area for kiddies, including the added incentives of a child's play area and big picnic lawn. **Surfers' Knoll** faces the ocean's waves from the opposite site of Spinnaker Drive.

Shore Things

- **Bike/skate rentals:** Cycles 4 Rent, 239 West Main Street, Ventura, 805/652-0462
- **Boat cruise:** Pacific Sailing, 1967 Spinnaker Drive, Dock D-10, Ventura, 805/658-6508

Map of Ventura County—Page 234

Ventura County

- **Dive Shop:** Ventura Dive 'n' Sport, Ventura Harbor Village, Ventura, 805/650-6500
- **Ecotourism:** Channel Islands National Park,1901 Spinnaker Drive, Ventura, 805/658-5730
- **Marina:** Ventura Harbor, Spinnaker Drive, Ventura, 805/642-8538
- **Pier:** Ventura Pier, 668 Harbor Boulevard, Ventura
- **Rainy day attraction:** San Buenaventura Mission, 211 East Main Street, Ventura, 805/643-4318
- **Shopping/browsing:** Ventura Harbor Village, Spinnaker Drive, Ventura, 805/644-0169
- **Sportfishing:** Harbor Village Sportfishing, 1449 Spinnaker Drive, Ventura, 805/658-1060
- **Surf shop:** Waveline Ventura, 154 East Thompson Boulevard, Ventura, 805/652-1168
- **Vacation rentals:** Harbor Realty, 1106 South Seaward Avenue, Ventura, 805/648-3068

Bunking Down

The place to stay in Ventura for the beach-obsessed is the **Holiday Inn Beach Resort** (450 East Harbor Boulevard, 805/648-7731, $$). This 10-story tower offers the best views of and closest proximity to the beach, beside Ventura Pier and U.S. 101. You couldn't ask for a better location, and the rooms take full advantage of this with balconies that overlook the water. It's a high-rise hotel, but the prices are fairly low (around $100–110 a night), especially compared with what you'd shell out for similar digs on the beach in Los Angeles County. One caveat: It's a contest between nearby U.S. 101 and passing trains (at 5 A.M.!) as to which noise source will most interrupt your sleep. The hotel offers earplugs to drown out the disturbances.

A modest notch down in location—and a modest step up in amenities—is the **Clarion Ventura Beach Hotel** (2055 East Harbor Boulevard, 805/643-6000, $$$). A block from the south end of San Buenaventura State Beach in a neighborhood removed from the downtown bustle, the rooms at this former Doubletree Hotel are spacious and well appointed, and a huge pool and hot tub are the attractive centerpiece of the interior courtyard. Just about any need can be met on the premises, from a drink at the Borneo Bar to a meal at the Gallery Restaurant.

Another respectable choice is the venerable and lately renovated **Pierpont Inn** (550 San Jon Road, 805/643-6144, $$), on seven beautifully landscaped acres atop a bluff overlooking Pierpont Bay. Built in 1908 and operated by the same family since 1928, the Pierpont Inn has east and west wings, plus the Bluff House, an eight-room building perched on the bluff directly overlooking the ocean, and two private cottages. Garden-view rooms go for $115–130 and ocean-view rooms for $130–145. The inn's 77 rooms include working fireplaces for those nights when the cold westerly winds blow off the ocean. The grounds are thick with flowers, and a path runs down the hill and under the freeway to the beach. A local landmark, the Pierpont attracts a faithful clientele.

Inn at the Beach (1175 South Seaward Avenue, 805/652-2000, $$) is a moderately upscale recent arrival with 24 Victorian-style guest rooms with French/Italian antiques and patios or balconies that overlook the ocean. At the south end of Seaward Avenue, it's just feet from the beach.

Finally, if you're traveling on a budget, the **Vagabond Inn** (756 East Thompson Boulevard, 805/643-2128, $) is clean, comfortable, and close enough to the action to have a footbridge to the beach and pier.

Coastal Cuisine

If it's really, really fresh seafood you want—so fresh it hasn't even been cooked—step up to **Sushi Marina** (120 South California Street, 805/643-5200, $$). It's the most swinging sushi bar this side of Hermosa Beach. When we ate there it stayed packed till its 10 P.M. closing with a young crowd of raw-fish addicts. Sushi

Ventura County

Marina serves some of the finest and freshest sushi we've had on the coast. The sushi dinner consists of six pieces each of California and tuna roll, plus half a dozen assorted sushi items, including such personal favorites as bonito, the roast beef of the sea. Sushi Marina has plenty of cooked selections, including teriyaki and sukiyaki, as well.

Out on Ventura Pier is a seafood restaurant where those without poles can still land a big fish. **Eric Ericsson's Seafood Restaurant** (668 Harbor Boulevard, 805/643-4783, $$$) grills some of the most bodacious fish fillets in Ventura. A refrigerated case filled with long, gigantic slabs of fish at their rainbow-hued finest—glistening crimson ahi, meaty white halibut, bright orange salmon—catches your eye as you enter. Another good view, onto Ventura Pier and the surrounding beach, awaits guests in the glassed-in dining room. Any number of fish specials—orange roughy, swordfish, halibut, salmon, ahi tuna, Pacific red snapper, mahimahi—are listed daily. Entrée prices average around $20, which includes chowder or salad, rice or potato, and vegetable. This is, you may notice, a full dinner. You are now on the Central Coast, which means that tab-inflating à la carte charges have, for the most part, been left behind, along with smog and traffic, in Los Angeles County. However, the large number of fried items at Eric Ericsson's is a tipoff that you've dropped a notch into another culinary zone. Our advice: stick to the fresh fish and seafood specials.

For lunch try **Franky's Place** (456 East Main Street, 805/648-6282, $), especially if you're poking around Ventura's Old Historic District. The booths are separated by pieces of sculpture set on pedestals, and the red-brick walls are covered with original oil paintings. The quality of the food matches that of the art—and it's healthy, to boot. Serving natural foods with a vegetarian emphasis, Franky's offers pita and croissant sandwiches, heaping salads, and great homemade soups.

Ventura Harbor has an unusually vibrant scene of its own, above and beyond the amenities on hand for the boating set. A boardwalk affords strollers a pleasant way to fantasy window-shop for yachts. It also offers more reality-based shops, a cute little play arcade (featuring Skee-ball, our favorite waste of time at the beach), friendly pubs, and open-air waterside eateries. We hooked an invigorating lunch at **The Greek at the Harbor** (1583 Spinnaker Drive, Suite 101, 805/650-5350, $$$), which has a magazine-sized menu of Greek staples (as well as belly dancing most nights and dancing waiters on weekends). The Aphrodite salad (jumbo shrimp, tomatoes, avocado, mushrooms, artichokes) was tasty and filling, and the golden calamari hit the spot. The Greek's musical soundtrack gave the scene a pleasant Mediterranean air.

Night Moves

Away from Southern California, the term "nightlife" generally takes on a less lustrous glow. Yet while downtown Ventura is no Sunset Boulevard in the party-down department, it's not entirely bereft of good times after dark. The restored **Ventura Theater** (26 South Chestnut Street, 805/653-0721) books a steady stream of middlingly popular national acts. The eclectic likes of Blondie, Steel Pulse, Alice Cooper, Jonathan Richman, the Misfits, and the former vocalist for Great White were among those advertised when we passed through town.

On the bar/club scene, we were pointed to a number of places, which we dutifully checked out. Our first stop was **Bombay Bar & Grill** (143 South California Street, 805/643-4404), where you might rock to a band with a handle like the Hound Dogs or dance to hip-hop records spun by a dude with a *nom de turntable* like DJ Pleazure. We passed.

More of the same urban swill (hip-hop deejays, male revues) is served at **Metro Night Club** (317 East Main Street, 805/653-2582), and we passed on that, too. Blues, swing, and

Map of Ventura County—Page 234

Talking Trash at the Beach

You just never know what might wash up on a California beach. But with our help, now you will. Setting aside a day for cleaning the beach was an idea pioneered in Oregon in 1984 and adopted by California in 1985. Traditionally, the beach cleanup day is held on a Saturday in September or October. Now some counties are doing it monthly.

Here is a random sampling of some of the more offbeat items that have been collected by maintenance workers and volunteer beach cleanup crews in recent years. We'd say everything but the kitchen sink has washed ashore—but several of those have turned up, as well.

aluminum outdoor lighting grate
an "E.T." hand
angel-food cake pan
athletic supporters
baby bathtub
baby pacifiers
bag of human hair
baggie of marijuana
bed springs
birth-control pills
bottom half of a set of false teeth
bowling ball
boxing glove
bungee cord
Bugs Bunny suit
camera
car parts
car windshield
cement park bench
cherry picker
Chicago Bulls cap
Christmas tree
couches
dead mouse in plastic bag
dead sheep
empty spools of cable
eyeglasses
family portrait
15-foot pipe

$50 bill
fireworks debris
fishing rods
Ford tractor
Frisbee
gear shift from a '54 Ford
Grateful Dead concert tickets
Gucci watch
hard hats
hypodermic needle
"I Love a Clean San Diego"
   bumper sticker
Japanese toilet bowl cleaner
Jehovah's Witness booklets
   (a 10-pound bag)
kitchen sink
La-Z-Boy recliner
life-size inflatable doll
loaded gun
logs the size of telephone poles
mail sack, undelivered
melted radio
milk jugs
miniature Bible
motorcycle
New Age prism
one white patent leather shoe
pickled pig's feet in jars
plastic squid

Ventura County

Map of Central California—Page 233

propane tank	toaster
prosthetic foot	TV
purse with credit cards and	20-gallon oil drum
identification	tweezers
radio	two lottery tickets (both winners)
rat named "Jack" interred in a	typewriter
small coffin	vandalized parking meters
shopping carts	voodoo dolls in jars
silk lei	vial of mystery liquid labeled
soggy screenplay	"Love Potion"
soiled diapers	washboard
stove	washing machine
surfboard	water heaters
tin of chewing tobacco	xylophone

The 12 most commonly collected items of trash on America's beaches—otherwise known as the Dirty Dozen—are listed below. Taken together, they account for two-thirds of the coastal debris picked up by volunteers on Coastal Cleanup Day. For shame, for shame—especially to the piggish smokers who drop their wretched butts in the sand. Here are the Dirty Dozen:

1. cigarette butts (22.55 percent)
2. plastic pieces (5.92 percent)
3. foamed plastic pieces (5.26 percent)
4. plastic caps/lids (5.22 percent)
5. plastic food bags/wrappers (5.11 percent)
6. paper pieces (3.97 percent)
7. glass pieces (3.41 percent)
8. glass beverage bottles (3.39 percent)
9. plastic straws (2.98 percent)
10. plastic beverage bottles (2.89 percent)
11. metal beverage cans (2.8 percent)
12. metal bottle caps (2.24 percent)

Since the program's inception, 507,000 Californians have picked up 7.5 million pounds of litter.

California beach cleanups are organized by the **California Coastal Commission,** with some corporate sponsorship. California Coastal Cleanup Days are held annually each September. If you want to participate, contact the California Coastal Commission, Adopt-A-Beach Program, 45 Fremont Street, Suite 2000, San Francisco, CA 94105, 800/COAST-4U.

Ventura County

Map of Ventura County—Page 234

novelty acts like the Maneaters and the Atomic Dogs are the fare served at **Nicholby's** (404 East Main Street, 805/653-2320), which has been voted "Ventura's #1 nightclub."

We decided to cut our losses and check out what was happening back at the **Borneo Bar** (2055 Harbor Boulevard, 805/643-6000) in our hotel, the Clarion Hotel Ventura Beach. The answer was "not much," so we threw in the towel.

There are a baker's dozen coffee houses in Ventura, including three Starbucks, where one can have a civilized good time in less hysterical surroundings. Several are clustered downtown on or near Main Street, including the **Busy Bee** (478 East Main Street, 805/644-4864), **Cafe Bella** (79 South California Street, 805/643-2171), and **Bagel Rock Cafe** (2781 East Main Street, 805/648-7625). And how can you not like a java joint called **Bad Ass Coffee Company** (204 East Thompson Boulevard, 805/641-2988)?

For More Information

Ventura Visitor and Convention Bureau, 89-C South California Street, Ventura, CA 93001, 805/648-2075, website: www.ventura-usa.com

Emma Wood State Beach

Emma Wood State Beach is attached to the north end of Ventura where U.S. 101 meets Old Rincon Highway. Emma Wood has campsites directly on the beach. The southern section of the park—designated Emma Wood **Group Camp** and located at the end of Main Street in Ventura—has four group sites for tent campers that can accommodate up to 30 persons each, plus an RV group site for up to 50 RVs. If you plan on coming, especially during the warmer months, a prior reservation through ReserveAmerica (800/444-7275) is an absolute necessity.

The **"North Beach"** section of the park has roughly 75 campsites along a threatened beach at which waves lap hungrily at a concrete seawall. It looks as if the campsites could easily be inundated by a big wave. Still, the place is often full because rarely does one get to sleep this close to the ocean. Plus, there's good surfing and fishing. Anglers cast for perch, bass, cabezon, and corbina. At low tide, kids and amateur biologists study the marine life in the tidepools. Bird-watchers find grebes, cormorants, curlews, willets, sandpipers, pelicans, and even a few songbirds and red-tailed hawks in the marsh at the southwest end of the beach.

The beach and campground are fascinating objects of study in and of themselves, as both appear imminently threatened by the ocean's merciless advance upon them. During a summer 2002 visit, we noticed that huge chunks had been chewed out of the seawall, and tree-sized drift logs had been hurled like toothpicks onto the beach. A ranger detailed all of the expensive fixes that have had to be done to date just to keep the place operative. We found ourselves wondering not if but when the state would have to cut its losses and forfeit Emma Wood State Beach to the elements.

Ventura County

Map of Central California—Page 233

Solimar Beach

At the south end of this tiny community, two miles north of Emma Wood State Beach along Rincon Parkway (a.k.a. Old Pacific Coast Highway), glimpses of the "old California" can be seen. Empty cars line the shoulder of the highway beside a mile-long seawall, their occupants straddling surfboards in the frothing ocean. There's no day-use fee, nor is there an official coastal access, because at the north end of the seawall lies the private "beach colony" of **Solimar Beach.** The not-so-pacific ocean waters beat relentlessly against the seawall and the thinning beach, leading one to suspect that this is an inevitably doomed stretch of road—not unlike patches of Old Pacific Coast Highway south of here that now rest in the big drink. Meanwhile, surfers paddle out to Solimar Reef, about 300 yards offshore, which provides a six-foot swell in winter.

Faria Beach

This minute town just north of Solimar Beach on Rincon Parkway/Old Pacific Coast Highway consists of a string of 30 residences facing the hungry ocean. The ocean's waves break directly on the cement wall upon which these doomed structures foolishly sit.

Faria Beach County Park offers 42 campsites in a dirt lot above the boulders that vainly hold back the ocean's encroachment. Faria (pronounced "fa-REE-ya") is a popular beach campground. Again, the access is almost too good. The nightly camping fee of $22 seems steep for what you get: a strip of sun-baked asphalt on a wave-rocked perch with no sand to stroll on. At the north end, the litter can get as thick as a town dump. On our latest visit, the pile of debris blowing about was a foul and shameful sight. This was despite the presence of a graffiti-festooned dumpster for trash disposal. Worse, a lot of non-camping ne'er-do-well youths looked to be engaged in some sort of *Porky's*-style weekend party antics. In all respects, the scene at Faria Beach is not our idea of a good time at the beach.

Surfers pay for day use to try their luck off Pitas Point. They make the strenuous hike up to the point with their boards. The "outside" break is for experienced hands, the "inside" for beginners. Sea kayakers were spied paddling around. But be forewarned: There are no lifeguards and there is no swimming, because there is no beach.

Seacliff

Rincon Highway passes through Seacliff, yet another private "beach colony." Public access is at **Hobson County Park,** which has a small, 31-site campground and picnic facilities. RVs are jammed so close together that privacy seems impossible. SUVs park at crazy angles, making it hard to negotiate the oval drive through the park. (The world, in our view, was not created with SUVs in mind.) Generators whir, kids shout, and music blares, but the campers seem blissfully unaware of these seeming annoyances. Beach erosion is severe here, and the park actually closes during heavy storms. In fact, Hobson looks to us to be one good meteorological jolt away from permanent closure. The reef here makes for good tidepool exploration at low tide, but swimming is out of the question.

The surfing is good at Seacliff, but it's a half-mile swim out to Seacliff Reef. Between Seacliff and Faria, **Rincon Parkway North** serves as a linear campground for RVs, which are allowed to pull over for the night for a modest charge. It's a bumper-to-bumper refugee camp of RVs—it's claimed there are 127 spaces, but it looked like more to us—squeezed onto a narrow shoulder of asphalt mere feet from

Ventura County

Nollan v. California Coastal Commission

James Nollan, a Ventura County landowner, made national headlines in 1987 by taking his property-rights case to the U.S. Supreme Court—and winning. The verdict in the case of *Nollan v. California Coastal Commission* was seen as a victory for developers and property owners, and as a setback for the commission by restricting one of its key strategies for providing greater coastal access to the public.

The site that ignited the legal imbroglio was a 3,600-square-foot beachfront lot in Faria Beach in rural northern Ventura County. On it sat a tiny, decrepit beach cottage owned by James and Marilyn Nollan. In 1982 the couple applied for permits to raze and replace it with a two-story beach bungalow. The California Coastal Commission (CCC), empowered to grant or deny permits for development along the ocean, routinely demanded public easements of landowners. In exchange for a permit, the CCC required the Nollans to grant a right of public access along a lateral strip of beach between the high-tide line and a seawall on their property. The area in question was 10 feet wide and ran the length of their property. The CCC wanted to make it easier for the public to pass between a public beach a quarter mile north of the Nollans' property and another that lay one-third mile south.

Under California law the public owns the shoreline up to but not above the mean high-tide line. That is to say, you can legally walk along the part of the beach that is always or occasionally inundated by waves, but not above it. The dry-sand part of the beach can be privately owned, and crossing it without prior permission is an act of trespass, if the landowner is so inclined. The CCC, in accordance with its mission to protect the state's coastline "as a natural resource belonging to all people," had for years and with uncontested success been imposing public-access dedication requirements upon permit-seeking property owners as a means of increasing public access to the beaches. Such conditions had been imposed upon 1,817 property owners through the end of 1984. Then came Nollan.

In Ventura County Superior Court, the Nollans challenged the CCC-issued development permit with the contested condition. After the Nollans won their case, the CCC appealed. The California State Court of Appeal reversed the ear-

Map of Central California—Page 233

Ventura County

lier decision, holding in favor of the CCC. Supported by the conservative Pacific Legal Foundation, the Nollans appealed to the U.S. Supreme Court, arguing that under the terms of the Fifth Amendment of the U.S. Constitution the CCC's demands for an easement constituted an unwarranted "taking" of private property. The clause in question comes at the end of the Fifth Amendment: ". . . nor shall private property be taken for public use without just compensation."

On June 26, 1987, in the last ruling handed down in the 1986–87 term, the Supreme Court held in favor of the Nollans. By a vote of 5–4, with Justice Antonin Scalia writing the majority opinion, the court ruled that granting public access to private property without compensation must be tied to a specific, justifiable public purpose. A condition placed on development, such as a grant of public easement, fails to pass the test of constitutionality if it "utterly fails to further the end advanced as the justification for the prohibition," said Scalia. In simpler language, if the CCC "wants an easement across the Nollans' property, it must pay for it."

The decision was a pivotal one in the area of private-property rights, pursued with vigor by the Rehnquist court with Justice Scalia at the forefront. The dissenting justices mustered strong arguments of their own, but the tilt of the conservative court opposes government limitations on private property development. The decision forced the CCC to reconsider its methods— which, in the long run, may have been more commendable in principle than constitutional in reality.

In the intervening years the Nollan case has turned out to have a less severe impact on government regulation than some had initially feared. Even the CCC tried to put a positive spin on the Supreme Court verdict, with its executive director claiming that "we're pleased the courts explicitly upheld the right of local and state governments to require public access and dedication as long as they can show a direct relationship between the project and the conditions."

As for the Nollans, it was all more a matter of principle than practice. They had been allowing people to cross their property for years and said they would continue to do so, even after the court decision. "As long as the people are not obnoxious, we would give them permission to walk back and forth," said Mr. Nollan.

Case closed.

Ventura County

Map of Ventura County—Page 234

highway traffic and overlooking an unusable, inaccessible beach. Pressed between traffic and a seawall, this is not beach camping at its most idyllic. Some folks just sit in chaise lounges and hang fishing poles over the seawall. Whatever floats your boat.

Oil Piers Beach

Among the more fascinating and eerie spectacles along the California coast are these four privately owned piers belonging to oil companies whose platforms you see on the offshore horizon. The longest pier leads to a man-made island, gussied up like a tropical paradise to disguise the oil-drilling pumps. Who's zooming who? **Oil Piers Beach** stretches south and north of the largest pier and provides some of the best surfing in California. (In fact, that's the only action these beaches attract.) It's something of a rite of passage to surf in the shadows of such industrial might. For those curious to catch a glimpse of this spectacle, park alongside Rincon Parkway/Old Pacific Coast Highway and poke your nose over the crest of the hill.

Mussel Shoals

Unlike the residential "colonies" to the south, Mussel Shoals is an actual town that sits on either side of the Pacific Coast Highway between Oil Piers Beach and the Santa Barbara County line. It's a threatened setting, with the surf literally rumbling the earth below one's feet. Abandoned segments of Old Pacific Coast Highway can be seen here, affording a sobering glimpse of what lies ahead for coastal planners.

North of **Mussel Shoals Beach** lies La Conchita Point, where the surf breaks close to the pier and onshore rocks. Needless to say, this one is for fearless experts only. The sight of someone taking a wave here is, like kung fu fighting, both exciting and a little frightening. North of the point is **La Conchita Beach,** which can be reached off the U.S. 101 shoulder via a riprap revetment. Plenty of surfers park beside the high-way between La Conchita and Rincon Point and lug their boards down to the beach. For everyone else, it's just not worth the trouble.

Bunking Down

For those who relish out-of-the-way overnight destinations, Mussel Shoals has a funky, out-of-the-way inn perched above the ocean. The name of this surfside haven is **Cliff House** (6602 West Pacific Coast Highway, 805/652-1381, $$$). At $115–195 per night, the rates are on the high side for surfers on safari but affordable for venturesome city sorts looking to make a romantic getaway. Crash here and you'll be lulled to sleep by waves that break against a seawall at the end of a grassy backyard festooned with tropical plants. There's a pool and ping-pong table out back and a restaurant (The Shoals) on-site.

Ventura County

Map of Central California—Page 233

Where's the Beach?

In the 1980s scientists Orrin Pilkey and Wallace Kauffman co-authored a book entitled *The Beaches Are Moving.* Pilkey is a renowned marine geologist and the director of the Center for the Study of Developed Shorelines at Duke University. He is something of a thorn in the side of developers and the U.S. Army Corps of Engineers, whose various projects have contributed significantly to the degradation of beaches and coastlines all over America. Were Pilkey to revise *The Beaches Are Moving* today, he might have to retitle it *The Beaches Have Moved.*

The problem of severe beach erosion has alarmed state and county officials. The beaches along U.S. 101 between Ventura and Santa Barbara have become badly eroded, and not just in front of homeowners' property, but at state and county parklands, too. At Hobson County Park, nine miles north of Ventura, the sea comes right up to the campground, where at one time it was buffered by a wide expanse of white, sandy beach. The problem of intensive erosion is also felt at Mussel Shoals, Solimar, Rincon, Emma K. Wood, and Faria Beaches.

It's a mostly human-made and partly natural disaster. From the human side the damming of streams and rivers has interrupted the supply of sand and sediment that replenishes the shoreline, especially during the high-flow winter storm season. Development along the coast—harbors, military bases, homes, and attendant beach-hardening structures such as jetties, seawalls, and breakwaters—has altered the southerly, longshore flow of sand, carrying it off the coast where it is forever lost in submarine canyons and depressions. Finally, nature itself goes through periodic cycles of enhanced storminess and erosion.

Current evidence strongly supports the theory of global warming, which may cause rising sea levels that will further inundate low-lying areas. That, too, might well have a human-engineered component to it, if by industrial and automotive release of "greenhouse gases" into the atmosphere we are contributing to a rise in global temperatures.

In any case, as we wandered along the narrow, rocky strips between sea and seawall at places like Rincon Beach, we found ourselves wondering, "Where's the beach?"

Ventura County

Map of Ventura County—Page 234

© ROBERT HULMES/CALTOUR

Chapter 5
Santa Barbara County

Santa Barbara County

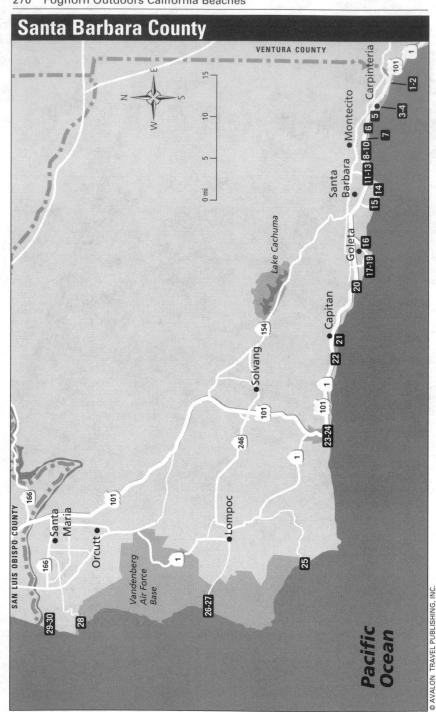

© AVALON TRAVEL PUBLISHING, INC.

Santa Barbara County Beaches

1 Rincon Point, page 278

Location: Rincon Parkway/Old Pacific Coast Highway at Ventura County line
Parking/fees: limited free roadside parking
Hours: sunrise–sunset
Facilities: none
Contact: none

2 Rincon Beach County Park, page 278

Location: Bates Road, off U.S. 101, three miles east of Carpinteria
Parking/fees: free parking lot
Hours: 8 A.M.–sunset
Facilities: restrooms and picnic area
Contact: Santa Barbara County Department of Parks and Recreation, 805/681-5650

3 Carpinteria State Beach, page 279

Location: From Highway 1 in Carpinteria, take Casitas Pass Road exit, turn right on Carpinteria Avenue and left on Palm Avenue, and follow it into the park.
Parking/fees: $4 entrance fee per vehicle. Camping fees are $13–22 per night, plus a $7.50 reservation fee.
Hours: 7 A.M.–sunset
Facilities: lifeguards, restrooms, showers, and picnic tables
Contact: Carpinteria State Beach, 805/684-2811

4 Carpinteria City Beach, page 279

Location: end of Linden Avenue in Carpinteria
Parking/fees: metered street and lot parking
Hours: sunrise–11 P.M.
Facilities: lifeguards
Contact: Carpinteria Community Services, 805/684-5405

5 Padaro Beach (a.k.a. Santa Claus Beach), page 279

Location: Santa Claus Lane in Carpinteria
Parking/fees: free roadside parking
Hours: sunrise–11 P.M.

Santa Barbara County

Map of Santa Barbara County—Page 270

Facilities: none
Contact: Santa Barbara County Department of Parks and Recreation, 805/681-5650

6 Loon Point Beach, page 280

Location: end of Padaro Lane in Padaro
Parking/fees: free parking lot
Hours: 8 A.M.–sunset
Facilities: restrooms
Contact: Santa Barbara County Department of Parks and Recreation, 805/681-5650

7 Lookout County Park, page 281

Location: end of Lookout Park Road in Summerland
Parking/fees: free parking lot
Hours: 8 A.M.–sunset
Facilities: lifeguards (weekends only), restrooms, and picnic tables
Contact: Lookout County Park, 805/969-1720

8 Miramar Beach, page 281

Location: at Miramar Resort Hotel, 1555 South Jamison Lane, in Miramar
Parking/fees: limited free street parking
Hours: 8 A.M.–sunset
Facilities: none
Contact: Santa Barbara County Department of Parks and Recreation, 805/681-5650

9 Hammond's Beach, page 283

Location: trail to beach from end of Eucalyptus Lane in Montecito Park
Parking/fees: free parking lot
Hours: 8 A.M.–sunset
Facilities: none
Contact: Santa Barbara County Department of Parks and Recreation, 805/681-5650

10 Butterfly Beach, page 283

Location: along Channel Drive, between Four Seasons Biltmore and Butterfly Lane, in Montecito
Parking/fees: free limited street parking
Hours: 8 A.M.–sunset
Facilities: none
Contact: Santa Barbara City Department of Parks and Recreation, 805/564-5433

Santa Barbara County

Map of Central California—Page 233

⬛11 East Beach, page 289

🚲 🌐 ⚄

Location: East Cabrillo Boulevard, between Ninos Drive and State Street, in Santa Barbara
Parking/fees: metered lot and street parking
Hours: 24 hours
Facilities: lifeguards, restrooms, showers, and picnic tables
Contact: Santa Barbara City Department of Parks and Recreation, 805/564-5433

⬛12 West Beach, page 289

Location: State Street at Stearns Wharf in Santa Barbara
Parking/fees: metered lot and street parking
Hours: 24 hours
Facilities: concession, lifeguards and restrooms
Contact: Santa Barbara City Department of Parks and Recreation, 805/564-5433

⬛13 Leadbetter Beach, page 290

🏄 ⚄

Location: Shoreline Drive, north of the Santa Barbara Harbor, in Santa Barbara
Parking/fees: metered parking lot
Hours: 24 hours
Facilities: concession, lifeguards, restrooms, and picnic tables
Contact: Santa Barbara City Department of Parks and Recreation, 805/564-5433

⬛14 Mesa Lane Beach (a.k.a. 1,000 Steps Beach), page 290

🏄 ⚂

Location: stairwell to beach at end of Mesa Lane in Santa Barbara
Parking/fees: free street parking
Hours: 24 hours
Facilities: none
Contact: Santa Barbara City Department of Parks and Recreation, 805/564-5433

⬛15 Arroyo Burro Beach County Park, page 290

🌐 ⚄

Location: two miles west of Santa Barbara, off Cliff Drive
Parking/fees: free parking lot
Hours: 8 A.M.–sunset
Facilities: concession, lifeguards, restrooms, and picnic tables
Contact: Arroyo Burro Beach County Park, 805/687-3714

⬛16 Goleta Beach County Park, page 295

Location: 5990 Sand Spit Road in Goleta
Parking/fees: free parking lot
Hours: 8 A.M.–sunset

Map of Santa Barbara County—Page 270

Santa Barbara County

Facilities: concession, lifeguards, restrooms, and picnic area
Contact: Goleta Beach County Park, 805/967-1300

17 Isla Vista County Park, page 296

Location: Del Playa Drive at Camino Corto in Isla Vista
Parking/fees: free street parking
Hours: 8 A.M.–sunset
Facilities: picnic tables
Contact: Santa Barbara County Department of Parks and Recreation, 805/681-5650

18 Santa Barbara Shores, pages 296–297

Location: south of Hollister Road in Isla Vista
Parking/fees: free parking lot
Hours: 8 A.M.–sunset
Facilities: none
Contact: Santa Barbara County Department of Parks and Recreation, 805/681-5650

19 Sands Beach (Coal Oil Point Natural Reserve), page 297

Location: end of Storke Road in Isla Vista, on the campus of the University of California at Santa Barbara
Parking/fees: Park in Isla Vista and walk across campus, or reserve a campus parking permit by calling the Natural Reserve System Office, 805/893-4127.
Hours: 24 hours
Facilities: none
Contact: Natural Reserve System Office, Marine Science Institute (Trailer 342), University of California at Santa Barbara, call 805/893-8000

20 Bacara Beach, page 297

Location: off Hollister Road five miles west of Goleta
Parking/fees: free parking lot
Hours: 8 A.M.–sunset
Facilities: restrooms and showers
Contact: Santa Barbara County Department of Parks and Recreation, 805/681-5650

21 El Capitan State Beach, page 298

Location: 15 miles northwest of Santa Barbara, off U.S. 101
Parking/fees: $4 entrance fee per vehicle. Camping fees are $13–22 per night, plus a $7.50 reservation fee.
Hours: 8 A.M.–sunset

Santa Barbara County

Map of Central California—Page 233

Facilities: concession, lifeguards (seasonal), restrooms, showers, and picnic tables.
Contact: California State Parks, Channel Coast District, 805/899-1400

22 Refugio State Beach, page 298

Location: off U.S. 101, 17 miles northwest of Santa Barbara
Parking/fees: $4 entrance fee per vehicle. Camping fees are $13–16 per night, plus a $7.50 reservation fee.
Hours: 8 A.M.–sunset
Facilities: concession, lifeguards (seasonal), restrooms, showers, and picnic tables
Contact: California State Parks, Channel Coast District, Gaviota Sector, 805/968-1033

23 San Onofre and Vista del Mar Beaches (Gaviota State Park), page 299

Location: .5 mile southeast of the main entrance to Gaviota State Park, off U.S. 101
Parking/fees: free roadside parking
Hours: 8 A.M.–sunset
Facilities: none
Contact: California State Parks, Channel Coast District, Gaviota Sector, 805/968-1033

24 Gaviota State Park, page 299

Location: 20 miles northwest of Santa Barbara off U.S. 101
Parking/fees: $4 entrance fee per vehicle. Camping fees are $13–22 per night, plus a $7.50 reservation fee.
Hours: 8 A.M.–sunset
Facilities: lifeguards (seasonal), restrooms, showers, and picnic tables
Contact: California State Parks, Channel Coast District, Gaviota Sector 805/968-1033

25 Jalama Beach County Park, page 300

Location: Take Highway 1 five miles north of Lompoc, then turn west onto Jalama Beach Road and follow it 10 miles.
Parking/fees: $5 entrance fee per vehicle. Camping fees are $16–22 per night.
Hours: 8 A.M.–sunset
Facilities: concession, lifeguards, restrooms, showers, and picnic tables
Contact: Jalama Beach County Park, 805/736-6316

26 Vandenberg Air Force Base Fishing Access, page 301

Location: Vandenberg Air Force Base, off Highway 1
Parking/fees: free weekend fishing access pass available from Vandenberg Air Force Base Game Warden; valid driver's license and California fishing license required
Hours: Saturday and Sunday, sunrise–sunset

Santa Barbara County

Map of Santa Barbara County—Page 270

Facilities: none
Contact: Vandenberg Air Force Base Game Warden, 805/606-6804

27 Ocean Beach County Park, page 301

Location: 10 miles west of Lompoc, via Ocean Park Road/Highway 246, in the town of Surf
Parking/fees: free parking lot
Hours: 8 A.M.–sunset
Facilities: restrooms and picnic tables
Contact: Ocean Beach County Park, 805/934-6123

28 Point Sal State Beach, page 301

Location: nine miles west of Guadalupe via Point Sal Road
Parking/fees: free parking lot
Hours: 8 A.M.–sunset
Facilities: none
Contact: California State Parks, Channel Coast District, La Purisima Sector, 805/733-3713

29 Rancho Guadalupe Dunes County Park, page 302

Location: eight miles west of Guadalupe, via Main Street/Highway 166
Parking/fees: free parking lot
Hours: 8 A.M.–sunset
Facilities: restrooms
Contact: Ocean Beach County Park, 805/934-6123

30 Guadalupe–Nipomo Dunes Preserve, page 302

Location: accessible through Rancho Guadalupe Dunes County Park (eight miles west of Guadalupe, via Main Street/Highway 166) or Oso Flaco Lake (four miles north of Guadalupe via Highway 1, then four miles west via Oso Flaco Lake Road)
Parking/fees: free parking lot
Hours: by reservation only
Facilities: restrooms
Contact: Dunes Center, Guadalupe–Nipomo Dunes Preserve, 805/343-2455

Santa Barbara County

Map of Central California—Page 233

Santa Barbara County

If you took all the best beach ingredients—sand, sun, surf, seclusion, and scenery, plus decent food and oceanfront lodging—and mixed them in a pot, you'd have Santa Barbara County. Even factoring in such negatives as offshore oil platforms, this county has been graced with an abundance of coastline to crow about. With the exceptions of private ranchland around Point Conception and a military installation, Vandenberg Air Force Base, Santa Barbara County is remarkably accommodating where the land meets the sea. The city of Santa Barbara is, in terms of geography, scenery, and climate, as close to perfect as any city we've encountered. If we could afford it, we might even move there to loll in the sun and play volleyball on the beach for the rest of our days.

The county begins at Rincon Point, a famed surfing spot, and ends at Guadalupe, a speck of a burg that provides access to the tallest sand dunes on the West Coast. In between these extremes exists a 100-mile slice of heaven on earth that encompasses the small-town appeal of Carpinteria (which boasts of having the "world's safest beach"), the urban amenities of Santa Barbara, and the timeless isolation of Point Sal State Beach. In the middle of the county is a holy trinity of state beaches—El Capitan, Refugio, and Gaviota—that are worth their weight in golden sand. Santa Barbara's central and north county beaches are so valuable, in terms of ecology and relative lack of development, that the federal government is looking at preserving 72 miles of coastline as Gaviota Coast National Seashore. We'd certainly second that proposal.

Map of Santa Barbara County—Page 270

Rincon Point and Rincon Beach County Park

Rincon is one of the best surfing spots in California. It used to be hard to access because of beach-hogging private homes in the area. However, there are now two well-maintained public accesses that will get you from the highway to the beach with relative ease and total legality. They are Rincon Point and Rincon Beach County Park. The long centipede-like parking lot of at **Rincon Point**—the more southerly of the two Rincon accesses, designated as a unit of Carpinteria State Beach—is a godsend to surfers. A well-graded dirt path at its south end worms its way between U.S. 101 and all the private beachfront homes en route to a U-shaped cove with a splendid view of the rugged mountains. One must then walk west around the point—which is just inside Ventura County and also accessible via Rincon Point Parkway—to find the waves for which Rincon is fabled.

Rincon is a classic right point break. It is also one of the best winter surf areas in the world because seasonal swells make for flawlessly shaped waves. You've got to know what you're doing, though, as the surf gets so rough

that even paddling out can be problematic. South of Rincon Point, a second and third point aren't as crowded and have the added feature of tidepools to explore if the waves aren't breaking. The cobblestone beach out here is pretty to look at but not conducive to wading or swimming. However, you don't have to come with the intention of surfing or swimming to appreciate the scenic beach and the shaded hike down to it. Bring a lounge chair and cooler, and watch a real-life surf flick unfold before your very eyes.

Directly across from the turnoff to Rincon Point is **Rincon Beach County Park,** a county-run facility with an overlook, picnic tables, and access to the beach via a winding wooden stairwell that descends a cliff face. Swimmers take the plunge north of the stairwell bottom, where a sign designates that 220 yards of beach have been set aside for swimmers only. Note that there are no lifeguards here. Nude sunbathers disrobe at the far north end of the beach. It's a mixed crowd (old, young, gay, straight) and a congenial scene.

Carpinteria

Many a coastal civic group has proclaimed its sandy land grant to be the "world's safest beach," but Carpinteria just might be the first beach to have been so ordained. Way back in 1602, Spanish explorers described it as *cosa segura de buen gente,* or "the safest beach on the coast." Nestled against the Santa Ynez Mountains on a fertile plain, Carpinteria is a small town (population 15,200) with big assets: beautiful, uncluttered beaches; pleasing Mediterranean climate; and a commanding view of the Channel Islands. The slope of the beach is gentle, with no sudden dropoffs or riptides, making for worry-free swimming.

The original inhabitants of the Carpinteria Valley were the Chumash, who utilized the extensive tar pits for pitch to seal their canoes. Their canoe-building enterprise gave rise to the town name, as Spanish conquistadors referred to it as a "carpentry shop." Carpinteria sits atop a huge pool of the black gold. Beneath the fertile soil in the valley lies a thick layer of tar, and below that, a sea of oil. Much industry in and around Carpinteria is related to petroleum production. Seven oil platforms are visible offshore, and many more fill the rich Santa Barbara Channel. Agriculture is pursued with equal gusto.

Santa Barbara County

Map of Central California—Page 233

To a vacationer's eye Carpinteria has the appeal of a quiet town with rural, slowpoke ways and naturally protected beaches. Some might even argue that Carpinteria is the last great undiscovered beach town in California. However, it is in the process of being discovered, and an upscale real-estate market is emerging. This feeds into the further privatizing of the shoreline, which is evident in the 12-mile stretch from Carpinteria to Santa Barbara, much of which is blocked off by mansions, residential "colonies," and "gated communities" (isn't that an oxymoron?). One place, Padaro, seems inordinately smitten with self-importance. The walls and trees surrounding it are peppered with "Absolutely No Trespassing" signs, and coils of razor-edged barbed wire top their castle walls.

One note of consolation: It seems that Padaro and its like are walled in on both sides. What glimpses we could catch of their shore revealed a lot of protective riprap and precious little beach. The town of Carpinteria itself, though, is unpretentious and laid back. It is so pleasantly livable that the less we say about it, the better for those who live there already.

Several years ago we noticed a sign—a small billboard, actually—staked into a grassy headland south of town. It read, "Buy The Bluffs: Small Town, Big Dreams." A grassroots group, the Citizens for Carpinteria Bluffs, worked to save the bluffs from developers and Union Pacific Railroad, which wanted to build a siding there. A drive up the bluffs, ending at a dirt lot, revealed why the locals were so interested in preservation. We got out of the car, walked to the edge of the cliff, and beheld one of the most stunning beach vistas in California—and one of the last tracts of coastal open space in southern Santa Barbara County.

In May 2002, a 52-acre tract of Carpinteria Bluffs that had been acquired by the group was officially dedicated in a day of celebration. This is great news, not just for this particular open-space parcel but as evidence of what a committed group of individuals can accomplish, even in the face of strong business and political interests that oppose preservation.

Beaches

Carpinteria State Beach is a 50-acre park with a mile-long sandy beach, large dunes, healthy tidepools, and 261 made-in-the-shade campsites. A pretty river courses through the park, descending from mountains that provide a scenic backdrop. It's Shangri-La at the shore, pure and simple. The only drawback is that passing trains can awaken sleeping campers in the middle of the night. An interpretive display on the Chumash is on the premises.

Adjoining it to the north is **Carpinteria City Beach.** A "bathing beach" at the end of Linden Avenue, this municipal beach is particularly safe because an offshore reef acts as a natural breakwater, preventing rip currents from forming. The broad, tree-backed beach bans dogs and surfing, but it's family friendly and has picnic tables and volleyball nets. You'll have to park at metered spaces on the surrounding streets or in a pay lot ($1 per hour, $5 all day). Some of the tar bubbling beneath the ocean floor (60 feet below the surface) seeps into the water and ends up on the bottoms of human feet, thus explaining the ubiquitous packets of "Tar Off" seen around town. Not to worry; it's part of a natural process, not an oil spill.

On the north side of Carpinteria, accessible via Santa Claus Lane, is **Padaro Beach** (a.k.a. Santa Claus Beach). Here's the drill: park your car on the side of the road, cross railroad tracks, and work your way over a wall of boulders and then through a small sand fence to get out onto the beach. A pretty beach it is, too: nice and flat, with coarse brown sand, looking north at the private colony of Padaro, protected from

Santa Barbara County

human invaders and the ocean's incursion by more boulders. Even with all that money, it's like they're living in some sort of prison. On the beach side, they're walled in by rocks, while on Padaro Lane, coils of razor wire prevent unwarranted access to the playpens of the rich and paranoid. Hey, they can have it—and here's hoping the next El Niño takes it.

A county beach access, **Loon Point Beach,** has been added in recent years, with a free parking lot among eucalyptus trees on Padaro Lane. It's a bit of a traipse to the beach that involves walking beside railroad tracks and then gingerly negotiating a rutted, gullied path down to the water. A quarter mile later, you're on a beautiful beach backed by yellow sandstone cliffs. The headland above it looks to be under development—no doubt another "luxury gated community" is on the way.

Bunking Down

Many overnight visitors to Carpinteria camp in the state park, one of the most scenic and well-shaded in all of coastal California. The town also gets its share of day-trippers at the city beach on summer weekends. Motels are few and scattered, but their number will no doubt increase as word gets out about this charming town. As it is, no motel sits directly on the beach, though you can make yourself comfortable several blocks away at the **Best Western Carpinteria Inn** (4558 Carpinteria Avenue, 805/684-0473, $$) or

Prufrock's Garden Inn (600 Linden Avenue, 805/566-9696, $$$$).

The latter, a romantic seven-room B&B, indeed takes its name from T.S. Eliot's elliptical poem "The Love Song of J. Alfred Prufrock." One does not expect to encounter abstruse literary references in modest Carpinteria, but we're not complaining. Rates are not cheap at either place, and rooms at the inn run in the stratospheric $200–300 range. If you're looking for cheaper digs in the same neighborhood, **Motel 6** (5550 Carpinteria Avenue, 805/684-8602, $) will leave the light on for you.

Coastal Cuisine

The usual assortment of pizza joints, taco huts, cafés, and delis typify Carpinteria's plain-cloth dining scene. You can charbroil your own fish at **The Palms** (701 Linden Avenue, 805/684-3811). The **Fish Barrel** (509 Linden Avenue, 805/684-2391) specializes in diversity, offering fish 'n' chips and Thai food on the same menu. The **Coffee Grinder** (910 Linden Avenue, 805/867-6015, $) will get your day off to a good start. If the coffee doesn't jolt you, the folk art will. For anything more ambitious head north to nearby Santa Barbara, which is one of California's culinary capitals.

For More Information

Carpinteria Valley Chamber of Commerce, 5320 Carpinteria Avenue, Carpinteria, CA 93013, 805/684-5479, website: www.carpcofc.com

Santa Barbara County

Summerland

The seaside village of Summerland (population 1,800) is a cat's whisker east of Montecito. The name summons visions of a place where everyone is on permanent vacation and the sun's always shining. Though small, Summerland has a pair of nice bed-and-breakfast inns, a good restaurant, a few antique shops, and two county-run beach accesses worth dropping by if you're passing through.

Beaches

Lookout County Park offers the option of picnicking on the wooded blufftop above or playing on the sandy beach below. This semi-isolated spot is the only public beach of any consequence between Carpinteria and Santa Barbara. Lifeguards are on duty on summer weekends only. Because of the isolation, nude sunbathers congregate on the sands south of here, unofficially known as Summerland Beach.

Bunking Down

The **Inn on Summer Hill** (2520 Lillie Avenue, 805/969-9998, $$$$) is a 16-room hotel/inn of-fering ocean views, full breakfast, canopy beds, and English country decor in its suites. Rates start at $229 per night. The yellow clapboard **Summerland Inn** (2161 Ortega Hill Road, 805/969-5225, $$) has fewer amenities than its competitor, but its 12 comfortable rooms go for about half the price ($99–190 in-season, and $30 less than that in the off season). It's a great deal, almost a bargain, on this pricey part of the coast.

Coastal Cuisine

Quaint and casual, the **Big Yellow House** (108 Pierpont Avenue, 805/969-4140, $$) is comfortably situated in a century-old Victorian mansion, offering home-style meals (steak, seafood, and pasta) and appetizing ocean views. Its culinary orientation is California-style home cooking, and it serves three meals daily.

For More Information

Santa Barbara Conference and Visitors Bureau, 1601 Anacapa Street, Santa Barbara, CA 93101, 805/966-9222 or 800/549-5133, website: www.santabarbaraca.com

Montecito

The main reason to come to the upscale village of Montecito is to stay at one of its several splendid hotel-resorts. From beachside beauties like the Four Seasons Biltmore Santa Barbara and the Miramar to the San Ysidro Ranch in the steep hills, the bywords here are money and luxury. If Santa Barbara is perceived as a bastion of high life brimming with comfort and money, then Montecito is an even more exclusive enclave. Coast Village Road is Montecito's Rodeo Drive, lined with expensive shops that bear names like Angel, Mischief, and Objects. On the real-estate market, unspectacular homes costing a cool million are not unusual, and $4 or $5 million for a house and lot with a view doesn't raise an eyebrow.

At one time a minor coda appended to Santa Barbara's seaside symphony, Montecito is now a full-fledged fugue in its own right. Currently the population is listed at 9,500. You can gauge the community's wealth not only by its inflated real-estate prices but by such everyday things as the cost of gas or a cup of coffee, and the lost-pet ad we saw affixed to local telephone poles. Instead of a beloved lab or housecat, the heartbroken owner was looking for an exotic red-billed parrot that had flown the coop.

Beaches

Miramar Beach is accessible from and named after the Miramar Resort Hotel, which fronts

Map of Santa Barbara County—Page 270

Santa Barbara County

You Stay, You Pay: The Incredible Inflated Hotel Resort Surcharge Scam

Have you ever noticed that the more you pay to stay somewhere, the less you get? It's almost as if an inflated room rate confers some sort of license to charge, in an à la carte fashion, for things that one might ordinarily expect to receive for free—e.g., a parking space for your car, use of the on-site exercise facility, or even (especially) daring to call out on the room phone. These add-ons can add up, especially when you factor in the lately popular energy surcharge ($3 night) or the cost of mandatory valet parking ($16–24 per night) or the unfathomable extras that are routinely tacked on to food and beverage items ordered through room service (inflated in-room menu charge plus 20 percent gratuity, plus $5 delivery fee, plus applicable taxes).

At one upscale resort, we calculated that a bowl of "mixed berries" would have set us back about $20, after all the surcharges were added to the listed fee of $10 for the miserly bowl of fruit. (For the record, $10 will fetch about four quarts of berries at a grocery store.) A cabana beside a pool at the same resort was going for a daily fee of $75–150. Also, use of the fitness rooms was complimentary, but a $25 daily fee for use of the locker room was applied. Can you realistically enjoy the former without the latter? Surely, even the wealthiest individual is going to notice the absurdity of being touched at every turn.

Here is our projection of the sorts of new fees that may show up as luxury-hotel surcharges in the future:

- minibar use-determination inspection fee
- beach recreation sand and crab hole disturbance fee
- scenic vista viewing assessment
- bedside pen-and-pad amenity replacement fee
- kiwi and honeydew melon decorative beveling charge
- toilet-paper origami end-sheet folding fee
- on-site fresh air consumption surcharge
- hourly television viewing charge
- shower and toilet wastewater-processing assessment
- foliage and shrubbery grounds-enhancement surcharge
- excretory-emergency bathroom-telephone usage fee
- window and mirror cleaning fee
- throwaway shower cap restocking charge
- room and hall vacuuming electricity-recovery surcharge
- robe and slippers laundering and rehanging fee
- valet car-insurance recovery surcharge
- semen-discharge linen restoration fee
- guest bill computation accountancy charge

Santa Barbara County

Map of Central California—Page 233

500 feet of prime, uncrowded ocean frontage. Trails lead to **Hammond's Beach,** a public beach slightly west of Miramar. These two beaches are mainly enjoyed by guests of the hotel or locals who want to escape the crowds in Santa Barbara. Both lie well off the beaten path. To get to Miramar and Hammond's Beaches, take Eucalyptus Lane to a small parking area at its end. Miramar is right here, while a trail leads from here to Hammond's Beach.

Butterfly Beach lies along Channel Drive between the "Biltmore Wall" (in front of the Four Seasons Santa Barbara Biltmore) and the end of Butterfly Lane. Butterfly Beach isn't much of a beach. In past years, it's been so eroded that we've seen the ocean lapping at the retaining wall. In 2002, there seemed to be a bit of a beach in place here. (We suspect beach renourishment.) In any case, an impressive contingent of coeds reposed in the sand. Behind the beach, the green, lovely grounds of the Biltmore provided a resplendent backdrop.

Incidentally, bicycling is a great way to get out and see the Montecito and Santa Barbara beachfront. A bike path runs from the Biltmore to the harbor area just north of Stearns Wharf, a distance of about four miles. Most hotels stock bikes for their guests. Alternatively, rent one at **Beach Rentals** (8 West Cabrillo Boulevard, 805/963-2524), across from Stearns Wharf in Santa Barbara.

Bunking Down

You'll find Santa Barbara's topmost hotels and resort properties in Montecito. The **Four Seasons Biltmore Santa Barbara** (1260 Channel Drive, 805/969-2261, $$$$) ranks at the top of the list. It is so posh and well established that it publishes its own folio-sized, book-length history. The premises teem with orange trees and fragrant botanical gardens, and the rooms are palatial. Graceful arches and brick walkways connect the villa-style buildings. The grounds are covered with Monterey cypress, blue gums, and parlor palms. The Four Sea-

sons Biltmore feels like a world unto itself—which, in a sense, it is, being situated directly on Butterfly Beach, out of range of traffic and in-town bustle. Amenities include a fully equipped fitness center, heated 50-meter outdoor pool and hot tub, and two on-site restaurants. Twelve-speed mountain bikes are cheaply rented to guests, which is good since standard room rates run—gulp—$475-520 nightly. Two nights at the Biltmore would pay our respective monthly mortgages!

Up the road apiece, a few miles into the mountains off San Ysidro Road, is the legendary **San Ysidro Ranch** (900 San Ysidro Lane, 805/969-5046, $$$$). It is a 540-acre resort ranch whose chief claims to fame are that Vivien Leigh and Laurence Olivier were married on the grounds and that JFK and Jackie honeymooned here. These events are preserved in framed clippings hung in the lobby area. Rest and relaxation without pomp or pretense is the philosophy here. The rooms are in bungalows strewn around the sprawling estate. Some have their own hot tub on a private deck. Nothing comes cheaply here: nightly rates range from $399 for a "canyon room" to $699 for a "deluxe cottage" to $1,350 for a two-bedroom suite to $1,875 for the "Kennedy Suite." If you've really got loot to burn, the Eucalyptus Cottage goes for $4,100 (no typo!) per night.

The ranch has its own stables, and guests can opt for any kind of horse ride, from a trail ride into the mountains to a "meditation walk" around the grounds. On the latter you close your eyes, bliss out, and let your equine bodhisattva lead you on a journey to the center of the mind. The ranch also offers spa services, such as massage, aromatherapy, and skin treatments. A menu of these, ranging from an hourlong massage to a full two-day schedule of indulgent therapies, will set you back anywhere from $145 to more than a grand.

Pets are welcomed and, somewhat ridiculously, pampered to the max. The "privileged pet" program includes peanut-butter canine cookies at check-in, VIP gifts upon arrival (rawhide chews, squeaky toys, personalized bowl), the pet's name hung on a wood-burned sign outside the cottage, doggie turn-down service, and Perrier for pets. Sound a bit excessive? It did to us, too. But maybe not to Pokey, Smoke, Chloe, Rexford, Fresca, and Sprite—some of the pooches whose names were entered in the pet guest register at the front desk.

The **Miramar Resort Hotel** (1555 South Jamison Lane, 805/969-2203, $$$) claims the technical distinction of being the only hotel on the beach in the area. That is to say, there's not even a street to cross to get to the sand. The hotel offers lodgers a choice of rooms, cottages, and bungalows at numerous price points, ranging $85–835. After being closed since September 2000, it reopened in spring 2003.

Closer to town, the **Montecito Inn** (1295 Coast Village Road, 805/969-7854, $$$$) has a bit of showbiz history attached to it. Charlie Chaplin and (though brochures don't mention him) the scandalized Fatty Arbuckle established the Montecito Inn in 1928. Its 53 rooms are decorated in French provincial style, while the lobby is a lake of Italian marble. The inn is three blocks from the beach. Chaplin's Little Tramp couldn't have afforded to stay here, but if you're solvent to the tune of $205 and up per night, they'll roll out the welcome mat.

A final word: While the standard rates quoted at the higher-end resorts might seem way out of your league, it's worth trolling around for special packages and deals. At the Montecito Inn, for instance, a "midweek special" will net you a room with a queen bed for $129 a night Sunday–Thursday.

Coastal Cuisine

All the best dining in Montecito is in the resorts and hotels. The menu at the **Stonehouse** at the San Ysidro Ranch (900 San Ysidro Lane, 805/969-5046, $$$$) for instance, will help you "rediscover the great foods of America," as the dining room's motto proclaims. Many of the herbs and vegetables used are organically grown on the premises. Entrées run about $20–40.

The Four Seasons Biltmore Santa Barbara has its own fine on-premises dining rooms as well: **La Marina** (1260 Channel Drive, 805/969-2261, $$$$) specializes in California regional cuisine (read: surf and turf items with creative, high-end sauces and accompaniments), such as roast sea bass with three vegetable purees, morel mushrooms and fava beans in a potato cage (let me out!). The more casual **Patio Restaurant** ($$$) serves a decadent Sunday-brunch spread from its glass-enclosed atrium.

Night Moves

The **Four Seasons Biltmore Santa Barbara** (1260 Channel Drive, 805/969-2261) has a nice, civilized lounge with a pianist. If you want anything more from your evening than the sounds of a well-groomed gent tickling the ivories amid the clinking of cocktail glasses, you'll have to head into downtown Santa Barbara, where you'll find nightlife to last till sunrise.

For More Information

Santa Barbara Conference and Visitors Bureau, 1601 Anacapa Street, Santa Barbara, CA 93101, 805/966-9222 or 800/549-5133, website: www.santabarbaraca.com

Map of Central California—Page 233

Santa Barbara

If you were to feed all the variables that govern quality of life into a computer, Santa Barbara might just top the list. All it takes is a day or two's exposure to the beaches, mountains, towering palm trees, Spanish architecture, and convivial bustle to become convinced that this is America's most nearly perfect setting for a city. This is true despite the very real problems (see "The Other Side of Paradise") that have beset the community over the years.

The reasons for Santa Barbara's good fortune are many, and geography is not the least of them. Santa Barbara (population 92,500) is encircled by the Santa Ynez Mountains, which cradle the city, staving off winds that blow down from the north. Twenty miles offshore, the Channel Islands intercept the Pacific swells, protecting the coastline. Santa Barbara is the only city in California that faces due south, running along a figurative ceiling that divides the Central and Southern California coasts. It is the northernmost city that maintains that sunny SoCal climate and vibe. The climate is moderate year-round: comfortably cool in summer, never too cool in winter, shirt-sleeve weather almost every day. Located between Los Angeles (92 miles southwest) and San Francisco (332 miles north), Santa Barbara embodies elements of both cities without suffering the extreme urban angst common to them.

This city is a human parade that makes State Street, the primary artery, seem like a nonstop Cinco de Mayo celebration. Our most recent visit to Santa Barbara coincided with this Mexican holiday, which has become, like St. Patrick's Day, another excuse for Americans to drink and party. College kids were out in force at happy hour and late into the night, although this is nothing unusual in Santa Barbara. Their whooping and whistling could be heard the length of State Street.

Other groups commingle in this open-air bazaar from first rays to last call. You'll see families on vacation, hooting happily as they pedal tandem bikes or duck into ice-cream shops for sugar fixes. Well-mannered, broadbellied bikers navigate gleaming, screaming Harleys. Perfectly togged yuppie couples stroll the streets on romantic getaway weekends. Young, free-spirited foreign visitors are drawn to Santa Barbara's figurative fountain of youth. At night, older folks turned out in dark suits and formal gowns make their way to the symphony or theater after dining at one of State Street's tony restaurants. You'll also see lots of homeless people.

We will grant you this: the homeless of Santa Barbara are more resourceful than the typical down-at-the-heels spare-changers in places like Santa Monica and San Francisco. On one of our visits, a homeless entrepreneur had constructed a folk-art installation on the sandy beach beside the pier. Decorative motifs included a tiny mirrored ball, sparkly adornments on flags, sawed-off plastic soda jugs, half-buried beer cans (possibly drained by the artist himself). The words "Welcome to Santa Barbara" were spelled out in raised block letters in the sand. We saw him chomping on a big hunk of watermelon when we first passed his environment; on our return, he lay prone inside a pup tent with his feet protruding from the end. He had placed a wicker basket below the pier railing to catch the change that grateful art lovers could lob into it from above. For better or worse, this sort of scene has become as much a part of the city's landscape as the Santa Barbara Mission.

Many who live here are activist-aesthetes who have made a mission of keeping their city clean, green, and out of the hands of those who'd turn it into an urban Disneyland at the drop of a bank loan. Public consensus ensures progressive stands on such issues as controlled growth and habitat preservation. Consequently,

Map of Santa Barbara County—Page 270

The Other Side of Paradise

Santa Barbara is a wonderful city. Seldom will you find such varied beauty—mountains, beaches, vineyards, hot springs—in such proximity, and with a perfect climate to top it all off. But the city, for all its magnificence, doesn't exist in a glass bubble. It is subject to the myriad stresses and strains that bear upon all American cities in these troubled times. It has fought many issues with the sort of diligence one wishes every community in America would muster. Nonetheless, this earthly paradise has had its share of problems, including:

Fire—On June 27, 1990, an arsonist set a fire on the brushy western outskirts of Santa Barbara that consumed 4,900 acres, destroyed hundreds of homes, caused $238 million worth of damage, and killed one person. The belt of blackened, scorched earth extended from the hills and down the canyons toward the ocean, racing through neighborhoods in northern Santa Barbara and Goleta.

Drought—In the 1970s Santa Barbara elected not to tie into water supplies imported from the Sierra via the State Water Project, fearing that more water would mean more unwanted development. In 1990 it paid a heavy price for its well-intended self-reliance. As California entered its fourth year of drought, with the dry summer season still to come, the city found one of its reservoirs empty and another only one-quarter full. The crisis forced the city to impose severe water conservation measures; its green parks and gardens then turned a dry, dead brown—just in time for the Painted Desert fire, described above.

Freeways and malls—For years Santa Barbara stubbornly defied progress by refusing to do anything about U.S. 101, which cut through the center of town. Residents also hotly debated the construction of a downtown shopping mall. Santa Barbara spent millions and convened nine civic commissions to study the mall and freeway projects. Their eventual implementation was a comedy of errors. By the time the city finally okayed the U.S. 101 project, the state had temporarily run out of funds to pay for it. Likewise, Santa Barbara dragged its heels on the downtown mall, losing commitments from key department stores. All's well that ends well, however. Freeway snarls are in the past, and the downtown mall is an improvement over what it replaced. But the projects did cause fallout, traumatizing and dividing the community for years.

Homelessness—Thanks to its temperate year-round climate, Santa Barbara attracts a sizable indigent population. They gather beneath palm trees by the beach, tilting back bottles and staring at the passing parade. Political correctness aside, their presence blights the area. The hue and cry over homelessness has gone on for many years, most famously in 1986, when an ordinance banning overnight sleeping in public was challenged by the late activist Mitch Snyder, who threatened to bring thousands of homeless folks to the streets of Santa Barbara in protest. The city council amended the ordinance to permit the homeless to sleep in vacant lots and parked cars—a move hailed as an act of "reasonableness and courage."

Offshore drilling—Oil rigs have physically polluted Santa Barbara's beaches and visually polluted the horizon. Nearly two-thirds of California's offshore oil and 85 percent of its natural gas is pumped from beneath the ocean in Santa Barbara and Ventura Counties. In 1969, Santa Barbara made national news and galvanized the environmental movement with a catastrophic spill from an offshore oil rig that befouled 150 miles of shoreline. Because of the spill, fishers in the Santa Barbara Channel lost 50 percent of their trawling grounds. Fast forward to 2002, when the Bush administration pushed for 36 approved but undeveloped oil leases off Santa Barbara County's coastline. The state of California, Santa Barbara and San Luis Obispo Counties, and 10 environmental groups have sued the Department of the Interior over the leases. Secretary of the Interior Gail Norton—a James Watt protégée—appealed a 2001 district court ruling that blocked drilling. On and on it goes.

Decommissioned oil platforms—The first oil rig went up in 1896, offshore of Summerland. Bigger platforms were erected in the 1940s and 1950s. By the late 1980s, the number had risen to 23. In the 1990s, the rigs began coming down as they reached the end of their useful lives. Four rigs in the Santa Barbara Channel were dismantled in 1996. That's good news because even when they're functioning properly, oil platforms produce pollution—each generating the equivalent of 7,000 cars driving 50 miles a day. Even when they come down, there are problems, such as what to do abut the heavy metal and hydrocarbon-contaminated shell mounds scraped off old platform legs.

Dirty beaches—Many of Santa Barbara County's beaches have had poor or failing grades for water quality, as reported in the Heal the Bay organization's beach report cards. Creek-mouth beaches are problematic during wet periods, when nonpoint source pollution washes into streams and out to sea, polluting nearshore waters. From April 2001 through March 2002, these Santa Barbara County beaches received failing grades during wet-weather periods: Carpinteria State Beach, Hammond's Beach, East Beach, Leadbetter Beach, Arroyo Burro Beach, Hope Ranch Beach, Goleta Beach, Refugio State Beach, Gaviota State Beach, and Jalama County Beach. The following beaches received grades of C or worse even in dry weather: Carpinteria State Beach (C), East Beach at Mission Creek (F), Leadbetter Beach (D), Refugio State Beach (C), Gaviota State Beach (D). Santa Barbara County needs to clean up its beaches.

Housing—There is a serious affordable-housing crisis in Santa Barbara. Much is made of the "chronic scarcity of well-designed, appropriately located housing for middle and lower income residents." When it comes to housing, Santa Barbara County is the least affordable in the state. Not only residents but businesses are being forced out by the squeeze. The median price for a home in Santa Barbara County's "South Coast" has lately reached $629,000. Ouch!

Santa Barbara County

Map of Santa Barbara County—Page 270

there's always some kind of battle being waged—city-hall caucuses and grassroots crusades aimed at saving parks and heading off the latest nefarious development proposal. Nonetheless, Santa Barbara can be a restful city. At least two beachcombers burned out from months of rambling around the lion's den of Southern California have found it to be so.

Santa Barbara exists in relatively easy harmony with its environment. Tourism is the closest thing to an industry. Block after block is filled with museums, galleries, theaters, libraries, bookstores, and historic buildings. Following a devastating 1925 earthquake, the city council established an architectural board of review that drafted a design code. Consequently, Santa Barbara was rebuilt in an appealing style that reflects the city's 200-year Spanish and Mexican heritage. Even gas stations and fast-food joints adhere to the stringent architectural code. Pipe roofs, terra cotta tile sidewalks, vanilla stucco walls, colorful mosaic blocks, arcades and walkways, wrought-iron railings, and flower-filled gardens confer a unified architectural signature. Even the benches are adobe.

The most visible example of this style is **Mission Santa Barbara** (2201 Laguna Street, 805/682-4713), established in 1786. Dubbed the "Queen of the Missions," it sits on a knoll overlooking the town. At close range it almost appears two-dimensional, like a Hollywood movie set. The grassy square before it is a greener green and the sky a bluer blue than your most vivid Kodachrome fantasy. The graceful Spanish Colonial facade is dressed in pink and white tones; behind it rise twin bell towers. The grounds include a museum and flower garden. Of the 21 Franciscan missions established throughout California, only Mission Santa Barbara remains active as a parish church.

Continuing into the hills along Mission Canyon Boulevard, you'll come upon **Santa Barbara Botanic Garden** (1212 Mission Canyon Road, 805/682-4726) and **Santa Barbara Museum of Natural History** (2559 Puesta del Sol

Road, 805/682-4711). The botanical garden encompasses 65 acres and 1,000 species of native California trees, flowers, shrubs, grasses, and annuals. The grounds are divided into environmental biomes (canyon, desert, arroyo, meadow, and woodland), each with its own trails. This lovely park plunges visitors back into pre-European, pre-condominium California. Inside the redwood grove everything is stilled to a profound, cathedral-like silence beneath huge boughs. Five miles of pathways wind through the garden. Admission is $5 for kids, $3 for seniors and teens, and $1 for kids.

The Santa Barbara Museum of Natural History offers geology and biology exhibits: a 33-foot model of a giant Pacific squid, planetarium, replica of a Chumash priest doing the "Seaweed Dance" (variations of which are performed nightly at the rock clubs down on State Street), and much more. Founded in 1916, it's impossible to miss: just look for the place with the 72-foot whale skeleton out front. Admission is $7 for adults, $6 for seniors and teens, and $4 for kids.

A walking tour of Santa Barbara's "Red Tile District" is recommended. Visitors can view 20 downtown buildings of historical and architectural interest in a 12-block stroll. (For a map and guide drop by the tourist information center at 1330 State Street.) One of the downtown "must-visits" is **El Presidio de Santa Barbara State Historic Park** (123 East Canon Perdid Street, 805/966-9729). Built in 1782, this was the northernmost of four military fortresses constructed by the Spanish along the coast. Two sections of the original Presidio quadrangle have survived earthquakes and are preserved as a park that forms the heart of Santa Barbara's El Pueblo Viejo Historic District.

Santa Barbara boasts arts-and-crafts galleries, plus a smattering of theater, symphony, and ballet. The city also has much to offer college kids and lower-rung culture vultures like ourselves. The heart of Santa Barbara—in terms of retail shops, restaurants, and nightlife—is State Street, from Los Olivos Street to Cabril-

Map of Central California—Page 233

lo Boulevard (on the waterfront). State Street has its share of pool halls, dive bars, and tattoo parlors, but for the most part it is in tune with the real-life needs of its collegiate, retiree, and tourist patrons. Recreationally, some of the most competitive volleyball in the state is played on the sand courts of East Beach. Within the county's borders are 20 U.S. Forest Service, California State Park, and Santa Barbara County Park campgrounds.

Down at West Beach, at the foot of State Street, lies Stearns Wharf, an old, broad-planked commercial pier on which the public can walk or drive. It is the oldest commercial pier on the West Coast. All day long, cars rumble slowly out and back along the weary timbers of the wharf. (You can park for a fee at pier's end.) The pier is home to a disappointing collection of long-lived seafood restaurants and shops, but it is worth a visit to catch a seabird's-eye view of the beach by day or a romantic glimpse at the twinkling lights of the city at night.

Last of all we'll mention the courthouse. If Mission Santa Barbara is the religious symbol of the community, then **Santa Barbara County Courthouse** is the town's most impressive secular landmark. Built in an elaborate Spanish-Moorish style and occupying a full city block, it looks more like a palace than a courthouse. This turreted treasure must be toured to be believed. It would indeed be an honor to pay a traffic ticket here. The crowning touch is the clock tower ("El Maridor"), atop which an observation deck offers a sweeping panorama of Santa Barbara.

Pondering the city from this vantage point, one cannot help but reflect on the perfect yin-yang of the setting: mountains and ocean, warm sun and cool breezes, college kids and golden oldies, Spanish Colonial architecture and contemporary Americana.

Beaches

Santa Barbara's south-facing beach runs in a long arc along Cabrillo Boulevard. Its 2.5 miles are divided into the plainly named **East Beach** and **West Beach.** These are calm-water beaches whose inland fringe is lined with huge, towering palms that list ever so slightly landward. You really can't improve on this setting, with the mountains, penetrating sunlight, and a hard-blue sky for a backdrop. There's ample parking in huge lots, but for a breezy, bracing, and gas-free tour we recommend the bike path that snakes along the beach zone. The beaches are sandy and broad, litter-free, and well-patrolled by lifeguards. Most everyone pedals or jogs the bike path at a relatively unhurried pace, savoring the sights. In-line skating moms can be seen pushing baby-joggers.

There are more sand volleyball courts on East Beach than anywhere else in California—except maybe Manhattan Beach. East Beach is also the site of Cabrillo Pavilion, a recreational center, bathhouse, and architectural landmark dating from 1925. Volleyball players, many of whom are seriously good, turn out in droves on weekends. On one Sunday in late spring, we saw kids braving the waves, shouting as they splashed around in frigid 60-degree water.

A few bum notes: Oil platforms are still visible offshore, though they are gradually being retired. In terms of health risks, the water at East Beach in the vicinity of Mission Creek has elicited warnings for elevated levels of coliform bacteria. In the spring of 2002, testing measured levels of over 11,000 coliform bacteria per milliliter of water. (Translation: oh, shit!) However, the beach in the vicinity of Sycamore Creek usually tests fine. To be safe, swim away from creek mouths (this is generally good advice anywhere). Polluted beaches are not a new story in Santa Barbara. In a rich irony, the self-styled coastal guru who calls himself "Dr. Beach" (a.k.a. Stephen Leatherman) in 2000 placed East Beach on his annual Top 10 list of world's best beaches as the beach was receiving failing grades from water-monitoring agencies for bacterial contamination. Parking at East Beach costs $2 for up to three hours or $7 for all day.

Santa Barbara County

You're supposed to self-pay, and don't think for a second they won't ticket you.

Some locals will cop an attitude and disparage these big, wide, breezy beaches as being "too touristy," but there's enough beach here for everybody. Landward of the bike path is a landscaped, grassy ribbon known as Palm Park. It's an appealing green complete with picnic tables and a lawn that's trimmed, weedless, and more comfortable than shag carpeting. Ask the homeless who while away the hours sitting in the midday sun.

West Beach, which is on both sides of Stearns Wharf, is wide but generally less used for sandy recreation than East Beach. At the far end of West Beach, around the 1,000-slip harbor and breakwater that protects it, the coast gets hillier, and small beaches are tucked into coves at creek mouths. **Leadbetter Beach,** off Shoreline Drive, adjacent to Santa Barbara Harbor, is a good board and windsurfing beach. It also makes a swell spot to pass the time watching boats sail in and out of the harbor. It's a popular place to party, and locals who avoid East and West Beaches claim it as their own. West of Leadbetter Beach, off Shoreline Drive at the end of Mesa Lane, is **Mesa Lane Beach,** another locals-only spot that maintains a comfortable distance from the hubbub of downtown Santa Barbara.

Two miles farther west, **Arroyo Burro Beach County Park** lies beneath the cliffs at the edge of a mesa at the mouth of Arroyo Burro Creek. It's a pretty spot, and a pretty popular one, complete with a picnic area, a surprisingly good restaurant (the Brown Pelican), and a sandy, crescent-shaped beach. Hang gliders launch from the cliffs above at Elings Park. The scene, particularly the striking geography, is like a scaled-down version of Black's Beach/Torrey Pines State Beach, in San Diego County.

Shore Things

• **Bike/skate rentals:** Beach Bike Rentals, 22 State Street, Santa Barbara, 805/966-2282

• **Boat cruise:** Santa Barbara Sailing Center, 133 Harbor Way, Santa Barbara, 805/962-2826

• **Ecotourism:** Captain Don's Whale Watching, 219 Stearns Wharf, Santa Barbara, 805/969-5217

• **Fishing charters:** Sea Landing Sportfishing, 301 West Cabrillo Boulevard, Santa Barbara, 805/963-3564

• **Marina:** Santa Barbara Harbor, 805/564-5433

• **Pier:** Stearns Wharf, State Street at West Cabrillo Boulevard, 805/564-5526

• **Rainy day attraction:** Santa Barbara Museum of Natural History, 2559 Puesta del Sol Road, 805/682-4711

• **Shopping/browsing:** La Cumbre Plaza, State Street and Hope Avenue, Santa Barbara, 805/687-6458; El Paseo, 812 State Street, Santa Barbara (California's oldest shopping mall!)

• **Surf shops:** A-Frame Surf, 3785 Santa Claus Lane, Carpinteria, 805/684-8803; Channel Islands Surfboards, 29 State Street, Santa Barbara, 805/966-7213; Surf Country, 5668 Calle Real, Goleta, 805/683-4450

• **Vacation rentals:** Coastal Getaways, 1086 Coast Village Road, Montecito, 805/969-1258

Bunking Down

Santa Barbara is not a cheap place to visit or vacation, so come prepared for some degree of sticker shock. An oceanfront favorite is **Harbor View Inn** (28 West Cabrillo Boulevard, 805/963-0780, $$$$). The beautifully landscaped mission-style inn overlooks Stearns Wharf and has its own outdoor pool and sundeck, plus an exercise room and sauna. The grounds are gorgeous and the renovated rooms large, airy, and appealing. There's marble everywhere, especially in the spacious, well-appointed bathrooms. Rates aren't cheap, running $150–350 per night in summer. Whatever you pay, keep in mind that you're right by the beach, the wharf, and the action along State Street. You could not be better suited in Santa Barbara, in terms of location and amenities.

Map of Central California—Page 233

Santa Barbara County

The **Santa Barbara Inn** (901 East Cabrillo Boulevard, 805/966-2285, $$$$) is a good choice within sight of the beach. Located east of the downtown bustle, it's quiet at the Santa Barbara Inn. Rooms are spacious and comfortable, and you're only a crosswalk away from East Beach and Cabrillo Pavilion. The three-story hotel has a sundeck, pool, and whirlpool, plus a pricey but highly rated on-site French restaurant, **Citronelle** (805/963-0111, $$$$).

A good distance away but well worth mentioning is **El Encanto Hotel and Garden Villas** (1900 Lasuen Road, 805/687-5000, $$$$). Nestled in the foothills overlooking Santa Barbara, El Encanto is a European-style inn brimming with informal elegance; it's worth the drive up the mountain. At night the town below glimmers like a distant field of flickering candles. Spread out on the grounds of El Encanto are the garden villas. A large pool and Japanese koi pond are set among a thick tangle of flowers and shrubs. A touch of class graces every aspect of El Encanto, where a casual California ambience tempers the European formality to a glow as rosy as a Pacific sunset. Room rates start at $209, and a deluxe suite can top $500 per night.

Between the mountaintops and ocean's edge are some less expensive motels where one can lie in for under $100 a night, but that is about the bottom-line limit in Santa Barbara. Our choice for the budget-minded, largely because of its location (a half-block from the beach, across from City Park), is **Santa Barbara Beach Travelodge** (22 Castillo Street, 805/965-8527, $$). Other serviceable and less costly beachside motels in the vicinity of West Beach include **Ocean Palms** (232 West Cabrillo Boulevard, 805/966-9133, $$), **West Beach Inn** (306 West Cabrillo Boulevard, 93101, 805/966-3904, $$), and **Best Western Beachside Inn** (336 West Cabrillo Boulevard, 805/965-6556, $$).

Coastal Cuisine

Every chef worth his or her salt mill wants to open a restaurant in Santa Barbara, which explains why there are somewhere in the neighborhood of 500 of them, from humble taco huts to formal fine dining. They publish brochures, flyers, and entire magazines about dining in Santa Barbara. Restaurants come and go on this highly competitive scene. The competition is ultimately too intense to allow everyone to make a go of it.

One solid survivor of the food wars is **Downey's** (1305 State Street, 805/966-5006, $$$$). Quality will always win out, and chef proprietor John Downey's philosophy of serving fine dishes made with fresh ingredients and no corner-cutting has served him well. It's a small restaurant, with about a dozen tables. Specializing in "sophisticated California cuisine," it has been judged by the Zagat Survey to be among the top 25 restaurants in California. Dinner here is meant to be an unhurried experience, lingered over and savored. Appetizers of note might include fresh deep-sea Santa Barbara mussels, served on the half shell in a smoky bacon vinaigrette. Entrée items can run the gamut from fresh catches, such as an extraordinary grilled Hawaiian escolar (a deep-sea dweller that occasionally turns up in tuna fishers' nets) to sliced breast of duck, grilled to a turn and served in cabernet sauce. Santa Barbara County wines are spotlighted on the wine list.

Original Enterprise Fish Company (225 State Street, 805/962-3313, $$$), a few blocks back from the beach on the west side of State Street, is our favorite place for seafood. The menu is a changeable list of fresh fish by location and type. It may include Alaskan halibut, Pacific swordfish, Hawaiian ahi, and Costa Rican mahimahi. The halibut, prepared your choice of four ways, is particularly affordable ($16.95, including salad, bread, and side item) and delicious. We tried it two ways—in a ginger-soy beurre blanc and crusted with sesame seeds and topped with spicy fruit salsa—and both were excellent. The restaurant occupies a cavernous old building with brick walls and exposed steel beams. The open cooking area at the center, with two huge smoking grills, is a show in itself. On our latest trip we had dinner at the Enterprise and then returned for lunch the next day. We would've eaten there again if duty didn't demand we check out some other places. **Brophy Bros. Clam Bar and Restaurant** (119 Harbor Way, 805/966-4418, $$$) is Santa Barbara's other great fish house. Its waterside location makes it a good place to head at sunset. **Piranha Restaurant & Sushi Bar** (714 State Street, 805/965-2480, $$$$) is the locals' choice for sushi. Over on Stearns Wharf, the **Harbor Restaurant** (210 Stearns Wharf, 805/963-3311, $$$) specializes in oak-grilled fish and seafood and offers the best ocean view in town.

Joe's Cafe (536 State Street, 805/966-4638, $) merits commendation for very different reasons. If you can appreciate an old-time saloon with padded booths, checkered tablecloths, and a long bar where food and drink are served in generous quantities, you'll love Joe's. Serving supper since 1928, it is Santa Barbara's oldest restaurant. The matchbook motto says it all: "Proud to be local and proud of our past." Mounted deer and moose heads look down on hungry diners awaiting the arrival of heaping, home-cooked blue-plate specials. More than once have we enjoyed the solid, stick-to-the-ribs grub: hot open-faced roast beef sandwiches, brisket of beef, combination seafood plates, and more. Take our clichéd advice and "Eat at Joe's."

A strong Mexican influence pervades Santa Barbara, and State, Haley, and Milpas Streets are lined with Mexican cantinas. Have at it, amigos, and may the best burrito win. For a hot tip on great, cheap Mexican eats, try **Super-Rica Taqueria** (612 North Milpas Street, 805/963-4940, $). Incidentally, the best day starter or eye opener is **Santa Barbara Roasting Company** (321 Motor Way, 805/962-5213, $), just three blocks from the beach near the corner of State Street and West Gutierrez. Great cof-

fee—especially iced drinks (try a white chocolate "Fred")—and baked goods are served in a relaxed, jazz-tinged atmosphere. We also dug the scene right off the beach at **Hot Spots Expresso Bar** (36 State Street, 805/963-4233, $), which is a combination coffeehouse, bakery, and Santa Barbara visitor center, with lots of racked travel literature that can be perused while you enjoy your java and croissant.

Of course, we haven't begun to cover the culinary possibilities in this cultured pearl of a town. Write the Santa Barbara Conference and Visitors Bureau or drop by the Information Stand at 1330 State Street for more detailed listings.

Night Moves

State Street in downtown Santa Barbara is a veritable Whitman's Sampler of fun after dark. Just wander by all the bars and clubs emitting decibels into the night and listen for something that catches your fancy. The street is a nonstop block party. Nobody seems to give a hoot about how loud the hoopla gets, and this laissez-faire attitude is a welcome change from the usual opprobrium.

We polled some local waitresses to get a reading on the hottest nightspots on Santa Barbara's changeable scene. They recommended **Velvet Jones** (423 State Street, 805/965-8676) for live music and **Q's Sushi A Go Go** (409 State Street, 805/966-9177) as the best place to party. Occupying a historic (ca. 1885) building, Q's has a dance floor, sushi bar, booths, and pool tables on its three floors. It has a sushi menu and a sick-of-sushi ("SOS") menu, too. Be forewarned of hefty covers and long lines. As for Velvet Jones, the likes of DJ Tabou and the Velvet Cage Dancers, Nogahyde *(sic)*, Thornlord, DJ Hogg, DJ Winner, and Lyricist Ize were performing when we hit town. We'll spare you a diatribe about the state of contemporary music and just say that we passed.

In our experience over the last 20 years, the

Map of Central California—Page 233

Post-Party Animals: Nightlife on the Sober Side

Back in the 1970s and 1980s, we partied like it was 1999. Now that 1999 has come and gone, we're less interested in "getting our freak on," as a hip-hop anthem from 2001 put it. One of us no longer drinks and the other imbibes rather sparingly—perhaps a beer now and then and a glass of red wine with a good dinner. Therefore, we've closely scrutinized the choices of nonalcoholic beverages at the beach. We're happy to report that night moves need not be stymied just because a person doesn't drink his or her body weight in draft beer.

In the past if you chose not to drink, you'd have to settle for club soda with lime (if you were lucky) or flat ginger ale. Those days are gone, thank god. The best part of sobriety is that you always get home okay and often with some money left in your pocket or purse. Moreover, you're able to function the next day while your fellow pub crawlers are shaking off a cruel hangover. Of course, the downside of sobriety is that you grow bored with the bar scene in less than an hour, realizing that the alligator mouths yammering and yapping on all sides aren't as clever as they seemed when you were under the influence. But that's another sidebar.

The original nonalcoholic beers on the market were bad enough to make one ponder tipping the bottle again. But over the years a batch of high-quality nonalcoholic brews have hit the bartop. They are not just palatable but tasty and refreshing. They're even less filling: 50 calories for a 12-ounce nonalcoholic beer versus 250 for the same amount of real beer.

Naturally, the Europeans make the best near-beers. Here are our favorites, in descending order of drinkability:

1. Kaliber
2. Clausthaler (Beck's)
3. Buckler (Heineken)
4. Coors Cutter
5. Old Milwaukee's NA
6. Sharp's (Miller; only if it's real cold)
7. O'Doul's (Budweiser; the least appealing, ordered only when there's no other choice.)

Note to bar owners: Get smart and start stocking nonalcoholic beer. It is a gold mine, because you can charge the same inflated prices as fortified beverages but don't have to pay alcohol taxes or fear you'll be sued for serving one beer too many to some barfly who drove his car through a wall.

Map of Santa Barbara County—Page 270

Santa Barbara County

supply of suds and sounds along State Street is dependably endless. You'll hear a little bit of everything while making the rounds of **Sharkeez** (416 State Street, 805/963-9680), **The Spot** (532 ½ State Street, 805/884-4085), **Calypso Bar & Grill** (514 State Street, 805/966-1388), the **Press Room** (15 East Ortega Street, 805/963-8121), the **Beach Shack** (742 State Street, 805/884-1107), and **O'Malley's** (513 State Street, 805/564-8904). We particularly like the eclectic CD jukebox at O'Malley's. Santa Barbara's nightlife choices just go on and oñ. Techno rules at the **Madhouse Martini Lounge** (434 State Street, 805/962-5516). There are also deejays at **Club 634** (634 State Street, 805/564-1069) and **Zelo** (630 State Street, 805/966-5792). Although it might seem as if there is nothing but techno and hip-hop being blasted into the ears of deaf (and dumb) college kids, there are alternatives, from the punky reggae party at the **Coach House** (110 Santa Barbara Street, 805/965-0789) to the mellower sounds at **Rocks** (801 State Street, 805/884-8485).

Home-brewed suds and good eats are found at **Santa Barbara Brewing Company** (501 State Street, 805/730-1040), where beer-making equipment is on view. Among the offerings, Santa Barbara Blonde and State Street Stout were to our liking. From the menu, we enjoyed the shrimp steamed in home brew. The place draws an attractive crowd of smiling faces.

At some point during your nighttime wanderings, angle out onto Stearns Wharf. This three-block wooden pier, built in 1872, widens into an over-the-water parking lot for all the people who have come to shop and dine at its restaurants. The longest-lived place on the wharf is the **Harbor Restaurant** (210 Stearns Wharf, 805/963-3311). Upstairs, the Harbor dispenses drinks and entertainment. Years ago it was described to us as a "one-night romance kind of place" by a bellhop who appeared to be in the know. Indeed, we later saw him off in a corner, deep in negotiations for a one-night romance. As for us, we were approached by a deranged woman who called us "fake preppies," insulted our clothes, refused to believe we weren't locals, asked for identification to prove otherwise, put one of our driver's licenses in her mouth, threatened not to return it, then made it abundantly clear she was available for the evening. One more story for (and from) the road.

For More Information

Santa Barbara Conference and Visitors Bureau, 1601 Anacapa Street, Santa Barbara, CA 93101, 805/966-9222 or 800/549-5133, website: www.santabarbaraca.com

Goleta

Goleta is an example of what we refer to as the "evil twin theory." For every lovely town that reins in development and maintains a high standard of living, there is another lurking nearby that lets such principles fall by the wayside. Santa Barbara's flip side is Goleta. With a population of 78,000, this next-door neighbor is nearly equal in size to Santa Barbara but doesn't attract a fraction of its publicity. In contrast to Santa Barbara's international reputation, Goleta is all but unknown to the outside world. That is because Goleta functions as a repository for those things Santa Barbara wishes to keep outside its city limits—mainly the University of California at Santa Barbara, the Santa Barbara Airport, and people who don't earn six-figure salaries.

This is no knock on higher education, you see. UC Santa Barbara is a fine school that turns out a lot of engineers, physicists, and surfers. But such is the nature of Goleta that the university located here nominally chooses to align itself with a city eight miles away. Goleta is essentially a seaside student colony. Its streets are dusty, its storefronts are generic, and the town has an overall look of plainness.

Map of Central California—Page 233

Santa Barbara County

The university is unquestionably the main attraction. The student body studies and lives here, and some of them surf at the base of the bluffs along which the school is situated. But for the most part they head into Santa Barbara to have fun. You should take their cue and do likewise.

Beaches

A terrific county park beach provides an oasis of escape from the strip-mall blues of Goleta. **Goleta Beach County Park** is a great spot in a gorgeous setting. Parking is free, and people come to picnic, play volleyball, toss horseshoes, and frolic in the water. Tables, hibachis, and open-air shelters are provided. The 29-acre park includes a long, thin pier; wide sandy beach; and more green acres than Hooterville. All in all, it's a very pleasant surprise.

Bunking Down

Your lodging choices in Goleta are pretty much brand-name chains, including a few nicely tended properties like the **Best Western South Coast Inn** (5620 Calle Real, 805/967-3200, $$) and the **Holiday Inn** (5650 Calle Real, 805/964-6241, $$).

However, a luxury resort has lately arrived on the scene. Four miles northwest of UCSB, **Bacara Resort & Spa** (8317 Hollister Avenue, 850/968-0100, $$$$) has its own beach away from the hubbub. Set along a rugged stretch of coastline 13 miles north of Santa Barbara—and technically in Goleta—Bacara is among the rarest of California species: a new luxury resort directly on the beach. Bacara is situated on two miles of coast. Its shoreline remains a wild beach—no grooming or cleanup—in deference to rare and endangered species like the globose dune beetle, the red-legged frog, and the monarch butterfly.

The Spanish mission–style buildings at Bacara are set back from the beach. You'll still get a nice view of the ocean, but the buildings don't infringe upon the dunes ecosystem. The re-

sort was designed to suggest the glamour of "old Hollywood" in the 1940s. This is most evident in the palatial lobby; the circular, clubby Bacara Bar; and the main pool. The approach to the pool, with the ocean behind it, is one of the more visually arresting sights at any California resort. We were impressed by the fact that on a spring weekend when the hotel was filled to capacity, the grounds were peacefully uncongested.

Room rates are what you'd expect at such a place, running $395–550 nightly, depending on location and view. The rooms are full of extra touches—robes, slippers, wide balconies, gas fireplaces. The Spa at Bacara occupies 42,000 square feet of pricey pampering (e.g., massages that cost $65 for 25 minutes).

The Bacara was built with wealthy executives and entertainment-industry types in mind. Even with a listing economy, there will always be an upper crust who can afford places like the Bacara and desire its rarefied air. We saw hip, Gatsby-esque types strolling to dinner at **Miro,** the fine-dining restaurant that displays three original Miro sculptures, plus wall-sized paintings executed after the style of great artists. In contrast to the mannerly old-money types who still don suits and ties for dinner, we saw a lot of L.A. playboys garbed in black with slicked-back hair and cell phones at the ready.

We've rubbed elbows with the rich and famous and have stayed at many of America's finest resorts. Even when we don't belong, we've gotten good at faking it. However, we felt somewhat out of our element at Bacara. No one made us feel that way; everyone was perfectly charming and gracious. It was just something we knew: serious money comes to let its hair down here. As they put it, "old Hollywood glamour" meets "new California dreaming" at Bacara.

Coastal Cuisine

Goleta Beach County Park has its own neat

Map of Santa Barbara County—Page 270

Santa Barbara County

The Battle over Haskell's Beach

Mention the words "Haskell's Beach" to Santa Barbara locals, and you might see tears forming in their eyes. For decades, Santa Barbara County residents knew a paradisiacal piece of the coast above Goleta as Haskell's Beach. It was a little slice of undefiled coastal habitat—a remote coast getaway enjoyed by those in the know. Now it is home to the ritzy Bacara Resort & Spa. These days, you'd never guess from strolling the peaceful grounds of this pricey resort that it was the site of a major battle between developers and environmentalists.

The debate over Haskell's dates back to a 1975 proposal by the Wallover Corporation (which bought the parcel in 1969) to build 153 townhouses on its coastal holdings. Wallover had been purchased by a New York banker and developer named Alvin Dworman, who was determined to develop the 73-acre coast parcel that came with his acquisition of the company.

After a futile attempt by the state of California to acquire the land for public recreation purposes in the late 1970s, Wallover partnered with the Hyatt Corporation, and a new proposal for a 524-room luxury destination resort was made in 1983. The Santa Barbara County Board of Supervisors was complicit in what followed, as they endorsed the rezoning of Haskell's Beach in 1985 as "Visitor-Serving Commercial." This action extended the Goleta urban planning area all the way out to this formerly deserted beach. While

little restaurant, the **Beachside Bar Cafe** (5905 Sand Spit Road, 805/964-7881, $$). It overlooks the water and serves fresh catches like local sea bass and ahi, plus everything from sandwiches to salmon *en papillote*.

For More Information

Goleta Valley Chamber of Commerce, 5730 Hollister Avenue, Goleta, CA 93117, 805/967-4618 or 800/646-5382, website: www.goleta valley.com

Isla Vista

Isla Vista backs right up against Goleta, and indeed the two are so inseparable that everything we said under "Goleta" suffices to cover Isla Vista as well in all categories—except beaches, of which Isla Vista has more options. Both Isla Vista and Goleta share campuses of the University of California at Santa Barbara. The main campus is at Goleta Point, in Goleta; the west campus is in Isla Vista, at Coal Oil Point. The town of Isla Vista (population 20,500) and its several beaches lie between the two points.

Beaches

For approximately 2.5 miles between Goleta Point and Coal Oil Point, the coast runs on a near-perfect east-west axis. Sand beaches are beneath the bluffs, beginning with **Isla Vista Beach,** accessible via stairways at several street ends. A grassy blufftop park, **Isla Vista County Park,** overlooks the beach. At this park you can lounge, read, and gaze seaward from ocean-facing wooden platforms.

One of Santa Barbara County's most recent coastal acquisitions is **Santa Barbara**

in the planning stages, the proposed development was called "the Santa Barbara Club Resort and Spa." In 1997, Hyatt—having grown wary of the economic risk—pulled out of the deal. Dworman forged onward, taking on all comers.

The fight to build or block the resort pitted Dworman and local pro-development forces against environmental and grassroots groups. Arguments against development included the fact that several protected and endangered species occupied the area. It became a battle royal. When the dust cleared, Dworman—a former Golden Gloves boxer—emerged victorious. But the brawl had been both ugly and costly. All told, there were 50 public hearings and three major lawsuits. The developers spent $11 million on public relations, legal fees, and permits.

The 360-room, $220 million Bacara Resort & Spa opened for business in September 2000. A lot is riding on its success, and not just the monetary investment made by Dworman and his backers. According to a November 2001 article in the *Santa Barbara News-Press*, "The economic viability of the Goleta Valley . . . will rely heavily on the success of the ritzy Bacara Resort & Spa, the area's largest generator of property tax revenue, a county official said."

As for the environmental denouement, one demoralized activist wrote, "Despite our best efforts, Haskell's Beach, as we know it, is gone. It is doubtful that it could be restored to its former beauty, were it possible to try. A tragedy of great magnitude has occurred at Haskell's Beach."

Shores, 118 acres of open space that abuts a golf course. Hiking trails skirt the coastal bluffs. You can access another beach, though not without difficulty, at the university-owned **Coal Oil Point Natural Reserve.** The reserve comprises mostly protected coastal wetlands, though the beach below the frontal dunes—plainly referred to as **Sands Beach**—is available to the public. Surfers call it **Devereaux's** (that's the name of the slough). All of these Isla Vista beaches are enjoyed by surfers who relish the fact they don't have to fight crowds to get super rides.

Just outside the Bacara Resort & Spa on Hollister Road is a new beach access, **Bacara Beach.** No doubt it was provided as part of the deal to construct Bacara Resort & Spa. These days, coastal development—when it is permitted at all—requires some kind of quid pro quo in the form of deeded public access by the developer. Bacara Beach—which occupies part of an area formerly known as Haskell's Beach (see sidebar)—has a playground, restrooms, showers, and free parking.

Night Moves

When you're done hitting the books, head to **Study Hall** (6543 Pardall Road, 805/685-0929) or **UCSBrews** (6549 Pardall Road, 805/968-5768). That is, if you're old enough, junior.

For More Information

Goleta Valley Chamber of Commerce, 5730 Hollister Avenue, Goleta, CA 93117, 805/967-4618 or 800/646-5382, website: www.goleta valley.com

Santa Barbara County

Map of Santa Barbara County—Page 270

El Capitan State Beach

North of Goleta, private ranchland dominates the terrain on both sides of U.S. 101. This prohibits any viable beach access, unless you savor the idea of being mauled by a steer while loping with your beach towel toward a stunning headland. Take time out instead to notice how your surroundings change as you proceed north. The distant peaks are higher, more jagged. The land is open, with rolling pasture between the ocean and mountains. The air even seems more breathable, and the winds blow with greater force. Road signs warn of "Gusty Winds."

Between Santa Barbara and Point Conception, the coastline runs east to west, and the beaches face due south. This keeps northern swells at bay, and anything else unpleasant is fended off by the Channel Islands. Ocean swimming is ideal here, and three of California's most appealing state beaches—El Capitan, Refugio, and Gaviota—can be found in a row along a nine-mile stretch.

The first of these is **El Capitan State Beach,** 15 miles northwest of Santa Barbara. To get here you'll pass beneath the U.S. 101 overpass and through a lovely grove of sycamore and oak trees, ending at a sizable campground. Nature lovers will enjoy exploring the many facets of this 133-acre park, including sea cliffs, tidepools, meadows, marine terraces, and canyons. A central stairwell cuts along the bluff to the beach below. It's a healthy strand with teeming tidepools. Swimming is safe, and good surfing is possible on winter swells. Surfcasting catches include perch, bass, and halibut. A trail for cyclists and hikers runs along the blufftop for 2.5 miles north to Refugio State Beach. A camp store is on the grounds, just in case you forgot sunscreen, potato chips, or "Tar Off" packets. There's also a boat launch ($5 per boat).

El Capitan State Beach was named for José Francisco de Ortega, the Spanish captain who scouted for the Portola expedition of 1769. Part of Ortega's old rancho serves as **El Capitan Canyon Campground** (11560 Calle Real, Goleta, CA 93117, 805/685-3887), a privately owned resort in a canyon on the other side of the highway. You can bunk down in a "deluxe safari tent" for $115-135 a night or opt for cabins that range $165-305 per night. Incidentally, the old Reagan Ranch is buried in the hills behind El Capitan.

For More Information

El Capitan State Beach, c/o Channel Coast District, California State Parks, 1933 Cliff Drive, Santa Barbara, CA 93109, 805/899-1400, website: www.parks.ca.gov

Refugio State Beach

The name of the park comes from Spanish explorer José Francisco de Ortega's once extensive rancho, La Nuestra Señora del Refugio ("Our Lady of Refuge"). From this refuge Ortega traded with pirates and smugglers until a band of French buccaneers came ashore, looted his mansion, and then burned it down. In the 1930s a chap named Nelson Rutherford opened a campground here. He built a house that still stands and granted public access to a mineral spring on the beach. When his private campground became too much for him to handle, he sold it to the state in 1950.

More than anything else, **Refugio State Beach** is a scaled-down version of El Capitan State Beach. Located 18 miles northwest of Santa Barbara and three miles above El Capitan, Refugio offers 80 tent campsites and a slightly rockier shoreline, with rich tidepools, a 1.5-mile-long beach, and a beautiful view of the Channel Islands from the bluff above the campground. Refugio has an added botanical dis-

Map of Central California—Page 233

tinction: enormous banana palm trees line Refugio Creek to the east, lending the land a tropical feel that is rare this far north. In recent years cliff erosion has threatened the sacred palms, 20 of which have been replanted farther inland. On one visit we saw a knot of surfers getting some good long rides up at the western end of the beach. We also saw people swimming in the freshwater lagoon formed where Refugio Creek enters the ocean.

For More Information

Refugio State Beach, c/o Gaviota Sector, California State Parks, 10 Refugio Beach Road, Goleta, CA 93117, 805/968-1033, website: www.parks.ca.gov

Gaviota State Park

Gaviota State Park lies six miles up the road from Refugio State Beach and 24 miles from Santa Barbara. It provides the last user-friendly access to the coast until Pismo Beach, 60 miles north. It's also the last viable glimpse of the Southern California coast before the elemental rawness of the Central Coast takes over on the far side of Point Conception. Gaviota takes its name from the Spanish word for seagull. It is here that Portola's gang came ashore and shot a seagull. (Don't get any ideas of your own.)

Gaviota offers full camping facilities (including showers and restrooms), isolation without danger, natural wonders, 5.5 miles of coastline, and easy access to the beach. The setting of this large and varied park is as unusual as it is beautiful. The rusting hulk of an ancient railroad overpass towers majestically over the beachhead, spanning two sheer walls of rock. Near the water 54 campsites are available, 36 of which have RV hookups. Located where Gaviota Creek empties into the ocean, the beach here is great for fishing, swimming, and beachcombing.

A fishing pier offers a three-ton hoist used to launch or haul power boats from the water. Away from the ocean Gaviota's 2,700 acres provide extensive hiking possibilities among the hills to the east. Hikers and backpackers can make their way to hot springs offering body-temperature water. An 11-mile trail crests at Gaviota Peak, a 2,458-foot promontory from which intrepid climbers can collect breathtaking coastline views as a reward for having made their way to the top.

A half-mile southeast of the main entrance to Gaviota State Park, adjacent turnouts have trails leading to clothing-optional cove beaches called San Onofre Beach and Vista del Mar Beach by name. Both lie on state-park property and do not offer facilities.

For More Information

Gaviota State Park, c/o Gaviota Sector, California State Parks, 10 Refugio Beach Road, Goleta, CA 93117, 805/968-1033, website: www.parks.ca.gov

Santa Barbara County

Map of Santa Barbara County—Page 270

Point Conception

Traveling north from central Santa Barbara County's three state-beach jewels—El Capitan, Refugio, and Gaviota—you have a choice. You can continue hugging the relatively inaccessible shoreline via Highway 1, or you can hit the freeway (U.S. 101), which cuts an inland swath.

If you choose Highway 1, you will be rewarded with Point Conception, a formidable jut of land 50 miles northwest of Santa Barbara that signals the geographical end of Southern California. There is no direct access to Point Conception, because private ranches swallow the Point Conception headland. These ranches—Bixby and Hollister, by name—are notoriously nasty to intruders, so be forewarned: we will not provide bail money should you be arrested with our book in hand. Still, getting to Point Conception is worth the difficult trek. As long as you stay below the high-tide line, you are within your legal right to walk to Point Conception via the beach. That doesn't mean you still won't be hassled by the sentinels at Hollister Ranch. The best way for a determined surfer to gain legal access to the waves at Point Conception is by boat. Intrepid beach hikers who want to see the point up close and personal can walk five miles south from Jalama Beach County Park.

Jalama Beach County Park

The beach at **Jalama Beach County Park** is small (a half-mile long, at most), but the campground is fairly large (110 sites, each overlooking the ocean) and set among 28 acres. Jalama draws anglers, surfers, windsurfers, hikers, bird-watchers, and whale-watchers. Surfers love Jalama Beach in the summer and often trek south to Point Conception in search of a perfect wave. Jalama Beach is very much out of the way, lying 55 miles northwest of Santa Barbara. One must turn west from Highway 1 onto Jalama Beach Road and drive 14 desolate miles to the park.

If you savor the thrill of beach hiking, you're in heaven. A mile north is Vandenberg Air Force Base (watch for missile fragments while beachcombing), and five miles south is Point Conception. The trail to Point Conception retraces the route of Juan Bautista de Anza, who brought 250 colonists from Mexico through here in 1775–76. Notably, they ended up founding San Francisco. It is safe to walk this trail only at low tide. The beach trail starts out wide but thins and disappears at times, forcing one to straddle seawalls and railroad tracks. Just north of the point is Point Conception Coast Guard Lighthouse, which has been warning boats away from this hazardous stretch of coast since 1856. Because it is a still-active lighthouse on government property, it is not a climbable landmark, so keep on trucking.

For More Information

Jalama Beach County Park, Star Route, Lompoc, CA 93436, 805/736-6316 (recorded information) or 805/736-3504 (park office), website: www.sbparks.com

Santa Barbara County

Lompoc

If you're up for another adventure after Point Conception, head out to **Ocean Beach County Park.** To find it follow Highway 1 through the sweet-smelling, flower-filled fields of Lompoc (pronounced lom-POKE). Highway 246/Ocean Park Road cuts west from the center (population 38,000), leading through Vandenberg Air Force Base. The road becomes curvier and bumpier with each of its 10 miles, finally giving out in a parking lot. Stop, look, and listen. Rusted railroad cars sit on an abandoned piece of track. The wind whistles through the sandy fields. You are officially in the middle of nowhere.

Ocean Beach County Park comprises 28 wetlands-bounded acres, embracing a broad, sandy beach and a lagoon at the mouth of the Santa Ynez River. The river mouth serves as a fragile riparian habitat for the California brown pelican and the least tern. A half-mile dirt path leads under the Southern Pacific Railroad trestle to a beach with healthy-sized sand dunes.

Vandenberg Air Force Base Fishing Access is the hard-core angler's El Dorado. Its beaches are reached out of a tiny blip on the mapmaker's radar called Surf, at the mouth of the Santa Ynez River. Vandenberg offers limited access (50 people per day, weekends only) to an eight-mile stretch of coast from the river to Purisima Point. No swimming or surfing—only fishing.

To obtain a fishing access, call the VAFB game warden (805/606-6804). Be prepared to give your name, license plate number, vehicle identification number, and a fishing license number for every occupant in your car. Fishing access permits are given to callers on a first-come, first-served basis for the coming weekend beginning the prior Monday morning. No calls are taken after noon on Friday.

For More Information

Vandenberg Air Force Base, Game Warden, Building 6335, 805/606-6804, website: www.vandenberg.af.mil

Point Sal State Beach

Another spot for the lonesome traveler in northern Santa Barbara County is **Point Sal State Beach,** a free day-use-only beach that takes nerves of steel and sturdy hiking boots to reach. To get to this windswept, two-mile stretch of coastal wilderness, take unpaved Brown Road (just south of Guadalupe) to Point Sal Road. The latter is "permanently closed" past a certain point, having been reclaimed by nature, necessitating a 4.5-mile one-way hike to the beach. Once you've made it this far, you might as well continue hiking along the beach to Mussel Point. The area has been likened to Big Sur.

Point Sal is a good surf-casting spot and, during the winter migration, a great whale-watching point. It is protected from the northwesterly winds that buffet the sand-dune ranges to the south. In other words, you don't have to hike the beach at a 45-degree angle.

An excellent hiking trail can be found in Point Sal. This vertigo-inducing five-mile trail can be treacherous, too, as it tiptoes along the tops of bluffs a hundred precipitous feet above the water. Down below, you can spot seals and sea lions on the rocks and hear them barking above the roar of the surf.

For More Information

Point Sal State Beach, La Purisima Sector, 2295 Purisima Road, Lompoc, CA 93436, 805/733-3713, www.parks.ca.gov

Santa Barbara County

Guadalupe–Nipomo Dunes Preserve

North of Lompoc, sand dunes rise along the coast like bare white mountains for 20 miles. They reach their highest peaks west of the ramshackle town of Guadalupe, and the highway doesn't go anywhere near them. To access the dunes you must follow Main Street/Highway 166 for eight miles out of Guadalupe to its end at the beach. Along the way Main Street passes the town cemetery, a few rugged fields, and an open range where cows graze oblivious to the gusty winds, chilly temperatures, and sand. A small parcel of beach is given over to **Rancho Guadalupe Dunes County Park,** where you'll find not much more than portable toilets, a parking lot, a seawall, and lots of wild, wind-blown beach.

Sand is everywhere. Sand blows over the road, obscuring it in places. Sand covers the parking lot. Sand forms a buffer between you and the beach. Sand gets in your eyes. This area—the first of three dune fields that make up a range of sand mountains known collectively as the **Guadalupe–Nipomo Dunes Preserve**—is owned and protected by the Nature Conservancy, which provides trail information and interpretive brochures. Since 1987, the conservancy has acquired 3,117 acres of dunes habitat. The area is of high ecological interest because of its overlap of southern and northern California coast habitats. Within these dune fields is a complex ecosystem made up of dune hollows, lakes, wetlands, and shrublands.

Meditative strolls can be taken among the dunes at various points along the 18 miles of coastline from here to Pismo Beach. Somewhere among all that sand is Mussel Rock, the highest dune on the West Coast. It is all sand, not rock, and stands 500 feet tall, give or take a few shifting grains. An arduous, ankle-sinking two-mile hike is required if you wish to see the biggest sand dune in the West. That might be your only recreation, because the ocean at the Guadalupe entrance to Nipomo Dunes is too rough for immersion. We saw no surfers, no swimmers, no picnickers, no fishers, and no lifeguards—nothing but sand, sand, sand. Enough to make Lawrence of Arabia feel at home.

In addition to the Guadalupe entrance off Highway 166, the Nature Conservancy maintains a second access point to the dunes and several hiking trails at Oso Flaco Lake. Four miles north of Guadalupe on Highway 1, turn left on Oso Flaco Lake Road and drive about four miles to the preserve. Parking costs $4, and the Nature Conservancy provides a map of the area at the entrance kiosk. A boardwalk through Nipomo Dunes leads 1.5 miles to the beach. Another trail, a seven-mile round-trip, winds along the shore of this pristine lake, which provides habitat for ducks, herons, and pelicans. Oso Flaco derives its name from the Spanish for "skinny bear," which is exactly what Portola's men killed here in 1769. There are no bears left, but there is a particularly secluded spot with a musical name, Hidden Willow Valley, where willows grow between the dunes. Bring a canteen and wear a hat.

This coastal preserve is one of the most remarkable in California, and because it's in the right hands, we can all sleep better. The entire Nipomo Dunes area has a history as fascinating as its terrain. These sands have been shifting for 20,000 years, embracing and covering any and all attempts at human habitation. Back in the 1930s, the dunes were home to the "Dunites," a ragtag army of artists, hermits, nudists, and writers who inhabited shacks among the ephemeral sands and published their own *Dune Forum* magazine. The area indeed lends itself to solitary artistic activity, and after an hour or so of hopping about shifting ground cover, one is put in mind of Kobo Abe's disturbing but brilliant novel *Woman in the Dunes.* Reading that book is as close as we'd like to come to living among all this golden sand, as

Map of Central California—Page 233

Guadalupe Dunes Disaster

It is a good thing that the Guadalupe Dunes have been frequented by only a handful of visitors over the past 30 years. It is a bad thing as to why this is so: the Union Oil Company of California (a.k.a. Unocal) maintained a 2,700-acre oil field among the Guadalupe–Nipomo Dunes dating back to the 1960s. At its peak, the oil field contained 215 separate wells that produced 4,500 gallons a day. Before the operation was shut down in 1994, however, a spill had been detected, and it was decided that it had been going on for quite some time, perhaps as far back as three decades. Estimates of the amount of petroleum product leaked into the sand over that time period range 8–20 million gallons, making it, by some people's yardstick, twice as big as the oil spill caused by *Exxon Valdez* in Alaska.

Unocal was charged with criminal activity because it tried to cover up the spills at its Guadalupe oil field while continuing to pump black gold. Once state officials and environmental groups got a whiff of the corporate malfeasance, the lawsuits flew. It is a constant source of amazement that no one ever goes to prison or has their corporate charter rescinded for such monstrous criminal acts—tantamount in our book to environmental terrorism. Rather, they get to agree to a compromise and settle for some seemingly arbitrary sum, much less than the actual damage done and ultimately passed along to customers.

In July 1998, Unocal ended five years of negotiating with the state and agreed to pay $43.8 million, one of the biggest settlements ever negotiated by the state attorney general's office. The money would cover penalties, natural resource damages, and injunctive relief to secure site cleanup. The Surfers Environmental Alliance has described the settlement as a "paltry token to the public," compared to the $425 million Exxon had to pay on its 1989 crude oil spill. Nonetheless, Unocal completed its mandated five-year cleanup in March 2001, after having been granted more than a thousand separate permits by the California Coastal Commission.

Not everyone agreed with this strategy, because the cleanup required Unocal to bulldoze an area the size of two football fields and several acres deep into the dunes to dredge all the contaminated sand—to destroy the dunes in order to save them, so to speak. The many different public and private landholders with a stake in the dunes' continued preservation have united under one umbrella organization called **The Dunes Center** (1055 Guadalupe Street, Guadalupe, CA 93434, 805/343-2455), which has a visitors center near the entrance to the preserve.

Santa Barbara County

Map of Santa Barbara County—Page 270

glorious as it is to look upon. Perhaps because of the deep isolation and rich legacy, Guadalupe Dunes attracts the occasional nude sunbather.

The Nature Conservancy operates the Dunes Center, a visitor center in Guadalupe that is open noon–4 P.M. on Friday, Saturday and Sunday. Staff serve as docents for hikes and bird walks into the dunes, sponsor workshops and other educational events, and work to preserve the dunes.

For More Information

The Dunes Center, Guadalupe–Nipomo Dunes Preserve, 1055 Guadalupe Street, Guadalupe, CA 93434, 805/343-2455, website: www.dunes center.org

Santa Barbara County

© ROBERT HOLMES/CALTOUR

Chapter 6
San Luis Obispo County

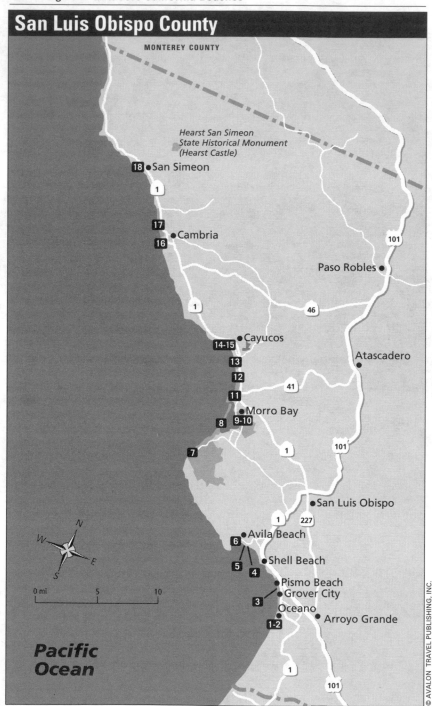

San Luis Obispo County

MONTEREY COUNTY

Hearst San Simeon
State Historical Monument
(Hearst Castle)

18 ● San Simeon

1

17
16 ● Cambria

1

101

Paso Robles ●

46

14-15 ● Cayucos

13

12

41

11

Atascadero ●

8 ● Morro Bay
9-10

7

101

● San Luis Obispo

1   227

6 ● Avila Beach

5   4 ● Shell Beach

3 ● Pismo Beach
● Grover City

● Oceano
1-2 ● Arroyo Grande

N
W   E
S

0 mi   5   10

1

Pacific
Ocean

101

© AVALON TRAVEL PUBLISHING, INC.

San Luis Obispo County Beaches

1 Oceano Dunes State Vehicle Recreation Area, page 314

Location: Enter the beach via access ramps at the end of Grand Avenue in Grover City and Pier Avenue in Oceano.

Parking/fees: $4 entrance fee per vehicle. Camping fee is $7 per night, plus a $7.50 reservation fee.

Hours: 8 A.M.–5 P.M.

Facilities: restrooms

Contact: Oceano Dunes State Vehicle Recreation Area, 805/473-7230

2 Oceano Dunes and North Beach (Pismo State Beach), page 317

Location: along Pier Avenue in Oceano

Parking/fees: $4 entrance fee per vehicle. Camping fees are $13–22 per night, plus a $7.50 reservation fee.

Hours: 8 A.M.–5 P.M.

Facilities: concession, restrooms, showers, picnic tables, and visitor center

Contact: Pismo State Beach, 805/489-1869

3 Pismo Beach (Pismo State Beach), page 317

Location: end of Pomeroy Street, at Pismo Beach Pier, in Pismo Beach

Parking/fees: Metered street and lot parking. Camping fee is $12–18.

Hours: 24 hours

Facilities: restrooms and showers

Contact: Pismo State Beach, 805/489-1869

4 Pirate's Cove, page 317

Location: From U.S. 101 south of San Luis Obispo, take Avila Beach Road exit and follow it two miles. Turn left on Cove Landing Road and follow it to the dirt parking lot on the right; a trail leads to the beach.

Parking/fees: free parking lot

Hours: sunrise–sunset

Facilities: none

Contact: none

5 Avila Beach, page 320

Location: Front Street between San Rafael Street and Harford Drive in Avila Beach

Parking/fees: free street parking

Hours: sunrise–sunset
Facilities: concession, lifeguards, restrooms, and showers
Contact: San Luis Obispo Port Authority, 805/595-5400

6 Olde Port Beach, page 322

Location: one mile north of Avila Beach, just south of Port St. Luis Pier
Parking/fees: free parking lot
Hours: sunrise–sunset
Facilities: restrooms
Contact: San Luis Obispo Port Authority, 805/595-5400

7 Montana de Oro State Park, page 325

Location: From Highway 1 north of San Luis Obispo take Los Osos/Baywood Park exit and drive west on Los Osos Valley Road, which becomes Pecho Valley Road, to the park entrance. Alternatively, from U.S. 101 three miles south of San Luis Obispo, take the Los Osos/Baywood Park exit. Drive 12 miles west on Los Osos Valley Road, which becomes Pecho Valley Road. Follow Pecho Valley Road to the park entrance.
Parking/fees: free parking lots. Camping fee is $7 per night, plus a $7.50 reservation fee.
Hours: sunrise–sunset
Facilities: restrooms and picnic tables
Contact: Montana de Oro State Park, 805/528-0513

8 Morro Dunes Natural Area, page 328

Location: Access the dunes via water taxi from the Embarcadero in Morro Bay.
Parking/fees: none
Hours: sunrise–sunset
Facilities: none
Contact: Morro Bay State Park, 805/772-2560

9 Bayshore Bluffs Park, page 326

Location: in Morro Bay at the west end of Bayshore Drive
Parking/fees: free parking lot
Hours: sunrise–sunset
Facilities: picnic tables
Contact: Morro Bay Parks Department, 805/772-6278

10 Morro Bay State Park, page 328

Location: From Highway 1 north of San Luis Obispo, take Los Osos/Baywood exit and drive west on Los Osos Valley Road for one mile. Turn right into park, which is along State Park Road in Morro Bay.

Map of Central California—Page 233

Parking/fees: $4 entrance fee per vehicle. Camping fees are $13–22 per night, plus a $7.50 reservation fee.

Hours: sunrise–sunset

Facilities: concession, restrooms, showers, picnic tables, and visitors center

Contact: Morro Bay State Park, 805/772-2560

▇▇ Morro Rock and Beach, page 328

Location: near Morro Bay Harbor, at the end of Coleman Drive in Morro Bay

Parking/fees: free parking lot

Hours: sunrise–sunset

Facilities: lifeguards and restrooms

Contact: Morro Bay Harbor Department, 805/772-6254

▇▇ Morro Strand State Beach (South), page 329

Location: along Highway 1 between Yerba Buena Avenue and Atascadero Road in Morro Bay

Parking/fees: Free parking lot. Camping fees are $13–16 per night, plus a $7.50 reservation fee.

Hours: sunrise–sunset

Facilities: restrooms and picnic tables

Contact: Morro Strand State Beach, 805/772-8812

▇▇ Morro Strand State Beach (North), page 329

Location: Studio Drive at 24th Street in Cayucos

Parking/fees: free parking lot

Hours: sunrise–sunset

Facilities: restrooms and picnic tables

Contact: Morro Strand State Beach, 805/772-8812

▇▇ Cayucos Beach, page 331

Location: In Cayucos access is via nine stairwells along Pacific Avenue, between First and 22nd Streets.

Parking/fees: free street parking

Hours: sunrise–sunset

Facilities: none

Contact: San Luis Obispo County Department of Parks and Facilities, 805/781-5930

▇▇ Cayucos State Beach, page 331

Location: Ocean Drive at Cayucos Road in Cayucos

Parking/fees: free street and lot parking

Hours: sunrise–sunset

Map of San Luis Obispo County—Page 306

Facilities: concession, restrooms, and picnic tables
Contact: San Luis Obispo County Department of Parks and Facilities, 805/781-5930

16 Moonstone Beach, page 333

Location: Moonstone Beach Drive between Leffingwell Landing and Highway 1 in Cambria
Parking/fees: free roadside parking
Hours: sunrise–sunset
Facilities: restrooms and picnic tables
Contact: San Simeon District, California State Parks, 805/927-2020

17 San Simeon State Beach, page 337

Location: San Simeon Creek Road at Highway 1
Parking/fees: free parking lot. Camping fees are $13–16 per night, plus a $7.50 reservation fee.
Hours: sunrise–sunset
Facilities: restrooms, showers, and picnic tables
Contact: San Simeon District, California State Parks, 805/927-2020

18 William R. Hearst Memorial State Beach, page 337

Location: end of San Simeon Road off Highway 1 in San Simeon
Parking/fees: $2 entrance fee per vehicle
Hours: sunrise–sunset
Facilities: concession, restrooms, and picnic tables
Contact: San Simeon District, California State Parks, 805/927-2020

Map of Central California—Page 233

San Luis Obispo County

One of the great joys of beach travel is discovering a stretch of coastline that has everything going for it and has been largely bypassed by the thundering herds. Such is the case with the Central Coast in general and San Luis Obispo County in particular.

This county begins at the remarkable Nipomo Dunes and ends north of San Simeon's Hearst Castle at the back door of magnificent Big Sur. The county takes its tenor from the town of San Luis Obispo, a scaled-down version of Santa Barbara set in an agricultural valley. From this jumping-off point, a visitor can easily access the county's extraordinary beaches.

Bunched together at the southern border are the "five cities": Arroyo Grande, Oceano, Grover Beach, Pismo Beach, and Shell Beach. The largest of these, Pismo Beach, is best known for the Pismo clam—which Euell Gibbons, in his beach survival guide *Stalking the Blue-Eyed Scallop,* called "a clam refined to the absolute ultimate." The area is also renowned for its broad dune fields, which are among the most extensive in the state. Oceano Dunes State Vehicle Recreation Area is the only place in California where one can legally drive on the beach. Shell Beach and Avila Beach offer enticing, cliff-hugging views and some splendid cove beaches. Because the pipes leading from Unocal's tank farm had been leaking for years, the town of Avila Beach and its central beach area were until recently reduced to oil-soaked rubble in what is one of the gravest environmental catastrophes ever to befall the California coast.

The visually arresting town of Morro Bay looks out on the marvelous monolith of Morro Rock, while Cambria's calling card is the romantic seclusion of Moonstone Beach. In between is the Western-themed town of Cayucos, which seems frozen in time.

Rolling hills and green valleys, clean air and comfortable temperatures, perfect sunsets, and more than 30 inland wineries in the Edna and Arroyo Grande Valleys serve to complement San Luis Obispo County's outstanding array of beaches.

Map of San Luis Obispo County—Page 306

Arroyo Grande

The 50-mile stretch of U.S. 101 from Santa Barbara to Pismo Beach passes through some extraordinary interior scenery, from the flower fields of Lompoc Valley to the forest surrounding Guadalupe. Suddenly, in a swooping series of hairpin turns, the highway descends to the coastal plain again, heading back toward the beach with the precision of a heat-seeking missile. Before reaching the ocean, the highway passes a crossroads called Arroyo Grande (pronounced "ah-ROY-yo GRAN-dee").

At this point, there is absolutely no question that you have left Southern California and entered the Central Coast. More Western than Californian, these towns are filled with less narcissistically body-conscious folks who go in for cowboy boots and motorbikes. Their homes aren't likely to be featured in *Architectural Digest,* nor are their wardrobes likely to turn up in the pages of *GQ.* Tentlike gingham dresses are spied as frequently as taut, bared midriffs on the women. Even the mountains that press against the towns are different, softer in tone and texture, less jagged, and covered with gray-brown whiskers.

Upon entering Arroyo Grande (population 16,000) you're reminded that California is many states rolled into one. Likewise, Pismo Beach is many towns that have incorporated into one. They call this midcoast mini-metropolis "the Five Cities." Following one another along U.S. 101, the towns begin at Arroyo Grande, move on to Oceano, Grover Beach, and Pismo Beach

proper, and end at Shell Beach. The manners and style vary somewhat from town to town, with Shell Beach representing the most overt stab at gentrification and Pismo Beach cut from plainer cloth, but each serves a prescribed role within the larger entity.

Arroyo Grande has, in recent years, been used as a backdrop for Hollywood film shoots. It has a pleasant hometown feel. The town center contains a few blocks of Victorian-era architecture, and its antique shops do a brisk business. Still, the best thing about Arroyo Grande is that it sends the Pacific Coast Highway shooting back toward the beaches. And given the unchecked growth and fast-food sprawl along its periphery, you're best advised to keep rolling westward.

Bunking Down

You'll notice soon enough that room rates drop once you round Point Conception and begin moving up the Central Coast. If you're laying over in Arroyo Grande, there's the attractive **Best Western Casa Grande Inn** (850 Oak Park Road, 805/481-7398, $), where rooms run $60–90. For that you get a pool, spa, gym, game room, plus breakfast, and you're only two miles from Oceano.

For More Information

Arroyo Grande Chamber of Commerce, 800 West Branch Street, Arroyo Grande, CA 93420, 805/489-1488, website: www.arroyograndecc.com

Map of Central California—Page 233

Oceano Dunes State Vehicle Recreation Area

Oceano Dunes is the only place on the California coast where it is legal to drive on the beach. That's right. From Oso Flaco at the north end of Nipomo Dunes, to Grover Beach—a distance of over four miles—cars are permitted on the beach. They call this the "Sand Highway." Its official name is Oceano Dunes State Vehicle Recreation Area, and it comprises 4,000 acres of sandy dunes and beaches. It can be accessed from Grover Beach and Oceano, two otherwise depressingly unzoned sprawl spigots whose elected officials should be ashamed of themselves The speed limit on the Sand Highway is 15 miles per hour, and

Dune Struck

The sand dunes in the Nipomo and Oceano area are the most extensive coastal dunes remaining in California. The material that forms these piles is washed into the ocean by rivers and creeks in the surrounding watershed. Deposits from this rich lode are carried by shore-paralleling ocean currents and then shaped into dunes by onshore winds. The prevailing winds here push sand particles into wavy crests that run north-south. The slope is gentle on the windward (west) side, steep on the leeward (east) side. As sand grains are blown over the crest of the dune from west to east, the high crests collapse, sliding leeward in what are called "slip-face" slopes.

The most stable dunes are those with vegetative cover—wildflowers, shrubs, and grasses that hold the sand in place by breaking the force of the prevailing winds. At Oceano Dunes the holdfast vegetation on the smaller, more stable dunes includes arroyo willow, California sagebrush, sand verbena, and bush lupine, as well as a nonnative European beach grass.

Most coastal vegetation is fragile and must survive in a harsh environment of desiccating wind, hot sun, and deep water table. These plants can be easily dislodged if disturbed by contact with visitors' feet or wheels. Once the top of the vegetative cover has been severed, the extensive root system that holds the sand in place dies off and the dune becomes vulnerable to massive shifting.

The key to keeping dunes in place is to leave them undisturbed. That is, do not blaze trails among the vegetation, and stick to areas that have already been traveled. Maybe we're just weird, but we've always wondered what kind of person could enjoy trampling vegetation while scooting around dunes atop a sputtering, gas-guzzling, noise-making machine.

On dunes like those at Pismo Beach, the biggest piles of sand are those that won't support vegetable cover. It is these places where all-terrain vehicles should be used (but not abused). Anyone caught driving through dune grasses deserves to be chopped up and fed to the Pismo clams.

Map of San Luis Obispo County—Page 306

S.L.O. County

 Dune Buggers

ATVs and OHVs are those three-wheeled gizmos that look like big-wheeled rider lawn mowers but are capable of considerably higher speeds. Like the Satanic ski-mobile and Jet Ski (er, personal watercraft), these vehicles have become the scourge of parks—and lovers of solitude—everywhere. They are as common in Oceano Dunes State Vehicle Recreation Area as sand fleas. They pointlessly churn the sand as their red-faced (and -necked) operators scale the sides of hills while risking rollover accidents. However, rather than dismiss them without trying them, we checked out the fleet and prices at a couple of venues in Oceano, with every intention of taking them out for a spin. But, as they say on *The Sopranos,* "fuggedabout it."

These things rent for upwards of $45 per hour! You can rent a car for a weekend for that! The big ones—recommended to us "beginners"—have five gears and no hand-clutch; the smaller ones go for $48 for two hours (there's a two-hour minimum at most places). No wonder all the fun-loving yahoos cart their own with them on trailers. And, as for the established speed limit of 15 mph, again you can "fuggedabout it." No driver—whether on an ATV among the soft hilly dunes or in a car on the flat hard beach—drives 15 mph or under. We, in fact, got in a veritable traffic jam going at least 35, unable to slow down lest we be rear-ended. And one obnoxious SUV owner—perhaps a redundancy—decided to "cut across Shorty" by taking a diagonal route past all the other cars toward the exit ramp. He had to be going 55 by the time he hit the asphalt. Someone could get killed out here! What a ridiculous way to spend a vacation!

In short, our advice is to park the car and simply walk on the beach. You will be much more richly rewarded. But look both ways before strolling in any direction.

you must drive in the hard-packed sand near the ocean's edge. Beginning at Post 2 in Oceano, all-terrain vehicles (ATVs) and off-highway vehicles (OHVs) are permitted on the dunes themselves, which stretch for almost a mile inland. Cars are not permitted on the dunes.

The tallest dunes have no vegetation holding them in place, and thus drift with the winds. A few tire tracks here and there aren't going to matter much. Although the state maintains other off-road recreational areas, Oceano Dunes is the only one directly on the coast. Thus, brigades of ATVs, OHVs, and "street legal"

vehicles converge on the park during summer weekends. When you come for a visit to Oceano Dunes, be prepared and always look both ways before crossing the beach.

Beaches

Oceano Dunes State Vehicle Recreation Area offers some of the most spectacular sand piles on the West Coast. You won't believe your eyes, especially when you're steering your car directly toward the ocean. Driving on the beach has a strange appeal, especially since it allows you to quickly cut away from the crowds and

Map of Central California—Page 233

find a quieter stretch of shoreline that's more to your liking. Keep an eye on your car, though. Some people fall asleep when high tide rolls in and . . . well, you can guess the rest. Also, be careful if you decide to go in the water, because there are no lifeguards.

Bunking Down

You can camp among the Oceano Dunes, but you are advised to make reservations in advance. The sites are primitive—basically, wherever you throw down your tent—and the number of campers allowed here at any one time is 1,000. You really don't need wheels to have fun. Plenty of excellent hiking trails traverse the dunes, inland lagoons, and a fascinating array of terrain.

You can pitch a tent at several more campgrounds in the area, too: the 64-site Oceano Memorial County Park (on Pier Avenue in Oceano), and two camps at Pismo State Beach.

For More Information

Oceano Dunes State Vehicle Recreation Area, 576 Camino Mercado, Arroyo Grande, CA 93420, 805/473-7230, website: www.ohv.parks.ca.gov

Pismo Beach, Oceano, Grover Beach, and Shell Beach

Pismo Beach is the heart and soul of the "Five Cities." The other four are Arroyo Grande, Oceano, Grover Beach, and Shell Beach. Pismo Beach and surrounding communities are the living embodiment of the area mascot, the Pismo clam. Both the towns and the clam are humble but majestic souls that have battled through bad times to emerge with bright prospects for the future.

Visitors are greeted by a spaceship-like sculpture of the Pismo clam at the Price Street exit off U.S. 101. The Pismo is the town's pride and joy, being one of the largest and most delicious clams on the West Coast. In fact, it's too tasty for its own good. In the mid-1980s the beleaguered bivalve found itself on the brink of extinction. For five years a law forbade any clamming of the Pismo, to allow them to replenish.

Other than the temporary loss of its clam, Pismo Beach has been blessed with natural gifts—dunes to the south; wide, hard-packed sand beaches in town; perfect year-round climate; and unsurpassable vistas from jagged headlands that spread north into Shell Beach. The biggest problem has been its image as a down-on-its-heels honky-tonk town. Take Shell Beach. This wealthier community ostensibly changed its name to get a separate post office (though it retains the same zip code and falls within Pismo Beach city limits). According to a local businessman, however, it really wanted to distance itself from Pismo Beach.

A Shell Beach businesswoman theorized that what's keeping Pismo from becoming a major vacation destination is its lack of an upscale shopping district. "Oh, you can buy things there," she rejoined, "but. . . ." Her "but" hung in the air, its silent aftermath implying that there's no Neiman-Marcus or New England seaport-themed shopping village in Pismo Beach. Maybe because shopping remains such a low priority for us, we're unable to grasp how a lack of boutiques is a drawback.

Our own theory about the town's image problem has nothing to do with shopping. It's the name. "Pismo" doesn't exactly roll off the tongue with a musical fanfare. But the name comes legitimately with the territory. As it turns out, *pismo* is a Chumash word meaning "blobs of tar that wash up on the beach." By the time the Spanish arrived, the Chumash had inhabited the area for 9,000 years. The Spanish had no problem with the name because for them

Map of San Luis Obispo County—Page 306

S.L.O. County

 ## Clamming for Pismos

No less an authority than Euell Gibbons honored the Pismo clam *(Tivela stultorum)*. In his 1964 beachcomber's bible, *Stalking the Blue-Eyed Scallop,* he wrote, "At the first bite I became a full-fledged convert to the Cult of Pismophagists, and I knew why Californians come year after year to do battle with the waves in order to get a bag of Pismos."

Since Gibbons sang his praise of Pismos, they were almost eliminated, due to over-clamming and shortsighted greed. Even then, he'd heard tales: "There are stories of local farmers gathering these clams by the wagon load by opening furrows across the beach at ebb tide with horse-drawn plows. Some . . . were sold on the market, but many a wagon load went back to the farms to fatten the pigs and chickens. . . . To hear of the way this vast wealth of clams was squandered is enough to make one weep."

But then so is the taste of a Pismo clam. Its flavor, plenitude, and size—it is one of the largest clams in the world—are what made it so popular. After a total ban on Pismo clamming in the mid-1980s, they have begun to return. The Pismo clam requires a rock-free sand beach and constant exposure to ocean waves. The beaches from Oceano to Morro Bay are ideal, with their pure sand and gradually sloping shoreline.

Pismo clams reach a length of five inches and weigh about a pound at maturity, after 4–7 years. A seven-incher is at least 15 years old. Some have lived to the age of 20 and weighed as much as five pounds. They are found in 1–3 feet of water at low tide, burrowing about a half-foot beneath the hard, wet sand. Finding them requires probing every few inches of the ocean floor with a clam fork, one with a five-inch clamming gauge. If a clam smaller than five inches is taken, it should be replaced with its shell opening toward the horizon.

The fun of Pismo clamming is that you have to spend your time knee deep in water. This means you get slapped around by the waves, too. "Ordinary clam digging might be poor sport," wrote Gibbons, "but this seeking the Pismo in the surf was wildly exhilarating. Not that the clams fight back. They don't need to. The clams merely lie quietly . . . and let the waves above do their fighting."

Now for the bad news. You cannot take any Pismo clams at any time in designated clam preserves, which include Pismo Beach and the Oceano Dunes and Nipomo Dunes areas. Pismos can be taken in Monterey and Santa Cruz Counties in season (September 1–April 30) with a limit of 10, five inches minimum. In short, you can take Pismo clams just about anywhere but Pismo Beach.

For information on the latest regulations regarding the taking of Pismo clams, contact the **California Department of Fish and Game,** Marine Region, 20 Lower Ragsdale Drive, Suite 100, Monterey, CA 93940, 831/649-2870.

Map of Central California—Page 233

pismo meant "a place to fish." Thanks to this semantic convergence, the town has a unique but not exactly mellifluous name.

Right now, Pismo Beach (population 8,500) has little to do with either tarry blobs or upscale shopping, but a lot to do with sand, surf, and beach. Happily, the town has begun to focus on its many natural blessings. The folks who flock here in the summer from the sweltering valleys aren't complaining. When the temperature exceeds 100 degrees inland, Pismo might as well be named Paradise. The hotter it gets in the valleys, the cooler it is in Pismo. The inland heat draws moist air off the ocean, bathing Pismo Beach in marine fog. This makes for endlessly varying cloud patterns and beautiful sunsets. Who wouldn't love such a setting, whatever the name?

Beaches

Pismo State Beach is a vast and lengthy swath of sand with access points covering 23 miles of coast and four of the "Five Cities." The state beach includes two campgrounds, **Oceano Dunes** and **North Beach.** Cars are allowed on the beach to the south (see "Oceano Dunes State Vehicle Recreation Area" earlier in this chapter), making it California's answer to Daytona Beach, Florida, without the bathing beauties. Thankfully, the beaches in Pismo Beach and Shell Beach are pedestrian only, with plenty of room for swimming, tanning, fishing, and surfing. The latter has grown so popular in recent years that an annual tournament is now held in Pismo. The namesake clam, meanwhile, slowly continues its comeback.

At the center of this modest scene is the Pismo Beach Pier, a 1,250-foot structure at the end of Pomeroy Street that is perfect for surf casting and surfer watching. The south side of the pier is one of the best surf spots in the county. What makes it so great is that it breaks left on the left side of the pier and right on the right side of the pier. El Niño storms brought high water that inundated the whole beach, lapping

at the bases of buildings and the street-end turnarounds, but Pismo Beach is building up again and looks little the worse for wear today.

The sea cliffs become more pronounced toward Shell Beach, where separate coves have been given names like **Turtle Beach** and **Pirate's Cove.** Several overlooks dot the blufftops along Seacliff Drive, and four of them have been designated city parks: Margo Dodd, Ocean, Memory, and Spyglass. Stairwells from the first two, on the southern edge of Shell Beach, lead down to small, secluded cove beaches.

On a final note we've lifted this pertinent quotation from (of all places) a Pismo Beach Chamber of Commerce brochure. It is from "Childe Harold's Pilgrimage," by that legendary beach bum, Lord Byron:

There is rapture on the lonely shore,
There is society, where none intrudes,
By the deep sea, and music in its roar:
I love not man the less, but Nature more.

Shore Things

- **Bike/skate rentals:** Pismo Bike Rentals, 519 Cypress Street, Pismo Beach, 805/773-0355
- **Dive shop:** Scuba Adventures Diving Center, 1039 Grand Avenue, Arroyo Grande, 805/473-1111
- **Ecotourism:** Kayaks of Morro Bay, 699 Embarcadero, Morro Bay, 805/772-9463
- **Marina:** Morro Bay Marina, 699 Embarcadero #11, Morro Bay, 805/772-8085
- **Piers:** Pismo Beach Pier, Pismo Beach; Port St. Luis Pier, Avila Beach
- **Rainy day attraction:** Hearst Castle, Hearst San Simeon State Historical Monument, San Simeon, 805/927-2020 or 800/444-4445
- **Shopping/browsing:** East Village, Cambria
- **Sportfishing:** Virg's Landing, 1215 Embarcadero, Morro Bay, 805/772-1222
- **Surf shop:** Central Coast Surfboards, 736 Higuera Street, San Luis Obispo, 805/541-1129
- **Vacation rentals:** Beachside Reservations, 640-A Dolliver Street, Pismo Beach, 805/773-0347

Map of San Luis Obispo County—Page 306

Bunking Down

Accommodations run the spectrum from seedy motels to luxury beach resorts. Most of the latter are found in Shell Beach, although the SeaVenture Resort has helped lift Pismo Beach's profile since the mid-1980s. **SeaVenture Resort** (100 Ocean View Avenue, 805/773-4994, $$$) is an ambassadorial representative of the kind of tony, upscale resort that's been popping up along the Central Coast, even in formerly honkytonk towns like Pismo Beach.

A few blocks from the pier at the end of quiet Ocean View Avenue, the SeaVenture is the kind of place where you'd like to take a load off and linger for a few days or longer. The resort is on a broad, sandy beach, but the rooms are so exceptional that one is almost tempted not to leave them. The walls and carpets are a soothing, deep green. Louvered doors open out onto balconies, each of which has its own hydrotherapy spa. Each room also has a fireplace with gas logs, as well as a wet bar, Sony CD clock radio, and a VCR. A continental breakfast is brought to each room in the morning, based on a checklist of preferences hung by guests on their doorknobs the night before. Bring some movies and CDs with you, eat on premises, and you'll never have to leave—or want to. Considering what you receive, especially compared to what you'd pay for an equivalent stay on the Southern California coast, rates (which begin at $119) are a bargain.

Cliffs at Shell Beach (2757 Shell Beach Road, 805/773-5000, $$$) is a five-story clifftop resort that offers luxury without excess. The setting—100 feet above the sea stacks on Turtle Beach—speaks for itself. The various on-premises amenities (large heated outdoor pool, sauna, well-groomed grounds and gardens, café and restaurant) complete the experience. Beach access is via a stairwell along the cliff face.

Back in Pismo Beach proper, another fine option is the **Best Western Shore Cliff Lodge** (2555 Price Street, 805/773-4671, $$), a well-tended hotel on stunning grounds. It comes with a heated pool. Not surprisingly, these three hotels also have the best restaurants in town attached to them.

The **Sea Crest Motel** (2241 Price Street, 805/773-4608, $$) is the best of the less expensive places. It's on the north side of Pismo, atop a cliff. A steep wooden stairwell leads to the sand. The grounds encompass a number of jagged promontories upon which one can watch the sun slip into the rough and tumble ocean.

The **Pismo Beach Hotel** (230 Pomeroy Street, 805/773-4445, $$) has been a local institution since 1937, but it's also been out of commission for a long time. Recently renovated and reopened by a new owner, it has the air of a European lodge, sans the high price tag. Moreover, it shares an address with the hippest coffee shop in town, the **Black Pearl** (230 Pomeroy Street, 805/773-6631, $), and it's only 200 yards from Pismo Beach Pier.

Coastal Cuisine

It used to be that in the Esperanto of road hunger, "Pismo" meant "mediocre." That is no longer true, as excellent dining spots are now serving fine fare from panoramic dining rooms. The **Shore Cliff Restaurant** (2555 Price Street, 805/773-4671, $$), in the Best Western Shore Cliff Lodge, offers good, fresh seafood dishes in a glassed-in dining room that takes in a sweeping view of the ocean from its perch. Order the calamari Galantine (Mexican squid fillet with crabmeat stuffing) or the fresh catch of the day. Shore Cliff has the best clam chowder in town. It's not the typical thick, floury stew, but more of a soup that lets the good taste of Pismo's finest shine through.

Fine dining can be had at the **Sea Cliffs Restaurant** (2757 Shell Beach Road, 805/773-3555, $$) in the Cliffs at Shell Beach resort. At one time the in-house spot was called Pismo Joe's, but the casual flavor was strangely inappropriate to the complex. Without much

Map of Central California—Page 233

S.L.O. County

fanfare the Sea Cliffs Restaurant chefs prepare some of the tastiest seafood on the Central Coast. Most of the seafood dishes are cooked on a mesquite grill. Lest we forget, you are now entering wine country. Several excellent wineries are within an hour's drive; ask your server for recommendations. The Sunday brunch here is a county-wide legend.

The **SeaVenture Restaurant** (100 Ocean View Avenue, 805/773-4994, $$$$) specializes in Cal-Asian cuisine: things like ginger-soy sauces and such fancy entrées as seared halibut with shiitake risotto and cashew pesto, Asian vegetables, red pepper coulis, and crispy soba. (Ye gods!) Other popular entrée items are champagne prawns and freshly shucked scallops. Get here early and receive a break on price with the Sunset Dinner menu. You'll also enjoy a great view of the ocean from the third-floor dining room. Happy hour (4 P.M.–7 P.M. daily) is a happening time here.

Finally, if you want a good, simple plate of fish 'n' chips—and who doesn't, now and then?—head to **Pismo Fish & Chips and Seafood Restaurant** (505 Cypress Street, 805/773-2853, $$). The fish is lightly battered and fried, and served good and hot. Pismo Fish & Chips and Seafood Restaurant has been run by a Danish family for decades, and they know their fish 'n' chips, fish dinners (13 kinds!), fish tacos, etc.

If you crave a break from fried fish, just say "Mo"—**Mo's Smokehouse** (221 Pomeroy Street, 805/773-6193, $$), that is. Mo's serves Virginia shredded pork, Memphis pork ribs, and hickory-smoked chicken in various combinations. Although it hit the spot as a break from our research-driven seafood inquiries, Mo's fare frankly pales next to the real thing back East. Still, by West Coast standards, Mo's is hot enough to have won awards the last eight years running.

The surfers and inlanders who come to Pismo Beach to play have their own routine of long-standing. According to an acquaintance of ours who grew up in San Luis Obis-

po, the perfect day in Pismo Beach is: hang out on the beach and surf by the pier; have a clam chowder in a sourdough bowl for lunch; hit the beach again in the afternoon; then chow down at McClintock's for dinner. F. **McClintock's Saloon and Dining House** (750 Mattie Road, 805/773-1892, $$$), which has a huge carved cowboy out front, serves great steaks, but local favorites also include onion rings with salsa and turkey nuts. (Yes, you read correctly.)

A final tip: For breakfast, grab a cinnamon roll at **Old West Cinnamon Rolls** (861 Dolliver Street, 805/773-1428, $). It won't do your diet any good, but you'll thank us just the same.

Night Moves

The daytime is really the right time in Pismo Beach. The town's social life centers around the pier and surrounding streets. The liveliest night spot in Pismo is **Harry's Cocktail Lounge** (690 Cypress Street, 805/773-1010), which has horseshoes for door handles and features live music—formerly country-and-western bands, then "contemporary rock bands," and now cost-cutting karaoke, two-man bands, and so-called live acts like a "retro disco" tribute band that was playing last time we were in town. They were from Los Angeles (natch) and called Rollercoaster, presumably after the Ohio Players' disco classic "Love Rollercoaster." But we deconstructed it differently, viewing the entire collegiate club scene as being on a giant roller coaster dropping down into worthless oblivion.

Harry's claim that "every night rocks" is a bit hackneyed by now, but it is the most popular nightspot in the area. Besides, many years ago John Madden met his wife at Harry's, and look how big he is now.

For More Information

Pismo Beach Visitor Information Center, 581 Dolliver Street, Pismo Beach, CA 93449, 805/773-4382, website: www.pismobeach.org

Map of San Luis Obispo County—Page 306

Avila Beach

Around the corner from Shell Beach, on the other side of San Luis Obispo Bay, is Avila Beach, a small village of about 300. Until the environmental disaster brought about by Unocal (see "Avila Beach: Oils Well That Ends Well"), Avila served as the sun-and-fun capital for students from California Polytechnic State University in San Luis Obispo. Then it became a veritable ghost town for two years, with Avila State Beach surrounded by construction fencing as bulldozers excavated oil-soaked sand to a depth of 80 feet. Having known what this beach looked like in happier times, it was downright eerie to see it in critical condition. Happily, it's been taken off the critical list and is presently on the mend.

North of Avila Beach is Port St. Luis Recreation Area, which includes a launching access at Olde Port Beach, commercial fishing pier, and coastal hiking trail. This 10-miler stretches from Avila to Montana de Oro State Park. It crosses land owned by Pacific Gas and Electric, which opened its Diablo Canyon nuclear facility in 1986 after years of litigation and engineering snafus. The Diablo Canyon Plant, like the one down in San Onofre, is on an earthquake fault. As a concession to the public (for jeopardizing its very existence?), PG&E has provided the Pecho Coast Trail. It can be accessed in Port San Luis, off Harford Drive. Along the trail you can see the **Port San Luis Lighthouse** (circa 1890), known as the "Victorian Lady" to locals. The Nature Conservancy leads hikes to the lighthouse, with reservations required (call 805/541-8735). A half-day hike goes to the lighthouse, and a full-day hike has Rattlesnake Canyon as its destination. One noteworthy part of the trail is an oak grove dedicated to Pat Stebbins, a California Coastal Commission director who died in 1990 after years of advocacy for public use of beaches.

The unsightly oil tanks that once dominated the backdrop from the highest peak above the town have been removed. The Unocal-polluted sand along the beachfront has been exhumed and hauled away, replaced by trucked-in sand that has weathered the past two winters well. The beachside promenade that had to be dismantled has now been replaced by a nice new boardwalk, attractive decorative planters, and numerous stairwells leading down to the wide, bionic beach. Volleyball nets have been restrung and expanded, and playground swings and a slide have been added for the wee ones. A portion of Front Street is now blocked off for pedestrians only.

All of these changes, of course, will not entirely solve the problems related to Unocal's malfeasance, but they at least relieve the scene of its most ominous symbols and open the door to a brighter future.

Although a local innkeeper complained that Unocal was dragging its feet—and we have no reason to doubt her—what we'd seen of Avila Beach three years ago, compared to what it looks like now, has to qualify as a minor miracle. It's certainly understandable why longtime townies, embittered by chronic corporate neglect, would think the transformation can't come quick enough. From our perspective, though, just seeing Avila opening its arms to visitors again is enough to warm the bivalves of our heart.

Beaches

To get to **Avila Beach** from either Shell Beach or U.S. 101, take Avila Beach Drive. It is the only road in and out of a circuitous rural stretch that requires your full attention. The collegians call it "Bust Road," because the cops wait along the shoulder after the bars close. When the town was undergoing its oily crisis in recent years, the Cal Poly students took to hanging out at Pirate's Cove, literally letting it all hang out at this clothing optional beach. They've only just begun trickling back onto the new, improved Avila Beach.

Avila Beach: Oil's Well That Ends Well

One of the more sordid sagas ever to take place along the California coast is the desecration of lovely Avila Beach by the Union Oil Company of California (Unocal), the same people who curried favor with the Taliban to build a pipeline across Afghanistan way back in the innocent days pre-9/11/01. Unocal has long had its way with this relatively defenseless village of 350. Were it just a matter of an oil leak and some contamination, the situation would be sad but solvable, perhaps serving as a cautionary tale that might make things better in the future.

Just as we suspected on our first visit to Avila Beach—once among our favorite beach towns on the Central Coast—the petroleum "tank farm" that once sat high atop a bluff above the town was not just an aesthetic blight but a ticking time bomb. The first detonation took place in 1989, when it was determined that the tanks had for years, if not decades, been dripping diesel and crude oil and gasoline from underground pipes leading to Unocal's industrial pier at Avila's harbor. The oil mixture built up beneath the postcard-perfect cove beach that defines this town, creating a toxic mound 10 stories high.

The cleanup, negotiated over a long period and finally begun in September 1998, was completed, for the most part, by the summer season of 2001. It necessitated Unocal's removal of 400,000 gallons of petroleum leakage and 100,000 cubic yards of sand, as well as the near closure of the only road into and out of the community (essentially shutting the town down for a year). Unocal also agreed to pay $18 million for cleanup and restoration. In addition, 20 beachfront homes and businesses—the downhome establishments that gave this town its appealing quaintness—were demolished. All of this cleanup was much more than Unocal was initially prepared to do.

The greatest fear of many longtime residents, while all this was going on, was not necessarily whether the environmental problem could be mitigated. It was what would be constructed on all that prime oceanfront real estate to replace what had been lost. After all, Unocal not only ruined the life of this village, it was allowed to buy the land on which the demolished houses stood while retaining its tank farm and its pier. In other words, Unocal could have reaped a profit from all this devastation. As one resident speculated back in 1998: "It's going to be high-rises; just another Newport Beach."

Though there are plans to build a 54-room hotel (designed to look like retro Avila), a conference center, and a series of California beach bungalows, none of this has yet come to pass. Indeed, though frayed about the edges, Avila Beach has survived the experience with its essential spirit intact.

Map of San Luis Obispo County—Page 306

S.L.O. County

A short distance north of Avila Beach is a crescent of darkened sand identified as **Olde Port Beach**. Our advice: Keep driving and have a meal at the Olde Port Inn Restaurant on the Port St. Luis Pier.

Bunking Down

Away from the ocean, among the woods along Avila Beach Drive, is a place that all weary travelers should be fortunate enough to stumble upon once in a lifetime. **Sycamore Mineral Springs Resort** (1215 Avila Beach Drive, 805/595-7302, $$$) is many things—gourmet restaurant (see the Gardens of Avila in "Coastal Cuisine"), place to stay, botanical haven, and a spiritual way station. But it is primarily a mineral-spring spa and has been since 1897. Here, for a reasonable fee ($40 for a half-hour, $60 for a full hour, $85 for 90 minutes), one can receive a professional massage and unlimited access to the natural hot springs. The friendly staff instantly makes you feel comfortable, and an hour later you will be too relaxed to get back in the car. This may mean staying overnight and eating dinner, neither of which is a punishing experience. In fact there's a package deal called "Rub, Tub, & Grub" that combines all of the above. The rooms are up in the woods, and each comes with its own mineral spa in a redwood tub. Eight hours of this and you could start your own religion. Or jump-start a dull marriage.

The **Inn at Avila Beach** (265 Front Street, 805/595-2300, $$) is the town's venerable beachfront mainstay. Having weathered the Unocal storm, the place deserves to thrive now. A pink stucco beach house with ocean-facing suites that have balconies, it is the best bird's-eye perch onto the sands of Avila.

Coastal Cuisine

The **Gardens of Avila** (1215 Avila Beach Drive, 805/595-7365, $$$) is at the lush Sycamore Mineral Springs Resort. The eclectic menu offerings range all over the globe, such as coriander-seared tuna with marinated cellophane noodles, baby leeks, and red miso-ginger sauce. Seafood items are the best bet, as the catch comes straight off the pier just down the road at Port San Luis. Be forewarned, unmarried couples: A local publication's readers recently voted Gardens of Avila "best place to propose."

The **Olde Port Inn Restaurant** (Port St. Luis Pier, 805/595-2515, $$$$) serves fish straight from the boats, too. Literally, you get the catch of the day. The restaurant's founder is Leonard Cohen (presumably no relation to the poet/singer). Cohen started the California Cio-Pinot Cook-off, an annual cioppino and pinot noir contest that benefits local charities. Dinner prices for seafood entrées start at $17.95, although fish 'n' chips and fish tacos from the à la carte menu run $8.95. The house special cioppino runs $23.95. And the view from the pier—well, you can't put a price on that. By the way, Cohen has turned the restaurant over to his son, also named Leonard. He has brought in a new chef who is introducing items like Cajun-blackened halibut with mango salsa. Not to worry, stalwart Olde Port fans: old standbys like fish tacos, shrimp quesadillas, and fish and chips are still on the menu.

Locals head to **Fat Cats Cafe** (Port San Luis, 805/595-2204, $) for breakfast, which is served 24 hours a day. Order *huevos rancheros* (ranch-style eggs) or a build-your-own omelette and enjoy the view of sailboats on the bay from the brick patio. Fat Cats serves lunch and dinner, too, and prices are very reasonable.

P.S.: If you want fresh seafood right off the boat to cook in your suite, Avila Bay Pier is the best place to shop.

For More Information

Pismo Beach Chamber of Commerce and Visitor Information Center, 581 Dolliver Street, Pismo Beach, CA 93449, 805/773-4382, website: www.pismobeach.org

Map of Central California—Page 233

San Luis Obispo

Like Santa Barbara, San Luis Obispo is the sort of town you don't want to just visit—you want to live there. The natural setting—a valley 2,000 feet below the Santa Lucia Mountains, bisected by a small river—blends perfectly with the culture and cuisine.

Although it is not directly on the beach, San Luis Obispo (pronounced "San LOO-iss Oh-Biss-poh" and called "S.L.O." for short) is a jumping-off point for numerous Central Coast getaways, including Pismo Beach, Avila Beach, Morro Bay, Cambria, and San Simeon. It is also a worthy destination in and of itself. The city has its own symphony and opera company, chorales, Mozart Festival, theater companies, and arts and crafts galleries.

That's just the half of it. San Luis Obispo (population 44,200) has an indefinable quality that transforms it from an otherwise pleasant crossroads into a real honey of a place. Perhaps it's the presence of California Polytechnic State University, with its hip, eco-minded student body of 11,000. In a college town the continuous stream of fresh blood and new ideas guarantees that daily life won't get stale. There are also the surrounding agricultural valleys, which once earned S.L.O. a reputation as a cow town. These days, the massive greenbelt seems downright magical, contributing to the healthy bustle of the town. Every Thursday a farmers market sets up on Higuera Street, and virtually the entire town attends. One can only hope that San Luis Obispo—located roughly halfway between Los Angeles and San Francisco—will continue to preserve the natural treasures that make it so unique.

Once the heart of **Mission San Luis Obispo de Tolosa,** the town has deep historical roots. The mission was the first in California to use red-tiled roofs as fireproofing against Native Americans' flaming arrows. The mission's church has been restored (782 Monterey Street, 805/543-6850), and the nearby **San Luis Obispo County Historical Museum** (696 Monterey Street, 805/543-0638) contains Native American and early settlement artifacts. Much of the rest of the town's architecture dates from the Victorian period. Careful planning and refurbishing has kept growth within tasteful bounds.

Walking is the best way to see the local history and architecture. Two suggested hikes offer a larger perspective on this setting. The first is a 1.5-mile round-trip trek up to Bishop Peak, which provides views of the town and the valley. The second is a one-mile walk through Poly Canyon on the university campus. Park across from the Fisher Science Building on Perimeter Road and roam among the wildflowers.

Another kind of touring is rewarding for those folks who, to paraphrase the late Orson Welles, drink no wine before its time. Forty wineries and vineyards are located in San Luis Obispo County. Among the best known of the bunch are **Edna Valley Vineyard** (2585 Biddle Rand Road, 805/544-9594) and **Corbett Canyon Vineyard** (2195 Corbett Canyon Road, 805/544-5800). Both are in the greater San Luis Obispo city limits. To find the rest, pick up a brochure at any area restaurant or motel.

Bunking Down

You may not look out upon sand and surf, but you will get a nice view in San Luis Obispo, no matter where you stay. For romantic getaways there are three excellent, slightly quirky places to consider. The **Madonna Inn** (100 Madonna Road, 805/543-3000, $$$) is best known for the simple reason there's no other place like it in California (or in the country, for that matter). Every one of its 109 rooms is decorated in a different style, and the architecture of the lodge itself is part Elizabethan, part gingerbread, part Victorian, part. . . . You get the idea. It's unabashedly eccentric, and the grounds are fun to stroll.

Equally delightful is the **Garden Street Inn**

Bed & Breakfast (1212 Garden Street, 805/545-9802, $$). Built in 1887 on land once owned by the mission, the Garden Street Inn is a Italianate Queen Anne–style house that's historic without being musty. It's also right in the center of the downtown historic area. Finally, the **Apple Farm Inn** (2015 Monterey Street, 805/544-2040, $$$) re-creates Victorian times with country classic styling, an attached mill house, and a restaurant that serves things like chicken and dumplings. Pass the apple pie, parson.

For budget-minded families, the **Vagabond Inn** (210 Madonna Road, 805/544-4710, $) offers a continental breakfast and the unique offer of "Kids under 19 stay free." Kids under 19?

Coastal Cuisine

Pete's Southside Cafe (1815 Osos Street, Railroad Square, 805/549-8133, $$) has the right pedigree. It began as a small café in Avila Beach. Now it's thriving as a fine diner that has an upstairs tamale bar. Its hallmark is Caribbean and Latin-American entrées, including a killer fish Veracruz. The paella Valencia wins "best of" awards yearly.

Night Moves

Nightlife in S.L.O. is anything but slow. It's a town full of college bars, with laughter and mug-clanging ringing out of every door front after dark. The most popular in town, **Mother's Tavern** (725 Higuera Street, 805/544-7575), charges a cover from those lured inside by the deejayed dance music. Here, you'll see valley cowboys trying to connect with Cal Poly coeds in a setting not designed for easy traffic flow. (It is a restaurant by day.)

More to our liking was **Brubeck's** (726 Higuera Street, 805/541-8688), which has a civilized upstairs bar with lots of mirrors allowing patrons to check out one another.

More appealingly raunchy is the downstairs **Cellar,** where the college crowd screams and shouts around a great jukebox. In between conversations they scribble graffiti on the walls. (It's encouraged.) There's no standing on ceremony here. Just shout out what you want; usually one word ("draft") will suffice. We were also told of a place that was popular with the thirty-something crowd. But what kind of fun can you have at the beach if you hang out with people our age? Give us arrested adolescents a hangout like the Cellar anytime!

Live music can be had at the **SLO Brewing Company** (1119 Garden Street, 805/543-1843). "Fine ales, food, and live music" are the calling cards. These days at SLO Brew, live music means reggae, a bit of blues, and acts with names like Functus, Bootie, Merago, Implant, and Joose w/Paloma. Hey, don't look at us; we've long since thrown in the towel when it comes to club life. Still, with 14 home brews on tap, any music will probably sound good in this place.

The best dance club, by general consensus, is **The Graduate** (990 Industrial Way, 805/541-0969). Each night features different types of music and dancing. For instance, Wednesday is "College Hump Night," Thursday is "Country Night with DJ Richy Rich" (yee-haw!), and Friday alternates between rock oldies and old-school disco/funk.

For More Information

San Luis Obispo County Visitors & Conference Bureau, 1037 Mill Street, San Luis Obispo, CA 93401, 805/634-1414, website: www.sanluisobispocounty.com; San Luis Obispo Chamber of Commerce, 1039 Chorro Street, San Luis Obispo, CA 93401, 805/781-2777, website: www.slochamber.org

Map of Central California—Page 233

Montana de Oro State Park

Just south of Morro Bay, near the small bayside towns of Los Osos and Baywood Park, Montana de Oro State Park spreads out across an immense swath of land. It faces the ocean for seven miles, from the Morro Sand Spit south. Spanish explorers named the area "Mountain of Gold" because of the golden poppies that cover its hills and terraces. Monarch butterflies nest in the eucalyptus October–March, adding to the gilded appearance. Today this 8,400-acre wilderness park is pure public-access gold, one of the great treasures of California's state-park system.

We quickly ran out of superlatives when trying to describe the park's assets and acreage. Simply ponder what is here: sand dunes, jagged cliffs, rocky coves, sea caves, and shallow reefs. There are 50 miles of trails for hiking, biking, and horseback riding. These trails traverse the inland canyons and mountains, as well as the shoreline, and provide a self-guided laboratory of geological and botanical diversity. On a clear day from the 1,845-foot summit of the Valencia Peak Trail, one can see 90 miles of coastline. People also come to fish, scuba dive, and tidepool along the rocky shore. For an unforgettably scenic four-mile round-trip hike, take the Bluff Trail, which runs from the visitor center to Grotto Rock, passing tidepools and cove beaches along the way.

Montana de Oro is a primitive park, with only 50 unimproved campsites and minimal facilities. That is precisely what keeps it pristine, despite increasing visitation as word gets around. And thus, we quietly encourage you to visit. To get there, from U.S. 101 three miles south of San Luis Obispo, take the Los Osos/Baywood Park exit. Drive 12 miles west on Los Osos Valley Road, which becomes Pecho Valley Road. Follow Pecho Valley Road to the park entrance. Alternatively, from Highway 1 north of San Luis Obispo, take Los Osos/Baywood Park exit and drive west on Los Osos Valley Road, which becomes Pecho Valley Road, to the park entrance.

Beaches

The beaches at **Montana de Oro State Park** are as wild as an unbroken colt, choked with rocky outcroppings and sea caves and pounded by a frothy, roiling surf. The coarse salt-and-pepper sand is not conducive to sunbathing, but the park and its coastline are ruggedly beautiful. Indefatigable surfers sometimes hike through the woods to the small beach at Hazard Canyon, where dangerous surf awaits.

The best beach is the sandy crescent at **Spooner's Cove** (named for the rancher and dairyman who was the former landowner), where there's a primitive campground. The cove takes up nearly half a mile of coastline and is worth a full day of exploration in itself. At the south end is a black pebbly sand beach wide enough to sunbathe on. Bring a pad to put under your towel, though, because the rocks will work their way into your back and buttocks. Splitting the cove in the middle is a rocky proscenium that allows the unique experience of walking out among the ocean waves and yet remaining high and dry, though this is not recommended for people with vertigo problems. Just to the north is another rocky cove beach backed by an enormous sea cave that begs to be explored. Signs warn of the possibility of getting trapped by fast incoming tides. Farther back from Spooner's Cove, you can see the limestone layers, hundreds of thousands of years old, from which this land was carved, and a trickling coastal stream, gurgling its pristine cool, clear water toward the ocean. This is as majestic a tableau of natural treasures as we've seen on any of our beach wanderings.

The only other campground in the park is a special area for equestrian campers, which must be reserved in advance. One deterrent to heavy visitation is that there is no potable water inside the park.

Map of San Luis Obispo County—Page 306

For More Information

Montana de Oro State Park, c/o San Luis Obispo Coast District, California State Parks, 1150 Laurel Lane, San Luis Obispo, CA 93401, 805/528-0513, website: www.parks.ca.gov

Los Osos/Baywood

The conjoined towns of Los Osos and Baywood (population 15,000) have grown in recent years, and they're on the verge of overdoing it as badly as the "Five Cities" franchise thicket in the Pismo Beach area. For now, though, Los Osos is an appealing stopover for visitors who don't fancy camping at Montana de Oro State Park.

Beaches

A tiny town park on Bayshore Drive sits off the south end of Main Street. **Bayshore Bluffs Park** abuts Morro Bay State Park; a stairway and graded path lead from the blufftop picnic area to the beach.

For More Information

Los Osos/Baywood Park Chamber, 781 Palisades Avenue, Los Osos, CA 93402, 805/528-4884, website: www.losososbaywoodpark.org/chamber

Morro Bay

Morro Rock is an enormous monolith, the remnant of an active volcano, that sits just offshore from the town of Morro Bay. It is the pet rock of the Central Coast and the "Gibraltar of the Pacific," and it dominates the landscape in these parts. It is inescapable, commanding, awesome. The rock is so much an icon that its likeness appears on anything having to do with Morro Bay, from postcards and tourist brochures to ashtrays and motel-room trash baskets. The Portuguese explorer Juan Cabrillo dubbed the rock El Morro ("Domed Turban") when he sailed into Estero Bay in 1542.

From a distance it looks like a bare, brown geodesic dome. It is one of seven volcanic peaks, known as the Seven Sisters, that run in a nearly straight line from San Luis Obispo to Morro Bay. Morro Rock is the most northwesterly of these intrusive plugs. Because it is offshore, it stands in bold relief and is the most spectacular to behold. Morro Rock rises 578 feet above sea level and weighs 20 million tons. Dating from the early Miocene period, it is estimated to be between 22 and 26 million years old.

Black Mountain, another of the Seven Sisters, rises close by in Morro Bay State Park. A paved road leads to **Black Mountain Lookout,** which, at 865 feet, is the highest point in the park. From here you are treated to a sweeping view of the coast. With its many different lithologies arrayed in a hodgepodge, this part of the Central Coast has been referred to as a "geological mulligan stew."

Morro Rock is composed of hard igneous rock that has outlasted the metamorphic rock of the Franciscan formation into which it intrudes. It looms above the landscape surrounding it, standing undaunted after millions of years. The only real threat to its well-being is humankind. Between 1891 and 1963 quarrying operations robbed Morro Rock of its sharp peak and some of its elevation. The volcanic rock and talus quarried off the rock were used to build breakwaters here and at Avila Beach, and to construct a causeway linking Morro Rock with the mainland. (It formerly stood 1,000 feet offshore.) After all that it was discovered that Morro's lava rock doesn't hold up to constant pounding by the sea. Moreover, quarrying was beginning to affect the fragile

There Otter Be a Law

In June 2002, biologists and vacationers began taking note of large numbers of dead sea otters washing up on the beaches of California's central coast. These sad sightings occurred shortly after the state's spring otter count had found that the species' populations were down by 1 percent from 2001, continuing a downward trend that dates back seven years, since the otters' population peaked in 1995 (the all-time low was hit in 1999).

Biologists suspect that the high death rates are due to starvation, disease, pollution, entanglement in fishing gear, and even shooting deaths. Something does smell fishy about the fact that most of the dead otters are young adults, the age group most vital for replacing the once plentiful numbers of this threatened species.

Morro Rock ecosystem. Nesting grounds for the rare and endangered peregrine falcon were being destroyed—as was the rock itself. By the time local residents demanded a halt to quarrying, more than a million tons of rock had been hauled away. Morro Rock was designated a State Historical Landmark and a Peregrine Falcon Reserve in 1968. These days you can drive up to its base and even halfway around it. Climbing the rock itself was banned in 1973, in deference to the birds.

The Morro Bay Power Station is another massive feature on the landscape. Its three 450-foot-tall smokestacks are directly across the road from Morro Rock, but you won't see them pictured on any postcards or promotional brochures for Morro Bay. They resemble enormous filter-tipped cigarettes, make a noise not unlike the drone in the film *Eraserhead,* and warm the nearby water by a few degrees. Between San Diego and Morro Bay we'd seen two nuclear power stations built on fault lines and now a power plant sited by one of the most wondrous natural features on the coast. When will they ever learn?

Its smokestacks aside, Morro Bay is a charming community of 10,350 friendly souls. People come to this less harried part of the coast

to lie back and watch Morro Rock or book a deep-sea fishing trip. With a sizable sport- and commercial-fishing fleet operating out of the breezy harbor, Morro Bay has the authentic flavor of a fishing village with minimal tourist trappings. A number of outfitters operate along the Embarcadero, Morro Bay's waterfront avenue. **Virg's Landing** (1215 Embarcadero, 805/772-1222) reels in the most anglers. It bustles like the floor of the stock exchange. Folks are constantly coming and going, booking trips and consulting the experts. A full-day trip runs $40. When the albacore are running, eager anglers flock to Morro Bay, and fishing fever takes over the town.

Every day, the commercial fleet sails in with fresh catches of salmon, albacore, ling cod, Pacific snapper, Alaskan halibut, and thresher shark. Morro Bay is one of the five largest estuaries in California and a biologically rich habitat. Visitors can partake of its bounty by boarding a water taxi from Virg's to the Morro Sand Spit, the four-mile peninsula that separates Morro Bay from the ocean. The 100-yard crossing will deposit you on a sand bank. It can be a mite uncomfortable on the spit "if the wind's blowin' like snot," according to our plainspoken skipper, so dress as you would for

Map of San Luis Obispo County—Page 306

a tornado. Once on the spit you can hike, dig for clams, surf cast, or bird-watch.

Still more soul-satisfying, nature-oriented activity can be found at **Morro Bay State Park,** attached to the southeastern end of town. It's a multiple-use recreation area with everything from campsites and hiking trails to a resort and an 18-hole golf course. A museum of natural history contains dioramas on nature, wildlife, and the area's early Chumash inhabitants. The marsh, located where Los Osos Creek enters Morro Bay, is home to 250 species of birds. The park is the site of a six-acre eucalyptus grove that serves as a rookery for great blue herons, which nest in the treetops from January to August. You can rent a canoe and paddle the quiet waters of the estuary or row out to the spit.

The Embarcadero runs for about a mile from Morro Rock to Morro Bay State Park. It is a highly walkable mile, passing bait-and-tackle shops and fish 'n' chip stands (serving local fish, they emphasize). At the corner of Morro Bay Boulevard and Market Street is the **Centennial Stairway.** This impressive redwood staircase descends to Fisherman's Memorial, a small harborside park with a 7,000-pound anchor as its centerpiece. The town's pride and joy is its Giant Chessboard, an outdoor game board whose dimensions are straight out of Alice in Wonderland. The redwood chessmen stand three feet tall and weigh 18 to 20 pounds each.

Morro Bay has been trying to pursue a slow-growth policy in the face of strong developmental pressure. As people flee Southern California with bulging retirement accounts and golden parachutes, keeping a lid on growth has proven difficult. The issue isn't just the usual desire to preserve an unhurried way of life and an unspoiled landscape. Water, or the lack of it, is the real limiting factor. Officials are concerned that overuse of dwindling water resources could cause underground aquifers to draw in salty seawater, ruining local water tables. Meanwhile, migrating Southern Californians have been steadily pricing Central Valley residents out of Morro Bay's housing market. In the late 1980s, housing prices jumped 40 percent in one year. With their deep pockets the Southlanders have simply outbid all other comers. Given the markets they're used to, they are paying prices that feel like bargains. Already the hills west of Main Street—a pretty tired-looking strip that runs alongside Highway 1 between Morro Bay State Park and Morro Strand State Beach—are crowded with homes.

Morro Rock itself presides benignly over the human activity at its base. It will still be standing long after the last fish 'n' chip shop has closed its doors. More than most communities Morro Bay takes a philosophical cue from this monolith, endeavoring to safeguard its essential qualities as a serene locale. The town refers to itself as a place "where the sun spends the winter." No matter what season, the view from Morro Bay is a fine one when the setting sun drops into the ocean. As the sun falls, train your eyes on Morro Rock, which takes on a bewitching range of hues and auroras. One evening around twilight we spied a small violet cloud hovering around the top of Morro Rock like a halo. Exquisite!

Beaches

If you love the beach, bay, and ocean, you will find Morro Bay an ideal place to drop anchor. The sand spit that extends north from Montana de Oro State Park like an arm ends with a fist-shaped protrusion that nearly chokes the narrow neck of the bay. It runs for four long miles and can be reached via water taxi (boarded at the Embarcadero in downtown Morro Bay) or by four-wheel drive from the south, where it joins the mainland at Montana de Oro. The spit is formally known as the **Morro Dunes Natural Area.** The dunes on the spit reach 85 feet in height.

Morro Rock and Beach, a small, crescent-shaped beach behind the breakwater, lies at the base of Morro Rock itself. Sun worshippers head here. Cataracts of spray fly off the top of the breakwater as waves thunder against it, but the water on the protected beach behind it is as calm as a rippled lake. Our advice: Enjoy the beach, but leave the breakwater alone. If you're tempted to scale the rocks for the view from the top, think twice about it. One afternoon years ago we hoisted ourselves up the breakwater's slippery, wet staircase of boulders. As we neared the top a longer-than-usual pause ensued between waves, and then a monster wave crested high above us. In the eerie seconds before we were washed down the wall of rock to the ground, we said our prayers. The gods were with us that day; we only got soaked, not severed on the rocks. Wetter than a pair of sea otters but otherwise unhurt, we changed into dry clothes and swore off climbing breakwaters.

Morro Strand State Beach is divided into two sections. The "south" section, formerly known as Atascadero State Beach, offers a 104-site campground. The smaller "north" section lies three miles north of town, off Highway 1. The beach is wide and runs for nearly two miles. RVs jam the campground, but the lack of shade might make Morro Strand State Beach South a little tough on tenters, who are better advised to check out Montana de Oro State Park. Morro Strand is an inviting day-use beach. Large waves roll lazily toward shore for a good distance, making for long rides. You can do everything on the beaches of Morro Strand but dig for clams, which is prohibited.

Bunking Down

Halfway between Los Angeles and San Francisco, Morro Bay is an ideal rendezvous point for residents of the two metropolises. The town is equipped with accommodations in all price ranges, from modest park-at-your-door motels to more resort-oriented facilities. The golden mean in Morro Bay would be someplace like the **Best Western Tradewinds** (225 Beach Street,

805/772-7376, $$), which is the closest lodging to Morro Rock itself and one short block from the waterfront.

The hotel of first choice has to be the **Inn at Morro Bay** (60 State Park Road, 805/772-5651, $$$). Located inside Morro Bay State Park, the inn is set back from the modest bustle of the Embarcadero. A luxury resort with a romantic atmosphere, its 100 guest rooms feature cathedral ceilings, gas fireplaces, country French decor, and outdoor decks overlooking the bay. The suite-sized rooms are filled with heavy, hand-carved furniture, and the brass-fixtured bathrooms come with a complimentary assortment of French soap. As lavish as it sounds, the Inn at Morro Bay has a cozy, country inn–style atmosphere.

Another fine choice is **Embarcadero Inn** (456 Embarcadero, 805/772-2700, $$), on the bay at the south end of town. The rooms are large, and the furniture cushiony. There are VCRs in the room and films at the front desk. Most rooms have a gas fireplace and an outdoor balcony, and the inn has a pair of indoor saunas. With its slate-colored, weathered-wood exterior, the Embarcadero Inn is the most distinguished-looking lodge on the waterfront.

The town of Morro Bay is outfitted with a number of plainer but perfectly comfortable and inexpensive motels. The **Harbor House Inn** (1095 Main Street, 805/772-2711, $) and **El Morro Lodge** (1206 Main Street, 805/772-5633, $) are both attractive, nicely maintained properties within walking distance of the waterfront.

Coastal Cuisine

Improvements are steadily being made along the waterfront as fading mom-and-pop joints inevitably give way to something more contemporary and, frankly, nicer. You'll find such successful newer arrivals as the **Otter Rock Cafe** (885 Embarcadero, 805/772-1420, $), a high-quality fast-food spot where you order at the window and carry your food to tables that look out over the water. At Otter Rock, baskets of fried seafood (fish, squid, oysters, scallops) and chips are served for under $10. Otter Rock Cafe also has a full bar and live entertainment on weekends.

Old reliables on the scene include the **Harbor Hut** (1205 Embarcadero, 805/772-2255, $$$) and the **Great American Fish Company** (1185 Embarcadero, 805/772-4407, $$$). Both are operated by longtime residents and serve freshly caught seafood. The Harbor Hut was the first restaurant on the waterfront in Morro Bay. It opened in 1948, serving chili and chowder in a small Quonset hut. Today it's a prosperous local institution where oysters are fixed a half-dozen ways. Daily catches from snapper to swordfish are fried, broiled, steamed, or sautéed, and combination surf-and-turf platters will assuage hearty appetites.

From an unfancy dining room overlooking Morro Harbor, the Great American Fish Company serves its namesake fish in mostly simple ways—i.e., grilled over mesquite or fried. The former option is indisputably healthier and arguably tastier, especially when you're talking about locally caught fish. Red snapper (moist, tender) and halibut (meaty, firm) are generally the freshest offerings caught by the local fleet, and a simple mesquite grilling (or Cajun-style blackening for a dollar extra) is preferred. Fish entrées run in the $12–15 range and come with a choice of two side dishes. Don't pass up the smoked albacore appetizer—a generous helping served with red-onion rings, crackers, and three sauces.

Moving upscale and away from the beach, the dining room at the **Inn at Morro Bay** serves Cal-nouvelle cuisine with a subtle French flair. You can count on fresh ingredients, superb preparation, a respectable wine list, excellent service, and a spectacular view of the bay. Entrée selection might include something like crab-crusted halibut with wild mushroom-asparagus ragout or lobster brûlée.

A perennial award-winner on Morro Bay's waterfront is **Windows on the Water** (699 Embarcadero, 805/772-0677, $$$), a great place for romancing couples. The restaurant's acronym is "WOW," and that's what you'll be saying when you dig into such entrées as prosciutto roasted salmon, especially if you've managed to snare a reservation at sunset.

Fish fans can indulge their yen for sushi at **Harada Japanese Restaurant and Sushi Bar** (630 Embarcadero, 805/772-1410, $$$). The must-stop place for breakfast is **Carla's Country Kitchen** (213 Beach Street, 805/772-9051, $), which serves knockout scrambled-egg dishes.

Night Moves

If you're hankering for a good dinner or a good time after dinner, go to **Rose's Landing Restaurant and Cocktail Lounge** (725 Embarcadero, 805/772-4441), a steak-and-seafood restaurant on the water that offers live entertainment on certain nights in summer.

For More Information

Morro Bay Chamber of Commerce, 880 Main Street, Morro Bay, CA 93442, 805/772-4467, website: www.morrobay.com

Map of Central California—Page 233

Cayucos

Cayucos is tucked into the head of a V-shaped cove formed where Cayucos Creek empties into the ocean. This town of 3,000 is an anomaly on the Central Coast. It doesn't look like it could give a hoot about tourism. It has the feel of an Old West town — which, in fact, it is. Its saloons look like real Old West saloons, because they are. No enormous infusions of cash have been pumped into Cayucos to restore, refurbish, revive, or revise. You'll find one central street (Ocean Avenue), with angle-in parking on both sides. Antique and gift shops predominate. An auto-repair garage on the north side of town has been here since 1932, which qualifies as ancient history on the West Coast. An enormous mobile-home park squats nearby. People come here to fish, decide they like the place, and stick around for a while.

Cayucos Pier, an old, planked affair that has all kinds of personality, has been around since 1875. Vendors push carts around the beachfront, selling such things as "churros" (long, greasy fried Mexican pastries rolled in sugar — mm-mm, bad). In Cayucos hot dogs and hamburgers outsell nouvelle cuisine. An unforgettable juxtaposition of signs that we noticed several years ago speaks volumes about the town. One by the town library announced the hours it was open: a mere two days a week. Next to it was a sign for a sporting-goods store, whose wares included "tackle, bait, amo *(sic)*, scuba gear."

Cayucos looks out over the placid waters of Estero Bay onto majestic Morro Rock, some five miles away. The little town lies in the proverbial shadow of Morro Rock and, hence, largely gets overlooked by those passing through the area. The Hearst Castle brings crowds to San Simeon, Morro Rock attracts tourists to Morro Bay, and romantic blufftop B&Bs draw couples to Cambria. However, nothing but empty ranchland and the town of Harmony (population 12) fills the 15 miles between Cayucos and Cambria. Cayucos is not a vacation destination per se, but if you want to experience a California beach town that has largely been left untouched, it fits the bill. In the words of a local who escaped a rat-race life decades ago, "What we offer is peace and serenity from the stresses of big-city life."

Beaches

Cayucos State Beach gets good waves and looks to be popular with boogie boarders, whom we've seen pitched into forceful forward rolls by sizable breakers. Anglers are in their glory on the 940-foot Cayucos Pier (built in 1875), which is surrounded by bait-and-tackle shops and lit at night. South of the state beach is **Cayucos Beach,** which can be accessed via nine stairwells along a 22-block stretch of Pacific Avenue. At its southern end, Cayucos Beach gives way to Morro Strand State Beach (North). This is the smaller, less developed section of the park.

Between Cayucos and Cambria along Highway 1 there are eight vista point turnouts where one can catch breathtaking ganders of the unsurpassably beautiful Central California coast.

Bunking Down

Don't come to Cayucos expecting to find pools, fireplaces, afternoon wine and cheese, and decanters of sherry. Most of the places here seem designed to meet the uncomplicated demands of those who have come to Cayucos to fish. Hence, kitchenettes are included with most rooms, so you can cook your catch. A couple of motels south of the town center rise above the no-frills standard. The most inviting of these is the **Beachwalker Inn** (501 South Ocean Avenue, 805/995-2133, $$$), which is only a block from the beach. Prices are a bit steep ($170 and up), but it must be a seller's market out here.

Coastal Cuisine

For seafood try **Sea Shanty** (296 South Ocean Avenue, 805/995-3272, $), which posts daily fresh-fish specials and is open seven days a week. Open since 1983, the Sea Shanty qualifies as a Cayucos institution that's popular with locals and vacationers alike. **Schooner's Wharf** (171 North Ocean Avenue, 805/995-3883, $$$) is under new ownership, and the new chef has made interesting changes to the menu, adding items like "surf trip halibut."

Night Moves

What longevity! **Old Cayucos Tavern** (130 North Ocean Avenue, 805/995-3209) has been serving cowboys and cowgirls since 1906. The atmosphere alone is priceless in this day and age of generic dance clubs and retro-chic bars. The tavern offers live music most nights.

For More Information

Cayucos Chamber of Commerce, 241 South Ocean Avenue, Cayucos, CA 93430, 805/995-1200 or 800/563-1878, website: www.cayucos-bythesea.com

Cambria

If there's a prettier setting for a beach in all of California than Cambria, we have yet to find it. Lying between Cayucos and San Simeon, Cambria is a shy princess knocking at the back door of Hearst Castle. Its motto says it all: "Where the pines meet the sea." A century ago Cambria was a thriving community of 7,000 souls who worked at whaling, mining, and farming. Today it numbers just slightly less than that, with a population of roughly 6,300, and there's little more going on than agriculture, arts and crafts, and a modest tourist trade. Those who visit here are mostly the spillover from San Simeon, plus enlightened travelers and couples on romantic getaways who can tell a genuinely quaint village from a contrived imitation. Part of the attraction of Cambria is its seclusion and wildness, and the townsfolk work to keep it that way. "Most of the residents have a slow-growth policy," explained a local innkeeper. "Some would call it a no-growth policy."

Many of the more recent arrivals are retiring creative sorts—artists, writers, and craftspeople—who have given Cambria something of the flavor of Laguna Beach without the hectic pace of Southern California. The town is divided by Highway 1 into East and West Villages. East Village is older, with many of its historic homes dating from the days when Cambria was known as "Slabtown," after the rough-

hewn boards from which they were built. It has all the shops and galleries, and it's a good place to while away the hours on a foggy morning as you're waiting for the sun to break through.

West Village is where the beaches are. To get there, disengage from Highway 1 at Moonstone Beach Road. Immediately you're in another world. You can see the steep, plunging mountains of Big Sur to the northwest, against a backdrop of flower- and grass-filled meadows. A string of cozy B&B-style motels/inns lines the landward side of Moonstone Beach Road. The preeminent feature in this landscape is the grassy, wildflower-strewn mesa that overlooks the beach. Trails crisscross the area right to the bluff edges, and people stroll at all hours. Take your pick—early morning, midafternoon, ruddy sunset, or by the light of the silvery moon. The scenery is always beautiful, and the variegated light plays on the panorama, revealing its many subtle facets.

Indeed, Cambria is the perfect spot for beach and nature lovers who aren't compelled to engage in frantic activities involving special equipment and sportswear. All you need in Cambria are walking shorts, a light sweater, tennis shoes, and maybe a camera—leave the rest to nature. It is hard to take a bad picture here. So come with your significant other, and prepare to savor some of the most breathtaking scenery and sunsets on the California coast.

Map of Central California—Page 233

Set among a native Monterey pine forest, Cambria is the sort of town that vigilantly eschews aesthetic breeches in the armor of good taste. In 1994, for instance, the townsfolk were up in arms about the possible arrival of a McDonald's. Reaction to this unwanted intrusion filled the front page of the local newspaper, spilling over into editorials and letters. One outraged local expressed the majority opinion: "The notion that something so insidious as a McDonald's chain restaurant may come to Cambria fills me with shock, anger, disgust, and disappointment."

More recently, Cambrians have banded together to check development before it chokes them. No two signs looked more welcome to us than the ones on Highway 1 approaching Cambria from the south: "Cambria Land Conservancy" and "Friends of the Ranchland." Both served to indicate that Cambrians, unlike those in Morro Bay and Pismo Beach, want to protect their golden egg before the yoke's on them. If this strikes outsiders as "burn the bridges" mentality, then so be it. Someone has to draw the line in the sand in California, especially if the government—local, state or federal—won't take necessary steps. We thank God for towns like Cambria (and Carmel and Santa Barbara), which are preserving some of their magic so that future generations can enjoy it.

Weather-wise, summer months are foggy—not the best time to visit the Central Coast, unless you're coming to escape the interior heat. September–October is usually picture-perfect: mild and clear, without blustery winds and choking fog. By the way, if you don't want to be pegged as a tourist, pronounce the town name "CAM-bree-ah", with a short "a" and the accent on the first syllable, as in "Camelot."

Beaches

Moonstone Beach runs for two miles until it tags up with San Simeon State Beach to the north. The coastline is rugged, with gnarled driftwood limbs and tangled mats of seaweed having been driven ashore. You can access Moonstone Beach at Leffingwell Landing, a quarter mile west of Moonstone Beach Drive's southern intersection with Highway 1. Moonstone Beach takes its name from the polished jade, agate, and quartz pebbles that collect in mounds here. On certain parts of the beach there is no sand, just heaps of these pea-sized stones.

A blufftop trail wanders above Moonstone Beach, extending from end to end. At some points, eroded indentations in the coastline have brought the ocean precariously close to the roadside. The paths above Moonstone Beach have had to adapt to the shoreward slumping of bluff materials. Waves rise in perfect form, then crash mightily on the rocks, sweeping over the stony shoreline. Surfers congregate up toward a point at the beach's south end. Everyone else just walks and watches. Who could ask for anything more?

Bunking Down

Cambria is the most romantic coast hideaway this side of Mendocino, and Moonstone Beach is the site of the choicest accommodations. All are in proximity to one another, and the decor, prices, and quality are fairly uniform among them. They all cost more or less the same: no less than $100 a night and, depending on time of year and demand for rooms, upward of $200 a night. Nearly all advertise "Pool * Fireplace * HBO" on their outdoor signs. And all are well maintained, quiet, and comfortable. We're partial to the **Sea Otter Inn** (6656 Moonstone Beach Drive, 805/927-5888, $$), which has gas fireplaces in all rooms, a heated pool, TVs with VCRs, and films for rent at the desk.

The **Best Western Fireside Inn** (6700 Moonstone Beach Drive, 805/927-8661, $$$) has the most units, and they are modern and well kept. Others that earn high marks and offer similar amenities include **Fog Catcher Inn** (6400 Moonstone Beach Drive, 805/927-1400, $$$) and **Sand Pebbles Inn** (6252 Moonstone Beach

Map of San Luis Obispo County—Page 306

Drive, 805/927-5600, $$$). The latter boasts English country decor, canopy beds, and a tea room where continental breakfast is served.

A newcomer to Moonstone Beach Drive, **Cambria's Pelican Suites** (6316 Moonstone Beach Drive, 805/927-1500, $$$), might just be the nicest hideaway of all. It's definitely the most elegant, featuring high beds with canopies. Comforters, carpeting, and wall coverings are coordinated in mauve and chocolate tones. A fine continental breakfast is served in the inn's warm, luxurious lobby. Cambria's Pelican Suites also gets a nod from us for spending $200,000 to save the riparian creek that runs through the property. All that and an extra-friendly staff add up to a winner in our book.

It pays to price-shop among the generally interchangeable venues on Moonstone Drive. By doing so on an early Sunday afternoon in May, we landed a deal at **Cambria Landing** (6530 Moonstone Beach Drive, 805/927-1619, $$$). For $75, which was well below the listed price, we got a comfortable room, free breakfast, a bottle of chardonnay, and access to two whirlpool tubs. Cambria Landing has the added bonus of being next door to Moonstone Beach Bar and Grill, which filled both our dinner and nightlife voids more than adequately.

Coastal Cuisine

A plentiful selection of nonfranchised restaurants can be found around town, both in East Village and out by Moonstone Beach. As one local put it, "We've already got **Main Street Grill** (603 Main Street, 805/927-3194, $). Who needs McDonald's?"

A long-standing favorite is **Brambles Dinner House** (4005 Burton Drive, 805/927-4716, $$$). It is so named because of the bramble bushes that run riot throughout the property, growing right up to the restaurant's windows. The Brambles is an old-fashioned English dinner

house. The walls are decorated with different patterns of china. Heavy red drapes hang in the windows, and the lights are turned down low. The house specialties run to surf-and-turf items prepared with a Greek flair. For dessert there's a rich, diet-busting cheesecake, as well as various flavors of ice cream frothed to a milkshake's consistency with liqueurs. We tried chocolate ice cream laced with amaretto, a concoction so tasty we were guiltily driven to hike off the calories on the trail overlooking Moonstone Beach.

Another East Village favorite is **Robin's** (4095 Burton Drive, 805/927-5007, $$), a gourmet vegetarian restaurant serving ethnic dishes prepared with locally grown organic produce.

Out on Moonstone Beach, the **Sea Chest Oyster Bar** (6216 Moonstone Beach Drive, 805/927-4514, $$$) does a raging business serving generous portions of Alaskan crab legs, among other things, to crowds that happily pile in to break bread and crab legs in good company. The **Moonstone Beach Bar and Grill** (6550 Moonstone Beach Drive, 805/927-3859, $$$), formerly the Moonraker, serves a variety of fare, but the best bet is the ever-popular pesto shrimp pasta and fresh mahimahi.

Night Moves

Go to **Moonstone Beach Bar and Grill** (6550 Moonstone Beach Drive, 805/927-3859) if you're thirsty for a nightcap. In general, though, like most villages on this wild and scenic stretch of coastline, more noise is made by ocean waves than human beings after 10 P.M. Knock off early and save your strength for a beach hike before breakfast.

For More Information

Cambria Chamber of Commerce, 767 Main Street, Cambria, CA 93428, 805/927-3624, website: www.thegrid.net/cambriachamber

Map of Central California—Page 233

San Simeon

Its owner christened it La Cuesta Encantada ("The Enchanted Hill"), but the world knows it better as Hearst Castle. The state park system formally refers to it as **Hearst San Simeon State Historical Monument.** Whatever you want to call it, the 165-room palace overlooking the ocean from the Santa Lucia Mountains is the Central Coast's gilded centerpiece. It's as simple as this: no visit to the area is complete without a tour of Hearst Castle.

San Simeon is castle country. Everything else—sun, sand, sea, and the mountains that roll down to it—takes a backseat to the incomprehensible enormity of Hearst Castle. The midcoast mountaintop hideaway was built by newspaper magnate William Randolph Hearst as a "carefully planned, deliberate attempt to create a shrine of beauty." One million people visit San Simeon every year, making it California's top state-run tourist attraction.

Hearst was one of America's wealthiest men when he commissioned work on the castle, portrayed as the tomblike "Xanadu" in Orson Welles's classic film *Citizen Kane,* the barely fictionalized biography that is a cornerstone of every college-level film-appreciation course. Born in 1863, Hearst was the sole heir to the nation's third largest fortune. His father, George Hearst, made his millions speculating in gold and silver mines, including the Comstock Lode. The elder Hearst turned his attention to real estate in the 1860s, gobbling up ranchland at 65 cents an acre. By acquiring adjoining land grants in the San Simeon area, he amassed a spread of 275,000 acres. In the later years of the 19th century, the family often embarked on summer retreats to San Simeon, living in a tent pitched on top of a 1,600-foot mountain they called Camp Hill.

William Randolph Hearst decided to build his dream castle on this site. He had not done badly for himself, thanks to his father's largesse. Hearst was given the *San Francisco Examiner* on his 24th birthday, and he went on to inherit the $11 million family fortune. He oversaw a vast media empire that grew to include 30 newspapers, 15 magazines, six radio stations, and several film companies. In all, he owned 94 businesses, employing 40,000 people. And yet history largely remembers Hearst as a yellow journalist whose papers' hysterical reportage helped start a war and elect a president.

His private passion for art collecting was greater even than his public passion for journalism and politicking. Hearst reportedly spent $1 million a year on artwork alone for 50 consecutive years. Some pieces date back 3,500 years, to the 18th Egyptian dynasty. He intended his castle to be a Louvre-like repository for his priceless collection of Mediterranean Gothic and Renaissance paintings, tapestries, and antique ceilings. Work was undertaken on the buildings and gardens in 1919. Hearst enlisted Julia Morgan, a renowned Berkeley-trained architect, to work for and with him. She agreed to devote two weekends a month to the Hearst manse, a project that kept her occupied for 20 years.

Hearst indulged every whim and desire that could be conceived, given virtually boundless economic resources. The crowning glory of the hilltop estate is La Casa Grande, the 115-room main house. It includes the gargantuan Refectory and Assembly Room (each filled with priceless art and artifacts), two libraries, and a movie theater. There's no place like home, especially when home is surrounded by 123 acres of exotic gardens, plus a line of 100-foot Mexican fan palms. Three guest houses—Casa del Mar, Casa del Sol, and Casa del Monte—adjoin the big house, as do huge indoor and outdoor swimming pools. Hearst, an animal fancier, made a virtual nature preserve of his estate, importing 90 species from around the world and allowing them to roam the hills and fields. To this day zebras and

Map of San Luis Obispo County—Page 306

Touring Hearst Castle

Four completely different daytime tours are offered of **Hearst Castle,** and in the spring and fall evening tours are available. The spruced-up visitors center includes the National Geographic Theater, which runs the large-screen companion movie *Hearst Castle—Building the Dream.* The state is to be commended for keeping admission fees reasonable. They have, in fact, decreased by a dollar since our last visit. This is despite the fact that the cost of upkeep is beyond belief now. For a yardstick, consider that it cost $3,000 per day to maintain the estate when the state took over in 1957. The tour guides we've had on our visits have all been well-informed and engaging speakers.

All tours involve about a half mile of walking and between 150 and 400 steps. Here's a quick overview of each tour, all of which also include the indoor ("Roman") and outdoor ("Neptune") pools:

• **Tour 1:** This is the General Tour, recommended for first-time visitors. It covers the ground floor of the main building, one of the guest houses ("La Casa del Sol"), and part of the gardens. Admission also includes a 40-minute film by *National Geographic.*

• **Tour 2:** On the Private Quarters Tour, visitors explore the upper floors of the main building, including two suites, study, guest rooms, library, kitchen, and pantry.

• **Tour 3:** The North Wing Tour consists of three floors of guest suites, one of the guest houses ("La Casa del Monte"), and a short film.

• **Tour 4:** The Garden Tour guides you through Hearst's gardens, as well as a guest house ("La Casa del Mar"), the wine cellar, and the "hidden terrace." The main building is not entered. This tour is offered April–October.

• **Tour 5:** The Evening Tour provides a nighttime glimpse of the castle on Fridays and Saturdays, March–May and September–December, as well as every night during some holiday periods, such as Easter and Christmas. The tour includes highlights from Tours 1, 2, and 4, and lasts two hours and 10 minutes.

For Hearst Castle tour reservations call 800/444-4445 or log on to www.hearst-castle.com. Alternatively, you can contact ReserveAmerica at 800/444-7275 or www.reserveamerica.com. Tickets for Tour 1— "Hearst Experience," which includes the National Georgraphic film—are $18 ($9 for those under 17). Tours 2, 3, and 4 cost $12 ($7 for those under 17), and evening tours run $24 ($12 for those under 17). Tickets may also be purchased at the Hearst Castle ticket office, open daily 8 A.M.–4 P.M. Reservations can be made up to eight weeks in advance for individuals and 12 weeks in advance for groups. Reservations for wheelchair-accessible tours can be made directly with Hearst Castle by calling 805/927-2020 at least 10 days in advance.

Map of Central California—Page 233

Barbary sheep, remnants of this bestiary, wander the grounds.

There is no end of jaw-dropping facts about the castle and tales about the celebrity aristocracy who were Hearst's constant guests during the gilded age of the 1920s and '30s. Artifacts on display include Greek and Roman temple relics, 2,000-year-old sarcophagi, millefleur tapestries from the north of France, and a Spanish castle ceiling (shipped overseas in 100 crates and reassembled at San Simeon). You hear of a storage room filled with fur coats, provided as a courtesy for female guests wary of catching a shiver in the cool mountain air after stepping out of the 345,000-gallon heated outdoor pool.

America is fascinated with "the Big Money" (to borrow a John Dos Passos book title), and that is what keeps the tourist buses chugging up the mountain day in and day out. Though we don't have a king and queen, we do have a palace, and its name is San Simeon. Seven years after Hearst's death in 1951, his heirs turned over the estate to the state of California in exchange for $56 million in tax breaks. Today, tours run like clockwork from 8:20 A.M.–3 P.M. (later in summer) every day of the year but Christmas, Thanksgiving, and New Year's Day. Tickets for the introductory "Hearst Experience" tour cost $18 per person. Tours 2, 3, and 4 are $6 less and night tours are $6 more. Kids under 17 get a big break on ticket prices. (For more information, see the sidebar "Touring Hearst Castle.")

Each tour lasts just under two hours and involves nearly equal amounts of walking and gawking. Visitors are shepherded around the grounds by smiling guides who remind you not to step off the indoor-outdoor carpet runners that keep tourist hoof prints off the priceless marble, tile, and wood floors. A word to the wise: Castle tours might be a little boring for fidgety young kids and culturally lowbrow adults. However, we'd recommend it without hesitation to travelers possessing any level of interest in art, architecture, or (of course) lifestyles of the rich and famous. Incidentally, the Hearst Corporation endures as a vast media empire, controlling newspapers, magazines, and book-publishing houses—not to mention 80,000 acres of land surrounding Hearst Castle.

The tiny village of San Simeon (population 250) lies beside the coast at the foot of Hearst's mountain. It exists mainly to serve the tourist population, and beyond a modest motel row, there's not much here. If you're planning on touring San Simeon—and it should be on your itinerary, if you've never done it—we'd recommend staying in Cambria, a short hop down the road and a more scenic and interesting place to bunk down.

Beaches

Although Hearst Castle eclipses everything around it, two public beaches in San Simeon offer something else to do when you're in the area. **San Simeon State Beach** is between Santa Rosa and San Simeon Creeks, abutting queenly Cambria to the south and providing 187 campsites and a day-use beach. Surfing is hit or miss, and swimming is for polar bears, but the diving is usually swell.

William R. Hearst Memorial State Beach lies at the foot of the Hearst property. The grounds include a lovely picnic area. There are two sections to this under-appreciated beach. To the north of the pier is a wide, protected cove beach backed by shade trees, a setting especially appealing to families. The stunning blue-green water here is calm enough that small craft and sailboats anchor right offshore. South of the pier is a much longer, rockier beach with rougher surf. This is more appealing to surfers and those who desire a bit more seclusion and have no qualms about removing their clothing. San Simeon Point protects Hearst Beach from the ocean's onslaught, but the real attraction is a 1,000-foot fishing pier, where anglers cast for snapper and rockfish or charter boats for deep-sea fishing trips.

From this vantage point you're in the old, often bypassed village of San Simeon. Formerly a whaling village, it is now just a small cluster of buildings on a short spur road off Highway 1. There's not much more here than an old schoolhouse and the oldest store in the state, Sebastian's General Store, which also houses the local post office.

Bunking Down

The first motel in the area was **San Simeon Lodge** (9520 Castillo Drive, 805/927-4601, $). Built in 1958, the year in which the state acquired the Hearst Castle, it offers serviceable accommodations and reasonable, family-friendly prices. A whole strip of motels has grown up alongside the year-round industry of castle touring. The **Best Western Cavalier Resort** (9415 Hearst Drive, 805/927-4688, $$) is the only oceanfront motel in San Simeon, boasting 900 feet of coastline, plus fireplaces, balconies, and other upscale amenities more common to Cambria than San Simeon.

The **California Seacoast Lodge** (9215 Hearst Drive, 805/927-3878, $$) puts a bit of Cambria's B&B-style amenities (country English decor, fireplaces, canopied beds) close to Hearst Castle. For the budget-minded a clean, new **Motel 6** (9070 Castillo Drive, 805/927-8691, $) offers economy and convenience.

Coastal Cuisine

Because they feed more than a million mouths a year, the restaurateurs of San Simeon take a similar approach toward hungry tourists: herd 'em in, fill 'em up, and move 'em out. They arrive by the busload before or after touring the house that Hearst built. One restaurant manager bragged to us about her restaurant's ability to feed literally thousands a day. The secret is to cajole them into eating from serve-yourself buffet troughs. "Don't

even let 'em see a menu," she told us. "They might get ideas."

San Simeon Restaurant (9520 Castillo Drive, 805/927-4604, $$), which adjoins San Simeon Lodge, has been around the longest and has the art of feeding the masses down to a science. One must heave open a veritable castle door to get inside. The dining room is filled with San Simeon memorabilia. The house specialty is prime rib, which suits the transient meat-and-potatoes crowd just fine.

At the other extreme is **Europa** (9240 Castillo Drive, 805/927-3087, $$), which would have better suited Hearst's kingly ambitions. In any case, this internationally flavored menu of beef, pasta, and fish specials is an attractive option if you're suffering from the all-you-can-eat blues.

The northernmost restaurant in San Luis Obispo County, the **Ragged Point Inn** (19071 Highway 1, 805/927-5208, $$$) just might be the most appealing place to dine on seafood. Without question, the setting—five miles north of San Simeon, on the southern edge of Big Sur—is hard to surpass. The inn also rents rooms, making Ragged Point a great spot for sedentary getaways.

Night Moves

William Randolph Hearst is dead, and after dark so is San Simeon. One viable choice is an evening tour of Hearst Castle (see "Touring Hearst Castle").

For More Information

San Simeon Chamber of Commerce, 250 San Simeon Avenue, Suite 2B, San Simeon, CA 93452, 805/927-3500, website: www.hearstcastle.org; San Simeon State Park, 750 Hearst Castle Road, San Simeon, CA 93452, 805/927-2020, website: www.parks.ca.gov

Map of Central California—Page 233

Point Piedras Blancas

Just south of the Monterey County line is Point Piedras Blancas, a vista point turnout you will not want to bypass in your haste to get to Big Sur. Although this detour offers no public beach access, it does offer a unique opportunity on the California coast to study the behavior of sea lions and seals in the wild. Adult elephant seals—so large they almost resemble manatees—are spotted here from late November to March. More frequently the beach below the viewing spots is dotted with the prone, twitching, snoozing, and honking bodies of weary California sea lions and harbor seals, as well as a few baby elephant seals (known as "weaners").

This Point Piedras colony of elephant seals is the fastest growing on the mainland of California. Informative placards describe the life cycles of these endangered sea mammals, and viewing perches let you peer nearly straight down at them in action. One placard described the fighting that often occurs among male elephant seals who are trying to protect their "harem" of females. A photograph of two bloodied studs accompanies the description, which prompted one young boy to ask his father if they were going to fight while we were watching them. "No, they only do that during mating season," the father explained. "What's mating mean?" the son queried, followed by silence, then a studiously delicate response, "That's when they are, uh, trying to find a girlfriend." As we are both fathers of young children, we noted the skill of this dad, for future use.

For More Information

Friends of the Elephant Seal, Central Coast, P.O. Box 490, Cambria, CA 93428, 805/924-1628, website: www.elephantseal.org

© ROBERT HOLMES/CALTOUR

Chapter 7
Monterey County

Monterey County

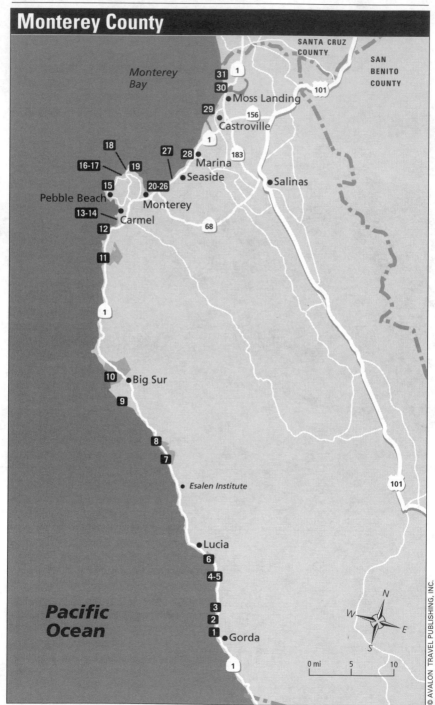

Monterey County

Pacific Ocean

SANTA CRUZ COUNTY
SAN BENITO COUNTY

Monterey Bay

31
30
● Moss Landing
29
Castroville
156
1
27 28
19 Marina
18
16-17
● Seaside
15 20-26
Pebble Beach ●
13-14 Monterey
Carmel
12
11
1

● Salinas
183
68
1
101

10 ● Big Sur
9

8
7

● Esalen Institute

● Lucia
6
4-5
3
2
1 ● Gorda
1

0 mi   5   10

N
W   E
S

© AVALON TRAVEL PUBLISHING, INC.

Monterey County Beaches

1 Willow Creek Picnic Area, page 355

Location: Milepost 61.5S/28.2N on Highway 1 in Big Sur
Parking/fees: free parking lot
Hours: sunrise–sunset
Facilities: restrooms, picnic tables, and fire pits
Contact: Big Sur Station, 831/667-2315

2 Jade Cove, page 355

Location: Milepost 59.8S/29.9N on Highway 1 in Big Sur
Parking/fees: free parking lot
Hours: sunrise–sunset
Facilities: none
Contact: Big Sur Station, 831/667-2315

3 Sand Dollar Picnic Area and Beach, page 355

Location: Milepost 59.3S/30.4N on Highway 1 in Big Sur
Parking/fees: free parking lot. Camping fee at Plaskett Creek Campground is $16 per night.
Hours: sunrise–sunset
Facilities: restrooms and picnic tables
Contact: Big Sur Station, 831/667-2315

4 Mill Creek Picnic Area, page 357

Location: Milepost 54.5S/35.2N on Highway 1 in Big Sur
Parking/fees: free parking lot
Hours: sunrise–sunset
Facilities: restrooms and picnic tables
Contact: Big Sur Station, 831/667-2315

5 Kirk Creek Campground, page 357

Location: Milepost 54.0S/35.7N on Highway 1 in Big Sur
Parking/fees: free parking lot. Camping fee is $16 per night.
Hours: sunrise–sunset
Facilities: restrooms and picnic tables
Contact: Big Sur Station, 831/667-2315

Map of Monterey County—Page 342

6 Limekiln State Park, page 357

Location: Milepost 52.1S/37.6N on Highway 1 in Big Sur
Parking/fees: $5 entrance fee per vehicle. Camping fees are $13–16 per night, plus a $7.50 reservation fee.
Hours: 8 A.M.–8 P.M.
Facilities: restrooms, showers, and picnic tables
Contact: Limekiln State Park, 831/625-4419

7 Julia Pfeiffer Burns State Park, page 357

Location: Milepost 37.0S/52.7N on Highway 1 in Big Sur
Parking/fees: $5 entrance fee per vehicle.
Hours: sunrise–sunset
Facilities: restrooms and picnic tables
Contact: Big Sur Station, 831/667-2315

8 Partington Cove, page 357

Location: Milepost 35.2S/54.5N on Highway 1
Parking/fees: free limited roadside parking
Hours: sunrise–sunset
Facilities: none
Contact: Big Sur Station, 831/667-2315

9 Pfeiffer Beach, page 358

Location: From Highway 1 in Big Sur, turn west onto Sycamore Canyon Road (Milepost 27.1S/63.2N) and follow for two miles.
Parking/fees: free parking lot
Hours: sunrise–sunset
Facilities: restrooms
Contact: Big Sur Station, 831/667-2315

10 Andrew Molera State Park, page 358

Location: Milepost 21.4S/68.3N on Highway 1 in Big Sur
Parking/fees: $4 entrance fee per vehicle. Camping fee (tents only) is $2 per person.
Hours: sunrise–sunset
Facilities: restrooms and picnic tables
Contact: Big Sur Station, 831/667-2315

11 Garrapata State Park, page 360

Location: Turnouts 13 and 14, just north of Garrapata Creek Bridge, on Highway 1 in Big Sur

Map of Central California—Page 233

Monterey County

Parking/fees: free roadside parking
Hours: sunrise–sunset
Facilities: none
Contact: Big Sur Station, 831/667-2315

12 Point Lobos State Reserve, page 363

Location: Riley Ranch Road, off Highway 1, three miles south of Carmel
Parking/fees: $5 entrance fee per vehicle
Hours: 9 A.M.–5 P.M. PST (9 A.M.–7 P.M. PDT)
Facilities: restrooms
Contact: Point Lobos State Reserve, 831/624-4909

13 Carmel River State Beach, page 368

Location: Scenic Road at Carmel Street, off Highway 1, one mile south of Carmel
Parking/fees: free parking lot
Hours: sunrise–sunset
Facilities: restrooms
Contact: Monterey District, California State Parks, 831/649-2836

14 Carmel City Beach, page 368

Location: end of Ocean Avenue in Carmel
Parking/fees: metered street parking
Hours: sunrise–10 P.M.
Facilities: restrooms and picnic tables
Contact: Carmel Department of Forests, Parks, and Beaches, 831/624-3543

15 Fanshell Beach, page 374

Location: Signal Hill Road at 17-Mile Drive in Pebble Beach
Parking/fees: $8 entrance fee per car to nonguests or nonresidents of Pebble Beach and its lodges
Hours: sunrise–sunset
Facilities: none
Contact: Pebble Beach Company, 831/647-7500 or 800/654-9300

16 Moss Beach, page 374

Location: north of Point Joe along Spanish Bay Road in Pebble Beach
Parking/fees: $8 entrance fee per car to nonguests or nonresidents of Pebble Beach and its lodges
Hours: sunrise–sunset
Facilities: none
Contact: Pebble Beach Company, 831/647-7500 or 800/654-9300

Map of Monterey County—Page 342

17 Spanish Bay, page 374

Location: behind the Inn at Spanish Bay, along the Spanish Bay Recreation Trail, in Pebble Beach
Parking/fees: $8 entrance fee per car to nonguests or nonresidents of Pebble Beach and its lodges
Hours: sunrise–sunset
Facilities: none
Contact: Pebble Beach Company, 831/647-7500 or 800/654-9300

18 Asilomar State Beach, page 377

Location: Sunset Drive between Asilomar and Jewel Avenues in Pacific Grove
Parking/fees: free street parking
Hours: sunrise–sunset
Facilities: restrooms and showers
Contact: Asilomar State Beach, 831/372-4076

19 Lover's Point, page 377

Location: Ocean View Boulevard at 17th Street in Pacific Grove
Parking/fees: free parking lot
Hours: sunrise–10 P.M.
Facilities: restrooms and picnic tables
Contact: Pacific Grove Parks Department, 831/648-3130

20 Shoreline Park, page 377

Location: Ocean View Boulevard between Lover's Point and Point Cabrillo in Monterey
Parking/fees: free street parking
Hours: 6 A.M.–10 P.M.
Facilities: none
Contact: Monterey Parks Department, 831/648-3860

21 Macabee Beach, page 386

Location: Prescott Avenue at Cannery Row in Monterey
Parking/fees: metered street parking
Hours: 6 A.M.–10 P.M.
Facilities: none
Contact: Monterey Parks Department, 831/646-3860

22 San Carlos Beach Park, page 386

Location: end of Reeside Avenue, between Cannery Row and Coast Guard Pier, in Monterey
Parking/fees: metered street parking
Hours: 6 A.M.–10 P.M.

Map of Central California—Page 233

Facilities: picnic tables
Contact: Monterey Parks Department, 831/646-3860

23 Del Monte Beach, page 386

Location: Park Avenue at Del Monte Boulevard near Wharf #2 in Monterey
Parking/fees: limited free street parking
Hours: 6 A.M.–10 P.M.
Facilities: restrooms
Contact: Monterey Parks Department, 831/646-3860

24 Monterey State Beach (Windows on the Bay), page 386

Location: north side of Wharf #2 off Del Monte Boulevard in Monterey
Parking/fees: limited free street parking
Hours: 9 A.M.–a half hour after sunset
Facilities: restrooms
Contact: Marina State Beach, 831/384-7695

25 Monterey State Beach (Beach Way Access), page 386

Location: end of Beach Way, off Del Monte Boulevard, in Monterey
Parking/fees: free parking lot
Hours: 9 A.M.–a half hour after sunset
Facilities: none
Contact: Marina State Beach, 831/384-7695

26 Monterey State Beach (Sand Dunes Drive), page 386

Location: south of Monterey Beach Hotel, at the end of Sand Dunes Drive off Highway 1, in Monterey
Parking/fees: free parking lot
Hours: 9 A.M.–a half hour after sunset
Facilities: restrooms
Contact: Marina State Beach, 831/384-7695

27 Monterey State Beach (Seaside), page 391

Location: north of Monterey Beach Hotel off Highway 1 in Seaside
Parking/fees: free parking lot
Hours: 9 A.M.–a half hour after sunset
Facilities: restrooms
Contact: Marina State Beach, 831/384-7695

Map of Monterey County—Page 342

Monterey County

28 Marina State Beach, page 395

🚶 ④

Location: end of Reservation Road in Marina
Parking/fees: free parking lot
Hours: 8 A.M.–a half hour after sunset
Facilities: restrooms
Contact: Marina State Beach, 831/384-7695

29 Salinas River State Beach, page 397

🚶 🎿 ①

Location: Portrero Road at Highway 1, one mile south of Moss Landing
Parking/fees: free parking lot
Hours: 8 A.M.–a half hour after sunset
Facilities: restrooms
Contact: Marina State Beach, 831/384-7695

30 Moss Landing State Beach, page 397

🚶 🎿 ③

Location: Jetty Road at Highway 1, north of Moss Landing Harbor, in Moss Landing
Parking/fees: $2 entrance fee per vehicle
Hours: 6:30 A.M.–a half hour after sunset
Facilities: restrooms
Contact: Marina State Beach, 831/384-7695

31 Zmudowski State Beach, page 397

🚶 🎿 ②

Location: end of Geiberson Road north of Moss Landing; follow signs from Highway 1 to beach
Parking/fees: free parking lot
Hours: 8 A.M.–a half hour after sunset
Facilities: restrooms
Contact: Marina State Beach, 831/384-7695

Monterey County

Monterey County

The coastline of Monterey County has inspired epic poems, novels, photographs, paintings, spiritual retreats, and nature cults. On a personal level Monterey County—especially Big Sur, its stunning geographical centerpiece—has never failed to reduce us beach bums to an awed silence. Intrepid travelers drive cliff-hugging Highway 1 through Big Sur; it is a veritable rite of passage for vacationers who want the true, uncut California experience. The experience is not unlike riding through the Louvre on a motorbike, with one geological masterpiece after another coming into view, varying enough in shape and size to keep things consistently breathtaking. The cove beaches of southern Big Sur meld into the raw contours and lofty peaks of the Ventana Wilderness and the exquisite beauty of northern Big Sur.

The sights don't stop here. The populous Monterey Peninsula has its own storehouse of treasures: the steep-sloped, blinding white-sand beach at Carmel; the calming stands of pine in Pacific Grove; and the strollable bayside in Monterey, with its pier, marina, and aquarium. Farther up the road, the population thins out, giving way to the wilderness beaches of rural Moss Landing and the fertile farmland surrounding Castroville.

Although much of the county is a purely visual delight (look, but don't touch), a number of jewel-like parklands can be found where land meets sea—in particular, Andrew Molera State Park and Point Lobos State Reserve. Don't just whiz through Monterey County like some harried, hotfooted tourist. Stop and smell the roses—and taste the artichokes, while you're at it.

Monterey County

Map of Monterey County—Page 342

Big Sur

Big Sur has inspired more verbiage than a dozen Norton anthologies. Poetry, prose, proclamations, postcards—you name it, and it has been written about Big Sur, one of the last great untamed, unregulated wilderness areas in the lower 48 states. Maybe it's the jagged rocks in the water. Or the crashing waves flinging cataracts of foam in the air. Or the portentous fog that hangs over land and sea. Or the enticing mystery of nature at its most inhospitable—a raw ocean backed by the Santa Lucia Mountains and Los Padres National Forest. "Harsh and lovely," wrote local novelist Lillian Bos Ross, "held fast to their ancient loneliness by a sheer drop of 5,000 feet by a shoreless sea." Whatever it is, one is never at a loss for words when describing Big Sur. Yet in the final reckoning, most attempts to describe it are inadequate.

Still, some noble efforts have been made. Robinson Jeffers wrote his most heroic verse while living here. Novelist Richard Brautigan

 Living with Big Sur

Other than glimpses gleaned from Henry Miller's later writings and curt chats with "hippie types" who camp here, we've never sated our fascination with, and fantasies about, what life in Big Sur must be like year-round. Maybe we're would-be utopians, longing for a community of 1,600 enlightened souls evenly spaced out along 90 miles of precipitous ridges and rugged shores.

With habitations out of sight of the road, chance encounters with Big Sur residents are pretty remote—that is, until we encountered a loquacious local at a Big Sur restaurant one evening. She was our "server," and when we told her of our longtime curiosity, she gladly entertained and enlightened us with tales of her life here. Articulate, witty, self-effacing and yet self-assured, she was not averse to telling all, in the best sense.

She came here from Pittsburgh, after getting a degree in social work that led to employment as a counselor. Deciding her long blonde hair and gentle spirit were not suited to life as a resident counselor at a state prison, she came to Big Sur, where she has resided ever since. She has lived in many homes, hopping from one rental to another as they became available, and camping in a tent when they did not. She even had the ultimate Big Sur experience of living in Henry Miller's former digs on Partington Ridge, a mystical place now in disarray that still attracts scores of rude interlopers. She is, in short, immersed in this seemingly invisible community, a gregarious soul living among hermits. She takes painting lessons from an elderly woman who serves as a sort of guru, and she wanders into the hills with her easel like Van Gogh at Arles. "So much comes up when you put oil on canvas," she says. "Who needs a psychiatrist?"

She also takes on "body work"—nutrition, health, hygiene, and massage. She grows herbs and English lavender, from which she makes medicinal po-

Map of Central California—Page 233

also mythologized the area, as did noted photographers Edward Weston and Ansel Adams, their visual record of Big Sur gracing many a coffee table. Nouveau salon painters continue the tradition of freeze-framing Big Sur, their efforts filling many a trendy gallery on the California coast.

We completely understand all the aesthetes' fascination and fixation with Big Sur. While researching this third edition, we happened to drive its length on one of the most glorious days in all creation. The sun was high, the sky hard blue, everything green and blooming, the air so clear that everything had a high definition almost to the point of hyper-realism. The natural world seemed more of a marvel and sanctuary than ever. Even the most devout atheist would have to give some ground to the notion of a divine creator in such a setting on such a day as this.

The Santa Lucia Mountains, which rise with near verticality from the waters edge, are harrowing and awesome to behold at any time, under any conditions. Yet they were particularly majestic on this day. Every turn in the road brought a new overlook onto the ocean

tions. In Big Sur no one agonizes over the issue of age as we do in the real world. Wrinkles betoken wisdom. What people do care about is privacy. And though it's not apparent to the naked eye, our server insisted that things are changing in changeless Big Sur. Upon one back ridge, 25 new homes have been built where there was just one when she first arrived. Rumors fly about celebrities buying property.

Stragglers and scavengers think nothing of poking around for intrigue or the ghost of Henry Miller. "As much as I love him, he is long gone," our Big Sur confidante said. She also bemoaned the high property taxes, reflected in her monthly rent, which force her to work three shifts at the restaurant. Then there's the summertime traffic snarl of tourists who take the spectacular drive along the Pacific Coast Highway and stop in for souvenir baubles, burgers, and whatnot.

Worst of all, the owner of the house where she lives—he's an organic agronomist in San Francisco—was threatening to kick her out of the apartment, allegedly to start a five-year agriculture experiment along the unblemished ridge. She'd been there five years herself, and "this was the first year the roof hasn't leaked," she says, exasperated but not embittered. She'll be okay, she insists. She has enough hooks in the community to keep a roof over her head. She can always go back to the tent life. "That was okay when I was young, but. . . ."

It doesn't seem fair, though we've seen it happen everywhere. People like our server, who have the lowest impact on the environment, are the renters. They're the ones who realize that life is temporary, so why try to own everything, mark off boundaries, chase money, and rearrange nature to please some acquisitive bug that is never pleased anyway? As for those who own real estate in Big Sur in these uncertain times, we humbly issue this request: Don't sell off the land. The rest of the world is a motel lobby. Predictable. Bland. Big Sur is heaven.

Map of Monterey County—Page 342

Monterey County

or scene of topographic wonder jutting above us. The forms are so incredible in their relation to one another that you sometimes feel as if you're wearing 3D glasses. Written large on a landscape that is inhospitable to habitation and highways—including that perilous marvel, Highway 1, etched into the cliffs and forever being repaired or rebuilt—it delivers a lesson in humility to a species that foolishly believes it can conquer all. Humankind will never tame this corner of creation—nor should we even dare to try.

From either end, the initial ascent into Big Sur is a roller-coaster ride like no other. You go up, up, up and then down, around curves and loop-de-loops, only to emerge with a vista that makes you feel as if you're on top of the world. Numerous turnouts make it possible to study the splendor. On a nice day, you might pull over and drink in nature's majesty for an hour or more. You might also choose to take a cigarette break, as many seem to do in a profound waste of fresh air. Each turn of the geographic kaleidoscope brings a new perspective. Green, folded mountainsides rise like fertile pinnacles toward heaven. The colors of the mountains change with the light and time of day, as does that of the water. Looking down on one cove, we saw brown, volcanic sand on the beach; agitated nearshore waters that had turned a sediment-stirred whitish-brown; a band of jade-colored water that reminded us of Florida's emerald coast; and, finally, the steely azure that typifies deeper Pacific waters.

Some sights are surreal. Certain offshore rock formations look like they were dropped here from outer space. Sheer mountain faces constantly cough up rocks onto the road, and yellow-and-black signs warn of slides. Work crews struggle to keep Highway 1 passable, especially after the winter rainy season, when running water further destabilizes nonvegetated cliff faces. There have been years when the road has been closed for months while Cal-Trans crews deal with cataclysmic rock slides

or the necessary re-bridging of some seemingly unbridgeable chasm. In places, the road looks like it's been Crazy Glued back together, and we could smell fresh asphalt on a few stretches. Highway 1 is high maintenance, and in some future decade, we imagine, they'll have to throw in the towel on it. On a per mile basis, Highway 1 is the costliest stretch of blacktop to maintain in all of California.

For all these reasons, CalTrans has found it necessary to devise a Big Sur Coast Highway Management Plan (CHMP). This is what they have to say about it: "The Big Sur CHMP . . . will establish a framework for continued safe and efficient operation of Highway 1 in a manner that preserves, restores, and maintains the natural and scenic characteristics of the corridor. . . . While intensive efforts are required to keep the highway open and safe, over time, some of the strategies employed are seen as having the potential to degrade the overall quality of the corridor. The management plan strives to achieve a consensus-based approach to developing sustainable management strategies that will ensure the long-term preservation of the special qualities that make Big Sur unique." In other words, hope to hell that someone doesn't turn off the funding spigot, or Highway 1 is history.

Notably, the flattest stretch, and the one that remains closest to sea level, is designated Pacific Valley. It lies between the communities of Gorda and Lucia, a distance of roughly eight miles. We could rhapsodize at length about every blessed mile of Big Sur, but we'll leave it to you to make your own discoveries, which is as it should be. The necessary stops, in our opinion, are Julia Pfeiffer Burns State Park and Andrew Molera State Park. Beyond that, just pull the car over whenever the mood and the view seize you. Bring plenty of film and make sure the your camera's batteries have enough juice in them to record the numerous pictures or lengthy videos you'll no doubt want to make. (When the batteries for our digital

Margaret W. Owings:
An Environmental Legacy

When Margaret Wentworth Owings died on January 21, 1999, California lost one of its greatest and most tireless coastal and ocean conservationists. In fact, when she was found dead of heart failure at Wild Bird, her clifftop home in Big Sur, she had just finished compiling her complete writings and artwork; the results were published as *Voice from the Sea: Reflections on Wildlife and Wilderness*. For the past 50 years, Owings fought to keep developers away from Big Sur and sat on the council of the Big Sur Land Trust.

The turning point in her activism, she once said, was when she saw a man shoot a sea lion for no reason but pointless bloodlust. Owings was founder and first president of Friends of the Sea Otter. She led a successful lobby to end bounty hunting of mountain lions in California. She was also a member of the Point Lobos League, which helped save the beaches between Carmel River and Point Lobos State Preserve. In addition, this tireless servant sat on the council of the Save the Redwoods League and was a member of the California Parks Commission (1963–69), a trustee of Defenders of Wildlife (1969–74), a board member with the National Parks Foundation (1968–69), a trustee of the African Wildlife Leadership Foundation (1968–76), a trustee of the Environmental Defense Fund (1972–82), and founder of the Rachel Carson Council.

In 1998 the National Audubon Society listed her among the 100 individuals who've done the most to shape the environmental movement, placing her in such stellar company as Jacques-Yves Cousteau, Lady Bird Johnson, and Morris Uddall. Almost everyone who visits Big Sur falls in love with it. Owings was one of those rare individuals who loved Big Sur so much she devoted her life to preserving it. A suggestion: Name a beach after her.

Monterey County

camera gave out just as we were entering Big Sur, we got reamed at a roadside shop to the tune of $8 for four AA batteries.) The same holds true for gas, which is both more expensive and less available in Big Sur than in the communities at either end.

On a cultural note, you'll want to stop at the Coast Gallery, which exhibits the watercolors of Henry Miller and prints of Marc Chagall. Miller, a Big Sur denizen for decades (he lived on Partington Ridge), was best known as a writer, though he painted with an almost religious zeal toward the end of his life. Filled with

rainbow-like hues, his celebratory paintings project a childlike wonder that is perfectly in keeping with his exuberant spirit. The Coast Gallery also sells lots of pricey, sleek animal sculptures, as well as books, gifts, coffee mugs, and decorative knickknacks; there's even a café. In terms of food, though, we'd recommend that you save your appetite for Ventana (if you want a great meal) or Nepenthe (if you want a great view).

Despite its obvious magnetism for artists and writers, it was not until itinerant savant and Brooklyn native Miller settled on Partington

Map of Monterey County—Page 342

Ridge in 1944 that Big Sur began gaining widespread notice. The same man who sparked obscenity trials with his erotica turned to watercolors here. About his new Canaan he wrote: "At dawn its majesty is almost painful to behold. That same prehistoric look. The look of always. Nature smiling at herself in the mirror of eternity."

Another writer, Jack Kerouac, came to Big Sur seeking solitude, briefly encamping here in 1960 to escape the wages of fame. He lit out for a shack in a Big Sur canyon and managed to capture a piece of it in his novel *Big Sur:* "Big elbows of rock rising everywhere, sea caves within, seas plollicking all around inside them crashing out foams, the boom and pound on the sand, the sand dipping quick (no Malibu Beach here). Yet you turn and see the pleasant woods winging upcreek like a picture in Vermont. But you look up into the sky, bend way back, my God you're standing directly under that aerial bridge with its thin white line running from rock to rock and witless cars racing across it like dreams! From rock to rock! All the way down the raging coast!"

Enough of artistic inquiry. A few geographic facts are in order to distinguish Big Sur the place from Big Sur the state of mind. Big Sur stretches, roughly, from the San Luis Obispo County line to the Carmel River, just above Point Lobos, a distance of 90 miles. It extends to the east beyond Ventana Wilderness. All told it covers 300 square miles (192,000 acres). The population of the region hovered around 1,000 for decades, a stability attributable to the high price of available land, scarcity of water, and the near impossibility of getting new structures approved under strict local ordinances. (The number of residents is now a whopping 1,600.) The largest part of coastal Big Sur—the part that most visitors see along the cliff-hugging Pacific Coast Highway—is privately owned. The town of Big Sur is not really a town but a sparsely settled strand of inns, restaurants, and residences, most of which are hidden on backcountry ridges. "No Trespassing" and "No Beach Access" signs are common, because the locals are hermits who don't want to be bothered.

The name Big Sur derives from a rare meeting of English and Spanish. "Sur" is taken from El Pais Grande del Sur, which means "The Big Country to the South." The name was bestowed by the Spanish at Carmel Mission in the late 1700s, denoting the impassable region along the coast. But many moons before the missions were built, the Esalen tribe inhabited the region. Their villages along the Big Sur Valley date back 3,000 years. They discovered an abundance of earthly delights at their disposal—plenty of fish and meat, as well as hot springs. Then the Spanish came to convert the contented Esalen to Christianity. The tribes died off soon thereafter. Today, one of the tribes' sacred springs is the centerpiece of the Esalen Institute, a spiritual organization that's blazing new trails in self-awareness.

The first-time visitor to Big Sur will take Highway 1 in and out. For all intents and purposes, this is the only road through here. Though a few back roads exist, only one—the sometimes inaccessible Nacimiento-Fergusson Road—actually pierces the mountains, connecting with U.S. 101, which lies 30 miles east. Other roads in the area are little more than dirt tracks, barely large enough for one car and best suited for four-wheel-drive vehicles.

The 91-mile passage through Big Sur on Highway 1 is as legendary as it is exhilarating. As a driving experience it is unsurpassed. In 1966 Lady Bird Johnson proclaimed it the nation's first Scenic Highway. Today, more cars and RVs lumber through Big Sur than Yosemite National Park each year. Like a naturally occurring roller coaster, Highway 1 varies in elevation from 20 to 1,200 feet, in width from 18 to 24 feet, and in scenic splendor from "Oh, wow!" to "Don't get too close!" to "Oh my GOD!!" Various points of interest along the road are designated not by address but by mile-

Map of Central California—Page 233

post from the south or north boundary. For example "Milepost 28S/63N" means that you are 28 miles from the northern boundary and 63 miles from the southern boundary. Since the winter storms of 1997 to 1998, the highway has taken major hits from floods and rock slides, and portions of it have been made one-lane only in order to do "seismic retrofit work." Be extra careful and patient. Hey, cut the ignition and dig the scenery.

Before embarking on this epic drive, take a few precautions. Fill the gas tank. Make sure the tires and brakes are in good shape. Drive from north to south, if possible—the most breathtaking views are seen that way. Let the passengers do all the ogling. If you want a closer look, 300 turnouts have been carved into the roadside for that purpose. Don't needlessly pass slowpokes; as the billboard says, "Risking Is Losing." En route, the constantly changing landscape will captivate and enrapture you. At points the road might even nauseate you. Bring crackers, soda, and motion-sickness medication in case of carsickness. Some places, particularly a handful of beaches, are well worth a side trip off Highway 1. Strap yourself in and enjoy the ride of a lifetime.

Beaches

The beaches of Big Sur include everything from rocky, sandless strips to coves whose sands range from beige to deep volcanic brown to coal black. You can view some of these coves from roadside turnouts, and they are as appealing as they are inaccessible. That is to say, some of the most amazing beaches in California cannot be physically reached, but they can be visually enjoyed from above.

Because we've organized this guidebook from south to north, the wonders of Big Sur will be described in that direction. (Both north and south mileposts are provided in the practical beach information below, however.) It will help to carry a map of Big Sur. A good one can be found in *El Sur Grande,* a newspaper-style guide that identifies all pertinent landmarks. Pick up a free copy while you're in the area; they're widely available. A good way to obtain Big Sur information is by calling **Big Sur Station** (831/667-2315). This multi-agency information service of California State Parks, the U.S. Forest Service, and CalTrans is housed in a brochure-filled office between Mileposts 46 and 47 in Big Sur. Of course, you'll want to be outfitted with the necessary maps and info before you reach that midpoint.

Some of the easiest coastal access in Big Sur can be found along a four-mile marine terrace at the south end, between Willow and Wild Cattle Creeks. **Willow Creek Picnic Area** and **Jade Cove** offer a scenic overview of the region's geologic treasures. Willow Creek is primarily a spot for a quick lunch. An access trail leads to a rocky cove beach, and the sizable rocks offshore are impressive to study. Jade Cove is worth a longer pause. At the Jade Cove access, you scale a stepladder over a fence and hike across a field of wildflowers to a dirt path that leads, via stumbling and sliding steps, down to a rocky beach. Visitors can scan the rocks and pebbles on shore for the mineral jade, specifically nephrite jade ("the stone of heaven"). Anything below the high-tide line is up for grabs, and some people make off with handsome hauls. As is always the case with a golden goose, though, people will pluck all the eggs. That is, amateur rock hounds and gallery-bound artists have picked so much of the nephrite, according to state authorities, that the Lands Commission is considering stepping in to monitor the activity. In 1971 divers took a 9,000-pound jade boulder worth $180,000.

Across the road from Jade Cove is the 43-site **Plaskett Creek Campground,** a National Forest facility that costs $16 per night. You'll need to make reservations as far in advance as possible if you wish to camp here. A half mile north of Jade Cove is **Sand Dollar Picnic Area and Beach.** It consists of tree-shaded picnic tables and a cove that can be reached by

Monterey County

Big Sur Land Trust

Monterey County

The future of Big Sur is a topic so hot that the locals have been burning up over it for the last two decades. At present Big Sur is an untamed wilderness, geographically and politically. The coastal lands are largely in private hands, while the interior mostly falls under federal jurisdiction as Los Padres National Forest. Despite efforts to have Big Sur declared a National Seashore—and thus, theoretically, protected in perpetuity—it is not presently controlled by any governmental body.

Flying in the face of those who say Big Sur should be federally protected, the Big Sur Land Trust (BSLT) works toward the goal of "retaining the land in its natural state" and "creating an effective private sector alternative for land preservation." To that end, BSLT has devised various creative ways by which locals can donate or set aside land without shafting their next of kin—i.e., through conservation easements, charitable remainder trusts, and life estates. To date, more than 20,000 acres of the Big Sur coast and the Monterey Peninsula have been protected by BSLT. A huge recent success story was the purchase by the Land Trust—in concert with the Nature Conservancy and the administration of California governor Gray Davis—of the Palo Corona Ranch, a 9,898-acre tract just south of Carmel that is the "gateway to Big Sur."

This success notwithstanding, arguments on both sides of the issue carry merit. The locals don't want Big Sur to become another playland like Yosemite and Yellowstone, overrun with tourists and RVs. They also don't want to be told what to do with their own land by outsiders—even well-known ones like Robert Redford and the late Ansel Adams, both of whom led battles on Capitol Hill to annex Big Sur in the 1980s. As a show of good faith, BSLT has adopted the stringent guidelines of the California Coastal Commission to ensure that no desecration of the land takes place. Still, the signs are there—"For Sale" signs on plots of land in southern Big Sur, that is—and the potential for exploitation exists with the selling of land from generation to generation.

Although we agree in spirit with Big Sur locals, one sentence in the Land Trust's glossy brochure gave us pause: "BSLT works in partnership with private landowners, assisting them in finding appropriate solutions for their particular land-use problems." Whether the Land Trust can exert any real control over the actions of private landowners, when push comes to shove, is very much the nagging question. On the other hand, as one local resident put it, "Why disturb what's perfect? Private property is a worthwhile idea in this area."

For more information, contact the Big Sur Land Trust, P.O. Box 221864, Carmel, CA 93922, 831/625-5523, website: www.bigsurlandtrust.org.

Map of Central California—Page 233

hiking across a field. The beach got stripped of its sand during a run of storm-filled winters. Natural processes have replenished it in the ensuing years, and it is one of Big Sur's real shoreline treasures—maybe the finest of the relatively rare number of accessible beaches along its southern 50 miles.

A similar setting exists at **Mill Creek Picnic Area,** although the beach is a bit rockier and the trail leading to it steeper. Another Forest Service campground can be found a half-mile up Highway 1 at Kirk Creek. Nestled against the Santa Lucia Mountains four miles south of the little town of Lucia, **Kirk Creek Campground** sits on bluffs overlooking the ocean, four miles south of Lucia. A steep, serpentine driveway leads to a small lot and a smattering of tables. You can scramble down a short path to a rocky shoreline with a sandy crescent just to the north. Trails also lead up into the Ventana Wilderness, where some long, satisfying hikes can be taken. Just make sure you've planned any trek so that you're back before nightfall. Being stuck on a primitive trail in the mountains of Big Sur when the animals start their nighttime stalking and screeching can be harrowing, especially for those lacking outdoor survival skills and experience.

Much of Big Sur, including beaches and campgrounds mentioned thus far this section, falls under the jurisdiction of the U.S. Forest Service. For more information, contact **Los Padres National Forest,** 6144 Calle Real, Goleta, CA 93117, 805/683-6711, website: www.r5.fs.fed.us/lospadres. For specific information on Ventana Wilderness—the 150,000-acre unit within Los Padres that includes part of the Big Sur coast and much of the Santa Lucia Mountains—contact the **Monterey Ranger District Office,** U.S. Forest Service, 406 South Mildred Avenue, King City, CA 93930, 831/385-5434. A detailed topographic map of Ventana Wilderness and a map of the entire Los Padres National Forest—including campgrounds and hiking trails—are available by mail from the Monterey Ranger District Office for $4.25 each. Specify which map(s) you are requesting, and make checks payable to "BSNHA."

Two miles north of Kirk Creek is a relatively recent acquisition, **Limekiln State Park.** Formerly a private campground, Limekiln was acquired by the state and opened to the public in the summer of 1995. Campsites are scattered in the redwoods and by the beach beneath a bridge at the mouth of Limekiln Creek, so-called for the remnants of historic lime kilns that lie a short distance up the creek (and can be hiked to). Frankly, the campsites aren't much—picnic tables and hibachis in a gravel lot directly beneath the bridge—but the natural setting is beyond compare. Limekiln Creek gurgles out of the mountains and then crosses a flat bed of gravel before emptying into the sea. Hiking trails extend into the mountains. Picnic tables at the ocean's edge make an enticing day-use area of Limekiln, too.

After a dozen or so miles of hairpin turns, you come upon **Julia Pfeiffer Burns State Park.** A 3,580-acre day-use park whose chief scenic attraction is **Waterfall Cove,** it is arguably the most spectacular and photographic spot on the Big Sur coast. Finding it requires a short hike along McWay Creek, which ends up plummeting 50 feet to the beach below. It is the only place on the California coast where a waterfall empties directly into the ocean. Major photo op here, and a lovely cove beach to boot. Divers submerge with joy into the 1,680-acre underwater reserve. Two environmental campsites are available, requiring a half-mile hike out to a bluff overlooking the ocean.

Partington Cove is the site of a 110-foot tunnel burrowed into the rock in the 1880s by pirates, who stashed their booty here. Later it served as a landing point for the early settlers and as a place for Prohibition-era bootleggers to bring liquor to shore. There is no official beach access at Partington Cove, but visitors can scoot down a steep path to the small beach. It is marked by an iron gate and black mailbox on the ocean side of the highway, 1.8 miles north of Julia Pfeiffer Burns State Park.

Two miles up the road is the **Coast Gallery** (Milepost 33S/52N, 831/667-2301), where local artists exhibit their work. What makes the Coast Gallery special is its extensive collection of original Henry Miller lithographs and watercolors. Miller devotees should also visit the Henry Miller Library (see sidebar), a few hundred yards up the road.

The first of Big Sur's truly great beaches lies five miles farther up the road. A poorly marked turnoff, Sycamore Canyon Road (Milepost 27.1S/63.2N), leads down to **Pfeiffer Beach.** The narrow two-mile dirt road takes you past inhabited Sycamore Canyon. Makeshift homes list among the trees like pine cones, testaments to the rough life still to be found in the wilderness (and a cautionary note to those who fantasize life here as an easy paradise). From the parking lot a quarter-mile path leads through cypress trees to the beach. Miracle of miracles, Pfeiffer Beach is a wide sandy beach, bashed by waves that rush through sea caves and arches to the shore in foamy torrents. A strong undertow discourages swimming. No camping or fires are allowed, either.

Though we've visited Pfeiffer Beach many times in years past, the area was closed when we came through in mid-2002 and had been for some time. A Forest Service day-use area, Pfeiffer Beach was undergoing road repair and site improvements, including new restroom facilities, paved parking for 63 vehicles, beach access trail, landscaping with native plants, and interpretive signing. The purpose for the improvements, according to ranger John Bradford, is to "replace aging facilities, minimize traffic congestion on Sycamore Canyon Road, eliminate random parking at the beach and along the road, reduce erosion and other impacts to the environment, and improve public health and safety conditions." The project was to be completed by December 2002, and the new, improved Pfeiffer

Beach day-use area should be up and running by the time you read this.

Another mile yields **Pfeiffer-Big Sur State Park** (Milepost 26.0S/63.7N), a splendid 821-acre retreat along the east side of Highway 1, at the foot of the Santa Lucia Mountains along the Big Sur River Gorge. Set among redwoods, oaks, and meadows, the park beckons campers (offering 217 developed sites along the pristine Big Sur River) and hikers (there are half a dozen trails in the park, ranging from one-third to four miles). There's also an inn (see "Bunking Down"). Some of the ancient, stately trees here predate the signing of the Magna Carta. Others, long dead, lie like toppled Greek columns in backwoods groves. One of the more memorable hiking trails leads to lovely Pfeiffer Falls. The Pfeiffers, whose names adorn so much around here, were the first European immigrants to permanently settle in this area, arriving in 1869.

Five miles north, another great parkland, **Andrew Molera State Park,** can be found. Molera allows public access to the ocean along a portion of Big Sur that is otherwise mostly held by El Sur Cattle Ranch, which restricts public access with barbed-wire fences and nasty signs (subliminal message: boycott beef). Andrew Molera State Park was named for the grandson of Juan Bautista Roger Cooper, the original owner of the ranch at Molera Point. It is speculated that Cooper used his "Ranch of the South" to import goods without paying the high customs in Monterey. Beyond that, Molera was a legitimate dairy man, famous for his Monterey Jack cheese. The largest state park in Big Sur, Andrew Molera's 4,800 acres feature scenic trails through former pastureland and alongside the Big Sur River, an area rich with bird life.

The beach at Andrew Molera is one of the few strollable sand strips in Big Sur. Still, it's rock-backed and pounded by rough surf that sucks much of the sand out to sea and makes for hazardous swimming. Worse, much of what

The Henry Miller Library

Could there be a more perfect setting than Big Sur for a literary legacy as exuberant as Henry Miller's? For years, even after Miller left Big Sur to live in semi-seclusion in Pacific Palisades, his good friend Emil White created and ran the **Henry Miller Library** out of his Graves Canyon home, where the library still exists today—a glimpse of green serenity along a dusty curve in the Pacific Coast Highway. White's archive consisted of his personal collection of Miller's books, mementos, and watercolors. A charming raconteur, White was also a factotum and screener of Miller's endless army of admirers, with a weakness for nubile flesh even more pronounced than Henry's. In some ways White's congeniality made him the unofficial greeter for the entire Big Sur community.

When White died in 1989 (Miller himself died in 1980), the Henry Miller Library was bequeathed to the Big Sur Land Trust. In 1997, the library became an independent organization whose mission is to champion Miller's literary and artistic legacy while also serving as a "cultural resource center" for artists, writers, musicians, and students. Concerts, workshops, and exhibits are held at the natural redwood amphitheater on the grounds, while readings and lectures are staged in the library. In keeping with Miller's renegade spirit, the 1999 West Coast Regional Championship Poetry Slam was held here.

Too many literary shrines are as stiff as the writer's cadaver. A painful shuffling of feet ensues while a wooden tour guide recites vital statistics as you stroll by the writer's roped-off pen and pencil set. There's no such formality here. The Henry Miller Library is a sort of "serve yourself" kind of place, the spirit of which is found in a "Notice to Visitors" that Miller wrote and posted on his own door. A facsimile of Miller's note sits outside the Miller library, gently offering such words of wisdom as, "When you come, be so kind as to check your neuroses and psychoses at the gate. Gossip may be exchanged during the wee hours of the morning when the gremlins have left. . . . Let us do our best even if it gets us nowhere. In the midst of darkness there is light."

The Henry Miller Library is at Milepost 29.7S/61.3N. It is open Wednesday–Sunday 11 A.M.–6 P.M. There is no charge to enter, and a small gallery and bookshop are on the premises. For more information contact the Henry Miller Library, Highway 1, Big Sur, CA 93920, 831/667-2574, website: www.henrymiller.org.

Map of Monterey County—Page 342

beach there is got washed away a few years back due to flooding on the Big Sur River. Lately the footbridges that cross the creek and trails that lead to the beach are in such disrepair that hiking to the ocean's edge isn't all that easy anymore. We tried in vain to find a place to ford the stream and pick up a beach path, but with no signs to guide us or ranger to ask, we gave up after poking around awhile. It's times like these that we wish the California State Park system would raise its rates again so that it would have sufficient operating revenue to keep a place like Andrew Molera in working order.

The seclusion seems to inspire a loss of inhibition, explaining a smattering of nudity at Andrew Molera State Park (as well as Pfeiffer Beach). A 60-site tent-only campground lies right above the ocean. Campers must pack in all gear on the half-mile trek from the parking lot. The campground is a big, grassy common area; there's a formal limit of 350 campers per night, but they try not to turn anyone away. Trails in the park allow for riverside, lagoonside, meadow, headland, and blufftop hikes. A private horse stable rents out the steeds for guided tours along what they call the "most spectacular ride in America." For reservations and information on horseback riding, call **Molera Trail Rides** at 831/625-8664.

Five miles north of Andrew Molera, the **Point Sur Light Station** shines a beacon on coastal history and continues to warn ocean-going vessels of the treacherous waters off Point Sur. Built in 1889 on a volcanic rock 361 feet above the pounding surf, Point Sur is the only functioning lighthouse on the California coast with all of its original buildings intact. The Stanton Center in Monterey displays its original Fresnel lens (it could be seen 23 miles out to sea); today the U.S. Coast Guard manages the station's automated light and fog signal. Guided tours of the lighthouse, which is on the National Register of Historic Places, are given by docents on weekends. (For information call 831/625-4419.)

Closer to the northern boundary of Big Sur— 5.4 miles above Point Sur, to be exact—Highway 1 crosses Bixby Creek Bridge, one of the West Coast's most photogenic spans. This concrete arch, a true engineering marvel, is 700 feet long and towers 260 feet above the creek. It was the longest bridge of its kind in the world when built in 1932. Back when the local sea otter population had almost dwindled to zero, it is believed that the sole surviving male—the one from whom all others are now descended—lived as part of a colony in the waters beneath Bixby Creek Bridge.

Six more miles bring yet another spectacular Big Sur parkland that screams out at passersby who think they've seen it all. **Garrapata State Park** lays claim to over four miles of coastline among its 2,879 acres. The trails that lead down to the rugged beaches wind through several different kinds of coastal vegetation, including cactus and redwood groves. Garrapata (which means "tick" in Spanish) is not for everyone, however, as the rough trails don't lend themselves to quick jaunts. The park trails are worth every step, offering spectacular views of the ocean, cavorting sea otters, and tidepools. Parking and day-use access to the park is free, but it is primitive. You pull your car over at either Turnout 13 (west side) or Turnout 14 (east side). The unmarked paths from Turnout 13 lead out to Sobranes Point and up to Whale Peak—a prime whale-watching promontory. As if to confirm our suspicions about the sort of hardy souls who'd seek this place out, the beach at Garrapata is a favorite with the clothing-optional set.

Finally, the northernmost access point on the Big Sur coast is Point Lobos State Reserve, a locale so extraordinary it warrants its own write-up, featured next in this chapter.

Bunking Down

A complaint we've often heard about Big Sur is that it's hard to get a foot in the door, so to speak. That is, people who don't want to rough

Map of Central California—Page 233

it by camping but still want to check out Big Sur are intimidated by the prospect of staying here. Fear not—there are plenty of places to stay. They've just been mandated into near invisibility. Built off the road, they blend into the landscape so well that if you speed through on the Pacific Coast Highway, you'll miss them. Do not look for glowing green "Holiday Inn" signs jacked 50 feet in the air. There are no brand-name motel chains to be found between San Simeon and Carmel. Accommodations run the gamut from primitive campsites to award-winning luxury lodges.

There are 10 campgrounds in the region, most on national forest or state park land. We've already discussed six of them that are set along or close to the ocean. Reserve all accommodations in Big Sur, campsites included, in advance. The best month to visit, everyone seems to agree, is October.

For those who don't want to camp but still want to give nature a great big bear hug in the morning, the 62-unit **Big Sur Lodge** (Milepost 26.0S/63.7N, 831/667-3100 or 800/424-4787, $$) is the answer. It's actually a number of semiprivate cottages—duplexes, triplexes, and larger—scattered among the trees in Pfeiffer-Big Sur State Park. Clean and comfortable, the rooms come with fireplaces, and some have kitchens. There's even a heated swimming pool, a comfortable place to soak among the cool air and redwoods. In-season rates for standard rooms are fairly reasonable ($99-179); add $30 for a fireplace or kitchen suite and $50 for both. Rates drop some after Labor Day.

Another isolated haven with roughly equivalent prices is **Lucia Lodge** (Highway 1, 831/667-2391, $$), comprising 10 spartan but well-maintained cottages that cling to the southern coast of Big Sur. Cabins are available on a first-come, first-served basis, with no reservations taken. No need to go elsewhere to eat, as there's a pleasant restaurant on the property.

Anywhere else but in Big Sur, the **Glen Oaks Motel** (Milepost 66N/25S, 831/667-2105, $) would be just another nondescript motel. Its typicality makes it stand out here. Actually, it's a clean "post adobe" not unlike any other roadside mom-and-pop motel with 15 rooms and two cottages. Speaking of mom, we had a tough time convincing the congenial matron to honor our reservation for a room with two beds here. But she eventually solved the problem with some last-minute room-shuffling. The two guys who pulled in after us weren't so lucky. They decided to make do with one bed, vowing to maintain "a discreet and dignified distance." Later we saw one of them dragging a chaise lounge into the room. Prices are ridiculously good for Big Sur (or anywhere, for that matter): $69 for a room with one double bed, $99-104 for two beds.

Then there's Ventana, a resort that exists on a whole other plane entirely. Do you want a honeymoon you'll never forget, or simply an unexcelled retreat from everything, including the usual romantic resort affectations? If the answer is "yes," then the **Ventana Big Sur Country Inn Resort** (Milepost 62.7N/28.3S, 831/667-2331, $$$$) is your window on the wilderness and one of the finest resting spots anywhere. Everything is arranged to enhance the embrace of solitude, from the exposed wood architecture to the fireplaces in the rooms, the meditative grounds strung out across two heaven-focused ridge tops, the serenade of birds, the almost noiseless leaping of deer through the underbrush. At check-in guests are issued a white, hooded terry cloth robe by a fellow who is as calm as a Zen master. After a day spent wandering around in your robe, you'll feel a little bit like a Zen master yourself. No wonder the motto here is "Nourish your spirit." (Follow your bliss, while you're at it!)

Further nourishing can be had at Ventana's health club, sauna, and library. An extensive array of massage services will cleanse away all worldly dust within you. Twelve masseuses are available, each with his or her

Monterey County

own special expertise. One advertised being "certified in Postural Integration Deep Tissue work," while another promised to "sculpt your body using a blend of techniques from deep tissue to subtle cranial work and energy balancing." (Decisions, decisions!) Needless distractions are kept at a minimum, which explains the ambivalence toward kids as guests. In the words of the innkeepers: "Ventana was designed and is operated as a retreat for adults. We do not have any activities for children and therefore we do not encourage people to bring them here. . . . Many people have come here for a few days expressly to get away from their own children." Ah, if only all resorts purporting to be "escapes" were so enlightened—and honest.

If you want company, a continental breakfast and afternoon wine-and-cheese buffet are served in the library and lobby. It's a spread of delights the likes of which you won't encounter anywhere else, including the best granola we've ever tasted. Relative to the peerless amenities and priceless peace and quiet, room rates at Ventana are reasonable. (They range $200–400 a night; there are 60 units in 12 buildings.) What is the sound of two beach bums smiling?

The newest arrival in Big Sur, and new arrivals are a glacial occurrence out here, is **Post Ranch Inn** (P.O. Box 291, 831/667-2200, $$$$). It opened for business in the spring of 1992— the first new resort to grace the Big Sur coast in more than two decades. The 30 cabins are spread among the redwoods along a ridge overlooking the ocean; some are designated "ocean houses," others "tree houses," for obvious reasons. Take your pick—woods or water?—and come prepared to pay handsomely for this splendid hermitage ($255–495 per night—ouch!).

Coastal Cuisine

No preprandial stroll can top the 10-minute walk from the Ventana Inn to the **Ventana Restaurant** (Milepost 62.7N/28.3S, 831/667-2331, $$$$). Lit by small shoe-level bulbs, the path crosses a woodland and ascends a ridge top with moon and stars above and wild game loping into the brush at ground level. The restaurant setting extends this sense of natural communion. Its understated elegance is conveyed in the lovely varnished wood and exposed beam interior. The dining room is surrounded by windows (*ventana* means "window" in Spanish) that look out on the 800-acre spread. It is staffed by folks who seem positively clairvoyant about your needs. An 18-page wine list offers rare and interesting California vintages, plus well-chosen and affordable ones, including a custom Ventana label chardonnay and riesling. The ever-changing menu is kept to a manageable size, offering artfully prepared appetizers and main courses. We supped contentedly on petit filet mignon with a fresh corn pudding sauce and grilled rainbow trout with fresh spinach and new potatoes. And we slept contentedly afterward. In fact, we paused on the pathway back to the inn to lie on our backs and look up at the night sky, with the moon shining brightly. Pure magic.

At **Nepenthe** (Milepost 62.2N/28.8S, 831/667-2345, $$) the Ambrosiaburgers roll out of the kitchen like beer barrels in Milwaukee. They're simply large burgers made of ground steak; Jack Kerouac referred to them as "Heavenburgers" in his underrated later novel *Big Sur*. While the food won't win any major culinary awards, people come to Nepenthe (it means "no sorrow" in Greek) for more than food. They come for the heavenly view, overlooking the ocean from a dazzling perch 808 feet above sea level. In fact, it is the view you're largely paying for, since no hamburger is worth $12.50 (add $1.50 for cheese), nor is a side of fries worth $6.75. In addition to the Ambrosiaburgers, Nepenthe serves a decent smoked salmon salad with lemon vinaigrette. For an appetizer, try the Castroville artichoke, poached, chilled, and served with balsamic vinaigrette. You can sit indoors, but unless a tempest is raging you will want to dine on the deck, with its matchless

Map of Central California—Page 233

view and gratis servings of fresh air. Originally an adobe and redwood house built by a student of Frank Lloyd Wright and bought as a wedding gift for Rita Hayworth by Orson Welles, Nepenthe has been run by the same family since 1949.

Across the street from the Glen Oaks Motel (see "Bunking Down") is the **Glen Oaks Restaurant** (Milepost 66N/25S, 831/667-2623, $$$), a surprisingly nice dining spot, with fresh seafood and pasta dishes in a rustic setting. Two other old reliables are **Deetjen's Big Sur Inn** (Milepost 60.8N/30.2S, 831/667-2377, $$$) and the **River Inn** (Milepost 66.5N/24.5S, 831/667-2700, $$$). Deetjen's is the more offbeat of the two, with a shrine to Robinson Jeffers taking up one entire corner. The Norwegian-style complex includes a 14-room inn and a restaurant that serves breakfast and dinner. The River Inn lies in the Big Sur Valley, where the Big Sur River discharges into the ocean. If you're driving from north to south, plan for an early-morning chowdown at the River Inn. Try the trout and eggs, as one of

us did many years ago during an unforgettable sojourn in the cool blue light of morning. The River Inn also includes an 18-unit motel, gas station, gift shop, and grocery store.

Night Moves

Nepenthe (Milepost 62.2N/28.8S, 831/667-2345) is as close to a public meeting spot as there is in this notoriously hermitic community. People nurse their drinks on the art-bedecked patio, warm their hands over a fire, and enjoy the views of the ocean and artwork, including a driftwood angel sculpture and eerie mosaic that are, like the restaurant, total originals.

Beyond that, Kerouac poetically stated in Big Sur, "There's the laughter of the loon in the shadow of the moon." In other words, stay where you are and savor the sounds of nature.

For More Information

Big Sur Chamber of Commerce, P.O. Box 87, Big Sur, CA 93920, 831/667-2100, website: www.bigsurcalifornia.org; Big Sur Station (information service), 831/667-2315

Point Lobos State Reserve

A rugged, primeval headland jutting out into fierce seas south of Carmel, **Point Lobos State Reserve** is billed as the "crown jewel of the California State Park system," a claim that's hard to dispute. The name derives from a much longer Spanish appellation that translates as "Point of the Sea Wolves." In the 1700s and 1800s, it variously served as a livestock pasture, abalone cannery, whaling station, and shipping point for coal mined nearby. At one point developers planned to subdivide it as Point Lobos City. Its purchase by a farsighted owner, A. M. Allan, forestalled such a fate. In 1933 Point Lobos was acquired by the Save the Redwoods League and donated to California to maintain as a parkland. Today it is jointly run by the state and the Point Lobos Natural History Association, whose volunteers

lead nature walks and staff the reserve's information station. Trailers and campers are prohibited, as is any kind of camping. The reserve is open 9 A.M.–6 P.M. daily and closes later in summer. Plan to arrive early, as the reserve has a "carrying capacity" of 450 people, and latecomers must wait to gain entrance.

The reserve occupies 554 land acres and 750 submerged acres. With the addition of the latter in 1960, Point Lobos became the first underwater reserve in the nation. Roads take you only so far into the park, which is fine, since Point Lobos begs to be explored on foot. Pick up a detailed map at the entrance station outlining 14 possible hikes. The Cypress Grove Trail, a three-quarter-mile loop, leads to the granite cliffs overlooking Pinnacle Cove and passes through one of two remaining natural

Monterey County

stands of Monterey cypress in the world. (The reserve was originally established to protect these gnarled wonders.) Skittering ground squirrels, fields of yellow lizard tails and apricot-colored sticky monkey flowers, and offshore rocks acrawl with sea lions and harbor seals are but a few of the sights to enjoy in this wild place.

Hikers who wish to traipse the perimeter should allow at least three hours to cover the six-mile trek from Bird Island to Granite Point. Beaches are tucked into several coves along the eastern side of the point's southern flank. Imagine our surprise to turn a corner on Bird Island Trail and catch sight of emerald green **China Cove Beach,** 100 feet below down a long staircase. At the mouth of Gibson Creek, where the Bird Island and South Plateau Trails run

out, you'll find Gibson Beach. It's separated from China Cove by Pelican Point and is another swell spot for launching a dive or braving a swim in frigid waters. Both can be reached via wooden staircases. The one-mile South Shore Trail yields its own bounty of rocky, shell-strewn beaches between Sea Lion Point and the Bird Island parking area, including **Hidden Beach, Weston Beach,** and **Sand Hill Cove.** Just be careful while wandering out on the rocks, and keep a mindful eye on the always unpredictable ocean.

For More Information

Point Lobos State Reserve, Highway 1, Box 62, Carmel, CA 93923, 831/624-4909, website: www.pt-lobos.parks.state.ca.us

Carmel

Among small American towns, Carmel is a celebrity. It can't travel to New York to appear on *The Late Show with David Letterman,* but in every other respect it fits the bill. Carmel is well known for being well known. It is a de rigueur stop on California bus-tour decathlons. Carmel's fame went into orbit when its most famous resident, Clint Eastwood, served a two-year term as mayor in the late 1980s. As is usually the case with a celebrity, strangers are drawn to it, desiring to bask in Carmel's limelight, as if proximity might confer some mysterious luster upon them as well.

Given its popular perception as a see-and-be-seen kind of place, Carmel can get mighty crowded. Cars gridlock the village streets and buses discharge an endless cargo of sightseers who clog the sidewalks. Attracted by its air of sophistication, foreigners descend on Carmel in droves, chattering in heavily accented English or their own native tongues. However, the universal truth that binds all visitors is that beyond a visit to an established historical landmark such as the Carmel Mission, no one can really figure out what to do in Carmel. Most

visitors amble up and down Ocean Avenue, munch on sweets, pose for pictures in front of rocks and trees, duck into quaint shoppes to ogle overpriced goods, and pause thrice daily for meals.

So why all the fuss? For starters Carmel is a gorgeous village, blessed with a natural setting that could turn any gutter-mouthed Dirty Harry into a beatific babbler like native son Robinson Jeffers. Carmelites refer to their community as "a village in a forest"—and that brief description neglects to mention the roiling ocean that crashes on the sugar-white sand of cypress-dotted Carmel City Beach. Nowhere in the world is the margin where land and sea meet as spectacular as it is in Monterey County from Carmel south through Point Lobos and Big Sur. That isn't just the lofty rhetoric of two itinerant beach bums; it comes close to being a verifiable truth. Moreover, the residents of Carmel are well educated, arts-savvy, and genuinely appreciative of their natural bounty.

So what's the problem? As bucolic as it may seem, the village of Carmel is swimming in

Map of Central California—Page 233

Mayor Clint

Things had gotten out of hand in Carmel: a developer might wait 10 years to get a building permit; the old guard and new arrivals had squared off and were at each other's throats; there was a lot of grumbling, differences of opinion— plenty of talk about change, but no action. Cleaning up this mess was a job that called for the biggest, toughest gunslinger on the Monterey Peninsula: Clint Eastwood.

Carmel's most famous celebrity resident ran for and won the position of mayor in 1986, garnering 75 percent of the vote. A typical headline in the world press: "Dirty Harry Wins Election!" Eastwood held the post for a single two-year term. To some his tenure was a raging success. To others it was a colossal headache, given all the tourists who suddenly descended on Carmel to catch a glimpse of its movie-star mayor. For two years they trampled the flower beds in front of city hall and knocked down curbside trees with their Winnebagos. "We don't want the kind of people that a movie draws," crowed one irate citizen.

Was he a good mayor? Depends on whom you ask. Many who wanted to see Carmel act with more dispatch on matters of growth and development were pleased to have him cut through the red tape. But there were dissenters, such as the Carmel resident who had this to say late in Eastwood's term: "Though he is mayor, he is seldom seen by most Carmel residents and business people except at monthly city council meetings. His assistant handles all his phone calls and generally refers problems to other city officials. . . . No one else as mayor would be allowed such a privilege. No one could escape severe criticism for such an obvious distortion of the normal give-and-take between the mayor and his electorate. Especially in such a small town."

Still, celebrity politicians make good copy. Those monthly city hall meetings became major tourist photo ops. Between all the neck-craning moms, pops, and paparazzi, the city had to move them to a large public hall. Eastwood fired back at his enemies in a weekly column for the *Carmel Pine Cone*. He referred to his opponents as "wolves and coyotes . . . pack animals that tear their victims apart." He refused to grant a variance to a resident who wanted to enlarge his home. The same person, a former council member, had once given Eastwood trouble over design plans for a building he wanted to construct downtown. One letter writer charged that at council meetings Eastwood "uses his gavel like a gun" to silence opposing views. One of his first acts as mayor was to replace four officials of the seven-member city planning commission with his own appointees. It was their "unfriendly" actions in denying him permission to build a retail-office complex next to Hog's Breath, his downtown Carmel restaurant, that drove him to run for mayor in the first place.

Having tasted political power, one wonders if Eastwood won't run for office again, this time at a higher level. How does President Dirty Harry sound to you?

Monterey County

contradictions. The election of "Mayor Clint" back in 1988 only let some of the most obvious ones out of the closet. Issues constantly being debated in this contentious community boil down to development vs. preservation, old (stodgy) vs. young (progressive), tourists vs. natives, and arts vs. sports. The last of these refers to what we perceive as an undeclared war between painters and golfers for the soul of Carmel, and the outcome will determine whether its future will be visionary or banal.

From a visitor's standpoint this can lead to mixed messages. They want you, but they don't want you. Or, put another way, they don't want you but they do need you. Carmel derives 60 percent of its operating revenue from tourism, while homeowners—mostly retirees—provide a meager 11 percent. Many Carmelites frankly and publicly disdain the locustlike invasions that overrun their streets. Yet tourism is a necessary evil in Carmel, so they've made a deal with the devil in the interest of keeping the money flowing.

Traffic coming into town is pure hell, backing up to Highway 1 as testy motorists inch their way along, engines and tempers overheating. Parking is scant. Buses are not allowed past a certain point, so they wheeze down a side street to a special bus-berthing spot, discharging their blinking passengers into the brilliant sunlight to hoof it about hilly Carmel. Wheezing themselves after a few paces, this army of day-trippers marches obediently into the business district, only to discover that the principal diversion in this faux country village is shopping. Ocean Avenue is a miracle mile of bakeries, bistros, galleries, and gift shops where you can score anything from gold chains to goat cheese.

The setup appears to go something like this: they want you to breeze into Carmel in the morning, while away the day dropping loot on gifts, antiques, and meals, and then blow out of town before night falls. If you haven't taken the hint, Carmel rolls up the sidewalks after

dark. Off of Ocean Avenue you'll find few streetlights to guide your steps, and the signs identifying street names are almost deliberately small, as if to confound and frustrate outsiders. Despite the tug of war between pro-growth, slow-growth, and no-growth factions, Carmel zealously guards its privacy while its denizens espouse a political outlook that comes closer to libertarianism than either of the mainstream political parties.

The denizens of Carmel are wealthy. They strongly defend their right to acquire and preserve without interference and regulations (except for those they impose on others). They have essentially burned their bridges to the outside world, leaving a narrow footpath into the village accessible only to those bearing the passport of a credit card and/or ready cash. Though such an outlook may seem peevish and elitist, even we cannot argue with the results (though we'd quibble with the philosophy). They have tended their community well, keeping vulgar commercialism at arm's length. For that you'll have to head up the peninsula, to Monterey or Seaside. Having viewed the entire coastline at close range, we'll concede that in certain cases enlightened despotism may be preferable to the unregulated rule of market forces. You see, they simply want Carmel to remain a pleasant seaside village. *Theirs.*

To that end Carmel has been buttressing itself against growth and development since day one. Carmel got its start in 1906 as a seaside colony populated by artists and academics who had been displaced by San Francisco's Great Earthquake. The village attracted a literary elite that included Jack London, Upton Sinclair, Sinclair Lewis, and Robinson Jeffers. Artists came as well. All were enchanted by the refreshing climate, gossamer sunlight, pine-forested hills, rugged cliffs, and powdered-sugar beaches of the Monterey Peninsula. From the beginning the citizens of Carmel banded together to ensure that their way of life would be preserved. Restrictive zoning ordinances

Map of Central California—Page 233

passed in the 1920s outlawed things that have become commonplace everywhere else, like tall buildings and neon signs. In 1929 Carmel wrote its guiding philosophy into the city charter: "The city of Carmel-by-the-Sea is . . . predominantly a residential city, wherein business and commerce are . . . subordinated to its residential character." Words alone are not enough to ensure such an outcome, so the town requires a permit for just about everything, from cutting down a bush to filming a movie scene. The result is governmental gridlock where nothing is granted, nothing gets done, and therefore nothing much changes.

Consequently, Carmel has the look—although crowds deny it the feel—of a rural English village. The same determined spirit not to yield to unchecked growth has remained viable throughout the century, although the composition of the town has shifted from artists to retirees. This is a polite way of saying that Carmel is evolving into a community that reveres golf tournaments more than Bach festivals. Still, there is a continuity between generations in that both resist the forces of change. Today, village preservation is pursued with an even greater twinge of fanaticism, since so much more can go wrong in the slipshod modern world. There are no street numbers in Carmel, for instance. No numbers means no addresses and, therefore, no mail delivery. The atavistic Carmelites must personally collect their mail at the local post office. When a small movement to number the houses of Carmel surfaced, an outspoken local newspaper and barometer of community opinion headlined its disparaging editorial, "What, a Subway Next?" When such issues arise, the battle cry becomes, "Save Carmel from Santa Cruz-itis!"

Carmel is a village of roughly 5,000 well-to-do souls—one-tenth the size of Santa Cruz—tucked into the lower left-hand corner of the Monterey Peninsula. It occupies exactly one square mile. The town starts at the top of a hill, where Ocean Avenue intersects Highway 1, and plunges steeply toward the ocean. It is along Ocean Avenue, as well as a block or two off the streets it crosses, that most of Carmel's upscale shops can be found. Inns and bed-and-breakfasts materialize closer to the water. Ocean Avenue gives out by Carmel City Beach, but the steep gradient continues down a hillock of pure white sand to the water's edge. Because traffic tends to snarl both in town and on weather-beaten Highway 1, particularly on weekends in season, you're best advised to park on the outskirts and walk into town. Be further advised that the retail shops in Carmel are not for the faint of pocketbook. Most of the older mom-and-pop shops have been squeezed out by places that can deal with $20,000 monthly rents for commercial space. A retailer must sell a hell of a lot of cashmere sweaters or pastel wall hangings to make ends meet, and you can believe that the cost of doing business in Carmel is passed along to the consumer.

Amid all this upscale merchandise, the old **Carmel Mission** remains an eminently worthwhile place for travelers to stop, rest, and refocus. Its full name is the Basilica of Mission San Carlos Borrodeo Del Rio Carmelo (cha cha cha). Constructed from 1793 to 1797, it was the personal favorite of the nine missions founded by Father Junipero Serra throughout California. The ambitious padre is, in fact, buried here. Architecturally, the mission is notable for its large, arcaded quadrangle, but there are also attractive gardens, informative exhibits, and a museum on the premises. A small donation is suggested. It is well worth it for the peace to be found inside the mission walls.

Carmel is indisputably a beautiful place, nestled among stands of pine and cypress against the ocean's indigo backdrop. It is a smogless village whose only drawback may be that too many people want to share in its natural bounty. For the lucky visitor who comes to stay for a few days or a week, Carmel makes a relaxing place to recharge the batteries in

Monterey County

splendid surroundings. Day-trippers with harried itineraries will catch only a fleeting glimpse of what makes Carmel special. Natives condescendingly abide the influx of outsiders while trying to control their numbers and minimize the impact on Carmel's all-important quality of life. The question is, how do you moderate the crowds without creating bad feelings and severing the economic jugular that allows the town to endure in its visitor-subsidized prosperity? They're debating that very question day by day, issue by issue, with great caution in Carmel.

Beaches

A wide crescent between forested points, **Carmel City Beach** is among the most stunning settings for a beach on any coast, in any part of the world. The first glimpse of this shoreline is unforgettable. As it nears the water, Ocean Avenue slopes sharply downhill, ending at a sandy circle with a Monterey cypress in the center. A heart-stopping plunge down steep-sloped dunes leads to the ocean. Carmel City Beach will mesmerize you with the clarity of the air and vivid brightness of the light; the impregnable points of land that jut out on either side, framing the beachfront; the wind-sculpted cypress trees perched atop the dunes, their agonized contortions a testament to adaptive fortitude; the inscrutable metallic blue of the churning sea; and, finally, the resounding cymbal crash of huge, unforgiving waves.

It is a rough beach to swim on, but a beautiful one to look at. The beach forms a sandy amphitheater upon which people sit and watch the sun set, listen to the crashing breakers, and enjoy a breathtaking tableau of sun, sea, sky, and cypress. People just tend to stare out to sea, mesmerized. Beachgoers spread out towels and blankets and sun themselves on windless indentations on the high dunes. Had we been plopped here unawares, we might have believed ourselves to be on a beach along the Côte d'Azur. On a sadder note, Carmel City

Beach appears to have suffered mightily at the hands of El Niño's destructive shoreline surgery. Lately, the beach looks like a wedding cake that's been half-eaten by an angry giant. It's steeper and narrower, as if the ocean is advancing upon the town.

If you're up for a walk, Scenic Road runs parallel to the ocean, affording blufftop views and occasional access to the beach via staircases. The southernmost of these leads to **Carmel River State Beach,** a 100-acre sanctuary on both sides of the mouth of the Carmel River. (More beach can be accessed south of here, off Ribera Road and Highway 1.) As the surf is hazardous and unpredictable, swimming is discouraged. Divers, however, enjoy exploring the offshore Carmel Bay Ecological Reserve. The Monterey pines and cypress are, incidentally, found nowhere else in the world.

Bunking Down

La Playa Hotel (Camino Real at Eighth Avenue, 831/624-6476, $$$) easily makes our short list of best places to stay at the beach in California. It is a comfy, sun-dappled paradise by the sea. On a quiet side street, with the hotel on one side and roomy bungalows on the other, La Playa sprawls across some of the choicest commercial real estate in Carmel. Purple bougainvillea crawl across the rooftops. The gardens outside the bungalows are a riot of flowers and greenery. An interior courtyard, fragrant with floral scents, encloses a pool. Carmel's amazing beach is a few short blocks away. In the style of the finest lodging places, La Playa creates the feel of a serene world-within-a-world that immediately relaxes visitors and drains away cares. The slapping of waves on the shore is audible from the open windows of the cottages. We stayed at a guest cottage named Log Haven, a two-story wooden house with a pair of sizable bedrooms, high-ceilinged living room with a fireplace and hardwood floors, fully equipped kitchen, upstairs sitting room, and lots of storage alcoves.

Map of Central California—Page 233

The guest cottages run quite a bit more than rooms at the hotel but offer enough room to accommodate several couples or a large family with no problem.

Another well-tended inn is the **Colonial Terrace Inn** (San Antonio and 13th Avenue, 831/624-2741, $$$). It's as close as any hotel gets to the beach in Carmel. The inn's seven buildings are decorated with heritage furnishings in the colonial style, and no two are alike. All rooms have gas fireplaces, some look out on the ocean, the gardens are beautiful, and a complimentary continental breakfast is served each morning.

Several enticingly low-key inns can be found in the heart of Carmel, along Ocean Avenue near the beach. Nestled amid the oaks and pines of old Carmel, **Lobos Lodge** (Monte Verde at Ocean Avenue, P.O. Box L-1, 831/624-3874, $$) is rustic on the outside and modern on the inside. Each of the 29 units is decorated differently, and all have fireplaces and patios. Some of Carmel's heart-of-the-village inns verge on the cutesy, such as the **Lamp Lighter Inn** (Camino Real and Ocean Avenue, 831/624-7372, $$), which is straight out of fairy-tale land. Its nine cottages have names like Hansel and Gretel and the Blue Bird Room and are painted to resemble gingerbread houses. The owner extends the fantasy by talking about the elves that play in the garden and referring to her associate as an "elf's helper." We were not certain she was playing with a full deck, but the Lamp Lighter Inn seems charming enough.

Up the hill from the beach, San Carlos Street is lined with inns and inn-like motels, such as the **Dolphin Inn** (San Carlos Street and Fourth Avenue, 831/624-5356, $$). Rooms are quiet and comfortable, extras like a pool, continental breakfast, and afternoon snacks are welcome, and it's great to be able to park your car and explore Carmel on foot from such a convenient location. The Dolphin Inn, incidentally, is one of seven "Inns by the Sea," an affordable assemblage of inns along the Monterey Peninsula with five properties in Carmel

and one apiece in Monterey and Pacific Grove. Call 800/433-4732 for more information about special rates.

South of Carmel, high on a hill overlooking the ocean, is **Highlands Inn** (Highway 1, 831/624-3801, $$$$). The inn is a historic property, built in 1916, renovated and modernized in recent years. It is a smooth-running, first-class resort popular with honeymooners (1,000 weddings are performed here annually) and anyone looking for a great escape in the rural highlands overlooking the ocean along the Central Coast. The view of the Pacific from the inn's Grand Lodge is splendid; it's as if you're on the bow of a ship suspended over the ocean. Each room is outfitted with a fireplace and vista deck. You will pay dearly for such pampering: rooms start at $265 a night and top off close to $700. Yes, it's a sharp upward climb to the Highlands Inn, both for the car and the pocketbook, but worth it if both are running smoothly.

A note for those seeking to travel economically: room rates in Carmel drop substantially during weekdays in winter.

Coastal Cuisine

We're partial to a couple of restaurants outlying the village of Carmel proper. **Rio Grill** (Rio Road and Highway 1, 831/625-5436, $$$) is an extremely popular Southwestern-themed restaurant in the Crossroads Shopping Center, a mile or so outside the village where the land begins dropping to the Carmel Valley floor. Caricatures by celebrity folk artist George Rodrigue—a relocated Cajun painter whose trendy "blue dog" is a recurring motif—fill the walls of the bar and lobby area. A jar of crayons on each table encourages adults to doodle and scrawl on paper tablecloths before the food arrives. And what food! Most entrées are grilled or cooked in a wood-burning oven. Selections range from hearty fare like rabbit, duck, chicken, and ribs to daily seafood specials.

We'd be neglectful if we didn't mention

Map of Monterey County—Page 342

the culinary houses of worship co-owned and operated by Carmel's most famous citizen, Clint Eastwood. By now all the world knows about **Hog's Breath** (San Carlos Street and Fifth Avenue, 831/625-1044, $$), the restaurant and saloon that is an in-town landmark. If you didn't know about Eastwood's involvement, the menu would quickly tip you off. Selections include the Dirty Harry Burger, the Sudden Impact (sausage, peppers, and cheese on a French roll), the Eiger Sandwich (roast beef), and the For a Few Dollars More steak dinner. (Hey, why not "Magnum Forcemeat"?) Tourists crowd in during the daytime and crane their necks in the unlikely hope of glimpsing Clint.

What the crowds don't know is that the restaurant was shut down for a spell in 1988 owing to health-code violations "too numerous to list," according to Monterey County health inspectors. The kitchen was described as "filthy," suggesting there was some veracity in the naming of the Dirty Harry Burger. The kitchen's sanitation problems were, they claim, partly due to bureaucratic delays in granting permits for renovation and enlargement. It was the owners' eight-year wait for permits that inspired Eastwood to run for mayor of Carmel. The restaurant has long since cleaned up its act, so cross Eastwood's name off the list of "Unforgiven"—at least in terms of his restaurant's kitchen problems. What he's trying to do to the Del Monte Forest up in Pebble Beach is another matter altogether.

Eastwood has also acquired **Mission Ranch** (26270 Dolores Street, 831/625-9040, $$$$), a historic property on the Carmel River. The house specialties are stick-to-the-ribs ranch food. The menu is heavy on steaks—barbecue, prime rib—though you'll find a few catch-of-the-day specials as well. The prime rib comes in either a regular or "ranch" cut, the latter suggested for Paul Bunyan appetites only.

Inside the village area Carmel is the site of pricey, intimate restaurants hidden on side streets—places like **Anton & Michel** (Mission Street, 831/624-2406, $$$) and **Sans Souci** (Lincoln Street between Fifth and Sixth Avenues, 831/624-6220, $$$$). Both are established restaurants serving gourmet European cuisine in a cozy, romantic setting. Another restaurant of long-standing, this one with a strong seafood emphasis, is **Flaherty's Seafood Grill** (Dolores Street and Sixth Avenue, 831/625-1500, $$$). At Flaherty's the fish and shellfish come right off local boats or are flown in fresh.

The **Grill on Ocean Avenue** (Ocean Avenue between Dolores and Lincoln Streets, 831/624-2569, $$$) offers an eclectic array of creative dishes—French and California cuisine with Japanese grace notes—bringing yet another unique range of flavors to the discriminating palates of Carmel.

If you're looking for a good meal for a reasonable tab, check out the **Clam Box** (Mission Street and Fifth Avenue, 831/624-8597, $$), which doesn't stand on ceremony but does dole out memorable dishes like rainbow trout *meunière* and prawns Newburg—not to mention the namesake clam preparations—for what qualify as rock-bottom prices in upscale Carmel.

The best for last: **Flying Fish Grill** (Carmel Plaza, 831/625-1962, $$$) served us one of the most inventive seafood dinners we've had on either coast. Run by genial Kenny Fukumoto, the Flying Fish is stylish without calling attention to itself, and the menu is short but sweet. We had eye-watering sashimi and lightly seared oysters (appetizers), escolar with roasted garlic and shiitake mushroom coulis, and the popular almond-crusted sea bass (entrées). Other tempting choices include black bean salmon and catfish. A reasonably priced wine list ($18–30 for a good bottle) is offered, as are artistically rendered desserts. Flying Fish is open for dinner only.

Night Moves

While wandering the darkened streets of Carmel in search of **Hog's Breath** (San Carlos Street and Fifth Avenue, 831/625-1044) one foggy night, we ran into a wizened old soul looking like the ghost of Ernest Hemingway. We asked for directions and he instructed us to follow him. "I've lived here 30 years, and I still get lost," he said. We trailed the kindly codger as he wound his way through back streets and alleyways. All the while he kept up a steady stream of chatter, muttering about Eastwood's restaurant-cum-watering hole, which he variously referred to as "Hog's Butt" and "Clam Breath." We followed him through a rear entrance into the courtyard of Hog's Breath. Without turning around or breaking stride, he bade us farewell for the night and exited through the front door.

There is virtually no other nighttime activity in the village of Carmel than the quiet boozing going on at Hog's Breath. It closes around 1 A.M., a little earlier or later depending on the crowd. We planted ourselves on the outdoor patio, where giant tree trunks gnarl their way out of the ground. The restaurant's interior is more intimate, with tables set off in alcoves for romantic tête à têtes. After a civilized drink or two, we groped our way back through the dark and fog to our inn, recalling the words of our self-appointed sage and sherpa: "The nightlife around here is strictly for the newly wed and nearly dead."

For More Information

Carmel Business Association and Visitor Information Center, San Carlos Avenue between Fifth and Sixth Avenues, P.O. Box 4444, Carmel, CA 93921, 831/624-2522, website: www.carmel-by-the-sea.com; Monterey Peninsula Convention and Visitors Bureau, 380 Alvarado Street, Monterey, CA 93940, 831/649-1770, website: www.monterey.com

Pebble Beach

We're not overly fond of Pebble Beach and the excessive privatization of its splendid coastline, so we'll be painlessly brief in our opprobrium. Pebble Beach is known for its two resorts (the Pebble Beach Lodge and the Inn at Spanish Bay), five golf courses (notably the Pebble Beach Golf Links), and the 17-Mile Drive (see sidebar, "The 17-Mile Drive: A Must to Avoid"). The origins of Pebble Beach as a resort date back to 1887, with the construction of the grand Del Monte Hotel and a private scenic drive that circled the property. In 1915 the grandnephew of telegraph inventor Samuel Morse oversaw a full-tilt series of "improvements" to the property, including the construction of the Lodge at Pebble Beach, the laying out of the Pebble Beach Golf Links, and the paving of the 17-Mile Drive.

Millionaires built seaside mansions on the property; the owner of one marble-faced palace went so far as to heat her private beach with underground pipes. In 1946 Bing Crosby began crooning a new tune as the impresario of an annual pro-am tournament played here that bore his name. (These days it's called the AT&T–Pebble Beach National Pro-Am Golf Championship.) In 1979 the whole shebang was sold to 20th-Century Fox. Then it went to a Japanese company. Now it's in the hands of a consortium headed by Pete Ueberroth (former baseball commissioner and 1984 Summer Olympics organizer), Dick Ferris (former United Air Lines chairman), Clint Eastwood (actor, ex-mayor, hard-line right-winger), and Arnold Palmer (former pro golfer). This gang of four has environmentalists in an uproar with their plans for an extensive expansion of commercial resort facilities and new residential lot subdivisions in Pebble Beach.

On July 26, 2001, the Pebble Beach Company filed 10 Development Project Applications with the Monterey County Planning Department. Among other things, these include plans for a new 18-hole golf course with

Map of Monterey County—Page 342

The 17-Mile Drive: A Must to Avoid

If you're headed to the Monterey Peninsula, chances are the 17-Mile Drive is on your itinerary. Almost everyone succumbs, believing that it is a not-to-be-missed scenic drive "through pine forests and groves of Monterey cypress and along a coastline of singular beauty."

You are wasting time and money if you shell out for the 17-Mile Drive. It would be a time-consuming bore if it were free, but the greedheads who live in Pebble Beach charge $8 for the dubious privilege of driving through their "private community." This is highway robbery. The money is not funneled into state or county coffers, nor does it benefit some worthy environmental cause. Instead, it goes to the private Pebble Beach Company. To add to the bottomless greed of it all, the brochure we were handed at the gate turned out to be a retail catalog for pricey golf wear from the Pebble Beach Lodge.

Year after year, the 17-Mile Drive remains a large draw, recommended as one of the top attractions on the Monterey Peninsula. The scenery is not nearly as striking as the hundreds of miles of public highways along California's coastline that can be driven for free. The drive through Big Sur—90 miles of mountainous coastal wonders without golf courses to distort the natural environment—puts the 17-Mile Drive to shame and doesn't cost a penny. Ditto for Sunset Drive in the adjacent congenial community of Pacific Grove.

When informed of our book venture, the crabby old gatekeeper barked: "If you quote from anything in the brochure, you've got to ask permission." Here's a quote from the brochure that says it all: "Fulfill your shopping desires by choosing from the ultimate in golf and tennis gear, jewelry, women's designer fashions, art, gift items, and more." We did not ask permission. Furthermore,

clubhouse, restaurant, parking lot, maintenance facility, pro shop, and 11 new hotel buildings that will house "golf cottages." The construction of the course would require the removal of approximately 9,000 trees. The Pebble Beach plunderers are also calling for major building additions at their Spanish Bay Resort and a new driving range and golf-teaching facility. They want to add a new building with 63 guest rooms at the Pebble Beach Lodge. They propose new residential lots and subdivisions around the property. The list goes on and on.

What makes it all so egregious is that Pebble Beach sits on the western side of the Monterey Peninsula in the middle of the Del Monte Forest, which is by far the largest and healthiest stand of Monterey pine forest left in the entire world. Pebble Beach is private and restricted, accessible only through five pay-to-enter gates along the 17-Mile Drive. As it is, 6,000 people live in the disappearing forest in and around Pebble Beach. In spite of the ecological value of this priceless island of Monterey pine forest, the Pebble Beach Company wants to develop almost all their remaining holdings in Del Monte Forest. If approved, it will be the largest single development in the history of the Monterey Peninsula in terms of homes, acreage, and destroyed pine forest. The population of Pebble Beach would increase by

Map of Central California—Page 233

we urge you to steer clear of Pebble Beach and stick to those parts of the coast that are, as they should be, free to all.

In fact, we'll save you the entrance fee into 17-Mile Drive. Climb in the car with us as we pay the $8, drive through the gate, and see the sights. First, you pass miles of what looks like any well-to-do suburban neighborhood in America, trailing fuming buses and a line of hoodwinked motorists. Along a stretch where the road hugs the coastline, they've erected signs pointing to photo ops like the "Restless Sea" and "Point Joe," which are attractive overlooks but nothing out of the ordinary for the Central Coast. But because the Pebble Beach Company has assigned names and numbers and charged money to drive past them, people believe they're experiencing something unique and worthwhile. Or maybe they don't, judging from some of the comments we overheard.

Eventually, you pass the Pebble Beach Golf Links, a study in the fine art of turning a pristine and endangered coastal forest into a denuded plain of heavily fertilized, close-cropped grass. We cruised onward. The sights were more sightless by the minute: earth-moving equipment, average-looking homes, charred trees. Even the "Lone Cypress"—the signature attraction of the 17-Mile Drive, and the pride and joy of Pebble Beach (it's part of the corporate logo)—is down on its heels, having become ridden with termites.

It seems that vandals tried to burn the tree, proving that there's no crime so perverse that someone won't eventually think to attempt it in California. Now termites have invaded the tree's charred, weakened ocean-facing side. Not to worry! The Pebble Beach Company's resource department is nursing a replacement Lone Cypress in a secluded spot while doing their best to shore up the original.

After a while, we couldn't wait to exit. We had a parting taunt ready for the gatekeeper, but a sign said "Do Not Stop at Gate" on the way out, presumably sparing the hired hands a chewing out from hotheaded tourists.

another 1,000 golf geeks, bringing with it additional environmental stresses.

The slate of proposed projects would develop more than one square mile—an area equal in size to the adjacent town of Carmel. If this sounds as ill-advised to you as it does to us, join the Concerned Residents of Pebble Beach and Monterey County in voicing your opinion to county supervisors. To learn more, point your browser to the nonprofit group's website at www.cr-pb.org.

With regard to Eastwood, Ueberroth, Ferris, and Palmer, we find ourselves wondering why these old farts can't be contented with the obscene riches they've already laid aside for themselves. Why do they have to mess with everything? Have any of them ever spent a day appreciating nature without conjuring ways to alter it for profit? Apparently, too much is never enough for an uber-capitalist.

If you've won the lottery or made a killing in the market, perhaps you can afford to stay at the **Lodge at Pebble Beach** ($500–675 per night) or swing a set of clubs on its famed golf course ($350 for 18 holes) or dine at one of its fine restaurants (four-course prix-fixe dinner, wine not included, $58 per person). If you share a standard ocean-view room, the cost of an overnight stay, game of golf, and dinner for two will total $1,491, plus beverages, taxes, and

Map of Monterey County—Page 342

gratuities. On the plus side they will refund the cost of passing through the 17-Mile Drive toll gate if you're staying at one of the lodges. That brings the pretax total of a one-night, one-meal, one-game stay down to $1,483 per couple.

Beaches

Believe it or not, there are actually some public beaches around Spanish Bay. No doubt they are a grudging concession from the developers exacted by the California Coastal Commission in exchange for permit approvals. From the junction of Asilomar Boulevard and Sunset Drive in Pacific Grove, a biking and hiking path called the Spanish Bay Recreation Trail leads through the forest behind the Inn at Spanish Bay, joining up with 17-Mile Drive and its procession of small cove beaches a short distance later. It also intersects a boardwalk that leads from the hotel lobby over the dunes and out to North and South **Moss Beach,** where you can sun yourself without spending a fortune (or a night).

The best surfing is found at **Spanish Bay**—"a half-mile of smooth beach surf," according to our bard of the longboard, Bank Wright—which frugal surfers get to by hiking from Asilomar State Beach. One of Pebble Beach's more notable cove beaches is **Fanshell Beach,** a north-facing sugar-textured sand beach at Signal Road and 17-Mile Drive. On the southern end of 17-Mile Drive—just north of Carmel City Beach—is another publicly accessible point, called **Stillwater Cove.** It has a tiny sand beach but is noted for its pier, which has a boat hoist. This is accessible via the private Lodge at Pebble Beach parking lot. Good luck. Call 831/625-8507 for boat information.

Bunking Down

Your choices are the **Lodge at Pebble Beach** (17-Mile Drive, 831/624-3811, $$$$) or the new kid on the block, the **Inn at Spanish Bay** (2700 17-Mile Drive, 831/647-7500, $$$$). In neither place will you lack for comfort. Each has a private beach, golf courses, tennis, pools, bikes, horses, health club, hiking trails, restaurants, stores, picnic tables, patios, balconies, and fireplaces. In addition the Lodge at Pebble Beach has a post office and bank. Are we leaving anything out? The Inn at Spanish Bay is described as the more "casual" of the two, which means you get a slight break on the room rate: $350–475 a night for a double room at the Inn at Spanish Bay versus $395–525 at the Lodge at Pebble Beach. A top-of-the-line suite at the latter goes for (brace yourself) $1,800 a night.

Coastal Cuisine

The celebrated restaurants at the Pebble Beach resorts are **Club XIX** (Lodge at Pebble Beach, 831/624-3811, $$$$) and the **Bay Club** (Inn at Spanish Bay, 831/647-7500, $$$$). Club XIX serves a French country menu, while the Bay Club tends toward northern Italian. Both are quite good, and both so expensive that (as the cliché goes) if you have to ask how much it is, you probably shouldn't be here. Dinner for two will cost around $90, exclusive of drinks, tax, and tip.

For More Information

Pebble Beach Company, 2700 17-Mile Drive, Pebble Beach, CA 93953, 831/647-7500 or 800/654-9300, website: www.pebble-beach.com

Map of Central California—Page 233

Pacific Grove

Pacific Grove is the shy but beautiful daughter of the Monterey Peninsula. Hidden by trees and cooled by steady winds off Monterey Bay, this modest seaside village values a sensible regimen of spiritual nourishment, moderate exercise, fresh food, and lots of beauty rest. She's not a bit covetous of her peninsular siblings' popularity. Pacific Grove is content to let Carmel, Pebble Beach, and Monterey deal with the vulgarities of fame.

This attitude comes with the territory. More hometown than boomtown, Pacific Grove has led a quiet, ascetic life since her birth in 1875 as a "Christian seaside resort." The original 100 acres of pine-, oak-, and cypress-covered wilderness that make up the central grid of the town were marked off by the Methodist Episcopal Church for use as a camp-meeting retreat. The first camp meeting was held on August 8, 1875, and the lots were sold in 30-by 60-foot increments—large enough to accommodate a substantial tent. But a crowd of 450 worshippers turned out, more than had been anticipated, and in the ensuing years still more arrived. When summer rolled around, Pacific Grove became a virtual tent city. At summer's end the wooden frames were left standing while the tents were unfurled and stored in Chautauqua Hall, a utilitarian wood structure built in 1879 for the "presentation of moral attractions."

With this many people seeking it out for solace, Pacific Grove could not remain a simple religious retreat for long. In 1889 a permanent, year-round population of 1,300 incorporated a square-mile area of woodlands, and the town was created. The tents disappeared, replaced by tiny board-and-batten cottages, some built directly on the old frames. Larger Victorian dwellings were also built. These homes, along with the original churches, Chautauqua Hall, and the Point Pinos Lighthouse, still stand in Pacific Grove as unpretentious reminders of a quiet past. Most of the homes have plaques on the front door that identify the original owner and the year of its construction. Today Pacific Grove's population hovers at around 17,500.

In terms of area, Pacific Grove embraces a choice corner of the wild Monterey Peninsula. You enter the town through a forest, and by the time you reach the seaside retreat you might as well have stepped back a century in time. This is not to imply that Pacific Grove is a spinster living among dusty hymn books and faded memories. On the contrary her original homes are in good repair and constant use as residences, inns, and offices—and their rising real-estate value has begun pricing this "last hometown" almost out of the reach of the middle-class folks that have always been its mainstay.

A full day can be spent hiking around Pacific Grove, admiring her restorations and resilience. An especially rewarding experience is the Pacific Grove Historic Walking Tour, an entertaining packet dispensed by the Chamber of Commerce from its neat little office at Forest and Central Avenues. Your efforts will be rewarded with a healthy perambulation and a thorough knowledge of Victorian-era California trivia.

The most informative tour stop is the **Pacific Grove Museum of Natural History** (165 Forest Avenue, 831/648-3116). Founded in 1881, it's one of the best of its size in the country. It's also free of charge, though you'll be moved to give a donation. In two floors of gallery space, every facet of Monterey County's rich natural history is showcased. This includes insects, rodents, birds (400 species), fish, reptiles, rocks, fossils, Native Americana, and the town's evocative symbol, the monarch butterfly *(Danaus plexippus)*.

A more appropriate mascot could not be found for Pacific Grove, which, when it gets

Map of Monterey County—Page 342

the slightest bit of boosterism, bills itself as "Butterfly Town, USA." Every year, thousands of orange-and-black monarchs migrate to the pine groves nearby. They arrive on November 1 and leave by March 1. On dull winter days they hang in thick clusters from the trees, but on warm, sunny days they swoop all over town. The city protects these fluttering critters, imposing fines of up to $1,000 for "molesting butterflies." This same ordinance asks citizens to "protect the butterflies in every way possible from serious harm and possible extinction by brutal and heartless people." If you don't want to be assaulted by a mob of angry matrons wielding antique butter churns, then you'd better leave the sweet little things be.

On the other hand, you may never see a monarch butterfly. They're gone by summer and are sometimes undetectable in winter. Their wings fold inward, so that only their neutral-colored undersides are visible. The distinctive, lovely markings are seen only by those with the patience to look closely. The same is true of Pacific Grove. The closer you look at it, the more its charming detail and coloring will be revealed.

The entire town gathers visitors in its warm embrace. Even at a gas station on Lighthouse Avenue where we stopped to ask for directions, the beaming, Ward Cleaver–like proprietor put his arms around our shoulders and said, "That would normally cost you a dollar, but I'm running a special today."

Beaches

For so understated a town, Pacific Grove is actually quite large in terms of area. Whereas the old historic neighborhoods can be pleasantly strolled in an afternoon, the ruggedly beautiful shoreline goes on for miles, especially in and around Asilomar State Beach. The beaches beg to be explored on bicycle. In fact, Pacific Grove is a peninsula within a peninsula. The terrain out here is relatively flat, the roads less traveled by cars, and the neighborhoods

safer than in Monterey. The Pacific Grove Bicycle Trail solves all your beachcombing problems. It starts at the south near Spanish Bay, cuts through Asilomar, Point Pinos, and Lover's Point, and then hooks up with the more heavily trafficked Monterey Bay Recreational Trail near the Monterey Bay Aquarium. The best place to rent wheels (or kayaks) is **Adventures by the Sea** (299 Cannery Row, 831/372-1807), directly on the beach at Lover's Point, just off the bike trail, which also rents kayaks, diving gear, and so forth for those who want to brave the bay. From there one can continue north, through Monterey and up to Seaside—quite a haul, though it gets progressively less meditative with each passing mile.

Back at Spanish Bay one comes face to face with the enmity that other Monterey Peninsula residents feel toward their Pebble Beach neighbors. This was once the most exquisite cove beach in the area, a favorite with locals, surfers, artists, and photographers. Now, it's the backdrop for a luxury resort (the Inn at Spanish Bay and its adjoining golf course, the Links at Spanish Bay), which, after years of heated legal dickering, was finally approved by the local zoning board. They must have been out of their sand bunkers! To make it worse, the beach at Spanish Bay is private. Why don't they just complete the deal by building a crocodile-infested moat around the compound? Ansel Adams, whose gallery is in Pebble Beach, would have been appalled.

There is a way to circumvent this privacy. Take the hiking trail at nearby Asilomar State Beach that leads, via a wooden boardwalk, to the Inn at Spanish Bay's parking lot. Continue walking, pausing long enough to thumb your nose at the resort. You will soon hook up with the Coastal Bluff Hiking Trail, which leads to Point Joe, the most scenic spot on the overly hyped 17-Mile Drive. You will be standing on the beach itself—not viewing it from some coerced overlook—and you will have saved $8, the pricey tariff to enter the

Map of Central California—Page 233

17-Mile Drive by car. The view? Imagine Ansel Adams's finest photograph.

Off Sunset Drive/Highway 68 and Asilomar Avenue, **Asilomar State Beach** is a meditative mix of rocky headlands, tidepools, and cove beaches. The beach is a half mile of sand backed by healthy grass-covered dune fields that stretch for hundreds of yards toward the Asilomar Conference Grounds. It's popular with surfers, divers, kite fliers, and sunbathers. Parking and day use are free at Asilomar State Beach.

The bike trail courses around the rocky headlands at Point Pinos and the Pacific Grove Shoreline Marine Refuge, a feast for the eyes. The beaches here are more for browsing than swimming, with many rich tidepools but sand and pebbles too coarse for bare feet. Pretend you're a seagull soaring above this buffet, which is probably what all those birders sitting in their cars with binoculars are doing. The waves create a teeming stew of fish, shells, kelp fronds, sea grapes, starfish, and sea grass. These are the same tidepools that inspired John Steinbeck and his hero, Doc Ricketts, in the novel *Cannery Row.* (Steinbeck: "It is a fabulous place: when the tide is in, a wave-churned basin, creamy with foam . . . but when the tide goes out the little water world becomes quiet and lovely, fantastic with hurrying, fighting, feeding, breeding animals.") His grandparents had a house nearby, now the modest **John Steinbeck Memorial Museum** (222 Central Avenue, 831/373-6976).

Speaking of literary inspiration, Robert Louis Stevenson spent many ecstatic hours in Pacific Grove, too. He sat out at Point Pinos—the entrance to Monterey Bay—perhaps staring longingly toward Tahiti. The **Point Pinos Lighthouse,** built in 1855, is the oldest light station in continuous service on the West Coast, guiding navigators through these sometimes rugged waters. The building, lenses, and prisms are all original, and they can be viewed by the public on Saturdays and Sundays, 1 P.M.–4 P.M. (For information call the lighthouse at 831/648-3116.)

Although surfers love Asilomar State Beach in the winter—when waves reach heights of eight feet—the heaviest bombers come to Point Pinos. Between Point Pinos and Lover's Point is an area known as "Boneyards"—though its official name is **Perkins Park**—where the surf breaks perilously close to the rocky headlands. Sit on one of the blufftop benches and watch the show, as do-or-die surfers consider this spot a must, especially at high tide.

Families gravitate to **Lover's Point,** a large, grassy area with volleyball courts, babies' swimming pool, snack bar, restrooms, and sandy beaches. (Sadly, this is where singer John Denver fatally crashed his experimental plane in 1997.) The surf here is nowhere near as rough as that at Point Pinos. The entire area is lined with grassy parks set on blufftops above the shore, along which runs the Monterey Bay Recreational Trail, a paved pathway for walkers and cyclists. This linear bayfront green passes and encompasses a series of small parks set back from the bay— including Berwick Park, Greenwood Park, and Andy Jacobsen Park. Collectively, the parks are known as **Shoreline Park** and offer access to pebbly pocket beaches here and there via short, sloping trails. Benches provide strollers with ample rest stops and offer further proof that Pacific Grove may indeed be the Monterey Peninsula's last real hometown. Finally, this same area—from Asilomar to Lover's Point—is a great promontory from which to watch whales migrate in the winter.

Also in the immediate area is a golfing opportunity par excellence, one of the few we wholeheartedly endorse at the beach. **Pacific Grove Municipal Golf Course** (77 Asilomar Boulevard, 831/648-3177) is a pleasant, low-key alternative to Pebble Beach's overpriced "links." It's truly a public course with the same stunning scenery. The fairway of the 16th hole, for example, runs alongside the Point Pinos Lighthouse. The greens fees are reasonable

Map of Monterey County—Page 342

Monterey County

($40 for 18 holes, as opposed to $300 at Pebble Beach), the staff friendly, and the manners decidedly casual.

Shore Things

• **Bike/skate rentals:** Adventures by the Sea, 299 Cannery Row, 831/372-1807; Pedal Stop, 99 Pacific Street, Monterey, 831/655-8687

• **Boat cruise:** Baywatch Cruises, 90 Fisherman's Wharf #1, Monterey, 831/372-7153

• **Dive shop:** Aquarius Dive Shop, 2040 Del Monte Avenue, Monterey, 831/375-1933, and 32 Cannery Row, Monterey, 831/375-6605

• **Ecotourism:** Chris' Whale Watch, Fisherman's Wharf, Monterey, 831/375-5951

• **Lighthouse:** Point Pinos Lighthouse, Pacific Grove, 831/648-3116

• **Marina:** Monterey Marina, foot of Figueroa Street, Monterey, 831/646-3950

• **Rainy day attraction:** Monterey Bay Aquarium, 886 Cannery Row, Monterey, 831/648-4888

• **Shopping/browsing:** Carmel Village, Carmel Business Association, Carmel, 831/624-2522

• **Surf shop:** On the Beach Surf Shop, 693 Lighthouse Avenue, Monterey, 831/646-9283

• **Vacation rentals:** San Carlos Agency, Inc., 26358 Carmel Rancho Lane, Carmel, 831/624-3846

Bunking Down

The **Asilomar Conference Center** (800 Asilomar Avenue, 831/372-8016, $$) might just be the best bargain on the Monterey Peninsula. Don't let the name put you off. A conference at Asilomar is as likely to be a quiet family retreat as a meeting of corporate eager beavers spouting sales figures and studying pie charts. Founded in 1913 by the YWCA as the premier "chautauqua" in California, the Asilomar Conference Center is now run on a nonprofit basis by the California State Park System. The original 11 buildings (all National Historical Landmarks) were designed by Julia Morgan, the San Francisco architect responsible for Hearst

Castle at San Simeon. They're spread out among 105 acres of Monterey pines and cypress, with wooden walkways leading across the dunes to the state beach. Facing due west, Asilomar is treated to stunning sunsets, and its 28 woodsy lodges have appealingly rustic names like "Willow Inn" and "Oak Knoll." Though conference facilities are available, guests need not be part of a group to come here. A full breakfast, served cafeteria-style in a large hall, comes with the room. It's like being back at camp.

The rest of the town's accommodations are similarly neat, trim, low-key and/or historic, making Pacific Grove the ideal place to stay if you're laying over on the peninsula. Options range from small motels like the **Larchwood Inn** (740 Crocker Avenue, 831/373-1114, $$) to the **Lighthouse Lodge and Suites** (1249 Lighthouse Avenue, 831/655-2111, $$). The former is next to Asilomar, while the latter is set among the shady acres close to Point Pinos Lighthouse, virtually guaranteeing a quiet vacation. Cute little mom-and-pop motels proliferate in the area around Asilomar, furthering the hometown ambience of Pacific Grove. Any one of them would make a fine place to drop your bags for a stay.

Pacific Grove is probably best known as a happy hunting ground for bed-and-breakfast inns, original Victorian homes that have been lovingly converted into lodgings. Several excellent ones include **Green Gables Inn** (104 Fifth Street, 831/375-2095, $$$) and **Gosby House** (643 Lighthouse Avenue, 831/375-1287, $$$). The Green Gables, a Queen Anne mansion built in 1888, is situated on a quiet cove, while the Gosby House is on the town's main thoroughfare. Both provide ideal escapes from modern civilization, offering more privacy than the average B&B amid trappings of quaint Victorian splendor that the old queen herself would definitely have approved. Gosby House has been an inn since it was built in 1887, its earliest guests having been pilgrims to the camp meetings. It has a quiet garden and courtyard,

Map of Central California—Page 233

and the 22 rooms (seven with private entrances) are filled with period furnishings, artwork, stuffed bears, and McGuffey's Readers. Both inns are reasonably priced ($100–170 per night at the Gosby House in season, $110–160 per night at the Green Gables Inn), considering what you get.

Coastal Cuisine

The Monterey Peninsula is now marketing itself, in a low-key way, as the "Provence of California," and indeed a revised approach to cuisine is developing around the abundant fresh local produce and seafood. It's little wonder when 80 percent of the world's broccoli is grown in the vicinity, as are large percentages of artichokes, grapes, lettuce, and ranch-raised game.

Fandango (223 17th Street, 831/372-3456, $$$) is the first of several restaurants to add to your dinner wish list. Run by the ever-pleasant (and present) Pierre Bain, Fandango resembles a villa in the south of France. Not surprisingly, the owner comes from a family restaurant tradition dating back 250 years in the Basque region. Prior to opening Fandango with his wife, Bain worked at Pebble Beach. Fandango has done so well that an upstairs dining room has been added and the patio has been converted to a private dining room.

The experience of eating here is top of the line, the menu prices eminently fair and affordable. As an appetizer, the Veloute Bongo Bongo is hard to top. It's a thick, hearty soup made from fresh spinach, oysters, and cognac. The house specialty is Paella Fandango (see sidebar, "Paella Fandango"), a veritable fishing boat of goodies including littleneck clams, scallops, calamari, shrimp, mussels, chicken, and much more. Other specialties include rack of lamb Provençal, Basque-style lamb shank, and mesquite-grilled salmon and swordfish.

The locals' favorite seafood venue is **Fishwife at Asilomar Beach** (1196 Sunset Drive, 831/375-7107, $$). The freshest catches are served with a Caribbean flavor and consistently win "Best Seafood" awards for the entire peninsula. The house specialties are snapper Cancun (seasoned with achiote and topped with salsa brava), prawns Belize, calamari abalone-style, fish chowder, and key lime pie. The setting is casual, the prices are right, and the line is often out the door. We recently visited Fishwife for an early lunch, slipping in before the line formed. The daily grill special featured wild Monterey Bay salmon, which has a rich, distinctive flavor. The pastas were tempting, too. Pasta Alfredo is cooked in a shellfish-based veloute sauce, sautéed with shallots, butter, and cream, and combined with crab, scallops, or shrimp (or in combination). The Portofino combines crab, shrimp, scallops, baby clams, calamari, and fresh fish. *Bueno!* The dinner menu is expanded with a mouthwatering group of "fisherman's bowls" that include the Bahamian bowl (snapper rubbed with Coral Key spices), Bayou bowl (catfish or snapper), Mazatlan bowl (jumbo shrimp), Cozumel bowl (tilapia), and others.

The Fishwife is so successful that a second restaurant has opened in Seaside (**Fishwife Seafood Cafe,** 789 Trinity Avenue, 831/394-2027, $$), the nondescript oceanfront town grafted onto the flanks of Monterey. Fishwife also publishes a popular collection of its recipes.

Another longtime favorite is **Tinnery at the Beach** (631 Ocean View Boulevard, 831/646-1040, $$), right on the water at Lover's Point. It's not exactly gourmet cuisine, but by Pacific Grove's standards it's affordable family dining. The Tinnery is staffed by friendly, wholesome locals, and the dining room has a peerless bay view. At sunset you can watch fishing boats returning to Monterey, and on clear days you can see as far as Moss Landing and Santa Cruz, on the far side of the bay. After you're as stuffed as a halibut, take an after-dinner stroll along Lover's Point before retiring to your room at the inn.

Yet another longtime resident of the Pacific Grove dining scene is the **Old Bath House**

Monterey County

Map of Monterey County—Page 342

Paella Fandango

Here's a recipe for Paella Fandango, one of the signature dishes served at Fandango in Pacific Grove. Fandango is among our favorite restaurants on the California coast. Chef Pierre Bain's recipe for this classic Spanish dish is easy to prepare and simply delicious. According to this paella guru, "If you follow the recipe, it turns out perfectly every time."

1/2 cup olive oil
1 large onion, chopped
2 cloves garlic, chopped
2 large tomatoes, diced
1 each red and yellow bell pepper, cut in strips
2 cups uncooked white rice
8 cups chicken broth
3 tablespoons fresh parsley, chopped
2 large pinches saffron threads
2 chicken breasts (cut into 4 to 5 pieces each)
1/2 pound chorizo sausage, cut into 1/2-inch slices
1/2 pound scallops
1/2 pound shrimp, peeled with tails intact
1/2 pound calamari
8 to 10 little neck clams
8 to 10 mussels
1 cup peas, fresh or frozen
salt, pepper, cayenne

In a Dutch oven, heat olive oil and add onion, garlic, tomatoes, and peppers. Sauté until limp. Add white rice and chicken broth, and bring to a boil. Add the parsley and saffron and cook for 20 minutes at a simmer. Add the remaining ingredients and cook until done, about 20 to 40 minutes. Season to taste with salt, pepper, and cayenne. Serves 8.

Monterey County

(620 Ocean View Boulevard, 831/375-5195, $$$$), a pricey place that does unusual things with seafood and game dishes. Eclectic appetizers include tempting exotica like house-cured salmon with pistachio-crusted goat cheese, and grilled prawns and wild boar sausage.

The aptly named **Passionfish** (701 Lighthouse Avenue, 831/655-3311, $$$) is making waves for its proclaimed dedication to "serving sustainable seafood." Cooks use only line-caught local fish—catches like wild Monterey Bay salmon—and local produce. On the night we visited (it's open for dinner only), six of 11 menu items were seafood, including wild salmon, halibut, escolar, and mahimahi. The artfully spartan interior design is a perfect complement to the fare, and the wine list has won awards from *Wine Spectator*.

Map of Central California—Page 233

To open your day, and perhaps even your mind, hit **Bookworks** (667 Lighthouse Avenue, 831/372-2242, $), Pacific Grove's best bookshop and a relaxed coffeehouse in the bargain. The shop has a decent collection of contemporary literature, classics, history and travel books, plus one of the largest and most passionately annotated displays of "staff picks" we bookworms have ever seen. In other words, they love the printed word at Bookworks.

Night Moves

Your after-dinner stroll along Lover's Point (originally, Lovers of Jesus Point) should suffice for nightlife in Pacific Grove. More by silent agreement than by local ordinance—though it was "dry" until 1972—Pacific Grove has no bars.

Nor will you find pool halls, nightclubs, discos, or beer joints here. About all you can do is quaff a drink to tepid lounge music at the Tinnery and the Old Bath House (see "Coastal Cuisine"). For anything more lively than this, head over to Monterey. In the ascetic spirit of Pacific Grove, we chose to pass up an evening of square-dancing at Crocker Hall in the Asilomar Conference Center. It just seemed too darned wild.

For More Information

Pacific Grove Chamber of Commerce, Central and Forest Avenues, P.O. Box 167, Pacific Grove, CA 93950, 831/373-3304; Monterey Peninsula Convention and Visitors Bureau, 380 Alvarado Street, Monterey, CA 93940, 831/649-1770, website: www.monterey.com

Monterey

If the Monterey Peninsula were a baseball team, Carmel would lead off and play second base, Pebble Beach would be the overpaid designated hitter, and Pacific Grove would be the utility infielder who exerts a stabilizing influence on the bench. Monterey would be the cleanup hitter, because that's exactly what it does. It cleans up after the tourists. This is no accident. By design Monterey draws the tourist hordes who roam the streets, starving, hysterical, clad in goofy clothing, looking for an angry fix of clam chowder.

Nothing is wrong with tourism. It gives people something to do two weeks a year and helps keep our temperamental economy afloat. It is also a "clean industry," for the most part, having a relatively minimal impact on the environment. Monterey's rich history, the restoration of the canneries, and the magnificent Monterey Bay Aquarium (see sidebar, "Monterey Bay Aquarium") are all part of the attraction. Unlike many tourist traps, Monterey actually has something to offer other than shopping and eating.

Still, in years past, we've felt that Monterey

was more of a tourist trap than it needed to be. At the same time, it's also true that in recent years the city has been changing for the better, especially on the water. An excursion to Monterey today is worthwhile, particularly when it's combined with side trips to Big Sur and other peninsular communities. That said, it is not exactly easy to find your way around the town of Monterey. Oh sure, it's the biggest town on Monterey Peninsula, but the layout of its streets and the web of exits that lead into it are confusing. It can be hard just to get from downtown to Cannery Row (or vice versa), even though they're close to each other.

Spread out around the curve of a harbor and groping inland, Monterey (population 31,500) is a contoured combination of the old and the really old. The center of the latter is historic Old Town, which can be toured with a decent pair of sneakers and a map. This section of Monterey has been taken over by the California State Park System (in conjunction with the Monterey History and Art Association), which does these sorts of things right. An excellent self-guided walking tour has been laid out, called

Monterey National Marine Sanctuary

Monterey Bay is the centerpiece of the largest protected marine area in the United States. Encompassing one-fourth of California's coastline, the **Monterey National Marine Sanctuary** stretches from the waters off San Simeon to the Golden Gate Bridge in San Francisco (with a 71-square-mile "raw sewage exemption zone" off San Francisco). In all, 5,312 square nautical miles—1.5 times the size of the largest national park in America—are protected from offshore oil and gas development, ocean dumping, sub-sea mining, agricultural runoff, and untreated sewage disposal. Although it would seem a good idea to protect all of our coastlines from the above encroachments, it's downright imperative to protect the rich ecosystem of Monterey Bay, which is:

- the permanent or seasonal home to 27 species of sea mammals, including endangered whales and threatened sea otters
- home to 345 species of fish, most of California's species of algae, and among the world's richest assemblage of invertebrate life
- the nesting area or sanctuary to 94 species of seabirds, some endangered.

We learned firsthand about the bay's invertebrate population one night. After an obligatory swing through Monterey's clubs and bars, we returned to our car, parked along Cannery Row's waterfront. There, in the water just offshore, we spied a veritable navy of fishing vessels. Pitch dark though it was on shore, it was bright as day on the bay. A circle of boats with powerful, mounted klieg lights eerily illuminated the surface of the water. They were fishing for squid, and this technique—using light to throw off their prey's biological clocks—brings them to the surface in search of food. Instead of finding a meal, these unsuspecting squid wind up as fried calamari strips on tourists' plates at Fisherman's Wharf.

The Monterey National Marine Sanctuary is a center for international research on marine life and marine ecology, encompassing 11 research institutions. Its mission is to monitor all activities impacting the marine area, including effluent from ships and land, development, and recreational uses, as well as monitoring the populations of aquatic species. Monterey Bay became the center of this sanctuary in 1992, when the federal government designated it as such after a 15-year wrangle. At present the sanctuary is managed by the National Oceanic and Atmospheric Administration (NOAA), but management may be transferred to a joint public-private venture.

Map of Central California—Page 233

"the Path of History," which allows visitors to explore the meticulously restored adobes, chapels, theaters, and pubs that make Monterey "the most historic city in California."

Monterey has several histories rolled into one. Founded in 1542 by Juan Cabrillo, it has been the capital of California on three separate occasions. It has also served as an international trading center, whaling mecca, giant industrial sardine cannery, and, finally, the place where the state of California was born. This historic event transpired at the Constitutional Convention of 1849, held in the still-standing Colton Hall. Soon after, gold was discovered up north. San Francisco swiftly became the preeminent city in California, leaving Monterey to ponder its past. The best place to begin a tour of the wonderful remnants of Old Town—and to pick up all the available free literature—is the **Monterey State Historic Park Visitor Center** (5 Custom House Plaza, 831/649-7118). Stop here to get acclimated, then start walking.

On the Path of History you'll see the original Custom House, where all imported goods were brought ashore and inspected before permission was granted to unload. Many a sea captain averted this procedure by off-loading on one of the islands south of Carmel, returning later to pick up the untaxed cargo. Also on the path is the state's first theater, still producing live drama when not serving ale and food under the name **Jack Swan's Tavern.** Other highlights include the **Pacific House** (an 1847 military storehouse, now an excellent museum of California history), the state's first kiln-fired brick house, the old whaling station, and the **Robert Louis Stevenson House.** Built in 1847, the Stevenson House is where the author lived when he was courting Fanny Osbourne, a married woman who vacationed here. Civil War buffs can see the house where William Tecumseh Sherman lived from 1847 to 1849, back when he was a man about town (before he torched Georgia). Even the historic houses that are not official

stops on the path have been commandeered for other functions—investment firms, real-estate offices, law offices, Mexican restaurants—leading us to turn an old cliché on its head: the more things stay the same, the more they change in Monterey.

One welcome addition to the waterfront that has rekindled interest in Monterey's history is the **Stanton Center.** This 18,000-square-foot structure is devoted to the rich maritime and European colonial history of the peninsula. Its centerpiece is the **Maritime Museum of Monterey** (5 Custom House Plaza, 831/373-2469). The museum focuses on the town's history as California's premier port, re-creating life aboard a ship, inside the Custom House, and at a lighthouse. Original artifacts, vintage photographs, and excellent documentary footage are used to convey these settings. The treasure is a two-story, five-ton Fresnel lens that served as the beacon at Point Sur Light Station for 100 years. A modest admission fee is charged ($3 for adults, free for kids), but the seven exhibit areas are a good return on investment. Next to the center in the outdoor plaza a performance space stages historic skits for the kids. The entire area is a successful compromise between doing justice to history and meeting tourist needs—a balance that Monterey itself has needed to strike for years.

The Stanton Center and its environs have gone a long way toward improving downtown Monterey, which was drastically altered by all the corporate development wedged onto the waterfront in the 1980s. The logjam of growth reconfigured the old street grids into a maddening and confusing maze. Ironically enough, this corporate strangulation discouraged locals from frequenting the downtown area. In the words of one entrepreneur, the ill-planned growth "castrated the town, sapping the vitality out of Alvarado Street, where things were once hopping all the time." But now the downtown is coming back, even if the electrical current that kept Alvarado humming has been

Monterey Bay Aquarium

The **Monterey Bay Aquarium** opened in 1984 with the expressed goal of "expanding public interest and knowledge and concern for the marine life of Monterey Bay and the ocean environment." In slightly less than two decades it has more than achieved its goal. In fact, it's a yardstick by which environmental education ought to be measured. With fresh and regularly changing exhibits, tanks full of living specimens, video and film footage, and live presentations, the aquarium re-creates the rich underwater habitat of Monterey Bay right outside its back door. A relief map we'd seen at the Pacific Grove Museum of Natural History showed how the bay plunges 300 feet straight down into an underwater canyon that eventually reaches 8,400 feet in depth. This nutrient-rich canyon nourishes a wide variety of marine species from which the aquarium draws its exhibits.

State-of-the-art does not mean virtual reality at Monterey Bay Aquarium. It means actual reality! That is, kids are allowed to watch real plants and animals do their things (everything from octopuses and sharks to sea slugs and barnacles). There's a kelp forest, sandy shore, coastal stream, reef, bat-ray tank, and a touch pool (the underwater equivalent of a petting zoo). Outdoor presentations take visitors into the surrounding waters for a fins-on experience in more ways than one.

Among the regular activities that visitors most enjoy is the daily feedings of sea otters (at 10:30 A.M., 1:30 P.M., and 3:30 P.M.). They are indeed irresistibly cute little critters. A sea otter, we learned, eats one-third of its weight in food every day (roughly the same fraction as the average Cannery Row tourist). Ac-

short-circuited by obstructive hotel complexes like the Doubletree.

To us there's no mystery about it. We've seen it a hundred times, in nearly every American beach town. If a community plays to its strengths—ocean, sand, and sun—it will never lose. If it goes too far toward accommodating entrepreneurial greed, replacing genuine atmosphere with gold-plated fakery, it will eventually pay the price for lost authenticity with diminished interest.

Take the two best-known attractions in town . . . please. They are Fisherman's Wharf and Cannery Row. Situated on opposite sides of a Coast Guard facility and 10 minutes apart by foot, they are similar in appeal—twin strips

of tourist flypaper around which buzzes an endless procession of dazed, confused humans whose wallets and purses are kept rather too busy buying clam chowder and souvenir baubles. Both were once the haunts of working men, clanging machinery, and ladies of the night. In short, they were raw places with a peculiar history all their own.

These days **Fisherman's Wharf** is easily the more appealing of the two areas, having been spruced up in recent years. Originally built by slave labor as a safe harbor for cargo-laden schooners rounding the horn from the east, the old Fisherman's Wharf was the center of the West Coast whaling industry. Since the late 1800s it has been the domain of a fleet of Si-

Map of Central California—Page 233

cording to a 2002 survey, only 2,139 of these otters are left in California. The otters who reside and cavort at the aquarium, to the immense delight and relief of all, were all injured or orphaned.

A current exhibit is "Jellies: Living Art," an aesthetic appreciation of these surprisingly (when seen in this light) beautiful creatures. One of the most fascinating exhibits is "Mysteries of the Deep," a display of deep-sea creatures taken from depths of over 3,000 feet in the bay. Normally, such creatures do not survive in captivity, but the aquarium spent $5 million and a decade of research to replicate the deep-sea environment, where no sunlight reaches, water temperature is close to 40 degrees, food is scarce, and water pressure is crushing. Up to 40 such rare species are on display now.

There's also a book and gift shop that is superior to any museum shop we've seen on any beach. An on-premises restaurant, the Portola Cafe (831/648-4870, $$), allows you to dine on crab cakes, calamari, prawns, grilled fish—that is, if the sight of cooked seafood delectables doesn't repulse you after having just admired them alive and well in their native habitat.

Admission to Monterey Bay Aquarium isn't cheap ($17.95 for adults, $14.95 for students and seniors, $7.95 for kids 3–12), but the facility is endlessly rewarding, warranting at least a half-day's studious wandering. You'll want to return year after year, too. The best deal is to become a member of the Monterey Bay Aquarium for $85, which allows an entire family—two adults plus all children or grandchildren 3–21—unlimited admission for a year. At the north end of Cannery Row in Monterey, the Monterey Bay Aquarium is open daily 10 A.M.–6 P.M. (from 9:30 A.M. in summer).

For more information contact the Monterey Bay Aquarium, 886 Cannery Row, Monterey, CA 93940, 831/648-4888, website: www.mbayaq.com.

cilian fishermen whose efforts made Monterey the sardine capital of the world. The seafarers have erected a shrine at the mouth of the harbor in honor of Santa Rosalia, their patron saint. Most of the old-family Italians who settled here eventually made a fortune in real estate. Oddly, the wharf doesn't exactly feel like a wharf. Walking its planks is more like strolling a downtown street, because shops and restaurants line both sides in an unbroken wall. Monterey's Fisherman's Wharf is unique among California pier/wharves because of this "closed in" feeling.

Cannery Row, on the other hand, has for years been a largely dubious tourist attraction, though the most excessive tourist bilking has begun to wane. You will want to poke your nose into the Coast Guard facility. Sea lions can be observed from the Coast Guard Pier, basking in the sun on the breakwater. These lazy-looking, heavy-lidded beasts lounge around like overfed tourists on a motel-room bed. Appearances are deceptive, though. The breakwater here is just a resting place on their annual migrations between Mexico and Canada. Feeding them is forbidden; they must catch their own calamari.

Beaches

Visitors come to Monterey for many reasons, but beaches are not one of them. Better beaches lie elsewhere on the peninsula (see Pacific

Grove and Carmel) and directly above it (see Seaside and Marina). The surf along the beaches of Monterey is too cold and hazardous for swimming, and the wind blows nearly nonstop, so don't wear that wacky straw hat you bought on Cannery Row, unless you want to see it wind up on the head of a sea lion.

Still, there is some coastal access and much in the way of watery recreation. Scuba diving, deep-sea fishing, ocean kayaking, sailing, and windsurfing are all popular pastimes, and local merchants can set visitors up with equipment rentals and instruction. The best spots for diving are **Macabee Beach, San Carlos Beach Park** (accessible along Cannery Row) and **Coast Guard Pier,** where you can swim alongside the sea lions and explore the rich marine life of Monterey Bay. And let's not forget the dive-bombing pelicans, who hit the water with a snappy report that sounds like a fastball smacking a catcher's mitt.

The best place for kids to hit the water is **Del Monte Beach,** along a lake in El Estero Park, on the other side of Del Monte Boulevard from the ocean. Ducks and migratory birds come here, and canoes and kayaks can be rented. There's also a toddlers' wading pool and the aptly named Dennis the Menace Play Area, designed by Hank Ketcham, the creator of that famous comic strip. It features innovative equipment and a real train engine for firsthand exploration.

Monterey State Beach offers several access points. A narrow stretch of sand known as **Windows on the Bay** can be found north of Fisherman's Wharf #2 (a municipal wharf built in 1926 for commercial fishing). Another unit lies a mile northeast, at the end of **Sand Dunes Drive.** This one is broader, sandier, and "dunier" than the first. Between these two points is **Beach Way Access,** which has a small free parking area at the end of Beach Way but no facilities.

The Monterey Bay Recreational Trail, a five-mile shoreline bike path that takes in the Monterey waterfront between Pacific Grove and Seaside, is a great way to get a ground-level feel for the town and the bay. It's particularly pleasant between San Carlos Beach Park and Fisherman's Wharf, passing through Fisherman's Shoreline Park.

Bunking Down

More than any other town on the peninsula, Monterey has welcomed large corporate hotels to set up shop. In fact, the Doubletree, Marriott, and Hyatt have been accused of undermining the town's essential character, and we'd have to agree that their soulless anonymity does nothing for Monterey beyond fattening the tax base. By far the best of the larger luxury hotels is **Hotel Pacific** (300 Pacific Street, 831/373-5700, $$$$), which blends in nicely with its neighborhood and is within easy walking distance of many attractions. Done up in peach tones, the Hotel Pacific has mastered the art of relaxed opulence. The architecture reflects the California mission style that is Monterey's architectural heritage. Even the layout is like that of a mission, with a series of discrete buildings constructed around four courtyards and linked with terra cotta–tiled pathways that pass beneath archways and beside adobe gardens.

The accommodations feel less like a hotel room than a real, open living space. Floors are either hardwood or adobe tiled. The second-floor library, where the hotel serves continental breakfasts in the morning and wine and cheese in the afternoon, contains a better selection of true literature (as opposed to best-seller dreck) than we've ever seen at a hotel or inn. An outdoor hot tub is hidden off to the side on an upper-floor landing. The town of Monterey itself spreads out on all sides, begging to be strolled. Yes, you pay for such convenience and elegance ($209–419 per night). But the Hotel Pacific, unlike some of its high-priced neighbors, exudes warmth and personality. It is the only place we've stayed where, in addition to the standard Gideon's Bible, a

Map of Central California—Page 233

copy of *The Teachings of Buddha* had been placed in the nightstand.

The most enjoyable bed-and-breakfast in town is the **Old Monterey Inn** (500 Martin Street, 831/375-8284, $$$$). Parental discretion is advised because this is a couples' getaway. Built as a private residence in 1929, it is set amid beautiful gardens of roses, begonias, ferns, and rhododendrons and a forest of giant California live oaks. It is an English country cottage whose 10 unique rooms have been given evocative, offbeat names (such as "Serengeti" and "Tattershall"). The proprietors, Ann and Gene Swett, are delightful hosts who make you feel that this is not just their home (as it has been for 25 years) but yours as well. When we arrived, we asked, "Where's the office?" Gene paused, reflected, smiled, and threw his arms out as he announced, "There is no office here." We immediately loved the place. Room rates include an elaborate home-cooked breakfast and a spread of wine and cheese in the afternoon. The Swetts know the area intimately, and their inn has won numerous awards.

The best beachfront hotel—indeed, the only place to stay on a sand beach in Monterey—is the **Best Western Monterey Beach Hotel** (2600 Sand Dunes Drive, 831/394-3321, $$). It is a banquet-sized lodge nestled among the healthy dunes beside Monterey State Beach, a formidable stretch of sand that extends north of here. The hotel was built in 1969, before the California Coastal Commission began automatically nixing such projects. As such it is an anomaly: a real beach hotel. It surely could not be built so close to the water in this day and age. Garden- and ocean-view rooms are available. Downtown Monterey is about two miles away. Waves crash with particular vigor here—all the better for lulling you to sleep at night.

Monterey Bay Inn (242 Cannery Row, 831/373-6242, $$$) is a pleasant, low-key lodge at the north end of Cannery Row. It nestles atop a rocky fold of land overlooking San Carlos Beach

Park. From our balcony we could watch sea otters frolicking in the shallows, birds flitting among the rocks, and divers plumbing the endlessly fascinating visual feast. The inn provides binoculars in each room (a nice, novel touch), free continental breakfast, hot tub and sauna, and safe parking space in a ground-level garage. It is very conveniently located. You're right on Cannery Row, and Fisherman's Wharf is only a 10-minute stroll up the bike path from the inn.

Of course there are scads more hotels and motels and inns all over Monterey. We've written about some of our favorites; if you would like a more extensive listing, contact the chamber of commerce and request a *Monterey Peninsula Hotel & Motel Guide*.

Incidentally, a flock of budget motels can be found in the vicinity of Seaside, Sand City, and Marina, the low-end burgs that lie northeast of Monterey. None are as inviting or as economical as they would have you believe. Mostly, they're a shabby row of generics held together by spackling compound that do business only as places fill up to capacity in the more desirable communities around the peninsula.

Coastal Cuisine

In years past Monterey did not have a dining scene worthy of its history as an international trading center. Mostly, it was run-of-the-mill fried fish, calamari strips, and "world-famous clam chowder" so pasty and thick a spoon would stand up in it. That all-you-can-eat mentality has magically transformed in recent years. The most telling sign can be witnessed on Old Fisherman's Wharf—that former dead zone for hunger pangs—where you can now get a decent, well-prepared meal. The dish of choice for tourists still seems to be that horrid chowder, served in hollowed-out "bowls" of Italian bread. Nonetheless, we did quite well for ourselves, stumbling on **Liberty Fish Company** (43 Fisherman's Wharf, 831/375-5468, $$), where the salmon smoking on the grill looked too good to pass up for lunch. It was excellent, perfectly singed and flavored, and served with a fresh salad. The marinated octopus salad looked good, too.

A few steps down the wharf is **Cafe Fina** (47 Fisherman's Wharf, 831/372-5200, $$), which is one step up in cuisine. The service surprised us with its quality, as did the house specialty, pasta Fina, a healthy and hearty plateful of shrimp over linguine. Better still is **Domenico's** (50 Fisherman's Wharf, 831/372-3655, $$$), an Italian classic of long-standing. Seafood and pasta, often in combination, are the prime entrées. Grilled sea bass, Dungeness crab, Monterey Bay prawns—you really can't go wrong. At **Gilbert's Red Snapper** (30 Fisherman's Wharf, 831/375-3113, $$$), the seafood comes reasonably priced and well-prepared—especially the grilled red snapper ($12.95) and that Central Coast staple, fish and chips ($10.95). **Rappa's End of the Wharf** (101 Fisherman's Wharf, 831/372-7562, $$$$) has been around since 1932. In addition to excellent seafood (pan-fried sand dabs, blackened red snapper, flame-broiled salmon, all local), there are great views and a free observation deck.

And that's only Fisherman's Wharf. Elsewhere, the cuisine has blossomed into a world-class act. The two most interesting we found—though there are many others—were **Fresh Cream** (99 Pacific Street, Heritage Harbor, 831/375-9798, $$$) and **Tarpy's Roadhouse** (2999 Highway 68, 831/647-1444, $$$). Fresh Cream serves French cuisine with a California touch (e.g., sautéed salmon on an artichoke puree), and it overlooks Monterey Bay, making it the most romantic dining spot in town. Chef Gregory Lizza has established a peerless reputation and has earned every possible accolade. It has been voted "Best Restaurant in Monterey County" for seven years running by readers of *San Francisco Focus*. Entrées are always inventive, and the restaurant begs repeated visits to properly sample such memorable preparations as sautéed halibut with sweet onion sauce, cabernet re-

duction and infused oil, and pan-seared ahi tuna with pineapple rum sauce.

Tarpy's Roadhouse serves up hearty American fare a few miles outside of town, on the road toward Salinas. Chef Michael Kimmel calls his approach "creative American country," which fortunately does not exclude seafood. In keeping with the quasi-rural setting, the menu choices are "from the ranch" (rabbit, veal, duck, beef) and "from the sea" (scallops, prawns, salmon). Seafood items from recent Tarpy's menus include salmon fillet with herb oil over asparagus and butternut squash risotto, and herb-crusted salmon with tomato-cucumber relish and lemon butter. The Dungeness crab cake and oak-grilled eggplant appetizers sent our taste buds soaring. Entrée-wise, they do things with rabbit that even magicians can't match. The oak-grilled ribs and bourbon-molasses pork chop are house specialties, but you're safe ordering any of the filling fare served here. There's even a meatloaf unlike any you've ever tasted; it's served with marsala-mushroom gravy on roasted-garlic whipped potatoes. The stone-house setting is as original as the eclectic art that lines the walls. The restaurant, incidentally, was named for Matt Tarpy, a local landowner from the 1800s who died protecting his property.

A favorite of locals is **Flavors Cafe & Grill** (807 Cannery Row, 831/646-8488), on Cannery Row. It's inexpensive and nonfranchised. Another well-kept secret beloved by locals is the **Trailside Cafe** (500 Wave Street, 831/649-8600, $), which is accessible only from the Monterey Bay Recreational Trail. It's a great spot for lunch or a cup of coffee, and you can eat inside or out.

For old time's sake we always take a meal at **Gianni's Pizza** (725 Lighthouse Avenue, 831/649-1500, $). The best way to find this institution is to follow your nose a few blocks up the hill from the dining dregs of Cannery Row. Family-owned and -run since 1974, Gianni's smells of homemade pasta, rich sauce, and fresh, oven-baked goods. While waiting for your pizza, try the

Canning Cannery Row

One path of history that you should avoid in Monterey is the one that leads through Cannery Row. Its past is indeed fascinating, but you will not find a genuine legacy here. With the shining exception of the Monterey Bay Aquarium, you will find a monument to bad taste and rampant consumerism. You will also find a degraded shopping zone that trades on the name of John Steinbeck so shamelessly as to sicken anyone who has read this great writer's work. You may find (as we did) money-grubbing Jesus freaks proselytizing on the street. You will certainly find anything and everything but a tribute to the hardworking blue-collar spirit of yesteryear.

Originally, Cannery Row was a line of packhouses where sardines were weighed, sorted, counted, and canned by guys and dolls who never dreamed that what they were doing to make ends meet would be glamorized decades later. The first canneries were built in the 1890s. By the late 1940s they were shut down because the bay and ocean were overfished and polluted. This was the place Steinbeck wrote about in his novel of the same name. Published in 1945, *Cannery Row* caught Monterey at the peak of its canning days, when 4,000 workers canned 237,000 tons of sardines in a year. Steinbeck saw Cannery Row as "a poem, a stink, a grating noise, a quality of light, a tone, a habit, a nostalgia, a dream. Cannery Row is the gathered and scattered, tin and iron and rust and splintered wood, chipped pavement and weedy lots and junk heaps."

This is not what exists along Cannery Row today. The shops here—many of which bear Steinbeck's name or a lame pun on one of his books' titles—are the sort of thing that you'd find at an amusement park: "old-fashioned" creamy fudge, jelly beans, and taffy. The "olde" arcade—one of the faithfully restored structures—has a depressingly musty feel. We witnessed a scene here that could have taken place at the sleaziest state fair sideshow.

Manning one of the booths was a gap-toothed, long-haired dude who was chatting with an equally disreputable-looking pal. He spotted a mother and her young kids coming his way. Suddenly assuming a loony expression and carny barker's voice, he importuned mom to shell out money to have her kids' likenesses emblazoned on a T-shirt or magazine cover. The clucking mom shooed her brood away from the affront, herding them toward a pie vendor.

Steinbeck expressed it best toward the end of his life, when he returned to see what had become of the Monterey he knew. "They fish for tourists now," he said forlornly. As if to echo Steinbeck's thoughts, on June 15, 1998, the National Trust for Historic Preservation named Cannery Row one of the nation's 11 most endangered historic places. In all fairness the city of Monterey has done what it can—putting up historic markers, offering tax incentives—but the developers can't be controlled. They are like rogue elephants that must be stopped. But how?

Map of Monterey County—Page 342

Monterey County

homemade garlic and cheese breadsticks—two or three of these will set you right! Gianni's is a family-style place in the very best sense.

Night Moves

Monterey will always hold a special place in the hearts of rock-and-roll fans. The first true rock festival took place here in 1967, later immortalized in the documentary *Monterey Pop*. Eric Burdon wrote a hit song about the event ("Monterey"), extolling the virtues of Flower Power two years before Woodstock. But the Monterey Pop Festival was a one-shot deal. It was the bastard son of the Monterey Jazz Festival, which is still held here each September at the Monterey Fairgrounds, a 24-acre field surrounded by oak trees. Blues fans gather for their own festival each June as well.

As for ongoing nightlife, Monterey holds the flickering candle for the entire peninsula. Those who just want to sip some unique suds should head to **Peter B's** (2 Portola Plaza, 831/649-4511, a microbrewery featuring six tasters for four bucks. Another option is "barking seal karaoke"; feel free to investigate.

The closing of Fort Ord—former home to thousands of restless military weekend party animals—has toned down the wildest excesses of Monterey's club scene. The two most viable venues for live rock and roll are **Doc's** (95 Prescott Street, 831/649-4241) and **Planet Gemini** (625 Cannery Row, 831/373-1449). Doc's, known for years as Doc Ricketts' Lab, is in the bottom of what was once the marine-life collecting lab of Doc Ricketts himself, the main character in John Steinbeck's Cannery Row. Besides being one of the few Cannery Row structures that has a legitimate connection with Steinbeck's legacy, Doc's features rock bands on a regular basis. The happy specimens who dance here nightly are a testament to the rejuvenating power of live rock and roll.

Sly McFly's Refueling Station (400-A Cannery Row, 831/649-8050) also offers live entertainment most nights and a full menu. Sly

has won "Best Blues Club" honors three years running—not that there's a slew of competition hereabouts for that particular niche. The area's most eclectic music venue (rock, blues, jazz, reggae) is the **Blue Fin Cafe** (685 Cannery Row, 831/375-7000), a third floor club-restaurant-pool hall that serves a decent full menu of burgers, pasta, and seafood and 22 types of beer. It also serves up a mixed bag of music, some live, some deejayed. For instance, Gene Loves Jezebel, a British New Wave band that was semi-obscure in this country even during its 1980s heyday abroad, was performing at the Blue Fin during our latest pass through the area. How many Gene Loves Jezebel fans, we wondered, could there be in Monterey in 2002? As regards the Blue Fin, we feel compelled to insert this disclaimer from a Monterey native who knows the nightlife inside and out: "It's a good place, but the service is just terrible. Every time I go there, I wish I hadn't—and I'm not hard to please."

We went to Planet Gemini to see an Eagles tribute band from Reno, Nevada. They were called Heartache Tonight (after one of the Eagles' songs), and they performed eerily accurate human-jukebox re-creations of the Eagles' old hits, bloodlessly studied right down to the 10-gallon hats they wore and the buzzard skulls and Old West totems that littered the stage. Some months later, one of us saw the Eagles perform on their overpriced, overhyped reunion tour. The upshot is that we paid a measly $3 to see Heartache Tonight play the Eagles' songs better than the Eagles did themselves for $100. Beyond all that Planet Gemini is a club in search of an identity, raving to techno and hip-hop one night and line-dancing to country music the next.

In downtown Monterey, we found a British-style pub, **Britannia Arms** (444 Alvarado Street, 831/656-9543), that proved to be a good spot to end a very long evening. It assuaged both our hunger pangs and our need to chill out after a full weekend of clubhopping. Decent

Map of Central California—Page 233

music was playing at reasonable volume as we ordered mugs of black and tan and plates of fish 'n' chips. So authentic were the grog and grub that we almost felt compelled to speak in faux British accents. Other popular downtown hangouts are **The Mucky Duck** (479 Alvarado Street, 831/655-3031), another British-themed pub; **Cibo** (301 Alvarado Street, 831/649-8151), an Italian restaurant and jazz bar renowned for its martinis; and **Viva Monterey** (414 Alvarado Street, 831/646-1415), a small but popular rock and roll club.

Monterey's nightlife is among the liveliest on the Central Coast. With part of Fort Ord

having been converted into a branch of the state university system, the town is hopping like never before. For an overview of Monterey's prolific club scene, pick up a copy of *Coast Weekly*, a free alternative weekly distributed all over the peninsula.

For More Information

Monterey Peninsula Chamber of Commerce, 380 Alvarado Street, Monterey, CA 93940, 831/648-5360, website: www.mpcc.com; Monterey Peninsula Visitors and Convention Bureau, 380 Alvarado Street, Monterey, CA 93940, 831/649-1770, website: www.monterey.com

Seaside

The town of Seaside straddles the coast between Monterey and Fort Ord like a fat flea sucking blood from its unwilling host. Believe it or not, Seaside (population 32,000) is actually as large as Monterey. In every other way, however, it is Monterey's inferior. The only reason a visitor would need to know about it is if you can't find lodging anywhere else on the Monterey Peninsula (see sidebar, "Full Moon over Monterey"). Full of one-star motels, fast-food stands, liquor stores, and a Super Kmart, Seaside looks like a Salvation Army warehouse for all the things that Monterey, Pacific Grove, and Carmel did not want.

Beaches

Parts of **Monterey State Beach** are in Seaside, on either side of the Best Western Monterey Beach Hotel. It's part of the same wild and windy beach that extends down from Marina, and you can't argue with the price—it's free.

For More Information

Seaside Chamber of Commerce, 505 Broadway Avenue, Seaside, CA 93955, 831/394-6501, website: www.centralbay.org

Sand City

Sand City is a tiny community of 184 souls on a narrow strip of sand between Highway 1 and the ocean. It was here that a planned 136-room oceanfront hotel and conference center was shot down by the California Coastal Commission in 1991, much to the consternation of locals in the tiny burg who'd hoped the hotel would aid their failing economy.

For More Information

Seaside Chamber of Commerce, 505 Broadway Avenue, Seaside, CA 93955, 831/394-6501, website: www.centralbay.org

Full Moon over Monterey

It was not our day. Or, should we say, night. Due to a clerical error on our itinerary, we showed up on the Monterey Peninsula late on a Saturday afternoon without hotel reservations. Every experience on the road, even a bad one, is useful to us in some way. The bad ones often turn out to be the most fun to write about. Besides, there are lessons to be learned from them. Perhaps you can benefit from our misfortune in this instance. The lesson is twofold: 1) Do not show up in popular vacation destinations on summer weekends without confirmed reservations; and 2) Double-check your itinerary for accuracy before leaving. Our botched Saturday night went down like this:

A day of reveling in the beauty of Big Sur had left us exhausted, so we were eagerly anticipating the turn of a key in a hotel room door and the opportunity to drop bags and collapse. Fatigue weighed heavy on us. Then we showed up in Monterey without a reservation and quickly found that the entire peninsula was booked solid. In Pacific Grove, Carmel, and Monterey the "No Vacancy" signs were glowing at every turn. Inquiries for advice on where to try next were met with words to the effect of "Go east, young men." East to Salinas, that is.

Salinas is a city 20 miles inland from Monterey. It is Steinbeck country, population 100,000. Imagine our surprise to discover that even the hotels and motels in Salinas were full. No room at the Comfort Inn. No room at fleabags with names like El Sombrero. One vacancy at the Holiday Inn Express: a smoking room with one bed for $105. No thanks; we weren't that desperate. We agreed that we would sleep in our car before paying $105 to pass the night in Salinas. We continued checking one motel after another. Upscale, low-rent, chains, independents—even a seedy property reeking of Indian curry. All were full. Packs of cowboys—or, rather, guys in cowboy hats—were hollering "yee-haw" in parking lots.

After an hour of chasing "No Vacancy" signs, we conceded defeat and swung out of Salinas. By now we were cruising past the broccoli fields of the Salinas Valley in a state of confused exhaustion as the day's final rays streaked the darkening night sky with a brilliant blaze of orange. We completed a circuitous loop through the area. We had begun in Monterey, proceeded to Salinas, and then headed northwest to the Castroville/Watsonville area before returning dejectedly to Monterey. This redundant trek added 100 pointless miles to our rental car. For the record, here are the main reasons we could not find a room:

1) It was the height of the summer season in Monterey—the 10th most popular tourist destination in California—on a Saturday that marked the first sunny weather in weeks.

Map of Central California—Page 233

2) Salinas was hosting the 85th annual California Rodeo that very weekend.

3) Laguna Seca State Park was the site of a car race.

4) Tourists, cowboys, and racing aficionados alike were all pressing upon the peninsula at the same time, and we were just two more bodies added to the overflow.

We tried the city of Marina, home to the decommissioned Fort Ord and now a virtual ghost town. The Travelodge, the Inn Cal—both large, both full. Grimly we drove south to Seaside, the town that sits like a boil on the ass of Monterey. There we found a strip of motels—good, bad, and ugly—flashing "No Vacancy" signs. The proprietor of one flyblown dive, chattering on a cell phone, said he'd heard there was one room left at another fleabag across the way. "Go, go!" he urged. Alas, we moved too slowly. Some other sucker snapped it up.

Good fortune smiled on us at last. The Bay Breeze Motel had one room left. One bed, $65. The room was spartan but clean. It would do. We made haste to throw the mattress on the floor, instantly creating two beds—and certain backache for the unlucky dupe who had to sleep on the box springs. We flipped for it. In no time we'd turned the motel room into a crash pad. It was like being in college again. We rested on our respective mattresses, heads reposing on thin, lifeless pillows as we reflected on the automotive nightmare of the last several hours. This is the darker side of traveling, the part where you pine for the comfort and safety of your bed back home.

Bay breezes blew cooling gusts of air through the window. The same breeze also carried the sounds of a couple who were arguing in Spanish in the parking lot. They were joined in disharmony by another squabbling couple. "You got a attitude problem," the male half of couple number two bellowed. "I be taking care of that," he vowed in menacing tones.

What was going on? We looked up into the night sky and beheld a radiant full moon. That explained why all hell was busting loose. We weren't going to get to sleep anytime soon, so we headed into Monterey for a bite to eat. We parked along Cannery Row, disembarking just in time to watch a yuppie couple laying into each other on the street. He yelled something. She yelled something back. "Bullshit!" he screamed, backing her against a wall. People turned toward them and froze, as if playing "statues." A stray dog got into the act, adding a loud, reproving "woof."

Cannery Row offered a miserable choice of dining options: jelly beans, hot dogs, and fudge; overpriced and overdressed hamburgers at a sports bar; and Sly McFly's Refueling Station. (Who could eat at a place with so silly a name?) The cheap scents drove us up the street to a family-run Italian restaurant off Cannery Row. Refueled by an eight-topping pie, we made our way back to our motel in Seaside. We woke up to a new morning, sun shining brightly, and a fresh start.

Monterey County

Map of Monterey County—Page 342

Marina

Marina is most notable for being home to Fort Ord, which lays claim to 28,500 acres of prime California coastland. Until 1993, when Defense Department budget cuts forced the phased closing of the base, the army infantry training center was home to thousands of service personnel and their families. It also encompassed two golf courses, shopping centers, housing developments, and miles of beaches. Obviously, the departure of so many folks has taken a toll on the local economy. But it wasn't as bad as the pro-military forces projected. Tourism has picked up the slack.

They still have a ways to go on this count. The

 ## Waiting for Fort Ord

A decade ago, thousands of people suddenly disappeared from the Monterey Peninsula, and they were replaced by dreams of a beachfront paradise. That is to say, the Department of Defense closed Fort Ord, a U.S. Army base located between the towns of Seaside and Marina, in 1993. The 28,500-acre military installation was the home of the 7th Infantry Division. The combined population of personnel and their family members topped 35,000, making it the largest city on the peninsula. That nearly empty base now commands some of the most coveted real estate on the California coast, including four miles of beachfront property, an 885-acre chunk of which was to have become Fort Ord State Park by 1998. Unfortunately, that park is still not open, and the big plans for developing much of the rest of the base are on hold as well.

The reason: Fort Ord is one large toxic waste dump. Throughout Fort Ord—which was, after all, an infantry training base and battle simulation center—ominous portents can now be found, including razor fencing, concrete roadblocks, barbed wire, and countless "Restricted Area" signs. Also found off the beaten track here are grim warnings about unexploded bombs, rockets, mortar shells, grenades, and bullets, as well as chemical spills. The military housing is off-limits, too, and probably beyond rehabilitation because of lead-based paint and asbestos used in its construction.

Nonetheless, Fort Ord is currently home to 5,000 remaining military personnel, as well as 900 college students at California State University, Monterey Bay (CSUMB). Big plans are still afoot, including a giant New Urbanism–style community, like Disney-owned Celebration, Florida. The driving philosophy of New Urbanism is to undo all the mistakes of urban planning over the past half-century, which have brought only suburban sprawl and soulless "edge cities" and gridlocked car traffic. A New Urbanist Fort Ord, like a state park at Ford Ord's beach, is a swell idea. Let's just hope that when and if it comes to fruition that this newfangled community won't (like Celebration, Florida) be just another exclusive enclave for the wealthy. Meanwhile, the beach at Ford Ord is still off-limits, unless you walk in from either Seaside or Marina.

Map of Central California—Page 233

towns of Seaside and Marina, between which Fort Ord is sandwiched, are pretty shoddy, as is the military installation itself. But Fort Ord's decommissioning has, in some ways, turned out to be a good thing. In fact, the Monterey Peninsula might be better off in the long run. Already a new branch of the state university system, California State University, Monterey Bay, opened in the fall of 1995 on the site of the former army base. Also in the cards is the razing of an army housing area and its replacement with 350 new homes. Two 18-hole courses at Fort Ord now belong to the town of Seaside.

As for the four miles of beaches that belonged to the military, these will become part of Fort Ord State Park. When it opens to the public, it will be the largest of the 12 state beaches along Monterey Bay. Though the 885-acre park was scheduled to open in 1998, it is still closed. We were told the beach will open as a day-use area in two years and that it would be five years before a campground would be available.

Beaches

The best beach access at the moment is **Marina State Beach**. With the sand a golden brown, the dunes rising gently, and no jagged rocks along the shore, Marina State Beach is as close to the look of a Southern California beach as you'll find along Monterey Bay. If this shoreline is any indication, Fort Ord's beaches will be real show-stoppers when they are open to the public. During the summer, when temperatures hover around 100 degrees in the valleys and deserts to the east, Marina State Beach is packed with sunbathers. The surf here is too rough for swimming, and the wind whips ferociously at times, explaining the hang-glider ramp that sits atop a big brown whale of a dune at the beach's center. A 2,000-foot boardwalk leads across the dunes to the beach. It is a compelling place to stroll and learn about dune vegetation, as accompanying charts explain the "good" (sand verbena, primrose, sagewort, lizard tail) and the "bad" (Hottentot fig, European dune grass) vegetation. Most of the stuff on the "bad" list consists of exotic species that were introduced for purposes of dune stabilization but overran the place, altering native ecosystems.

For More Information

Marina Chamber of Commerce, P.O. Box 425, Marina, CA 93933, 831/384-9155, website: www.centralbay.org

Castroville

Castroville lies a whisper to the east of the beach. It's not on the coast per se, but it's close enough to merit mention. Besides, we're fond of artichokes, and Castroville (population 6,700) is the artichoke heart of America. "What we do here in Castroville is grow artichokes" is how a local chamber of commerce representative plainly put it to us. The entire town marches to the beat of a different vegetable. They are completely devoted to the 'choke, which is a tasty if unusual plant. (Actually, it's a flower.) Between Monterey and Half Moon Bay, we've enjoyed many a Castroville artichoke, dunking them in mayonnaise, butter, or vinaigrette as if they were green potato chips.

If you're in Castroville, you should stop and eat the artichokes. The main house of artichoke worship is the **Giant Artichoke** (11261 Merritt Street, 831/633-3204, $$). The cooks do everything that can be done to an artichoke. They serve it fried with garlic mayonnaise, steamed with butter, boiled into artichoke soup, placed atop beef patties with Monterey Jack cheese (the Castroville Burger), and baked into quiches. The smart way to go if you're a true devotee is the Artichoke Sampler, which offers a taste of everything. But don't pass up

Monterey County

Map of Monterey County—Page 342

Salinas: A Side Trip to Steinbeck Country

Though Salinas is not on the ocean, it makes a great day trip for visitors to the Monterey Peninsula, primarily because it is the hometown of John Steinbeck. The half-hour drive east on Highway 68 cuts through massive agricultural tracts and enters this pleasantly cluttered "cow town" at the heart of fertile Salinas Valley. The setting of many of Steinbeck's novels—including *East of Eden* and *Tortilla Flat*—Salinas is an authentic slice of Western life that has grown into a sizable city but has changed relatively little in atmosphere from the days when the author lived here.

The best place to start is the **National Steinbeck Center** (1 Main Street, 831/796-3833), a state-of-the-art museum devoted to the life of one of our greatest writers. In addition to having the definitive collection of Steinbeck artifacts, exhibits on his life, and guides to walking and driving tours of Salinas, the center has actual artifacts from the master's life. For example his camper, "Rocinante" (featured in one of our favorite road books, *Travels with Charley*), is on permanent display, as are stage settings that bring the other books to life. The museum is open 10 A.M.–5 P.M. daily; admission is $7.95 for adults and $5.95 for children ages 13–17. These prices, it seems to us, have been unduly inflated to take advantage of the Steinbeck centenary in 2002.

Not far away is **John Steinbeck House** (132 Central Avenue, 831/424-2735), the Victorian-era home dating from 1897 where Steinbeck was born (in 1902) and raised. In addition to the preserved shrine (entrance is free), a dandy little restaurant is on the premises. There are two seatings for lunch, at 11:45 A.M. and 1:15 P.M.; call ahead for reservations. Serious Steinbeck scholars will want to visit the **John Steinbeck Library** (350 Lincoln Avenue, 831/758-7311), a full-fledged public library with the author's archives housed in a separate wing. These include books, manuscripts, tapes, correspondence, clippings, and photographs. The library is open Monday–Saturday, and the archives are open by reservation only.

To celebrate its native son, Salinas holds an annual **Steinbeck Festival** the first week in August that includes lectures, films, tours, panel discussions, and live dramatizations of his work. Another wildly popular event in Salinas is the **California Rodeo,** held the third week in July. One of the nation's largest and most celebrated, the rodeo packs the peninsula every year.

Finally, for lovers of roadside oddities, check out the sculpture on the lawn of the Salinas Community Center (940 North Main Street). Created by Claes Oldenberg and entitled *Hat in Three Stages of Landing,* it features three cowboy hats, each weighing 3,500 pounds.

For more information on Salinas, contact the **Salinas Valley Chamber of Commerce,** 119 East Alisal Street, P.O. Box 1170, Salinas, CA 93902, 831/757-7611, website: www.salinaschamber.com.

the seafood entrées as well: calamari, snapper, you name it.

The produce and seafood in the area couldn't be fresher. We whiled away part of an afternoon at local produce stands, savoring the sights and smells of just-picked vegetables bulging in the bins. We felt healthier just looking at them. Of course we purchased artichoke-decorated T-shirts. Every year the town hosts the Artichoke Festival. Posters scattered around town urge support for various candidates for the title of Artichoke Queen. Would you believe that Marilyn Monroe won the title of Artichoke Queen back in 1947?

For More Information

Castroville Chamber of Commerce, 11272 Merritt Street, Castroville, CA 95012, 831/633-6545, website: www.centralbay.org

Moss Landing

There's not much to Moss Landing, a harborfront community of 500 in northernmost Monterey County. It is quickly passed through, unless you're hunting for beaches. Three state beaches—Salinas River, Moss Landing, and Zmudowski—lie within striking distance. So does another prominent coastal feature: Elkhorn Slough. It is a long slough that stretches seven miles inland, harboring a variety of wildlife. Visitors can tour it via guided sea-kayaking trips and marine biologist-led pontoon-boat tours. You'll see harbor seals, sea otters, shore birds, and more. For additional information, contact **Elkhorn Slough Safari** (831/424-3939). Moss Landing also has a safe T-shaped harbor that's used by pleasure boaters.

Beaches

Just south of Moss Landing, beach mavens will find **Salinas River State Beach.** It is a haunting, windswept location that is fairly inhospitable unless you come dressed and prepared for it. A wooden walkway leads from the parking lot to the beach. A sign warns "Swimming and Wading Unsafe," and the heavy chop on the water does look daunting. The beach is broad and sandy, with steep dunes. On one visit we saw a few intrepid anglers braving gale-force winds while a sailboat seemed on the verge of capsizing. All we saw on a return visit several years later was a shivering group of migrant workers and a clump of college coeds who were dancing in gale-force winds. The former were drinking and the latter grooving to boom-box music. The 518-acre **Salinas River Wildlife Refuge** adjoins the beach to the south. Though Salinas River State Beach occupies a very rural setting, the smokestacks of a nearby power plant are visible.

Next up is **Moss Landing State Beach,** which offers access to Elkhorn Slough, rewarding nature lovers with a close look at coastal wetlands. The beach itself is broad and windswept, the surf rough and dangerous, the view (onto power-plant smokestacks) not the best. But Elkhorn Slough is not to be missed.

The sign pointing the way to **Zmudowski State Beach,** the last beach in Monterey County, lies a few miles north of Moss Landing. Be forewarned: When you make the turnoff from Highway 1, you're still quite a ways from the water. The road to Zmudowski skirts fields of artichokes and Brussels sprouts. On the beach a sign warns: "Danger: Intermittent Waves of Unusual Size and Force." That is in addition to blasts of wind of unusual size and force. Zmudowski, like Moss Landing State Beach, is a good place for clamming and surfing. The only folks we saw on the beach, though, were a family trying to picnic while getting sandblasted silly. For your average beachgoer, Zmudowski really isn't worth the effort it takes to get there.

Monterey County

Coastal Cuisine

The hot spot for seafood in Moss Landing is **Phil's Fish Market and Eatery** (7640 Sandholdt Road, 831/633-2152, $$$). You can get charbroiled salmon, shark, ahi, albacore, halibut, and more, or grilled snapper, sole, sand dabs, and squid steak. The "lazyman's cioppino" is famous, as are the clam chowders.

Specialties at **Moss Landing Deli Cafe** (421 Moss Landing Road, 831/633-3355, $$) include squid and eggs, crab cakes, and deep-fried artichokes. Don't leave town without trying the oysters and prawns, served with homemade sauces, at **Moss Landing Oyster Bay** (413 Moss Landing Road, 831/632-0119, $$). Prices are fair, portions are large, and the ambience is local. The restaurant serves some of the best seafood in Monterey County, and the crab sandwiches (made with Dungeness crab) are a total treat.

For More Information

Moss Landing Chamber of Commerce, 8071 Moss Landing Road, P.O. Box 425, Moss Landing, CA 95039, 831/633-4501, website: www .monterey-bay.net/ml

Map of Central California—Page 233

© ROBERT HOLMES/CALTOUR

Chapter 8
Santa Cruz County

Santa Cruz County

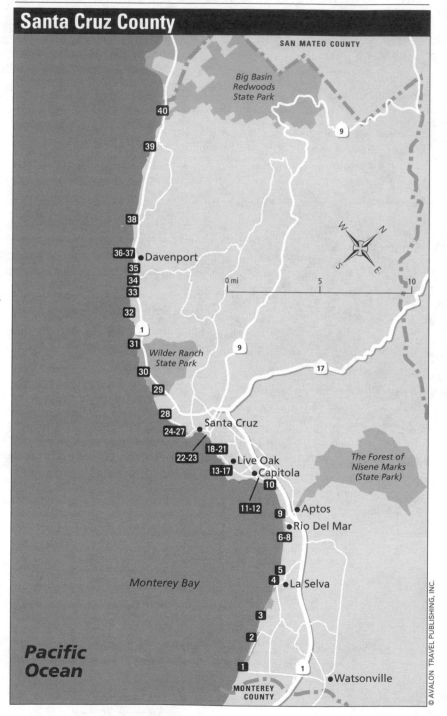

Santa Cruz County Beaches

■ Palm Beach (Sunset State Beach), page 410

🚴 🚶 ⛷ ③

Location: From Highway 1 in Watsonville, follow Beach Road five miles west to the beach.
Parking/fees: $3 entrance fee per vehicle
Hours: 7 A.M.–a half hour after sunset
Facilities: restrooms and picnic area
Contact: Sunset State Beach, 831/763-7063

■ Sunset State Beach, page 410

🚴 ⛺ 🚶 ⛷ ④

Location: From Highway 1 in Watsonville, turn west onto Sunset Beach Road and follow it to the beach.
Parking/fees: $5 entrance fee per vehicle. Camping fees are $13–16 per night, plus a $7.50 reservation fee.
Hours: 7 A.M.–a half hour after sunset
Facilities: lifeguards, restrooms, showers, and picnic tables
Contact: Sunset State Beach, 831/763-7063

■ Manresa Uplands (Manresa State Beach), page 410

⛺ 🚶 ④

Location: end of Sand Dollar Drive, off San Andreas Road, in La Selva
Parking/fees: $5 entrance fee per vehicle. Camping fees are $13–16 per night, plus a $7.50 reservation fee.
Hours: 7 A.M.–a half hour after sunset
Facilities: restrooms, picnic tables, and showers
Contact: Manresa Uplands State Beach, 831/761-1795

■ Manresa State Beach, page 410

⛷ ④

Location: end of Manresa Beach Road, off San Andreas Road, in La Selva
Parking/fees: $5 entrance fee per vehicle
Hours: 7 A.M.–a half hour after sunset
Facilities: lifeguards and restrooms
Contact: Manresa State Beach, 831/724-3750

■ Lundborgh Beach (a.k.a. Trestle Beach), page 410

⛷ ③

Location: Park at Manresa State Beach and walk north.
Parking/fees: none
Hours: sunrise–sunset
Facilities: none
Contact: none

Santa Cruz County

Map of Santa Cruz County—Page 400

6 Hidden Beach, page 411

Location: From Rio Del Mar Boulevard in Aptos, turn left on Townshend Drive and then left on Cliff Drive and follow it to the park.
Parking/fees: none
Hours: sunrise–sunset
Facilities: restrooms and picnic tables
Contact: Santa Cruz County Parks Department, 831/454-7900

7 Seascape Park, page 411

Location: From Rio Del Mar Boulevard in Aptos, turn left on Sumner Avenue and follow it to the beach.
Parking/fees: free parking lot
Hours: sunrise–sunset
Facilities: restrooms and picnic tables
Contact: Santa Cruz County Parks Department, 831/454-7900

8 Rio Del Mar Beach (Seacliff State Beach), page 411

Location: end of Rio Del Mar Boulevard in Aptos
Parking/fees: $5 entrance fee per vehicle
Hours: sunrise–10 P.M.
Facilities: restrooms and showers
Contact: Seacliff State Beach, 831/685-6500

9 Seacliff State Beach, page 411

Location: end of State Park Drive, off Highway 1, in Aptos
Parking/fees: $5 entrance fee per vehicle. Camping fees are $13–22 per night, plus a $7.50 reservation fee.
Hours: sunrise–10 P.M.
Facilities: concession, lifeguards, restrooms, showers, and picnic tables
Contact: Seacliff State Beach, 831/685-6500

10 New Brighton State Beach, page 412

Location: end of Park Avenue, off Highway 1, between Aptos and Capitola
Parking/fees: $5 entrance fee per vehicle. Camping fees are $13–16 per night, plus a $7.50 reservation fee.
Hours: sunrise–10 P.M.
Facilities: concession, lifeguards, restrooms, showers, and picnic tables
Contact: New Brighton State Beach, 831/464-6330

Map of Central California—Page 233

11 Capitola City Beach, page 414

Location: along the Esplanade, at end of Capitola Avenue, in Capitola
Parking/fees: metered street and lot parking
Hours: 24 hours
Facilities: lifeguards, showers, and restrooms
Contact: Capitola Public Works Department, 831/475-7300

12 Hooper's Beach, page 414

Location: foot of Wharf Road in Capitola
Parking/fees: metered street and lot parking
Hours: 24 hours
Facilities: none
Contact: Capitola Public Works Department, 831/475-7300

13 The Hook, page 416

Location: East Cliff Drive at 41st Avenue in Live Oak
Parking/fees: metered street and lot parking
Hours: sunrise–sunset
Facilities: none
Contact: Santa Cruz County Parks Department, 831/454-7900

14 Pleasure Point, page 416

Location: East Cliff Drive at 32nd Avenue in Live Oak
Parking/fees: metered parking lot and permit-only street parking
Hours: sunrise–sunset
Facilities: restrooms and showers
Contact: Santa Cruz County Parks Department, 831/454-7900

15 Moran Lake Beach and Park, page 416

Location: East Cliff Drive at 26th Avenue in Live Oak
Parking/fees: $5 entrance fee per car on weekends and holidays from Memorial Day to Labor Day; free parking at other times
Hours: 8 A.M.–sunset
Facilities: restrooms, showers, and picnic tables
Contact: Santa Cruz County Parks Department, 831/454-7900

16 Corcoran Lagoon Beach, page 416

Location: East Cliff Drive between 22nd and 23rd Avenues in Live Oak
Parking/fees: permit-only street parking

Map of Santa Cruz County—Page 400

Santa Cruz County

Hours: sunrise–sunset
Facilities: restrooms
Contact: Santa Cruz County Parks Department, 831/454-7900

17 Sunny Cove, page 416

Location: East Cliff Drive at 17th Avenue in Live Oak
Parking/fees: permit-only street parking
Hours: sunrise–sunset
Facilities: none
Contact: Santa Cruz County Parks Department, 831/454-7900

18 Lincoln Beach, page 416

Location: East Cliff Drive at 15th Avenue in Live Oak
Parking/fees: permit-only street parking
Hours: sunrise–sunset
Facilities: restrooms
Contact: Santa Cruz County Parks Department, 831/454-7900

19 Twin Lakes State Beach, page 421

Location: East Cliff Drive at Seventh Avenue in Santa Cruz
Parking/fees: metered street and lot parking
Hours: 8 A.M.–10 P.M.
Facilities: lifeguards and restrooms
Contact: California State Parks, Santa Cruz District, 831/429-2850

20 Santa Cruz Harbor Beach, page 421

Location: East Cliff Drive at Fifth Avenue in Santa Cruz
Parking/fees: metered street parking
Hours: sunrise–sunset
Facilities: concession, lifeguards, and restrooms
Contact: Santa Cruz Harbor, 831/475-6161

21 Seabright Beach (a.k.a. Castle Beach), page 421

Location: in Santa Cruz at the end of Seabright Avenue
Parking/fees: metered street parking
Hours: 24 hours
Facilities: concession, lifeguards, and restrooms
Contact: Santa Cruz Marine Safety Division, 831/420-6015

Santa Cruz County

Map of Central California—Page 233

22 Main Beach (a.k.a. Santa Cruz Beach), page 421

Location: in Santa Cruz along Beach Street, east of the Municipal Wharf
Parking/fees: metered lot and street parking
Hours: 24 hours
Facilities: lifeguards and restrooms
Contact: Santa Cruz Marine Safety Division, 831/420-6015

23 Cowell Beach, page 423

Location: in Santa Cruz along Bay Street at West Cliff Drive, west of the Municipal Wharf
Parking/fees: metered street and lot parking
Hours: 24 hours
Facilities: lifeguards and restrooms
Contact: Santa Cruz Marine Safety Division, 831/420-6015

24 Steamer Lane, page 423

Location: in Santa Cruz at Lighthouse Point off West Cliff Drive
Parking/fees: metered street parking
Hours: 24 hours
Facilities: none
Contact: Santa Cruz Marine Safety Division, 831/420-6015

25 Lighthouse Field State Beach, page 424

Location: in Santa Cruz at Point Santa Cruz along West Cliff Drive
Parking/fees: metered street parking
Hours: sunrise–sunset
Facilities: restrooms and picnic tables
Contact: Santa Cruz Surfing Museum, 831/420-6289

26 Its Beach, page 425

Location: West Cliff Drive between Lighthouse Field State Beach and Natural Bridges State Beach in Santa Cruz
Parking/fees: metered street parking
Hours: 24 hours
Facilities: none
Contact: Santa Cruz Marine Safety Division, 831/420-6015

27 Mitchell's Cove, page 425

Location: West Cliff Drive between Lighthouse Field and Natural Bridges State Beaches in Santa Cruz

Santa Cruz County

Map of Santa Cruz County—Page 400

Parking/fees: metered street parking
Hours: 24 hours
Facilities: none
Contact: Santa Cruz Marine Safety Division, 831/420-6015

28 Natural Bridges State Beach, page 425

Location: West Cliff Drive at Natural Bridges Drive in Santa Cruz
Parking/fees: $5 entrance fee per vehicle
Hours: 8 A.M.–sunset
Facilities: concession, restrooms, picnic tables, and visitor center
Contact: Natural Bridges State Beach, 831/423-4609

29 Wilder Ranch State Park, page 429

Location: two miles north of Santa Cruz, off Highway 1
Parking/fees: $5 entrance fee per vehicle
Hours: 8 A.M.–sunset
Facilities: restrooms and visitor center
Contact: Wilder Ranch State Park, 831/423-9703

30 Four Mile Beach (Wilder Ranch State Park), page 429

Location: four miles north of Santa Cruz, off Highway 1
Parking/fees: free roadside parking
Hours: 8 A.M.–sunset
Facilities: restrooms
Contact: Wilder Ranch State Park, 831/423-9703

31 Red, White, and Blue Beach, page 430

Location: Scaroni Road at Highway 1, seven miles north of Santa Cruz; look for red, white, and blue mailbox
Parking/fees: $7 entrance fee per person. Camping fees are $12–16 per night.
Hours: 10 A.M.–6 P.M. (4 P.M. in winter)
Facilities: restrooms
Contact: Red, White, and Blue Beach, 831/423-6332

32 Laguna Creek Beach, page 430

Location: Laguna Creek Road at Highway 1, seven miles north of Santa Cruz
Parking/fees: free roadside parking
Hours: 6 A.M.–10 P.M.
Facilities: none
Contact: Santa Cruz County Parks Department, 831/454-7900

Map of Central California—Page 233

33 Panther Beach, page 430

Location: off Highway 1, eight miles north of Santa Cruz; look for turnouts
Parking/fees: free roadside parking
Hours: 6 A.M.–10 P.M.
Facilities: none
Contact: Santa Cruz County Parks Department, 831/454-7900

34 Yellowbank Beach, page 430

Location: off Highway 1, eight miles north of Santa Cruz; look for turnouts
Parking/fees: free roadside parking
Hours: 6 A.M.–10 P.M.
Facilities: none
Contact: Santa Cruz County Parks Department, 831/454-7900

35 Bonny Doon Beach, page 430

Location: Bonny Doon Road at Highway 1, nine miles north of Santa Cruz
Parking/fees: free parking lot
Hours: 6 A.M.–10 P.M.
Facilities: none
Contact: Santa Cruz County Parks Department, 831/454-7900

36 Davenport Beach, page 431

Location: off Highway 1 in Davenport, 11 miles north of Santa Cruz
Parking/fees: free roadside parking
Hours: 6 A.M.–10 P.M.
Facilities: none
Contact: Santa Cruz County Parks Department, 831/454-7900

37 Davenport Landing Beach, page 431

Location: 13 miles north of Santa Cruz off Highway 1 in Davenport
Parking/fees: free roadside parking
Hours: 6 A.M.–10 P.M.
Facilities: none
Contact: Santa Cruz County Parks Department, 831/454-7900

38 Scott Creek Beach, page 431

Location: 14 miles north of Santa Cruz off Highway 1 in Davenport
Parking/fees: free roadside parking
Hours: 6 A.M.–10 P.M.

Santa Cruz County

Map of Santa Cruz County—Page 400

Facilities: none
Contact: Santa Cruz County Parks Department, 831/454-7900

39 Greyhound Rock Fishing Access, page 432

Location: Highway 1 at Swanton Road in north Santa Cruz County
Parking/fees: free parking lot
Hours: 6 A.M.–10 P.M.
Facilities: restrooms and picnic tables
Contact: Santa Cruz County Parks Department, 831/454-7900

40 Waddell Creek Beach, page 432

Location: one mile south of the San Mateo County line, along Highway 1
Parking/fees: $1 entrance fee per vehicle
Hours: 6 A.M.–sunset
Facilities: restrooms
Contact: Big Basin Redwoods State Park, 831/338-8860

Santa Cruz County

Map of Central California—Page 233

Santa Cruz County

For beachy symbolism you can't beat this fact: the first east-west road encountered in southern Santa Cruz County is called Beach Road, and it leads to Palm Beach. The beach due north of it is called Sunset Beach. Santa Cruz County is something of a throwback to the beachy mind-set of Southern California. You start seeing things like jailbait in bikinis, rowdy dive bars, a surfer's shrine and museum, a seaside amusement park, and people of all ages wearing anything from tentlike bathing suits to daring two-pieces to nothing at all. Yes, there's lots of nudity in Santa Cruz, especially on the remote north county beaches.

The coastline varies from upscale villages in the south to the boardwalk-town playland of Santa Cruz to the vastness and isolation at the north end of the county. The shapes and sizes of the beaches vary as widely as the people who populate them. There exists everything from tiny coves that only privileged handfuls know about to broad, sandy expanses where hard-fought volleyball games get played while surfers compete for wave-riding privileges.

Santa Cruz County is home to UC Santa Cruz and coastal playpen for the populated burgs of the Santa Clara Valley, located up and over the Santa Cruz Mountains. The city of Santa Cruz is one of the most liberated places on the planet, in terms of lifestyles. It's the urban equivalent of one of those "mystery spot" attractions where gravity doesn't behave the way it does elsewhere. (Perhaps not coincidentally, there is a mystery spot three miles north of town.) Cut off from the rest of the world by geography, Santa Cruz has evolved a distinct character of its own—one in which the alternative has become mainstream.

Santa Cruz County

Map of Santa Cruz County—Page 400

Sunset State Beach

Santa Cruz County is a wonderland of unspoiled beaches in jaw-dropping settings. Some are confined to coves, while others run for great distances along a regular shoreline. Beaches are pressed against staggering backdrops that include sheer cliff faces and steep, vegetated dunes.

The public beaches begin with Palm Beach. Taking the Beach Road turnoff from Highway 1, you'll traverse five miles of bumpy backroads that pass farmers' fields. **Palm Beach** (a unit of Sunset State Beach) is well off the beaten track and offers two completely different settings separated by a whale of a dune ridge. The first is a grove of eucalyptus trees whose limbs provide a fragrant canopy for a scattering of picnic tables. It is a calm, shaded environment protected from stiff winds by high, humpbacked dunes. Cross the dunes and it's a different scene: warm sun, wide sandy beaches, and breakers rolling ashore in perfect sets, urged along by seemingly ceaseless breezes. Palm Beach borders the Pajaro River Bike Path, a nine-mile route that runs along the watercourse that divides Santa Cruz and Monterey counties. Close by is Pajaro Dunes, a development of condos and homes too near this unspoiled beach for our liking.

Up the road lies the main entrance to **Sunset State Beach.** It has more facilities—paved parking lots, covered picnic tables, and developed campsites. A cliff-hugging road zigzags down to the campground and the beach. Cultivated fields border the park. Monstrous silver drift logs have washed ashore. Whether you're looking down at the beach from the vantage point of the bluffs or up from the water's edge, Sunset State Beach offers breathtaking scenery. It's lifeguarded and popular with day visitors and overnight campers alike. The surf, alas, is hazardous, but that doesn't deter crowds from frolicking on the ample strand.

For More Information

Sunset State Beach, San Andreas Road, Watsonville, CA 95076, 831/763-7062, website: www.parks.ca.gov

La Selva

A little community that's snug as the proverbial bug in a rug nestles off Highway 1 between the wilds of southern Santa Cruz County and the reappearance of civilization in Aptos. La Selva boasts its own public library and surf shop. You may see (as we did) handwritten signs urging you to slow down. You can't get to the beach directly from town, but a blufftop park offers a spectacular coastal overlook. We watched four horses and riders gallop around free as the breeze on the wide, sandy, private expanse below.

Beaches

Manresa State Beach is a dual-access park. The **Manresa Uplands** unit offers walk-in tent camping in a scrub-and-shrub setting and beach access from a smallish parking lot. Stretch those calf muscles before sallying forth, because 170 steps lead down the stairs to the beach. Crumbly, light brown sandstone bluffs loom behind the beach. The main entrance to Manresa is more accessible—a mere 55 steps down to the beach. Lots of folks surf and sunbathe and giggle in the sand.

Next up is private La Selva Beach, and above it is **Lundborgh Beach,** which lies in front of a train trestle. It is public, but you can get to it only by walking north from Manresa State Beach, being careful while crossing La Selva Beach, lest you rile the locals who own the property.

Map of Central California—Page 233

For More Information

Santa Cruz County Conference and Visitors Council, 701 Front Street, Santa Cruz, CA 95060, 831/425-1234 or 800/833-3494, website: www.santacruzca.org

Aptos

Eight miles south of Santa Cruz, Aptos is a study in contradictions. It's a charming, quiet village, and a bustling, harried town (population 9,500). It's a friendly place but one where people lose patience when something gets in their way. For example, shortly upon arriving in Aptos one slightly chilly July afternoon, we encountered: 1) a punk at Rio Del Mar Beach boxing a plastic barrier meant to keep cars off the beach while his friends clapped and cheered; 2) a blasé and unhelpful clerk at the local post office who sold us a cardboard box but adamantly refused to provide us a strip of tape to seal it; and 3) a typically impatient freeway flyer who leaned on his horn and flashed his lights because we apparently interfered with his God-given right to exceed the speed limit.

Nerves jangled by our brief foray into the part of Aptos that lies east of Highway 1—the part where all the strip malls are—we rolled down Rio Del Mar Boulevard's long incline, which deposited us on Rio Del Mar Beach. This side of Aptos is just what the doctor ordered—a flat, open beach; pretty neighborhoods tucked into green, viny hills; and a handful of motels and restaurants within view of the water.

Beaches

Rio Del Mar Beach is the center of the action in Aptos. Located at the end of Rio del Mar Boulevard, the sand is so wide you'll work your calf muscles into oxygen deficit traipsing across it to the water's edge. If you wish to escape the summer crowds, a turn from Rio del Mar Boulevard onto Summer Avenue or Townshend Drive will lead to **Seascape Park** and **Hidden Beach,** respectively. These two county parks plopped among residential developments merit the names "Hidden" and "Seascape." Parking is minimal—20 spaces at Seascape and 8 at Hidden Beach— but if you can snag a spot, you'll be rewarded with access to the less visited side of Aptos' lengthy strand. Both parks also have playgrounds and picnic tables.

Lying just a short, hikable distance west of Rio Del Mar Beach is **Seacliff State Beach.** This is the site of a real curiosity: the *Palo Alto,* an old World War I supply boat that never saw active duty and now serves as an extension of the fishing pier. Towed here in 1929, it was a kind of pleasure palace—dining, dancing, what have you—before going financially bust two years later and then literally breaking up in a storm. Lashed to the end of the fishing pier, it's open to visitors, who can mount a few rusty steps onto its deck and toss a line into the water or just poke around. The park is heavily used by anglers, picnickers, and campers. Commercial facilities include a bait-and-tackle shop and snack bar that dispenses homemade sandwiches. The beach is reached by a steep, winding road. It has 26 choice campsites with full trailer hookups right by the water, and you'd better believe they are rarely vacant. A bike path links Rio Del Mar and Seacliff State Beach.

Bunking Down

Beach lovers flock to the **Rio Sands Motel** (116 Aptos Beach Drive, 831/688-3207, $$), which takes pride in being "100 steps to the beach." Give or take a few footfalls, that seems accurate. An unusually comfortable motel, the Rio Sands is on a quiet side street. Some rooms are actually suites with small kitchens, comfy bedrooms, and living area with couch, TV, and balcony. An outdoor spa nestles in a peaceful courtyard garden. All that for $119–159 a night

Map of Santa Cruz County—Page 400

in season—a bargain (more so if you request an AAA discount). The **Seascape Resort** (1 Seascape Resort Drive, 831/688-6800, $$$$) perches on bluffs overlooking the ocean. As if the setting weren't sufficient, the resort gilds the lily with golf, tennis, spa, and other ways to drop a bundle.

Coastal Cuisine

For starters, Aptos has one of the finest restaurants in Santa Cruz County, the **Bittersweet Bistro** (787 Rio Del Mar Boulevard, 831/662-9799, $$$$). The look is casual elegance, the style is American bistro with Mediterranean influences, and the sauces and presentation are exquisite. Freshly caught seafood and organic local produce are highlighted.

You can't get any closer to the ocean than **Cafe Rio** (131 Esplanade, 831/688-8917, $$$), a modern-looking wood-and-neon place that has good fresh seafood and is a stone's throw from the beach. Then there's **Cafe Sparrow** (8042 Soquel Drive, 831/688-6238, $$$), a cozy continental hideaway that offers grilled chicken, lamb, veal dishes, and a solid wine list.

Night Moves

Most night moves are made in the direction of Capitola and Santa Cruz. Aptos maintains more of a village atmosphere than its noisy neighbors. Still, **Cafe Rio** (see "Coastal Cuisine") does have a nice bar and a semblance of life after dark.

For More Information

Aptos Chamber of Commerce, 7605-A Old Dominion Court, Aptos, CA 95003, 831/688-1467, website: www.aptoschamber.com

New Brighton State Beach

Between Aptos and Capitola is **New Brighton State Beach,** which is reachable via the Park Avenue exit off Highway 1. Signs point the way into a tree-shaded glen, beyond which lie high, grass-covered dunes and a flat, sandy beach. New Brighton, which faces due south, is spared the prevailing winds that mercilessly wrack other stretches of the Santa Cruz coast. This area was originally known as China Cove or China Beach, from a time in the late 1800s when Asian fishermen dragged the water with fishing nets. Tall beach grasses and thick, scrubby vegetation hold the steep dunes in place. At the foot of the dunes is a gravel road used by joggers, and hiking trails line the cliffs. New Brighton has a mile's worth of coastline, which is excellent for surf fishing and clamming. Behind the dunes, 112 developed campsites burrow beneath stands of pine and cypress.

For More Information

New Brighton State Beach, 1500 Park Avenue, Capitola, CA 95010, 831/464-6330, website: www.parks.ca.gov

Map of Central California—Page 233

Capitola

Many who work in Santa Cruz prefer to live In Capitola, Aptos, or Soquel, the upscale villages that lie just southeast of town. These seaside towns look like botanical gardens compared to parts of Santa Cruz. Capitola—or Capitola-by-the-Sea, to be accurate—is south of Highway 1 and east of 41st Avenue, a heavily trafficked road lined with shopping centers and gas stations. The easiest way to get to the heart of Capitola and its city beach is to take the Bay Avenue exit off Highway 1 and proceed south until you start smelling suntan lotion.

Capitola (population 10,000) is built around a broad, sandy cove. The Esplanade runs along the water, and Capitola Avenue parallels it for a few blocks. All the town's best shops, restaurants, and action can be found here. After a few laps around the shopping district, it becomes clear that Capitola is a melange of well-to-do young professionals, coffee-drinking bookworm/artist types, and beach bums and bunnies who have driven down for the day from UC Santa Cruz, San Jose, and points inland. Indeed, Capitola and Santa Cruz are the northernmost outposts of the classic California beach life.

There's only one snag when it comes to enjoying this cold-water Acapulco: parking. "Going to Capitola today?" a Santa Cruz merchant asked with raised eyebrows. "Good luck finding a parking space." Prepare to drive in circles and then pounce when a car pulls away from a meter. Considerable gas is wasted by a wagon train of frustrated drivers playing "musical parking spaces." There's a large, metered public lot on Capitola Avenue a few blocks from the beach behind City Hall (25 cents for half an hour, 8 A.M.–8 P.M. daily), but that too fills quickly and you may find yourself driving in circles waiting for someone to leave. Moreover, the spaces are too narrow to fully accommodate today's wide-body SUVs. If you're not up for an extended hunt for a parking space,

miles of state beaches run from Capitola down to the Monterey County line. Incidentally, we had the thought that being a tow-truck driver in Capitola would make a lucrative occupation.

There used to be a lot more beach in Capitola than there is now. The beach profile changed with the construction of jetties at the Santa Cruz Small Craft Harbor in 1985. Due to alterations in the littoral current, Capitola's beaches washed away that winter. Capitola City Beach was subsequently restored with trucked-in sand and protected by a jetty built south of Capitola Fishing Wharf. But that jetty has itself triggered a domino effect, starving beaches beneath the Grand Avenue cliffs (south of Capitola City Beach) and causing erosion and property loss. All of which goes to prove you'll never create anything but disaster by messing with nature.

Capitola is a pretty village, with attractive homes nestled into the hills and ravines along Soquel Creek. Way back in 1869 Capitola came to life as a campground retreat. In 1894 came the Grand Capitola, a palatial resort hotel comparable in its heyday to San Diego's Hotel del Coronado. Financial troubles prompted the hotel to close in 1929, and some suspected arson when a fire destroyed the building that December. Today, Capitola supports a modest tourist industry and entertains large numbers of Santa Clara Valley day-trippers fleeing the scorching summer heat. On nice weekends—and except for stormy winter days, just about all of them are—Capitola swells to overflowing. It's a great beach town in miniature, with a small, crescent-shaped public beach, modest 600-foot fishing wharf, and a lagoon near the mouth of Soquel Creek known as "Little Venice," where paddle boats are rented.

Beaches

We're a little concerned about Capitola. The beaches are shrinking, while traffic to and

Santa Cruz County

Map of Santa Cruz County—Page 400

people on them keep growing. Still, when it's healthy or recently replenished with sand, **Capitola City Beach** is one of the loveliest beaches in a county blessed with an abundance of them. Jam-packed with bodies, it attracts surfers, collegians, families, valley girls and guys, and more. The beach is about a quarter mile long and 100 yards at its widest point. At times every square foot is packed with sprawling, lounging bodies and volleyball players.

The surrounding shopping area is full of stores that display trendy merchandise (designer swimwear, arts and crafts) and tend to the hunger pangs of the perambulating beach crowd. You might see musicians playing for spare change or artists displaying their wares (e.g., watercolors of beach scenes) along the walkway by the beach. Occasionally the ocean water gets bacterially contaminated by runoff from Soquel Creek, but this is not usually a problem in the dry months of May through September. Generally, Capitola City Beach is clean and safe. Folks even hang out at night. Concrete benches line the Esplanade, and strollers come to breathe the salt air and meditate to the musical mantra of the sea's waxing and waning. One evening we spied a man wearing only a pair of red Speedos and a shower cap bolt across the beach on a mission: a midnight swim. Disbelieving spectators shouted advice and encouragement as the polar bear disappeared into the inky darkness where night and ocean meet: "Buddy, you're gonna freeze." "Go, go!" "Damn, he went in." He returned dripping wet but none the worse for wear, climbing into his van and turning on the heater.

Capitola also has another sandy crescent, known as **Hooper's Beach,** just west of its fishing wharf at the end of a stairwell. It's been dog-friendly since 2000, after the locals clamored for a legal beach for Fido to run on.

Bunking Down

Capitola isn't exactly a vacationers' mecca, but there are a few places to stay. Two are side by side near the Capitola Fishing Wharf, overlooking the beach and bay. One of them, the **Capitola Venetian Hotel** (1500 Wharf Road, 831/476-6471, $$), has an interesting history. It's next door to the Venetian Court, California's first condominium development. At the time of its construction in 1920, the word "condominium" didn't exist to describe the concept of individual ownership of apartment-style, stucco-and-tile cottages. Over the years the Venetian—at the mouth of Soquel Creek, an area known as "Little Venice"—has taken its share of direct hits during winter storms. Still, most owners seem determined to remain and rebuild, probably because you can't get any closer to the ocean or the heart of Capitola. And the units are beautiful, as are the flowery grounds around them.

Adjacent to the Capitola Venetian is the 10-unit **Harbor Lights Motel** (5000 Cliff Drive, 831/476-0505, $$), which provides balconies, deck chairs, and complete kitchens. If you don't mind not being right on the ocean, the **Inn at Depot Hill** (250 Monterey Avenue, 831/462-3376, $$$$) is a sumptuous bed-and-breakfast just up the hill.

Coastal Cuisine

All conversations about dining in Capitola inevitably begin and end with **Shadowbrook** (1740 Wharf Road, 831/475-1511, $$$), a romantic dining spot that's been around since 1947. Set along Soquel Creek in a quiet, residential part of Capitola, Shadowbrook serves seafood, prime rib, and other tasty fare in an elegant yet comfortable setting. Getting there is half the fun. To reach the restaurant you must park in a lot above it and then make the descent via a red cable car that's been a fixture since 1958. There are half a dozen different dining rooms, including the Wine Cellar and the garden-view Greenhouse. Speaking of wine cellars, Shadowbrook has an extensive one—amazingly, the restaurant lost only a bottle or two in the '89 quake, thanks to prescient earthquake-proofing only a year or

Map of Central California—Page 233

so earlier—and bartenders also mix some tasty liqueur-spiked coffee beverages.

Capitola is also home to a top-quality sushi restaurant called **Sushi Capitola** (820 Bay Avenue, 831/462-3381, $$$). Among the 20 or so rolls offered are the rock 'n' roll (eel, avocado, cucumber, fish eggs) and tuna kamikaze (tuna, avocado, fish egg).

If you're looking for gourmet takeout, head to **Gayle's Bakery and Rosticceria** (504 Bay Avenue, 831/462-1200, $). It's worth fighting the crowds to peruse the selection of sandwiches, salads, meats and cheeses, appetizers, and desserts.

As for the beach scene, **Ristorante Il Pirata** (201 Esplanade, 831/462-1800, $$$) is the place to be on busy weekends, by the look of the crowded deck and long line out front. With reasonably priced items like *pesce alla griglia* (grilled fish) going for $16.50, we can see why.

Night Moves

At night the area surrounding Capitola City Beach becomes a popular promenade. Several square blocks of Spanish-style stucco exteriors are bathed in cursive neon script. Couples stroll shoulder to shoulder with youths who wander between coffee shops, pizza parlors, and the beach. By 9 or 10 P.M., several mild-mannered restaurants make a Clark Kent–style changeover into nightclubs. Two old reliables are **Margaritaville** (321 Esplanade, 831/476-2263) and **Zelda's** (203 Esplanade, 831/475-4900). The former was the liveliest place we ducked into, having the decided plus of an outdoor deck overlooking the water. Down the street is Zelda's, a restaurant that offers live entertainment once the kitchen shuts down. One night we heard a local singer-guitarist have a respectable go at the blues.

For More Information

Capitola Chamber of Commerce, 716-G Capitola Avenue, Capitola, CA 95010, 831/475-6522, website: www.capitolachamber.com

Live Oak

The private community of Live Oak has a string of beaches—mainly larger named and smaller unnamed coves—between 41st Street in Capitola and the Small Craft Harbor in Santa Cruz. Live Oak is a leafy, tree-lined burg nestled between Capitola and Santa Cruz; it escapes most of those towns' traffic problems. On the other hand, East Cliff Drive can get pretty congested on weekends as surfers and beachgoers vie for limited parking. Their solution to this is a "parking by permit only" system. That is to say, you can't park at any of the Live Oak beaches without paying for a permit. They can be purchased from a white, parked van on East Cliff Drive at Ninth Avenue. It's marked "Parking Permits Sold Here." Nonresident parking permits cost $5 per day, $30 for the summer, and $20 for the rest of the year.

Beaches

Live Oak does its best to make the beachgoing experience difficult for outsiders. The following sign can be seen all along East Cliff Drive in Live Oak:

WELCOME TO LIVE OAK BEACHES
No Glass Containers
No Littering ($1,000 Fine)
No Alcoholic Beverages
No Fire On Beaches
No Camping
Dogs On Leashes
No Burning Pallets

If you can find parking and observe all the rules, this is a pleasant stretch of cove beaches, with benches overlooking the ocean from East Cliff Drive and paths or stairs leading

Santa Cruz County

Map of Santa Cruz County—Page 400

down to the sandy crescents below. Many are outposts for surfers and tidepoolers. Live Oak Beach is the most accessible and widest drape of sand hereabouts, but do have that parking permit in hand and good luck finding a spot.

Beaches can be accessed via paths or stairs at the ends of avenues along East Cliff Drive in Live Oak, between the Santa Cruz Small Craft Harbor and 41st Avenue. **The Hook** is a premium wave-riding spot at 41st Avenue; ditto for **Pleasure Point,** at 32nd Avenue. The bluffs above make a premium surf-watching spot as well. Around Pleasure Point lies **Moran Lake Beach and Park,** the next sizable drape of sand. People come here mostly to sunbathe and walk dogs; its flat expanse is protected from the wind by large rocks at either end. **Corcoran Lagoon Beach** is backed by the body of water that provides its name. Tidepools can be found on the east side, accessible from a path at East Cliff Drive and 21st Avenue. **Sunny Cove** draws bodysurfers and boogie boarders, while **Lincoln Beach** attracts picnickers and more contemplative sorts.

For More Information

Santa Cruz County Conference and Visitors Council, 701 Front Street, Santa Cruz, CA 95060, 831/425-1234 or 800/833-3494, website: www.santacruzca.org

Santa Cruz

Santa Cruz County

Santa Cruz marches to the beat of a different drummer. It is one of the most free-thinking, footloose, and liberal communities in the world. In order to decipher the various drumbeats, one really has to get to know the area, and that takes time. Although we pride ourselves on being able to accurately size up a town pretty quickly, Santa Cruz gradually unveils itself in layers, resisting hasty or expeditious conclusions. To understand Santa Cruz you must get in the flow and go with the flow. But which flow to go with? That's the problem.

The social geography of this city, like the physical terrain in the area, varies according to location. The municipal wharf, boardwalk, and main beach area, for instance, combine the Southern California beach-town mentality and the Jersey Shore boardwalk sensibility. Imagine Asbury Park, New Jersey, coupled with Huntington Beach, California. Surfing and volleyball rule on Cowell Beach, just west of the boardwalk by the Santa Cruz Municipal Wharf. Beach volleyball games go on from sunup to sundown on this favored spot, where world-class volleyball tournaments are staged. Meanwhile, surfers vie for large, tubular waves that roll ashore on this south-facing beach.

We witnessed a scene at Cowell that will be forever emblazoned in our memories. Two young, curvaceous beach babes carrying surfboards forded the knee-deep mouth of the San Lorenzo River and then walked along Santa Cruz's Main Beach between West Cliff and East Cliff Drives. We watched incredulously as the girls, wearing only bikinis while most of the guys were zipped into wet suits, paddled out to the waves at Cowell Beach. What made this so remarkable was the fact that, on this windy afternoon in late March, the water temperature registered only 51 degrees. We'd always heard that 20 minutes exposure to 55-degree water provokes the onset of hypothermia. Deciding to test the waters, we waded in up to our calves. This brief immersion caused numbness followed by pain shooting up our legs. How did they do it? Is it a simple matter of growing accustomed to frigid water, or were these nubiles some sort of bionic aliens with surfboards? Forget the summer 2002 surfer-girl flick *Blue Crush;* these Santa Cruz hotties were the real deal.

A late-afternoon run along West Cliff Drive was more our speed. It is here that Santa Cruzans' intense pursuit of fitness can best be observed.

Map of Central California—Page 233

West Cliff Drive is an ideal place for strolling, running, skateboarding, in-line skating, dog-walking, surfing (and surfing-as-spectator-sport), people-watching, and reverent contemplation of one of nature's grandest temples: the wild, steep, and fluted edge of the Pacific Ocean. For all these reasons West Cliff Drive is one of the can't-miss highlights of the California coast. Seemingly everyone has a bicycle, surfboard, skateboard, or "animal companion" in tow. Those that don't are jogging or gazing meditatively upon the ocean from park benches.

West Cliff Drive follows the undulating coastline of Santa Cruz, with steep, indented cliffs and cove beaches at their bases. Signs read "Warning! Cliff Edges Are Dangerous," as if the danger weren't self-evident. Protective steel barriers keep the public from getting too close to the edge along some sections of West Cliff Drive. This is the site of Steamer Lane, one of the most legendary surf spots on the West Coast. Surfers by the score bob atop boards at various localized breaks, tightly clustered and divvying up rides according to a rigid pecking order. Small pocket beaches (e.g., Its Beach) can be accessed via stairways, and these are particularly popular with dog owners. In fact, it's a veritable canine free-for-all on some of these sandy crescents, as they bark and bask and scamper and test the water and check one another out.

The other part of Santa Cruz where the social geography's a little different is downtown along Pacific Avenue. This is where the town's alternative heart and soul beats loudest. It lies at the figurative intersection of Woodstock Nation and Desolation Row. The area is known as Pacific Garden Mall, and it is Santa Cruz's answer to Venice, California, or the Lower East Side of Manhattan. Here, penniless urban bohemians must countenance increasing incursions by upscale merchants. Franchises for the upwardly mobile like The Gap lie close to bars and coffeehouses where the less prosperous nurse their mugs for hours. Out on the street the downright destitute congregate in packs or mill solitarily. Human nutcases can frequently be seen muttering and gesticulating wildly to no one in particular. Santa Cruz is benignly tolerant of its homeless population, and they are a fact of life here, though we've detected increasing rancor on the subject.

Some of the kids who aren't yet homeless look as if they're apprenticing at it. You'll find more wool caps on the streets of Santa Cruz than anywhere this side of Saskatchewan. There are also acres of tattooed skin, sadistic metal piercings, hair sprouting from every orifice (though often shaved right off the head), oversized thrift-shop clothing, lit cigarettes, and vacant or malcontented stares. These are the visible retorts of the economically disfranchised—some by circumstance, others by choice. All the same, Pacific Avenue has received a partial makeover during the dot-com and Dow-driven prosperity of the 1990s. Lights have been strung in the trees that line the street, making nighttime glimmer like Christmas, and big construction projects bring new parking garages and office space to downtown Santa Cruz. All of this makes the contrast between the high and low end, with relatively little in between, that much more pronounced. A *New York Times* article from 2002 reported Santa Cruz's housing crunch and skyrocketing prices for real estate, with extremely modest one-bedroom "starter homes" going for $450,000. Even though the dot-com bubble has burst, Santa Cruz remains an almost prohibitively expensive place to live. How does a student or surfer dude make ends meet here?

Even though its essential character was severely altered by the dot-com revolution, Santa Cruz remains a very determined eddy swirling against the American mainstream. It is indeed a puzzling, intriguing, and contrary place—even Highway 1 can't make up its mind what to do, boldly entering the city from the south and then becoming a confusing maze of turns and exits. Suffice it to say that Santa Cruz—which means "Sacred Cross"—is many things.

Santa Cruz County

Map of Santa Cruz County—Page 400

Scenes from Santa Cruz

A community as fluid and freewheeling as Santa Cruz is hard to explain. That is to say, it can't truly be "captured" in a conventional essay. So we're offering this mosaic, based on things we saw and heard during our most recent visit.

A homeless man who looks like Popeye begs for change from a guy with his nose buried in a book at a sidewalk café. The bookish coffee-drinker ignores the pleading, which prompts the bum to press his case even harder. A middle-aged earth mother at another table chides the homeless man for bothering the coffee-drinker who wants to be left alone. She then hands the bum some change and they say "God bless you" to each other. Another homeless man, who's muttering nonsense as he drifts down the sidewalk, pauses to lean over the rail and purr "You're beautiful" to a college girl, who scowls and looks disgusted.

Two extremely hirsute hippies in ponchos and jeans are playing the Beatles' "Across the Universe" on flute and guitar for strollers on Pacific Avenue in downtown Santa Cruz. Up the street, by a faded old Volkswagen van whose door has been slid open, one hippie dude strums madly on an acoustic guitar while his pal bangs time on the VW's side panel. Over in Capitola, yet another musical duo is trolling for change by playing spacy fare like Pink Floyd's "Wish You Were Here." A smoldering cigarette hangs from the heavy-set keyboardist's lips.

Three sushi chefs at a popular Japanese restaurant take a break from their knives to admire a vintage automobile that has entered the parking lot. "Wow . . . a 1968," one exclaims before they resume with the tuna fillets and rice balls.

A lanky fellow sporting a giant plastic pig nose pedals a bicycle down Front Street. He is wearing a white sanitation worker's uniform. The words "Make Your Mark" are scrawled on the back in green paint.

Santa Cruz's answer to the Addams Family enters a restaurant at dinner hour. The glowering, taciturn father has the rugged, unsmiling demeanor of a bounty hunter. The tall, witchy mother sports black capri pants more appropriate to a teenager's figure. A silver ring pierces the goth-girl daughter's lower lip, and a web of longshoreman's tattoos covers every inch of her arms. And you thought the Osbournes were a case study in psychopathology.

"Everybody's being nice and mellow out there in traffic today," exclaims a deejay on a jam-packed Sunday afternoon. "There's been some fender-benders down in Monterey, but nothing to report in Santa Cruz. Keep it up!"

Map of Central California—Page 233

A couple of teenage boys are attempting the pointless feat of riding skateboards down a narrow rail that runs beside Longs Drugs. Not surprisingly, one takes a hard fall and winds up face down on the sidewalk, writhing in pain.

A spare-changer on a park bench is deep in conversation with another bum. He earnestly entreats, "Why are all the whores suddenly going to church?"

A local weekly asks people on the street a timely, topical question and prints selected responses. Recently they queried, "Has the sex scandal involving priests affected your view of the Catholic church?" A UC Santa Cruz student's reply: "I think they are using the scandals to create a media hype to distract people from the real issues of war."

Over on Santa Cruz Boardwalk, a cross-section of humanity mills around the arcade and food stands. They range from morbidly obese women with braying children tugging at their beefy thighs to a tie-dyed, salty-dog old hippie smoking a cigarette and staring into the cosmic void. The screams of riders being hurled around the Hurricane compete with the accompanying strains of "Hanky Panky," by Tommy James and the Shondells.

Two hip, young German couples check into a motel on Ocean Street, overpaying without complaint. Do these fun-seeking foreigners head for the beach and boardwalk? No. They are later spied huddling around the two-star motel's tiny, kidney-shaped pool, looking bored and confused.

Three surf bums are carrying surfboards from their cheap, utilitarian motel room. With visions of Steamer Lane no doubt dancing in their heads, they climb into a van, turn the key in the ignition, and—nothing. Dead battery. Someone left the interior light on all night long. Talk about a turn-down day.

A young boy is marching ahead of his family toward the ocean, proudly carrying a toy boat. He suddenly drops the boat, holds his nose and exclaims, "PU! It smells like the beach."

Signs of the Times:
• "Trespassers will be eaten." —sign on a chain-link fence surrounding a house near the beach
• "MUMI NATION . . . Santa Cruz art phunk . . . bring beer goggles, photon beams, and dancing shoes . . . $3." —flyer affixed to telephone pole
• "Free" —one-word offer taped to discarded box springs propped against a fence
• "No Skateboarding." —a jagged line has been scratched through these words with a key on a sign listing forbidden activities in a hotel parking lot
• "Is It Too Old-Fashioned to Have Integrity?" —Santa Cruz graffiti

Map of Santa Cruz County—Page 400

It's a patchwork of lifestyles, politics, land-forms, and roads that converge to make up the largest seaside resort north of Santa Barbara. The base population of 55,000 swells on week-ends with crowds from Silicon Valley, San Jose, and San Francisco.

From the start the town was marked by mys-terious events. The mission built here in 1791, Mission la Exaltacion de la Santa Cruz, van-ished without a trace. It was somewhere near the San Lorenzo River and was perhaps swal-lowed by it. To this day the river is subject to destructive flooding. A replica of the mission has been built outside of town, but few go out of their way to see it. That is just as well, be-cause Santa Cruz turned away from spiritual matters in 1865, when the first public bath-house was built on the beach.

A boardwalk, dance hall, and casino were added, bolstered by a lucrative logging econ-omy that transformed the quiet town into a re-sort. A roller coaster and carousel followed. The crowds began arriving when the railroad company feverishly promoted a "Suntan Spe-cial," which deposited visitors from San Fran-cisco and San Jose on the main beach at Santa Cruz. This inspired railroad stations to be built up and down the coast, paralleling what is today Highway 1. The original roller coaster and carousel—the latter with beautiful mounts designed and painted by Charles Looff in 1911—are still in service, and many of the fine Vic-torian homes of the logging moguls still stand.

The San Lorenzo River snake-dances through town before emptying into the ocean south of Main Beach. Santa Cruz is a busy proletarian beach resort at this end of the river. Upriver, Santa Cruz is more upscale and suburban. Everywhere else, the town is a hotbed of lib-eralism and laissez-faire lifestyles. New Age free-thinkers seem to hold sway here to a greater degree than any other community in America (save, perhaps, Bolinas). We took a politi-cal/philosophical reading from two bumper stickers spied on different cars within minutes of each other: "Visualize Industrial Collapse" and "Never Drive Faster Than Your Angel Can Fly."

Still, for a supposedly peaceable haven, you don't always feel safe in Santa Cruz, especial-ly after dark. The city has an underside, as do most places where eccentricities are not only tolerated but encouraged. We overheard un-nerving snatches of conversation around town on such subjects as "urban warfare." You'll see squadrons of loiterers affecting a punky-hippie look that bespeaks poverty and defi-ance. It's the same all over: tousled cataracts of hair spilling out from under wool caps; morgue-like black clothes draped over hunched shoulders; wispy nature trails of facial hair; metal piercings affixed to lips, nostrils, cheeks, and other anatomical parts. One night, we spied a gaggle of such specimens gathered out-side a club where a band was mangling a Jimi Hendrix song—all too appropriately, "I Don't Live Today."

Here's a scene we'll never forget. One af-ternoon, we watched a '60s acid casualty offer running, unsolicited commentary on a young street musician's performance: "It's not that you can't play, man. You play pretty good. It's just that you're not utilizing your talent to any creative, original purpose." The fact that the singer was wearing a red clown's nose as he strummed his earnest folk tunes lent some cre-dence to the hippie elder's critique.

The liberal melting pot in this left-of-center burg is the University of California, Santa Cruz, which occupies a green, 2,000-acre campus northeast of town. Founded in 1965, UC Santa Cruz is set on a former cattle ranch that's now home to an arboretum of rare plants and groves of redwood trees. The buildings are hidden among the trees, making this one of the best-concealed institutions of higher learning on the planet. The sports mascot is the banana slug, the campus restaurant is called the Whole Earth (serving "Thai-style Tofu and Veggies"), narra-tive evaluations are given instead of grades, and

Map of Central California—Page 233

courses have borne names like "The Pursuit of Truth in the Company of Friends" and "Female Masturbation." All levity aside, it is heartening to find a university that isn't just a mill for business degrees. Student-led tours are available through the admissions office Monday–Friday; for reservations call 831/459-4008. To get to UC Santa Cruz, take Highway 1 to Bay Street, then head north and follow the signs. And now, follow us to the beaches of Santa Cruz.

Shore Things

• **Bike/skate rentals:** Bike Rental Center, 131 Center Street, Santa Cruz, 831/426-8687
• **Dive shop:** Aqua Safaris Scuba Center, 6896 Soquel Avenue, Santa Cruz, 831/479-4386
• **Ecotourism:** Venture Quest, 125 Beach Street, Santa Cruz, 831/427-2267
• **Marina:** Santa Cruz Harbor, 135 Fifth Avenue, Santa Cruz, 831/475-6161
• **Pier:** Santa Cruz Municipal Wharf, Beach Street, Santa Cruz, 831/420-6025
• **Rainy day attraction:** Santa Cruz Surfing Museum, Mark Abbott Lighthouse, West Cliff Drive, Santa Cruz, 831/429-3429
• **Shopping/browsing:** Pacific Garden Mall, Pacific Avenue, Santa Cruz
• **Sportfishing:** Santa Cruz Sportfishing, North Santa Cruz Harbor, Dock H, Santa Cruz, 831/426-4690
• **Surf report:** 831/464-3233
• **Surf shop:** Santa Cruz Surf Shop, 753 41st Avenue, Santa Cruz, 831/464-3233
• **Vacation rentals:** Bailey Properties, 106 Aptos Beach Drive, Aptos, 831/688-7009

Beaches

Santa Cruz has numerous beach-access points, though some are in residential areas with limited parking. Only savvy locals know about some of the more hidden coves, and each beach seems to be claimed by a different crowd. Starting on the east side of town, **Twin Lakes State Beach** is a popular 86-acre park that lies between Corcoran Lagoon and the **Santa Cruz**

Harbor Beach, at Santa Cruz Small Beach Harbor. On the west side of the yacht basin is **Seabright Beach**—though sentimental locals still prefer the name **Castle Beach**—where the most popular pastimes along the mile-long strand are volleyball by day and bonfires at twilight. There's a small lighthouse at the east end and a rock jetty. Nice, tubular waves break on a sloping, brown-sand beach. There are plenty of families, lots of room, and a little concession stand out here. We couldn't help but notice, however, that the sand is littered with charred wood chips from beach bonfires.

Despite all the attractive options that lie east of the San Lorenzo River, you'll probably wind up on **Main Beach** if you're not a local. As the name suggests, it's the longest and widest strand in town—the "main" beach—and it fronts the famed Boardwalk. Accommodations are clustered close by. Touristy though it is, Main Beach and the Boardwalk should be strolled and experienced. It's a real slice of life and a full-tilt funtime arcade unique along the West Coast.

The **Santa Cruz Boardwalk** has been spruced up since the 1980s. Back then it looked like the setting for a Bruce Springsteen song about hard times on the Jersey shore. Today it's much improved. Neptune's Kingdom, a clean if generic arcade, is a recent addition. Parents can toss down schooners of beer upstairs while their progeny destroy galaxies on video games downstairs. A "historium" justifies the nautical motif with a few educational placards. Outside in the bright sun, beach bums have their pick of things to ride, eat, and play, including our old boardwalk favorite, Skee-ball. We copped some plastic skull rings this time out.

The Sky Glider ski lift carried us high above the frivolity, providing an incredible panorama of the town, beach, and ocean. Caterpillar cars dipsy-doodle on the roller coaster next door, allowing total strangers to share moments of gleeful terror. A multitude of food stalls sell typical beach fare, and an equally

Santa Cruz County

Map of Santa Cruz County—Page 400

Best of Santa Cruz

Our most recent visit to Santa Cruz coincided with the publication of "The Goldies"—a listing of readers' best-of's for 2002 in numerous categories, compiled by the city's excellent arts and entertainment weekly, *Metro Santa Cruz*. We've written about places and things we like in Santa Cruz, so now we'll turn the podium over to the folks who actually live there. Here are Goldies awarded in selected categories, reprinted from *Metro Santa Cruz*. All are in Santa Cruz, unless otherwise noted.

Beaches/Outdoors

Best Beaches: Seabright, Main Beach, and Natural Bridges
Best Bike Rides: West Cliff Drive, Wilder Ranch, and Forest of Nisene Marks
Best Bird-watching Spots: Elkhorn Slough, Natural Bridges, and Neary Lagoon
Best Hiking Spots: Wilder Ranch, Forest of Nisene Marks, and Pogonip
Best Sunset-watching Spots: West Cliff Drive, Natural Bridges, and Porter Meadow
Best Surf Spots: Steamer Lane/Cowell Beach, Pleasure Point, and The Hook
Best Surf Shops: O'Neill, 110 Cooper Street, 831/469-4377; Pacific Wave, 1502 Pacific Avenue, 831/458-9283; Santa Cruz Surf Shop, 753 41st Avenue, Capitola, 831/464-3233; and (tie) Paradise Surf Shop, 3961 Portola Drive, 831/462-3880

Nightlife

Best Bars: Club Dakota, 1209 Pacific Avenue, 831/454-9030; Red Room, 1003 Cedar Street, 831/426-2994; and Crow's Nest, 2218 East Cliff Drive, 831/476-4560
Best Microbreweries: Seabright Brewery, 519 Seabright Avenue, 831/426-2739; Santa Cruz Brewing Company, 516 Front Street, 831/429-8838; and Boulder Creek Brewery, 13040 Highway 9, Boulder Creek, 831/338-7882

large number of rides will help you lose it. The rides have names like Giant Dipper and Chaos. One spinning capsule holds riders suspended upside down at its apogee for several seconds, then flings them back to earth in a frightening blur. Do people really pay for this sort of torture? Apparently so, judging from the crowds, laughter, and screams. If you're buying by the ride, these stomach churners can add up, so go for a day pass. In sum, Main Beach is a classic boardwalk scene that from a distance— say, from Lighthouse Point or Municipal

Wharf—conveys an airy, nostalgic quality, almost like it's been frozen in time.

If boardwalk revelry isn't your kids' idea of fun, two options remain. First, lengthy psychological testing. (What child doesn't love being suspended upside down a hundred feet above the ground?) Second, take the **Santa Cruz Steam Train.** It's a turn-of-the-century locomotive that leaves from the back of the boardwalk arcade and travels inland through a redwood forest and along the San Lorenzo River canyon. It stops at Roaring Camp, a former gold-min-

Map of Central California—Page 233

Best Dive Bars: Rush Inn, 113 Knight Street, 831/435-9673; Asti, 715 Pacific Avenue, 831/423-7337; and Brady's Yacht Club, 413 Seabright Avenue (no phone)
Best Happy Hours: El Palomar, 1336 Pacific Avenue, 831/425-7575; Crow's Nest, 2218 East Cliff Drive, 831/476-4560; and Seabright Brewery, 519 Seabright Avenue, 831/426-2739
Best Live Music Clubs: The Catalyst, 1011 Pacific Avenue, 831/423-1336; Moe's Alley, 1535 Commercial Way, 831/479-1854; and Kuumbwa, 320-2 Cedar Street, 831/427-2227
Best Places to Dance: Blue Lagoon, 923 Pacific Avenue, 831/423-7117; The Catalyst, 1011 Pacific Avenue, 831/423-1336; and Club Dakota, 1209 Pacific Avenue, 831/454-9030
Best Singles Bars: Blue Lagoon, 923 Pacific Avenue, 831/423-7117; Club Dakota, 1209 Pacific Avenue, 831/454-9030; and Crow's Nest, 2218 East Cliff Drive, 831/476-4560

Restaurants

Best Coffeehouses: Union, 120 Union Street, 831/459-9876; Cafe Pergolesi, 418 Cedar Street, 831/426-1775; and Starbucks (various locations) (What, the generic chain Starbucks over Santa Cruz Coffee Roasting Company? What's going on here?!)
Best Seafood: Riva Fish House, 500 Municipal Wharf, 831/429-1223; Crow's Nest, 2218 East Cliff Drive, 831/476-4560; and Stagnaro's, 59 Municipal Wharf, 831/423-2180
Best Sushi: Mobo Sushi, 105 River Street, 831/425-1700; Shogun, 1123 Pacific Avenue, 831/469-4477; and Takara, 1800 Soquel Avenue, 831/457-8466

Miscellaneous

Best Place to Be Hassled by Homeless People and Then Have Your Tax Money Go to Put Them Up for the Night: Santa Cruz

ing area. It's a great half-day excursion. (Call 831/335-4484 for fares and schedules.)

At the north end of the oceanfront, on the other side of the municipal wharf, is **Cowell Beach.** Years ago, a Miss California pageant held here had to be canceled because spectators pelted the contestants and each other with raw meat. Now the main competition at Cowell is an annual volleyball tournament. Volleyball and surfing rule at Cowell. It's almost an unstated imperative that you must be doing something athletic on this beach. Few just lie around.

Some of the best surf California has to offer can be found above Cowell Beach, along West Cliff Drive at a rocky area called **Steamer Lane.** Only the best and bravest surf here, because the swells reach mountainous heights and threaten to hurl their fearless riders against the cliff bases or fillet them on rocks that barely jut above the surface. Surfers who aren't in the water sit on the rocks, waiting their turn. Everyone else stands on the edge of an eroding cliff, watching nervously, taking photographs, and creating an intimate community based on fear

Map of Santa Cruz County—Page 400

or sadism. Waves slam against the shore, sending spray upward. Before the fence was erected, onlookers were occasionally washed over the edge to their deaths.

The state allocated funds to create **Lighthouse Field State Beach,** a 10-acre open space that overlooks Steamer Lane. This spared it from a threatened development (conference center and hotel), which galvanized Santa Cruz environmental groups. An integral part of Lighthouse Field—which stretches west of the bluffs—is the **Santa Cruz Surfing Museum,** in

Young and in the Way

Picture the scene: a bunch of gray, balding hippies sitting around agonizing about the problems of today's youth. Though this may sound like the plot to an ill-advised sequel to *The Big Chill,* it really happened in Santa Cruz.

If you thought the youth-culture tidal wave that created grunge was a tough nut to crack, get a load of the teens on the loose here. They aren't all spare-change artists (yet) or surf punks, like their big brothers were. They are, however, loud. They are angry, ugly, and bored. And they are everywhere, though they have no place to go. They are not allowed in the bars (too young). They are often refused service in the cafés (too scruffy). They are attracted to the rundown areas of beach communities such as Santa Cruz, where they can squat in quarters unfit for rental.

Youth-as-enemy should have a familiar ring in Santa Cruz, where the city council is made up of erstwhile hippies, socialists, and protesters who still wear the battle scars of their civil disobedience. Ponder the irony of aging hippies trying to bust the chops of today's youth. Underneath it all nothing has changed, really, except for the wardrobes. Thirty years ago it was long hair, tie-dyed T-shirts, headbands, patchouli, unkempt facial hair, bells, beads, and bangles. Now it's shaved heads, wool caps, jackboots, tattoos, pierced body parts, and grossly oversized clothing. Today's punks spray paint angry slogans on walls—often one-word epithets like "bile"—and hang out. Therein lies the rub. Santa Cruz is sick and tired of them hanging out.

This issue hit home at Vertigo, a downtown café. Angry homeowners claimed that petty crime and physical assaults in the neighborhood had increased. The youths allegedly pissed on lawns, sidewalks, and shrubbery, showing little respect for the mostly elderly residents. They dealt drugs and made noise. The owner was aware of the problems and took steps to cooperate with the police. But he can't solve society's problems, and alas, Vertigo was shut down by the city council's ex-hippies.

Such problems are, of course, not unique or new to Santa Cruz. For decades the town has been a repository for society's discards. But these youths, the old guard contend, are different. Nastier. More menacing. With no place to hang out, they're even more pissed off than usual. The problem has not been solved, just pushed aside—like the kids themselves.

Map of Central California—Page 233

the **Mark Abbott Lighthouse** (West Cliff Drive, 831/429-3429). Like the California Surf Museum in Oceanside, this is an imperative stop. Photographs adorn the walls—of people riding hollowed-out 16-foot longboards, of 19 surfers crammed inside a woodie—and videos and news clippings document the sport's rich history. The centerpiece is a shrine where the ashes of 18-year-old Mark Abbott are interred beneath a pile of rocks and shells. This young man challenged the sea and lost, but the war rages on at Steamer Lane. The bookshop here has a great selection of surf and beach publications. Interestingly, Lighthouse Point, on which it sits, is regarded as the northernmost end of Monterey Bay.

Nearby **Its Beach** is popular with dog owners, who are allowed to unleash their canines in the morning and evening. The same goes for **Mitchell's Cove**, another patch of sand that does a disappearing beach trick during winter months when storms scrub the shore clean. Most years it reappears when fair weather rebuilds the beaches.

If you're not yet beached out, follow West Cliff Drive to **Natural Bridges State Beach**, named for an offshore arch. Though no lifeguards patrol the beach, it's considered safe, and chaperoned tots wade giddily in the foaming waves. The 65-acre park includes trails through coastal scrub meadow habitat. Visitors can study marine life at **Joseph M. Long Marine Laboratory and Aquarium** (100 Shaffer Road, 831/459-4308), a working research facility with an aquarium full of sea urchins, sea sponges, abalone, anemones, and starfish. There's also a sea lion–viewing perch, as well as the skeleton of a blue whale. It's a cheap way to educate the kids and learn something yourself. (The laboratory is open Tuesday–Sunday 1 P.M.–4 P.M.)

West Cliff is the best place in town to walk, run, bicycle, skateboard, in-line skate, watch surfers, observe sunset, meditate, contemplate, exercise a dog, meet a friend, whatever. We always make a point of running along West Cliff Drive from Cowell Beach to as far as our legs will carry us. Something about the cornucopia of interesting people and the cliff-hugging scenery makes this one of the more exceptional aerobicizing locales in coastal California.

On a final note, lifeguards are on duty at Santa Cruz city beaches from Memorial Day to Labor Day and on weekends only in spring and fall.

Bunking Down

The motel scene in Santa Cruz, like the scene around the boardwalk and arcade, has steadily been improving. In the past, sobering stories were whispered about oceanfront motels here—tales of crime, degeneracy, noise, odors, overcrowding of rooms, and substance abuse. Our favorite story: A teenager steps out to get a soda one evening, leaving his grandmother in the motel room with the door unlocked. He lingers awhile on the boardwalk. When he returns, he finds a derelict passed out in bed next to Grandma, who has somehow slept through it all. Then, there's the tale of the "hippie" (they use that word a lot) who lived for a month inside a hotel elevator.

We've informally inventoried hotels and motels near Main Beach, where rooms plunge to under $40 in the dead of winter and get jacked up to $129 and more in summer at places with letters missing from their signs. Some Santa Cruz innkeepers are reluctant to quote hard-and-fast prices, especially on busy summer weekends, when they charge whatever the market will bear (see sidebar, "Room Rate Roulette").

The best-situated hotel in Santa Cruz, if not the whole of California, is the **West Coast Santa Cruz Hotel** (175 West Cliff Drive, 831/426-4330, $$$$). Formerly the Dream Inn, this 10-story lodge overlooks the Santa Cruz Municipal Wharf, Cowell Beach, and the Pacific Ocean, whose plunging waves will lull you to a deep, restful sleep. The view alone is worth the price of the rooms, which are not so much

Room Rate Roulette in Santa Cruz

There's a game that gets played in Santa Cruz in the summer months and on nice warm weekends the rest of the year. We call it "room rate roulette." It's a game of chance in which motels and guests each look to secure the best price, from their perspective. Motels want to charge as much as they can, while guests want to spend as little as they have to. There is nothing unusual about this. What makes the situation in Santa Cruz unique is the fluidity of the prices. It verges on being a barter system. If you know this, you can save some money.

A Santa Cruz motel owner tipped us off to this years ago. There are a lot of motels in Santa Cruz. Sometimes there are more would-be guests than rooms, and other times it is the other way around. Things can get interesting either way. When rooms are tight, people scramble from motel to motel checking out availability and happily paying an inflated price for a roof over their heads. When rooms are readily available, they will peruse motels for the lowest price. If you've come without reservations, you'll quickly learn if it's a buyer's or seller's market.

On a sunny Saturday afternoon in mid-May—a great beach day—"Vacancy" signs were up all over town. Motel lots looked to be half to two-thirds full. Occupancy rates were high enough that motels weren't giving rooms away but not so full that lodgers couldn't afford to check out their options. It made for an interesting dynamic. We had a room, but as an experiment we inquired about prices at a number of motels along Ocean Street and Riverside Avenue. Many others were doing likewise. We'd run into the same faces in different lobbies.

It soon became clear that prices fluctuate according to traffic and can be ne-

extravagant as extremely comfortable. The ocean-facing deck on the third floor has a heated pool and spa. One memorable night after the sun went down, we watched transfixed from the hot tub as a full moon illuminated the night sky. You can't put a price on moments like these, which might be a good thing since room rates run around $188 per night. For those on a bit more of a budget, **Holiday Inn Express** (600 Riverside Avenue, 831/458-9660, $$) lies just two blocks away and costs half as much, with a free breakfast thrown in.

We've also stayed at a posh resort that's not on the water but overlooks it from the hills above Santa Cruz. As we made the steep ascent to **Chaminade** (1 Chaminade Lane, 831/475-

5600, $$$$), a deer loped in front of our car. It seems as much a nature preserve as a hotel, and it gets high marks for its mountainside setting. We also liked the villa-style rooms and unparalleled quiet within. If Chaminade is a more meditative retreat than your typical hotel and conference center, that's because the compound used to be a monastery. Chaminade's Library dining room, incidentally, serves an award-winning weekend brunch.

Coastal Cuisine

Santa Cruz has a varied dining scene—everything from fast food to health food, from seafood restaurants on the wharf to taco stands on side streets. The Santa Cruz Municipal Wharf is

Map of Central California—Page 233

gotiated. "What are you looking to pay?" was a refrain we'd hear while leaving a lobby after being quoted a rate. It's like visiting a car lot, where a prospective buyer might start to walk away and the salesperson suddenly becomes pliable and even a little vulnerable beneath the slick, hardball exterior. The difference is that, unlike car lots, many Santa Cruz motel lobbies reek of Indian spices.

We were quoted prices ranging $65–130. Do the math: the lower rate is half the higher one. The cheapest rate we were quoted was at Inn Cal, an unfancy if perfectly fine motel on Ocean Street a half-mile from the beach and boardwalk. The highest were in the immediate vicinity of the beach, where we were quoted a fixed price of $129 at the AAA-rated Carousel, ideally situated on the corner of Riverside Avenue and Beach Street, and a range of $99–129 at Super 8 Motel, where they'd hung flower baskets to counter the chain's lowbrow image. The median price was $89. If you don't like what you hear, then feel free to barter, if you've got the stomach for it. Don't be afraid to leave if you don't like what you see, and don't cave in to hard-sell tactics.

FYI, room rates drop drastically during the week, especially outside the summer months. They must have long winters in Santa Cruz. The sign out front of a Travelodge advertised "low winter rates"; the date we saw this was May 13. It should also be pointed out that Santa Cruz is a popular beach town. Don't come expecting a Ritz-Carlton or even a three-star Holiday Inn. People come to Santa Cruz to party, and motel rooms reflect this reality. They're not filthy or uninhabitable, but they've seen a lot of use by family vacationers and hordes of party people. It's not far different from the scene at boardwalk towns along the Jersey Shore or in Myrtle Beach, South Carolina. In terms of California coast towns, however, Santa Cruz stands alone in this regard.

the place to go for a seafood meal with a view. This huge, bulky wharf extends 3,000 feet into the ocean. There's usually plenty of parking; you collect a ticket at the entrance gate and pay by the hour. Take your pick of sit-down restaurants with picture windows that face the ocean. A longtime wharf favorite is **Stagnaro Brothers** (Municipal Wharf, 831/423-2180, $$). A restaurant and a fish market, Stagnaro's motto is "Caught today, cooked today." You can eat your catch in a casual atmosphere or take it to go. Red clam chowder is a house specialty; it's a hearty concoction that cuts the chill when a cold wind is blowing off the ocean.

Though locals might disparage the wharf for being too touristy, they've got no qualms about

walking the planks to dine at **Riva's Fish House** (500 Municipal Wharf, 831/429-1223, $$), which draws hordes of residents and visitors alike. We won't elaborate on what the menu at a fish house on a wharf might look like (use your imagination). Just know one thing: If you don't get here early, prepare to leave your name and wait.

Once, on a squalling January afternoon, we had a memorable lunch at the **Miramar** (552 Municipal Wharf, 831/423-2666, $$). We ate sole meunière, salad, and fresh bread while watching monstrous winter waves threaten to pound the wharf to smithereens. Gazing out the windows while gale-force winds blew the rain sideways, we could see an ocean kayaker

Map of Santa Cruz County—Page 400

being tossed around like a bath toy. Then came a run of big waves. Each giant breaker struck the pier with a sound like a bowling ball scattering tenpins. The wharf would shudder, and overhead lights swayed. We found ourselves wondering how the pier could endure such abuse. And yet the Santa Cruz Municipal Wharf has been standing since 1914.

Santa Cruz's most popular waterfront restaurant is the **Crow's Nest** (2218 East Cliff Drive, 831/476-4560, $$), near Twin Lakes State Beach and the Small Craft Harbor. It get its fish from the fleet next door, has easy access to the beach, and is family friendly. Wednesdays it holds a clambake on the beach. Crow's Nest is also a big singles hangout and nightclub.

A favorite eatery near the Boardwalk is **Beach Street Cafe** (399 Beach Street, 831/426-7621, $), a good bet for breakfast or lunch. While basking in the friendly chatter, enjoy the framed collection of Maxfield Parrish prints, one of the largest in the United States. Good coffee, great omelettes. For morning muffins, hit **Rebecca's Mighty Muffins** (514 Front Street, 831/429-1940, $). Some are healthy, others are sinfully good, and still others try to be a little of both. Our faves: raspberry poppyseed cheesecake, cranberry orange pecan, and chocolate chip cheesecake.

For killer Mexican food, head to **El Palomar** (1336 Pacific Garden Mall, 831/425-7575, $$), where you can choose from two eating areas: a fancy dining room with high-end Mexican seafood dishes and a stand-up taco and alcohol bar. At the latter, you can scarf down unbelievable snapper and scallop tacos. Soft corn tortillas are hand-pressed before your very eyes from a mound of dough. It's a bustling room in which a terrific quick meal can be made from several soft tacos and a Mexican beer or two.

Another Mexican favorite is **Rosie's Rosticeria** (495 Lake Avenue, 831/479-3536, $), by the Yacht Harbor and very reasonably priced. For something completely different try **Vasili's Greek Food & Barbeque** (1501 Mission Av-

enue, 831/458-9808, $$), which serves a terrific roast chicken in lemon, olive oil, and artichoke hearts. The most beloved sushi restaurant in Santa Cruz is **Mobo Sushi** (105 South River Street, 831/425-1700, $$$), where they're reverential of their craft and very creative. Rolls include the Crop Burning (avocado, cucumber, shiitake, cilantro, spicy sauce) and the Pink Caddy (unagi, hamachi, sake, ebi, spicy sauce). A sushi platter will net delicacies like bonito and some of the reddest tuna you'll ever see.

Santa Cruz Coffee Roasting Company (1330 Pacific Avenue, 831/459-0100, $) is a coffee bar in the true sense of the word. You select a type of coffee (e.g., "Steve's Smooth French"), then servers place a paper filter inside a Melita-style cone, spoon fresh-ground coffee, and pour boiling water over the grounds. You wait as your mug fills, drop by aromatic drop. Additives include the usual cream and sugar, plus such healthy alternatives as soy milk and honey.

One of the best breakfasts or brunches in town is served at **Zachary's** (819 Pacific Avenue, 831/427-0646, $). How's this for a morning jump-starter: smoked chicken-apple sausage, eggs, home-fried potatoes, and homemade bread, all for $6.95.

Night Moves

Santa Cruz is a party town. People listen and dance to any type of music—live, taped, synthesized, loud, soft, garage, grunge, Glenn Miller. It doesn't matter. Clubs are scattered around town, catering to a cross section of locals and party animals from over the mountains.

Two of the most popular and longest-lived are the **Crow's Nest** (2218 East Cliff Drive, 831/476-4560) and the **Catalyst** (1011 Pacific Avenue, 831/423-1336). The Crow's Nest turns the second floor of its seafood restaurant into a happy danceteria, and after the plates are put away, it cranks up the volume. Occasionally the club features live acts, but mostly it's decent deejayed music—one night we could hear James Brown's "I Feel Good" as we ap-

Map of Central California—Page 233

Santa Cruz County

proached blocks away—and the dance floor is jam-packed. It's a thirty-something crowd, though not a somnolent one.

The Catalyst is a former bowling alley transformed into a world-renowned venue for alternative music. More collegiate and liberalized, it's a cavernous clubhouse with two floors, several rooms, and bars everywhere you turn. The Catalyst has a long and storied history. It's a favorite venue of Neil Young, who's been known to break in new material and/or bands here. On one visit we saw the Latin Playboys, a spin-off of Los Lobos. Good band, great venue.

Much of downtown Santa Cruz, along Pacific Avenue, had to be rebuilt or renovated after the 1989 earthquake. It's generally an okay place to stroll around. We're not going to romanticize it, though, because the area sometimes has the unnerving aura of an urban DMZ compounded by rampant homelessness. Here's a quasi-amusing vignette: One morning we stumbled upon a bum changing clothes on the grounds of our hotel beside a sign that read "Panhandlers Are Not Welcome and Will Be Prosecuted." So it goes in Santa Cruz.

Downtown you will find good bookshop, coffeehouses, and bars filled with locals. True to its name, **99 Bottles of Beer on the Wall** (110 Walnut Street, 831/459-9999) offers 99 brands of beer. If you really want to bend elbows with the locals, stroll the lower end of Pacific Avenue, where you'll find such dive bars as the **Asti Cafe** (715 Pacific Avenue, 831/423-7337). The Asti and its neighbors have cold beer, blaring jukeboxes, milling crowds, and an atmosphere as loud and lascivious as the bars where we misspent our college years. The Asti gets extra points for carding one of us.

For More Information

Santa Cruz County Conference and Visitors Council, 701 Front Street, Santa Cruz, CA 95060, 831/425-1234 or 800/833-3494, website: www.santacruzca.org

Wilder Ranch State Park

Wilder Ranch State Park is one of California's most intriguing oceanfront parks. It opened in the early 1990s. For the century prior to the acquisition of nearly 5,000 acres by the state in 1974, the ranch was operated as a farm by the Wilder family. About 900 acres are still under cultivation, with one-eighth of the nation's Brussels sprouts grown inside park boundaries. Twenty-two more acres have been set aside as a cultural preserve, and many of the original Wilder family buildings stand intact.

Most of the trails and acreage lie north of Highway 1, up in the hills, which rise to 800 feet. But it's the stretch of Wilder Ranch seaward of the highway that is attractive to beach bums. There are six named beaches inside the state park. One way to view them is to hike the Ohlone Bluff Trail, a majestic 2.5-mile footpath that runs along the shoreline. From the park office take Old Cove Landing Trail for 1.2 miles to the beach, where it meets Ohlone Bluff Trail. Wilder Beach is an off-limits preserve for the endangered snowy plover. Other beaches appear as separate coves below the blufftop, and the names are as appealing as the scenery: Fern Grotto Beach, Sand Plant Beach, Strawberry Beach, Three Mile Beach, and Four Mile Beach.

Logically enough, **Four Mile Beach** (the most popular) is four miles north of town, off Highway 1. Start measuring the distance from Highway 1 at Mission Street in Santa Cruz, and at four miles look for a rut-filled parking lot. A 10-minute walk across railroad tracks and past a wetlands leads to the beach. Clothed and nude beachcombers and surfers use Four Mile by day, and teen hell-raisers show up after dark.

In addition to Ohlone Bluff Trail, 34 miles of scenic backcountry trails wind through the inland hills and valleys. These trails are popular

Santa Cruz County

with horseback riders and mountain bicyclists. No camping is allowed. Guided tours and hands-on demonstrations of ranch life are offered on the weekends; reservations are required.

For More Information

Wilder Ranch State Park, 1401 Coast Road, Santa Cruz, CA 95060, 831/423-9703, www.parks.ca.gov

Red, White, and Blue Beach

Red, White, and Blue Beach is a private nude beach off Highway 1, five miles north of Santa Cruz. (Keep an eye out for the mailbox with the patriotic color scheme.) A day-use fee is charged, and overnight camping costs $12–16 per night. As is customary on California's nude beaches, you must be 21, married, or accompanied by parents to be allowed onto the beach, where there are disrobing facilities and volleyball nets. The beach is open 10 A.M.–6 P.M. in summer and 10 A.M.–4 P.M. the rest of the year. Unless you're camping, you have to be gone by closing time. Red, White, and Blue Beach is a third of a mile long. A warm, sunny day can draw a crowd of 500 or so, most of whom exercise the no-clothing option.

Bonny Doon Beach

Beginning about seven miles north of Santa Cruz, a series of cove beaches can be accessed along Highway 1, including **Laguna Creek Beach, Panther Beach, Yellowbank Beach,** and **Bonny Doon Beach.** Each requires hiking across a bluff and down to the beach—often a steep scramble down a loosely consolidated sea cliff. The best known, Bonny Doon, is nine miles north of Santa Cruz, at Milepost 27.6 on Highway 1 at Bonny Doon Road. (Up in the hills is the bucolic little settlement of Bonny Doon.) Laguna Creek, Panther Beach, and Yellowbank Beach lie 1.7, 1.3, and 1.0 miles south of Bonny Doon, respectively. These are legendary party spots on weekend nights—especially during full moons, when all-night raves are staged on the sands of Four Mile and Panther beaches.

Now an officially recognized coastal access, Bonny Doon offers paved, angle-in parking along the ocean side of Highway 1. Signs warn against parking between 10 P.M. and 6 A.M. After crossing railroad tracks and descending a dirt path, you come upon an absolutely stunning beach that resembles a natural amphitheater, with cliffs on either side that keep the winds at bay. The remoteness of the site and the protection afforded by the encircling cliffs have made Bonny Doon one of the premier nude beaches on the California coast. It is also one of the friendlier haunts of the bare-assed set, who congregate by the cove at the north end. The other beaches in this daisy chain are equally endowed with sheltering cliffs and desirable isolation.

A word of caution about the beaches of northern Santa Cruz County: Their character tends to change after dark from a nude Dr. Jekyll to an intoxicated Mr. Hyde. Nighttime is when young party animals from the Santa Clara Valley come to raise hell. They build bonfires on the beach, drink themselves senseless, and litter the sand with glass, garbage, and puke. One high-schooler told a reporter for the *San Jose Mercury News,* "We party at Bonny Doon. You have to walk down a hill, and cops don't go down there. So you light a bonfire and drink until you can't walk. A lot of times people just spend the night; they're way too drunk to walk back up the hill." For years the authorities have attempted to curb this behavior. They've ticketed cars parked on the shoulders of Highway 1 at night. They've broken up many a beachside bacchanal, some of

Map of Central California—Page 233

which have attracted upward of a thousand kids. But there's only so much they can do. Youth must have its fling.

The dark side of all this is fights, drunk driving, falling off cliffs, drownings, and murder. Even during daylight hours we've seen some pretty thuggish-looking characters hanging around these north county pullouts. Auto breakins are another problem—don't leave valuables inside your car or trunk. Watch your step, watch the company you keep, and don't drink and drive. Don't ever come out here alone. Enough kids have been hurt or died that the authorities and general public are unamused by alcohol-related lawbreaking, even if it is part of the perceived adolescent rites of passage.

Davenport

For such a little place, Davenport (population 200) has several worthwhile attractions. It is home to the Davenport New Cash Store—a one-of-a-kind restaurant, bakery, bed-and-breakfast, and art gallery. In winter and early spring, the town is one of the premier spots in Northern California to watch gray whales as they make their way from feeding grounds in the Arctic to breeding grounds in Mexican lagoons and back again. Davenport is also the site of a giant, Depression-era cement plant. The decayed pilings of a massive, 3,000-foot wharf, from which the plant loaded its product onto ships, list in the water. For beach fanatics, the main attraction is a trinity of sandy accesses: Davenport Beach, Davenport Landing, and Scott Creek Beach.

Beaches

From the highway it's a short dash to the huge expanse of sand at **Davenport Beach.** The healthy dune structure makes a scenic backdrop for a beach hike, where the only threat to your serenity might be the occasional hang glider leaping from a bluff above. Incidentally, a half mile south is Davenport Cove (a.k.a. Shark's Tooth Cove), a spot frequented by nude beachgoers.

Davenport Landing Beach is accessed via Davenport Landing Road, a loop road one mile north of town. Parking beside the road is permitted 6 A.M.–10 P.M., but there's only room for about 20 cars. It's a lot easier to get to than Bonny Doon and its neighboring accesses. A short hike leads down a gradually sloping embankment, revealing cliffs at either end of a scenic cove. On a perfect Thursday in late July, we had the beach to ourselves.

The prettiest of the three coastal settings in Davenport is **Scott Creek Beach,** where Scott Creek trickles across a sandy delta into the Pacific. When we visited, surf casters were digging the scene (though no fishing is allowed in the creek itself). Windsurfers frequent both Davenport Landing and Scott Creek. There's a lovely pond and wetlands on the east side of Highway 1 at Scott Creek, and the quarter-mile beach lies between bluffs on the west side.

Bunking Down

For a real getaway, book a room at **New Davenport Bed & Breakfast Inn** (Highway 1 and Davenport Avenue, 831/425-1818, $$), whose rooms are behind the New Davenport Cash Store and above the restaurant.

Coastal Cuisine

The **Davenport New Cash Store** (Davenport Avenue, 831/426-4122, $$$) is a gourmet restaurant, bakery, pottery gallery, and bed-and-breakfast inn rolled into one. The culinary emphasis is on creative seafood and pasta dishes, as well as local wines. Breakfast, lunch, and dinner are served.

For More Information

Santa Cruz County Conference and Visitors Council, 701 Front Street, Santa Cruz, CA 95060, 831/425-1234 or 800/834-3494, website: www.santacruzca.org

Santa Cruz County

Map of Santa Cruz County—Page 400

Greyhound Rock Fishing Access and Waddell Creek Beach

The angler's Nirvana in these parts is **Greyhound Rock Fishing Access,** 28 miles north of Santa Cruz in the middle of nowhere. Developed by the State Department of Fish and Game, Greyhound Rock features a trail and stairwell that lead down to the beach from paved parking lots right off Highway 1. The pathway is a real doozy, descending steeply to the beach. Greyhound Rock sits offshore, deflecting waves that wrap around it in such a way that a triangular beach has formed onshore. There is a picnic table and overlook up top if you don't want to huff and puff down to the water.

Waddell Creek Beach is bounded by Big Basins Redwood State Park, an enormous parkland (18,000 acres) that extends into the Santa Cruz Mountains. An overnight stay in the inland campground is an attractive proposition. Big Basin offers outdoors enthusiasts 80 miles of backcountry hiking trails, waterfalls, and tent sites—145 at base camp, plus 40 walk-in sites.

The beach at Waddell Creek is usually quite windy, making it a favorite spot for windsurfers and hang gliders. A self-guided nature center offers insight on local flora and fauna, including a sobering note about dwindling steelhead and rainbow-trout populations, which once spawned happily in Waddell Creek. One more observation: The parking lot at Waddell Creek is deeply rutted and sits on unconsolidated bluffs that look to be slumping shoreward at an alarming rate. Just above Waddell Creek, Highway 1 passes some of the most menacing, erosion-prone cliffs this side of Big Sur. It's a high-hazard area for slides as the dark brown cliff faces—nearly vertical and shorn of vegetation—periodically slump and fail. A pile of rubble typically accumulates at the bottom. Keep your foot on the gas pedal through here.

For More Information

Big Basin Redwoods State Park, 21600 Big Basin Way, 831/338-8860, www.parks.ca.gov

Santa Cruz County

© ROBERT HOLMES/CALTOUR

Chapter 9
San Mateo County

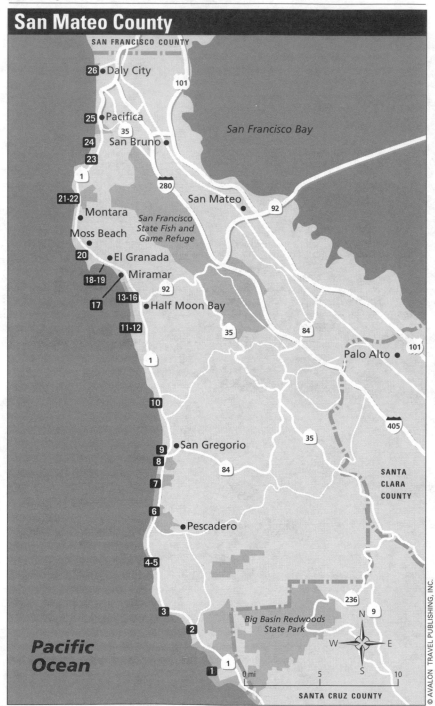

San Mateo County

SAN FRANCISCO COUNTY

26 ● Daly City

101

San Francisco Bay

25 ● Pacifica

35

24   San Bruno ●

23

1

21-22

● Montara

San Francisco
State Fish and
Game Refuge

San Mateo

92

280

Moss Beach

20

● El Granada

18-19   ● Miramar

92

17   13-16   ● Half Moon Bay

35

84

101

Palo Alto ●

11-12

1

405

10

SANTA
CLARA
COUNTY

9   ● San Gregorio

35

8

7   84

6

● Pescadero

4-5

236

N

3   9

Big Basin Redwoods
State Park

W   E

2

S

1   *Pacific
Ocean*

0 mi   5   10

1

SANTA CRUZ COUNTY

San Mateo County

© AVALON TRAVEL PUBLISHING, INC.

San Mateo County Beaches

1 Año Nuevo State Reserve (New Years Creek and Bight Beach), page 441

Location: New Years Creek Road off Highway 1, 26 miles south of Half Moon Bay
Parking/fees: $4 entrance fee per vehicle. The fee for guided elephant seal walks, offered December 15–March 31, is $4 per person.
Hours: 8 A.M.–sunset, with special hour restrictions for seal viewing areas; check with the park for details.
Facilities: restrooms, picnic tables, and visitor center
Contact: Año Nuevo State Reserve, 650/879-2025

2 Gazos Creek Access, page 442

Location: Gazos Creek Bridge at Highway 1, 22 Miles South of Half Moon Bay
Parking/fees: free parking lot
Hours: 8 A.M.–sunset
Facilities: restrooms
Contact: Año Nuevo State Reserve, 650/879-2025

3 Pigeon Point, page 442

Location: Pigeon Point Road at Highway 1, 20 miles south of Half Moon Bay
Parking/fees: free parking lot. Lodging fees at Pigeon Point Lighthouse Hostel are $15–18 per night.
Hours: 7:30 A.M.–9:30 P.M.
Facilities: restrooms and showers
Contact: Pigeon Point Light Station State Historic Park, 650/879-0633

4 Bean Hollow State Beach, page 442

Location: 18 miles south of Half Moon Bay off Highway 1
Parking/fees: free parking lot
Hours: 8 A.M.–sunset
Facilities: restrooms and picnic tables
Contact: California State Parks, Bay Area District, 415/330-6300

5 Pebble Beach, page 442

Location: 17 miles south of Half Moon Bay off Highway 1
Parking/fees: free parking lot
Hours: 8 A.M.–sunset
Facilities: restrooms and picnic tables
Contact: California State Parks, Bay Area District, 415/330-6300

San Mateo County

Map of San Mateo County—Page 434

6 Pescadero State Beach, page 443

Location: 14.5 miles south of Half Moon Bay along Highway 1
Parking/fees: $4 entrance fee per vehicle at north lot; free parking at central and south lots
Hours: 8 A.M.–sunset.
Facilities: restrooms and picnic tables
Contact: Pescadero State Beach, 650/879-2170

7 Pomponio State Beach, page 443

Location: 12 miles south of Half Moon Bay on Highway 1
Parking/fees: $4 entrance fee per vehicle
Hours: 8 A.M.–sunset
Facilities: restrooms and picnic tables
Contact: California State Parks, Bay Area District, 415/330-6300

8 San Gregorio State Beach, page 444

Location: 10.5 miles south of Half Moon Bay on Highway 1
Parking/fees: $4 entrance fee per vehicle
Hours: 8 A.M.–sunset
Facilities: restrooms, picnic tables, and fire pits
Contact: California State Parks, Bay Area District, 415/330-6300

9 San Gregorio Private Beach, page 444

Location: end of dirt toll road, 100 yards north of junction of Highways 1 and 84
Parking/fees: $5 per car or $2 per person entrance fee
Hours: 10 A.M.–7 P.M. (9 A.M.–sunset on weekends)
Facilities: restrooms
Contact: none

10 Martins Beach, page 445

Location: Martins Beach Road and Highway 1, six miles south of Half Moon Bay
Parking/fees: $5 entrance fee per vehicle
Hours: 6 A.M.–5 P.M. (6 P.M. on weekends and later in summer)
Facilities: restrooms and picnic tables
Contact: Martins Beach, 650/712-8020

11 Cowell Ranch State Beach, page 446

Location: From Highway 1, three miles south of Half Moon Bay, follow the dirt road for a half mile to the parking lot and staircase to the beach.
Parking/fees: free parking lot

San Mateo County

Map of Central California—Page 233

Hours: 8 A.M.–sunset
Facilities: restrooms
Contact: Half Moon Bay State Beach, 650/726-8820

12 Pelican Point Beach, page 446

Location: Miramontes Point Road at Highway 1, two miles south of Half Moon Bay
Parking/fees: free roadside parking. Camping fees at Pelican Point RV Park are $18–27 per night.
Hours: sunrise–sunset
Facilities: restrooms, showers, and picnic tables
Contact: Pelican Point RV Park, 650/726-9100

13 Francis Beach (Half Moon Bay State Beach), page 446

Location: end of Kelly Avenue, off Highway 1 in Half Moon Bay
Parking/fees: $4 entrance fee per vehicle. Camping fees are $13–16 per night (Francis Beach) and $75 per night per group site (Sweetwood Group Camp).
Hours: 8 A.M.–sunset
Facilities: restrooms, showers, and picnic tables
Contact: Half Moon Bay State Beach, 650/726-8820

14 Venice Beach (Half Moon Bay State Beach), page 446

Location: end of Venice Boulevard, off Highway 1 in Half Moon Bay
Parking/fees: $4 entrance fee per vehicle
Hours: 8 A.M.–sunset
Facilities: restrooms and picnic tables
Contact: Half Moon Bay State Beach, 650/726-8820

15 Dunes Beach (Half Moon Bay State Beach), page 446

Location: end of Young Avenue, off Highway 1 in Half Moon Bay
Parking/fees: $4 entrance fee per vehicle
Hours: 8 A.M.–sunset
Facilities: restrooms and picnic area
Contact: Half Moon Bay State Beach, 650/726-8820

16 Roosevelt Beach (Half Moon Bay State Beach), page 446

Location: From the end of Young Avenue at Dunes Beach, off Highway 1 in Half Moon Bay, follow the park road north to Roosevelt Beach.
Parking/fees: $4 entrance fee per vehicle
Hours: 8 A.M.–sunset

San Mateo County

Map of San Mateo County—Page 434

Facilities: restrooms
Contact: Half Moon Bay State Beach, 650/726-8820

17 Miramar Beach, page 448

Location: end of Mirada Road in Miramar, two miles north of Half Moon Bay
Parking/fees: free street parking
Hours: half hour before sunrise to half hour after sunset
Facilities: none
Contact: none

18 El Granada Beach (a.k.a. Surfers Beach), page 449

Location: between Mirada Road and East Breakwater at Pillar Point Harbor, three miles north of Half Moon Bay off Highway 1
Parking/fees: metered parking lot at Pillar Point Harbor
Hours: half hour before sunrise to half hour after sunset
Facilities: none
Contact: none

19 Pillar Point, page 450

Location: along Capistrano Road, four miles north of Half Moon Bay off Highway 1
Parking/fees: metered parking lot
Hours: sunrise–sunset
Facilities: restrooms and picnic tables
Contact: Pillar Point Harbor, 650/726-5727

20 James V. Fitzgerald Marine Reserve, page 452

Location: end of California Avenue, off Highway 1 in Moss Beach
Parking/fees: free street parking
Hours: sunrise–sunset
Facilities: restrooms and picnic tables
Contact: James V. Fitzgerald Marine Reserve, 650/728-3584

21 Montara State Beach, page 453

Location: Second Street at Highway 1 in Montara
Parking/fees: free parking lot
Hours: 8 A.M.–sunset
Facilities: restrooms
Contact: California State Parks, Bay Area District, 415/330-6300

San Mateo County

Map of Central California—Page 233

22 Gray Whale Cove State Beach (a.k.a. Devil's Slide), page 455

Location: between Montara and Pacifica, at Devil's Slide off Highway 1
Parking/fees: $6.50 entrance fee per person ($7.50 on weekends)
Hours: 8 A.M.–sunset
Facilities: restrooms and picnic tables
Contact: Gray Whale Cove State Beach, 650/728-5336

23 Pacifica State Beach, page 457

Location: Highway 1 between Crespi Drive and Linda Mar Boulevard in Pacifica
Parking/fees: free street parking
Hours: 24 hours
Facilities: restrooms and showers
Contact: California State Parks, Bay Area District, 415/330-6300

24 Rockaway Beach, page 457

Location: end of Rockaway Beach Avenue, off Highway 1 in Pacifica
Parking/fees: free parking lot
Hours: 24 hours
Facilities: none
Contact: Pacifica Parks, Beaches, and Recreation, 650/738-7381

25 Esplanade Beach (a.k.a. Sharp Park), page 457

Location: along Beach Boulevard in Pacifica
Parking/fees: free street parking
Hours: 24 hours
Facilities: restrooms
Contact: Pacifica Parks, Beaches, and Recreation, 650/738-7381

26 Thornton State Beach, page 458

Location: end of Thornton Beach Road in Daly City
Parking/fees: free street parking
Hours: sunrise–sunset
Facilities: none
Contact: California State Parks, Bay Area District, 415/330-6300

San Mateo County

Map of San Mateo County—Page 434

San Mateo County

I f the Santa Cruz coast is like a mop-topped surfer, his grungy edge tempered by a basically sunny disposition, then the San Mateo coast is a grizzled veteran of the sea—maybe a steely-eyed fisherman or salty dog. The rocky shoals and heavy fogs along this 55-mile shoreline have long put the fear of shipwrecks in sailors' hearts, and the steep, shifting terrain in the Devil's Slide area has tossed both a coastal railroad and a highway into the Pacific.

The perfectly appealing towns of Half Moon Bay, Princeton, Moss Beach, Miramar, El Grenada, and Montara exemplify the other side of the San Mateo coast. There's also the wild isolation of Año Nuevo State Reserve, home to a huge colony of seals, and a string of state beaches—Bean Hollow, Pescadero, Pomponio, San Gregorio, Half Moon Bay, and Montara. It is a land of grazing cattle and green fields of vegetables that love the cool fogs that shroud the area.

With San Francisco to the north, San Jose and the Santa Clara Valley to the east, and Santa Cruz to the south, San Mateo County exists in a sort of urban-to-rural transition zone. Despite its proximity to populated areas, geographical isolation makes it a tough commute. That has held in check the explosive growth that is so evident elsewhere on the coast. That's not to say the San Mateo Coast, especially Half Moon Bay, isn't growing. Lately, especially on weekends, we've found traffic to be knotty and slow-moving all over town—a sure sign of inundation. Let's hope they can keep a lid on it.

The beaches themselves are too cold and hazardous for swimming, and the only beauties you'll see sunbathing here are northern elephant seals at Año Nuevo State Reserve. The blubbery darlings are the largest pinnipeds in this hemisphere, reaching 16 feet in length. In addition to seal-watching, San Mateo County offers low-impact pastimes—tidepooling, strolling, fishing, camping, birding, and whale-watching—on its raw and elemental shoreline.

San Mateo County

Map of Central California—Page 233

Año Nuevo State Reserve

Año Nuevo State Reserve is first and foremost a wildlife refuge. It is the mainland rookery of the northern elephant seal. Peak population of the playful pinnipeds at Año Nuevo is 3,000. Second, it is a park open to human visitation. Just north of the Santa Cruz County line and 55 miles south of San Francisco, the reserve's 4,000 acres include scrub-covered coastal hills and rocky intertidal beaches. A rustic white barn serves as visitor center, museum, gift shop, and ticket counter for guided seal walks.

The shoreline consists of sandy coves and rocky headlands, with one of California's largest surviving dune fields bordering the wildlife protection area. Visitors can hike to a point from which they might spy seals playing on the beach or on offshore chunks of rock. One elongated outcrop is particularly surreal, as several abandoned buildings stand on it. Rocks and buildings alike are covered with seals and cormorants and stained with their droppings, giving it the peculiar appearance of a Hollywood stage set overtaken by wildlife.

The tangy air, crashing waves, and barking seals make for an enchanting nature experience. From the parking lot past the entrance station, it's a short hike to the silty, V-shaped, drift-log strewn **New Years ("Año Nuevo") Creek Beach,** via the gullied New Years Creek Trail. It's a 1.6-mile hike out to Point Año Nuevo, but the trail has been closed past the 0.9-mile mark. A section of the park south of Cascade Creek is off-limits to visitors during seal breeding season (December 15–March 31), though guided tours of small groups are conducted by volunteer naturalists at this time. These walking tours cover three miles and take 2.5 hours. **Bight Beach** is another seals-only playground by the sea. It lies between South and North Points, backed by a vast dune field covering 350 acres. Humans are allowed out here by permit only April–November.

There are two more beach accesses off Highway 1 at the north end of Año Nuevo's landholdings. You'll see two small lots on the west side of the highway, from which trails lead fourtenths of a mile across a meadow to these **North Año Nuevo Beaches.** There are no facilities here—nothing more than free parking, garbage cans, and sandy, deserted beaches.

Whale-watching, bird-watching, clam-digging, and surf casting are other popular activities. In addition to elephant seals, other marine mammals—harbor seals, northern fur seals, sea lions, and sea otters—make their home here for at least part of the year. California gray whales pass Point Año Nuevo during their winter migration. Año Nuevo's rocky, south-facing beach runs along a mile of curving coastline. Surfers have been known to catch a wave off the point, which breaks best in summer, but they must face the ever-present threat of shark attacks. Sharks are natural predators of seals, and are therefore found in greater number at Año Nuevo. Is a well-formed wave worth that kind of risk? Apparently, some surfers think so.

For **Año Nuevo Guided Walk** reservations call 800/444-4445. Reservations are required for walks, offered December 15–March 31, and can be made anytime on or after October 20. To watch a live webcam of seals frolicking on the shores of Año Nuevo, log on to www.parks.ca.gov/popup/main.asp.

For More Information

Año Nuevo State Reserve, New Years Creek Road, Pescadero, CA 94060, 650/879-2025, website: www.parks.ca.gov

San Mateo County

Map of San Mateo County—Page 434

Gazos Creek Access

Stairs lead to a lagoon and beach by Gazos Creek Bridge, six miles north of the Santa Cruz County line on Highway 1. The creek meanders into the sea at **Gazos Creek Access**. The parking lot is on a bluff overlooking the broad, sandy, semicircular cove beach. Behind it rise the redwood canyons of Gazos, Whitehouse, and Cascade Creeks, combined into the undeveloped acreage of Año Nuevo State Park. The Pigeon Point Lighthouse is visible to the north.

Pigeon Point

The 115-foot-tall **Pigeon Point Light Station** has been guiding mariners since 1872. Because so many ships have sunk off the point, the lighthouse remains a vital navigational aid. It is the second tallest structure of its kind in California and the tallest one still in operation. Also on the site is a hostelry where you can stay for a pittance out on the wild edge of the San Mateo coast. The lighthouse and hostel are on Pigeon Point Road, off Highway 1 about 20 miles south of Half Moon Bay and 27 miles north of Santa Cruz. Due to concerns over the lighthouse's structural safety, tours are not currently being given, though the grounds remain open. There's good tidepooling in the vicinity of **Pigeon Point,** and gray whales can be sighted on their annual migration during spring months.

Bunking Down

The **Pigeon Point Lighthouse Hostel** (210 Pigeon Point Road, Pescadero, 650/879-0633, $) occupies bungalows that formerly accommodated Coast Guard families. There are private rooms for couples and families, as well as dormitory-style bunkrooms for travelers who are game for a communal experience. Rates run $15–18 per person; a private room costs $15 more. The former Fog Signal Building now serves as a recreational lounge for overnighters. A big hot tub overlooking the ocean is available for rental. South of the lighthouse, a trail leads to Gazos Creek Beach.

For More Information

Pigeon Point Light Station State Historic Park, 210 Pigeon Point Road, Pescadero, CA 94060, 650/879-0633, website: www.parks.ca.gov

Bean Hollow State Beach and Pebble Beach

A shelf of rocks divides **Bean Hollow State Beach,** one of the more wild and scenic stretches of coastline in San Mateo County, into broad coves. Raw, elemental beach wilderness is the main feature at Bean Hollow, which lies 18 miles south of Half Moon Bay. It's mostly rocky surf, save for small, sandy coves at **Pebble Hollow** and **Arroyo de Frijoles Beach,** at the south end of Bean Hollow.

A nature trail connects Bean Hollow with **Pebble Beach,** a mile to the north. A helpful brochure, which can be picked up in boxes at either end of the trail, is keyed to numbered posts along the way, and the basic geology, ecology, and marine biology of the area are conveyed in easy-to-follow text. One of the more interesting facts we learned has to do with coastal bluff erosion. Where the sandstone is soft, cliffs can retreat as much as 22 feet per year. Living proof of this can be seen in the rerouting of the trail that's been necessitated by the shoreward retreat of the bluffs.

San Mateo County

Pebble Beach derives its name from the crop of smooth, rounded pebbles found at surf's edge. One theory holds that it is the site of a former stream mouth whose pebbly remnants were bound up in the sandstone-conglomerate overlay in the recent geological past. You're encouraged to admire the pebbles but to leave them where they lie. The sandstone in this vicinity takes on a distinctive orange hue. Rare, lacelike formations called tafoni are carved into the coastal rocks. Offshore, the roiling surf whips up an oozy froth.

Pescadero State Beach

There are three beach-access points at **Pescadero State Beach,** a mile-long beach 14.5 miles south of Half Moon Bay. The best access is the northernmost lot at Pescadero Creek, where a small day-use fee is collected. The south one has a larger parking lot perched at bluff's edge, overlooking the raging sea. The parking lot, formerly a bumpy and pothole-riddled disaster, has been scraped and had new gravel laid. All three lots offer access to **Pescadero State Beach Marsh Preserve,** on the east side of the highway, where hiking trails wander through one of the most significant freshwater/brackish coastal marshes in California. It is a critical resting place on the Pacific flyway. A bird checklist is available to visitors. Free ranger-led marsh walks are offered on Saturday at 10:30 A.M. and Sunday at 1 P.M. throughout the year, weather permitting. Meet at the parking lot on Highway 1 just south of Pescadero Creek. Look for a sign that reads: "Pescadero State Beach Marsh Preserve." No reservations are necessary.

The beaches of Pescadero represent the San Mateo coast at its wildest: rough surf, rocky beach, nearly leveled headlands that people explore for close encounters with nature in extremis. Breakers violently pound rocky outcrops. The rough-and-tumble setting is perfect for sunset watching, as the ocean's acrobatics provide a dramatic soundtrack for the sun's disappearing act. If you're fearless and sure-footed, stroll out onto the points of rock that extend seaward in defiance of the waves' relentless pounding. It is haunting and undeveloped out here, and one roadside sign says it all: "Next Gas 35 Miles."

Coastal Cuisine

The "historic" community of Pescadero, a tiny hamlet a few miles inland, is in the heart of a rural area renowned for its trout fishing. At **Duarte's Tavern** (202 Stage Road, 650/879-0464, $$), a former stagecoach-era saloon, locals flock for seafood and gossip. Pronounce it DOO-arts, or they'll know you're from out of town. Hell, they'll probably know that anyway.

Pomponio State Beach

Pomponio State Beach, 12 miles south of Half Moon Bay, is the smallest of the trio of state beaches located in the sparsely populated midsection of San Mateo County. The broad, semicircular beach is not as stunning as San Gregorio or as expansive as Pescadero, but neither is it as heavily visited. It is a sandy creek-fed beach flanked by grassy bluffs, with a cove and a narrower strip of sand running north of it. Pomponio takes its name from a Native American outlaw who lived in a nearby cave during Spanish rule. There are picnic tables in the green grass above the beach.

At its southern end Pomponio is a clothing-optional beach that's a bit hard to reach. If you're walking along the water line, this stretch is accessible from the parking lot only at low tide, lying .7 mile to the south. The other way in is to walk north the same distance from Pescadero State Beach.

Map of San Mateo County—Page 434

San Mateo County

San Gregorio State Beach

San Gregorio State Beach is a great spot for hiking. Scenic paths wander atop mustard-colored sandstone bluffs overlooking the ocean, and the beach itself is wonderfully wide at the mouth of San Gregorio Creek. Away from the creek, it narrows dramatically in both directions, hemmed between ocean and bluff. The beaches of San Mateo County—and San Gregorio in particular—are amazing to behold. The topography is rugged, the ocean chilly and tempestuous. Solitary beach hiking is an inviting activity, though you are advised to keep an eye on tides and sleeper waves. One evening around sunset in May, we hiked up a trail that skirted the cliff's edge south of the creek. From this awesome promontory, we watched the sun set—a magnificent spectacle that resulted in this sincere, if perhaps overstated, notation: "Greatest experience of life: Sunset over San Gregorio."

On a weekend afternoon in late summer, the broad apron of beach below the parking lot was packed with all kinds of folks: a church youth group playing games on the beach; families of every ethnic origin gathered around picnic baskets; college students basking in the sun; and little children charging madly about. However, not a soul braved the water. On a windy March weekday in another year, by contrast, San Gregorio was empty, and a bitter wind chilled us to the marrow. A winter's worth of storms had turned the expansive creek mouth beach into what looked like a graveyard for drift logs.

The paved parking lot at San Gregorio costs $2 to enter. Just up the hill, south of the bridge over San Gregorio Creek, people park on the shoulder of Highway 1 and enter for free along paths that lead down to the beach. Being ardent supporters of California State Parks, we encourage one and all to ante up their fair share and spare the crumbling bluffs their destructive footsteps.

San Gregorio Private Beach

San Gregorio Private Beach is clothing optional. It's not just any old nude beach, though. San Gregorio Private Beach claims to be America's oldest nude sand beach, having catered to naturists for six decades. Located below steep bluffs, San Gregorio offers an expansive stretch of scenic beauty. In addition to true-blue au naturel aesthetes, some prurient opportunists apparently couple in driftwood lean-tos, referred to as "sex condos." There's plenty of beach to go around out here—two long, lonesome miles of it. Crowds numbering upward of 500 let it all hang out on summer weekends. Straight couples and families congregate at the south end.

Some avoid the charges ($5 per car or $2 per person) by parking along the roadside and making the treacherous hike down via trails. Such high-impact intrusions are no doubt responsible for accelerating bluff erosion. Be a sport and enter where you ought to. As an option, you can hike north along the beach for half a mile from San Gregorio State Beach.

San Gregorio Private Beach is at the end of a dirt toll road 100 yards north of the intersection of Highways 1 and 84, near the crossroads community of San Gregorio.

San Mateo County

Map of Central California—Page 233

Martins Beach

The fact that science-fiction writer H. P. Lovecraft coauthored a short story called "The Horror at Martin's Beach" shouldn't put you off of this prime fishing spot in San Mateo County. **Martins Beach** is a private fishing cove; you pay a $5 toll to enter the road and cast a line. There's an on-site store that's open in summer, plus restrooms and picnic tables. **Martins Beach** (650/712-8020) lies six miles south of Half Moon Bay, off Highway 1 at the end of Martins Beach Road.

Half Moon Bay

At the rate it's growing, Half Moon Bay may soon be Full Moon Bay as suburban sprawl pushes down from San Francisco (30 miles north) and over from Silicon Valley (30 miles southeast). Formerly a nub in the middle of the rural San Mateo Coast, where Highway 1 meets Highway 92, the quaint, seaside town served as an overflow valve for stressed-out urbanites fleeing the congested Bay Area. However, strict coastal zoning regulations, limitations in sewer capacity and water supply, and the hassles of living here—which is to say, the hassle of commuting from here—have regulated the influx somewhat.

The community itself has implemented a three percent per year ceiling on growth. In its pursuit of slow growth, Half Moon Bay is occasionally assisted by flooding and landslides, which have closed Highways 1 and 92 from time to time. Still, the area is growing and ill-prepared to handle the influx. The long-range view is that Half Moon Bay and its neighboring communities are facing "overwhelming transportation, economic, and environmental problems," according to a 1998 report. Already the area is badly bogged down by traffic, and it feels less like a "getaway" than a crowded suburban adjunct of San Francisco and Silicon Valley.

Half Moon Bay (population 16,400) is at the heart of an area known as Coastside—a string of towns along the central San Mateo County coast. In addition to Half Moon Bay, Coastside includes El Granada, Miramar, Princeton, Moss Beach, and Montara. The combined population of these and a few inland hamlets is growing. Much of the land along the foggy coast is used for growing artichokes, Brussels sprouts, pumpkins, and flowers. Luxury Cape Cod–style developments have gone up, contrasting with the modest dwellings of agricultural workers. The once-present aura of tranquillity has been disturbed, and the future is uncertain. Much depends on how accessible the area becomes as improvements to the primary arteries are made. Many who live here don't want to see it change, but already Highway 92 has been widened, and plans are afoot to bore a new hole through the mountains to make Highway 1 more passable through Devil's Slide, between Half Moon Bay and Pacifica.

The oldest community in San Mateo County, Half Moon Bay has already been gentrified. Art galleries, trendy boutiques, and sophisticated eateries like Pasta Moon and Sushi Main Street have taken up residence alongside San Mateo County Farm Supply and Cunha's Country Store. This is a small town attracting an increasingly wealthy population. Half Moon Bay is an appealing weekend destination, offering comfortable bed-and-breakfasts, urbane restaurants, upscale shopping, and an opportunity to chill out. And we mean chill out.

Emplaced in a natural setting of waves and sand backed by rolling brown hills and jutting headlands, the Coastside area is appealingly raw and strikingly beautiful. Frequently buried beneath a ceiling of coastal overcast, Half Moon Bay wears a gray, austere look. Heavy fogs

San Mateo County

carry as much as a million gallons of water shoreward per hour. Temperatures are unvarying: highs in the 60s, lows in the 40s. Precipitation varies a lot, however. May through mid-October is the dry season, while mid-October through April is rainy.

Beaches

Cowell Ranch State Beach, which lies three miles south of town, opened to the public in 1995. Getting to the beach requires a half-mile hike and a descent down a steep staircase, all of which ensures more privacy than you'll find on the beaches up in Half Moon Bay. **Pelican Point Beach,** about two miles south of where Highways 1 and 92 meet in Half Moon Bay, has a bit more to offer. The private campground has 84 campsites for tents and RVs, as well as beach access.

The big enchilada in these parts is **Half Moon Bay State Beach,** a 2.3-mile stretch of shoreline in Half Moon Bay proper. It has four named beaches: Francis, Venice, Dunes, and Roosevelt (from south to north). Theoretically, the six-mile Coastside Trail connects these beaches, running along the marine terrace above the water. It's used by joggers, bicyclists, and walkers. However, the trail is discontinuous, owing to bluffside erosion and the ocean's encroachment. Attempting to run its length one morning, we found ourselves stymied by sudden endings and reroutings. It's a lovely path to be sure, but one that is (like the coast itself) under siege, particularly at the north end. An equestrian trail runs parallel to the Coastside Trail. Horses can be rented by the hour at private stables in Half Moon Bay.

Francis Beach is the largest and most popular unit. It is reached by heading west along Kelly Avenue (off Highway 1) and then turning right on Balboa Boulevard, which leads to the gated entrance. A field of grassy short bluffs above the beach is studded with picnic tables. Picnicking families and their victuals

draw a crowd of hungry shorebirds that squawk for handouts and forage through garbage cans like a scene from Alfred Hitchcock's *The Birds.* Wave erosion and human feet have carved gullied paths down to the beach. From the sandy strand, it's another sharp drop to where the waves wash up. The steep gradient and strong backwash make this look to be an unsafe beach for swimming. Water temperatures hover just above 50 degrees, and hypothermia is almost guaranteed without a wet suit. Still, crowds descend on Francis Beach to camp, picnic, and play games at the beach.

A gravel road leads out to **Venice Beach,** which has a large parking lot and is a popular spot for horseback riding. **Dunes Beach** and **Roosevelt Beach** are smaller points of entry accessed from the same road (Young Avenue). Between Venice and Dunes is the **Sweetwood Group Camp,** a tent-only group campsite that can accommodate up to 50 persons and 12 vehicles. Close by are the **Sea Horse Ranch and Friendly Acres Horses and Rentals** (2150 Highway 1, 650/726-2362), where a 90-minute horse ride on the beach costs $40; add $10 for a barbecue dinner.

Shore Things

• **Bike/skate rentals:** Half Moon Bay Bike Rentals, 648 Kelly Avenue, Half Moon Bay, 650/712-4499
• **Ecotourism:** Pescadero State Beach Marsh Preserve, Pescadero, 650/879-2170
• **Lighthouse:** Pigeon Point Light Station, Pescadero, 650/879-0633; Montara Point Lighthouse, Montara, 650/728-7177
• **Marina:** Pillar Point Harbor, Princeton by the Sea, 650/726-5727
• **Pier:** Romeo Pier, Pillar Point Harbor, Princeton-by-the-Sea, 650/726-5727
• **Rainy day attraction:** gallery hopping, Main Street, Half Moon Bay
• **Shopping/browsing:** Main Street, Half Moon Bay
• **Sportfishing:** Riptide Sportfishing, H Dock,

San Mateo County

Pillar Point Harbor, Princeton-by-the-Sea, 650/747-8433

• **Surf shop:** Half Moon Bay Board Shop, 3032 Cabrillo Highway North, Half Moon Bay, 650/726-1476

• **Vacation rentals:** Del Mar Properties, 270 Main Street, Half Moon Bay, 650/712-6800

Bunking Down

The Beach House (4100 North Cabrillo Highway, 650/712-0220, $$$$) is a relative newcomer to Half Moon Bay. It's a modern, well-equipped (with fireplaces and CD changers), inn-like hotel that looks out on Princeton Harbor from the far north end of Half Moon Bay. The Coastside Trail—a scenic godsend to walkers, bikers, and runners—begins right out the Beach House's back door. The rooms are described as "ocean lofts," and they're not quite suites but more spacious than typical digs at hotels or inns. You can prop yourself up on pillows in bed and gaze out the picture window onto the harbor—not an unpleasant proposition. You can also cook a meal, listen to CDs, watch a film on the VCR, or warm up by the fire. In short, all the bases are covered at this ultramodern inn.

The posh **Half Moon Bay Lodge** (2400 South Cabrillo Highway, 650/726-9000, $$$$) is another recent arrival. It's part of the Woodside Hotels and Resorts collection, which is an assurance of quality. Rooms have an elegant, European feel. The Half Moon Bay Golf Links (two courses) and the beach are nearby. One cool morning we sat in the gazebo-covered outdoor whirlpool and soaked before heading off to grab the free continental breakfast. It's a relaxing place to de-stress on the San Mateo Coast. And the staff will happily point you to all the best restaurants in town, too.

The old Victorian buildings of Half Moon Bay have been preserved, and a few have been put to use as bed-and-breakfast inns. The most lavish of these is **Mill Rose Inn** (615 Mill Street, 650/726-8750, $$$$), a pricey,

overblown but romantic retreat in Half Moon Bay's Old Town district surrounded by an English country garden. They pamper you to the nines here: robes, wine and cheese, tubs for two, outdoor spa in a white gazebo, and so on. Roses are everywhere. Honeymooners, take note. Another denizen of the bed-and-breakfast scene is the **Old Thyme Inn** (7979 Main Street, 650/726-1616, $$), done in Queen Anne style with an herb garden and more affordable prices.

Half Moon Bay also has a couple of newer arrivals in the motel category, namely a **Ramada Ltd.** (3020 Cabrillo Highway, 650/726-9700, $) and a **Holiday Inn Express** (230 South Cabrillo Highway, 650/726-3400, $$). At the other extreme is the lately arrived **Ritz-Carlton Half Moon Bay** (1 Miramontes Point Road, 650/712-7000, $$$$), also by the golf links and perched on bluffs overlooking the ocean. This 261-room lodge, needless to say, is *le plus ultra* along the San Mateo Coast.

Coastal Cuisine

Since the restaurants of Half Moon Bay serve the discriminating palates of many who live (or once lived) in San Francisco, there is a respectable dining scene here. Topping the list is **Pasta Moon** (315 Main Street, 650/726-5125, $$$), where linguine with scallops and other seafood-pasta combos are worth raving about. **San Benito House** (356 Main Street, 650/726-3425, $$$) is a turn-of-the-century inn and restaurant known for California cuisine in a French country setting. San Benito was the original name of the settlement at Half Moon Bay. **Cetrella** (845 Main Street, 650/726-9040, $$$) serves Mediterranean cuisine and has a great bar and wine cellar. This recent arrival serves such entrées as local halibut over a corn, fava bean, and cherry tomato succotash (healthy!) and Catalonian shellfish stew.

Gourmet takeout fare or eat-in can be had at **Two Fools Cafe and Market** (408 Main Street, 650/712-1222, $$). **Main Street Grill**

San Mateo County

(435 Main Street, 650/726-5300, $) serves the best home-cooked breakfast and lunch on the San Mateo coast—everything from omelettes and sourdough French toast to burgers and microbrewed beers.

Raw fish addicts will want to head to **Sushi Main Street** (696 Mill Street, 650/726-6336, $$$). You can judge a sushi bar by its rolls, and Sushi Main Street's are killer. The local favorites are Half Moon Bay (artichoke heart, avocado, radish, sprouts) and Princeton-by-the-Sea (albacore, ginger, green onion). And dig the Hawaiian special: tuna, avocado, macadamia nuts. The restaurant also has hot entrées (tempuras, teriyakis) and clay pot specials.

On a more budget-conscious note, **Three Amigos** (200 South Cabrillo Highway, 650/726-6080, $$) will have you doing handstands and hat dances over its Mexican food. Go for the chicken fajita burrito, a hearty handful of grilled poultry strips and all the other Mexican essentials stuffed inside a flour tortilla. At first glance, it looks huge enough to feed a party of five, but one hungry gaucho can put it away without much trouble.

Night Moves

The **Half Moon Bay Inn** (401 Main Street, 650/726-5997), a dimly lit tavern smack dab in the center of town, is where the locals come to bend an elbow. The bar at the aforementioned **Cetrella** (845 Main Street, 650/726-9040) is a great place to sip wine or microbrewed beer. Alternatives in the communities north of Half Moon Bay include **Miramar Beach Restaurant** (131 Mirada Road, 650/726-9053) and **Moss Beach Distillery** (Beach and Ocean Streets, Moss Beach, 650/728-5595).

For More Information

Half Moon Bay/Coastside Chamber of Commerce, 520 Kelly Avenue, Half Moon Bay, CA 94019, 650/726-8380, website: www.halfmoonbaychamber.org

Miramar

Miramar is more remarkable for what it used to be than what it is. It was once the site of the Palace Miramar, a seaside resort hotel (circa 1916) with an indoor saltwater plunge. During Prohibition, Miramar served as the dropoff point for bootleg liquor shipped down from Canada. Local rumrunners paddled out to meet the large ships and carry the hooch to shore under cover of darkness. The Miramar Beach Inn (circa 1918) was designed and constructed as a Prohibition roadhouse and, it is rumored, bordello. These days, the same building does business as the Miramar Beach Restaurant, a rustic eatery and music club with great ocean views. Miramar itself (population 400) is a sweet nothing of a town: a few residential streets running parallel to a beach that disappears rapidly as high tide approaches.

Beaches

Miramar Beach adjoins El Granada Beach (see next entry), which runs up to the breakwater at Pillar Point Harbor. The breakwater, built in 1959, has caused massive erosion on the beaches south of it. It interrupts the natural, shore-parallel movement of sand down the coast and focuses greater wave energy on the beaches, resulting in accelerated sea-cliff erosion. Parts of Mirada Road have been destroyed, and the highly erodable cliffs have retreated an estimated 90 feet since the harbor construction project. Life is a beach, unless you live downdrift of a breakwater or jetty, in which case life is a shrinking beach.

Bunking Down

The **Cypress Inn** (407 Mirada Road, 650/726-6002, $$$) is a bright, contemporary B&B outfitted in Southwestern decor. The three-story, 12-room inn was built a stone's throw from the ocean in 1989, and every comfort-

San Mateo County

able room has a fireplace, balcony, and view of Miramar Beach.

Coastal Cuisine

The **Miramar Beach Restaurant** (131 Mirada Road, 650/726-9053, $$$) was revamped some in the 1990s. It still has the sturdy, solid look of dark wood and brass, but the menu has been expanded and updated. In addition to grilled steaks and seafood, you can order linguine with cracked crab and bay shrimp or salmon in puff pastry.

Night Moves

Surprisingly, for a town that's just a blip on the coastal radar, Miramar boasts two revered music spots. **Miramar Beach Restaurant** (131 Mirada Road, 650/762-9053) tends to book the remnants of San Francisco bands that stood the world on its ear in the 1960s and are somehow scraping by today. During one of our treks through the area, former members of Moby Grape, the Doobie Brothers, and the Sons of Champlin were all booked.

The other side of Mirada's musical coin is the **Bach Dancing and Dynamite Society** (Mirada Road, 650/726-4131), an oceanfront beach house whose owner and impresario, Peter Douglas, hosts 26 Sunday afternoon concerts a year—mainly jazz and the classics. You can bring your own wine and picnic on the deck while the band plays.

For More Information

Half Moon Bay/Coastside Chamber of Commerce, 520 Kelly Avenue, Half Moon Bay, CA 94019, 650/726-8380, website: www.half moonbaychamber.org

El Granada

El Granada is a mostly residential town of 5,500 arrayed in semicircular roads on the east side of Highway 1. It has a touch of everything for the tourist: a nice, comfy inn that's a five-minute stroll from the beach (**Harbor View Inn,** 51 Avenue Alhambra, 650/726-2329, $$), a good continental bistro that offers live jazz and classical music on weekends (**Cafe Classique,** 107 Sevilla Avenue, 650/726-9775, $$$), and El Granada Beach.

Beaches

El Granada Beach is wide, but the short bluffs behind it suffer erosion when winter storms do their damage. Sometimes the sea chomps through the riprap and into the roadway, necessitating repairs. Pillar Point Harbor (see next entry) has brought increased commerce to Coastside but made a mess of the beaches next door. Still, water-sports enthusiasts—boogie boarders, ocean kayakers, and surfers—have fun just below the east breakwater, an area known as **Surfers Beach.**

For More Information

Half Moon Bay/Coastside Chamber of Commerce, 520 Kelly Avenue, Half Moon Bay, CA 94019, 650/726-8380, website: www.half moonbaychamber.org

San Mateo County

Princeton-by-the-Sea and Pillar Point

The cliffs of Pillar Point form a protective shield enfolding the development known as Pillar Point Harbor. The Army Corps of Engineers built two breakwaters in 1961, further protecting the harbor and allowing expansion to its present size of 369 berths. Surrounding the harbor is the community of Princeton-by-the-Sea (population 1,000), an unpretentious scattering of Cape Cod-type homes that were here long before the faux New England architectural theme became an overplayed cliché on the California coast. Princeton is a quiet town along Harbor Road, which curves off and rejoins Highway 1. Pillar Point is a real working harbor whose 180-boat fishing fleet lands 10 million pounds of fish a year.

Not surprisingly, there are some terrific seafood restaurants in the area—probably the best grouping of them between San Francisco and Santa Cruz. Still, the harbor complex doesn't appear to be prospering the way its developers might have hoped. A huge, glassed-in harborfront retail complex, complete with cushy hotels and restaurants, never got beyond the planning stages.

Beaches

Half Moon Bay made headlines in 1994 when a world-class surfer was killed while riding a 18-foot wave at a break called Maverick's, offshore of **Pillar Point** (see sidebar). Maverick's is not for the timid or inexperienced, but the word is out—both about the size of waves when

Surf's Way, Way Up at Maverick's

Maverick's is where the most fearless wave-riders in the world come to play Russian roulette with Mother Nature. Hawaiian surfer Mark Foo, considered the greatest big-wave rider of them all, met his match two days before Christmas 1994 when he disappeared inside an 18-foot wave. His splintered surfboard and 36-year-old body were found floating in the harbor an hour later. Foo's premature exit made national headlines and was the subject of multiple magazine articles that helped put Maverick's, big-wave riding, and the larger notion of "extreme sports" on the map. The whole spin wasn't so much "what a senseless tragedy" but "awesome wave, dude!" As a result, the winter wave-riding scene at Maverick's regularly receives national coverage. Now it's been formalized into a competition—bearing the macho name "Men Who Ride Mountains"—underwritten by the surfboard maker Quiksilver.

So what's all the fuss about? Maverick's lies beyond the cliffs along the north shore of Pillar Point, where huge swells from far-distant storms create waves as high as 40 feet four or five times a year during the winter storm season. It is a quarter-mile, half-hour paddle out to this ferocious, open-ocean break. (Most surfers get there by boat.) Risks associated with Maverick's—aside from the obvious one of falling off a mountain of water and being driven to the ocean floor until drowned—include shark attacks and being filleted on the nearshore rocks. The *San Francisco Chronicle* has branded Maverick's "the wildest, heaviest, most dangerous big-wave spot on

Map of Central California—Page 233

they're breaking, and their lethal potential. Unless you're a world-class daredevil, just stay onshore and look for whales or at surfers. Pillar Point is a prime location for whale-watching December–March.

Bunking Down

But for the west-facing coastline, the **Pillar Point Inn** (380 Capistrano Road, 650/728-7377, $$$) might make you think this is Massachusetts rather than California. This stately gray Cape Codder has 11 rooms filled with feather beds and decor accenting local history.

Coastal Cuisine

Princeton scores high marks with regard to food, since seafood makes a quick passage from fishing boats to restaurant kitchens in this area.

For terrific fried seafood in comfortably funky surroundings, duck into **Barbara's Fishtrap** (281 Capistrano Road, 650/726-7049, $$). You may have to wait in line, and Barbara's doesn't accept credit cards or reservations.

Another local institution is the **Shore Bird Restaurant** (390 Capistrano Road, 650/728-5541, $$$). The building is a replica of a house on Cape Cod, copied down to the minutest detail. Overlooking the harbor and surrounded by a garden and a white picket fence, the Shore Bird looks more like a prosperous sea captain's home than one of the area's most popular dining spots. The restaurant specializes in fresh, broiled fish preparations.

You really can't go wrong anywhere around the harbor. We made a good, simple midday meal of clam chowder and sourdough bread

---

earth." There's even a risk involved in watching this madness from the tall, slippery cliffs at Pillar Point.

Maverick's is not for the timid or inexperienced, which is why it's fortunate the spot has a no-nonsense gatekeeper in Jeff Cook, who discovered it back in 1975. The surfing competition at Maverick's runs from the beginning of November to the end of January, is by invitation only, and is limited to 20—most of them Northern Californians with plenty of prior experience at Maverick's. Still, this is extreme sports in extremis: a surfing event where wave height and water temperature reach unfathomably high and low points, respectively, nearly meeting somewhere in the 40s and testing the most indomitable competitor's will to power.

All this danger is courted for what amounts to chump change in the world of professional sports. As Mark Foo griped shortly before his death, "We're out there risking our lives for nothing, or maybe a few thousand bucks, while some overweight guy is standing over a three-foot putt for half a million dollars." Money isn't even a factor in the minds of most who surf Maverick's, however. It's the challenge of those big waves and the indescribable rush of what is almost a certifiable act of insanity.

If you want to watch the goings-on at Maverick's on big-wave days, take West Point Road to the U.S. Air Force Radar Tracking Station at Pillar Point. Park at the small lot by the marsh and follow the trail out to the bluffs, where surfers will be visible in the distance. If the lot is full (and it probably will be) you might have to park down at Pillar Point Harbor and walk an hour to the site. You see, nothing about Maverick's is easy.

San Mateo County

at **Ketch Joanne's** (25 Johnson Pier, Pillar Point Harbor, 650/728-5959, $$$), a complex that includes a bar/restaurant, fish market, and open-air seafood barbecue grill. As usual, the list of fresh fish goes on and on.

Night Moves

You can grab a beer or drink at **Ketch Joanne's Harbor Bar** (17 Johnson Pier, Pillar Point Harbor, 650/728-5959), but for anything more you'll need to head up to Moss Beach or down to Miramar. Hey, see if *you* feel like partying after a hard day of hauling fish onto the deck of a wave-tossed boat.

For More Information

Half Moon Bay/Coastside Chamber of Commerce, 520 Kelly Avenue, Half Moon Bay, CA 94019, 650/726-8380, website: www.half moonbaychamber.org

Moss Beach

Tucked off Highway 1 six miles north of Half Moon Bay, Moss Beach (population 4,200) is another in a string of inviting Coastside communities. It's got a New England–village feel, but in a natural and not voguish way. Remnants of the little town's rum-running history survive at Moss Beach Distillery, a Prohibition-era roadhouse that's endured as a popular restaurant and landmark. The chief natural attraction of Moss Beach is James V. Fitzgerald Marine Reserve, which runs for three miles below the bluffs between Pillar Point and Montara.

Beaches

We had a queasy feeling about Moss Beach, which is formally known as the **James V. Fitzgerald Marine Reserve.** We tried to enter from the parking lot at Moss Beach Distillery, but a sign announced the closure of the trail into the reserve. Crumbling cliffs, washed-out trails—same old story. We somehow fumbled our way onto the beach, later discovering there's an easy access from the reserve's well-marked parking lot. (Follow signs from Highway 1.) It was a weird stretch of sand that smelled of seaweed and was covered with black gunk that looked like asphalt chunks. At low tide the ocean pulls back to reveal acres of tidepools, the reserve's big draw. You can investigate on your own or take a ranger-led walk. For information on times and places, call the reserve at 650/728-3584.

In the end we discovered that Moss Beach does have its charms. We explored a trail leading up one of the southern cliffs and found ourselves in a large, eerie cypress forest. From there we took a staircase down to a lovely, secluded beach. No complaints, honest.

Bunking Down

The **Seal Cove Inn** (221 Cypress Avenue, 650/728-7325, $$$) is a recently constructed English manor house that overlooks the ocean in a setting of cypress and wildflowers. It's the kind of comfortably luxurious place that draws people who come to decompress from life in the city—you know, kick back, light a fire, read a book, and get sane again.

Coastal Cuisine

The **Moss Beach Distillery** (Beach Way and Ocean Boulevard, 650/728-5595, $$$) is celebrated for its great beachside location, its history, and its possession by ghosts. There's a long story that goes with this, centering around the legend of the Blue Lady, a married woman who died in a car wreck en route to meet her lounge-lizard boyfriend here 75 years ago. Now they both supposedly haunt the place—as does the lounge lizard's distraught wife, who leapt to her death upon learning of his infidelity.

Beyond this amusing nonsense, which is occasionally goosed up with ghostly "special effects," the Moss Beach Distillery offers a

San Mateo County

superb coastal view and serves entrées that run the gamut from pasta and steak to a host of fresh seafood specials. The prevailing culinary approach is uncomplicated but serviceable. And don't you just love the address: the intersection of Beach Way and Ocean Boulevard, evoking a figurative seaside paradise where we should all be so lucky to spend the rest of our days.

Night Moves

The **Moss Beach Distillery** (Beach Way and Ocean Boulevard) is the place to come for an afternoon libation or a late-evening nightcap. The outdoor patio is stocked with deck chairs and heavy blankets. Order a drink, tuck yourself in, and watch the sunset—if you're lucky enough to catch one. If you eventually start seeing double, it may have nothing to do with ghosts.

For More Information

Half Moon Bay/Coastside Chamber of Commerce, 520 Kelly Avenue, Half Moon Bay, CA 94019, 650/726-8380, website: www.half moonbaychamber.org

Montara

Montara was conceived at the turn of the century as an artists' colony by a bohemian magazine publisher from San Francisco. However, his grand plans for a seaside community of creative types never took hold, and the artists were displaced by bootleggers. Today, Montara has reclaimed some of its intended character. It's another likable link in the Coastside chain—a nice place to visit or live. Unless, of course, you have to commute over Devil's Slide.

As luck would have it, we spent our last day of beachcombing for an early edition of this book at Montara. The gods were with us that August afternoon, because the sunset we witnessed was one for the ages—our solar going-away present, we figured. For about 10 wonderful minutes, people spontaneously dropped what they were doing—be it surfing at Montara State Beach or dining on surf-and-turf at the Chart House—to watch the last sublime rays before the sun dropped from sight. Oddly enough, the sky was cloudy except for a narrow clearing of blue just above the horizon. All of a sudden a brilliant gold band of light appeared between the cloud bank and the ocean. The sun glowed a fiery red-orange as it made its brief but stunning sojourn, dipping behind the horizon with a final flicker and twinkle that drew whoops and applause. It was, we offer with no irony, a religious experience. Ah, California.

Beaches

Montara State Beach is the hippest beach in San Mateo County. That's not saying a lot, really. From Montara south to the Santa Cruz County line, less than 30,000 people live along the coast, and relatively few of them are self-consciously hip. Some pick artichokes and Brussels sprouts. Others make real-estate deals or work in Silicon Valley. Then there are retirees and the second-home wealthy. Montara, for some anomalous reason probably having to do with proximity to Pacifica and San Francisco, draws a younger crowd. They play games on the beach—volleyball, Frisbee, paddleball—as if down on Santa Cruz's Cowell Beach rather than knocking on the back door of Fogtown. Waves are good, if inconsistent. The scene is cool, the water cold.

Bunking Down

Many years ago, we stayed at the **Farallone Inn** (1410 Main Street, 650/728-8200, $$) back before it got its massive facelift. Suffice it to say that it needed it, and now it's a modernized, refurbished wonder. All nine rooms have decks and hot tubs, yet there are still

Devil's Slide: A Hell of a Headache

Highway 1 negotiates a treacherous and unstable passage between Pacifica and Montara known as Devil's Slide. It has always been subject to short-term closures for various reasons, but during January 1995, in the midst of a considerable rainy spell, the road at Devil's Slide essentially slipped off its hinges. A four-mile section of Highway 1 through Devil's Slide was immediately closed and remained so for 158 days. This added delays of up to two hours for Coastside commuters who were forced to take Highway 92. Then the debate began: Repair the existing road? Blast a tunnel through the mountain? Build an inland bypass?

Highway engineers and environmentalists have been locked in a pitched battle over Devil's Slide since the 1960s. CalTrans would like to pursue the inland option, cutting across McNee Ranch State Park, but the Sierra Club filed suit to protect the parkland. Environmental groups want to see a tunnel drilled through San Pedro Mountain, which separates Montara and Pacifica. CalTrans argued that would be prohibitively expensive and a geological gamble. Environmentalists argued that the bypass would scar the landscape, silt the watershed, and subject drivers to dangerous fog much of the time. The business community viewed the environmentalists as bleeding-heart obstructionists and pressed to have the 4.3-mile bypass built for the sake of business as usual. "We'd much rather have a safe road than another state park," groused a restaurant manager, echoing the prevailing sentiment.

However, the voters of San Mateo County won the day, overwhelmingly approving the tunnel option by a 76–24 margin in November 1996. The California Coastal Commission certified it a year later. The plan that CalTrans will in all likelihood carry out calls for construction of a 4,000-foot-long double-bore tunnel through San Pedro Mountain. The current projected cost of construction is $272 million—more than double the 1996 estimate. In April 2002, the Federal Highway Administration approved the Environmental Impact Statement for the project, taking it one step closer. CalTrans guesses that construction will begin in summer/fall 2004 and take three years to complete. Once the tunnel has opened, the abandoned stretch of Highway 1 at Devil's Slide will be deeded to San Mateo County for use by bicycles and other nonmotorized traffic.

Just remember that until the tunnel is built, the devil still has the upper hand at this dangerous slide area.

San Mateo County

Map of Central California—Page 233

reminders of its 1908 heritage. **The Goose and Turrets** (835 George Street, 650/728-5451, $$) is a rambling house with a lot of character. You can walk to the beach or lie in the garden hammock, reading and daydreaming about the four-course breakfast that's served every morning. If you're living on a shoestring, you can board cheaply at **Montara Lighthouse Hostel** (Highway 1 at 16th Street, 650/728-7177, $).

Coastal Cuisine

Steve's Blue Pacific Restaurant (Seventh Street and Highway 1, 650/728-5209, $$) is the kind of place that locals like to keep to themselves and out-of-towners wouldn't think to visit without being tipped off. Well, consider yourself tipped. Barbecue is the specialty, and the smoked entrées—prime rib, baby-back ribs, beef bones—rule. You can also order charbroiled salmon, halibut, and prawns.

The Foglifter (8455 Highway 1, 650/728-7905, $$) is another locals' favorite whose rather ramshackle facade belies the cozy dining room and excellent seafood and Italian fare within. The local **Chart House** (8150 Highway 1, 650/728-7366, $$$) is a landmark, overlooking and sharing a parking lot with Montara State Beach. It's high-quality surf-and-turf fare from a franchise that's got the best seaside locations in California. When Devil's Slide shuts down Highway 1, this is where the "Road Closed" signs go up.

For More Information

Half Moon Bay/Coastside Chamber of Commerce, 520 Kelly Avenue, Half Moon Bay, CA 94019, 650/726-8380, website: www.half moonbaychamber.org

Gray Whale Cove State Beach

Strange as it may sound, the state of California is a partner in the nude-beach business. **Gray Whale Cove State Beach** (a.k.a. **Devil's Slide**) is privately managed on state-owned land as a clothing-optional beach. There are restrooms, pop machines, even a hot-dog stand (though it's up to you to bring the buns, if you know what we mean). Here's the drill at Gray Whale Cove: park on the east side of Highway 1, hike down to the small, 800-foot cove, pay your money, and let it all hang out. Gray Whale Cove, incidentally, has recovered nicely after the beach-stripping ravages of El Niño.

Pacifica

Pacifica is not just one small city but a conglomeration of nine separate townships and subdivisions that came together in 1957. For this reason it is not your average municipality. There is no center of town, per se, and each area retains something of an independent personality. There is considerable parkland and wonderful ocean views from the upper elevations of Milagra Ridge and Sweeney Ridge. Pacifica's chief problem, as regards tourism, is that it lies in the long shadow of San Francisco. Somehow, "If you are going to Pacifica/Be sure to wear some flowers in your hair" just doesn't have the same ring.

No one in their right mind is going to make Pacifica (population 40,000) a vacation destination—not with San Francisco's overwhelming abundance of culture, architecture, and activities so close by. Residents of San Francisco who are looking for a weekend getaway simply pass through Pacifica—if they pass through town at all—en route to the Half Moon Bay area. This is somewhat ironic, since Rockaway Beach served as "the Playground for San Francisco" for a good portion of the last century.

San Mateo County

Map of San Mateo County—Page 434

Gone with the Waves: El Niño's Impact on California Beaches

Back in August 1997, *Time* magazine posed the question "Is It El Niño of the Century?" That was well before the full effects of the weather-altering phenomenon had been felt across the Americas. In its aftermath, many would agree that the winter of 1997–98 was indeed the mother of all El Niños. It brought intense flooding to North Dakota, prolonged drought and heat to Texas, deadly twisters to Tennessee, drought and wildfire to Florida. It also brought hellacious downpours to the California coast, and the battering wrought some lasting changes to the beaches. El Niño's legacy includes eroded beaches, landslides, road closings, and property damage.

Before getting into impact, we'll summarize the El Niño phenomenon. *El niño* is Spanish for "Christ child," so called because it generally appears around Christmas. It is triggered by the cessation of trade winds, which triggers an unusual warming of the Pacific Ocean along the equator. Normally, these winds cause the ocean to tilt two feet higher on the Asian side of the Pacific. That tilt causes cold, deep, nutrient-enriched water to upwell along the Peruvian coast as the ocean restores equilibrium across its basin. During an El Niño event, however, trade winds weaken and warmer water piles up in the eastern Pacific. The thermocline—the divide between warmer surface water and colder underlying water—breaks down. When trade winds weaken and the thermocline dissolves, eastern Pacific fisheries go into sharp decline and meteorological havoc breaks loose. All of the accumulated energy in the ocean and atmosphere fuels huge storms—and that's exactly what California got lashed with for months.

Beaches were drastically reconfigured along the California coast, with the stretch between Big Sur and Marin County particularly hard-hit. In Carmel, a formerly wide, white mountain of sand is noticeably steeper and narrower. At Stinson Beach, more than a million cubic yards of sand were stripped from the shoreline. In Southern California, Cardiff State Beach has been rendered a beachless wreck of buckled concrete and twisted metal. South Carlsbad State

San Mateo County

Then there are ever-present problems with Devil's Slide, the high-hazard area that links Pacifica with the rest of San Mateo County. Of all the locations on the California coast, Pacifica was hit hardest by El Niño. Nature's unkindest cut came in March 1998, when houses along Esplanade began teetering at the edges of coastal bluffs that had eroded 30 feet shoreward in two weeks. The unstable, rain-soaked cliffs crumbled, and waves lapping at their bases further accelerated erosion. Ten houses collapsed or had to be destroyed.

Beaches

Pacifica does have a few things going for it: a

Map of Central California—Page 233

Beach is a sea of cobbles lying below collapsing bluffs. San Diego County alone needs 30 million cubic yards of sand to replenish its beaches in the wake of El Niño. The beach at Capitola, in Santa Cruz County, lost 200 feet of width (later replenished with replacement sand). Storm-driven drift logs piled up along the beaches of Northern California. In terms of property damage, the biggest loser was Pacifica, where 10 homes fell into the ocean or had to be destroyed.

Ideally, the bright side is that El Niño's torrential rains were supposed to replenish the beaches with a fresh supply of sand scoured from all the rushing creeks and rivers. The reality is that much of that desperately needed sediment remained trapped behind dams. Once again, humankind found a way to eliminate the silver lining to an undeniably dark cloud. However, all is not bad news. Cowell Beach, in Santa Cruz, is healthier than it was before El Niño, and a couple of pocket beaches popped in the coves along West Cliff Drive in its aftermath. Many say that California's coastal waters are cleaner.

The what's-wrong-with-this-picture scenario became more skewed farther up the West Coast, where semitropical fish like yellowfin tuna and blue marlin were suddenly being caught by anglers off the coast of Washington state. Those species had never before been seen in the normally frigid waters of the Northwest. The California Fish and Game Department, noting the unusual influx of warmwater species like mahimahi, reported that "El Niño Brings Great Opportunity for Anglers." Further confounding the good news, bad news routine was the fact that the Pacific mackerel, a fish that feeds on juvenile forms of the already embattled salmon species, were among those showing up in increased numbers.

Meanwhile, certain beaches and stretches of coastline are clearly still hurting, having been stripped of their sandy mantle by a combination of factors. Several of them are clearly human-driven—for instance, the beach-narrowing effects of jetties, groins, and seawalls, and the sediment-starving impacts of dams along California's rivers. Even the unusually fierce El Niño event of 1997–98 is blamed by some on human activities. That is to say, some scientists believe that El Niño was far stronger than normal because of the role global warming has played in altering atmospheric chemistry. This is a scary thought. If it ever gets to the point that there is no longer any such thing as "a day at the beach," we may have only ourselves to blame.

San Mateo County

restaurant-motel complex at Rockaway Beach and a fishing pier at Sharp Park where salmon are there for the taking. Fall and winter are particularly nice times to visit; it's generally sunny, with moderate temperatures.

Some of the biggest winter waves on the Central Coast roll ashore on the cocoa-colored sands of **Rockaway Beach,** whose build-ings are protected from the intrusive surf by rip-rap boulders. About a half mile south lies **Pacifica State Beach,** whose light brown sand and calmer waters provide sharp contrast. Pedro Point provides partial protection from another big, dangerous wave break. **Esplanade Beach** (a.k.a. **Sharp Park**) is a little over a mile north of Rockaway. Drainpipes poke

Map of San Mateo County—Page 434

the ocean at either end of the dark-sand beach, adding to the drab setting. A concrete pier that only an angler could love sits up at the north end. The lure at Sharp Park is fishing, both from the 1,020-foot **Pacifica Pier** (650/355-0690) and the beach. Catches include salmon and striped bass (in summer), plus rock bass, surf perch, and jacksmelt. It is claimed this pier is the only place in California where you can land a salmon without a boat.

Bunking Down

A complex of motels and restaurants at Rockaway Beach would like to project a resort aura. Yet a certain tentativeness pervades the area, as if they're afraid it all might wash away. And well it might. The long-standing Lighthouse Hotel has had its ups and downs up until a 1998 renovation and reincarnation as **Best Western Lighthouse Hotel** (105 Rockaway Beach Avenue, 650/355-6300, $$$). It's a perfectly serviceable, 92-unit motel; prices run $115–225, depending on time of year. There's also a Victorian-style **Days Inn** (200 Rockaway Beach Avenue, 650/359-7700, $$)—one of the nicer franchises in that generally downscale chain— at Rockaway Beach.

Coastal Cuisine

The **Moonraker** (105 Rockaway Beach Avenue, 650/355-6300, $$$) has been a romantic favorite for three decades but lost some of its reputation and fell on hard times for a while. Now it's back on the upswing as part of the Best Western Lighthouse Hotel complex. **Nick's Restaurant** (100 Rockaway Beach Boulevard, 650/359-3900, $$$) takes its fine-dining rep seriously, with a tuxedo-clad wait staff bustling about. A local landmark, Nick's is also attached to a motel (the Seabreeze, a modest little 20-room job). Nick's serves three meals a day, seven days a week.

Night Moves

In addition to being a restaurant, **Nick's** (100 Rockaway Beach Boulevard, 650/359-3900) is a cocktails-and-dancing kind of place, with live music on weekends. It's like stepping into the past, back when Rockaway Beach was San Francisco's playground and not the overlooked footnote it is today.

For More Information

Pacifica Chamber of Commerce, 225 Rockaway Beach #1, Pacifica, CA 94044, 650/355-4122, website: www.pacificachamber.com

Daly City

A sizable backdoor suburb of San Francisco, Daly City (population 103,650) offers unsightly evidence of the area's insatiable need for bedrooms. It was Daly City that inspired folksinger Malvina Reynolds to write "Tiny Boxes," a derisive commentary on mass-produced housing projects: "Tiny boxes, little boxes, and they're all made out of ticky-tack." Not much has changed since Reynolds' lampoon from the 1960s except more tiny boxes have gone up and a verse about cheesy condos could be added. Tightly packed together, running up and down the hillsides, they look like plastic Monopoly houses. Some of them are built

right along the San Andreas Fault. Talk about living dangerously!

Beaches

Thornton State Beach lies below steep coastal bluffs and is best accessed by walking down from Fort Funston or up from Mussel Rock City Park. A hiking trail follows the blufftop. People sometimes scramble down the cliffs to reach the sand, though this is not recommended because of the history of landslides. The main attraction on Thornton Beach is surf casting. The beach is all but useless for any other purpose during the summer months, which are foggy and cold. It does become more hospitable in the fall—which is the real summer out here—when temperatures warm and the sun breaks free of its fog-induced funk.

For years Thornton State Beach has been closed; its status is in limbo. It hasn't recovered from 1982–83 winter storms that wiped out the beachside parking and facilities. These notations are from a 1982 U.S. Geographical Survey El Niño Coastal Erosion Map: "Severe beach and cliff erosion . . . Landslide damaged highway . . . Road to parking lot of Thornton State Beach downdropped about 7 meters [al-most 23 feet] along headwall scarp of pre-existing landslide. The state park facilities were permanently abandoned."

Daly City has been wanting to improve access, via hiking trails, to what is a perfectly fine, if landslide-prone, beach. Don't think about swimming, though: too cold, too dangerous.

For More Information

Greater Daly City Chamber of Commerce, 335 Gellert Boulevard, Suite 230, Daly City, CA 94015, 650/991-5101, website: www.daly city-colmachamber.org

San Mateo County

© ROBERT HOLMES/CALTOUR

Northern California

Chapter 10
San Francisco County

Northern California

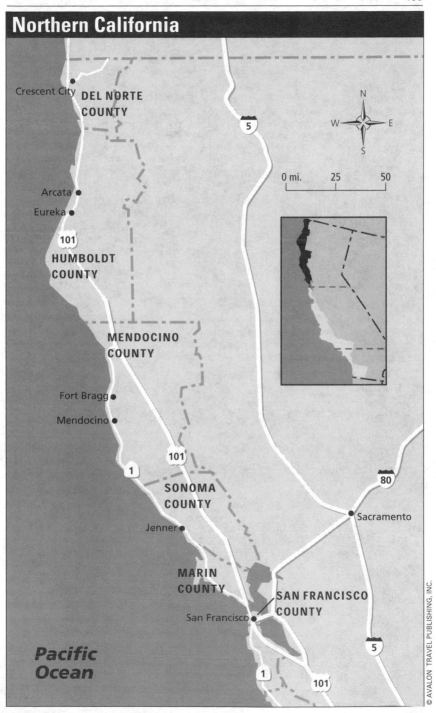

Crescent City

DEL NORTE COUNTY

Arcata

Eureka

101

HUMBOLDT COUNTY

MENDOCINO COUNTY

Fort Bragg

Mendocino

101

1

SONOMA COUNTY

Jenner

MARIN COUNTY

SAN FRANCISCO COUNTY

San Francisco

Sacramento

80

5

1

101

5

N
W — E
S

0 mi.   25   50

Pacific Ocean

© AVALON TRAVEL PUBLISHING, INC.

San Francisco County

San Francisco County

© AVALON TRAVEL PUBLISHING, INC.

San Francisco County Beaches

Burton Memorial Beach, page 470

Location: south of Fort Funston at Skyline Boulevard/Highway 35, near San Mateo County line
Parking/fees: free parking lot
Hours: 6 A.M.–one hour after sunset
Facilities: none
Contact: Golden Gate National Recreation Area, 415/556-0560

Fort Funston Beach, page 470

Location: off Skyline Boulevard/Highway 35, one mile north of San Mateo County line
Parking/fees: free parking lot
Hours: 6 A.M.–one hour after sunset
Facilities: restrooms and picnic tables
Contact: Golden Gate National Recreation Area, 415/556-0560

Ocean Beach, page 470

Location: Great Highway, between Cliff House and San Francisco Zoo, in San Francisco
Parking/fees: free street parking
Hours: 6 A.M.–10 P.M.
Facilities: restrooms
Contact: Golden Gate National Recreation Area, 415/556-0560

Lands End, page 470

Location: From Geary Boulevard in San Francisco turn north onto Merrie Way and park on street. Follow Lands End Trail to beach.
Parking/fees: free street parking
Hours: 6 A.M.–one hour after sunset
Facilities: none
Contact: Golden Gate National Recreation Area, 415/556-0560

China Beach, page 470

Location: Seacliff Avenue at El Camino Del Mar in San Francisco; trail leads to beach
Parking/fees: free limited street parking
Hours: 6 A.M.–one hour after sunset

San Francisco County

Map of San Francisco County—Page 464

Facilities: lifeguard, restrooms, showers, and picnic tables
Contact: Golden Gate National Recreation Area, 415/556-0560

6 Baker Beach, page 471

🏃 🗑 ☀️4

Location: west end of Gibson Road, near southwest corner of Presidio, in San Francisco
Parking/fees: free parking lot
Hours: 6 A.M.–one hour after sunset
Facilities: restrooms and picnic tables
Contact: Golden Gate National Recreation Area, 415/556-0560

7 North Baker Beach, page 471

🏃 🗑 ☀️2

Location: walk north from Baker Beach
Parking/fees: free parking lot (at Baker Beach)
Hours: 6 A.M.–one hour after sunset
Facilities: none
Contact: Golden Gate National Recreation Area, 415/556-0560

San Francisco County

Map of Northern California—Page 463

San Francisco County

While one can easily leave their heart in this remarkable city-county, we left our footprints in the sand. That's right. The city by the bay has an unheralded side to its personality. The eight-mile stretch of ocean coastline from the San Mateo border to the Golden Gate Bridge is all public land, and much of it is fronted by sand.

An ocean beach in San Francisco, you say? No, not just an ocean beach, but Ocean Beach, a four-mile strand that stretches from Daly City to an old landmark, the Cliff House. This beach has it all—sand dunes, sea walls (dressed up by WPA murals from the 1930s), walkways, promontories. So where are all the swimsuit-clad beachgoers? Well, the plain fact is that San Francisco's beaches don't see very many days of sunshine or wind-free warmth. Especially during the summer months, the shoreline fog is so thick you need a divining rod to find the water. And when you do, the frigid, tempestuous waves roar their disapproval. The riptide-prone Ocean Beach is flat-out dangerous, having claimed the lives of many unwary swimmers over the years.

If you stay dry and enjoy the view, you'll be fine. No city in America is blessed with such awe-inspiring ocean vistas as San Francisco. The view from the Presidio's coastal trail north toward the Golden Gate Bridge and the Marin Headlands is one that everybody should lay eyes on during their lifetime. There are even a couple of beaches—Baker Beach and China Beach—where one can sunbathe in relative comfort. They're around the protective bend of Lands End.

Map of San Francisco County—Page 464

San Francisco

San Francisco really doesn't belong in this book. Coming to this magnificent city for its beaches is like going to Las Vegas for its libraries—no doubt they exist, but they hold a very low priority among visitors, and they're far from being the best examples of their kind. The beaches of San Francisco just aren't the sorts of places you'd want to spend a lot of vacation time. The water's cold, the surf rough, the wind stiff, the fog chilling. That said, it's also true that on one of those rare golden days when the sun is out and the wind has subsided to a whisper, there's no more glorious place to be, especially at sunset.

But back to the original point. We would have preferred to bypass San Francisco and left this splendid city to the myriad travel books devoted exclusively to its manifold assets and activities. However, the city does have beaches, so we'll dutifully cover that aspect of its geography forthwith. Just don't expect more than a quick overview of San Francisco's waterfront, because 400 miles of Northern California coastline remain ahead of us.

If you're coming here be sure to pack warm clothes. Just because it's summertime, don't think you can get away with wearing shorts and a T-shirt. In the words of Mark Twain, "The coldest winter I ever spent was a summer in San Francisco." Dress as you would for autumn in New England; wear long pants and keep a sweater tied around your neck. And if you venture here in the winter, make sure you pack an umbrella—the rainy season typically extends November–March.

Before hitting the beaches, we should say a few words about **Fisherman's Wharf,** that working dock turned tourist trap. It's overrun by disposable-camera-toting outsiders and shunned by locals. All the same, there are a few good reasons for dropping by—and an equal number for not sticking around too long. Come to stroll the bayside streets, dodging the low-

rent vendors' plaints if possible. We're fond of the seafood takeout counters lined outside the wharfside restaurants. For three or four bucks, you can grab a cup of crab, shrimp, lobster, or squid topped with a tangy dollop of cocktail sauce and a squeeze of lemon. The protein will fortify you for hiking around Nob Hill, Russian Hill, and all the other hills in this vertically inclined city when you tire of the waterfront. If you're looking for a more substantial meal, Italian-surnamed seafood restaurants are plentiful.

Shopping opportunities abound, although there is a distinct low-end aspect to the Fisherman's Wharf retail experience. Along Taylor Street, which runs down to the wharf, we had unsettling flashbacks of Venice Beach in Southern California. Sidewalk peddlers hawk T-shirts, sunglasses, sweatshirts (the Unholy Trinity of street sales), and assorted junk and gimcracks. At the other end of the spectrum, visitors with a ready line of credit will want to explore the maze of shops and boutiques at the **Cannery** (a former Del Monte produce-packing plant) and **Ghirardelli Square** (a converted chocolate factory). East of Fisherman's Wharf is **Pier 39,** a teeming bazaar that draws a zombiefied crowd of browsers and buyers. Fat, overfed sea lions bob about the green water, barking at tourists for handouts. The crowd-pleasing pinnipeds have mutated from intelligent, vigorously active creatures into slovenly pier bums, much like their human counterparts. This, of course, is no way to experience San Francisco, unless you're completely lacking in imagination and curiosity.

Other wharf-area attractions include ferry rides and tours of islands in the bay, which leave from Piers 41 and 43 ½. The National Park Service conducts trips to **Alcatraz** (415/546-2805), the small, jutting island on which a grim-looking former federal penitentiary housed America's most hardened felons, including the

Map of Northern California—Page 463

Golden Gate National Recreation Area

This amazing park encompasses 75,398 acres (114 square miles) spread across three counties: San Mateo, San Francisco, and Marin. The **Golden Gate National Recreation Area** (GGNRA) is a veritable urban greenbelt that ensures this growing metropolitan area will never want for recreational lands in natural settings. In conjunction with the similar-sized holdings of Point Reyes National Seashore up north, it puts San Francisco in the enviable position of having more dedicated parkland close at hand than any other major city in the United States. The citizens of San Francisco should be dancing in the street about this backyard windfall, established by an act of Congress in 1972.

Eight miles of San Francisco's ocean-facing coastline fall under the domain of the GGNRA, providing green space and beaches to urban dwellers. The 1,500-acre Presidio, until recently a military installation, has been added to the park. In Marin County the GGNRA holdings are vast, running the length of the county in a band that follows Highway 1 and taking in everything from the Marin Headlands and Muir Woods to Stinson Beach, Olema Valley, and Tomales Bay. A 1,014-acre tract in San Mateo County, Sweeney Ridge, is a recent addition. GGNRA holdings include historic sites (Alcatraz Island, the Cliff House, various seacoast fortifications) and scenic treasures (redwood forests, mountains, bays, and beaches). In total, there are 28 miles of shoreline and 100 miles of trails. In addition, the National Park Service conducts regular tours and educational events at sites throughout the system. These can range from guided hikes and bird-watching expeditions to hands-on seminars on how to go crabbing in the bay.

For more information, contact the Golden Gate National Recreation Area, Fort Mason, Building 201, San Francisco, CA 94123, 415/561-4700, website: www.nps.gov/goga.

In addition to park headquarters at Fort Mason, there are visitor centers at Cliff House (415/556-8642), Fort Funston (415/239-2366), the Presidio (415/561-4323), Alcatraz (415/705-1042), Pacifica (650/355-4122), Fort Point (415/556-1593), the Marin Headlands (415/331-1540), and Muir Woods (415/388-2596). You can also call GGNRA for information on Stinson Beach's weather (415/868-1922), Alcatraz Island boat transportation (415/546-2700), and the National Maritime Museum (415/556-3002).

Bird Man and Al Capone. If you go, be sure to rent one of the audiotape tours available at the park; narrated by former wardens and prisoners, it paints a realistic and compelling portrait of life on the Rock.

Angel Island, a 760-acre island that actually lies within Marin County waters, serves as a more idyllic state park offering panoramic views of San Francisco from a trail that leads to the top of Mount Livermore (781 feet). Picnicking, tent camping, hiking, and biking can all be enjoyed on **Angel Island** (call 415/435-1915 for ferry schedules and fares). Ferries also make frequent crossings to the bay-hugging,

San Francisco County

Map of San Francisco County—Page 464

picturesque Marin communities of Sausalito, Tiburon, and Larkspur.

Shifting our attention toward the eastern side of this boxy peninsula, the piers of the Embarcadero take over, offering deep-water berthing in one of the world's great natural harbors.

Highly recommended to all who want to tour the city by automobile is the 49-Mile Scenic Drive. You can begin at City Hall (Van Ness Avenue and McAllister Street) or pick it up at any other point en route. Just follow the blue-and-white seagull signs and allow plenty of time to eyeball San Francisco's scenic sights and heights. An annotated outline of the route can be obtained at the **Visitor Information Center** (Hallidie Plaza, at Powell and Market Streets), which is a great place for a visitor to stock up on maps, brochures, and tourist tips.

Beaches

Much of San Francisco's coastline belongs to the Golden Gate National Recreation Area, the vast tri-county federal parkland that is managed by the National Park Service. This includes the eight-mile stretch from the San Mateo county line to Aquatic Park, east of Golden Gate Bridge. Four miles' worth, from the county line to Point Lobos, faces the ocean, running along a nearly perfect north-south axis. Coming up from the south, this area encompasses **Burton Memorial Beach** (which straddles San Mateo and San Francisco Counties), **Fort Funston Beach** (a popular launch site for hang gliders), and **Ocean Beach** (a long, flat stretch of beach paralleled by the Great Highway).

People come to Ocean Beach to park and watch the sun set; to fish on the beach or surf the often sizable waves; and to jog, walk, bicycle, and in-line skate along pathways that run on both sides of the Great Highway. Unspoiled and impressively empty, the beach is regrettably unsafe for swimming—too rough and too cold. In fact, a combination of factors create deadly riptides. On the California coast,

88 percent of all lifeguard rescues are attributable to riptides. Ocean Beach, which is the worst for riptides, has no lifeguards! If all this hasn't convinced you not to swim at Ocean Beach, ponder this statement made in May 2002 by Francis Smith, a UC Berkeley graduate student who's studied riptides: "Ocean Beach is the most hazardous and dangerous piece of shoreline associated with an urban environment in the whole United States." He noted that more than a dozen people had drowned there in 1998 alone.

As you drive north from Ocean Beach, the road begins to rise, meeting a San Francisco landmark, the **Cliff House.** A jaw-dropping overview of Ocean Beach can be had from the deck of the Cliff House. Tourist buses choke the area around the Cliff House with gassy fumes. The tourists pile out to gawk at the bird- and seal-covered rocks offshore and browse the shops, museums, and restaurants before moving on to the next stop. The Cliff House Visitor Information Center, run by the National Park Service, is a good place to stock up on brochures, books, and maps covering the recreational opportunities of the Golden Gate National Recreation Area, from visiting forts to hiking ridgetops to camping on the beach. Parking is available along Point Lobos Avenue, the Great Highway, and El Camino Del Mar.

The remains of the Sutro Baths, a turn-of-the-century natatorium, lie below the sandstone bluffs. Trails crisscross the knobby area known as **Lands End** between the Cliff House and China Beach. It's a fascinating place to explore, with paths running down to the ocean, through tunnels, and up and over the bluffs. The beach at Lands End is found at the bottom of a steep path. It's not worth the trouble or the risk to scuttle down, although the paths above it afford good overlooks.

Around Lands End the coastline runs east for a short distance before making a sharp turn north again to the foot of the Golden Gate Bridge. **China Beach** is tucked into a rel-

Map of Northern California—Page 463

atively safe, protected pocket of beach. It is a small sandy cove that is lifeguarded in summer. China Beach lies below all the gorgeous stucco homes that line El Camino Del Mar in the exclusive Seacliff District. Park on the street and make the steep descent via a path or a paved service road (for handicapped parking only) to the beach.

In terms of size, China Beach has nothing on **Baker Beach,** a 1.5-mile ribbon of sand that runs all the way up to Golden Gate Bridge. The *San Francisco Bay Guardian* calls Baker Beach "America's most popular urban nude beach, drawing local residents and tourists whenever the weather is sunny, plus a smattering of winter dichards." We won't argue with them; their annual list of California's nude beaches is going on 30 years old and is among our favorite reading material. Wonderful views of the photogenic steel span and the Marin Headlands can be had here. Everyone we saw, though, was otherwise engaged: figures sleeping on the beach, couples groping on the sand, picnickers at tables under the protected windbreaks of cypress groves, anglers casting lines into the water. **North Baker Beach** sheds its inhibitions and becomes an almost exclusively nude beach. Should you happen to wander off in that direction, don't be surprised if you stumble onto a colony of beachgoers as naked as seals.

Rounding out the city's shoreline are **Marina Green** (managed by the San Francisco Parks and Recreation Department), **Crissy Field** (a popular launch site for windsurfers east of the Golden Gate Bridge in the decommissioned Presidio), and **Aquatic Park** (a celebration of all things maritime). Marina Green is a broad bayfront green space used by outdoor-minded San Franciscans as a place to do a little bit of everything: bicycling, jogging, walking, Frisbee-tossing, and kite-flying. It's San Francisco's latter-day equivalent of the traditional village green, serving as a gathering place for celebrations and rallies, not to mention being a good place to hang out on a nice day.

Aquatic Park lies between Marina Green and Fisherman's Wharf. It's protected by two piers and a breakwater. The 1,850-foot Municipal Pier is great for fishing. Onshore, there's the **National Maritime Museum** (415/556-2904), tourable ships, more green space, and a small sandy beach. (Don't base your vacation around the latter, though.) The square-rigger *Balclutha,* built in Glasgow in 1886 and docked at **Hyde Street Pier** (415/556-6435), can be toured for a fee. It is one of seven vessels belonging to the maritime museum, which also houses model ships and seafaring artifacts. It's all part of the **San Francisco Maritime National Historical Park** (415/556-3002), which is headquartered at Hyde and Beach Streets, on the west side of Fisherman's Wharf.

Bunking Down

You want to stay at the beach? We've got just the place for you. It ain't fancy, but it's clean and at the beach—and that's what this book is all about. It's **Roberts-at-the-Beach Motel** (2828 Sloat Boulevard, 415/564-2610, $), where you're invited to "sleep by the sea." Roberts is a block off the Great Highway, near the San Francisco Zoo and Golden Gate Park. Two blocks farther landward on the same street is a **Days Inn** (2600 Sloat Boulevard, 415/665-5440, $$), offering a modicum of brand-name dependability. Actually, we found our room and its furnishings quite comfortable. Also close to the beach is the **Oceanview Motel** (4340 Judah Street, 415/661-2300, $), which is unfancy but clean, safe, and accessible to Ocean Beach and Golden Gate Park.

Another find close to the beach—very close, in fact, to the Cliff House, Lands End, and the Presidio—is **Seal Rock Inn** (545 Point Lobos Avenue, 415/752-8000, $$), an older hotel that makes up in location what it lacks in amenities.

Do you want to feel like a rock star? Stay at the **Phoenix Hotel** (601 Eddy Street, 415/861-3109, $$). It's a tropical-themed hotel with a hip restaurant (Backflip) and simple, reasonably priced rooms ($100 and up) whose

San Francisco County

tasteful tackiness is part of the fun. All of the rock bands have stayed here at one time or another. If you're queasy about location, you may want to look elsewhere, though, as it's on the edge of the Tenderloin district. Down by touristy Fisherman's Wharf, you'll find a wide range of places to stay. On the high end there are humongous 500-room towers run by **Sheraton** (2500 Mason Street, 415/362-5500, $$$$) and **Hyatt** (555 North Point Street, 415/563-2218, $$$$), as well as less impressive (and less expensive) properties by **Holiday Inn** (1300 Columbia Avenue, 415/771-9000, $$$), **Ramada Inn** (590 Bay Street, 415/885-4700, $$$), and **Howard Johnson** (580 Beach Street, 415/775-3800, $$$). You know what you're getting with those kinds of places—a guarantee of quality within a narrow standard of deviation. All are within three blocks of Fisherman's Wharf. You'll pay dearly to stay near the wharf, but you'll pay dearly to stay anywhere else in San Francisco, too.

Slightly outside the area, between Fisherman's Wharf and the Financial District, are four affiliated motor inns of late-model vintage that offer a real break on price and value (around $80 a night, year-round). They're strung along busy Lombard Avenue, with **Cow Hollow Motor Inn** (2190 Lombard Street, 415/921-5800, $$) close to Marina Green, and **Lombard Motor Inn** (1475 Lombard Street, 415/441-6000, $$) close to Fisherman's Wharf. In between you'll find **Coventry Motor Inn** (1901 Lombard Street, 415/567-1200, $$) and **Chelsea Motor Inn** (2095 Lombard Street, 415/563-5600, $$).

If you're looking for more of a bed-and-breakfast experience, you might try **Marina Inn** (3110 Octavia Street, 415/928-1000, $$), a 40-room hotel on the corner of Lombard, behind Fort Mason in the Marina District. For a fuller array of accommodations in the Bay Area, lay hands on the latest lodging guide published by the San Francisco Convention and Visitors Bureau.

Coastal Cuisine

San Francisco rightly enjoys a reputation as an epicurean paradise. There are more than 3,300 restaurants in the City by the Bay. Since detailed coverage of a subject so large is well beyond the scope of this book, we've narrowed our commentary to restaurants in the vicinity of Fisherman's Wharf and out by Ocean Beach. Even there we've been selective.

Numero uno out by the beach has to be the **Beach Chalet Brewery & Restaurant** (1000 Great Highway, 415/386-8439, $$$), where Golden Gate Park meets the ocean. What could be better than knocking back a schooner of home-brewed California Kind Ale or Golden Gate Park Porter on the Thursday evening "surf night"—featuring live music by a spinoff of the Bay Area's great Mermen—after a dinner of seared salmon and sea scallops while you watched the sun set?

Up where Point Lobos Avenue meets the Great Highway sits a San Francisco institution, the **Cliff House** (1090 Point Lobos Avenue, 415/386-3330, $$$). Five different structures have occupied the same site since its inception in 1863. One burned down when a boatload of nitroglycerin crashed into the cliff on which it sits. The latest edifice is physically quite secure, though locals often sniff that its culinary reputation isn't as firmly grounded. Visitors, dazzled by the glorious views and the old San Francisco ambience, don't seem to care.

The Cliff House is a multilevel complex with a popular bar and two completely different restaurants. Downstairs is more seafood oriented, with an art deco interior. Upstairs the menu is broader, with pasta, veal, and beef dishes available in addition to seafood. The bar at the Cliff House, incidentally, has an extensive appetizer/deli-sandwich menu, if you just want to drop in for a drink and a snack. If you're coming for dinner, the house favorite dish is crab Louis, and we've had a bouillabaisse here that rivals any we've ever tasted. In the cards for the Cliff House is a major renovation that will restore the land-

Map of Northern California—Page 463

mark to its 1909 appearance and bring it up to code. Administrators with the Golden Gate National Recreation Area, which manages the property, warn that if it doesn't happen, Cliff House will have to close.

Also near the beach, a hole-in-the-wall restaurant turns out the best ribs and barbecue this side of Oakland. **Leon's BBQ** (2800 Sloat Boulevard, 415/681-3071, $$) has a real downhome neighborhood vibe to go with the hearty servings of ribs and 'Q. So come on in for some home-cooked chow and leave with an "I Porked Out at Leon's BBQ" bumper sticker.

The Fisherman's Wharf area has long served as a punching bag for food critics, who insult it directly when they don't ignore it entirely. This is a little unfair. Sure, the area in general is a tad tacky, with a scuzzy commercial underside whose carnival aura is more reminiscent of Times Square than a working wharf and fish market. But some of the restaurants of long-standing do a good job of serving quality seafood.

A. Sabella's (2766 Taylor, 415/771-6775, $$$), for instance, dates back to the 1920s, when Antone Sabella—whose father ran a retail market on Fisherman's Wharf—opened a restaurant on this spot. Sabella's is still run by Antone Sabella (albeit the founder's grandson). Fittingly, the menu's pièce de résistance is a dish named after the founder: Antone, a swordfish concoction baked in a beurre blanc, stuffed with deviled shrimp, and topped with parmesan cheese and white sauce. The crab legs (sautéed, fried, or Bordelaise) and crab cioppino (simmered with shrimp and shellfish) also are excellent. Sabella's rates high in our book for the food and the view—three stories above the Fisherman's Wharf hubbub, with an unobstructed outlook on the bay.

Another good bet on the wharf is **Scoma's** (Pier 47, 415/771-4383, $$$). San Francisco's highest-grossing restaurant, it attracts crowds for one reason (well, besides location): dependably fresh, well-prepared seafood. Scoma's signature dish is a little bit of culinary inspiration called Shellfish Sec, a symphony of seafood in a light wine sauce. The combination seafood cocktail (crabs and prawns), the Louis salad, and the sautéed entrées are also highly recommended. Scoma's has its own fish-receiving station, complete with off-loading and a processing operation that goes 16 hours a day. You can wander over and look at what might turn out to be your dinner being cleaned and filleted.

Elsewhere near the water, seafood fans flock to the **Pier 23 Cafe** (The Embarcadero, Pier 23, 415/362-5125, $$), whose alfresco dining patio and lively atmosphere attract a young, hip crowd on nice days. Other popular spots include **Scott's Seafood Grill**, which has locations in the Marina District (2400 Lombard Street, 415/563-8988, $$$) and in the Financial District (3 Embarcadero Center, 415/981-0622, $$$), and **Cafe Pescatore** (2455 Mason Street, 415/561-1111, $$$), a small Italian seafood restaurant excelling at such creative concoctions as ravioli stuffed with minced scallops and covered with a tomato-garlic cream sauce.

Before we leave the subject of seafood, we have to break our vow about not straying from the water's edge when it comes to restaurants. It's an ironic fact of life that when San Franciscans crave food with fins, they head inland. Here's the lowdown on four of the best fish joints in town: the venerable **Tadich Grill** (240 California Street, 415/391-1849, $$$), which claims to be California's oldest restaurant in continuous operation; its younger neighbor **Aqua** (252 California Street, 415/956-9662, $$$), a decidedly upscale and pricey Financial District favorite; **Hayes Street Grill** (320 Hayes Street, 415/863-5545, $$$), a more casual Civic Center eatery; and the **Swan Oyster Depot** (1517 Polk Street, 415/673-1101, $$), where a friendly staff plunks down incredibly fresh, simply prepared seafood on its long lunch counter.

Frankly, you'll find excellent and creative seafood dishes in nearly all of the better restaurants in town. Culinarily speaking, this is a city in love with the denizens of the ocean (and

San Francisco County

lakes and rivers and bays). Finally, we can't exit San Francisco without saying a word about sourdough bread. Some of the best mass-produced sourdough bread to be had is at **Boudin Sourdough Bakery & Cafe** (156 Jefferson Street, 415/928-1849, $), which brings us back to Fisherman's Wharf. There are also Boudin locations at Pier 39 and Ghirardelli Square.

Night Moves

San Francisco is often touted as the most cosmopolitan city in America, and it's certainly one of the most open-minded. Contained within its borders is a little bit of Paris, Rome, Vienna, Sodom, and Gomorrah. Everything from ballet to bondage bars can be located on its fog-shrouded streets after dark. You really don't need us to tell you where or how to have a good time in San Francisco, so we'll just offer a few stray observations before calling it a night.

The tavern at the **Cliff House** (1090 Point Lobos Avenue, 415/386-3330) is patronized and enjoyed even by famously tourist-wary San Franciscans (at least when they have out-of-town guests in tow). With its log-burning fireplace and "oh, wow" views, this is a must-visit place to drain a coffee mug or wine glass. Down at Fisherman's Wharf, another favorite tourist haunt, **Lou's Pier 47** (300 Jefferson Street, 415/771-0377), presents live blues acts, none of them too darn spectacular.

It's a yuppie world now, and the fact is evident in most every neighborhood, even in North Beach, that traditionally working-class, Italian neighborhood that was the old stomping ground of the Beat Generation. (Incidentally, North Beach used to mark the actual shoreline before landfill was used to extend the city by half a mile out to its present location at Fisherman's Wharf and the Embarcadero.) Today, this landlocked beach is a grab bag of brass-encrusted cafés, coffeehouses, bars, and bookstores. If you'd like to walk in Jack Kerouac's footsteps, try the following, which were beat-generation hangouts in the 1950s and still

retain an air of authenticity: **Caffe Trieste** (609 Vallejo Street, 415/392-6739), **Mario's Bohemian Cigar Store** (566 Columbus Avenue, 415/362-0536), **Tosca Cafe** (242 Columbus Avenue, 415/391-1244), and **Vesuvio's** (255 Columbus Avenue, 415/362-3370). The last two establishments are near the famed **City Lights Bookstore** (261 Columbus Avenue, 415/362-8193), still run by the venerable poet and scene patriarch, Lawrence Ferlinghetti (who was anointed San Francisco's poet laureate in 1998).

Looking for a decent rock club in this music-crazed city? Well, **Bottom of the Hill** (1233 17th Street, 415/621-4455) is San Francisco's answer to New York's CBGB. It's the only real mid-sized rock venue in S.F. and, like CBGB, tends to stack the bill with no-name acts. Still, it gets some good cult favorites, like Lou Barlow (of Sebadoh), Of Montreal, Interpol, Isis, and others known to those who keep their ear to the ground.

Bimbo's 365 Club (1025 Columbus Avenue, 415/474-0365) is a marvelous relic of San Francisco's martini-swilling past, dating back to 1931. Red velvet everywhere, it's the definition of swank, with one of the best sound systems on the West Coast. Catch a show here if you can. The eclectic bookings range from Apples in Stereo to Sergio Mendes—now that's a spread!

Finally, you can hope that someone good is playing at the **Great American Music Hall** (859 O'Farrell Street, 415/885-0750), one of the prime rock venues in the country and a San Francisco landmark. While you're at the show, look up and admire the ornate ceiling.

Beyond this overview, you're on your own in this great big city. Grab a local paper and have at it.

For More Information

San Francisco Convention & Visitors Bureau, 201 Third Street, Suite 900, San Francisco, CA 94103, 415/974-6900, website: www.sfvisitor.org; San Francisco Visitor Information Center, Hallidie Plaza (lower level), 900 Market Street, San Francisco, CA 94103, 415/391-2000

Map of Northern California—Page 463

San Francisco County

© ROBERT HOLMES/CALTOUR

Chapter 11
Marin County

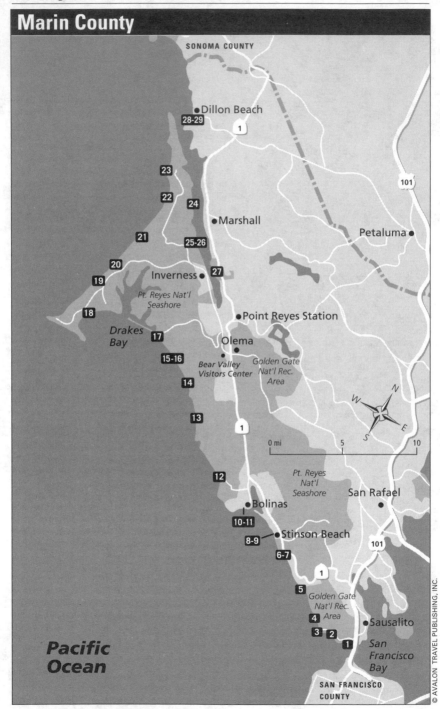

Marin County

Marin County Beaches

Marin County

1 Kirby Cove, page 484

⛰️ 🥾 🚻 ③

Location: From U.S. 101 north of Golden Gate Bridge, take Alexander Road exit to Conzelman Road in the Marin Headlands and follow it to Kirby Cove.

Parking/fees: free parking lot. Camping is free; obtain permit from National Park Service.

Hours: 24 hours

Facilities: restrooms and picnic tables

Contact: Marin Headlands unit of Golden Gate National Recreation Area, 415/331-1540

2 Bonita Cove, page 484

🥾 🚻 ③

Location: From U.S. 101 north of Golden Gate Bridge take Alexander Road exit to Conzelman Road. Bonita Cove is at the southwest tip of Marin Headlands and can be reached via a hiking trail from Battery Alexander.

Parking/fees: free parking lot

Hours: 24 hours

Facilities: none

Contact: Marin Headlands unit of Golden Gate National Recreation Area, 415/331-1540

3 Rodeo Beach, page 484

🥾 🚻 ③

Location: From U.S. 101 north of Golden Gate Bridge take Alexander Road exit to Bunker Road and follow it to Rodeo Beach.

Parking/fees: free parking lot

Hours: 24 hours

Facilities: restrooms and picnic area

Contact: Marin Headlands unit of Golden Gate National Recreation Area, 415/331-1540

4 Tennessee Cove, page 484

🥾 🚻 ③

Location: end of Tennessee Valley Road, off Highway 1 in Mill Valley; follow trail from parking lot to beach

Parking/fees: free parking lot

Hours: 24 hours

Facilities: none

Contact: Marin Headlands unit of Golden Gate National Recreation Area, 415/331-1540

5 Muir Beach, page 485

🚴 🥾 🚻 ④

Location: Pacific Way at Highway 1 in Muir Beach

Parking/fees: free parking lot

Hours: 9 A.M.–10 P.M. (summer); closing hours vary between 7 P.M. and 9 P.M. the rest of the year.

Map of Marin County—Page 476

Marin County

Facilities: restrooms and picnic tables
Contact: Stinson Beach Ranger Station, 415/868-0942

6 Steep Ravine Beach, page 485

Location: off Highway 1, two miles south of Stinson Beach
Parking/fees: free limited roadside parking. Camping fees are $11–13 per night, plus a $7.50 reservation fee. Cabin rentals are $30 per night, plus a $7.50 reservation fee.
Hours: 7 A.M.–10 P.M. (summer); closing hours vary between 6 P.M. and 9 P.M. the rest of the year.
Facilities: restrooms and picnic tables
Contact: Mount Tamalpais State Park, 415/388-2070

7 Red Rock Beach, page 486

Location: Highway 1 near Milepost 11, about 1.5 miles south of Stinson Beach. A trail leads to the beach from a roadside turnout.
Parking/fees: free limited roadside parking
Hours: 7 A.M.–10 P.M. (summer); closing hours vary between 6 P.M. and 9 P.M. the rest of the year.
Facilities: none
Contact: Mount Tamalpais State Park, 415/388-2070

8 Stinson Beach, page 487

Location: 20 miles north of San Francisco, on Highway 1 in Stinson Beach
Parking/fees: free parking lot
Hours: 9 A.M.–10 P.M. (summer); closing hours vary between 7 P.M. and 9 P.M. the rest of the year.
Facilities: concession, lifeguards, restrooms, and picnic tables
Contact: Stinson Beach Ranger Station, 415/868-0942

9 Seadrift Beach, page 487

Location: off Seadrift Drive north of Stinson Beach
Parking/fees: free street parking
Hours: 9 A.M.–10 P.M. (summer); closing hours vary between 7 P.M. and 9 P.M. the rest of the year.
Facilities: none
Contact: Stinson Beach Ranger Station, 415/868-0942

10 Bolinas Beach, page 489

Location: From Highway 1, 4.5 miles north of Stinson Beach, turn west onto Olema-Bolinas Road and follow it into Bolinas. Turn left onto Wharf Road and follow it to the beach.
Parking/fees: free street parking
Hours: 24 hours
Facilities: none
Contact: Bolinas Beach Utility District, 415/868-1224

Map of Northern California—Page 463

⓫ Agate Beach, page 489

Location: From Highway 1, 4.5 miles north of Stinson Beach, turn west onto Olema-Bolinas Road and follow it into Bolinas. Turn left onto Elm Road and follow it to the beach.
Parking/fees: free parking lot
Hours: 24 hours
Facilities: none
Contact: Bolinas Beach Utility District, 415/868-1224

⓬ Palomarin Beach, page 493

Location: From Highway 1, 4.5 miles north of Stinson Beach, turn west onto Olema-Bolinas Road and follow it 1.8 miles. Turn right onto Mesa Road and continue 4.5 miles to a gravel parking lot. Hike to the beach from Palomarin trailhead.
Parking/fees: free parking lot
Hours: 24 hours
Facilities: none
Contact: Point Reyes National Seashore, 415/663-1092

⓭ Wildcat Beach, page 493

Location: Hike more than five miles from trailheads at Palomarin, Five Brooks, and Bear Valley Visitor Center at Point Reyes National Seashore. Consult park map for details.
Parking/fees: free parking lots. Camping is free; obtain permit at Bear Valley Visitor Center.
Hours: 24 hours
Facilities: restrooms and picnic tables
Contact: Point Reyes National Seashore, 415/663-1092

⓮ Kelham Beach, page 492

Location: Hike 4.8 miles from Bear Valley Visitor Center at Point Reyes National Seashore. Consult park map for details.
Parking/fees: free parking lots
Hours: 24 hours
Facilities: picnic table
Contact: Point Reyes National Seashore, 415/663-1092

⓯ Sculptured Beach, page 492

Location: Walk east at low tide only from Santa Maria Beach at Point Reyes National Seashore. Consult tide tables and park map for details.
Parking/fees: free parking lots
Hours: 24 hours
Facilities: none
Contact: Point Reyes National Seashore, 415/663-1092

Map of Marin County—Page 476

16 Santa Maria Beach, page 492

Location: Hike nine miles from Bear Valley Visitor Center or 2.5 miles from Point Reyes Hostel at Point Reyes National Seashore. Consult park map for details.
Parking/fees: free parking lots. Camping is free; obtain permit at Bear Valley Visitor Center.
Hours: 24 hours
Facilities: restrooms and picnic tables
Contact: Point Reyes National Seashore, 415/663-1092

17 Limantour Beach, page 492

Location: From Highway 1 in Olema, turn onto Bear Valley Road and follow it one mile. Turn onto Limantour Road and follow it to the beach.
Parking/fees: free parking lot
Hours: 24 hours
Facilities: restrooms
Contact: Point Reyes National Seashore, 415/663-1092

18 Drakes Beach, page 493

Location: From Highway 1 in Point Reyes Station, turn west onto Sir Francis Drake Highway and drive 15.5 miles to turnoff for Drakes Beach. Follow signs to beach.
Parking/fees: free parking lot
Hours: 24 hours
Facilities: concession, restrooms, showers, picnic tables, and visitor center
Contact: Point Reyes National Seashore, 415/663-1092

19 Point Reyes Beach South, page 493

Location: From Highway 1 in Point Reyes Station, turn west onto Sir Francis Drake Highway and drive 16 miles to the turnoff for South Beach. Follow signs to beach.
Parking/fees: free parking lot
Hours: 24 hours
Facilities: restrooms
Contact: Point Reyes National Seashore, 415/663-1092

20 Point Reyes Beach North, page 493

Location: From Highway 1 in Point Reyes Station, turn west onto Sir Francis Drake Highway and drive 13 miles to turnoff for North Beach. Follow signs to beach.
Parking/fees: free parking lot
Hours: 24 hours
Facilities: restrooms
Contact: Point Reyes National Seashore, 415/663-1092

Map of Northern California—Page 463

Marin County

21 Abbotts Lagoon, page 494

Location: From Highway 1 in Point Reyes Station, turn west onto Sir Francis Drake Highway. At a fork 2.5 miles north of Inverness, bear right onto Pierce Point Road and drive three miles to Abbotts Lagoon parking lot. A two-mile hiking trail leads to the beach.
Parking/fees: free parking lot
Hours: 24 hours
Facilities: restrooms
Contact: Point Reyes National Seashore, 415/663-1092

22 Kehoe Beach, page 494

Location: From Highway 1 in Point Reyes Station, turn west onto Sir Francis Drake Highway. At a fork in the road 2.5 miles north of Inverness, bear right onto Pierce Point Road and drive five miles to Kehoe Beach parking lot. A half-mile trail leads to the beach.
Parking/fees: free parking lot
Hours: 24 hours
Facilities: restrooms
Contact: Point Reyes National Seashore, 415/663-1092

23 McClure's Beach, page 494

Location: From Highway 1 in Point Reyes Station, turn west onto Sir Francis Drake Highway. At the fork in the road 2.5 miles north of Inverness, bear right onto Pierce Point Road and drive nine miles to McClure's Beach parking lot. A half-mile trail leads to the beach.
Parking/fees: free parking lot
Hours: 24 hours
Facilities: restrooms
Contact: Point Reyes National Seashore, 415/663-1092

24 Marshall Beach, page 494

Location: From Highway 1 in Point Reyes Station, turn west onto Sir Francis Drake Highway. At the fork in road 2.5 miles north of Inverness, bear right onto Pierce Point Road, drive 1.5 miles, and turn right onto L Ranch Road. Drive 2.5 miles to Marshall Beach parking lot. A 1.5-mile hiking trail leads to the beach.
Parking/fees: free parking lot
Hours: 24 hours
Facilities: restrooms
Contact: Point Reyes National Seashore, 415/663-1092

25 Hearts Desire Beach (Tomales Bay State Park), page 494

Location: From Highway 1 in Point Reyes Station, turn west onto Sir Francis Drake Highway.

Map of Marin County—Page 476

At the fork in the road 2.5 miles north of Inverness, bear right onto Pierce Point Road and drive one mile to Tomales Bay State Park entrance.

Parking/fees: $4 entrance fee per vehicle
Hours: 8 A.M.–sunset
Facilities: restrooms, picnic tables, and fire grills
Contact: Tomales Bay State Park, 415/669-1140

26 Shell Beach, page 494

Location: Hike south along Tomales Bay for four miles via Johnstone Trail from Hearts Desire Beach (see above entry) or park at the end of Camino del Mar, off Sir Francis Drake Highway, and follow a half-mile trail to beach.
Parking/fees: $4 entrance fee per vehicle at Tomales Bay State Park; free parking lot at the end of Camino del Mar
Hours: 8 A.M.–sunset
Facilities: none
Contact: Tomales Bay State Park, 415/669-1140

27 Alan Sieroty Beach, page 495

Location: at Millerton Point on eastern shore of Tomales Bay, 4.5 miles north of Point Reyes Station off Highway 1
Parking/fees: free parking lot
Hours: 8 A.M.–sunset
Facilities: restrooms and picnic tables
Contact: Tomales Bay State Park, 415/669-1140

28 Lawson's Landing, page 499

Location: end of Marine View Drive, south of Dillon Beach off Highway 1
Parking/fees: $5 entrance fee per vehicle. Camping fee is $13 per night.
Hours: 7 A.M.–sunset
Facilities: concession, restrooms, showers, and picnic tables
Contact: Lawson's Landing, 707/878-2443

29 Dillon Beach (Lawson's Resort), page 499

Location: Beach Avenue in Dillon Beach, off Highway 1 near Sonoma County line
Parking/fees: $5 entrance fee per vehicle
Hours: 8 A.M.–6 P.M. (7 P.M. on weekends)
Facilities: concession, restrooms, and picnic tables
Contact: Lawson's Resort, 707/878-2094

Map of Northern California—Page 463

Marin County

B y general consensus Marin County signals the beginning of Northern California. The leap over the Golden Gate Bridge marks a psychological and geographical break from the rest of the state. Marin County heralds the beginning of a particularly stunning stretch of coastline. From the Marin Headlands to the Oregon border, the scenery changes around every mind-boggling bend in the road. Several divergent factors have shaped Marin County: the San Andreas Fault, which runs through the county; Mount Tamalpais, which forms a formidable, albeit lovely, barrier to easy access; an entrenched hippie ethos that dates back to a mass exodus from San Francisco's Haight-Ashbury district in the late '60s; and a tradition of environmentalism that dates back to the county's most celebrated citizen, John Muir.

Because much of the shoreline is federal parkland, falling either to Golden Gate National Recreation Area or Point Reyes National Seashore, the Marin County coast is as pristine as you'll ever find close to a major metropolitan area. The expenditure of effort and difficult passage to these beaches makes the rewards of arrival all the greater. What this does, as devotees of Marin County know full well, is separate flighty tourists from real travelers. This, in turn, keeps things relatively peaceful for the hardy souls who live in windswept west Marin. Although most San Franciscans in search of fun converge on Stinson Beach, the real spirit of place can be found at Point Reyes Peninsula—truly a land apart from the rest of the continent.

Map of Marin County—Page 476

Marin Headlands

The Marin Headlands unit of the Golden Gate National Recreation Area (GGNRA) stares down San Francisco from the north side of the Golden Gate Bridge. It used to be U.S. Army land, and the remnants of forts and batteries dot the terrain. For purposes of this book, we'll provide a brief perusal of the beaches, beginning with Kirby Cove (near the foot of the bridge), proceeding west to Point Bonita, then heading northwest to Muir Beach.

The best way to get a handle on the headland's scenic heights is to follow Conzelman Road. Cross the Golden Gate Bridge into Marin County on U.S. 101, take the Alexander Avenue exit, then make a left turn into GGNRA territory, where you'll pick up Conzelman Road. It is a twisty, windy, sometimes one-way corkscrew that works its way out to Point Bonita Lighthouse, providing some incredible vistas en route.

Kirby Cove is half a mile from where you pick up Conzelman Road. Marin County's geographical counterpart to San Francisco's Baker Beach, it's identifiable by a locked gate in front of a dirt road leading to the beach. There's a narrow, quarter-mile beach and a cave that people like to explore. They also tend to get naked out here, which is pretty much the case with most of the GGNRA beaches. The park service looks the other way, so to speak, unless they get complaints.

There are some fairly difficult-to-find beaches in the vicinity of **Bonita Cove,** which is broken by rocky points into a trio of pocket beaches. Notably, they are composed of wave-pulverized pillow lava. "The more inaccessible, the better" is how nude beach aficionados look at it, and all three beaches are frequented by those who like to recreate au naturel.

Moving on, **Rodeo Beach** is the most accessible beach in the headlands, but it's just a pebbly cove. The sand is a brown-black color, partly composed of volcanic material, and the beach is dominated by an impressive whitish outcropping at its south end. To the east is pristine Rodeo Lagoon, encircled by hiking trails. A number of disused buildings from the old Fort Cronkite facility complete the coastal tableau, giving the area the sort of frozen-in-time atmosphere of an *X Files* episode. An inviting coastal hiking trail extends in either direction along the headlands. As we hiked north toward the next beach, Tennessee Cove, we found a group of surfers taking waves into what appeared to be a sheer cliff face. Nearby, a tiny cove invites exploration, though it is reachable (and dangerously so) only by sea. As we hiked north, the quiet and fog—pierced by the mournful ring of a buoy's bell and the occasional wave breaking in the distance—embraced and intoxicated us. Bird calls and the lonesome sound of wind whipping through the dry vegetation added to the air of mystery. This is the sort of place that explains the fixation in Marin County with all things New Age. How can one not be visited by meditative thoughts when surrounded on all sides by such a paradise? We watched transfixed as waves repeatedly washed over a rock. Could staring at crystals be far behind? The old coast road ends in a gully between Rodeo Beach and Tennessee Cove, an apt reminder of the fleeting nature of human existence. We'll stop before we start sounding Krishnamurti.

The beach at **Tennessee Cove** is backed by a pond with still more bird life. Getting there requires a two-mile hike from the Tennessee Valley parking area. The next accessible stretch of sand is Muir Beach (see next entry). There's plenty more to do in the Marin Headlands—camping, hiking, horseback riding, visiting seacoast fortifications—than this brief synopsis can touch on. The tri-county Golden Gate National Recreation Area (see sidebar in the San Francisco chapter) is the largest urban park in the world and deserving of a full-length travel guide in its own right.

Map of Northern California—Page 463

For More Information

Golden Gate National Recreation Area, Marin Headlands Visitor Center, Building 948, Fort Cronkite, Sausalito, CA 94695, 415/331-1540

Muir Beach

Not only did he have a stand of redwoods dubbed after him, but pioneering environmentalist John Muir rated a beauty of a beach that bears his name. Signs along the impossibly serpentine Highway 1 point to **Muir Beach,** which is within the Golden Gate National Recreation Area and linked to various other Marin Headlands units via the 35-mile Coastal Trail. To reach the beach from the parking lot, which is small and often filled, visitors must cross a rocky field and a bridge that spans a small lagoon. The more adventuresome opt for a makeshift series of boards and stepping stones instead. The stream is, fittingly, called Redwood Creek.

Framed by a creek and dense, green woods, Muir Beach provides a striking setting even when the elements are inhospitable. A lucky few have been allowed to build homes on the hillside that overlooks the beach. The architecture is all dark wood and low-scale, like an old California bohemian enclave. Frequently windy and draped in fog, Muir Beach does have its serene days—especially during Indian summer, when things warm up. The iffy weather, by the way, hasn't stopped the area from being unofficially partitioned into clothed and clothing-optional beaches. The former is what

you walk to from the parking lot. The latter is reached by walking north along the main public beach, across a lagoon, and over a rockpile.

On a sunny day in late June, the wind was blowing so hard that people were huddled in hooded sweatshirts and jackets. Other regular visitors include grosbeaks, warblers, loons, grebes, and gray foxes.

Coastal Cuisine

Muir Beach is the site of a unique Marin County dining and lodging establishment, **Pelican Inn** (10 Pacific Way, Muir Beach, CA 94965, 415/383-6000, $$$). As authentic-looking as any place in the Cotswolds, the large, Tudor-style building houses a pub and restaurant on the ground floor and seven small guest rooms upstairs. Rooms are snug and appointed with quaint British touches. The pub, as the throng of locals can attest, is just the sort of place you'd want to knock back a pint of Guinness or a warming glass of port on a chilly day. The food is good, hearty (if somewhat pricey) pub fare: bangers and mash (sausage and potatoes), fish 'n' chips, and the like. The Pelican also serves a popular Sunday brunch, and there's a lovely patio out back for alfresco dining on balmy days.

Steep Ravine Beach

At **Steep Ravine Beach** you can experience a sensation unique on the California coast: tiptoeing into the water at low tide to sit in warm springs that percolate through the ocean floor. Visitors can tent camp or stay in one of 10 rustic cabins here, with prior reservations.

Steep Ravine is a little more foreboding if you're day-tripping—a wild, rocky, sandless

beach that necessitates a steep, mile-long hike off Highway 1. (They don't call it Steep Ravine for nothing.) To reach the oceanfront look for dirt pullouts and a road with a locked gate, two miles south of Stinson Beach. If you're camping, you can drive part of the way there. If not, you must park along Highway 1 and hoof it.

Map of Marin County—Page 476

Red Rock Beach

Red Rock Beach has been touted as the coast's friendliest and most popular nude beach. That's friendly as in, "C'mon down, take your clothes off and stay awhile." We stumbled upon it by accident many years ago. It's 1.5 miles south of Stinson Beach and is identified by a dirt parking lot by the side of Highway 1. Fairly sizable though it is, we found the lot full, with overflow lining both sides of the road. There are no signs for it, nor is the beach visible from the road. We saw a trail leading down, so we took it. Imagine our surprise to round a corner at the bottom and find ourselves facing a pack of naked bodies. They looked to be having great fun, flinging Frisbees and letting it all hang out. There were more people here, in fact, than at the huge public beach we'd just left. The beach is a quarter-mile cove on state-park property. No one bothers the skinny-dippers (or vice versa). The path to the beach is fairly steep and takes about 15 minutes each way to walk. If you wear nothing else, bring a good pair of walking shoes.

Stinson Beach

Stinson Beach is where San Francisco goes when it wants to enjoy a day at the beach. Stinson is a flat, sandy three-mile break in the action between the Marin Headlands and the sea cliffs of Bolinas. Big crowds turn out on weekends when the sun is shining and the air is calm, especially in the months between summer's foggy chill and winter's stormy surliness. There's a bargain aspect to Stinson Beach that no doubt adds to its popularity. It is part of the Golden Gate National Recreation Area, administered by the National Park Service. Unlike the state beaches, which charge day-use fees of up to $5, Stinson is absolutely free.

The beach and the small town that surrounds it are nestled at the base of Mount Tamalpais in a storybook setting. You must earn your passage to this sandy wonderland, and the price to be paid is carsickness. The easiest way here is via Highway 1 (also known as Shoreline Highway or "Dramamine Drive"), which disengages from U.S. 101 near Mill Valley. The road follows the curves and contours of Mount Tamalpais, passing south of Muir Woods. The horseshoe curves will make you queasy. On any given turn you may encounter a snorting Greyhound Ameri-Cruiser or a house-sized RV with its wheels in your lane, so drive carefully. It's worth the risk for the panoramic views along the cliff edges, from which more ocean is visible than anywhere outside of a window seat on an airplane.

A long descent leads into the small town of Stinson Beach (population 772), which has a bit of everything for day-trippers and passers-through: a grocery store, gas station, antique shop, bookstore, surf shop, restaurants, and a few small roadside motels. With a rise of mountains providing a dramatic backdrop, pure Marin County air to breathe, and a wide white-sand beach to play on, Stinson Beach is well worth the curves nature throws in your path to get there. Indeed, on a good day it looks and feels like a Southern California beach scene, though one that leaves itself open to more rarefied pursuits like "Shakespeare at Stinson."

Beaches

We've seen **Stinson Beach** in all kinds of weather: forbiddingly gray and chilly, on the one hand, and sunny and warm, on the other. On nice days crowds swell to 15,000 and traffic backs up on Highway 1. Still, the enormous parking lots appear capable of taking on all comers. Stinson is a great spot for surfing and has one of the North Coast's best outfitters,

Map of Northern California—Page 463

Marin County

Live Water Surf Shop (3450 Highway 1, 415/868-0333). Fall and winter are best for surfing, though we've seen monster waves breaking in summer, too.

Walking north from Stinson Beach, you eventually come to a hidden jewel known as **Seadrift Beach**. (It can also be reached via Scadrift Drive). This lovely sand beach fronts an upscale subdivision called Seadrift, mostly weekend homes protected by a seawall. Despite local perception, this is not a private beach, so wander on it to your heart's content.

Shore Things

• **Bike/skate rentals:** Cycle Analysis, Main Street, Point Reyes Station, 415/663-9164
• **Boat cruise:** Delta Charters, 3020 Bridgeway, Sausalito, 415/332-3291
• **Dive shop:** Pinnacles Dive Center, 875 Grant Avenue, Novato, 415/897-9962
• **Ecotourism:** Point Reyes Bird Observatory, Point Reyes National Seashore, 415/868-1221; Muir Woods National Monument, 415/388-2595
• **Lighthouses:** Point Bonita, Marin Headlands, Golden Gate National Recreation Area, 415/331-1422; Point Reyes Lighthouse, Point Reyes National Seashore, 415/663-1092
• **Marina:** Sausalito Harbor, 415/499-5000
• **Rainy day attractions:** Bay Area Discovery Museum, 557 McReynolds Road, Sausalito, 415/289-7295; Bay Model Visitor Center, 2100 Bridgeway Boulevard, Sausalito, 415/332-3871
• **Shopping/browsing:** Bridgeway Boulevard, Sausalito
• **Surf report:** 415/868-1922
• **Surf shop:** Live Water Surf Shop, 3450 Highway 1, Stinson Beach, 415/868-0333
• **Vacation rentals:** Oceanic Realty, 3468 Highway 1, Stinson Beach, 415/868-0717

Bunking Down

Our inn of first choice, Casa del Mar, was recently sold by its owners and is now a private residence. This leaves the pickings somewhat lean here, though the 70-year-young **Stinson Beach Motel** (3416 Highway 1, 415/868-1712, $$) is a good choice. It's small (seven units) and features a lush garden setting. Prices fluctuate dramatically from room to room ($85–200). The location (two blocks from the beach) can't be beat, but what really won us over is the fact that the manager is named Frodo. If your name is Bilbo or Gandalf, you may be eligible for a discount.

A unique place to stay in Stinson Beach is **Patterson Sand Castle Bed and Breakfast Inn** (28 Calle del Pinos, 415/868-1652, $$$), which has all of one room. It's large, airy, romantic, and close enough to the ocean to hear the waves. The house is a landmark, built by the inventor of the Popsicle, Francis Epperson, in 1949. Yes, it looks like a miniature castle. No, it's not built of Popsicle sticks.

Given the lack of accommodations in Stinson Beach, your best bet is to call **Oceanic Realty** (415/868-0717). This company has an extensive listing of beach houses for vacation rental, and many are surprisingly affordable, starting at $700 per week.

Coastal Cuisine

The Parkside Cafe and Snack Bar (43 Arenal Avenue, 415/868-1272, $$) is a friend to snacking surfers and serious eaters alike. The café serves three meals a day, with dinners tending toward Italian fare. The snack bar's hamburgers have been warming the bellies of beach bums for 50 years. The **Stinson Beach Grill** (3465 Highway 1, 415/868-2002, $$) is the place to go for that West Marin County favorite, barbecued oysters, as well as pasta and seafood. Another casual Stinson Beach eatery, the **Sand Dollar** (3458 Highway 1, 415/868-0434, $$), serves fresh local seafood, and you can dine outside on the patio or inside by the fireplace. In 1999, new owners extensively remodeled and expanded the restaurant and gussied up the menu. Don't worry; seafood is still the Sand Dollar's specialty.

Map of Marin County—Page 476

Marin County

Night Moves

The **Sand Dollar** (3458 Highway 1, 415/868-0434) has the town's most popular bar and its only real nightlife. The beach itself remains open till 10 P.M. in summer. Since there are fire pits and picnic tables, maybe this is the place to party.

For More Information

West Marin County Chamber of Commerce, 11431 Highway 1, Suite 15, P.O. Box 1045, Point Reyes Station, CA 94956, 415/663-9232, website: www.pointreyes.org

Bolinas

If Bolinas had a town motto, it might be "Go away." Residents really don't want the world to beat a path to their door, and while they're not openly hostile, neither are they openly hospitable. There's the issue of the road sign, for instance. To get to Bolinas, you must turn off Highway 1 onto Olema-Bolinas Road, just north of Bolinas Lagoon (about 25 miles north of San Francisco). If you don't know what you're looking for, you won't know where to turn. Not only is there no marker pointing to Bolinas, but the very road sign identifying Olema-Bolinas Road is usually missing, a tradition that started in the late 1960s and continues to this day. Between 1970 and 1990 hard-core Bolinas isolationists ran off with 36 road signs. (There must be quite an interesting collection somewhere.) Transit officials have announced that they will not install any more signs.

So who needs signs? To get to Bolinas turn west from Highway 1 at a fork by the lagoon, approximately five miles south of Olema and four miles north of Stinson Beach. (If this page is missing from the book, you'll know that someone from Bolinas ripped it out.) Follow the eucalyptus trees into town. If you somehow make it here, you may think you've stumbled into a '60s time warp. The denizens of Bolinas look like survivors who fled the Haight-Ashbury in the late '60s. Remnants of this lost clan populate the rugged coast from Marin County all the way up to Oregon. Bolinas, being closest to their spawning ground, is one of their strongholds.

Hallmarks of the Haight-Ashbury mentality are everywhere: a multicolored, cabalistic rendering of the sun painted in the street, bearing the legend "Super Solstice to All"; a bakery/café that prides itself on being the area's "only all-organic flour bakery"; and a fleet of vehicles so ragged it's a miracle their engines turn over. We saw one antique Plymouth parked at the curb with three flat tires and rusty rims. To the windshield was pinned a tow order from the Marin County Sheriff's Office, on which the owner scrawled this response: "If you tow this car there will be trouble." On a nearby billboard was this notice: "'71 VW Bus For Sale. Leaving town and need to sell. $1,700 or best offer."

It's all part of the eccentric appeal of a community that hasn't gone for the corporate land grab and cutesy boutiquing that has elsewhere stripped the California coast of its natural look and heritage. That's "community" in the best sense, with everyone looking after everyone else. The Community Store dominates the main drag and the "Bolinas Community Mural Project" dominates the sides of the old wooden building. The bulletin board contains snapshots of local surfers and announcements of local events, including "reggae dances" at the local one-room library. Bolinas has a bad rap as a hermitic, misanthropic enclave. Not true; to a person, the people we met here were friendly. They simply desire their privacy, know they live in a special place, and want to keep it that way— as do most genuine communities in America that are ceaselessly pestered by the agents of homogeneity. Peevish though they may appear, the natives of Bolinas are easily understood and forgiven their eccentricity. Long may they live!

Map of Northern California—Page 463

Bolinas Lagoon Needs Restoring

The greatest treasure of Bolinas is its lagoon, a 1,100-acre tidal estuary that teems with wildlife—well, for now, anyway. Located between Stinson Beach and Bolinas, the lagoon is rapidly filling up with sediment. Although its demise is not imminent, something must be done soon about the problem. Sedimentation is nothing new, having begun in the 1880s when redwoods in the area were logged. But the process has accelerated in the last two decades, as nearby hills are overgrazed and overdeveloped, and runoff from both accumulates in the lagoon.

The Marin County chapter of Surfrider describes the situation: "If not corrected, the opening of the lagoon could close off within 50 years. Once the opening closes, the lagoon will stagnate. Vegetation will die, the marine mammals and sea birds will leave, and the sand bars that produce the great waves will disappear." Nobody wants this to happen—not boaters, fishers, swimmers, sunbathers, or surfers—but not everyone agrees on the solution. The (gulp) Army Corps of Engineers released a Draft Feasibility Report and Draft Environmental Impact Report for the extensive dredging project it proposes, and six different options have been offered. Public hearings have been heated, but a compromise appears to be shaping up. Dredging will likely begin in 2004 and last into 2005.

A coalition, the **Bolinas Lagoon Foundation,** has formed to save the lagoon, which is blessed by some of the largest migratory bird populations in Northern California, as well as a healthy population of harbor seals. The foundation has mounted an impressive consciousness and fundraising campaign. To learn more, contact the Bolinas Lagoon Foundation, P.O. Box 444, Stinson Beach, CA 94970, website: www.bolinaslagoon.org.

There's not much for an outsider to do in Bolinas, particularly the kind of tourist who's looking to spend hours at a shopping mall or shoot 18 holes of golf. Still, if you're even mildly curious, Bolinas is worth the side trip. One incentive is **Point Reyes Bird Observatory,** atop Bolinas Mesa. While you're in town, be sure to stop at Bolinas Bay Bakery & Cafe and pick up picnic supplies—sandwiches, salads, wholesome organic goodies—to take out to Point Reyes.

Beaches

To get to **Bolinas Beach,** follow Olema-Bolinas Road to Wharf Street, which ends at a concrete ramp by a pile of riprap that holds a section of the eroding spit in place. If you come out here, make sure you're proficient at three-point turns, because there is no turnaround at the end of Wharf Street. We suspect this is just one more effort to discourage visitation. The south-facing beach looks across Bolinas Lagoon, a nature preserve for migratory waterfowl, toward Stinson Beach. Bolinas Beach ends at a jetty. The shoreline narrows precipitously on the south side of the lagoon, where waves lap hungrily at the base of the bluffs.

Facing the ocean full-on is **Agate Beach,** whose principal attraction is access to **Duxbury Reef,** an offshore mass of rock where marine

Marin County

and intertidal life can be observed. It can be reached by parking at the end of Elm Road and descending a stairway to the beach. It's evident that the forces of nature are doing more damage to Bolinas than any feared tourist influx. The sea cliffs upon which Bolinas rests are made not of sandstone but mudstone, a more erosive material. Geologist Gary Griggs describes the Bolinas sea cliffs as "one continuous plane of landslides."

Bunking Down

For all its isolation Bolinas has a number of inns and guest houses, including **One Fifty-five Pine** (Box 62, 415/868-2721, $$), a beach cottage overlooking the ocean, and **Blue Heron Inn** (11 Wharf Street, 415/868-1102, $$), a small Victorian cottage above a restaurant, lounge, and espresso bar in the center of town. The guest rooms at **Thomas' White House Inn** (118 Kale Road, 415/868-0279, $$) also have funky charm and dynamite coastal views.

Coastal Cuisine

The aforementioned **Bolinas Bay Bakery & Cafe** (20 Wharf Street, 415/868-0211, $$) takes pains to prepare things the healthy way, using organic flour and greens, and stressing vegetarian preparations. The salads are great: curried tuna, tofu, and eggplant in Asian barbecue sauce, raspberry poppyseed coleslaw—you get

the idea. Baked goods include loaves of "Stems and Seeds" bread (a nine-grain, three-seeded whole wheat), sun-dried tomato and Parmesan sourdough bread, and poppyseed custard cake. The owners are not doctrinaire vegans, either. You can order a hamburger (made from Bolinas-raised, natural ground beef) or smoked baby-back ribs (the porkers, too, have had a natural upbringing). They also make great pizzas, pastas, soups, and a pesto croissant stuffed with spinach, walnuts, and six cheeses. Never in our experience has health food seemed so decadent.

Night Moves

Smiley's Schooner Saloon (41 Wharf Road, 415/868-1311) jumps to the beat of live bands on weekends, many of them survivors of the golden age of the San Francisco scene. You might catch New Riders of the Purple Sage, Commander Cody, Maria Muldaur, or Barry Melton—the old guitarist for Country Joe and the Fish, who now works as a public defender. Incidentally, Smiley's runs a little hotel with guest rooms up the hill from the saloon.

For More Information

West Marin County Chamber of Commerce, 11431 Highway 1, Suite 15, P.O. Box 1045, Point Reyes Station, CA 94956, 415/663-9232, website: www.pointreyes.org

Point Reyes National Seashore

The wilderness area known as Point Reyes is a geological island. It is an island arc that hitched a ride across the Pacific Ocean and slammed into the North American plate, becoming part of the great state of California many millions of years ago. The tectonic fun and games continue to this day, as the Pacific and North American plates engage in the geological equivalent of sumo wrestling. Sooner or later, immense pressure builds along fault lines and the plates slip past each other—an

adjustment known as an earthquake. During the cataclysmic San Francisco quake of 1906, whose epicenter was in the Marin County town of Olema, the Point Reyes Peninsula moved 16 feet in 45 seconds. Even when the San Andreas Fault isn't throwing a seismic temper tantrum, it propels the hook-shaped peninsula northwesterly at the rate of two inches per year. No wonder the National Park Service has made "A Land in Motion" Point Reyes's official slogan.

Map of Northern California—Page 463

All this continental drift has helped create California's most unusual coastal landmass. Point Reyes is one of only seven National Seashores in the United States and the only one on the West Coast. It's separated from the rest of California by the San Andreas Fault, which runs through Marin from Bolinas Lagoon to Tomales Bay. Inverness Ridge contributes to Point Reyes's distinct climate zone. East of the ridge the weather is like that of the inland valleys. West of the ridge the land is frequently blanketed in thick, blinding fog, pelted with rains of biblical intensity, and blasted by stiff, chilling winds. They blow as high as 100 miles per hour out by the lighthouse at land's end. It's as if nature is trying to scare human beings away, screaming, "You've got all that other land to play with, but this is mine!" At least one Point Reyes lighthouse keeper was driven mad by the relentless winds.

Gusty though it may be, Point Reyes is a land of natural beauty, abundant flora and fauna, and rich history. Before venturing onto the peninsula, stop at **Bear Valley Visitor Center,** the main entrance to the National Seashore, off Highway 1 in Olema. Maps and advice are freely dispensed, and the well-stocked bookshop includes numerous titles about Point Reyes. There are other visitor centers at Drakes Bay and Point Reyes Lighthouse, but Bear Valley is the best place to get your bearings. All three visitor centers are open 9 A.M.–5 P.M. weekdays and 8 A.M.–5 P.M. weekends; call 415/663-1092.

Point Reyes is a hiker's paradise, crisscrossed with 147 miles of trails. To whet your appetite try the 0.7-mile Earthquake Trail, which traverses the San Andreas fault line outside the Bear Valley Visitor Center. A reconstructed Miwok village is on the grounds. Point Reyes is one of the world's prime birdwatching meccas. Over 450 avian species have been spotted here, including such waterfowl as curlews, coots, buffleheads, and loons. (Don't they sound like a wacky bunch?) At the south end of the shore is **Point Reyes Bird Observatory** (415/868-1221), a nonprofit research center with a small museum and large database on bird sightings.

On a clear day the drive from Bear Valley to the beaches of Point Reyes is as scenic as any in the state. Around every bend a new and fascinating wrinkle in the land materializes. Forests give way to meadows, which yield to dunes and marshes. Hawks soar above hills and fields, looking for mice rustling in the grass. Herons stand like ghostly sentinels in the wetlands. Deer and elk bound nervously out of the shadows. Cows graze stiffly in the buffeting winds. The only signs of human habitations on the peninsula are these still-operating dairy farms, the remnants of the private landholders left from 1962, when the area was declared a National Seashore.

Based on its history, one could argue that Point Reyes is the real New England. In 1579 Francis Drake (not yet "Sir") beached his ship, the *Golden Hinde,* on the peninsula to make repairs and gather supplies before heading back to England with a load of Spanish plunder. He met a peaceful tribe of hunters and gatherers, the Miwok, who'd lived here for centuries. Since the cliffs above the coast vaguely resemble Dover, a homesick Drake dubbed his find "Nova Albion" ("New England"). He claimed the land in the name of Queen Elizabeth and asserted his rights by leaving behind "a plate of brasse, fast nailed to a great and firme post."

That's about as far as the English influence went, because the Spanish were the next to step up to the Pacific plate. In 1603 they swung for the fences, naming the land mass La Punta de Los Reyes (after the Feast of the Three Kings) and pressing the Miwok into forced labor in the missions farther inland. (If Native Americans ever hit up Spain for reparations, they'd have a strong case.) After California became a state in 1850, the large land grants were divvied into several ranches—hence, the herds of cattle you still see out here.

Map of Marin County—Page 476

Everyone who lives within 200 miles of Point Reyes has their own secret spot. We couldn't possibly do justice to it all, so we'll confine our comments to the beaches and hope that intrepid travelers will ferret out the other goodies that lie inland (creeks, hills, forests, pools, mountain trails). With 74,000 acres of pristine wilderness, there's no end of things to do.

On a sad note, the largest fire in 65 years charred 12,000 acres on Point Reyes and destroyed 40 homes in Inverness in the fall of 1995. Roughly a fifth of the park became a blazing tinderbox when an illegal campfire set by four teenagers erupted into a raging wildfire on October 3. The Vision Fire, as it came to be known, closed the park for two weeks. It took a firefighting team of 2,000 to bring the blaze under control. To this day, remnants of the fire are still visible along Limantour Road.

Beaches

Beachcombers may find it rough going, but those who like it wild and woolly will be in their glory on this rugged peninsula. There are 30 miles of wilderness beaches on Point Reyes. They're hazardous for swimming but wonderful for hiking, sunning, and seeking solitude. The beaches of Point Reyes can be reached from three park entrances: Mesa Road (off Olema-Bolinas Road), Limantour Road (off Highway 1 near Olema), and Sir Francis Drake Boulevard (off Highway 1 south of Point Reyes Station).

The best and safest beaches are on the southern half of Point Reyes, where they're sheltered by the peninsula's protective hook. The arm that extends back toward mainland California—officially known as Point Reyes—acts as a sort of windbreak and jetty and explains why Drake chose to land here rather than the wild shore to the north. The quickest access to the southern beaches is Limantour Road, a lovely route that winds through the town of Inverness and passes Point Reyes Hostel before ending at Limantour Beach.

Limantour Beach offers good swimming in calm waters and picnicking without gale-force winds. In the 1950s a Carmel-type commercial development (Drakes Beach Estates) was on the drawing board until distressed conservationists intervened to save Limantour, arguably the peninsula's most idyllic spot. Limantour Spit protects the rich and varied Estero de Limantour, and inland trails skirt its shoreline. Bring the binoculars for whale- and bird-watching.

Other beaches exist south of Limantour, but they are accessible only by park trails. The first of these wilderness beaches is **Santa Maria Beach,** where the primitive but popular Coast Camp lies behind a sandy ridge. To get there walk south for 1.5 miles from Limantour Beach or hike 2.5 miles over dunes and past marshes along the Coast Trail from its trailhead at Point Reyes Hostel. (The Coast Trail stretches for 16 miles, from the hostel to the Palomarin parking area, near Point Reyes Bird Observatory.)

Sculptured Beach lies 1.3 miles south of Santa Maria, and it too lies off the Coast Trail. It is more of a visual delight than a swimming hole, with sea caves, sea stacks, and crumbling ocher cliffs providing a rugged setting. (Be careful not to get stranded against the cliffs by a rising tide.) Those who like to live dangerously can proceed around a rubbly point at low tide to another cove, the aptly named **Secret Beach.**

Back on the Coast Trail, **Kelham Beach** lies 2.3 miles south of Sculptured Beach, around Point Resistance. Continue another 0.7 mile and you can crawl through a sea tunnel at Arch Rock (but only at low tide). A backpackers' dream, Wildcat Camp, lies 3.5 miles farther down the trail. A shorter hike to Wildcat Camp can be had by departing from Five Brooks Parking Area, five miles south of Olema on Highway 1. The camp lies 5.7 miles west of Five Brooks, via Stewart Trail (as opposed to 10.5 miles via the Coast Trail from Point Reyes

Map of Northern California—Page 463

Hostel). Wildcat Camp occupies a grassy meadow near a small stream. **Wildcat Beach,** another cliff-backed wilderness wonder, lies at the end of a short spur trail.

There's one more named beach on the south flank of Point Reyes National Seashore. **Palomarin Beach** lies west of the Palomarin parking area, just above Bolinas, off Mesa Road. This parking area is the southern trailhead for the Coast Trail. Wildcat Camp lies 5.5 miles north and Coast Camp is 13.2 miles north. Got all that? If not, pick up a Point Reyes trail map at **Bear Valley Visitor Center.** Palomarin Beach is narrow (a minus) and isolated (a plus), and leashed dogs are permitted (another plus).

The most popular beach on Point Reyes is **Drakes Beach.** Though located on the peninsula's south side, it is reached by way of a completely different route than Limantour Beach. Backtracking to Inverness, pick up Sir Francis Drake Boulevard and drive 18 miles to Kenneth C. Patrick Visitor Center, a well-appointed facility. From here, easy hikes are available through three different beach habitats—shore, lagoon, and bluff. The beaches and dunes are postcard perfect. Heck, you can even swim here sometimes, though we certainly don't have the cold-water tolerance for it.

The second most popular attraction on the peninsula is around the bend from Drakes Beach, where Sir Francis Drake Boulevard ends at the lighthouse. It's a great and often busy spot for viewing migrating whales and birds, especially at Sea Lion Overlook. The trek out to **Point Reyes Lighthouse** (built in 1870) requires descending 300 steps (which means ascending 300 steps on the return). It's not for everyone, and on a foggy, blustery day it's really not for anyone. A great alternative to the lighthouse is Chimney Rock, which lies at the tip of Point Reyes's hook. Getting here requires a 1.5-mile hike, but it's worth every step. In winter over 20,000 gray whales have been counted passing this checkpoint. Just don't let the idyllic panoramic view fool you.

In the teeming waters below the rocks lie the remains of countless ships that have wrecked in the smothering fog, the second thickest in America. (Cape Disappointment, in Washington state, has the thickest fog.)

To our thinking, the beaches north of the lighthouse are the hidden treasures of Point Reyes National Seashore. However, be aware that these beaches can be imposing, whipped by winds and waves and fog like something out of a Shakespearean tragedy. The water is subject to severe undertow and sneaker waves (the kind that hit when you least expect), and the bluffs are subject to erosion. Be careful when trekking here, and check tide tables to make sure you won't be trapped by high tide. The only lifeguards are the tule elk, and they'll probably laugh demonically at you like creatures from a Far Side cartoon.

Even so, we strongly recommend visiting the northern beaches. The closest to the lighthouse are **Point Reyes Beach North** and **Point Reyes Beach South,** reachable from accesses several miles apart on Sir Francis Drake Boulevard. Combined, they account for a 10 miles of raw, unsullied wilderness beach. When the weather cooperates, the area is a paradise for walkers, photographers, artists, and picnickers—but always an inferno for swimmers and surfers.

We leave you with a few more beaches on the north shore. The best swimming in this region is not in the ocean but on the beaches of Tomales Bay. The water is warmer and much safer. (See Tomales Bay State Park, next.) Out on the ocean beaches—well, we'll defer to the National Park Service. The posted warning at the trailhead leading to Kehoe Beach says it all: "The 19-mile northwestern shore of Point Reyes National Seashore is unsafe for swimming, surfing, or wading. Do not enter the water. This warning applies to all beaches from Tomales Point south to the Point Reyes Headland, including McClure's Beach, Kehoe Beach, Abbotts Lagoon, North Beach, and South Beach. Cold water, rough surf, and loose footing make

Marin County

hazardous swimming conditions, but there are more serious dangers. Rip currents, sharks, and sneaker waves are constant threats."

Another panel adds that fatal attacks by great white sharks were reported five different years between 1960 and 1977. Don't say you haven't been warned. Hiking out to these beaches provides jaw-dropping glimpses of nature in the raw. A bracing two-mile walk, for instance, leads to **Abbotts Lagoon.** The 0.6-mile path to **Kehoe Beach** passes mountainous dunes, towering bluffs, variegated vegetation, and (if you're lucky) baby-blue skies dotted by silver-lined clouds. Locals prefer Kehoe because you can bring dogs out here.

Kehoe Beach has a counterpart across Inverness Ridge on Tomales Bay. **Marshall Beach** is the only bay beach within Point Reyes National Seashore. It's hard to get to, requiring a four-mile drive off Sir Francis Drake Boulevard and a somewhat dreary 1.5-mile hike from the parking lot. It's worth the trouble only if you want to save the niggling entrance fee at Tomales Bay State Park, where you can drive your car right to **Hearts Desire Beach.**

From the parking lot at the end of Pierce Point Road, a half-mile trail leads to **McClure's Beach.** At low tide explorers are beckoned by tidepools and beautiful water-sculpted driftwood. (A beach to the north, toward Tomales Point, is unofficially known as Driftwood

Beach.) Again, be careful while walking the beaches. Stay away from the water's edge, and don't even think about swimming. If the threats of shark's teeth and sleeper waves don't deter you, then bear in mind that the average water temperature is a bone-numbing 55 degrees.

Bunking Down
One of the nation's most splendidly sited hostels is **Point Reyes Hostel** (P.O. Box 247, Point Reyes Station, CA 94956-0247, 415/663-8811, $). It has 44 beds, wood stoves, and complete kitchens. A modest fee of $12 per night is charged. Be sure to call ahead for reservations, for it is a popular hostel. Other accommodations are readily available in nearby Olema, Point Reyes Station, and Inverness.

Coastal Cuisine
You can grab a snack at **Drakes Beach Cafe** (Kenneth C. Patrick Visitor Center, 415/669-1297, $), which is open Friday–Tuesday 11:30 A.M.–4 P.M., "weather permitting." Your only other options lie outside the park at restaurants and grocery stores in the surrounding communities.

For More Information
Point Reyes National Seashore, Bear Valley Road, Point Reyes, CA 94956, 415/663-1092, website: www.nps.gov/pore

Tomales Bay State Park

Tomales Bay State Park consists of 1,840 acres adjoining the National Seashore on Point Reyes Peninsula. This super state park lies east of Inverness Ridge along Tomales Bay, which provides safe beaches with calm currents and water that can reach 80 degrees by summer's end. Clamming at low tide (limit of 50 with a fishing license) and surf casting (no license needed) are popular activities. Camping is no longer allowed, and overnight parking of cars is prohibited. The most visited of the sheltered, warm-

water wonders along Tomales Bay is **Hearts Desire Beach.** It is flanked by **Indian Beach** and **Pelican Beach,** which lie north and south, respectively, via half-mile trails. Farther down is **Shell Beach,** a locally popular destination reached by a four-mile hike from Hearts Desire or a half-mile walk from a nearby parking lot. The 6.5-mile Jepson Trail cuts through one of the few remaining virgin stands of Bishop pine. On the other side of Tomales Bay, along Highway 1 between Point Reyes Station and

Marshall, is the state park's Millerton Point unit. There's a west-facing bay beach, **Alan Sieroty Beach**, and a picnic area.

For More Information

Tomales Bay State Park, 415/669-1140; www.parks.ca.gov

Olema

Olema was more populous in the 1870s than it is in the new millennium. Although hardly a bustling metropolis, it is a major West Marin crossroads (Highway 1 meets Sir Francis Drake Boulevard) and gateway to Point Reyes National Seashore. Bear Valley Visitor Center lies one-third mile west of town. The word *olema* means "coyote" in the language of the native Miwok. The area attracted counterculture types in the 1960s, including the Youngbloods, who recorded a musical retort to country singer Merle Haggard's hippie-baiting "Okie from Muskogee," which they entitled "Hippie from Olema."

This inauspicious crossroads, incidentally, was the epicenter of the San Francisco earthquake of 1906, when the ground jumped 16 feet in less than a minute. A fashion/jewelry store in Olema calls itself The Epicenter. This reality might have something to do with the fact there hasn't been a population boom out here, which helps to keep Olema pleasantly low-key. Horseback riding is available at **Five Brooks Stable** (415/663-1570).

Bunking Down

The **Olema Inn** (10000 Sir Francis Drake Boulevard, 415/663-9559, $$) has been around since 1876, standing proudly at the crossroads. It's a pretty three-room inn with a garden setting and a pleasant ground-floor restaurant. It merits a literary footnote, too, having been patronized by Jack London and John Steinbeck. Nearby stands another bed-and-breakfast, **Roundstone Farm** (9940 Sir Francis Drake Boulevard, 415/663-1020, $$), which occupies a 10-acre horse ranch in the hills overlooking the Olema Valley and Tomales Bay. Built in 1987, this five-room B&B comes with solar heating and skylights. Another recent addition to the local lodging scene, the **Point Reyes Seashore Lodge and Conference Center** (10021 Highway 1, 415/663-9000, $$$), provides travelers and business folk with modern conveniences such as whirlpool baths, wet bars, and a choice of accommodations in luxury cottages or the main lodge.

Coastal Cuisine

The restaurant at the quaint and inviting **Olema Inn** (10000 Sir Francis Drake Boulevard, 415/663-9559, $$$) has a Cal-Mediterranean slant (e.g., calamari with cilantro pesto) and a fine wine list. Tomales Bay oysters, Petaluma duck, and vegetarian dishes are other menu staples. The **Olema Farm House** (Highway 1, 415/663-1264, $$) is an all-American kind of place, serving steak, chicken, and seafood to hungry families.

For More Information

West Marin County Chamber of Commerce, 11431 Highway 1, Suite 15, P.O. Box 1045, Point Reyes Station, CA 94956, 415/663-9232, website: www.pointreyes.org

Map of Marin County—Page 476

Point Reyes Station

Point Reyes Station lies along Highway 1, which follows the San Andreas Fault. As you enter from the south, the road makes a sharp left turn, passing a few blocks of stores. This is the heart of Point Reyes Station (population 400), which is the center of provisioning for Point Reyes Peninsula. Here the New West meets the Old West for a showdown on Main Street, where you'll find art galleries alongside a saddle shop and feed store. Times have changed, as galleries outnumber feed stores. Still, when the noon whistle blows, it's not a whistle but a mechanized "moo." Point Reyes Station makes a convenient, centralized point of entry into the National Seashore. It has a smattering of inns, good restaurants, even a hint of nightlife.

Bunking Down

Try calling **Inns of Marin** (415/663-2000), a referral-and-reservation lodging service for the West Marin area. You will want to stay in a bed-and-breakfast inn out here. In fact you have little choice in the matter, as the rural landscape practically mandates the B&B experience. We had a memorable stay at **Thirty-Nine Cypress** (39 Cypress, 415/663-1709, $$), a single-story redwood home overlooking pastures, marshlands, and the fringes of Inverness Ridge. **Holly Tree Inn** (3 Silverhills Road, 415/663-1554, $$) is a four-roomer near park headquarters on a 19-acre estate overlooking Tomales Bay.

Coastal Cuisine

The **Station House Café** (11180 Main Street, 415/663-1515, $$) is one of the most celebrated gourmet restaurants along this stretch of the coast. It's warm, comfortable, and unpretentious on the inside, offering live music on Sunday afternoons and piped-in jazz the rest of the time. The real virtuosity is in the kitchen. For starters try some oysters. They couldn't be fresher, having been raised close by on Tomales Bay. They're served several ways: broiled

in garlic and butter, barbecued with a tasty sauce, and served raw with spicy cocktail sauce. Entrées run from beef, raised organically on a North Coast ranch, to vegetarian plates. Seafood dishes might include salmon broiled with saffron cream sauce or halibut cooked to a delicate turn and served with yellow-pepper vinaigrette. Such accompaniments as pureed beet-ginger tart round out the attractively presented dinner items. Save room for dessert. The lemon pot de crème is a nice grace note to an exceptional meal. Service is friendly and attentive, and the clientele—as is often the case in West Marin County—offers an interesting study in rugged and eccentric individualism. In other words, the joint's got character, as well as great food. The Station House is open seven days a week and serves three meals.

Night Moves

When the sun is hanging low in the sky, Point Reyes Station resembles the backdrop from the old *Gunsmoke* series. Rather than draw a six-gun and start plugging varmints, head to the **Western Saloon** (Main Street, 415/663-1661), a local institution. It's got the obligatory long wooden bar with brass rail and gunmetal-gray cash box. Every now and again (or so we were told) someone gets real drunk and rides a horse into the Western. Pool tables, pinball games, and an eclectic jukebox provide other diversions. A bumper sticker above the cash box reminds imbibers that "Nobody's Ugly After 2 A.M." They wouldn't add our McDonald's gift certificate to the grubstake pinned to the wall, but the Western is a very hospitable place.

The **Station House Café** (11180 Main Street, 415/663-1515) is a civilized place to hoist a few and has live weekend jazz to boot. A more recent arrival is **Cafe Reyes Roastery & Pub** (Main Street, 415/663-8368), which also has live entertainment on weekends.

Map of Northern California—Page 463

A Horse Is a Horse—
Unless It's from Marin County

The residents of Point Reyes move to the beat of a different drummer. We were told by one of the first people we met out here that West Marin County was "different" from East Marin County—or anywhere else, for that matter. We didn't quite understand until we came across a news story in the local weekly. The headline read "Community Rallies to Save Hurt Horse." How nice, we thought, a quiet country town is deeply concerned about a fallen plow mare. Then we read further. The horse was a purebred equestrian jumper. When something spooked it in an open field, she sustained the kind of leg injury that usually signals a trip to the glue factory.

However, the paper reported that an "animal communicator" was called in from Inverness. Through "conversations" with the fallen filly, the expert concluded that she had a "very positive attitude about her recovery and was determined to walk again." This gave the horse's owner the courage to hang in there with her steed. Another expert was brought in to administer acupuncture and herbal salves. A third healer strode out from the wings to massage the beast. We never did learn if the plucky filly recovered, but the tail—er, tale—speaks volumes about life in West Marin County.

For More Information

West Marin County Chamber of Commerce, 11431 Highway 1, Suite 15, P.O. Box 1045, Point Reyes Station, CA 94956, 415/663-9232, website: www.pointreyes.org

Inverness

In the words of a local innkeeper, "Inverness runs at two speeds: dead slow and stop. Usually, it's the latter." Slow or no, Inverness (population 600) provides a convenient and idyllic bayside base for exploring Point Reyes Peninsula. The town offers easy access to Tomales Bay. Contact **Blue Waters Kayaking** (12938 Sir Francis Drake Boulevard, 415/669-2600) about kayak rentals.

Bunking Down

The **Golden Hinde Inn and Marina** (12938 Sir Francis Drake Boulevard, 415/669-1389, $$) offers inn-like comforts (continental breakfast, fireplaces) in a motel setting (comfortable rooms, TVs, showers, pool) directly on Tomales Bay. The adjacent marina serves as a boat launch and berthing spot. The inn also rents kayaks and offers guided kayak tours around Tomales Bay. Rates are very reasonable ($75–99), and some units have kitchens, which might come in handy if you catch your own dinner.

On the bed-and-breakfast front, there's the venerable **Blackthorne Inn** (266 Vallejo Avenue, 415/663-8621, $$$), which has been called a carpenter's fantasy because of its ornate construction from redwood, cedar, and Douglas fir milled right on-site. In addition to its architectural charms, the inn has a 2,500-square-foot sundeck

Map of Marin County—Page 476

and hot tub, and a glassed-in, upper-story room dubbed the Eagle's Nest. Nearby, **Manka's Inverness Lodge** (Argyle Street, 415/669-1034, $$$) has eight cozy guest rooms and two cabins in a secluded, woodsy setting.

To find out about other inns, cottages, and B&Bs scattered around Inverness and surrounding communities, call **Inns of Point Reyes** (415/663-2000) or **Point Reyes Lodging** (415/663-1872). While you're at it, request hiking and day-trip guides.

Coastal Cuisine

Because the median income of Inverness is relatively high and many of the townsfolk are restaurant-going retirees, the local dining choices are varied and of good quality. They run the culinary gamut from Cal-nouvelle to Czech. At **Barnaby's by the Bay** (12938 Drake Boulevard, 415/669-1114, $$), the restaurant at the Golden Hinde Inn, there are always plenty of freshly harvested mussels and oysters on hand. You'll also find applewood-smoked ribs, chicken, and seafood (including crab cioppino).

Vladimir's Czechoslovakian Restaurant (12785 Drake Boulevard, 415/669-1021, $$$) is interesting because of its owner. A self-proclaimed "mechanical genius" and "extremely hard worker," Vladimir Nevl is a Czechoslovakian expatriate who skied his way to freedom in 1948 after the Communist takeover. He came to Inverness and opened his eatery in 1960. Every entrée bears his name: Vladimir's Garlic Lamb Shank, Vladimir's Beef Tongue, etc. Another Czech-inspired restaurant is **Manka's Inverness Lodge & Restaurant** (30 Callendar Way, 415/669-1034, $$$). On the site of a former hunting lodge in the hills above the bay, the small, rural-chic restaurant is highly regarded even by snobby San Francisco food critics. It specializes in game dishes (e.g., rabbit-walnut sausage, pan-seared elk loin) and local seafood.

For More Information

West Marin County Chamber of Commerce, 11431 Highway 1, Suite 15, P.O. Box 1045, Point Reyes Station, CA 94956, 415/663-9232, website: www.pointreyes.org

Marshall

Marshall is a blink-and-you-miss-it town of 500 along the eastern shore of Tomales Bay. The seafood specialty in West Marin County is barbecued oysters. More than half the state's commercial shellfish farms are in Marshall. The local bivalves come in two varieties: Hog Island (more freshwater than saline, mild flavored, best eaten raw on the half shell) and Johnson's (saltier, better suited to roasting and slathering with barbecue sauce). You can't lose either way.

Bunking Down

If you want to drop anchor in Marshall, then the **Inn at Tomales Bay** (22555 Highway 1, 415/663-9002, $$$) is your place, as all rooms look out on the bay.

Coastal Cuisine

Oysters are served in restaurants all over the county, but no one does 'em better than **Tony's Seafood Place** (18863 Highway 1, 415/663-1107, $$). One gray afternoon we sat on the outdoor deck and watched a guy standing over a charcoal brazier, basting the bubbling bivalves with a sweet-spicy barbecue sauce. Were they ever good! Nearby is **Tomal Saka Tomales Bay Kayaking** (22555 Highway 1, 415/663-1743), which offers kayaking classes, rentals, and tours, including a "culinary kayaking adventure."

For More Information

West Marin County Chamber of Commerce, 11431 Highway 1, Suite 15, P.O. Box 1045, Point Reyes Station, CA 94956, 415/663-9232, website: www.pointreyes.org

Map of Northern California—Page 463

Dillon Beach

Dillon Beach is the northernmost beach in Marin County. A subdivision of second homes and vacation rentals sprawls upon the hills overlooking the tip of Point Reyes. The big draws are **Lawson's Landing,** a private campground at the mouth of Tomales Bay where you can rent boats and dig for clams, and Lawson's Resort, a private day-use beach on the ocean. You can surf cast, tidepool, or pokepole at **Lawson's Resort** (1 Beach Avenue, 707/878-2094, $), which also has a general store and restaurant. For curious readers, "pokepoling" involves sticking a 14-foot-long bamboo pole fitted with hook and leader under the crevice of rocks at low tide in order to catch eel, cabezon, and so forth.

Bunking Down

Open-meadow camping is available at **Lawson's Landing** (137 Marine View Drive, 707/878-2443, $). The operators run a barge over to a sand bar at low tides (approximately 7–10 days per month), where folks dig for giant clams. Barge rides are $3 per adult and $2 per child. **Dillon Beach Vacation Rentals** (707/878-9011) is the place to call for home and cottage rentals in the area.

© ROBERT HOLMES/CALTOUR

Chapter 12
Sonoma County

Sonoma County

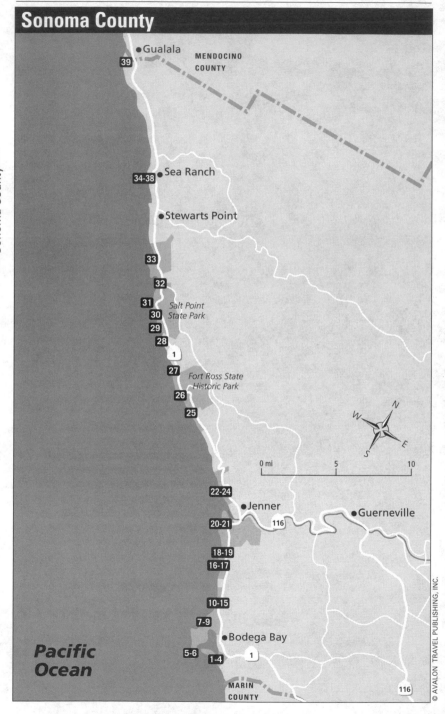

Sonoma County

Gualala
39
MENDOCINO COUNTY

34-38 Sea Ranch

Stewarts Point

33
32
31
30
29
28
1
27
Salt Point State Park

Fort Ross State Historic Park
26
25

0 mi   5   10

22-24
Jenner   Guerneville
20-21   116

18-19
16-17

10-15

7-9
Bodega Bay
5-6   1-4   1

Pacific Ocean

MARIN COUNTY   116

© AVALON TRAVEL PUBLISHING, INC.

Sonoma County Beaches

1 Pinnacle Gulch, page 512

Location: 20600 Mockingbird, off Highway 1 in Bodega Bay; trail leads to beach
Parking/fees: $3 entrance fee per vehicle
Hours: sunrise–sunset
Facilities: restrooms
Contact: Sonoma County Regional Parks, 707/565-2041

2 Doran Beach Regional Park, page 512

Location: end of Doran Beach Road, off Highway 1 in Bodega Bay
Parking/fees: $3 entrance fee per vehicle. Camping fee is $16 per night.
Hours: sunrise–sunset
Facilities: concession, restrooms, showers, and picnic tables
Contact: Doran Beach Regional Park, 707/875-3540

3 Bird Walk Access Point, page 512

Location: 355 Highway 1 in Bodega Bay
Parking/fees: $3 entrance fee per vehicle
Hours: sunrise–sunset
Facilities: none
Contact: Sonoma County Regional Parks, 707/565-2041

4 Campbell Cove, page 512

Location: off East Shore Road along the western mouth of Bodega Bay Harbor
Parking/fees: free parking lot
Hours: 8 A.M.–one hour after sunset
Facilities: restrooms and picnic tables
Contact: Sonoma Coast State Beaches, 707/875-3483

5 Westside Regional Park, page 512

Location: From Highway 1 in Bodega Bay, turn west onto Bay Flat Road and follow it to Westside Road. The park entrance is off Westside Road at Bodega Bay Harbor.
Parking/fees: $3 entrance fee per vehicle. Camping fee is $16 per night.
Hours: sunrise–sunset
Facilities: restrooms and picnic tables
Contact: Westside Regional Parks, 707/875-3540

Sonoma County

Map of Sonoma County—Page 502

6 Bodega Head, page 512

🚶 ④

Location: From Highway 1 in Bodega Bay, turn west onto Bay Flat Road and follow it to Westside Road. Bodega Head is at the end of Westside Road.
Parking/fees: free parking lot
Hours: 8 A.M.–one hour after sunset
Facilities: restrooms
Contact: Sonoma Coast State Beaches, 707/875-3483

7 Bodega Dunes, page 515

⛰ 🚶 ⑤

Location: one-half mile north of Bodega Bay, off Highway 1
Parking/fees: $4 entrance fee per vehicle. Camping fees are $13–16 per night, plus a $7.50 reservation fee.
Hours: 8 A.M.–one hour after sunset
Facilities: restrooms, showers, and picnic tables
Contact: Bodega Dunes Campground, 707/875-3483

8 South Salmon Creek Beach, page 515

🚶 ④

Location: 1.5 miles north of Bodega Bay, along Highway 1, at mouth of Salmon Creek
Parking/fees: free parking lot
Hours: 8 A.M.–one hour after sunset
Facilities: restrooms
Contact: Sonoma Coast State Beaches, 707/875-3483

9 North Salmon Creek Beach, page 515

🚶 ③

Location: two miles north of Bodega Bay off Highway 1, on the north bank of Salmon Creek
Parking/fees: free parking lot
Hours: 8 A.M.–one hour after sunset
Facilities: restrooms
Contact: Sonoma Coast State Beaches, 707/875-3483

10 Miwok Beach, page 517

🚶 ②

Location: 2.5 miles north of Bodega Bay, off Highway 1; trail leads to beach
Parking/fees: free parking lot
Hours: 8 A.M.–one hour after sunset
Facilities: none
Contact: Sonoma Coast State Beaches, 707/875-3483

11 Coleman Beach, page 517

🚶 ②

Location: three miles north of Bodega Bay, off Highway 1; trail leads to beach

Map of Northern California—Page 463

Sonoma County

Parking/fees: free parking lot
Hours: 8 A.M.–one hour after sunset
Facilities: none
Contact: Sonoma Coast State Beaches, 707/875-3483

12 Arched Rock Beach, page 517

Location: 3.3 miles north of Bodega Bay, off Highway 1; trail leads to beach
Parking/fees: free parking lot
Hours: 8 A.M.–one hour after sunset
Facilities: none
Contact: Sonoma Coast State Beaches, 707/875-3483

13 Carmet Beach, page 517

Location: 3.8 miles north of Bodega Bay, off Highway 1; trail leads to beach
Parking/fees: free parking lot
Hours: 8 A.M.–one hour after sunset
Facilities: none
Contact: Sonoma Coast State Beaches, 707/875-3483

14 Schoolhouse Beach, page 517

Location: four miles north of Bodega Bay, off Highway 1; trail leads to beach
Parking/fees: free parking lot
Hours: 8 A.M.–one hour after sunset
Facilities: none
Contact: Sonoma Coast State Beaches, 707/875-3483

15 Portuguese Beach, page 517

Location: 4.3 miles north of Bodega Bay, off Highway 1; trail leads to beach
Parking/fees: free parking lot
Hours: 8 A.M.–one hour after sunset
Facilities: restrooms
Contact: Sonoma Coast State Beaches, 707/875-3483

16 Gleason Beach, page 517

Location: 4.8 miles north of Bodega Bay, off Highway 1; trail leads to beach
Parking/fees: free parking lot
Hours: 8 A.M.–one hour after sunset
Facilities: none
Contact: Sonoma Coast State Beaches, 707/875-3483

Map of Sonoma County—Page 502

Sonoma County

17 Duncan's Landing, page 517

Location: five miles north of Bodega Bay, off Highway 1; trail leads to beach
Parking/fees: free parking lot
Hours: 8 A.M.–one hour after sunset
Facilities: none
Contact: Sonoma Coast State Beaches, 707/875-3483

18 Wright's Beach, page 516

Location: six miles north of Bodega Bay off Highway 1
Parking/fees: $4 entrance fee per vehicle. Camping fees are $13–16 per night.
Hours: 8 A.M.–one hour after sunset
Facilities: restrooms and picnic tables
Contact: Sonoma Coast State Beaches, 707/875-3483

19 Shell Beach, page 516

Location: seven miles north of Bodega Bay off Highway 1
Parking/fees: free parking lot
Hours: 8 A.M.–one hour after sunset
Facilities: restrooms
Contact: Sonoma Coast State Beaches, 707/875-3483

20 Blind Beach, page 517

Location: along Goat Rock Road, off Highway 1 near mouth of Russian River, south of Jenner
Parking/fees: free parking lot
Hours: 8 A.M.–one hour after sunset
Facilities: restrooms
Contact: Sonoma Coast State Beaches, 707/875-3483

21 Goat Rock Beach, page 517

Location: end of Goat Rock Road off Highway 1 near the mouth of Russian River, south of Jenner
Parking/fees: free parking lot
Hours: 8 A.M.–one hour after sunset
Facilities: restrooms and picnic tables
Contact: Sonoma Coast State Beaches, 707/875-3483

22 North Jenner Beaches, page 517

Location: Access trails lead to beaches along a two-mile stretch of Highway 1 between Jenner and Russian Gulch.

Map of Northern California—Page 463

Sonoma County

Parking/fees: free roadside turnouts
Hours: 8 A.M.–one hour after sunset
Facilities: none
Contact: Sonoma Coast State Beaches, 707/875-3483

23 Russian Gulch, page 517

Location: 25 miles north of Jenner off Highway 1; trail leads to beach
Parking/fees: free parking lot
Hours: 8 A.M.–one hour after sunset
Facilities: restrooms
Contact: Sonoma Coast State Beaches, 707/875-3483

24 Vista Point, page 517

Location: Meyers Grade Road at Highway 1 four miles north of Jenner
Parking/fees: free parking lot
Hours: 8 A.M.–one hour after sunset
Facilities: restrooms and picnic tables
Contact: Sonoma Coast State Beaches, 707/875-3483

25 Fort Ross Reef, page 519

Location: eight miles north of Jenner, off Highway 1
Parking/fees: $4 entrance fee per vehicle. Camping fee is $13 per night, which includes admission to Fort Ross State Historic Park and Salt Point State Park.
Hours: 8 A.M.–one hour after sunset
Facilities: restrooms and picnic tables
Contact: Fort Ross State Historic Park, 707/847-3286

26 Fort Ross Cove, page 519

Location: 11 miles north of Jenner, off Highway 1, at Fort Ross State Historic Park
Parking/fees: $4 entrance fee per vehicle
Hours: 10 A.M.–4:30 P.M. (buildings), sunrise–sunset (grounds)
Facilities: restrooms, picnic tables, and visitor center
Contact: Fort Ross State Historic Park, 707/847-3286

27 Timber Cove, page 520

Location: 12 miles north of Jenner, off Highway 1
Parking/fees: $6 entrance fee per person. Camping fees are $19–21 per night.
Hours: 8 A.M.–sunset
Facilities: concession, restrooms, showers, and picnic tables
Contact: Timber Cove Campground, 707/847-3278

Map of Sonoma County—Page 502

Sonoma County

28 Stillwater Cove Regional Park, page 521

▲ ⤳ 🏃 ④

Location: 16 miles north of Jenner, at 22455 Highway 1
Parking/fees: $3 entrance fee per vehicle. Camping fee is $16 per night.
Hours: sunrise–sunset
Facilities: restrooms, showers, and picnic tables
Contact: Stillwater Cove Regional Park, 707/847-3245

29 Ocean Cove, page 521

▲ ⤳ ③

Location: 17 miles north of Jenner, off Highway 1
Parking/fees: $5 entrance fee per vehicle. Camping fee is $14 per night.
Hours: 9 A.M.–6 P.M. (weekdays), 8 A.M.–8 P.M. (weekends)
Facilities: concession, restrooms, showers, and picnic tables
Contact: Ocean Cove Store and Campground, 707/847-3422

30 Gerstle Cove (Salt Point State Park), page 521

▲ ⤳ 🏃 ⑤

Location: 18 miles north of Jenner, off Highway 1
Parking/fees: $4 entrance fee per vehicle. Camping fees are $13–16 (tents and RVs) and $50 (group camp) per night.
Hours: 8 A.M.–sunset
Facilities: restrooms, picnic tables, and visitor center
Contact: Salt Point State Park, 707/847-3221

31 Stump Beach (Salt Point State Park), page 521

⤳ 🏃 ③

Location: 19 miles north of Jenner, off Highway 1
Parking/fees: free parking lot
Hours: 8 A.M.–sunset
Facilities: restrooms and picnic tables
Contact: Salt Point State Park, 707/847-3221

32 Fisk Mill Cove (Salt Point State Park), page 521

⤳ 🏃 ④

Location: 20 miles north of Jenner, off Highway 1
Parking/fees: $4 entrance fee per vehicle
Hours: 8 A.M.–sunset
Facilities: restrooms and picnic tables
Contact: Salt Point State Park, 707/847-3221

33 North Horseshoe Cove (Salt Point State Park), page 521

⤳ 🏃 ③

Location: 21 miles north of Jenner, off Highway 1
Parking/fees: free parking lot

Map of Northern California—Page 463

Sonoma County

Hours: 8 A.M.–sunset
Facilities: none
Contact: Salt Point State Park, 707/847-3221

34 Black Point (Sea Ranch), page 524

Location: Highway 1 at Milepost 50.8; trail leads to beach
Parking/fees: $3 entrance fee per vehicle
Hours: sunrise–sunset
Facilities: none
Contact: Gualala Point Regional Park, 707/785-2377

35 Pebble Beach (Sea Ranch), page 524

Location: Highway 1 at Milepost 52.3; trail leads to beach
Parking/fees: $3 entrance fee per vehicle
Hours: sunrise–sunset
Facilities: none
Contact: Gualala Point Regional Park, 707/785-2377

36 Stengel Beach (Sea Ranch), page 524

Location: Highway 1 at Milepost 54.0; trail leads to beach
Parking/fees: $3 entrance fee per vehicle
Hours: sunrise–sunset
Facilities: none
Contact: Gualala Point Regional Park, 707/785-2377

37 Shell Beach (Sea Ranch), page 524

Location: Highway 1 at Milepost 55.2; trail leads to beach
Parking/fees: $3 entrance fee per vehicle
Hours: sunrise–sunset
Facilities: none
Contact: Gualala Point Regional Park, 707/785-2377

38 Walk-On Beach (Sea Ranch), page 524

Location: Highway 1 at Milepost 56.5; trail leads to beach
Parking/fees: $3 entrance fee per vehicle
Hours: sunrise–sunset
Facilities: none
Contact: Gualala Point Regional Park, 707/785-2377

Sonoma County

Map of Sonoma County—Page 502

39 Gualala Point Regional Park, page 524

Location: one mile south of Gualala at 42401 Highway 1
Parking/fees: $3 entrance fee per vehicle. Camping fee is $16 per night.
Hours: 6 A.M.–sunset (8 A.M.–sunset in winter)
Facilities: restrooms, showers, picnic tables, and visitor center
Contact: Gualala Point Regional Park, 707/785-2377

Sonoma County

Sonoma County

Sonoma County affords a travel experience not unlike a slow-motion replay of Big Sur. In this part of Northern California, one typically negotiates a series of winding bends in the road as vistas of rocky headlands and vast ocean come into view. Every so often you come upon a town. Actually the town is likely to be a brief scattering of well-hidden homes and ramshackle tackle huts that cling like barnacles to the rocks above the roaring Pacific or along the banks of a clear, cool river.

In other words, the concept of the California beach getaway must be modified in Sonoma County. Fishing villages include Bodega Bay and Jenner. Both are former logging and fur-trading centers that fell into blissful sleepiness early in the 20th century, when the trees and otters went thataway. Slowly these outposts have reawakened as fishing holes and coast retreats to soothe the frayed nerves of urban dwellers who make regular pilgrimages here.

This isn't to say Sonoma County has no beaches. On the contrary, the southern third of the county is one large state beach—a 16-mile series of coves collectively known as Sonoma Coast State Beaches. They're excellent for fishing and tidepooling but not for swimming or even wading; an unexpected wave may knock you off your feet and a rip current will finish the job. No lifeguards are posted at any of Sonoma's beaches, so watch your step wherever you comb.

The flip side of this state-beach enclave is Sea Ranch, a private development that claims the northern third of Sonoma County's coast. There exist public accesses to some of the cove beaches along Sea Ranch—not obtained without litigation, of course—but the overall feeling is that no welcome mat has been rolled out. With so much beach to go around, who needs 'em anyway? Along the middle third of the Sonoma coast, beaches are associated with the scattered hamlets that cling to river-mouth coves.

Map of Sonoma County—Page 502

Bodega Bay

After bypassing the Point Reyes Peninsula, Highway 1 rejoins the coast at Bodega Bay, Sonoma County's busiest harbor and pleasure port. So many fishing boats use Bodega Bay that several large marinas are kept active, and the main boat-launching ramp is six lanes wide.

The harbor could not have been planned any better than the way Mother Nature drew it up. Bodega Head is a slug-shaped headland that protects the harbor from the west. The sand spit known as Doran Beach Regional Park provides a sort of tonsil in the harbor's throat, protecting it from the south. A drive to the top of Bodega Head is an absolute must, as the view is a stunner. Don't let a gale-force wind deter you, either. The harder it's blowing, the more awesome the scenery.

Bodega Bay Harbor hasn't always been a smooth-sailing operation. The inner bay, near the warehouses and docks, has had a recurrent problem with silting. A deep-water dredge performed in 1943 created a channel that could service a large fishing fleet. By the 1950s Bodega Bay was processing a million pounds of fish, 900,000 pounds of crab, and 400,000 pounds of albacore a year. Nowadays Bodega Bay (population 1,000) primarily serves as a port for recreational and smaller-scale commercial fishing, as its fortunes have waned in tandem with dwindling catches in the overfished ocean. Still, anglers do their best to snare what's left. Deep-sea fishing boats are expelled seaward past Doran Beach, and no resident salmon or rock cod is safe, especially in the waters off Tomales Point.

Bodega takes its name from a Spanish word meaning "resting place." Our idea of rest in Bodega Bay was to let others do the fishing while we ate seafood and hiked the beaches. Incidentally, Bodega Bay was the setting for Alfred Hitchcock's terrifying film *The Birds*. In fact, you can visit the schoolhouse immortalized in the movie.

All visits, of course, should begin at the wharf, a beehive of activity where you can charter a fishing boat or simply order a seafood dinner at one of the restaurants that continually receive fresh catches.

Beaches

Doran Beach Regional Park can be reached by turning off Highway 1 onto Doran Park Road. Your landmark will be the Best Western Bodega Bay. Continue past the hotel and to a couple of areas to park and play along the bay. The best of these is the Cypress area. It's a picturesque setting, with plenty of small craft at anchor, bobbing on the bright blue water. Doran, a county beach with a $3 day-use fee, features an extensive bayside campground (no RV hookups). There are also places to picnic, clean fish, and launch boats. **Westside Regional Park,** another county-run facility, is on the inner, harbor-facing side of **Bodega Head.** It's got much the same menu of amenities: boat launch, picnic tables, campsites (no RV hookups), sand beach. Sonoma County also obliges hikers with coastal-access trails at **Pinnacle Gulch** (below Bodega Bay, off Highway 1; follow signs to trailhead) and **Bird Walk Access Point** (on the east side of the bay, on Highway 1).

Trails crisscross Bodega Head. The longest leads through thick dunes to South Salmon Creek Beach (see next entry). A shorter trail leads east across Bodega Head to **Campbell Cove,** a harbor beach with a boardwalk leading to an observation deck overlooking a small lagoon known as "Hole in the Head." Another trail leads to the top of the headland, providing stunning views of the ocean, bay, harbor, and migrating whales. Aquatic mammals pass south in December and January and return north in March and April. Trails lead down the bluffs to small, scenic coves. Winter waves and weather can be ferocious, so come prepared for a walk on the wild and windy side. Dress warmly!

Map of Northern California—Page 463

The University of California operates its **Marine Biological Research Lab** on Bodega Head. It is open to the public for tours on Fridays only 2–4 P.M.; call 707/875-2211 for information. Just in case you're wondering, there are nude beaches in Sonoma County, but they're all along the Russian River, whose waters are considerably more inviting than the frigid, treacherous coastal beaches.

Shore Things

• **Bike/skate rentals:** Bodega Bay Surf Shack, 1400 Highway 1, Bodega Bay, 707/875-3944
• **Dive shop:** Bodega Bay Pro Dive, 1275 Highway 1, Bodega Bay, 707/875-3054
• **Ecotourism:** Bodega Head, Westside Road, Bodega Bay, 707/865-3291
• **Marina:** Mason's Marina, 1820 West Shore Road, Bodega Bay, 707/875-3811
• **Pier:** Lucas Wharf, 595 Highway 1, Bodega Bay, 707/875-3522
• **Rainy day attraction:** Fort Ross State Historic Park, 19005 Highway 1, Fort Ross, 707/847-3286
• **Shopping/browsing:** Ocean View Center, 2001 Highway 1, Bodega Bay
• **Sportfishing:** Bodega Bay Sportfishing Center, 1500 Bay Flat Road, Bodega Bay, 707/875-3344
• **Surf report:** 707/875-3944
• **Surf shop:** Bodega Bay Surf Shack, 1400 Highway 1, Bodega Bay, 707/875-3944
• **Vacation rentals:** Bodega Bay and Beyond, 913 Highway 1, Bodega Bay, 800/888-3565

Bunking Down

Each of the 78 large rooms at the **Best Western Bodega Bay Lodge** (Highway 1, 707/875-3525, $$) has a balcony overlooking the bay and Doran Beach. Amenities include pool, spa, sauna, gym, and fireplace. A free breakfast comes with the room, and dinner can be had on premises at the Ocean Club. A slightly more upscale hostelry is **Inn at the Tides** (800 Highway 1, 707/875-2751, $$$), which offers the

same peerless water views and the Bayview Restaurant and Lounge. The earth-toned lodge blends nicely into the landscape, and the views of the harbor and Bodega Head make this a cozy hideaway.

Bodega Bay Lodge and Spa (103 Coast Highway, 707/875-3525, $$$) is the largest resort-style lodging on the Sonoma coast. The lodge itself has 84 rooms, each with its own fireplace. The expansive grounds also offer fishing and access opportunities on Doran Beach, a fitness center with full-service spa, a heated swimming pool, and an excellent on-site gourmet restaurant, the Duck Club. Once you check in, there's no real reason to leave. A complimentary wine hour is held in the rustic lobby each day 5–6 P.M. There's a guest library here, as well. One of the more literary inns we've ever stayed at, Bodega Bay Lodge and Spa stocks its rooms with books (good ones, too), as well as CD players, TVs, and VCRs. It's equipped as an ideal weekend escape from the harried Bay Area. Vacationers from all over would be well advised to savor the splendid Sonoma-coast scenery from these tony digs.

Sonoma Coast Villa (16702 Coast Highway, 888/404-2255, $$$$) is another luxury enclave in the Bodega Bay area. The 12-room inn's Mediterranean-flavored terra-cotta architecture, terraced gardens, expansive grounds, and numerous amenities (spa, putting green, swimming pool) make it a peaceful hideaway for those who can afford it. Rooms generally run $245–325 per night. Proprietor Cy Griffin has thoughtfully designed a website outlining the best places and activities in Bodega Bay and west Sonoma County. Log onto www.bodegabayvisitors.com for some insightful tips on wine-tasting, golfing, horseback riding, gallery-hopping, and beachwalking.

Coastal Cuisine

Along the shores of Bodega Bay sits **Tides Wharf** (835 Highway 1, 707/875-3652, $$$),

Map of Sonoma County—Page 502

Sonoma Coast Safety Check

If you want to maintain a healthy relationship with the ocean on the rugged North Coast, you have to treat it with respect. We came upon the following guidelines for doing just that. They seem so sensible and appropriate to all of Northern California that we've included them here, in abbreviated and paraphrased form, for your safety:

• The ocean is not a large lake or a bubbling creek. It's rough, powerful, and frigid.
• When you're down below a bluff, you can't be seen or heard from above. Children, in particular, should not be allowed to climb down alone.
• Always consult tide tables if you plan to hike along the beach. Advancing tides can pin you to the base of a bluff with nowhere to escape.
• Bluff and headland trails are cut into erodable, soft rock. Before descending any trail, study the terrain and waves from above. Pay special heed to the force and size of incoming waves.
• Never turn your back on the ocean.
• If you're hit by a large, unexpected wave don't try to save anything other than yourself (i.e., drop your camera, backpack, paintbrush).
• Don't go beachcombing or exploring clifftops alone.
• Beware of poison oak, which thrives all over the North Coast.

a complex that includes a fish market, restaurant, bar, and gift shop. When it was discovered that the original pilings on which it was built were slowly sinking, Tides Wharf received not only a new foundation but a complete makeover in 1998. The new, improved Tides Wharf has a clean, airy look—particularly the dining room, with its big glass picture windows, hardwood floors, and exposed-beam ceiling. The emphasis at Tides Wharf is on fresh seafood served with light sauces that subtly accentuate the taste of the fish or shellfish. Local catches include Pacific red snapper, ling cod, and petrale sole. We sampled the sole, which are small, delicate fillets served either pan-fried or dore style (dipped in egg wash, sautéed, and served with a creamy lemon-butter sauce). The sweet, fork-tender calamari steak is prepared parmesan style, with cheese and tomato sauce, but chefs will also do it dore style, at your request.

Crab cioppino is a house favorite that consists of a goodly quantity of shellfish (shrimp, scallops, mussels, and a whole Dungeness crab) swimming in a spicy tomato-based sauce that is sopped up with hunks of toasted Italian bread. The seafood brochette and prime rib also come highly recommended. The appetizer menu includes salmon and albacore, both smoked in-house to a delicate turn, and a real standout called popcorn shrimp: medium-sized rock shrimp from Washington that have been rolled in herbed bread crumbs, pan-fried, and served with a dipping sauce made of butter, wine, garlic, and cayenne pepper. An extensive listing of desserts includes Charleston chocolate truffle, a dense wedge of divine decadence, and New Orleans–style bread pudding topped with praline sauce.

Tides Wharf's wine list is well-chosen and reasonably priced, especially the house label wines, which are made for the restaurant by

Map of Northern California—Page 463

Adler-Fells winery. The house chardonnay is crisp, buttery, and refreshing, and is as good a bottle as you'll ever order for $20. The bar serves terrific local microbrews, including Russian River Abbey Ale, a ruddy ale that goes down smoothly, and a super-dark oatmeal stout. The **Duck Club** (103 Coast Highway, 707/875-3525, $$$) bills its fare as California French cuisine, which means that it freely draws upon two culinary worlds. The large windows of the restaurant open onto windswept dune fields and tidal flats where deer can often be seen wandering. (Fortunately, venison is not on the menu.) Roast crispy duck with ginger sauce and candied orange is the signature dish here, and the chef and sous chef are renowned for innovative combinations of sweet and spicy sauces. For appetizers, you can't miss with Jerusalem artichoke fritters with roast garlic lemon aioli and a cup of Bodega Bay fog chowder. We feasted on ahi tuna with soy, sake, and ginger and achiote-marinated mahimahi. The fabulous Duck Club cuisine—along with the wafting strains of Frank Sinatra, which set a clubby mood—proved to be the perfect sweet-and-spicy tonic we needed after a long day's drive on the winding roads of Northern California. The Duck Club, in short, kept us from, um, "quacking up" on what turned out to be the last night of another long and eventful exploration of California's remarkable coastline.

For More Information

Bodega Bay Chamber of Commerce, 850 Highway 1, Bodega Bay, CA 94923, 707/875-3422 or 800/905-9050, website: www.bodegabay.com

Bodega Dunes and Salmon Creek Beach

Bodega Dunes is one of the last intact dune fields in California. The sandy wonders have been preserved in a park that includes a 98-site campground where campers can pitch tents or park RVs beneath a canopy of pines and firs. Enormous dunes, covered with a profusion of swaying grasses, protect the campground from offshore winds. A zigzagging wooden walkway leads over the dunes to **South Salmon Creek Beach,** which runs for roughly three miles, from the mouth of Salmon Creek to Mussel Point on Bodega Head. Being directly connected with the Bodega Dunes, South Salmon Creek Beach is the broader, lengthier strand. Parking is located south of Salmon Creek, while park headquarters is located on the creek's north bank. **North Salmon Creek Beach** lies at the bottom end of a 10-mile run of Sonoma Coast State Beaches, a grouping of wild and forlorn accesses, each of which has its own turnout and path to a fan-shaped cove beach.

All sorts of compelling reasons are offered against swimming here, including a strong backwash, rip currents, and sleeper waves. The camping is as good as it gets at the beach, but leave the swimsuit at home; the average water temperature on Sonoma coast beaches is between 48 and 52 degrees. If you don't die of hypothermia or get gnawed to bits by a great white, you might wind up filleted on the rocks by an oversize wave. So what can you do on a beach like this? Put on a hooded sweatshirt, walk along the shoreline, and "visualize world peace" (to borrow a bumper sticker message we saw in the parking lot). We did our bit for global harmony by giving a vacationing German family a ride from the beach back to their campsite. They left us a car full of sand in return.

A dune restoration project was recently completed at South Salmon Creek Beach. After being denuded of their native vegetation, studded with ecosystem-altering invasive plant species, and generally abused for a century, the dunes have mostly been restored. The project involved reshaping the dunes, reintroducing native flora, and laying down boardwalks to minimize damage from humans. A good idea and money well spent; the results speak for themselves.

Map of Sonoma County—Page 502

Sonoma County

Sonoma Coast State Beaches

You've heard of ghost towns. Well, Sonoma is a ghost county. Travelers who are sick of crowds, development, and predictable vacations will find the Sonoma coast appealing, but the beaches here can be a bit, well, ghostly. These lonely and wild stretches of sand are pleasurable to ponder from a blufftop but can be daunting at close range, especially in the wrong kind of weather.

Collectively known as the Sonoma Coast State Beaches, the 16-mile stretch from Bodega Bay to just north of Jenner offers over 5,000 acres of public land, 1,000 acres of which are dunes and the rest coastal bluffs, with more than 20 units overseen by the state park staff. Here's a list of beach accesses, moving from south to north:

- Bodega Bay
- Campbell Cove
- Bodega Dunes Campground
- South Salmon Creek Beach
- North Salmon Creek Beach
- Miwok Beach
- Coleman Beach
- Arched Rock Beach
- Marshall Gulch
- Carmet Beach
- Schoolhouse Beach
- Portuguese Beach
- Gleason Beach
- Duncan's Cove
- Rock Point
- Duncan's Landing
- Pacific View
- Wright's Beach
- Furlong Gulch
- Shell Beach
- Blind Beach
- Goat Rock Beach
- Russian Gulch

That's an average of one beach-access point every two-thirds mile. To get to each requires a hike of varying length and an often harrowing descent to the beach. We've taken a gander at several over the years but have by no means trekked out to all of them. Several, such as Rock Point, aren't beaches at all but headlands overlooking the ocean. The Willow Creek Unit isn't even on the ocean, lying upstream of Willow Creek and several miles from the coast. Granted, it's confusing. We're not sure we've nailed down the Sonoma Coast State Beaches, but our accounting is as comprehensive as any official listing. Incidentally, in deference to the endangered Western snowy plover, dogs are not allowed on any of the Sonoma Coast State Beaches south of Coleman Beach or on Goat Rock Beach.

To make this discussion manageable, we'll focus on units that are more heavily used, have facilities, or are distinctive in some way. From the south, the first Sonoma Coast State Beach access is **Bodega Dunes,** one of the two coast campgrounds (see Bodega Dunes and Salmon Creek Beach) on state land. The second can be found at **Wright's Beach,** six miles north. There are fewer campsites here than at Bodega Dunes, but they're directly on the beach.

Shell Beach is favored by beachcombers, tidepoolers, anglers—and geologists. Yes, this particular beach stands out among the Sonoma Coast pack for its geological revelations. Dr. Terry Wright has described the rocky coast at Shell Beach as a place "where the complex structure and rocks of the Franciscan Complex lie out like a smorgasbord for hungry geologists. It is a classic field area, world-famous for its perfect exposures of an incredible variety of rocks and structures." Moreover, because it lies along a sheltered inlet, "it is a pleasant place to visit even on the most windswept days."

We walked out to Shell Beach for a good, close look. It's a straight shot off Highway 1 to the parking lot above Shell Beach. From here you can descend the steep, partially paved path to the beach or wander across the blufftops

Map of Northern California—Page 463

to **Goat Rock Beach** via Kortum Trail, a 2.6-mile hike. There are many cormorants in the area; apparently, these dark, long-necked birds like this spot. Human visitors should exercise great caution, though. One sign reads: "The surf at this beach has caused the death of many people who were simply walking the shoreline." Those pesky sneaker waves. There's more: "The cliffs along this coast have caused many deaths." It's a pretty spot. Just keep an eye on the ocean, the tides, and your footing.

Portuguese Beach is good for rockfishing and surf casting. **Duncan's Landing** is the place to go if you fancy drowning. Otherwise known as **Death Rock,** it's the single most dangerous spot on California's deadliest stretch of coastline: the 16 miles between Bodega Head and Russian Gulch. **Goat Rock Beach** lies just south of the Russian River mouth. You can walk down to this hard, black-sand beach from Goat Rock Road. Goats used to graze on the massive offshore rock; now Goat Rock is inhabited by harbor seals and seabirds and is off-limits to humans. The best time to visit is April–August, when waves are less menacing and seals are mating.

The other Sonoma Coast State Beaches—**Schoolhouse, Gleason, Miwok, Arched Rock, Carmet, Coleman,** and **Blind Beach**—are more for surf casters and solitary souls. Sure, they're marvelous to look at and fully deserving of the melodic names bestowed upon them. But after slipping and sliding down long, steep paths to get at several of them, we're more inclined to pull the car over and enjoy the view from a safe distance.

For More Information

Sonoma Coast State Beaches, 707/875-3483, www.parks.ca.gov

Jenner

Jenner's physical setting on the mouth of the Russian River is nothing short of regal, with the town bravely clinging to the cliffs along the river and the curves of Highway 1. From vista points south of town, you can watch this undammed California river roll into the Pacific. Pull over and enjoy an area that is rich in history and scenic beauty. Russian fur trappers originally named the river Slavyanka, meaning "Russian girl," but the name was too much of a mouthful for English-speaking tongues, and it was renamed Russian River.

Later settlers used this stretch of Highway 1, carved into the jagged clifftops in 1875, as a logging trail. Redwoods were floated down the Russian River toward the sea, where they were loaded onto boats and wagons. If you're interested in learning more, the **Jenner Visitor Center** (Highway 1, 707/865-9433) delves into Sonoma Coast history in greater detail, though it's open only on weekends.

North out of town drivers ascend Jenner Grade, one of the most dramatic stretches of highway on the California coast. It rivals even Big Sur for vertigo-inducing thrills and chills as one ascends its steeply graded switchbacks. Do we need to add "Fasten your safety belt"? If you'd like to gather your wits before tackling this driving challenge, Jenner and environs offer several fine restaurants and inns burrowed off the highway.

Beaches

The state owns much of the coastal land north of the Russian River mouth. Several beaches between Jenner and **Russian Gulch,** known as the **North Jenner Beaches,** are reachable by steep coast-access trails down eroding bluffs. **Vista Point** is a relatively new overlook, picnic spot, and beach-access point four miles north of Jenner, where Meyers Grade Road meets Highway 1.

Navigating the North Coast

We hate to sound like a couple of biddies, but driving the North Coast of California requires a focused mind and a steady pair of hands to see you safely through. North of Bodega Bay, Highway 1 hugs the rugged, rolling contours of the coastal cliffs, sending vehicles soaring skyward, twisting around hairpin turns, and edging precariously toward cliffs with drops of hundreds of feet and no guardrail. If the topography doesn't unnerve you, then Highway 1 might send roaming cattle or fully laden lumber trucks in your path. Indeed, this section of the Coast Highway is even more treacherous and difficult than the legendary Big Sur. Not to say that it doesn't have its rewards, mainly in the form of unobstructed views of wild, pristine coastline unrivaled anywhere in the world.

Unless God is your copilot, you might want to ponder the following driving tips. We picked them up from local sources and through personal experience on our many coastal forays:

- As this two-lane road is the only north-south route on the coast, Highway 1 bears a fair amount of traffic. Don't get involved in a test of wills or a drag race with those driving too fast or slow for your liking. Pull off the highway into one of the many turnouts and overlooks that have been carved into the roadside or wait patiently for slowpokes to do so.
- State law prohibits holding up more than five vehicles in a row. If you've got a convoy trailing you, pull over to the side to let 'em by.
- Don't try to pass. A double-yellow line is plastered on most of Highway 1 for good reason, and straightaways are scarce.
- Stay alert at night and in the frequent fog. Keep an eye out for wildlife, especially deer and cattle.
- Turn on your headlights in the fog, using normal (not high) beams. This not only helps you see better, but also allows oncoming traffic to better see you.
- Watch out for the many bicyclists who use the road. This requires extra caution from drivers because little shoulder room exists and there's no margin for error. One small mistake could mean somebody's life. In 1995, a friend died while cycling the Pacific Coast Highway in Northern California. He was hit from behind by a car whose driver did not even see him. RIP, Tom Sinclair.

Bunking Down

Sea Coast Hide-A-Ways (21350 Highway 1, 707/847-3278) is the biggest vacation-home rental agency in town. All the rentals are clean and comfortably furnished, with full kitchens. Many travelers opt for **River's End** (Highway 1, 707/869-3252, $$), a full-service operation that boasts an excellent restaurant, boat-rental agency, general store, bar, campground, and eight-room lodge. The remodeled cabins at River's End hug the cliffs and offer stupendous ocean views. Another restaurant/lodge operation is **Murphy's Jenner Inn** (10400 Highway 1, 707/865-2377, $$). You can choose between bed-and-breakfast–style rooms and suites at River House (on the Russian River) or

Map of Northern California—Page 463

Longfellow's Landing (by a creek). In addition, Jenner Inn rents out a cabin (sleeps eight) and handles private home rentals.

Coastal Cuisine

River's End (11048 Highway 1, 707/865-2484, $$$) is one of the premier restaurants on the Northern California coast. The fare tends toward hearty game dishes—rabbit, duck, quail, venison—and seafood, all prepared with Germanic flair, assembled with local ingredients, and pungently flavorful. We can heartily recommend the coconut-covered prawns and plump Pacific oysters. A splendid meal is guaranteed, but try to make reservations well in advance.

The view of the ocean from the restaurant and the deck that encircles it is a kind of visual dessert. River's End restaurant is open Thursday–Monday, while the inn is open seven days a week.

Jenner's other restaurant of note is **Jenner Inn** (10400 Highway 1, 707/865-2377, $$$), which offers seafood, vegetarian, and beef dishes; a full bar graced by a stone fireplace; and, on weekends, live jazz, classical, and New Age music.

For More Information

Sonoma Coast Visitor Information Center, Russian River Region, 14034 Armstrong Woods Road, Guerneville, CA 95446, 707/869-9212 or 800/253-8800, website: www.sonoma.com

Fort Ross

The most historic site in the area is Fort Ross, a 1,160-acre Russian stronghold 11 miles north of Jenner. Not to worry, Joint Chiefs: Fort Ross was abandoned by the Russians in 1841. The original Russian settlers came to the California coast searching for new sources of fur (mainly sea otters) and food for the enrichment of the Tsarist Russian empire. They landed in Bodega Bay in 1809 and held all the coastal land from there to this site, building the fort in 1812 out of local redwood. Eighty Native American Aleuts and 25 Russian fur trappers kept the Spanish at bay while the job was completed. Fort Rossiya was also a base for growing wheat to supply Russian colonies in Alaska. The Russians, unlike the Spanish, did not try to suppress Native American culture or subjugate the natives. Instead, they intermarried with the local tribe (the Kashaya Pomo) and traded extensively with them. Even today, the largest collection of Pomo artifacts is stored in a museum in St. Petersburg, Russia.

At **Fort Ross State Historic Park** (19005 Highway 1, 707/847-3286), restored and reconstructed buildings include barracks, a stockade, a Russian Orthodox chapel, blockhouses, and the commandant's residence. An on-site museum is open daily 10 A.M.–4:30 P.M. A "Living History Day" is held the last Saturday in July, re-creating a typical day at the fort in 1836. Bring your own Stoli?

Beaches

Just beyond Fort Ross's front gate is **Fort Ross Cove**, a small beach frequented by shell collectors. A nearby garden filled with exotic plants is a popular picnicking spot. An underwater park for divers, designated **Fort Ross Reef**, sits offshore. Three miles south is Fort Ross Reef Campground. Trails from the campground lead to coves and beaches in the area.

Bunking Down

If you want to stay overnight but not inside a tent, the **Fort Ross Lodge** (20705 Highway 1, 707/847-3333, $$) offers accommodations with ocean views, fireplaces, patios, hot tubs, complimentary wine, and coastal access.

Sonoma County

Timber Cove

Timber Cove is the site of a couple of unrelated and dissimilar operations. One is a restaurant with vacation home rentals, the **Timber Cove Inn** (21780 Highway 1, 707/847-3231, $$$$), at which you'll pay between $195 and $600 for a two-night stay (that's the minimum). Timber Cove has 49 rooms in all, spread out on a 26-acre headland. Units range from small cabins to three-bedroom homes; some are down by the ocean, others up in the redwoods. The on-site restaurant has a French-Continental menu that's on the expensive side.

The other is the **Timber Cove Campground** (21350 Highway 1, 707/847-3278), which has a 40-site tent and RV campground. The campground provides all that's needed for fishing and boating: rentals, launches, licenses, tackle shop. At the inn you may be shocked to discover a 72-foot obelisk by the late sculptor Benjamin Bufano, entitled *The Expanding Universe.* Ponder that while you're watching whales go by; a major moment of clarity can't be far behind.

 ## We Brake for Cows

Highway 1 through Sonoma County is cow country. The critters wander all over the place like acid-dosed Woodstock hippies trying to find the freeway shoulder they parked their van on. During one passage through coastal Sonoma, we were coming around a mountain when we suddenly came screeching to a halt. A big black cow was standing in our lane, staring us down like a Bergmanesque apparition of death. Pea-soup fog was draped around the beast's neck like a shawl, rendering it nearly invisible. We skidded to a stop inches from its steaming nostrils. The cow slowly, carefully appraised the situation, then lumbered aside to let us pass. *Moove,* it seemed to say. We pulled around the bovine obstruction and continued on our journey. Had an RV come rumbling around the bend at that moment, Sonoma would have been one head of cattle poorer and the world one beach book lighter.

On a recent visit we counted no fewer than nine cattle meandering along Highway 1. Three of them clung to an inside curve, barely off the shoulder, pressed against the cliffs. Others nonchalantly clomped across the road. It was a vertical plunge of hundreds of feet to the ocean, and a sheer wall of rock rose high above the road. How did the cows get there? How would they get back to wherever they came from? Clearly they pose a danger to unwary motorists, particularly the guy trying to prove how well his new sports car can handle the curves. We had to wonder how many cars have tumbled over the cliffs in Sonoma County over the years, with Elsie's face their last conscious memory.

Map of Northern California—Page 463

Stillwater Cove Regional Park

Four miles north of Fort Ross is lovely **Stillwater Cove Regional Park,** a county-run facility that is often passed without a second look by tourists hellbent on making Mendocino before nightfall. It's more popular with locals, who are given discounts on the day-use and camping fees. The appeal is obvious. A looped hiking trail leads along Stockoff Creek, through a small forest, and down to a cove frequented by abalone divers.

Bunking Down

Near the park is **Stillwater Cove Ranch** (22555 Highway 1, 707/847-3227, $). Coastal accommodations in Sonoma County are few and far between, and rarely are they priced this reasonably. Some units go for $55-65 midweek and a little more on weekends. "We're for the kind of travelers who can't afford to stay on this otherwise premium-priced stretch of the coast," said the perky proprietress. Actually, the place is not so much a ranch as an assortment of rustic units and a dairy-barn bunkhouse. The ocean is right across the highway, making this a good spot for fishing, whale-watching, hiking, and enjoying the uncommonly good restaurants between Jenner and Gualala. Stillwater Cove Ranch doesn't serve meals, and all but a handful of rooms lack cooking facilities.

Salt Point State Park

This is another heaven-sent state park, the perfect way station on the North Coast for those who want a bit of everything. Among its 5,970 acres, **Salt Point State Park** has seven miles of rugged shoreline with dozens of hard-sand cove beaches, as well as hiking trails that head inland and reach elevations of 1,000 feet in the foothills. There are both coastal (Gerstle Cove) and upland (Woodside) campgrounds. The former is situated by the **Gerstle Cove Underwater Reserve,** a diving and tidepooling spot with 30 improved sites. The latter is a bit farther removed, offering 109 sites, both improved and primitive.

Beaches

A rewarding hike from a roadside parking lot leads out to **Stump Beach.** It's a two-miler that meanders along the blufftops to a lovely cove beach that derives its name from the driftwood that washes up here, much of it the residue of a dying logging industry. Nearby is **Gerstle Cove,** an ecological preserve that was one of California's first underwater parks. It's a prime whale-watching site December-April. Two more beaches—**Fisk Mill Cove** and **North Horseshoe Cove**—lie off Highway 1, one and two miles north (respectively) of Stump Beach. Fisk Mill has facilities, and an entry fee is charged. North Horseshoe Cove costs nothing, and nothing is provided—except, of course, an exceptionally scenic beach.

April-June the 300-acre **Kruse Rhododendron State Reserve,** a mile inland from Salt Point State Park, is ablaze with multicolored rhododendrons. These showy shrubs were planted to replace a forest of firs that was destroyed by fire. The reserve is also noteworthy for its extensive system of hiking trails covered with foliage ranging from rhododendrons to redwoods.

Bunking Down

A mile south of Salt Point State Park is **Salt Point Lodge** (23255 Highway 1, 707/847-3234, $), a contemporary motel with reasonable rates, broad grassy lawn, playground equipment, sundeck, sauna, and a hot tub. The management also runs a small restaurant serving three meals a day. Across the road is **Ocean Cove** (Highway 1, 707/847-3422), a privately owned beach and bluff at which guests can camp, fish, and dive for abalone.

Map of Sonoma County—Page 502

Sonoma County

Stewarts Point

Two roadside curiosities converge at the historic site of Stewarts Point, overlooking Fisherman's Bay. One is **Stewarts Point Store** (3200 Highway 1, Sea Ranch, 707/785-2406), a nifty general emporium on Highway 1 that's truly a relic from a bygone era. From the mid-nineteenth to the early twentieth century, so-called doghole schooners turned this rugged shore into a busy port town that serviced the logging trade. The only trustworthy way to haul the timber from the north woods was by sea, with the cargo being loaded primarily via cables tied from the

 ## Bobbing for Abalone

Swathed in a shell of mother-of-pearl, endowed with a delectable taste, the abalone is one of the most prized denizens of the deep along the California shoreline. It belongs to the mollusk clan, a large phylum that includes more than 100,000 species of invertebrates such as squid, clams, oysters, mussels, snails, and octopuses. The abalone is one of the largest mollusks, ranging 4–10 inches in width. Any abalone 10 inches or larger is lovingly dubbed "a hubcap" by divers, and the world's record, taken in 1993 off the Humboldt coast, was 12 $^5/_{16}$ inches across, 9 $^3/_4$ inches wide, and weighed 11 $^3/_5$ pounds.

Eight of the world's 100 abalone species dwell along California's coast, though "dwell" could be interchanged with "dwindle" because they've been hunted, poached, and harvested to near extinction. The most in demand is the state's indigenous red abalone *(Haliotis rufenscens)*. Prime catches of red abalone are worth anywhere from $50 to $80 apiece, with the retail price for its meat topping $100 per pound.

Abalone live on rocks in shallow water along rugged shorelines, clinging tenaciously to their perches and feeding on algae. The couch potatoes of the sea-life set, abalone are so stationary that they're often covered with other organisms. To wrest them from their resting places one needs a pry bar—a miniature crowbar available in bait-and-tackle and dive shops. Humans have long valued the abalone for its tasty meat and its beautiful oval shell, but we're not the only ones who dig these crazy mollusks. Sea otters, who eat one-third their body weight daily, also relish abalone. Once they've pried the shell loose, they smash it open on the rocks and scoop out their bounty.

Thankfully, commercial abalone harvesting is banned north of San Francisco. Even though only recreational harvesting is allowed along the North Coast, more than two million pounds of red abalone is taken for sport each year. Bagging one or two is a regular rite of vacation passage for some waders and divers.

Not surprisingly, because abalone has been depleted to near extinction south of San Francisco, the abalone along the North Coast (particularly in

Map of Northern California—Page 463

bluffs to the anchored ships. Most of the lumber ended up in San Francisco, where the redwood was incorporated into Victorian homes and the Douglas fir was used for schooners. The doghole schooners were so named because they had to be nimble enough to anchor in bays that were just big enough, as the sailors used to say, "for a dog to turn around in."

The store and an abandoned stagecoach-stop hotel are all that remain from these colorful times. As you pass the turnoff to Tin Barn Road, look east for the second curiosity. You'll spy **Odiyan,** a Tibetan Buddhist monastery, as anomalous as the Russian Orthodox chapel at Fort Ross. It's not open to the public.

Sonoma County) are subject to poaching and illegal harvesting. Indeed, a 16-man abalone poaching ring, working in Sonoma and Mendocino counties, was broken up by the state Department of Fish and Game in 1999, resulting in stiff prison sentences and tighter surveillance of this dwindling treasure. So tempting is the quest for abalone that in December 2000 a member of the state's abalone preservation advisory board was arrested for poaching in Sonoma County, having been found with 129 illegally caught abalone worth $10,000.

If, after all this, you still want to bag abalone along the North Coast, here are a few pointers:

• Wear a wet suit. The water temperature ranges 48–52 degrees most of the year.
• Have a valid fishing license in plain view on your person, preferably in a clear, waterproof pouch.
• It is illegal to use scuba equipment to catch abalone; it has to be done with snorkel and mask or by wading, stooping, and groping by hand along the bottom.
• Use a seven-inch measuring bar to make sure the abalone shell is of legal size. Return anything smaller.
• Use a proper pry bar. Improper tools can break the shell and kill the abalone immediately, which is a total waste.
• Never wade or dive alone.
• Wait for a minus tide (–1/0-foot or better).
• Check rocky kelp beds first. This is where abalone are most often found.
• Take only your legal limit of three per day (because of the unsustainable harvesting, the limit was lowered from four in 2001) and 24 total for a calendar year.
• A $12.60 reporting card is required for taking abalone.

Abalone may be taken April 1–June 30 and August 1–November 30. The season is closed during the month of July. State game wardens will bust you good and proper if you break the law. Fines start at $500 for the first abalone over the legal limit and are $250 per abalone above that.

If you see a person or group of people whom you suspect are illegally harvesting abalone, call the state's toll-free, 24-hour tip line for fish and wildlife violations (888/334-2258). Rewards are offered as an incentive. For the latest news about abalone along the North Coast, contact the **Sonoma County Abalone Network,** P.O. Box 3801, Santa Rosa, CA 95402, website: www.abalonenetwork.org.

Map of Sonoma County—Page 502

Sea Ranch

The last 10 miles of coastline in Sonoma County belong lock, stock, and barrel to a private development known as Sea Ranch. It's a planned, 5,500-acre community for the second-home wealthy. Originally, Sea Ranch met stiff resistance from the California Coastal Commission and environmental groups. At one time this land was part of a 17,500-acre Mexican land grant, Rancho de Herman, and a former sheep ranch. The developers finally compromised, allowing five coastal-access footpaths across the property. Each trail is about a quarter-mile long and leads to a cove beach, but a posted set of stringent rules governing hikers just about kills whatever fun you might have along the way.

In all fairness, Sea Ranch has won awards for its environmentally sensitive architecture and planning. All of the houses—wood-shingled and built low to the ground—blend in with the pines and fir trees. Still, the lengthy privatized expanse of Sea Ranch and its golf course strike us as an indefensible appropriation of so much of this grandly desolate stretch of the coast.

Beaches

The cove beaches here include, from south to north: **Black Point, Pebble Beach, Stengel Beach, Shell Beach,** and **Walk-On Beach.** They are all pretty much the same, and the short trails that cross the Sea Ranch property to them are heavily regulated. We walked to the end of three Sea Ranch trails before throwing in the beach towel. There are no facilities, save for portable restrooms at the trailheads.

Bunking Down

Some of the houses at Sea Ranch can be rented, or you can lie in at the **Sea Ranch Lodge** (60 Sea Walk Drive, 707/785-2371, $$$), a 20-room retreat whose plentiful windows look out on the ocean. There's also a restaurant and lounge with a fireplace and solarium.

For More Information

Sea Ranch Lodge, P.O. Box 44, Sea Ranch, CA 95497, 707/785-2371, website: www.sea ranchlodge.com

Gualala Point Regional Park

The 125-acre **Gualala Point Regional Park** is in Sonoma County, where it looks across the Gualala River at the town of Gualala in Mendocino County. Gualala Point is fenced off from Sea Ranch, which deeded the land for the park. Every 50 yards or so you are reminded of this fact by signs warning against trespassing on private property. Still, the views of the river mouth, ocean, and town of Gualala are rewarding. Tuck your $3 entrance fee into the self-pay box and, before setting out for the beach, peruse the visitors center's collection of relics from the days when Gualala was a logging port. A trail leads to Gualala Point, which offers spectacular views of the rocky coastline. A campground (no RV hookups) lies on the east side of Highway 1, beside the Gualala River. For park information, call 707/785-2377.

Map of Northern California—Page 463

© ROBERT HOLMES/CALTOUR

Chapter 13
Mendocino County

Mendocino County

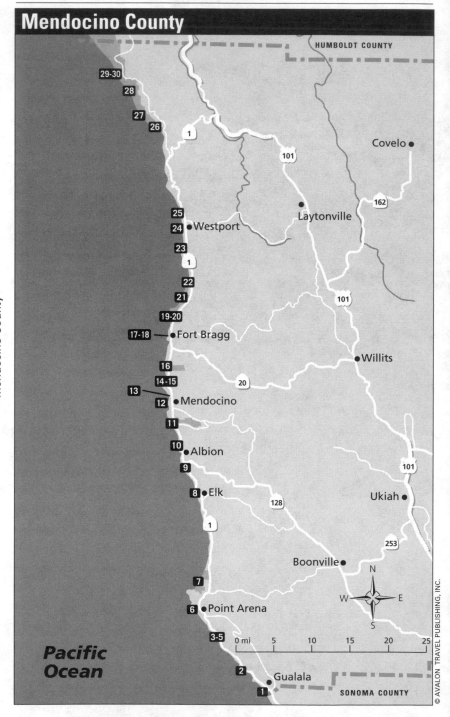

Mendocino County Beaches

❶ Gualala River, page 535

Location: Follow dirt access roads off Highway 1 at the north bank of Gualala River, in Gualala.
Parking/fees: free parking lot
Hours: 24 hours
Facilities: none
Contact: Gualala Kayak Rental, 707/884-4705

❷ Anchor Bay Beach (a.k.a. Fish Rock Beach), page 537

Location: at Anchor Bay Campground, off Highway 1, four miles north of Gualala
Parking/fees: $1 entrance fee per vehicle, plus $1 per person. Camping fees are $21–23 per night.
Hours: 7 A.M.–7 P.M.
Facilities: concession, restrooms, and picnic tables
Contact: Anchor Bay Campground, 707/884-4222

❸ Schooner Gulch Beach, page 538

Location: Schooner Gulch Road at Highway 1, 35 miles south of Point Arena; trails lead to beach
Parking/fees: free roadside parking
Hours: 24 hours
Facilities: none
Contact: Mendocino District, California State Parks, 707/937-5804

❹ Bowling Ball Beach, page 538

Location: From Schooner Gulch Road at Highway 1, 35 miles south of Point Arena, follow Bowling Ball Beach trail to the beach.
Parking/fees: free roadside parking
Hours: 24 hours
Facilities: none
Contact: Mendocino District, California State Parks, 707/937-5804

❺ Ross Beach (a.k.a. Moat Creek Access), page 538

Location: 25 miles south of Point Arena off Highway 1
Parking/fees: free parking lot
Hours: 24 hours
Facilities: none
Contact: Mendocino District, California State Parks, 707/937-5804

Mendocino County

6 Arena Cove Beach, page 538

Location: in Point Arena at the end of Port Road, off Highway 1
Parking/fees: free parking lot
Hours: 24 hours
Facilities: concessions and restrooms
Contact: Arena Cove Pier, 707/882-2583

7 Manchester State Park, page 539

Location: From Highway 1 north of Point Arena, Stoneboro, Kinney, and Alder Creek Beach Roads lead to different sections of Manchester State Park.
Parking/fees: $4 entrance fee per vehicle. Camping fees are $13–16 per night, plus a $7.50 reservation fee.
Hours: 24 hours
Facilities: restrooms and picnic tables
Contact: Mendocino District, California State Parks, 707/937-5804

8 Greenwood Creek State Beach, page 539

Location: mouth of Greenwood Creek, off Highway 1 in Elk
Parking/fees: free parking lot
Hours: 24 hours
Facilities: restrooms and picnic tables
Contact: Mendocino District, California State Parks, 707/937-5804

9 Navarro River Beach Access, page 539

Location: From Highway 1 two miles south of Albion, turn west on Navarro Bluff Road and follow it to the beach.
Parking/fees: free parking lot. Camping fee is $5 per night.
Hours: 24 hours
Facilities: restrooms
Contact: Mendocino District, California State Parks, 707/937-5804

10 Albion Flat, page 541

Location: 10 miles south of Mendocino on Highway 1, at the mouth of the Albion River
Parking/fees: $5 per person entrance fee. Camping fee is $15 per night.
Hours: 6 A.M.–5 P.M.
Facilities: concession, restrooms, picnic tables, and showers
Contact: Albion River Campground and Fishing Village, 707/937-0606

Mendocino County

Map of Northern California—Page 463

11 Van Damme State Park, page 545

Location: in Little River three miles south of Mendocino, off Highway 1
Parking/fees: $4 entrance fee per vehicle. Camping fees are $13–16 (tents and RVs) and $37 (group camp) per night, plus a $7.50 reservation fee.
Hours: 24 hours
Facilities: restrooms, showers, and picnic tables
Contact: Mendocino District, California State Parks, 707/937-5804

12 Mendocino Headlands State Park, page 545

Location: on headlands overlooking the ocean in Mendocino
Parking/fees: free parking lots
Hours: 24 hours
Facilities: none
Contact: Mendocino District, California State Parks, 707/937-5804

13 Russian Gulch State Park, page 545

Location: two miles north of Mendocino off Highway 1, at the mouth of Russian Gulch Creek
Parking/fees: $4 entrance fee per vehicle. Camping fees are $13–16 (tents and RVs) and $30 (group camp).
Hours: 24 hours
Facilities: restrooms, showers, and picnic tables
Contact: Mendocino District, California State Parks, 707/937-5804

14 Caspar Headlands State Reserve, page 548

Location: Five miles north of Mendocino, turn west from Highway 1 onto South Caspar Drive, then turn onto Headlands Drive and follow it to the reserve.
Parking/fees: free roadside parking
Hours: 24 hours
Facilities: none
Contact: Mendocino District, California State Parks, 707/937-5804

15 Caspar State Beach, page 548

Location: Point Cabrillo Road/Old Highway 1 at the mouth of Doyle Creek in Caspar, across from Caspar Beach RV park
Parking/fees: free parking lot. Camping fee is $16 per night at Caspar Beach RV Park.
Hours: 24 hours
Facilities: concession, restrooms, showers, and picnic tables (at Caspar Beach RV Park)
Contact: Mendocino District, California State Parks, 707/937-5804, or Caspar Beach RV Park, 707/964-3306

Map of Mendocino County—Page 526

Mendocino County

16 Jug Handle State Reserve, page 549

🏃 ④

Location: 15 miles north of Caspar, off Highway 1
Parking/fees: free parking lot
Hours: 24 hours
Facilities: restrooms and picnic tables
Contact: Mendocino District, California State Parks, 707/937-5804

17 Noyo Harbor, page 551

⚓ ①

Location: end of Noyo Harbor Drive at the mouth of the Noyo River, in Fort Bragg
Parking/fees: free parking lot
Hours: 24 hours
Facilities: restrooms and showers
Contact: Noyo Harbor Pier, 707/964-0167

18 Glass Beach, page 551

🏃 ①

Location: end of Elm Street in Fort Bragg
Parking/fees: free street parking
Hours: 24 hours
Facilities: none
Contact: none

19 Pudding Creek Beach (MacKerricher State Park), page 551

🚲 🏃 ③

Location: end of Pudding Creek Road, off Highway 1 in Fort Bragg
Parking/fees: free parking lot
Hours: 24 hours
Facilities: none
Contact: Mendocino District, California State Parks, 707/937-5804

20 Virgin Creek Beach (MacKerricher State Park), page 551

🚲 🏃 ④

Location: Highway 1 at Virgin Creek in Fort Bragg
Parking/fees: free parking lot
Hours: 24 hours
Facilities: none
Contact: Mendocino District, California State Parks, 707/937-5804

21 MacKerricher State Park, page 553

🚲 ⛺ 🏃 ⑤

Location: three miles north of Fort Bragg on Highway 1
Parking/fees: free parking lot. Camping fees are $13–16 per night, plus a $7.50 reservation fee.
Hours: 24 hours

Map of Northern California—Page 463

Mendocino County

Facilities: restrooms, showers, and picnic tables
Contact: Mendocino District, California State Parks, 707/937-5804

22 Seaside Creek Beach, page 553

Location: one mile north of Ten Mile River on Highway 1
Parking/fees: free roadside parking
Hours: 24 hours
Facilities: none
Contact: Mendocino District, California State Parks, 707/937-5804

23 Chadbourne Gulch, page 553

Location: two miles south of Westport on Highway 1
Parking/fees: limited free roadside parking
Hours: 24 hours
Facilities: none
Contact: Mendocino District, California State Parks, 707/937-5804

24 Wages Creek Beach, page 553

Location: 17 miles north of Fort Bragg, off Highway 1 in Westport
Parking/fees: $10 entrance fee per vehicle. Camping fee is $18 per night.
Hours: 10 A.M.–5 P.M.
Facilities: restrooms, showers, and picnic tables
Contact: Wages Creek Beach Campground, 707/964-2964

25 Westport-Union Landing State Beach, page 553

Location: three miles north of Westport, off Highway 1
Parking/fees: free parking lot. Camping fees are $13–16 per night, plus a $7.50 reservation fee.
Hours: 24 hours
Facilities: restrooms and picnic tables
Contact: Mendocino District, California State Parks, 707/937-5804

26 Usal Beach (Sinkyone Wilderness State Park), page 556

Location: From Highway 1 three miles north of Rockport, turn onto Usal Road/County Route 431 and follow it for six miles to Usal Campground. A spur road leads to the beach.
Parking/fees: $4 entrance fee per vehicle. Camping fee is $7 per night, plus a $7.50 reservation fee.
Hours: 24 hours
Facilities: restrooms and picnic tables
Contact: Sinkyone Wilderness State Park, 707/986-7711

Mendocino County

Map of Mendocino County—Page 526

27 Little Jackass Creek Beach (Sinkyone Wilderness State Park), page 557

Location: From Highway 1 three miles north of Rockport, turn onto Usal Road/County Route 431 and follow it for six miles to Usal Campground. Hike north on Lost Coast Trail for 7.5 miles to Little Jackass Creek Camp.
Parking/fees: $4 entrance fee per vehicle. Camping fee is $7 per night, plus a $7.50 reservation fee.
Hours: 24 hours
Facilities: none
Contact: Sinkyone Wilderness State Park, 707/986-7711

28 Bear Harbor Beach (Sinkyone Wilderness State Park), page 557

Location: From U.S. 101 in Garberville, take Redway exit and turn west on Briceland Road. Proceed for 28 miles to Orchard Camp and hike south on Lost Coast Trail for 0.4 mile to beach.
Parking/fees: $4 entrance fee per vehicle. Camping fee is $7 per night, plus a $7.50 reservation fee.
Hours: 24 hours
Facilities: none
Contact: Sinkyone Wilderness State Park, 707/986-7711

29 Needle Rock Beach (Sinkyone Wilderness State Park), page 557

Location: From U.S. 101 in Garberville take Redway exit and turn west on Briceland Road. Proceed for 26 miles to Needle Rock Visitor Center and hike on Needle Rock Beach Trail for 0.2 mile to beach.
Parking/fees: $4 entrance fee per vehicle. Camping fee is $7 per night, plus a $7.50 reservation fee.
Hours: 24 hours
Facilities: restrooms and picnic tables
Contact: Sinkyone Wilderness State Park, 707/986-7711

30 Jones Beach (Sinkyone Wilderness State Park), page 557

Location: From U.S. 101 in Garberville take Redway exit and turn west on Briceland Road. Proceed for 25 miles to Jones Beach Camp and hike Jones Beach Trail for 0.3 mile to beach.
Parking/fees: $4 entrance fee per vehicle. Camping fee is $7 per night, plus a $7.50 reservation fee.
Hours: 24 hours
Facilities: none
Contact: Sinkyone Wilderness State Park, 707/986-7711

Map of Northern California—Page 463

Mendocino County

Mendocino County's 130 miles of coastline extend from the unpretentious town of Gualala to the southern end of what is justifiably known as the Lost Coast. Between these borders are some of the state's most appealingly romantic retreats. Then there's Fort Bragg, the county seat and a hardworking center of commerce.

Southern Mendocino County extends the splendid isolation of Sonoma County. The two regions are often lumped together under the nickname "Mendonoma." Low-key and perfectly appealing towns—Gualala, Anchor Bay, Point Arena, and Elk—appear every 10 scenic miles or so, each with its own quiet charm. At Albion, north of where Highway 128 funnels into Highway 1, the tone gets more upscale. Albion, Little River, and Mendocino are bona fide "destinations," to borrow a travel-industry term that signals good food and wine, fine lodging, views, shopping, art, attractions, recreation, and culture. At its northernmost end Mendocino County has no cultural appeal and needs none, because most of it is pristine wilderness.

The beaches are as varied and fascinating as the towns. As usual, the state of California has been kind to the coast, preserving exceptional locales such as Manchester State Park, Van Damme State Park, Mendocino Headlands State Park, Jug Handle State Reserve, MacKerricher State Park, Westport-Union Landing State Beach, and Sinkyone Wilderness State Park. Interestingly, though, the California Coastal Commission cites Mendocino County as one of two locales (Malibu being the other) that need more public-beach accesses. The flip side of Mendocino County's romantic allure is the palette of possibilities it affords those who love to play outdoors in glorious country such as this.

Rubes with a View

Mendocino County

You can always tell when the wrong sort of city slickers come to the North Coast. They're the ones who talk too loudly and wear purple designer polo shirts and loud pullovers advertising the tourist attraction where they spent their vacation last year. All the while they so desperately try to manifest the self-importance of young, upwardly mobile sorts who have made their money too quickly in some dubious profession in which nothing useful is produced.

One night we had the pleasure of dining at a restaurant with the most stunning view of the Pacific Ocean on the North Coast. We had the additional pleasure of being seated at a table close to a window that looked out to where a river flows into the ocean at a rocky cove. It was just before sundown, and the sky was bathed in a heavenly orange-pink glow that would render most people quiet and grateful for the view.

Next to us, at the best table in the house, sat a couple who were neither quiet nor grateful. The man ran his mouth at a volume that was just loud enough to interrupt our peaceful thoughts, and the woman nodded and giggled goofily—his wife, we thought at first, then quickly realized he was cheating on his wife. He spent his dinner hour at this coveted perch boisterously recounting the dirty jokes his colleagues had told him on the golf course that afternoon. After those witticisms were exhausted, he gamely charged on to jokes he'd heard at work the previous week.

From there the conversation moved on to the usual list of suspects: Robert Blake, Martha Stewart, Michael Jackson. Then he embarked on tales of last winter's ski expeditions and a boringly detailed deconstruction of his golfing game.

In between each mindless volley of chitchat and coarse laughter, there was conspicuous silence, as they stared vacuously at their wine glasses. Joke, story, giggles, then empty silence. Meanwhile, the sun was going down and the unfolding scene was one we'd like to think will greet us in heaven after our lifetime of good works.

At the same time another couple was seated at a table by the window. He was a burly guy wearing a New York Giants T-shirt, sunglasses dangling on a designer cord (sunglasses at night?). His gal pal wore a pink sweatshirt that said "BEVERLY HILLS CALIFORNIA." They loudly ordered martinis and began guzzling, and he let out a belch. Lovely.

These two couples obviously came all the way up here from some stressed-out urban center. They spent $250 for a room, another $150 for a meal. They are sitting at the best tables in the nicest restaurant on the North Coast. It is sundown on a perfect day. The music is playing softly. And they are missing it all.

Map of Northern California—Page 463

Gualala

Gualala (properly pronounced WAH-la-la) is a town without airs. The stuffy manners observed next door at Sea Ranch are of no use here; in fact, they're out of place. The only birdies Gualalans shoot have wings, and the carts they tend to ride are manufactured by Harley-Davidson.

Gualala has the wide-open feel of the Old West, to which it bears a legitimate connection. Gualala was once a thriving mill town, but when the forests were depleted, it fell to other means of making a living, including fishing for salmon and trout. The Gualala River runs parallel to the ocean for two miles here, creating an odd beachfront (makes sense that *gualala* is a Native American word meaning "where waters meet").

The source of Gualala's Old West flavor is the town's centerpiece, the Gualala Hotel. This flaking, rusting, creaking structure sits on Highway 1, exhibiting the rakish charm of a frontier saloon. It has operated as a triple-threat bar, inn, and restaurant since before the Great Earthquake of 1906 hit San Francisco. (We found ourselves wondering how this ramshackle old place survived that destructive temblor.)

Entering Gualala, one feels compelled to hitch the car to the post out front, hop the dusty wooden steps, and say, Stetson in hand, "I'd be much obliged iff'n you'd point me to the nearest livery, stranger." Because Gualala is more of a sloppy, let-it-all-hang-out kind of place than its neighbors, the town has witnessed a steady influx of growth, as evidenced by the countless "Land For Sale" signs dotting the countryside. Though all the new business no doubt boosts the local economy, it can only mean that sweet, antiquarian Gualala will eventually turn trendy, especially when the inevitable occurs—i.e., when the Gualala Hotel succumbs to old age.

One sign of the new wave can be found diagonally across the street from the venerable hotel. It's a slick modern inn (opened in August 1994) that boasts urbanite-friendly amenities like cable TV, while obscuring the roadside view of the Gualala River. (For shame, for shame.) Be that as it may, Gualala has so many more natural charms that one need only do what the native Gualalans do. That is, shrug your shoulders and go on about your business.

Beaches

Gualala's beaches start below the Mendocino County line, a mile south of town, with **Gualala Point Regional Park,** which shares a fence with Sea Ranch (see writeup in the Sonoma County chapter). In Gualala itself the **Gualala River** forms a broad lagoon, making it difficult to get to the sand spit that fronts the Pacific. One way around this is to take to the water in a kayak and paddle back and forth between the river and ocean. Darn, left yours at home? Try **Adventure Rents** (39175 Highway 1, 707/884-4386) for kayaks, canoes, and "hybrid" bikes. If you've a mind to dive for a dinner of abalone, **North Coast Scuba** (38820 Highway 1, 707/884-3534) rents gear and sells abalone licenses.

Bunking Down

If you're in an adventurous, devil-may-care mood, the **Gualala Hotel** (Highway 1, 707/884-3441, $) is a relatively inexpensive blast from the past. The place desperately pines for a coat of paint, but as one guest wrote in the ledger, "Nostalgia is good for the soul." When we arrived, no one was at the front desk, a weather-beaten table. A hand-lettered sign advised us to "Register for rooms with the bartender." We did just that, negotiating our tariff with a curt but efficient hostess at the bar. The digs aren't grand here—a clean room with shared baths and a ceiling so high you couldn't touch it with the aid of a trampoline—but the comforting cloak of history more than makes up for any lack of luxury. By contrast, what experience

Mendocino County

could you have at the slick, modern inn across the road that could possibly rival the slice-of-life you'd enjoy at the Gualala Hotel for only $48–60 per night?

Farther up Highway 1, the tariff and comforts increase considerably at **St. Orres Bed & Breakfast** (36601 Highway 1, 707/884-3303, $$$). This inn is an architectural wonder that offers an incomparably meditative North Coast experience on its 42 acres of rolling woods and gardens. St. Orres was designed by owners Eric and Ted Black, and built on the foundation of the old Seaside Hotel. The Blacks capture the flavor of the earliest Russian settlers with rustic and somewhat exotic elegance. The inn was constructed from 100-year-old timber. The eight European-style rooms have double beds and shared baths, some with views of the forest, some of the ocean. Just beyond the hotel are 12 hand-crafted cottages of varying size, price ($100–225 per night), and levels of amenities.

The **Old Milano Hotel** (38300 Highway 1, 707/884-3256, $$) is an atmospheric North Coast lodge (circa 1905) directly above the ocean on a blufftop. The Milano has nine guest quarters, all well tended and intimate, including a lovely cottage and a real railroad caboose.

Coastal Cuisine

St. Orres must have been the patron saint of good taste. The **St. Orres Restaurant** (36601 Highway 1, 707/884-3335, $$$) offers one of the finest and most distinctive dining experiences on the California coast. Set inside a cathedral-like dining room, it is part of a structure suggestive of the area's Russian roots. You won't believe your eyes when you pass the onion domes of St. Orres—Moscow on the Pacific?—on a bluff along the east side of Highway 1. The food is exceptionally well prepared and competently served. A meal starts with homemade garlic bread and the soup of the day. Entrées might include steelhead and salmon, or such game items as a stuffed wild boar

chop or rabbit. The kitchen utilizes fresh ingredients from on-premises gardens, as well as local-produce farms and ranches. In addition to the à la carte selections, St. Orres offers a $30 three-course, prix-fixe dinner special. This place is wildly popular, so make your reservations well in advance.

The restaurant at the **Gualala Hotel** (Highway 1, 707/884-4840, $) is the class act of that operation. Old and endowed with a weathered dignity, the dining room dishes up healthy North Coast cuisine such as rigatoni with white beans and tomatoes, as well as heartier fare like chicken and game dishes. If we had to prioritize what to do on the premises of the Gualala Hotel, we'd eat, drink, and sleep, in that order.

Night Moves

If you're headed to Gualala for a romantic getaway, you don't need any advice from us. But if you want to bathe in the sloppy friendliness of a hard-drinking saloon, welcome to the **Gualala Hotel** (Highway 1, 707/884-4840). The scene that greeted us one Saturday night was, no doubt, typical of what has been going on here for a century (after all, this was a favorite haunt of writer Jack London): Four members of a motorcycle club stand at the bar, laughing uproariously over a novelty-store item called "Spotted Owl Helper." (In case you haven't noticed, folks in logging country aren't overly fond of this particular feathered friend.) Two more bikers quietly play Pac-Man. A tanned young man with impossibly blond tresses and an earring regales his aging yuppie companions with tales of his acting career down in Los Angeles.

Three enormous women in glowing polyester slacks perch on consecutive bar stools and discuss ostrich racing, smoking to beat the Surgeon General. An elderly man sits alone at a corner table, nursing a beer and a grudge. The jukebox plays "Suzie Q" by Creedence Clearwater Revival (the long version).

Map of Northern California—Page 463

The heads of moose, deer, and bear adorn the walls, as do various large fish. Photographs document the expeditions that led to these game trophies. One picture shows a dead fish being offered a Hamm's Beer. Another shows a man hanging upside down from a fish scale.

We hung around the bar for a while, then called it a night, since we faced a long drive south the next day. We shouldn't have bothered; the noise and laughter kept us up till the wee hours. For our money, the bar at the Gualala Hotel just might be the wildest hangout between San Francisco and the Oregon border.

For More Information

Redwood Coast Chamber of Commerce, P.O. Box 338, Gualala, CA 95445-0338, 707/884-1182 or 800/778-5252, website: www.gualala.org

Anchor Bay

Four miles north of Gualala, tiny Anchor Bay (population 175) has more going on than its size would suggest. A small rocky cove, Collins Landing, is on the property of the Serenisea Ocean Cabins; access requires permission. **Anchor Bay Beach** (a.k.a. Fish Rock Beach) can be reached via **Anchor Bay Campground** (35400 Highway 1, 707/884-4222). This is a .75-mile-long sand beach and campground complex comprising 66 sites on a tall bluff shaded by redwoods. Camping costs $25 per night; day use is a modest $1 per person plus $1 per vehicle. Interestingly, the area is in a nearly fogless five-mile zone of coastline known as the Banana Belt.

Bunking Down

Laying claim to a cove beach and tidepools is **Serenisea Ocean Cabins** (36100 Highway 1, 707/884-3836, $$). These 25 vacation homes and four cabins in Anchor Bay bring you closer to the beach than any lodge in the area at daily rates that run $80–180. Anchor Bay is also home to the **Whale Watch Inn** (35100 Highway 1, 707/884-3667, $$$). Admittedly the inn stretches the B&B concept a bit by including two-person whirlpool baths, breakfast in bed, condo units, golf, and tennis. But the setting is magnificent, and trails lead down to a private beach.

For More Information

Redwood Coast Chamber of Commerce, P.O. Box 338, Gualala, CA 95445-0338, 707/884-1182 or 800/778-5252, website: www.gualala.org

Point Arena

This sleepy burg of quaint homes, old-time theater, and Main Street–type businesses has been blessed with more than its share of coastside delights, which include a six-mile stretch of sandy and rocky cove beaches and a scenic, historic lighthouse.

When it was incorporated in 1908, Point Arena could rightly be called a city. The busiest port on the North Coast, it was a rollicking place with saloons, cathouses, banks, and shootouts on the main drag. Schooners steamed up from San Francisco daily, and off-duty loggers came out of the woods to make this their Sin City. Some old buildings have survived (Victorian homes, the town theater), but many were destroyed in the 1906 earthquake. The original wharf was obliterated by storms in 1983, and a brand-new **Point Arena Pier** has since been built on Arena Cove.

The population of Point Arena hovers at around 500. The most interesting remnant of the area's history is **Point Arena Lighthouse** (707/882-2777). Admission is $3 for adults and $1 for kids under 12, and the museum is open daily 11 A.M.–2:30 P.M. (10 A.M.–3:30 P.M. on summer weekends). It's set on the end of a windswept headland, two miles out on Lighthouse Road. The drive to the lighthouse is one of the most amazing on the North Coast, passing through pastureland that ends abruptly at the lip of the raging Pacific. The lighthouse, a blinding white monolith, is pinned against a blue backdrop. Built in 1870, it employed a powerful Fresnel lens, which is still installed but no longer operable. To see this remarkable piece of engineering requires a six-story ascent (145 steps), but it's worth every huff and puff. The view is spectacular, and the guides are friendly and informative. Some of the tourists, on the other hand, can be a pain in the ass, like the pushy woman who nearly shoved us down the circular metallic stairs in her haste to get by.

For more lengthy ruminations on coastal ecology and maritime history, don't miss the excellent museum housed in the Fog Signal Building next door. The lighthouse and museum's setting is timeless enough to have been used as the backdrop for the Mel Gibson movie *Forever Young,* a romantic weeper about a cryogenically preserved World War II bomber pilot who, after being thawed out, seeks his long-lost, lighthouse-dwelling love. Yeah, right.

Beaches

The most accessible beaches in the area are, from south to north, **Schooner Gulch Beach, Bowling Ball Beach,** and **Ross Beach.** Schooner Gulch embraces 70 acres of headlands, and a short trail leads to tidepools and a driftwood-covered beach. Bowling Ball is a great beachcombing spot, dotted by black, rounded stones (hence the name), but you must park on the highway shoulder to get to it. ("Park facing south only on Highway 1," reads the warning sign.) At low tide you can walk south from Bowling Ball to Schooner Gulch. **Moat Creek Access,** better known as Whiskey Shoals to the surfers who come here, provides access to Ross Beach. You park in a dirt lot and follow a trail down the cliff. Just north

of Point Arena Lighthouse, off Miner Hole Road, you can park near the south bank of the Garcia River, a steelhead fisherman's favorite that's also the wintertime home of tundra swans. From here a path leads to a sandy beach at the river's mouth.

Flanking the Point Arena Pier is **Arena Cove Beach.** Some of the best waves on California's North Coast can be found here, but because of the razor-sharp offshore reef this spot's strictly for experts. Diving for abalone and chartered sportfishing expeditions are big here as well.

Bunking Down

At the **Point Arena Lighthouse** (45500 Lighthouse Road, 877/725-4448, $$$), three homes on the property are available as vacation rentals, with proceeds going to the nonprofit lighthouse preservation society. Each has 1,400 square feet of space, three bedrooms, two baths, a fully equipped kitchen, fireplace, and television. You'll only have to bring sheets, pillow cases, and towels. For $170 a night in an unbeatable setting, it's a steal.

One step up is the **Coast Guard House** (695 Arena Cove, 707/822-2442, $$$), a restored 1901 Cape Codder that was once a lifesaving station and is now a snug bed-and-breakfast inn. Less adventurous, but equally comfortable, is the **Wharf Master's Inn** (785 Port Road, 707/882-3171, $$$), overlooking the pier at Arena Cove. Three separate structures provide surprisingly lush amenities (hot tub, private deck, Victorian appointments), given the spartan fisherman's setting below.

Coastal Cuisine

A pleasant restaurant beside the Point Arena Pier, the **Galley at Arena Cove** (707/882-2189, $$) is made airy and light by its spacious, second-floor setting. The seafood is taken straight from the adjoining fisherman's pier—which is, incidentally, the only boat-launch facility between Bodega Bay and Fort Bragg.

Map of Northern California—Page 463

For More Information

Fort Bragg–Mendocino Coast Chamber of Commerce, 332 North Main Street, P.O. Box 1141, Fort Bragg, CA 95437, 707/961-6300 or 800/726-2780, website: www.mendocino coast.com

Manchester State Park

Manchester State Park lies at the point where two creeks and the San Andreas Fault make a break for the ocean. The 1,400-acre preserve offers five miles of broad, mocha-colored sand backed by dunes matted with thick grass and wildflowers. Manchester provides good steelhead fishing in the winter and some of the best surf casting in Mendocino County all year long. Perhaps the most notable thing about the beach is that it looks like a graveyard for driftwood. The whitened logs are the skeletons of dead trees that have washed onto the beach like soldiers killed in a maritime invasion. Picnickers and sunbathers use the logs as windbreaks. They come in handy, especially in summer, when stiff winds make for harsh beachcombing.

Part of the thrill is the drive out to Manchester. Three roads provide access to the beachfront. On the way out you pass an AT&T relay station that is the trans-Pacific link for undersea phone service to Hawaii and the Far East. The old cable was replaced in 1989 by a fiberoptic job, allowing the Aloha State the dubious benefits of pay TV.

The park's Kinney Road entrance leads to a campground offering 48 primitive sites that are snapped up quickly. Anglers and birdwatchers, in particular, like to stay here. The beach is a 15-minute walk from the camp. Wintering swans, pelicans, godwits, killdeer, and surf scoters (a type of sea duck) delight birders in this area.

Other beach accesses lie at the ends of Alder Creek and Stoneboro Roads. The latter is typical of what is meant by beach access on this hardy stretch of the coast. From the highway you drive 1.6 miles through cow pastures, park in a dirt lot, and hike humpbacked dunes to the sea. Incidentally, a vista point at Mallo Pass Creek (four miles north of Manchester) affords a magnificent panorama of the ocean, as well as the forests and creek canyons to the east and north. Bring the camera.

For More Information

Manchester State Park, 41500 Kinney Lane, Manchester, CA 95459, 707/882-2463, website: www.parks.gov.ca

Elk

Elk used to be known as Greenwood in the boomtown days of logging and fishing. The lumber business closed down around these parts in 1932, and nowadays Elk is awash in bed-and-breakfast inns, with nature being explored rather than exploited. This town of 500 may seem out of the way but is easy to reach, as Highway 128 meets Highway 1 just five miles north of here.

Beaches

The appeal of Elk is obvious at **Greenwood Creek State Beach**, just north of town. It is a 47-acre park with a sandy, mile-long cove beach, sea stacks, and cliffs. Park free in the lot across from the Elk Store and hike a quarter mile along a headland to the beach. Once a redwood mill flourished here. The cove beach at Greenwood Creek offers all sorts of activities: driftwood collecting, ocean kayaking, steelheading, wildlife observation, picnicking, walking the beach, or just staring at the sea.

North of Elk is **Navarro River Beach Access,** where yet another of the North Coast's pristine waterways empties into the ocean—almost.

Mendocino County

Like the scene in Gualala, the river here runs parallel to the ocean for a long way, providing double the beach pleasure. But the Navarro stops just shy of the Pacific, either defying the laws of nature or making a lie of the Pete Townshend song "The Sea Refuses No River." Primitive camping is permitted; open sites lining the bluff are available to intrepid tenters. The fishing in the river and from the shore is good, but the wind can be ferocious. The drive to the beach along Navarro Bluff Road is a curious one. Rickety, abandoned homes line the roadway, including a forlorn, boarded-up hotel called Navarro-by-the-Sea.

Bunking Down

By our count, you've got your choice of five bed-and-breakfasts in tiny Elk. One of the best is the **Elk Cove Inn** (6300 Highway 1, 707/877-3321, $$). Lying just north of Greenwood Creek, this collection of romantic cottages is one of the few North Coast B&Bs that offer direct beach access; just take a set of stairs down to the water's edge. Another fine oceanfront lodge is the **Sandpiper House Inn** (5520 Highway 1, 707/877-3587, $$). Built in 1916, the Sandpiper offers a secluded beach, lovely gardens and grounds, and a view that'll knock your socks off. The palatial **Harbor House Inn** (5600 Highway 1, 707/877-3203, $$$$) is a replica of the California timber industry's exhibit hall at the 1915 Panama-Pacific International Exposition. The six guest rooms and four cottages are luxuriously appointed and command wonderful views of the coast and gardens. Rates run $195–315 per night, which include breakfast and a four-course dinner at the inn's fabulous restaurant.

Coastal Cuisine

The café at **Greenwood Pier Inn** (5928 Highway 1, 707/877-9997, $$) serves healthy California garden cuisine. The inn itself, a playful, 11-room, cliff-clinging wonder, is worth a visit as well. Two tables a night are set aside at the well-regarded **Harbor House** (5600 Highway 1, 707/877-3203, $$$) for nonguests of the inn. The restaurant serves a $35 prix-fixe menu; advance reservations are essential. At the other end of the scale, the **Roadhouse Cafe** (6061 Highway 1, 707/877-3285, $) serves all the usual staples for breakfast and lunch, plus a few more imaginative dishes (e.g., omelettes packed with goat cheese, red peppers, and garlic) that put them a cut above the usual home-cookin' joint.

Night Moves

For a relaxed, end-of-day drink, if not an entire meal, try **Bridget Dolan's Irish Pub** inside yet another of Elk's B&Bs, the **Griffin House at Greenwood Cove** (5910 Highway 1, 707/877-3422, $$).

For More Information

Fort Bragg–Mendocino Coast Chamber of Commerce, 332 North Main Street, P.O. Box 1141, Fort Bragg, CA 95437, 707/961-6300 or 800/726-2780, website: www.mendocinocoast.com

Mendocino County

Albion

Perhaps because one of Northern California's rare east-west roads (Highway 128) meets Highway 1 just south of here, Albion has a more grown-up feel than its pleasant but snail-like neighbors to the south. We mean grown-up in the sense of being overseen by an enlightened community. This is our delicately worded way of saying that we rejoiced at being able to begin the day with a decent cup of coffee and a current daily newspaper.

Yes, there's more to distract the city-bred along the Mendocino coast from Albion north to Fort Bragg. More than that, one gets the feeling that the local citizens have a firm grip on what will become of their towns: the quality of life, the sustainability of local economies, and so forth. These are places where big-city dwellers feel more comfortable. The lodging and dining tariffs rise accordingly—but not that much higher, and the full North Coast experience is worth every buck.

Albion has a storied past that only reinforces its adulthood. Portuguese, Spanish, Russian, and English sailors took turns plying the coastal waters here in the 1600s. Many versions of how the town came to be called Albion are told, but the most frequent is that Francis Drake briefly moored here after naming California "New Albion" (Anglophiles will remember that Albion is one of England's historic nicknames), annexing it in the name of good Queen Bess. It's the same tale they spin at Point Reyes, leading us to suspect that Drake said that to all the bays.

In 1850, after a crew from San Francisco arrived to salvage a wrecked trading vessel, the city slickers got a hankering for the region's redwood-studded forests. Fresh from their Gold Rush feeding frenzy, they soon turned Albion into a logging center, with a large wharf and sawmill. The latter was capable of manufacturing 4,000 board feet of wood a day. Then shipping bowed out to railroads, which bowed out to trucks, and the last log was milled here in 1928.

Fishing followed as the new boom industry, but when catches dwindled along the North Coast, Albion turned to tourism. Two of the earliest tourists were John Dillinger and Pretty Boy Floyd, both of whom hid out in this quiet village. In the late '60s Albion became an early home of renegades of a different stripe—counterculture dropouts, who also erected a beachhead up in Mendocino. (Does anyone but us remember Cat Mother and the All-Night Newsboys' second album, *Albion Doo-Wah?*)

The setting could not be more ideal for getaways. The highway winds through redwoods, then rounds the crest of a rugged headland, crossing a majestic steel-and-wood trestle over the beautiful Albion River and emptying into the ocean alongside a scenic harbor and quiet village. Above this backdrop—with waves crashing on the jagged sea stacks—the sound of a foghorn fills the air every 30 seconds. Instead of being bothersome, as you might think at first, the foghorn insinuates itself into your stay here. After a while you are lulled into a state of perfect, uncomplaining complacency.

Beaches

At the mouth of the Albion River, in the shadows of the spectacular cliff-spanning bridge, a sandy river-mouth beach known as **Albion Flat** provides easy access to the ocean. It's mainly for anglers and boaters who cast off from the nearby boat dock. Canoe rentals are also available here. The beach is not for swimming, but surf-casting and rock-fishing opportunities are plentiful. Nearby **Albion River Campground** (3540 North Highway 1, 707/937-0606, $) offers tent and RV camping. Full-hookup RV camping can be had at **Schooner's Landing** (33621 Albion River North Side Road, 707/937-5707, $), east

Mendocino County

of Albion Flat. The latter operation offers all sorts of diversions: hiking, picnicking, boat launching, and swimming.

Bunking Down

One of the North Coast's true jewels is the **Albion River Inn** (3790 Highway 1, 707/937-1919, $$$), which can be seen from the road as Highway 1 passes north over Albion River Bridge. The view of the ocean and Albion Cove from these 20 New England–style, cliff-top cottages is spectacular. The rooms are cozy, the foghorn sings its deep-throated lullaby, and the 10 acres of gardens and grounds offer ample opportunities for strolling and daydreaming. You are guaranteed to regenerate from any of the stresses that brought you here.

Coastal Cuisine

If you don't stay in one of the cottages, you should at least eat at the restaurant at the **Albion River Inn** (3790 Highway 1, 707/937-1919, $$$), a truly remarkable place where the food matches the view. The restaurant predates the inn (which was launched in 1982) and is part of the original complex that opened in 1916. Its founder, Carl Larsen, built a smithy out of wood salvaged from the *Girlie Mahoney,* an ill-fated steamer than happened to be carrying 400,000 feet of lumber when she went down in the cove. The haul eventually spawned a general store and a restaurant (how's that for recycling?) that quickly became a North Coast staple. It was the Harbor Lights in the 1950s,

the Windjammer in the 1960s, the Blacksmith Inn in the 1970s. Now the Albion River Inn, the restaurant is nestled inside Larsen's lovingly renovated original structure.

Always a great family dining spot, the Albion River Inn has emerged as one of the finest gourmet eateries in Northern California. The menu changes daily to reflect what's freshest in the local seafood and produce markets. The Pacific Rim bouillabaisse, for example, bathes clams, mussels, rock shrimp, and other deep-sea delights in a lemongrass, tomato, and fennel broth. A scrumptious sea-bass dish we tried was sautéed with artichoke hearts and Madeira wine. Snuggled into a rocky pocket atop a cliff, the restaurant is staffed by friendly, sharp-witted locals, and the extensive wine list features the products of fine local vineyards, many accessible via Highway 128. The Albion River Inn offers a taste of the good life at a fair price—a feast for the eyes, stomach, and soul.

Night Moves

There's a small bar at the **Albion River Inn** (3790 Highway 1, 707/937-1919). Barring that, Mendocino lies 10 miles up the road. We made do with the foghorn's serenade and the view over the cliffs from the inn.

For More Information

Fort Bragg–Mendocino Coast Chamber of Commerce, 332 North Main Street, P.O. Box 1141, Fort Bragg, CA 95437, 707/961-6300 or 800/726-2780, website: www.mendocinocoast.com

Mendocino

The communities of Mendocino and Fort Bragg are about 10 miles apart. They form a sort of North Coast yin and yang, based on their respective appeals. The rap goes something like this: Mendocino is artsy-craftsy, while Fort Bragg is working-class. Mendocino is boutiques; Fort Bragg is hard goods. Mendocino is secluded bed-and-breakfast inns;

Fort Bragg is roadside motels. Mendocino is Cafe Beaujolais; Fort Bragg is Taco Bell. Mendocino is couples; Fort Bragg is families. You get the idea.

This has been the situation for years, though of late there's been a symbiosis between these two seeming opposites as they grow together in discernible ways. Still, change comes slowly to this section of the coast. The locals scrutinize every permit application as if adding a few more units to a B&B were tantamount to erecting Trump Tower in the pristine wilderness. (Seriously, we've been told you must meet 44 terms and conditions to get a zoning or use permit up here.) You've got to love their attitude, simply because it works. Essentially, a few more inns have materialized on the highway between Mendocino and Little River in the past decade, and that's about all.

To get a proper handle on Mendocino, it helps to think of it as a kind of impressionistic painting. Perspective is the key. Observed at close range, the town appears to be a pleasant rural outpost of scattered wood-frame houses and postcard-quaint inns. As one pulls back to observe the big picture, though, Mendocino reveals itself to be a town with a vision. And to grasp that vision, one has to understand the people who live here.

Mendocino's roots date back to the mid-1800s, when California's first redwood mill was built on the banks of the Big River. This slow-moving river empties into the ocean beneath the steep headlands on which Mendocino was founded. The community enjoyed nearly a century of prosperity as a lumber town, followed by decades of decline in the wake of the sawmills' closing. In the 1950s it was discovered by artists and dropouts drawn from the burgeoning cities, especially San Francisco. Rising apartment rents and the stodgy middle-class conformity of the postwar era drove more sensitive souls into the countryside to seek sanctuary. To those who were searching for another way to live—closer to nature, in an environment more conducive to contemplation—Mendocino exerted a magnetic pull. The old, abandoned wood houses came cheaply, the rugged Northern California coast was quiet and rarely visited, and the natural beauty of Mendocino's coast and forest lands provided a constant source of inspiration.

With the founding of the Mendocino Arts Council in 1959, the character and mission of the community became official, and art remains a rallying point for the loose-knit denizens of this town. In the 1960s the area became a refuge for counterculture types who found the increasingly drug-plagued, crime-ridden streets of Haight-Ashbury too congested for their liking. The Sir Douglas Quintet had a Top 40 hit in 1969 with a song entitled "Mendocino," which put this little North Coast speck on the map (at least in the eyes of the counterculture). Its chorus perfectly caught the stoned, soulful flavor of the times: "Mendocino, Mendocino, where life's such a groove you'll blow your mind in the morning."

Amazingly, things haven't changed so very drastically since those halcyon days. Mendocino remains a place where a life of reflection can be lived on relatively modest means. Artists can scrape by without selling out, musicians and film people find seclusion, and lesser cultural aspirants can, at the very least, manage to keep a roof over their heads. For instance, we spied a run-down pickup truck by the side of the road, whose owner advertised his wares in juvenile hand-lettering on the side panels: "Firewood and Donkey Dung." There's also a downside to this sylvan scene. Mendocino is still getting invaded by San Franciscans. Yet instead of solitude-seeking '60s transcendentalists, it's been infested by homeless and often drug-addled derelicts. "Ex-cons, street crap from Union Square" is how one disgusted innkeeper referred to the newcomers, who can be seen ambling aimlessly about the village center.

Size-wise, Mendocino is home to about 1,300 people in town and 9,000 out in the woods. In Fort Bragg the number of townies and woodsfolk is 6,000 and 6,000. One thing both communities share is clean air. The National Clean Air Monitoring station is located in Mendocino County. After passing over thousands of miles of open ocean, the air is the freshest you'll ever breathe, and the nation's

Map of Mendocino County—Page 526

Canoeing the Big

The longest unspoiled estuary in Northern California is the **Big River,** which spills into the Pacific Ocean just south of Mendocino. Its pristine riverine marshes, canyons, and streambeds are vital to the regional ecosystem. The river's first eight miles are tidally influenced—that is, subject to the ebb and flow of the ocean. If you time it right you can paddle upriver with an incoming tide and return on an ebbing one.

To explore the Big River, one needs a canoe. Speedboats and personal watercraft are banned (thank God), as is developing the river's banks, damming its flow, or turning the mouth into a harbor. For our fearless trip into the unknown, we procured an outrigger at **Catch A Canoe & Bicycles, Too!,** whose redwood and fiberglass craft are designed by a local artisan. The outriggers can be steered by foot controls and will not flip over. They also cut through the water at great speed with minimal effort. In our rented outrigger, we experienced that rarest of pleasures in this day and age: a clean, teeming river, tall trees on both banks, nesting birds, blue skies, and total silence from manufactured contraptions.

Catch A Canoe also rents and sells canoes, kayaks, and mountain bikes equipped with shocks for riding the wilderness trails in Jackson National Forest or Van Damme State Park. It provides bike racks and maps if you want to take your rentals farther up or down the coast. For more information contact Catch A Canoe & Bicycles, Too!, Highway 1 and Comptche-Ukiah Road, P.O. Box 487, Mendocino, CA 95460, 707/937-0273.

standard for clean air is measured by that sampled in Mendocino. That in itself makes the place an appealing destination. The sunsets are yellow and gold, not brown as they are in more sooty locales.

There's more good news: wildlife is making a comeback in the area. Salmon are returning to some of the local rivers. Ospreys, red-tailed hawks, and peregrine falcons have been sighted in increased numbers. Habitat protection is paying dividends. It feels good to pass along some positive news in the environmental realm for a change.

Like much of the remote North Coast, you have to really want to be in Mendocino to make it worth the drive over winding roads, trailing RVs driven by slow-moving tourists unused to the curves. Then there's the weather. Mendocino is frequently shrouded in fog and, in winter, heavy rains. These coastal fogs don't creep in on little cat's feet, either (like in Carl Sandberg's poem "Fog"); they clop in on heavy cattle hooves.

Somehow, this is part of Mendocino's allure as a romantic hideaway. The cool, gray days of summer provide a good excuse to stay inside a cozy room and light a fire. The phrase is overused, but Mendocino truly is a place to get away from it all. The town makes a convenient base for exploring the wineries of Mendocino and Sonoma Counties during the day. The high points in the calendar year are the **Annual Summer Fair** and the **Mendocino Music Festival** (held in July over 10 days), but you can be sure there's always something art-worthy going on in town. Outdoors enthusiasts also find plenty to do, including hiking, canoeing, fishing, and diving for abalone. Miles of beaches and parklands in and around Mendocino beg to be explored on foot. But the best thing about Mendocino is that you really don't have to do anything at all.

Beaches

Yes, there are beaches way up here, especially north of Mendocino at places like MacKerricher State Park, where they run for mile after unbroken mile. In Mendocino per se, the beach is less accessible and remarkable than the headlands that back up against them. **Mendocino Headlands State Park** runs north from the banks of the Big River. Narrow, linear headlands extend out from the mainland like serpents' tongues. Trails skirt the bluffs, and you can peer over the side to the beaches at their bases, way down below. Be careful, though: The Mendocino Headlands remain a work in progress, a symphony of rock carved by the relentless rhythm of waves. A wide, sandy beach exists on the south bank of the Big River. However, we'd recommend finding a place to perch high up on the fissured headlands, where you can stare out to sea and, in season, look for whales.

Three miles south of Mendocino in Little River (population 412) is **Van Damme State Park.** This 2,100-acre park spreads inland for four miles from its small, sandy beach. At the mouth of the Little River, this beach is among the best abalone-diving spots on the North Coast. Inland, Van Damme encompasses a sword-fern canyon and a forest of stunted conifers. Van Damme's 10 miles of hiking trails and cool, shaded, 84-site campground make it a popular place, especially during the relatively warm, dry months May–September. We did some hiking at Van Damme through the cool, shady woods. One thing that caught our attention was the posted "Mountain Lion Warning." If you encounter a mountain lion, you are instructed to "convince them that you are not prey and that you may be dangerous." Funny, it had never before occurred to us to try to reason with a mountain lion.

Two miles north of Mendocino is **Russian Gulch State Park,** which is home to serene redwood groves and an open beach where Russian Gulch Creek runs into the ocean. A big attraction is Devil's Punchbowl, a blowhole that's 100 feet long and 60 feet deep. The force of incoming waves funneling through this collapsed sea cave creates geysers and noisy explosions. Another natural wonder is a 36-foot waterfall. Thirty choice campsites are situated along the creek inside a canyon forested with second-growth redwoods, as well as firs, hemlocks, oaks, and laurels. Again, as demand is far greater than supply, reservations are necessary. Skin diving and rock fishing are the main activities pursued on the beaches at Van Damme and Russian Gulch.

Shore Things

• **Bike/skate rentals:** Catch-a-Canoe & Bicycles, Too!, Highway 1 and Comptche-Ukiah Road, Mendocino, 707/937-0273

• **Dive shop:** North Coast Scuba, 38820 Highway 1, Gualala, 707/884-3534

• **Ecotourism:** Jug Handle State Reserve, Caspar, 707/937-5804; Van Damme State Park, Little River, 707/937-5804

• **Horseback riding:** Ricochet Ridge Ranch, 24201 North Highway 1, Fort Bragg, 707/964-7669

• **Lighthouse:** Point Arena Lighthouse, 45500 Lighthouse Road, Point Arena, 707/882-2777

• **Marina:** Noyo Harbor, Fort Bragg, 707/947-0167

• **Pier:** Noyo Harbor Pier, Fort Bragg, 707/964-4719

• **Rainy day attraction:** Point Arena Lighthouse & Museum, 45500 Lighthouse Road, Point Arena, 707/882-2777

• **Shopping/browsing:** Mendocino Art Center, 45200 Little Lake Street, Mendocino, 707/937-5818

Map of Mendocino County—Page 526

Mendocino County

• **Sportfishing:** Tally Ho Sportfishing, North Harbor Drive, Fort Bragg, 707/964-2079
• **Surf Shop:** North Pacific Designs, 1250 North Main Street, Fort Bragg, 707/961-0314
• **Vacation rentals:** Mendocino Coast Reservations, 1000 Main Street, 707/937-1000

Bunking Down

On the inn scene the trend in Mendocino is away from cloned Victoriana and toward more contemporary, original, and nature-oriented presentations. The secret to survival in the bed-and-breakfast business these days is quality. People want the vacation experience to be immediate and intense. "People want to be plushed," said one innkeeper.

You can certainly get plushed at **Stanford Inn by the Sea** (Highway 1 at Comptche-Ukiah Road, 707/937-5615, $$$$). High on a hillside overlooking the ocean, it strikes a perfect balance between a four-star hotel and a cozy B&B. Rooms are spacious and decorated with unfinished, knotty-pine walls, four-poster beds, and wood-burning fireplaces. A bottle of wine is provided, as are confections from a local chocolatier. Logs are stacked by the hearth, along with instructions on how to build a fire. Stanford Inn by the Sea strikes the perfect match between rusticity and luxury.

In the morning guests head to the **Ravens,** the on-site restaurant (with vegetarian emphasis) for breakfast. Ravens serves wonderful dinners, too. During the day, guests can enjoy the enclosed pool and sauna, or check out the organic garden and greenhouse (Big River Nurseries) on the premises. At the foot of a gravel drive leading down to the river's edge is another of owner Jeff Stanford's businesses: Catch-a-Canoe & Bicycles, Too! (see sidebar "Canoeing the Big"). There's not much you can't do here—including relaxing in the most rejuvenating sort of atmosphere.

Joshua Grindle Inn (44800 Little Lake Road, 707/937-4143, $$$) is a two-story captain's house a short walk from the village. The grounds are a riot of flowers and shrubbery. Rooms are quite comfortable, whether in the main house or the rustic buildings out back. A full hot breakfast is served each morning.

Just south of Mendocino in the town of Little River, the **Stevenswood Lodge** (8211 Highway 1, 707/937-2810, $$$) impresses with its gleaming, polished hardwood floors and air of newness. Individual rooms are outfitted in light woods with natural finishes and named for the nineteenth-century founders of the town. A Japanese poi garden offers a peaceful setting out back. Deer and other forest critters wander to the edge of the property. The operative philosophy at the lodge is to bring the outdoors inside via windows and skylights that capture the streaming rays.

Breakfast is home cooked and tremendous: baked muffins the size of catcher's mitts, eggs Benedict, bowls of fruit salad. Another plus is the fact that owner Robert Zimmer's brother runs an art gallery in Mendocino. The spillover from the gallery winds up on the lodge walls, in the halls, in the rooms, even in a small, on-site showroom—all very attractive, all for sale.

Also in Little River is the **Heritage House** (5200 North Highway 1, 800/235-5885, $$), which has 66 cottage rooms spread among 37 verdant acres and has been used as a Hollywood film backdrop (see also "Night Moves"). **Little River Inn** (Highway 1, 888/466-5683, $$) owns the distinction of being Mendocino's oldest (circa 1853) lodge.

Coastal Cuisine

Cafe Beaujolais (961 Ukiah Street, 707/937-5614, $$$), a restaurant with a world-class reputation, is in the heart of Mendocino. The English country-cottage decor creates a casually elegant environment, from the hardwood floors and floral print wallpaper to the subtle background music. The café has its own bakery, which turns out extraordinary breads, such as Red Seal rye, Mendocino sourdough (made from white and rye flours), and nine-grain Australian sunflower-

Map of Northern California—Page 463

Cafe Beaujolais

Cafe Beaujolais has been one of the premier gourmet dining experiences on the North Coast for the last quarter of a century, and it has survived a change in its longtime ownership during this decade. Cafe Beaujolais is in a house surrounded by a flower garden. The walls are painted avocado green and adorned with framed black and white nature photographs. Jazzy New Age guitar CDs waft through the restaurant. It is a peaceful, relaxing setting, and if you've braved the drive up U.S. 101 and over on the curvy, mountainous Highway 128, you will greatly appreciate the calming atmosphere.

The signature dish is sturgeon, which is dipped in egg wash and gently sautéed. It is served atop a healthy array of pasta and vegetables—mushrooms, snow peas, beet chunks—and generously sauced with a truffle essence reduction that is extremely flavorful. Our second choice would be halibut served atop risotto with mixed vegetables and a creamy Alfredo-style sauce. Beaujolais also serves organic meats from Nieman Ranch. Delectable appetizers include jumbo sea scallops in a chicken liver essence reduction and minced rabbit with brandied prunes and toasted walnuts. The best desserts are such light, fruity concoctions as blueberry cobbler with buttermilk ice cream and three sorbets (passionfruit, blood orange, mango). The menu changes with the seasons, but the items are uniformly delicious and creative. The restaurant has published three cookbooks, the most essential of which is *Evening Food,* by Christopher Kump (whose father founded the Culinary Institute of America).

seed bread. Among the many stellar entrées is oven-steamed sturgeon with a sauce of garlic, lemon, tomato, olive oil, and herbs. Cafe Beaujolais also serves meat and game "from animals raised humanely in a free-range environment." There's a good selection of local wines, and they do neat things with coffee, too. All in all, Cafe Beaujolais, which serves dinner nightly and brunch on weekends, offers a top-notch North Coast dining experience.

The owners of **955 Ukiah** (955 Ukiah Street, 707/937-1955, $$$) have built their restaurant into something special through hard work and vision. The accent is continental, the culinary offerings pure poetry, bearing up the elaborate menu descriptions. The salmon, for instance, is poached in a "mirror-like bouillon," while the free-range chicken is "serenely cap-

tivated by a sauce of wild mushrooms." You, too, will be serenely captivated by the food and ambience at 955 Ukiah.

Night Moves

In the informed opinion of a local innkeeper, the **Heritage House** (5200 Highway 1, 707/937-5885) still mixes the best drinks on the coast. It also has one of the best views, not to mention fine food and lodgings on a 37-acre spread. Heritage House is in Little River, a few miles south of Mendocino. **MacCallum House** (Albion Street, 707/937-5763), a century-old Victorian mansion that does double duty as a classy restaurant and B&B, has a small but sociable bar in a parlor to the left of the main hall. It's called the **Grey Whale Bar & Café,** and if you don't feel up to the culinary extravaganza

Mendocino County

across the hall, you can opt for the bar's menu of burgers and pub grub.

Finally, if you feel up for something wilder than an after-dinner drink, make for the **Caspar Inn,** four miles north of Mendocino (see the entry below).

For More Information

Fort Bragg–Mendocino Coast Chamber of Commerce, 332 North Main Street, P.O. Box 1141, Fort Bragg, CA 95437, 707/961-6300 or 800/726-2780, website: www.mendocinocoast.com

Caspar

Caspar is a friendly ghost of a town far enough west of Highway 1 to escape most of its bustle. During its lumber-milling heyday, Caspar was a bustling town of 500—the first on the coast, in fact, to get electricity. Now it's little more than a dot on the map off the main road, though it's got a viable artistic community and is home to several galleries. Beyond that, little Caspar also scores big on two counts: beaches and nightlife. Read on.

Beaches

The state has acquired several acres of the crumbling, fissured **Caspar Headlands State Reserve.** The headlands, at the end of Headlands Drive, can be visited only with an entry permit, obtainable at the State Park District Office at Russian Gulch State Park. Is it worth the trouble? Probably not, since the impressive headlands in nearby Mendocino are open to all without red tape. **Caspar State Beach** sits at the head of a long, bottleneck-shaped bay where Doyle and Caspar Creeks empty into the Pacific. Bookended by low bluffs, it's a sandy beach accessible from Point Cabrillo Road (also known as Old Highway 1).

Bunking Down

If you want to bunk down in Caspar, camping is the best (and maybe only) option. **Caspar Beach RV Park** (14401 Point Cabrillo Road, 707/964-3306, $) features 100 sites (56 with full hookups) and ocean frontage in a wooded, creekside setting. It's also got everything a camper might need: camp store, showers, coin-operated laundry, and playground.

Coastal Cuisine

There's a small café, **Oscar's at Caspar** (Caspar Road, 707/964-0602, $), beside the venerable Caspar Inn (see "Night Moves"). At Oscar's the accent is on fresh, healthy food for eat-in or takeout.

Night Moves

The **Caspar Inn** (Caspar Road, 707/964-5565) is one of the last true vestiges of the '60s. A night here is what hanging around the funky clubs and ballrooms of San Francisco in its late-'60s prime might have been like. The inn books live bands, true hair-to-the-waist anachronisms that like to boogie. We were blown away here by a band called Clan Dyken. What a pleasant surprise to find out that live, organic rock and roll still lives in nooks and crannies like the Caspar Inn.

It is a scene that's almost impossible to describe. The friendly crowd really gets into dancing. We had to back up a few paces when a floor full of eager dancers began encroaching on our turf with their frantic footwork. Clan Dyken had 'em on their feet for hours with original songs that could have passed muster with Jefferson Airplane and some other San Francisco Scene–era bands. The crowd lost itself in dancing, from the Latino fellow who assayed some rather formal-looking flamenco steps to the hirsute dude who was practically dancing sideways, shaking his mane as he grew ever more consumed by the music. If you have trouble finding the Caspar Inn, just look for the place that's got cars parked on the street out front in both directions.

Map of Northern California—Page 463

For More Information

Fort Bragg–Mendocino Coast Chamber of Commerce, 332 North Main Street, P.O. Box 1141, Fort Bragg, CA 95437, 707/961-6300 or 800/726-2780, website: www.mendocino coast.com

Jug Handle State Reserve

Now we know how mountain climbers feel when they get within reach of a legendary peak. Here at this 769-acre park, we ventured onto the farthest point of a fingerlike headland, striding cautiously toward the inviting horizon of blue ocean water and jagged, reddish brown sea stacks. It became a test of nerves to venture all the way out. We wobbled onto our knees and crept forward, shivering as it became clear, with the wind whipping us, that if we weren't careful, we could fall over the side and get smashed to bits.

Jug Handle State Reserve gets our vote for most exciting beach promontory on the North Coast. Several of these slivers of land poke way out into the ocean, and we hereby warn you to prepare yourself for a sudden bout of vertigo. In addition to these remarkable blufftops, the reserve offers a 2.5-mile nature trail that leads up an ecological staircase of marine terraces through 500,000 years of geological history. The lowest (youngest) of the five terraces bears the full brunt of the ocean waves. The next one is covered in sea grass and wildflowers, the third one supports a pygmy forest, and the fourth and fifth ones have taller, more mature forests. You can't imagine the majesty of Jug Handle State Reserve. It simply must be seen!

Bunking Down

The small but pleasant **Jug Handle Beach Country Bed & Breakfast Inn** (32980 Gibney Lane, 707/964-1415, $$) is within viewing distance of these coastal headlands. The inn was built in 1883 and is far enough away from the bustle of Fort Bragg to make for a quiet getaway.

Fort Bragg

"I'm fond of saying that Fort Bragg is poised on the verge of greatness," contends Colette Bailey, who runs the venerable Grey Whale Inn. At her suggestion, we joined her for an early-morning walk along an abandoned log-haul road that runs along the ocean toward MacKerricher State Park. It was 7 A.M., and she was keeping an Olympic pace while offering a running commentary on Fort Bragg. En route we passed dozens of like-minded walkers out for their morning jaunt by the sea. They're here each day like clockwork. We labored to keep up, waddling like the friendly pack of ducks whose path we had crossed earlier.

Colette may have a point about Fort Bragg's bid for better days. Unlike many boutiqued-to-death coastal destinations, Fort Bragg has the feeling of a real working community. In fact, the town (population 6,500) is defined by the delicate balance that's struck between its two largest industries—timber and tourism. (The big employer in these parts is the lumber giant Georgia Pacific.) At this point, the two are neck in neck in terms of revenue generated. As far as which provides more tax money to the municipal coffers, tourism is way ahead, with the bed tax in large part funding it. There are many more guest rooms in Fort Bragg than Mendocino, and these are geared toward travelers across the spectrum—not just couples, but families and those traveling on business. It's also becoming a popular place for retirees to settle. They're moving in and building big homes, infusing much-needed cash into the local economy.

Mendocino County

Revitalization is underway not just in economic terms but aesthetically as well. Artists who have been priced out of Mendocino have moved to Fort Bragg, and the town has been receptive to their arrival. The **Fort Bragg Center for the Arts** (337 North Franklin Street, 707/964-0807) provides regular doses of culture and cheap studio rents for the army of artisans who are replacing the lumberjacks. The arts come to the people on "First Friday," a monthly tour of local galleries and studios.

The appeal of the area is easy to understand. Fort Bragg isn't completely dominated by hermitic, offbeat types as is Mendocino. It's just a working town that's mending its nets and looking to rebound. Fort Bragg has the largest port between San Francisco and Eureka, and it's the largest coastal city along that same stretch.

For anyone who lives in the mountains and valleys to the east or along the coast in either direction, Fort Bragg is a vital service and provisioning center. With that comes the good (cheaper prices on rooms and meals), the bad (slipshod commerce, strip malls), and the ugly (Georgia Pacific's timber mill, which hogs much of the beachfront and belches steam and smoke on one and all).

Money has been pumped into the town and its various attractions, bed-and-breakfast inns and antique shops have boomed in recent years, and an influx of new immigrants has added a likable ethnic mix. One cultural event we passed up—but only because we were farther up the road when it took place—was Cow Chip Bingo. Here's how it works: a local football field is divided into 500 squares. Contestants lay claim to squares for $5 apiece. Three cows are turned loose onto the field to graze and (you guessed it) make cow pies. The owner of the square first plopped in wins $1,500, second $1,000, and third $500. Unless one is intimate beyond imagination with the excretory habits of cows, our guess is it's a game of chance, not strategy.

Though referred to as "historic" Fort Bragg in all the tourist literature, the town's history can be summed up in two sentences: A fort was established here in 1857 to keep the nearby Native Americans in check and closed seven years later. Timbering and railroads arrived in 1885 and have been leading industries ever since. From this they've managed to create a 28-stop walking tour of historic sites (mostly restored Victorian homes and inns). To visitors, the biggest attraction is the **Skunk Train**, an authentic re-creation of the logging railroad that ran from Fort Bragg to Willits, 40 miles inland. The train consists of observation cars hauled by a diesel logging locomotive. It makes several round-trips to Willits and Northspur (the midway point) daily. Your best bet is the three-hour round-trip to Northspur, which runs along the Noyo River through redwood forests and mountains. The Skunk Train Depot is at the foot of Laurel Street. Call 707/964-6754 or 800/77SKUNK for information; round-trip fares to Northspur cost $27 for adults, $14 for kids.

Finally, a parting comment on the North Coast weather, which applies to Fort Bragg, Mendocino, and surrounding coastal destinations. You can always tell how hot it is inland by how heavy the fog is on the coast. When they're sweating in Sacramento, they're putting on sweaters in Mendocino. The inland heat creates a temperature differential that sucks cool, moist air off the ocean, bathing the northern coastal counties in fog. It almost never rains in the summer, but overcast is common. It generally burns off by midday, but gray skies can linger for weeks.

Fort Bragg and its environs receive their warmest weather in September and October, when the mercury can climb to 80 degrees. The months of December through February are the height of the rainy season. Because the coastal environment is so strongly influenced and moderated by the ocean, temperature extremes in either direction are rare. They may

Map of Northern California—Page 463

get a frost or two each winter and a dusting of snow every half-dozen years, but that's the worst of it. Autumn is really the ideal time to come, because of the Indian summer weather: clear and warm.

Beaches

The state park system provides access to the best beaches in the vicinity: Jug Handle State Reserve (two miles south) and MacKerricher State Park (three miles north). The **Pudding Creek Beach** access, at the south end of Mac-Kerricher State Park, is the closest to a classic sand beach that Fort Bragg has to offer. Here, Pudding Creek trickles into the ocean, and a small dirt parking lot allows limited (and free) entry. You must walk under a condemned train trestle, but the mountain of sand is inviting. The waves break invitingly, too, but a sign warns of "Recurring Rip Currents." No lifeguards are on duty.

One creek-mouth north is **Virgin Creek Beach,** a wide, sandy beach that draws local crowds. An unmarked pulloff by the side of the road is your only clue about this one. Both Pudding Creek and Virgin Creek Beaches lie along the eight-mile log-haul road now used by joggers, walkers, and bicyclists. Elsewhere in Fort Bragg the beach pickings are slim. Georgia Pacific, incidentally, guards its beachfront property with the ferocity of pit bulls, surrounding it with fencing, barbed wire, and "No Trespassing" signs (not realizing the irony that no one in his or her right mind would want to trespass). More ironic, however, is that this pro-America company patrols its compound with foreign-made trucks. It was Georgia Pacific, remember, who waved the American flag while lobbying to cut first-growth timber. The public beach next to this property, **Glass Beach,** is a mess, suffering from proximity to the lumber mill, although it is bounded by a marsh on the other side. Allegedly, you can scavenge for wave-polished pebbles and glass bits at Glass Beach, but it looks none too inviting.

The west end of **Noyo Harbor** (accessed via Noyo Harbor Drive, next to the bridge off Highway 1) is home to a tiny cove beach bordered by rock jetties that hold open the river's mouth. It's quite a setting, though mostly for viewing. The Pacific waves break loudly against the jetties, and the bridge span arches dramatically in the background. Be careful on the jetties if you choose to fish from them, as they are slick.

Bunking Down

It's true that rooms are cheaper and more plentiful in Fort Bragg than in the coastal towns to the south, but you get what you pay for. That is, for a few dollars more, you can have a total North Coast experience in Mendocino, Little River, Albion, or Elk. Still, a fair number of nice and new Fort Bragg motels provide the sort of dependably simple ambience and comfort many road-weary travelers crave. In that regard, the **Best Western Vista Manor Lodge** (1100 North Main Street, 707/964-4776, $$) and the **Quality Inn Seabird Lodge** (191 South Street, 707/964-4731, $$) are your best bets.

The **Grey Whale Inn** (615 North Main Street, 707/964-0640, $$) was the first bed-and-breakfast in Fort Bragg and has been a North Coast landmark for years. The handsome, four-story building used to be the general hospital for the area, once boasting 36 beds. With such a background, it's no surprise that the inn is very wheelchair accessible, with wide ramps running throughout. The rooms are large, impeccably decorated, and immaculately maintained. Walls are paneled with broad redwood planks. Beds are covered with homey quilts. There's a game room downstairs with a pool table and a television. Each morning, a mouthwatering breakfast is served, including such goodies as a breakfast strudel of spinach and sun-dried tomatoes layered in a custard of bread and eggs. Croissants, fresh fruit salad, yogurt, granola, a special blend of coffee, and cinnamon-flavored hot tea round out the meal. The Grey Whale offers 14 rooms, ranging from "French country simplicity" to suites and penthouses with fireplaces and refrigerators. A few years ago, a woman who was born here when it was a hospital returned to spend her wedding night at the Grey Whale.

The closest lodge to the beach access at Pudding Creek is **Pudding Creek Inn** (700 North Main Street, 707/964-9529, $$), a well-heeled little Victorian manor that offers a full buffet breakfast and an enclosed garden court.

Coastal Cuisine

An influx of foreign immigrants has given Fort Bragg a much-needed shot of diversity in the food department. The most interesting newcomer, and one of the great finds on the Mendocino coast, is **Viraporn's Thai Café** (500 South Main Street, 707/964-7931, $). It's owned and operated by a native of the Phrae province in northern Thailand. She prepares every dish using fresh, authentic ingredients. Her chicken lemongrass soup and *pad Thai* will rescue you from all those burgers you've eaten elsewhere in Fort Bragg. Viraporn's is open every day but Tuesday.

Ye olde Fort Bragg–style chowdown can still be had at **Round Man's Smoke House** (137 Laurel Street, 707/964-5954, $), which offers the North Coast's best smoked salmon, albacore, and cod, as well as salmon and turkey jerky. Sample tastings are encouraged.

For breakfast and lunch you can't go wrong with **Schat's Bakery and Café** (360 North Franklin Street, 707/964-1929, $). If you want fish, go where they reel 'em in. Overlooking busy Noyo Harbor is the **Cliff House** (1011 South Main Street, 707/961-0255, $$), where they dish out fresh local seafood on four dining levels.

Less touristy and more local in flavor is **The Wharf** (780 North Harbor Drive, 707/964-4283, $$), which is perched over the water beneath the Noyo River Bridge, among the ramshackle flotsam of the fishing trade. The nautical bustle and sea breezes will transport you to a proverbial Treasure Island of the tummy on the back of a freshly grilled salmon steak.

Night Moves

The **North Coast Brewing Company** (444 North Main Street, 707/964-2739) is a friendly pub that has been winning awards every year for its home-brewed ales and stouts. Try the Scrimshaw Pilsner, Red Seal Ale, and Old No. 38 Stout. The pub grub is quite good, too, including smoked fish and stump-sized burgers that would sate the hungriest lumberjack's appetite.

For More Information

Fort Bragg–Mendocino Coast Chamber of Commerce, 332 North Main Street, P.O. Box 1141, Fort Bragg, CA 95437, 707/961-6300 or 800/726-2780, website: www.mendocinocoast.com

Map of Northern California—Page 463

MacKerricher State Park

Mendocino County hugs the coast for 130 miles, much of it an inaccessible stretch of sea cliffs and tiny pocket beaches. **MacKerricher State Park,** however, is a North Coast anomaly, offering a broad, mostly sandy beach that runs for eight uninterrupted miles. MacKerricher's lengthy expanse and shoreline equestrian trail are ideal for horseback riding. Guided rides can be arranged just outside the park at **Ricochet Ridge Ranch** (707/964-7669). Bicyclists, joggers, and walkers make use of the old logging road that runs through the park. Anglers find good fishing around the headlands and in Lake Cleone. You can do just about everything but swim in the 50-degree water.

A boardwalk leads out from the main parking lot of the state park to **Laguna Point,** a stunning promontory from which to view migrating whales and harbor seals. At low tide the tidepools are chock full of life, but at high tide the Pacific waves pound the point with profound fury. We watched in amazement as the lush and beautiful marine vegetation just rolled with the ceaseless punches.

Elsewhere on the premises is **Lake Cleone,** a 15-acre freshwater lake stocked with trout. It's a popular duck haven, too. The sand on the beach itself is large-grained and blackish in color. The hard-packed granules make for great bike riding. The beach runs unbroken from Pudding Creek (in Fort Bragg) north to Ten Mile River.

Westport

North of Fort Bragg, Highway 1 continues along the coast before pulling away to join U.S. 101 at Leggett. Along this stretch lies a quartet of accessible beaches clustered in the vicinity of a one-horse town called Westport (population 300).

Beaches

Starting from the south, **Seaside Creek Beach** is at the mouth of Seaside Creek. Parking is by the side of the road. Offshore sea stacks are visible, and driftwood lines the sandy beach. **Chadbourne Gulch** is the keeper—a mile-long, sandy beach that's good for sunning, surfing, and surf casting. There's lots of beach to wander, though not much room for cars, which must park on the highway shoulder. At high tide the beach becomes none too wide itself. These creek-mouth beaches of northern Mendocino County are very angler-friendly, being good places for netting smelt, catching steelhead, and foraging for abalone.

The next two are prime North Coast camping spots. **Wages Creek Beach** is a privately run campground with sites along the creek overlooking the ocean. A half mile north of Westport, it primarily draws RV nomads and anglers. **Westport-Union Landing State Beach,** three miles north of Westport, offers blufftop camping at seven campgrounds along its two-mile ocean frontage. Trails and stairs lead to a primarily rocky beach; the sandy, quarter-mile-long beach that begins at the mouth of DeHaven Creek on the park's south end is known as Pete's Beach. Westport-Union Landing can be a raw spot indeed in winter, when stormy weather and rough seas pound the bluff bases, sending wave spray soaring 50 feet in the air, all the way up to campground level. Divers, tidepoolers, and surf casters especially seem to enjoy this primitive, sea-swept environment.

Bunking Down

If camping sounds a little austere but being near this wild and rocky coast holds some appeal, you can always opt for comfort and proximity to nature by staying at one of the

Let's Get Lost: A Side Trip to Sinkyone Wilderness State Park

We were looking for **Usal Road** (a.k.a. Mendocino County Road 431). Even so, we didn't notice the turnoff when we came upon it while driving along Highway 1. It was right there, just like the maps said, three miles north of Rockport, which itself was little more than a crossroads. But it came up suddenly, in a silent way, requiring almost a complete doubling back to the left. We saw it too late and had to turn around on Highway 1 at the next opportunity for a re-approach from the north. This time, we did it. Then we stopped, read the signs, and got nervous.

Usal Road is a one-lane dirt road that negotiates the mountains of the King Range. It zigs and zags for roughly 25 miles along the Lost Coast, an awesome wilderness of jagged mountains that plunge precipitously to the ocean. Usal Road is all ups and downs and sharp turns and curves and very little straight-away. It is pure hell on a car's brakes and transmission. Signs warn that the road is not recommended for RVs and trailers and may be impassable in the winter months owing to mud and washouts. (Our advice, if you do venture up Usal Road, is to carry a cell phone and AAA's "Supernumber" for roadside assistance: 800/222-4357.) The road is not very well maintained by the county, we were later told by a woman up in Shelter Cove. We have some sympathy for the county on this matter, because the road is basically unmaintainable. However, our innkeeper in Mendocino the night before assured us that we could make it through if we took it easy. "Don't go over the side," he said half-jokingly.

We were driving a rental car, so we braved it. We managed to drive about seven miles into the heart of the Lost Coast, reaching **Usal Beach**. These were seven of the hardest, longest miles we've ever driven. It took nearly an hour. Along the way, our dust-covered late-model Mazda Protégé sputtered and groaned as it rolled up and down the rutted roadway. Each hairpin turn sent our hearts into our stomachs. Would we encounter an SUV on a blind curve? Would we hit a pothole that might crack an axle? Would the brakes give out?

At one point, about 4.5 miles from Highway 1, the road hugs the cliff's edge for half a mile, edging along a sheer drop of a thousand feet to the churning ocean. These afford high-altitude ocean vistas that rival the best in Big Sur. They lie less than five miles off the main road, yet we felt that relatively few eyes had ever gazed on—and fewer still had ever actually set foot on—these pristine black-sand beaches. The ocean stretched out to eternity. We had never seen so much ocean arrayed before us. It looked like a vast sheet of rippled tin foil, extending to a luminous horizon where ocean and sky blended in silvery unity. The drive along Usal Road, and the repair bill you may incur as a result, is worth the trouble just to lay eyes on this view of the Pacific Ocean. Trust us. We pressed on for another two difficult miles, finally reaching signs an-

Map of Northern California—Page 463

Mendocino County

nouncing the entrance to **Sinkyone Wilderness State Park.** This is one of the remotest outposts in the state-park system. The park offers campsites, a beautiful wilderness beach, and the southern trailhead for the Lost Coast Trail, which extends for 22 miles up to Mattole River. Some, but not much, information is posted on a board. Vehicles park here and people fill out the necessary form to hike the Lost Coast Trail. On a gorgeous midweek day in May, we saw no one camping or on the beach.

Usal Beach lies just north of a nerve-wracking bridge that requires positioning one's wheels on elevated wooden tracks to make a successful crossing. That done, we turned west on Beach Road and followed it to an impromptu parking lot of sand and rocks. Usal Creek enters the ocean here in a series of meandering curves. A few picnic tables are scattered around. The beach is beautiful and rugged, made up of spongy dark volcanic sand. The beach face is steep, and powerful waves run up its face. We thought of a newspaper article that had been posted on the information board. It warned of "rogue waves"—waves of sudden and unpredictable size that can swamp swimmers, hikers, and boaters—and told of a recent incident in which a group of hikers was washed off the beach in the vicinity of Shelter Cove. In one year, 13 people were drowned by rogue waves near Point Reyes alone.

In this wild, dangerous and unconquerable place, we reveled in the beauty. The air, having passed across 3,000 miles of open ocean, was as clean as any on earth. The day was perfect.

We debated the wisdom of continuing on Usal Road to Shelter Cove. We had come only seven miles, and 19 more lay before us. At this rate, it would take two or three more hours to get there, the good Lord willing, and already it was 5:30 P.M. Providence interceded at that moment in the form of an SUV that came rumbling down from Shelter Cove. We asked the driver if Usal Road was passable in that direction, and he strongly recommended against driving it. He ruefully noted that the road was muddy and deeply rutted north of here. On one particularly hazardous stretch, he incurred nasty dent in his Explorer when it plunged into a pothole. Imagine what that might do to our low-to-the-ground compact car. No thanks, we opined, retracing our steps back to Highway 1 and then taking the long way to Shelter Cove: north to Leggett, where we picked up U.S. 101, and then up to Garberville and west to Shelter Cove. This meant another 70 miles of zigzagging, up-and-down roads, but at least they were paved and, for the most part, well-graded.

In a way, we were glad it worked out the way it did, because on the return trip we got to see a bit of nature in the raw. A furry black figure darted across the road. It was a black bear cub. It hid behind and then climbed a tree. The curious critter poked its head around the tree and stared at us for a few minutes. Cute as the dickens, it looked like something out of a cartoon. It finally slid down and darted into the forest. Soon after that we saw an eagle swoop down and snare a meal out of a tree. These were majestic visions, and they would not have happened had we not chanced the road less taken.

Mendocino County

bed-and-breakfast inns scattered about the area. This part of the coast is uncrowded and unhurried. If you're serious about getting away, you couldn't do better than Westport. Our picks: **Howard Creek Ranch** (40501 Highway 1, 707/964-6725, $$) and **DeHaven Valley Farm Country Inn and Restaurant** (39247 Highway 1, 707/961-1660, $$), both of which offer oceans and mountains for a backdrop.

With 10 and 8 rooms respectively, these are the largest inns in Westport; others are smaller but just as charming.

For More Information

Fort Bragg–Mendocino Coast Chamber of Commerce, 332 North Main Street, P.O. Box 1141, Fort Bragg, CA 95437, 707/961-6300 or 800/726-2780, website: www.mendocino.coast.com

Sinkyone Wilderness State Park

Sinkyone Wilderness State Park occupies the northwest corner of Mendocino County. Three miles north of Rockport on Highway 1, pick up Usal Road/County Road 431 and continue six miles to Usal Campground. Access to the north end of the park is gained from the Humboldt County town of Redway. Pick up Briceland Road, which leads to a visitor center and campgrounds at Needle Rock 36 miles away. Be advised that roads within the park are only seasonally passable to most vehicles.

In a sense, this is a new one on us: a park you can't get to. At least some of the time, that is. Two roads lead into Sinkyone: one from Rockport in Mendocino County, one from Redway in Humboldt County. Both are steep, winding, and difficult to negotiate under the best of circumstances—and flat-out impassable when the rains are heavy. RVs and trailers are out of the question all the time. Cars and pickups will get you there from March to October. Four-wheel drives are best for getting around the rugged terrain of an area that's colloquially known as the Lost Coast.

So what's the attraction? Try 7,300 acres of deep coastal wilderness that even Highway 1 fails to penetrate. There are 10 primitive, hike-in campsites, and one at which you can park your vehicle. The Lost Coast Trail zigs and zags for 22 miles along Sinkyone's coastline, sometimes at sea level and other times atop ridges at elevations of 800 feet.

The steep mountains rise to heights of 1,800

feet and support a diverse array of plants, from second-growth coastal redwoods and California laurels to grasslands, meadows, and shrubs. The region was heavily logged for a century—from 1888 to 1986, the last owner being Georgia Pacific. Now the land is recovering and reverting to a wild state. It's hard to believe that in the midst of this now-empty country, Georgia Pacific and its forerunners created bustling company towns at Wheeler and Usal, which were burned to the ground by the lumber company in 1969 to eliminate liability problems from leaving the old buildings standing. Prior to the timberfest, this land was the home of the Sinkyone people, and the story of their subjugation is another sordid chapter in the history of the abuse of native populations.

Today, the old ranches and lumber camps are abandoned and overgrown. Except for a small visitors center at Needle Rock House, a former rancher's home, Sinkyone Wilderness State Park has little more than trails and gravel roads running through it. Camping is first-come, first-served, and you must bring your own water and firewood. The most interesting campground is at **Bear Harbor Cove**, site of a former dog-hole port where lumber was shipped. Wilderness permits are required to hike the Lost Coast Trail between **Usal Beach** and Bear Harbor. They cost $3 a night and are obtainable at the Usal Beach Campground or Needle Rock Visitor Center.

Down by the ocean, black sand and coarse

Map of Northern California—Page 463

gravel beaches lie at the mouths of creeks. Between them the beach narrows to a thin ribbon of dark volcanic sand. Primitive beachfront sites are strung out along the Sinkyone shoreline. From south to north there's **Little Jackass Creek Beach** (visited by as many seals as humans), **Bear Harbor Beach** (good tidepooling), **Needle Rock Beach** (long, hikable shoreline), and **Jones Beach** (cove beach at the end of a steep trail).

For More Information

Sinkyone Wilderness State Park, P.O. Box 245, Whitehorn, CA 95489, 707/986-7711, website: www.parks.ca.gov

Mendocino County

Map of Mendocino County—Page 526

© ROBERT HOLMES/CALTOUR

Chapter 14
Humboldt County

Humboldt County

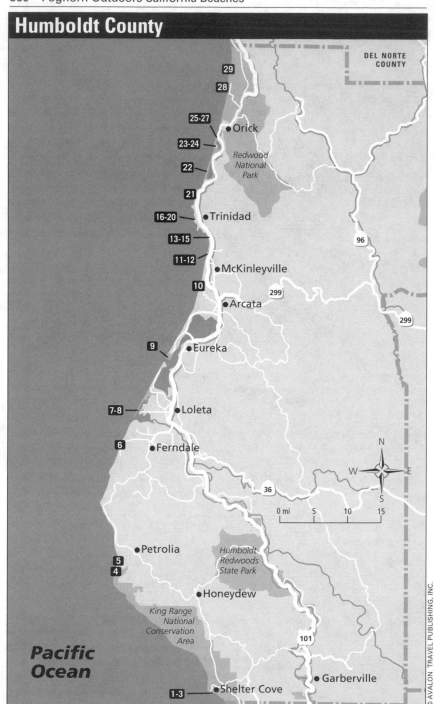

Humboldt County Beaches

1 Dead Man's Beach, page 570

Location: From Shelter Cove, take Shelter Cove Road to Machi Road, which leads to Lost Coast Landing marina. Hike south from the marina.
Parking/fees: free parking lot (Shelter Cove Deli and Campground)
Hours: 24 hours
Facilities: none
Contact: Arcata District Office, King Range National Conservation Area, 707/825-2300

2 Shelter Cove, page 570

Location: Take Garberville/Redway exit off U.S. 101 in Garberville. Follow Briceland-Thorne Road to Shelter Cove Road and continue to Shelter Cove.
Parking/fees: free parking lots. Camping fees are $15-25 per night.
Hours: 24 hours
Facilities: concession, restrooms, showers, and picnic tables
Contact: Shelter Cove Deli and Campground, 707/986-7474

3 Little Black Sands Beach, page 570

Location: Wave Drive at Dolphin Drive, just north of Point Delgada in Shelter Cove
Parking/fees: free street parking
Hours: 24 hours
Facilities: none
Contact: Arcata District Office, Bureau of Land Management, 707/825-2300

4 Black Sands Beach, page 570

Location: from the end of Beach Road in Shelter Cove to the mouth of the Mattole River
Parking/fees: free parking lot
Hours: 24 hours
Facilities: none
Contact: Arcata District Office, Bureau of Land Management, 707/825-2300

5 Mattole River Beach (a.k.a. Lighthouse Road Beach), page 574

Location: end of Lighthouse Road, at mouth of Mattole River, five miles west of Petrolia
Parking/fees: free parking lot. Camping fee is $5.
Hours: 24 hours
Facilities: restrooms and picnic tables
Contact: Arcata Resource Area, Bureau of Land Management, 707/825-2300

Humboldt County

Map of Humboldt County—Page 560

6 Centerville Beach County Park, page 577

Location: end of Centerville Road, five miles west of Ferndale
Parking/fees: free parking lot
Hours: 24 hours
Facilities: restrooms
Contact: Humboldt County Parks Department, 707/445-7651

7 Crab County Park, page 578

Location: From Loleta, take Loleta Drive to Cannibal Island Road and continue west to the park.
Parking/fees: free parking lot
Hours: 24 hours
Facilities: restrooms
Contact: Humboldt County Parks Department, 707/445-7651

8 South Spit and Jetty, page 578

Location: From U.S. 101 10 miles south of Eureka, take Hookton Road to Table Bluff Road. At Table Bluff County Park turn north on South Jetty Road and drive to the jetty.
Parking/fees: free parking lot
Hours: 24 hours
Facilities: none
Contact: Humboldt County Parks Department, 707/445-7651

9 Samoa Dunes Recreation Area, page 580

Location: From Highway 255 in Eureka drive to North Spit. Turn left on New Navy Base Road and follow it to Samoa Dunes.
Parking/fees: free parking lot. Camping fees are $12 per night.
Hours: 24 hours
Facilities: concession, restrooms, showers, and picnic tables
Contact: Arcata Resource Area, Bureau of Land Management, 707/825-2300, or Samoa Boat Launch County Park, 707/445-7652

10 Mad River Beach County Park, page 585

Location: From U.S. 101 north of Arcata, take Janes Road exit and follow signs to the park.
Parking/fees: free parking lot
Hours: 24 hours
Facilities: restrooms and picnic tables
Contact: Humboldt County Parks Department, 707/445-7651

Humboldt County

Map of Northern California—Page 463

⓫ Clam Beach County Park, page 587

Location: From U.S. 101 north of McKinleyville, take the Clam Beach exit and follow it to the park.

Parking/fees: free parking lot. Camping fee is $8 per night.

Hours: 24 hours

Facilities: restrooms and picnic tables

Contact: Humboldt County Parks Department, 707/445-7651

⓬ Little River State Beach, page 587

Location: U.S. 101 at Little River, four miles north of McKinleyville

Parking/fees: free parking lot

Hours: 24 hours

Facilities: none

Contact: Little River State Beach, 707/488-2041

⓭ Moonstone Beach, page 588

Location: From Main Street in Trinidad turn south on Scenic Drive and follow to Moonstone Beach Road, which leads to the beach.

Parking/fees: free parking lot

Hours: sunrise–sunset

Facilities: none

Contact: Humboldt County Parks Department, 707/445-7651

⓮ Houda Point, page 588

Location: one-half mile north of Moonstone Beach on Scenic Drive in Trinidad

Parking/fees: free limited roadside parking

Hours: sunrise–sunset

Facilities: none

Contact: Humboldt North Coast Land Trust, P.O. Box 457, Trinidad, CA 95570

⓯ Luffenholtz Beach, page 589

Location: From Main Street in Trinidad, turn south on Scenic Drive and drive two miles; trails lead to the beach.

Parking/fees: free roadside parking

Hours: sunrise–sunset

Facilities: none

Contact: Humboldt County Parks Department, 707/445-7651

Humboldt County

16 Baker Beach, page 589

Location: From Main Street in Trinidad, turn south on Scenic Drive and drive one mile; trails lead to the beach.
Parking/fees: free roadside parking
Hours: sunrise–sunset
Facilities: none
Contact: Humboldt North Coast Land Trust, P.O. Box 457, Trinidad, CA 95570

17 Indian Beach, page 589

Location: Follow a marked trailhead to Indian Beach from the intersection of Edwards and Main Streets in Trinidad.
Parking/fees: free roadside parking
Hours: sunrise–sunset
Facilities: none
Contact: Humboldt North Coast Land Trust, P.O. Box 457, Trinidad, CA 95570

18 Trinidad Head, page 589

Location: west end of Edwards Street in Trinidad
Parking/fees: free parking lot
Hours: 7 A.M.–5 P.M.
Facilities: concession and restrooms
Contact: Trinidad Harbor, 707/677-3625

19 Trinidad State Beach, page 589

Location: From Main Street at Stagecoach Road in Trinidad follow signs to the beach
Parking/fees: free parking lot
Hours: sunrise–sunset
Facilities: restrooms and picnic tables
Contact: North Coast Redwoods District, California State Parks, 707/445-6547

20 College Cove, page 589

Location: From Main Street in Trinidad turn onto Stagecoach Road. Pull into the dirt parking lot a quarter mile on the left. Trails lead to College Cove South and College Cove North.
Parking/fees: free parking lot
Hours: sunrise–sunset
Facilities: none
Contact: North Coast Redwoods District, California State Parks, 707/445-6547

Humboldt County

Map of Northern California—Page 463

21 Agate Beach (Patrick's Point State Park), page 590

▲ 🚶 🏃 ⑤

Location: From U.S. 101 five miles north of Trinidad, take Patrick's Point Drive exit and follow signs to the park.
Parking/fees: $4 entrance fee per vehicle. Camping fees are $13–16 per night, plus a $7.50 reservation fee.
Hours: 8 A.M.–sunset
Facilities: restrooms, showers, picnic tables, and visitor center
Contact: Patrick's Point State Park, 707/677-3570

22 Big Lagoon County Park, page 590

▲ 🚶 ③

Location: U.S. 101 at south end of Big Lagoon, seven miles north of Trinidad
Parking/fees: $1 entrance fee per vehicle. Camping fee is $12 per night.
Hours: 24 hours
Facilities: restrooms and picnic tables
Contact: Humboldt County Parks Department, 707/445-7651

23 Dry Lagoon (Humboldt Lagoons State Park), page 592

▲ ③

Location: U.S. 101 at Dry Lagoon, 13 miles north of Trinidad
Parking/fees: free parking lot. Camping fee is $7 per night; register at Patrick's Point State Park.
Hours: sunrise–sunset
Facilities: restrooms and picnic tables
Contact: North Coast Redwoods District, California State Parks, 707/445-6547

24 Stone Lagoon (Humboldt Lagoons State Park), page 592

▲ ③

Location: U.S. 101 at Stone Lagoon, 14.5 miles north of Trinidad
Parking/fees: free parking lot. Camping fee (boat-in sites) is $7 per night, plus a $7.50 reservation fee.
Hours: sunrise–sunset
Facilities: restrooms and picnic tables
Contact: North Coast Redwoods District, California State Parks, 707/445-6547

25 Freshwater Lagoon (Redwood National Park), page 592

▲ ③

Location: U.S. 101 at Freshwater Lagoon, three miles south of Orick
Parking/fees: free roadside parking. Camping is free; register at Redwood Information Center, one mile north.
Hours: 24 hours
Facilities: restrooms
Contact: Redwood Information Center, Redwood National Park, 707/464-6101, ext. 5265

Humboldt County

26 Redwood Creek Beach (Redwood National Park), page 592

Location: Two miles south of Orick, off U.S. 101
Parking/fees: free parking lot
Hours: 24 hours
Facilities: restrooms and picnic tables
Contact: Redwood Information Center, Redwood National Park, 707/464-6101, ext. 5265

27 Orick Fishing Access (Redwood National Park), page 593

Location: end of Hufford Road, off U.S. 101, two miles west of Orick
Parking/fees: free parking lot
Hours: 24 hours
Facilities: none
Contact: Redwood Information Center, Redwood National Park, 707/464-6101, ext. 5265

28 Gold Bluffs Beach (Prairie Creek Redwoods State Park), page 593

Location: From U.S. 101 three miles north of Orick, take Davison Road turnoff and follow it to the beach.
Parking/fees: $4 entrance fee per vehicle. Camping fees are $13–16 per night, plus a $7.50 reservation fee.
Hours: sunrise–sunset
Facilities: restrooms, showers, and picnic tables
Contact: Prairie Creek Redwoods State Park, 707/464-6101, ext. 5301

29 Carruthers Cove Beach, page 594

Location: From U.S. 101 five miles north of Orick, turn onto Drury Scenic Parkway/Old U.S. 101 and drive seven miles. Fork left onto Coastal Drive. At signs for Carruthers Cove Trail, park and hike to the beach.
Parking/fees: free roadside parking
Hours: 24 hours
Facilities: none
Contact: Prairie Creek Redwoods State Park, 707/464-6101, ext. 5301

Humboldt County

Map of Northern California—Page 463

Humboldt County

They call it Humboldt County, but we think a better name would be *Humbled County*. We certainly were humbled by all there was to do and see in this vast natural wonderland. Everything seems bigger up here, and not just the towering redwoods. Humboldt County also has 100 miles of coastline; the tallest peak on any continental margin in the United States (King Peak, at 4,086 feet); and two lengthy shoreline hikes, the Lost Coast and Coastal Trails, which wander the beaches for 50 and 30 miles, respectively. If you come here, allow plenty of time to drink in the immense natural beauty of the redwoods and beaches, and lose yourself in the foggy mysteries of a world apart.

Humboldt County comprises three counties in one. The southern third is part of the Lost Coast—a place where mountains rise right out of the ocean and roads swing inland, as if afraid to venture near the rugged shoreline. Shelter Cove is the most accessible point on the Lost Coast, but even it requires a 24-mile drive from U.S. 101 over narrow, curving, and steeply graded roads. Your reward is a black-sand beach that seemingly runs to infinity in either direction.

The middle portion of Humboldt County is a verdant place of river valleys, pastureland, embayments, and deep woods. It's also home to the population centers of Ferndale (a Victorian village), Eureka, Arcata, McKinleyville, and Trinidad, which spread along a 30-mile stretch of U.S. 101. Lengthy sand spits and wild, dune-covered beaches characterize the coast through here.

The northern third of Humboldt is redwood country. Redwood National Park and Prairie Creek Redwoods State Park occupy much of the acreage, with a little stagecoach stop called Orick being the only human settlement between Trinidad and the Del Norte County line. West of Orick is Gold Bluffs Beach, one of the most stellar settings for a beach anywhere in the world.

Humboldt County

Shelter Cove

Shelter Cove lies at the heart of the Lost Coast, a remote and staggeringly beautiful region occupied by Sinkyone Wilderness State Park and the King Range National Conservation Area. Although a few unwary home builders have stumbled onto Shelter Cove, whose population is 350, it still deserves to be described as "lost."

It lies a mere 24 miles west of Garberville, but these are 24 trying miles, particularly approaching the coast. The road is paved but unmarked, and it meanders and curves, ascending and descending. Eventually it reaches a peak high in the King Range and the ocean pops into view—one of the most mesmerizing first

 ## "Lamb Lips of Oblivion": Hibernating among the Humboldt Hippies

Once we crossed the line into Humboldt County, a change occurred in more than just the natural landscape. Having barely survived a tortuous, aborted attempt to traverse Usal Road, we followed U.S. 101 inland as it pulled northward away from the coast and entered the cathedral-like dusk of redwood groves. En route, we passed roadside attractions like the **Grandfather Tree,** the **Famous One-Log House** (hollowed from a single 2,100-year-old redwood log), **Legend of Bigfoot,** and **Confusion Hill.** The last of these was the home of the world's largest redwood chainsaw sculpture and the "Gravity House."

Finally, we arrived in Garberville, the jumping-off point for **Shelter Cove** and the main provisioning outpost for southern Humboldt County. Although this town of 2,000 provided a welcome place to chill out and refuel, we were struck with an unmistakable sense of deja vu. The town center was spotlessly clean, but this was primarily because a lanky dude with a gray, ZZ Top–style beard and wool cap yanked tightly over his wildly matted hair was pulling a one-man litter patrol, stooping every few feet to pick up a cup, cigarette butt, can, or wrapper. Down the street, we found a music shop that advertised "Freak Brothers Comics." Then we stumbled into a used record haven where we bought a mint condition copy of the Steve Miller Band's first album, *Children of the Future* (for $5!) and some comic books. We perused an art co-op, a bead shop, several cafés (one entirely vegetarian), a restored cinema, a recycled clothing store, a head shop, and a gift emporium that "introduces your inner child to your outer adult." Wares included Native American hand drums, prayer sticks, medicine staffs, tie-dyed shirts, and sarongs. The wafting odor of patchouli and musk conjured memories of rock festivals from our misspent '60s youth. In short, Garberville was a flashback to all the things we loved about the '60s.

Two miles down the road in Redway, however, we came upon some children of God who'd taken a wrong turn on their way back to the garden (to

Map of Northern California—Page 463

Humboldt County

glimpses of the mighty Pacific on the entire West Coast. If it's not shrouded in fog, the ocean glistens brightly in the distance like a diamond choker. From here a long, heart-stopping grade drops down to sea level. You can buy a T-shirt at the Shelter Cove Deli that celebrates the fact you survived the passage.

Shelter Cove is spread out on land surrounding a natural harbor between headlands in the King Range. About 400 houses have been built out here in a slow-going development of what used to be a giant sheep ranch. The ranch owner sold his tract back in 1965 for a quarter-million dollars; it was resold for $900,000 to a development company that subdivided it into 1,300 smallish (given the rural location) lots. The homes that have gone up here are mainly incongruously large dwellings built by retirees

rephrase lyrics from Joni Mitchell's immortal "Woodstock"). What we saw and sniffed almost literally made us sick. Three people—a dude and two chicks—were crammed into the front seat of a Subaru station wagon tightly stuffed with provisions; mounds of gypsy peasant attire, seemingly ripped off from a Goodwill bin; a few stringed instruments, pressed against the back window; and other assorted, unidentifiable junk. The vehicle was so full you couldn't have fit a fly inside. Not that a self-respecting fly would want to be a passenger therein.

We walked within five feet of the car, encountering a stench so profoundly overwhelming that it knocked us back on our heels. The nauseating odor was a mix of sweat, urine, nameless secretions, and the slight tangy hint of scented candles, with which they no doubt illuminated their squatters' digs. It was like a roving homeless encampment, a latter-day version of the Joad family without the dignity. They were the most unkempt human beings we'd ever seen who weren't passed out across an urban sewer grate. The car's engine screamed with the effort to depart the gas station convenience store, wobbling away as if on its last legs. As they passed us, the driver—who wore a filthy, rainbow-hued cap and looked completely out of his gourd—gave us a wordless "hail-fellow-well-met" nod, as though we were kindred spirits from the Humboldt backwoods. Did we really look that bad after a month on the road?

On the way out to Shelter Cove, we tuned in the local community radio station, which featured a dopey New Age priestess reciting and interpreting inane verse by an understandably obscure feminist poet. The first words we heard were "moccasin flowers." The woman beatifically chirped verses of poetry in a smiley, hippie-chick monotone while we laughed hysterically. She droned on about lilies and roses and snakeskins, about the "crackling lick of the sun" and "lamb lips of oblivion."

As we came over the crest of **Paradise Ridge,** we flicked her off and focused on the heart-thumping 2,000-foot plunge toward the Pacific Ocean. This was an epic poem unfolding before our eyes and, thankfully, no words were needed. The figurative essence of patchouli oil was quickly replaced by the acrid, real-life odor of overheating brakes. We were, like, freaking out, man.

Humboldt County

Map of Humboldt County—Page 560

from points south. They move to Shelter Cove with the best intentions, get the heebie-jeebies from all the isolation (think of *The Shining*), and then try to unload their haunted homestead onto the next ocean-loving retiree.

As the pleasant old bird who ran a seaside motel where we stayed put it, "The population here is 350, if they're all here at once. The rental homes are nearly always rented because the retirement age people don't stick it out here. They build these big houses but they don't think it through. They get out here and get homesick and are far from their families and there's no medical help for a hundred miles. I probably wouldn't be here myself if I hadn't already been here forever."

And isolated it is. Unique on the California coast, you must drive for an hour to get to a bona fide grocery store or movie house. The King Range, with peaks that rise to heights of 4,000 feet, separates Shelter Cove from civilization. Try as they might to lure people here by putting in a small airstrip while continuing to subdivide and sell as best they can, the area is simply too distant to be attractive to urbanites, even those who toy with the fantasy of fleeing civilization.

You wonder why they even try, because the realtors' half-assed efforts—as well as the most forlorn nine-hole golf course we've ever seen—give the area an unfair aspect of a place that's gone to the dogs. (Come to think of it, there are a lot of unleashed canines in Shelter Cove and, for that matter, all over Humboldt County.) Softening that impression is **Mal Coombs Park,** a nifty, bluff-hugging promenade at the foot of Machi Road on the south end of town. Here you'll find informational kiosks, a boat launch, some tidepooling and rock fishing opportunities, and a miniature, singularly photogenic, lighthouse. Blink your eyes and you'd think you were in a Maine fishing village.

Shelter Cove does have a marina, several small motels, a couple of restaurants, all the solitude you can stand (and then some), and black-sand beaches that will dazzle and delight the intrepid beachcomber.

Beaches

Shelter Cove is the site of some lengthy black-sand beaches, including a 24-miler known as **Black Sands Beach.** On a sunny day you'll rarely find a beach more beautiful than Black Sands Beach, at the northwest edge of town and accessible via Humboldt Loop and Beach Road. The sand is coarse, gravelly, and coal colored. The beach is extremely wide by the parking lot and then narrows up the coast. It continues north for 24 miles and is firm enough for good hiking. In fact, the beach links up with a trail through the Sinkyone Wilderness to form the nearly 50-mile Lost Coast Trail, which runs from Usal Campground to the Mattole River. If you're in search of plentiful solitude on a true wilderness beach, you can do no better than this stretch of the Lost Coast. Closer to the center of town, a short trail in the vicinity of Pelican's Landing restaurant leads to **Little Black Sands Beach,** a favorite of locals. The sand is volcanic in origin, hence the color.

Our own favorite beach, and a shoo-in for a coastal Top 10 list, is **Dead Man's Beach.** This gem sits at the south end of town, beginning at the Shelter Cove Deli and Campground. Park in one of the lots by the marina, follow the cement boat-launch ramp down to the beach, and walk south along the broadly curving cove past some spectacular scenery. Cliffs rise behind the narrow strip of sand, while breakers thunder ashore. Small waterfalls cascade over the sheer rock face to the beach below. Surfers are fond of the waves at Dead Man's Beach about a half mile south of the boat launch. They'll drive their four-wheel-drives (everybody's got one here) along the beach, tide permitting. The tidal exchange can be extreme—as great as eight feet—so consult a tide chart before attempting to walk or drive.

Map of Northern California—Page 463

A recent 1.5-mile hike on Dead Man's Beach suggested how the place got its name. After chugging south through relatively stable and wide sand, along seaweed, dead starfish, and dead crab-snarled patches and over rounded pebbles and boulders, we turned around when a headland blocked our path. Retracing our steps became an adventure we hadn't expected. The tide was coming in and the formerly wide beach left us barely two feet of walking space that wasn't under water—and nowhere to scramble against a sheer cliff face. As we hustled out of there, we talked out the script idea for a film called *The Lost Coast,* a teen-exploitation film à la *Blair Witch Project.* In our script, a pack of spoiled rich kids on a beach-camping adventure get trapped against a cliff by a rising tide and find themselves at the mercy of rogue waves, a deadly winter tempest, and angry rattlesnakes. (Yes, we were told to watch out for rattlesnakes, which sun themselves on the beach here.) Our can't-miss Hollywood pitch would sound something like this: "Eight hiked in but only three walked out and just one of them could tell about the unspeakable horrors they encountered. . . ." We've obviously spent too much time in Los Angeles.

Simply for viewing purposes, there's also **Seal Rock National Conservation Area,** where the watery mammals can be spied bobbing in the surf among the folds of a protective cove at the north end of town.

Bunking Down

We put in for the evening at the **Shelter Cove Beachcomber Inn** (412 Machi Road, 707/986-7551, $). It's a small place—just six individual units—that's comfortable and functional. Rooms include a kitchen, TV, and enough beds to sleep 3–6 people. If you're arriving late, the proprietress may (as she did for us) leave a note on the office door, informing you which unit in which to rest your weary head. She collected the tariff the next morning. A nice touch, we thought.

The **Shelter Cove Bed and Breakfast** (148 Dolphin Drive, 707/986-7161, $$) has two first-floor suites with ocean views and hot tubs, two small upstairs rooms with balconies, and a large, though viewless, downstairs room. Upon request (a bow to Shelter Cove's isolation), the owners can arrange for home-cooked meals to be delivered to your room. Another lodging alternative is **Shelter Cove Marina and Campground** (492 Machi Road, 707/986-7474, $). RVers venture out here to land's end to deep-sea fish, dive for abalone, and enjoy the solitude.

Coastal Cuisine

The on-premises deli at the **Shelter Cove Deli and Campground** (492 Machi Road, 707/986-7474, $) serves the best fish 'n' chips we've ever had. Lest this sound like hype, let us assure you we were skeptical. "Are the fish 'n' chips any good?" we queried without conviction while peering hungrily at the sandwiches (particularly the hearty Surfer's Sub) in the deli case. "Are you kidding?" the matron behind the counter responded. "We caught it fresh this morning." Indeed, the generic term "fish 'n' chips" just can't do justice to the basket of fried black snapper that had been pulled from the ocean hours earlier. They'll ask if you want tartar or cocktail sauce with it, but a splash of lemon or malt vinegar will do just fine.

For More Information

Shelter Cove Information Bureau, 412 Machi Road, Shelter Cove, CA 95589, 707/986-7069, website: www.sheltercoveca.com

Humboldt County

King Range National Conservation Area

The King Range National Conservation Area is a massive tract of public land administered by the federal Bureau of Land Management (BLM). It occupies 52,000 acres in southwest Humboldt County, extending for 35 miles between Whale Gulch and Mattole River, and up to six miles inland from the Pacific Ocean. Indeed, there is little in this corner of the county that isn't federal land—just the town of Shelter Cove and some scattered holdings in the mountains.

Black Sands Beach (see Shelter Cove) is a lengthy strand of coarse, pitch-black volcanic sand that runs without interruption from Shelter Cove to the Mattole River, a sandy, 24-mile traipse. This primeval North Coast beach is backed by the jagged peaks of the relatively youthful King Range. The jump in elevation from sea level to 4,086 feet—the height of King Peak, the highest point on any shoreline in the continental United States—occurs in less than three miles.

Backpacking is possible both along inland mountain trails and the beach. For a thrilling

Riding with the King: A Drive through the King Range National Conservation Area

Since we survived the first seven miles of Usal Road with only our rental car the worse for wear (see "Let's Get Lost" in the Mendocino chapter), we decided to brave the gravel road from Shelter Cove north through the King Range. Though the road surface was easier to navigate than the rutted mess on Usal Road, the drive was in some ways even more treacherous.

The rainy season had just ended, but rivulets were still subject to appearing across the gravel and dirt surface. In fact, we had to ford six separate streams en route along the aptly named Wilder Ridge Road. In places, the entire undercarriage of our car was under water and our curses filled the otherwise perfectly still air. At some of these crossings, we'd have to stop and size up the situation: Do we try to rumble over the big dry rocks on the left and maybe dent the car beyond repair, or should we opt for the flatter, wetter course on the right and possibly plunge over the side to our deaths?

The BLM map by which we were navigating included a couple of notes in tiny script about "RVs and trailers not advised for this section." The writing on all of the roadside signs—some of which would have been desperately needed without a map—had been obscured by bullet holes, presumably the work of inebriated hunters (though hunting is illegal here) or other backwoods maniacs. The map's misleadingly straight line from Shelter Cove to Honeydew in no way tipped us off to the countless double-backs and zigzags that sent gravel and rocks and dust flying and tumbling in our wake. All in all, it was a white-knuckle experience and a royal pain in the chassis. But, ah, the views!

Map of Northern California—Page 463

Humboldt County

experience, hike the Lost Coast Trail north from Shelter Cove for exactly five miles, then pick up Buck Creek Trail, which runs for 2.5 miles in a zigzagging northeast direction before approaching the 3,290-foot summit of Saddle Mountain. Back at sea level, you'll pass offshore rocks inhabited by sea lions, seals, and marine birds. Other sights include the remains of shipwrecks and the abandoned **Punta Gorda Lighthouse.**

Camping is permitted anywhere on the beach. **Mattole River Beach** (see Petrolia) is the site of a primitive campground. Away from the beach, BLM maintains four campgrounds in the King Range: **Wailaki** (nine campsites) and **Nadelos** (six), which lie east of Shelter Cove near the Humboldt-Mendocino County line, and **Tolkan** (nine) and **Horse Mountain** (nine), in the southern third of the park, about 1.5 miles inland.

May–October are the best months to come, as the torrential rains of winter tend to wash out roads and dampen spirits. Some parts of the King Range get deluged with 200 inches a year of precipitation. Be mindful of encroaching tides while walking the beach. High tides can strand unwary hikers in coves, and sleeper waves—individual waves of extraordinary size that appear out of nowhere—can wash the unsuspecting out to sea. Carry and consult tide tables, available at local stores, and never turn your back on the ocean.

For More Information

Arcata Resource Area, Bureau of Land Management, 1125 16th Street, Room 219, Arcata, CA 95521, 707/825-2300, website: www.ca.blm.gov/arcata/king_range.html

Honeydew and Petrolia

They've paved the state road that leads to Honeydew! This is big news in Humboldt County. You can now make the incomparable drive from Shelter Cove to Honeydew and on to Petrolia, and finally land in beautiful, Victorian Ferndale. This is one of the great scenic drives in America (75 total miles), passing forests, farmland, mountains, meadows, and beaches. Honeydew (population 500) and Petrolia (population 400) are small towns—dots on the map, really—out in the middle of nowhere. Mailboxes are few and far between. The road is narrow and uneven but drivable—almost all of it is paved.

To get to Honeydew from the highway, take U.S. 101 to the Mattole Road turnoff and then drive west 21 miles to Honeydew. Petrolia lies 15 miles northwest of Honeydew along the same road. At Petrolia, you either pick up Lighthouse Road, which runs out to Mattole River Beach, or proceed up to Ferndale via Mattole and Wildcat Roads.

To get to Honeydew from Shelter Cove—

which is what we were attempting to do as we worked our way up the coast—takes a bit more effort. From Shelter Cove Road, the turnoff to Honeydew is about halfway between Shelter Cove and Garberville. The opening up of the area to more than four-wheel-drive vehicles was, as we understand it, the culmination of an effort to drive some particularly tenacious pot growers out of the area. Cultivators of "Humboldt Gold," they were as entrenched in these mountains as rattlesnakes and would go to extremes to keep the outside world at bay. Stories are told of shots fired at unfamiliar vehicles and booby traps strung across hiking trails to scare off narks and even innocent folks enjoying the outdoors.

A 1990 government campaign called Operation Greensweep employed helicopters, infrared photography, and armed troops to identify hemp fields in the mountainous wilderness and flush the growers from their lairs. In 1999, the federal Bureau of Land Management heard testimony from eyewitnesses concerning the

Map of Humboldt County—Page 560

Humboldt County

environmental and human harm caused by the marijuana eradication program. One woman "described how her daughter, Blossom, was upset after encountering a gun-toting Operation Greensweep guardsman in camouflage gear, who refused to identify himself," according to the Drug Reform Coalition Network.

You can still see the remnants of the pot growers' anti-authoritarian ilk here and there, gazing at passersby with reddened eyes from the front porches of listing houses. More unsettling is the sight of abandoned cars pocked by bullet holes by the side of the road. It's probably not a good idea to look too hard or linger too long around here.

In the way of services, there's a general store at Honeydew and a handful of places to fill up with gas, food, and supplies in Petrolia. And whatever you do, please drive slowly for the sake of the quail who scoot across the roads around here. We very nearly wiped out a brood of the sweet critters after rounding a curve near Petrolia.

Beaches

Much of the drive described herein circumnavigates the interior of southern Humboldt County. But for a six-mile stretch along Mattole Road, just north of Petrolia in the direction of Ferndale, it follows the coast at sea level. And what a stretch of coast it is: gigantic sea stacks; extruded basalt formations on the inland side; a sea that's colored foamgreen close to shore and metallic blue farther out; dark-sand beaches that beg to be walked. This is cattle country, and the beasts cross the road at their leisure, looking quizzically at passing cars.

The ocean views, particularly as the road makes a perpendicular turn and dizzying northward ascent toward Ferndale, are the equal of any on the coast. Beach access can allegedly be gained along Mattole Road via gated paths that cross private land. Park beside the road whenever you can find a bit of

dusty shoulder. We, however, never found the reputed pullouts.

There's one prominent, accessible beach worth mentioning. At a fork in the road, Petrolia lies to the right along Mattole Road, while Lighthouse Road follows the Mattole River till it meets the ocean. At the mouth of the river is an enormous wild wonder of a beach. The locals have fenced in the parking lot with gigantic driftwood trunks, silvery and skeletal, to discourage ATVs (all-terrain vehicles) from tearing up the beach. A colorful mural of a beach scene includes this legend: "We love our beach. Please respect it. Beaches are important to everyone." Attached is a notation that **Mattole River Beach** (a.k.a. Lighthouse Road Beach) has been "adopted by the Mattole Union 3rd, 4th, and 5th grades."

The beach is a wide delta formed by the gravelly river. On one late-summer day, we watched the wind blowing up fearsome whitecaps. No sane person would go near this churning surf—that is, if anyone could even get to it in the teeth of a nonstop wind that seems to blow unimpeded all the way from China. The lone beach bum (besides us) was fighting to keep a kite under control. Chalk up one more wild and beautiful beach for the seemingly endless coast of Northern California.

Mattole River Beach falls within the King Range National Conservation Area. You are welcome to toss up a tent or park a camper in the open area out here, though facilities are primitive: chemical toilets, picnic tables, and fire rings. You must bring your own water. A so-called "iron ranger" has been installed, and you're asked to pay $5 a night on the honor system. Depending on your perspective, the Lost Coast Trail, which extends south to Shelter Cove and Sinkyone Wilderness State Park, either begins or ends here.

To the north of here, along the shoulder of Mattole Road, some dirt turnouts have been provided. Most folks content themselves with an appreciative glance at the scenery from a

Map of Northern California—Page 463

parked car, but at one turnout a worn path leads out to the wind-whipped beach for those made of sterner stuff. One rock formation at the center of this coastal tableau resembles an ocean liner, and a similar series of suggestive, Rorschach test–like sea stacks lend a ghostly appearance to this extension of the Lost Coast. The accessible shoreline ends at Cape Mendocino, where a gumdrop-shaped outcropping slams the door on any further ventures northward all the way up the coast to Ferndale's Centerville Beach. A quick snapshot of the beach is about all you'll want to take here, although the benign madness of surfers was once again proven to us, as we saw two intrepid wave-riders toting boards across the headland toward the sea just south of Cape Mendocino.

Bunking Down

In Petrolia the **Lost Inn** (Mattole Road, 707/629-3394, $$) makes a great getaway for those who crave privacy well off the beaten path. The inn features a three-room suite that includes a glassed-in porch and private garden where guests can sit among the flowers and marvel at the splendid isolation of it all. The Lost Inn is one block from Petrolia's General Store and seven miles from Mattole River Beach.

You can also camp in the sand at **Mattole River Beach.** The price is right (free, unless you want to make a $5 donation), though you must bring your own water or treat the nonpotable water from the campground spigot.

Coastal Cuisine

Duck into the **Hideaway Bar and Grill** in Petrolia (Mattole Road, 707/629-3330, $) for a burger, taco, and/or brew. It's at Lindley Bridge, on the banks of the sparkling Mattole River.

For More Information

Garberville-Redway Area Chamber of Commerce, 773 Redwood Drive, P.O. Box 445, Garberville, CA 95542, 707/923-2613 or 800/923-2613, website: www.garberville.org

Ferndale

Hollywood descended upon Ferndale in the summer of '94 to film the medical thriller *Outbreak,* a frankly terrible film about a virus that runs amok through a rural population. There hadn't been such excitement in Ferndale since the 1992 earthquake. The streets of this tiny village (population 1,300) of restored Victorian homes and step-back-in-time stores were jammed with trailers and people. Celebrity sightings were reported all over Ferndale and nearby Eureka, where crew and cast—including Dustin Hoffman, Carrie Fisher, and Rene Russo—were staying. The townsfolk were eating it up and so were we, just coincidentally in town to research the first edition of this book.

Normally, life in Ferndale moves at a snail's pace. All visitors should be prepared to reset their timepieces back. Be advised, though, that you don't lose an hour; you lose a century. You think we're exaggerating? Imagine this: Virtually every structure in Ferndale looks much like it did 100 years ago. They are cleaned, polished, and freshly painted right down to their elaborately carved woodwork. The whole town has been designated a state historical landmark (Number 883, to be precise). In the beginning the primary source of income in these parts was dairy farming, and the local creameries were so productive that Ferndale became known nationally as "Cream City." The wealth that flowed from the cows' udders built the ornate town-and-country residences, nicknamed "Butterfat Palaces," in the 1880s.

Today, Ferndale—which touts itself as "the prettiest painted place in the America Northwest"—has got everything for a weekend getaway. You can bed down at the Gingerbread Mansion, among the most celebrated bed-and-

Humboldt County

Litter Longevity

Even along unpaved, isolated, and deserted Usal Road, we saw the occasional can or bottle decorating the landscape. Six miles deep into Sinkyone Wilderness State Park, we saw cigarette butts littering the trails. Putting aside the absurd contradiction of sucking on a cancer stick while hiking in the wilderness, the tossing of a cigarette here is more than just a litter problem. It could start a forest fire, especially during the dry and lately drought-ridden summer seasons. Apparently, we weren't the only ones who noticed this disconnection from reality. At the camp registration kiosk for the park, the following chart was posted for all to contemplate.

How Long Does Litter Last?
- cigarette butt: 1–5 years
- wool socks: 1–5 years
- plastic-coated paper: 5 years
- plastic bag: 10–20 years
- nylon fabric: 30–40 years
- leather: up to 50 years
- tin can: 50 years
- aluminum can and tab: 80–100 years
- plastic six-pack holder: 100 years
- glass bottle: 1 million years
- plastic bottle: indefinitely

Humboldt County

breakfast inns along the North Coast, and walk a mere block downtown to dine or stroll from shop to shop. Ferndale is packed with antique stores, art galleries, old-fashioned candy emporiums—just the sort of shopping district you'd expect to find in a town swathed in a Victorian mantle. It also has a quaint little museum, run by the local historical society, where you can learn all about the area via exhibits that run the gamut from earthquake seismometers to a reconstructed barbershop.

On the earthquake front, there was a whole lotta shakin' goin' on in Ferndale and environs on April 25 and 26, 1992. Between 11:06 A.M. on April 25 and 4:18 A.M. on April 26—a span of only 17 hours—three separate earthquakes rocked Cape Mendocino. The first (and largest)

measured 7.1 on the Richter scale and had its epicenter five miles southeast of Petrolia. The second and third, which came during the night, measured 6.6 and 6.7, respectively, and were centered off the coast. Geologists rank them among the most powerful quakes ever to shake California, with an acceleration force measured at 2.25 G. For comparison's sake the Loma Prieta earthquake that hit San Francisco and Santa Cruz in 1989 had a peak acceleration force of only 0.646 G and an equivalent Richter scale reading of 7.1. No wonder buildings were toppled and fires broke out in the villages of Scotia and Rio Dell.

If you look closely there's an object lesson in what will eventually happen to beachfront real estate on a young, geologically active coastline

Map of Northern California—Page 463

(i.e., California). The road leading up to the empty naval facility near Centerville Beach offers a pullout and a magnificent overlook. Study the abandoned roadway, much of which has eroded and crumbled into the ocean. Look at the retreating cliffs. Imagine your beach house perched precariously on the edge. As one of our coastal geology professors used to say, "If you can see the ocean, it can see you, too."

Beaches

Centerville Beach County Park, five miles west of Ferndale via Centerville Road, is a sizable swath of sand bordered by farmers' fields. The expansive beach is covered with driftwood and deep, soft, dirty-brown sand. We watched thunderous breakers roll ashore on an otherwise calm July afternoon. It is a great beach for barefoot strolling up the coast, beyond where the eye can see in the salty mist kicked up by the roiling surf. Upon returning, we noticed that the only footprints in the sand were ours.

It is desolate out here. En route to the beach one day we braked in front of an old, abandoned farmhouse—not to wax nostalgic about the cobwebs on the porch swing, but because a flock of geese chose that moment to waddle across the road.

Bunking Down

The Gingerbread Mansion (400 Berding Street, 707/786-4000, $$$) is the most striking example of Ferndale's elegantly playful Victorian style. Its eye-popping brown and orange exterior, fanciful wedding-cake moldings, and storybook gardens have made it the best known and most photographed of Ferndale's structures. Owner Ken Forbert is an antiques hound, dating back to his college days in San Francisco. Many rooms have authentic claw-foot bathtubs on raised platforms; one has an old Victorian fainting couch perched beside it. The ambience is gracious yet relaxed. Tea is served at four in the afternoon. Breakfast is a real undertaking, served at long, decorated tables at the appointed hour with a hot egg dish complementing an array of fruit, pastries, homemade granola, coffee, and tea.

Another B&B that lets visitors steep themselves in the Victorian flavor of the town is **Shaw House Bed-and-Breakfast Inn** (703 Main Street, 707/786-9958, $$). Built by the founder of Ferndale in 1854, the inn is the oldest house in Ferndale; it was modeled after Hawthorne's House of the Seven Gables. The six attractive guest rooms have private baths, and the gardens, gazebo, and fish pond lend visual interest to the one-acre property. In the morning, guests greet the day with an elaborate breakfast spread.

Coastal Cuisine

Curley's Grill (460 Main Street, 707/786-9696, $$$) now occupies the site of an old favorite restaurant of ours, Bibo and Bear. Curley's fresh California bistro cuisine has made it a hot spot to eat in town, with a menu that ranges from burgers, steaks, and fries to grilled polenta and shrimp Dijon.

Another choice for fine dining in Ferndale is the **Victorian Inn** (400 Ocean Avenue, 707/786-4949, $$), which offers an extensive and varied menu—from salmon to steak, scampi to spanokopita—in an attractive building (circa 1893) that also does business as a lodging house.

For More Information

Ferndale Chamber of Commerce, P.O. Box 325, Ferndale, CA 95536, 707/786-4477, website: www.victorianferndale.org/chamber

Humboldt County

Map of Humboldt County—Page 560

Loleta

Loleta is a sweet morsel of a town that will make you say "cheese." It occupies the center of Humboldt's dairy-farming country, between Ferndale and Eureka. Situated in a valley on the fertile delta of the Eel River, it provides an idyllic setting where cows graze and time passes slowly.

The little hamlet's calling card is the **Loleta Cheese Factory** (252 Loleta Drive, 707/733-5470). You can tour the facility and sample its wares: award-winning Monterey Jack and cheddar cheese, among others. A gift shop sells local wines and aged cheeses. Beyond the draw of its cheese factory, Loleta is notable mainly for the access that it and the neighboring pin-sized communities of Fernbridge and Beatrice provide to the ocean, bay, and river.

Beaches

Anglers will go batty over the rock jetty at **South Spit and Jetty** (reached from Beatrice via Table Bluff Road), the bayfront beaches of **Crab County Park** (off Cannibal Island Road, four miles west of Loleta), and the delta of the Eel River (accessible from a maze of roads out of Ferndale). For a panoramic stroll, take the Hookton Road exit from U.S. 101 to **Table Bluff County Park.** Parking is free and hiking trails along the bluff afford nice views of the ocean, which batters the South Spit of Humboldt Bay, and the Eel River Delta. The Eel River, federally classified as a Wild and Scenic River, is California's third largest, carrying 10 percent of the state's annual runoff.

For More Information

Loleta Chamber of Commerce, P.O. Box 327, Loleta, CA 95551, 707/733-5666

Eureka

Eureka is a Greek word meaning "I've found it!" It's also the state motto of California, one that derives from Gold Rush days. In years past, were your opinion of the city based solely on the first impressions made as you entered from the south on U.S. 101 North, you'd have assumed the meaning of Eureka had changed to "I've lost it!"

While the retail corridor at the south of Eureka hasn't gotten much more palatable over the past five years—the town, in fact, added another depressing mall to the mix of billboards, guide wires, smoke and fumes from paper mills, and motel after motel offering cheap rooms—the city itself has lately worked hard to restore itself to what it once was: the pearl of the North Coast. In the process, it has begun to work its way into our hearts. We, in fact, have come to love the place. Had Ulysses S. Grant been stationed here today,

he'd have never written, as he did in 1854 while at nearby Fort Humboldt, "You do not know how forsaken I feel here!"

The visual madness at the south end of the city is an unfair gauge of Eureka's true charm. Perhaps it just seems more jarring after a drive through the Avenue of the Giants, the 31-mile stretch of U.S. 101 that passes through the majestic Humboldt Redwoods State Park. Keep pressing north on U.S. 101 and until you round a bend in the road (Broadway) that reveals the other Eureka—the city that inspires a joyful "I've found it!"

For a quick and helpful orientation, stop by the **Eureka Chamber of Commerce** (2112 Broadway) or the **Humboldt County Convention and Visitors Bureau** (1034 Second Street). You will be directed to historic **Old Town,** the bayfront area that extends from C to M Streets between 2nd and 3rd Streets. Old Town has been diligently restored and is surprising in its size and vitality. Armed with a *Eureka Visitor Map,* you'll willingly leave the wheels behind and re-enter the age of foot traffic. And you get a sense of how Eureka must have been in the 1850s, when it was the most important port city for the thousand miles between San Francisco and Seattle.

A principal site on this walking tour is the **Carson Mansion** (2nd and M Streets), which the Smithsonian calls "one of the most exuberant houses built in 19th-century America." Part Victorian and part fairy-tale castle, the house was constructed for William Carson, the lumber baron whose redwood empire opened up the North Coast. The mansion was erected during lulls in the logging season by the bossman's own lumberjacks and was completed in 1885, after three years of labor. The crazy-quilt array of gables, columns, and ornamental woodwork somehow manages to blend together. Look and admire, but don't enter. It's a private men's club called the Ingomar now.

Across the street from Carson's former digs is the **Pink Lady** (202 M Street), another example of money's-no-object Victoriana. The gaudiness of this Pepto Bismol–pink Queen Anne–style structure may give some viewers visual indigestion. Once a wedding gift from Carson to his son, the Pink Lady is now an art gallery featuring the work of local artists.

Many other structures in and around Old Town have historic value, representing the period when Eureka was the "King of the Pacific Northwoods" and the "Heart of the Redwood Empire." The town got its start in 1850 from the fallout of the Gold Rush. The diggings were slim along the Trinity and Klamath Rivers, but the felling of redwoods provided plenty of work for able-bodied men. Within four years of its founding, Eureka was home to seven sawmills, and 140 schooners were kept busy carting away lumber from Humboldt Bay to points south. In their leisure time the lumbermen came to Eureka, a brawling, boozing, and brothel-filled respite from the monotony of sawing logs.

In some ways Eureka is still King of the Northwoods. Despite the imperilment of the lumber trade all over the northwest, logging has endured in Eureka, though overforesting and cheap lumber from Canada have taken a toll. If you listen to the lumberjacks, Redwood National Park has denied job-hungry timbermen the largest chunk of what trees remain in Humboldt County. It's this area, in fact, that provoked former president George Bush's specious remark about "being neck deep in spotted owls."

In recent years the city has turned elsewhere to fill the economic void. Arty types have begun flocking here in growing numbers. Their reasons are varied, but most have grown tired of where they came from and simply want to escape.

Eureka, like Mendocino, is set in a gorgeous and non-distracting environment where artists feel free to actualize their visions. Galleries, bookshops, and cultural events thrive in this city, thanks in part to the enlightened presence of Humboldt State University in nearby Arcata. Much of the original art and crafts on display in the local galleries are quite striking and unique to this locale, as transplanted, university-trained artists blaze new trails in landscape painting while local folk artists continue to produce their remarkable handmade wares.

The best site for the latter is the **Wooden Garden** (317 2nd Street), a menagerie of politically charged pieces created by local sculptor Romano Gabriel over a 30-year span. Other examples reflect the spirit of the location even more closely. The history of the region's ecology and its indigenous peoples can be explored at the **Clarke Memorial Museum** (240 E Street, 707/443-1947), which has a world-class collection of Native American basketry and artifacts. These items are housed—safely, one can be certain—in the historic Bank of Eureka Building (circa 1912).

Humboldt County

The newly restored Carnegie Library Building is now home to the **Humboldt Cultural Center** and the **Morris Graves Museum of Art** (636 F Street, 707/442-0278), a world-class venue for painting, sculpture and performance arts. Also, a rich benefactor has pumped money into restoring the waterfront, which forms the northern edge of Old Town Eureka. The result brilliantly pulls the city's scenic harbor into the fabric of this up-and-coming destination spot.

The annual two-day **Blues by the Bay** festival each July has begun to put Eureka on the itinerary of any self-respecting blues giant, as well as any blues fan in the country. Eureka gives us anything but the blues. As we entered the city, the local FM station was playing a long piece of sitar music—with nary a commercial break or explanation—and as we left two days later, the same station was playing recent releases from a plethora of local area bands, including one all-woman band that sounded better than the Go-Go's. Wish we'd caught their name.

Located 284 miles north of San Francisco, Eureka is nestled on the shores of Humboldt Bay—the second largest enclosed bay in California and the center of the region's recreational and commercial fishing. Thirty million pounds of fish are harvested annually in these waters. The fleet docks at the **Woodley Island Marina,** just across the Samoa Bridge from Old Town on Highway 255. Eureka's water-related history can be explored at the **Humboldt Bay Maritime Museum** (1410 2nd Street, 707/444-9440), a collection of nautical artifacts housed in a replica of the oldest house in town (circa 1854).

Beaches

The easiest way to explore the Humboldt Bay area is by boat. The best tour is the **Humboldt Bay Harbor Cruise,** operated by the Maritime Museum. A narrated, 75-minute tour aboard the M/V *Madaket* (the oldest

operating passenger ship on the West Coast, circa 1910) leaves regularly from the foot of C Street, off Waterfront Drive (707/444-9440). **Woodley Island Marina** is a great viewing station for harbor seals and egrets, and the adjoining promenade has a number of interpretive placards.

Nearby Samoa Island is the site of **Samoa Dunes Recreation Area,** a broad expanse of dune fields and beaches at the southern tip of the North Spit, which angles down from Arcata. It is one of the projecting fingers that enfold and protect Humboldt Bay. A 300-acre parcel of Samoa Dunes falls to the Bureau of Land Management, while Humboldt County maintains a boat launch and a bayside campground.

A stiff breeze often blows off the water, which sculpts the dunes into sloping, windswept shapes. The berm is sufficiently hard-packed to allow for jogging or easy beach hiking. Kite flying, collecting driftwood, and bird-watching are popular activities out here. At low tide the remains of the USS *Milwaukee,* a destroyer beached in a 1917 rescue attempt, can be seen offshore.

The south spit of Humboldt Bay, a four-mile-long strand that ends at a jetty built in 1891, is maintained by the county. Access for cars is limited and a key is needed from the Humboldt County Parks Department (707/445-7651) to enter the locked gate. Bluffs to the south can be explored by foot at Table Bluff County Park (see Loleta writeup). A local organization called **Friends of the Dunes** (P.O. Box 186, Arcata, CA 95518, 707/444-1397) publishes an excellent brochure that exhaustively covers the beaches and dunes along Humboldt Bay.

Shore Things

• **Bike/skate rentals:** Sport & Cycle, 1621 Broadway, Eureka, 707/444-9274
• **Boat cruise:** Humboldt Bay Harbor Cruise, Humboldt Bay Maritime Museum, Eureka, 707/444-9440

Map of Northern California—Page 463

Humboldt County

- **Ecotourism:** Arcata Marsh and Wildlife Sanctuary, I Street, Arcata; Humboldt Redwoods State Park, U.S. 101 and Highway 254, Weott, 707/946-2264
- **Lighthouse:** Trinidad Head Lighthouse, Trinidad
- **Marinas:** Bob's Boat Basin, Trinidad Harbor, Trinidad, 707/677-3625; Humboldt Bay Harbor Recreations, 601 Startare Drive, Eureka, 707/443-0801
- **Pier:** F Street Dock, foot of F Street, Eureka
- **Rainy day attraction:** Humboldt Bay Maritime Museum,1410 2nd Street, Eureka, 707/444-9440
- **Shopping/browsing:** Old Town (from C to M Streets and 1st to 3rd Streets), Eureka
- **Sportfishing:** King Salmon Charters, 1875 Buhne Drive #67, Eureka, 707/442-3474; Trinidad Bay Charters, Trinidad Harbor, Trinidad, 707/677-3625
- **Surf shop:** Humboldt Surf Company, 817 H Street, Arcata, 707/822-2680
- **Vacation rentals:** Trinidad Vacation Rentals, Trinidad, 707/677-0246

Bunking Down

The celebrated **Hotel Carter** (301 L Street, 707/444-8062, $$$) actually embraces three properties: the 23-room hotel itself; **Carter House,** the awesome Victorian home that sits catty-corner to the hotel at 1033 3rd Street; and **Bell House,** the 1890 cottage adjacent to Carter House (call 707/445-1390 for information on these two last properties). Hotel Carter is a yellow neo-Victorian with large rooms and modern amenities. Some come equipped with whirlpool baths. A nightly wine-and-cheese hour is provided for guests. The classy comforts and warm glow of Hotel Carter are unrivaled on the North Coast.

Carter House, the most traditional of the three buildings, is where the stars of *Outbreak* chose to stay while it was being filmed down the road in Ferndale. Interestingly, it was built in 1982 as an exact replica of a beloved Victo-

rian inn, the Murphy House in San Francisco, which was razed to make room for a high-rise. It's an attractive place where the wooden beams and walls in the living area receive and reflect sunlight in a way that is positively magical. As in the adjacent Bell House, wine and cheese is set out every evening, followed by tea and cookies a few hours later. Both homes have large living areas and a common kitchen for the use of guests, along with TVs and VCRs in each room. Our room at Bell House broke with the code of Victoriana and was decorated in a contemporary mode.

The **Eureka Inn** (518 Seventh Street, 707/442-6441, $$) is a bird of a different feather. The sprawling, Tudor revival–style inn opened in 1922 as a symbol of Eureka's booming fortunes. It has since been designated a National Historic Place. The anomalous English architecture, set in an otherwise nondescript neighborhood, only adds to its imperturbable grace. The 150-room building carries its age well; constant efforts are made to keep the building in good repair and equipped with modern amenities like a heated pool and hot tubs. The rooms themselves are spacious and comfortable enough for British royalty.

A setting of elegant Victoriana can be had at **An Elegant Victorian Mansion** (1406 C Street, 707/444-3144, $$). Yep, that's really the name of this restored, four-room mansion, a National Historical Landmark built in 1888. Not the least of the inn's charms are the enthusiasm and dedication to detail of its owners.

Coastal Cuisine

Restaurant 301, the on-premises dining room at Hotel Carter (301 L Street, 707/444-8062, $$$), is among the most distinctive on the North Coast. The list of appetizers and entrées is kept to a manageable one page, but the items constantly change, reflecting chef Robert Szolnoki's indomitable imagination. Those ingredients not grown at Hotel Carter's own garden three blocks from here are

Humboldt County

acquired from local farms, and the seafood on the menu is as fresh and local as it can be. For appetizers, we've had Hogg Island oysters topped with a swipe of Smokey Jim's BBQ sauce or served in a deliciously floral Caledonia butter. Equally heavenly appetizers include a fava bean with prosciutto dish and Dungeness crab and bay shrimp fritters with fresh herbs and lemon beurre blanc. Even the seven-grain cakes were out of this world!

The roster of entrées is big on creatively sauced grilled items, such as rock cod with hazelnuts, lemon, and dill; filet mignon glazed with burgundy and served with peppered cheese sauce; and coffee-rolled grilled salmon on polenta. All were superb. The wine list is extensive, and Hotel Carter's owner, Mark Carter, genially hovers about the premises. At the drop of a fork, he'll gladly share his encyclopedic knowledge of California wines. A house pastry chef creates a short list of nightly temptations, as well.

Wherever you dine in Eureka, whether it be in a historic old building or a seafood grill by the water, your surroundings are as vital to the experience as the food itself. Both seem tailored to remind you of the town's hard-working past. Take the **Samoa Cookhouse** (Samoa Road, 707/442-1659, $$). Across the bridge on Samoa Island, it is the last surviving cookhouse in the West. Food is served camp style, and though the words "all you can eat" are never mentioned in the literature, you won't leave here hungry. There's no menu. One set price. No à la carte. No wine list.

It starts innocently enough, with salad you toss yourself in a large bowl. This is quickly followed by soup, ladled from a black kettle.

Top Universities for Beach Lovers In California

From south to north, here are some of California's finest colleges—as well as great places to cultivate a tan and improve your surfing skills.

- **University of California at San Diego** (UCSD)—This institute of higher learning perches atop cliffs overlooking Black's Beach in La Jolla.
- **Long Beach State University**—The student bodies hang out in Belmont Shore (a.k.a. "Horny Corners") and party like it's 1999.
- **Pepperdine**—We include this college overlooking Malibu, despite the fact it hired right-wing "special prosecutor" Ken Starr, who did his biased best to topple President Bill Clinton.
- **University of California at Santa Barbara** (UCSB)—Actually, it's in Goleta, which is Santa Barbara's lesser neighbor, but the surf spots are hard to beat.
- **California Polytechnic State University**—Study engineering in the near-perfect community of San Luis Obispo. All the Poly dollies and dudes hang out at Avila Beach.
- **University of California at Santa Cruz** (UCSC)—This is about as "alternative" a state university as you'll ever find, and it's a short drive to the Santa Cruz Boardwalk and Steamer Lane.
- **Humboldt State University**—Bring plenty of flannel to this school in Arcata.

Humboldt County

Map of Northern California—Page 463

Gigantic hunks of bread appear next. Then come bowls full of peas, kidney beans, and mashed potatoes and gravy, trailed closely by fried chicken, sliced ham, or whatever else the main courses happen to be. You'll even be offered seconds. Order iced tea, and an entire pitcher materializes. Warm apple pie baked in a big metal pan was placed on the table at the end of the meal. Actually, this is how (and where) the lumberjacks were fed in Eureka's timber heyday. Prices for lunch and dinner are low, given the quantities of food served. As one whiskered and suspenders-clad old-timer proclaimed, "If you leave here hungry, it's yer own dang fault."

Lazio's Seafood (327 Second Street, 707/447-9717, $$) is another local institution. It's been serving seafood since 1944, though the family's roots in the fishing industry go back as far as 1889, when Lorenzo Lazio started a wholesale fish operation in San Francisco. Lazio's is filled with seafaring paraphernalia. Take your time poring over the extensive menu, which includes crab legs Lazio and salmon cannelloni. Don't be afraid to order plain old broiled seafood, as it's fresh enough not to need doctoring with sauces. The broiled salmon is especially fine. Pacific oysters on the half shell are plump and gamy, quite different from their East Coast cousins. They are something of an acquired taste—and we quickly acquired a taste for them.

A newer arrival on the seafood scene is the **Sea Grill** (316 E Street, 707/443-7187, $$), an Old Town eatery that posts a lengthy list of catches and ways you can have it prepared (sautéed, grilled, charbroiled, broiled, poached, or deep-fried). The fact that sturgeon and Dungeness crab were both on the menu caused our fins to perk up.

Cafe Marina (Woodley Island Marina, 707/443-2233, $$) serves decent food along with the best view in town: across the bay onto Old Town Eureka from Woodley Island. A listing of available seafood items is handed customers along with a regular menu. You can't go wrong with grilled or broiled petrale sole or ling cod.

If you're fried on seafood, head to another Old Town favorite, **Smokey Jim's BBQ** (307 Second Street, 707/443-4554, $). It's a classy hole-in-the-wall with its own character and an absurdly good barbecue sauce (mild or spicy) that's slathered on ribs, chicken, and beef brisket. Prices are fair and portions ample.

Finally, how could we ignore a bakery and café called **Ramone's?** In tribute to the departed singer (RIP, Joey) and bassist (RIP, Dee Dee) of one of our favorite punk-rock bands, we suggest that you start your morning at one of three Ramone's restaurants in Eureka (or the ones in Arcata and McKinleyville). The Ramone's in Old Town Eureka is at 209 E Street (707/445-2923). Another good morning port o' call is **Humboldt Bay Coffee Company** (211 F Street, 707/444-3969), also in Old Town.

Night Moves

Six Rivers Brewing Company (325 2nd Street, 707/268-3893) is as nice a brewhouse as we've seen in California. Having successfully offered North Coast locals a great new haven up in McKinleyville, the company has opened a venue in Old Town Eureka by restoring an old building, leaving the brick walls intact and exposed, adding a second floor (with pool tables) and comfortable padded wooden booths, not to mention the nice touch of an overstuffed sofa and lounge chairs off to the side. This feels like a real pub, not a faux nostalgic one. There's live music with no cover charge, and locals have responded to the gesture, if the crowd we saw on a Thursday night was any indication.

This was a rainbow coalition of North Coast types: longhairs in wool caps, lithe young women displaying bare midriffs, clean-cut jocks, grungy guys wearing backwards baseball caps (we heard one of these no-accounts affecting

Humboldt County

a gangsta rapper's delightful vocabulary, older Earth Mother types, and purebred yuppies. The pool table was doing land office business upstairs while a band played an inventive set of folk rock, tossing an obscure early Pink Floyd song into the mix. All in all, it was as healthy a night scene as we'd yet witnessed north of San Francisco.

Civilized imbibers should head to the smoke-free **Lost Coast Brewery** (617 4th Street, 707/445-4480), which specializes in microbrewed beers (especially English-style ales) plus the usual complement of sports-bar amenities: pool tables, dart boards, big-screen TVs, lunch and dinner items, and happy hour specials.

Club West (535 5th Street, 707/444-2582) is a North Coast approximation of a Southern California dance club. What you get is an eclectic mix of folks who've come to shake their booties. You'll see lonesome cowboys in Western wear, working girls dragging on cigarettes from barside perches, college kids who have wandered over from Arcata, well-groomed yuppies, and straights and gays (depending on the night) out to make the scene.

For More Information

Eureka Chamber of Commerce, 2112 Broadway (U.S. 101), Eureka, CA 95501, 707/442-3738 or 800/356-6381, website: www.eureka chamber.com; Humboldt County Convention and Visitors Bureau, 1034 Second Street, Eureka, CA 95501, 707/443-5097 or 800/346-3482, website: www.redwoodvisitor.org

Arcata

Humboldt Bay merges with Arcata Bay at its northern end, where the waters balloon inland. It would be an ideal setting for a small town. But Arcata is not all that small a town, and its fairly nondescript outlying development runs in a rough L shape around the top of the bay and up U.S. 101. Like Eureka, Arcata got its start as a depot and base (then called Union) for the Trinity Mountain gold fields. But it quickly became a booming lumber town, and evidence of its past lines the bayshore—warehouses, factories, slag heaps, smokestacks, and the like. Close by these industrial eyesores are the boxlike homes of the employees. On a gray day it resembles a scene from George Orwell's *The Road to Wigan Pier,* his impassioned study of working-class life.

Arcata, however, is not just another burned-out mill town. Rounding the bend away from the factories, visitors discover an attractive city in transition and an impressive oasis of higher learning. Humboldt State University, one of the oldest branches of the state system, is here. The school's academic emphases include forestry management, environmental science, and marine biology. When these programs bloomed on university campuses nationwide, Humboldt State was an early and much-imitated model. The school is also oriented toward the arts, as one glance at the bohemian student body will make clear (lots of black clothing and plaid flannel). All in all, the students have found that nexus between nature and creativity.

The forest is never far from their hearts. The school teams are called the Lumberjacks, and the dorms are the Jolly Giant Commons. The campus itself is on a large, grassy knoll east of the highway. Its 140 acres afford ample space for 7,500 students to roam, and the public is invited to enjoy the excellent natural-history museum. Just don't come here for a business degree.

The university pumps new blood and innovative ideas into the town. One is the **Arcata Community Forest,** a 600-acre preserve of second-growth redwoods that is the only city-owned forest in the state. Ten miles of trails crisscross the forest for the benefit of hikers, bicyclists, and horseback riders. Another great idea is the **Arcata Marsh and Wildlife Sanctuary,** a 75-acre haven created from a former landfill and industrial site (at the foot of I Street). It's been transformed into one of the state's best bird-watching areas, with a hiking trail running through the many different ecosystems (bay, marsh, pond, foothills, streams). This restored marsh is fertilized by the Arcata sewer system—an ingenious way of recycling waste into something green and clean.

The town of Arcata (population 16,200) also beams with pride over its local artists, whose work is showcased on the premises of many businesses and along a self-guided Mural Tour. Arcata's most intriguing cultural event is the **Kinetic Sculpture Race,** which takes place each year in late May. It's difficult to explain the rules or point of this extravaganza, a 35-mile cross-country race that passes over hills and dunes from Arcata to Ferndale. To qualify, all vehicles must be navigable pieces of sculpture. Beyond that, whether it's pumped, paddled, or pushed doesn't matter. The Kinetic Sculpture Race, which celebrated its 33rd anniversary in 2002, is emblematic of the town's spirit.

June–October an open-air farmers market takes over Arcata Plaza on Saturdays. The fresh local produce, flowers, and baked goods are enough to make you want to sink your own roots in lovely Arcata.

Beaches

The beach nearest Arcata is as hard to fathom as a piece of kinetic sculpture. The 90-acre **Mad River Beach County Park** is aptly named—at least the "mad" part, because this is an area where sand and sea, rivers, creeks, and lagoons come together with an almost primitive fury. The roads are a little out of whack, making the whole experience seem rather mad in the British sense as well. To get to Mad River, take the Janes Road exit from U.S. 101, then turn right on Heindon Road, left on Iverson Road, and right on Mad River Road. It sounds simple on paper, but all are farm-hugging back-roads. Try to follow the signs, because the thrill of the chase is half the fun.

At the end of Mad River Road, the beach overwhelms lucky visitors with its size and beauty, extending in both directions as far as the eye can see. The undertow here is treacherous, but the fishing is good. Three different types are available in this unusual mix of habitats: salmon and steelhead fishing in the river, surf casting for perch, and net fishing at night. A boat launch and an equestrian staging area are also provided. We watched gaggles of anglers standing around driftwood fires while their unattended poles stood upright in the sand. We also saw some very wet animal companions merrily sloshing around the creeks that one must cross on this wide beach to get to the ocean. Oh, yes: Memorize the route you took out here or you may make an unintentionally lengthy side trip through the dairy lands west of Arcata, as we did.

The **Lanphere-Christensen Dunes Preserve** is just south of here, at the west end of Lanphere Road. It's part of the Mad River Slough. No fee is charged for access to either.

Bunking Down

The **Hotel Arcata** (708 Ninth Street, 707/826-0217, $$) is a good, centrally located place to drop your suitcase. Unveiled as the town plaza's showplace in 1915, Hotel Arcata was one of the finest inns of its size on the coast. But when a financial downturn hit town in the 1980s, the hotel fell into disrepair. The likable three-story structure has been restored to its original grandeur and has been augmented with hot tubs, a sauna, and a swimming pool.

At the north end of town, on Valley West Boulevard (off U.S. 101), a strip of motels and restaurants bear dependable, franchised names. The **North Coast Inn** (4975 Valley West Boulevard, 707/822-4861, $$), an erstwhile Travelodge, has comfortable, well-maintained rooms and a health-club area whose centerpiece is a large heated indoor pool.

Humboldt County

Coastal Cuisine

Try **Abruzzi** (780 7th Street, 707/826-2345, $$$) for Italian and **Folie Douce** (1551 G Street, 707/822-1042, $$) for creative fine dining. The nice thing about both places is that they have less expensive options to high-end dinner entrées, if you're looking to economize. Folie Douce, for instance, serves wonderful, wood-fired pizzas. Abruzzi, in the basement of a block-sized building known as Jacoby's Storehouse, specializes in fresh fish and pasta dishes inspired by the cuisine of Abruzzi in central Italy. Should you want something simpler—appetizers, sandwiches, or grilled fare—the **Plaza Grill** (780 7th Street, 707/826-0860) is upstairs, on the third floor.

Night Moves

The heart of Arcata is its plaza, a square formed by G, H, 9th, and 10th Streets. Here you'll find the restored Arcata Hotel; restaurants, cafés, and coffeehouses; record stores; a village green where Arcatans sit cross-legged and contemplate the passing scene; and an assortment of bars and nightclubs. There's live music at **The Alibi** (744 9th Street, 707/822-3731), **Plaza Grill** (780 7th Street, 707/826-0860), and **Jambalaya** (915 H Street, 707/822-4766). A few more options: **Humboldt Brewery** (856 10th Street, 707/822-2739) for local microbrews and **Sacred Grounds Organic Coffee Roasters** (686 F Street, 707/822-0690) for righteous java fixes.

Several years back we caught a local band at the Alibi called Barking Dogma. The line-up included four women (two of whom played sax), a drummer, and a guitarist who looked like Frank Zappa and composed all the music. The crowd danced vigorously to their witty, complex compositions, hanging tough even through frequent meter changes. The band was having as good a time as the crowd. Nights like these up and down the California coast have helped restore our faith in rock and roll as an organic means of communication that thrives in small clubs, away from big bucks and disfiguring hype.

On weekends students have been known to engage in a colorful ritual known as "ring around the plaza." It involves downing a beer, a margarita, or some other libation in each of the bars that surround the plaza. Of course the raised drinking age has greatly reduced the number of legal contestants. In summer, nightlife is notably less frenetic. Still, there's the delightful **Minor Theatre** (1013 H Street, 707/822-5177), a lavishly restored 1915 structure with three screens showing current, classic, and art films. And even those weary fans who have rightfully grown sick of professional baseball should check out the **Humboldt Crabs,** a semipro team that plays its home games at **Arcata Ballpark** (9th and F Streets, 707/826-2333). The Crabs play 43 home games a year, and tickets cost $4 for adults and $1 for kids. Go Crabs!

For More Information

Arcata Chamber of Commerce, 1062 G Street, Arcata, CA 95521, 707/822-3619, website: www.arcata.com/chamber

Humboldt County

McKinleyville

Once called Minorsville—after Isaac Minor, owner of the local general store—the town of McKinleyville took its present name in 1901, after President McKinley's assassination. This is a town that fancies itself a holdover from the Wild West. It's got a tradition in which horses have the right of way, and the annual **Pony Express Days Celebration** (first weekend in June) is the biggest event in town.

Behind the macho image, however, McKinleyville offers little to the traveler, lying well off the highway and consisting mainly of drab dwellings and a homely town center. Don't be fooled by the "Tourist Information" signs pointing toward McKinleyville from U.S. 101. It's a bum steer to a little A-frame info stand way the heck off the highway.

Beaches

West of McKinleyville is the first spot above San Francisco where U.S. 101 runs directly beside the ocean. Two beach access points sit right off the highway. **Clam Beach County Park** is a sizable swath of sand with 100 RV and tent sites for camping, and picnicking areas at its north and south ends. Getting to the beach is no easy matter. A short path over tall dunes reveals a broad expanse of mostly flat, grassy dune fields extending to the ocean. A small creek must be forded, and logs have been laid across it for that purpose, serving as wooden stepping-stones.

Solitary figures press against the wind as they make their way across the desolate landscape. Though you can comb for driftwood and dig for razor clams, the real appeal of Clam Beach is for the equestrian set. Hitching posts have been provided at various spots along Hammond Trail, which runs along the

coast from Mad River north to Murray Road. Dogs, too, enjoy charging around the stark expanse, such as the pair of St. Bernards we saw emerging from the creek completely soaked and sandy but happy. Clam Beach takes its name from the once plentiful Pacific razor clams found here. It is now a nesting area for the threatened Western snow plover.

Little River State Beach is more of the same: 112 undeveloped acres of dunes, driftwood, and broad, hard-packed sand. At the north end Little River trickles through the sand, creating a boundary between this beach and Trinidad's Moonstone Beach.

Bunking Down

A **Holiday Inn Express** (3107 Concord Drive, 707/840-9305, $$) has opened in McKinleyville in recent years. It is within a mile of Clam Beach County Park.

Coastal Cuisine

Typical of McKinleyville's Old West mind-set is **Niveen's** (2145 Central Avenue, 707/839-3417, $), a large, friendly restaurant with an American flag proudly waving out front. The menu is as large as the room: burgers, steaks, Mexican, Italian, little of this, little of that.

On the edge of town, **Six Rivers Brewery** (1300 Central Avenue, 707/839-1400, $$) is a homemade burger and homebrewed beer kind of place. Surprisingly lively, it provides the most palatable nightlife in these rural parts.

For More Information

McKinleyville Chamber of Commerce, 2196 Central Avenue, P.O. Box 2144, McKinleyville, CA 95519, 707/839-2491, website: www.mckinleyville.net

Humboldt County

Trinidad

Summer in Trinidad is like spring in many other places. The air is crisp and clean, the sky is a sweet baby blue, the wind blows like March's proverbial lion, and the ground is covered with a colorful carpet of wildflowers. It never really heats up to a summer swelter here in Trinidad. Actually, the phrase "here in Trinidad" is misleading. Trinidad is not so much a single place you can point to as a jumble of hills, headlands, coves, and coastline. As a result, there is a tremendous diversity of beaches and headlands to explore, making Trinidad an ideal place to bring both hiking shoes and beach blankets.

Briefly, Trinidad and its natural harbor were first sighted by the Portuguese explorer Sebastian Cermeno in 1595. He did not come close to land for fear of the pointed rocks. The Tsurai (pronounced CHER-eye) who inhabited the region were probably just as glad he kept his distance. On June 11, 1775, they weren't so lucky: the Spanish explorer Don Bruno de Hezeta anchored in the bay, came ashore, and promptly declared that all his eye beheld belonged to Spain. It was Trinity Sunday when he staked his claim, and thus the area was called La Santisima Trinidad.

During Gold Rush days, the town boomed, reaching a population of 3,000 and serving as the seat of what was then Klamath County. Trinidad flourished again as a mill town in the 1870s, and once more in the 1920s as a whaling port. When each of these industries bit the dust, so did the town. The current population is around 500.

Today, Trinidad is home to artists and other lovers of solitude. With its abundant natural beauty—stunning and variegated beaches, coves, headlands, and offshore rock formations—it is not hard to understand Trinidad's appeal to those with creative temperaments (such as Captain Beefheart, who is rumored to live up here) and folks with a yen for the outdoors.

Beaches

The beaches begin north of the Little River Bridge, along Scenic Drive. Starting at the river, **Moonstone Beach** sits below what was formerly Merryman's restaurant and is now out of business. (Rock trivia fans, take note: Captain Beefheart and the Magic Band's worst album, *Unconditionally Guaranteed,* was rehearsed up here at Merryman's, and the reclusive Beefheart—one of rock's true geniuses—has lived in the Trinidad area for many years.) Word has it that the restaurant will reopen under a new name and management. One thing's for sure: It looks out on one of the most picture-perfect locations on the California coast. A small spur, Moonstone Beach Road, runs down to the beach, where there is parking in a gravel lot.

Moonstone Beach falls under county jurisdiction, and it's plenty popular with an eclectic mix of beachgoers. On the large, sandy delta over which the Little River meanders before meeting the sea, it's studded with sea stacks. Families come to picnic on the beach behind the rocks, which afford protection from the wind. Kids swim and play in the shallow creek waters, which are safer and warmer than the ocean. Surfers hungrily eye the waves that form off the point. We even saw a bicyclist pedaling on the hard-packed sand.

Moving north on Scenic Drive, we found a real hidden treasure at **Houda Point.** Thanks to the Humboldt North Coast Land Trust, public access has been provided here, though there is only limited roadside parking. Still, if you negotiate the somewhat shaky series of steps down to the water, you will find a visual paradise. Just offshore is Camel Rock, a humped outcrop popular with surfers, because the waves break nicely out far from shore. It is also home to the largest breeding colony of Leach's petrel in California, as well as a nesting area for gulls, cormorants, and black oyster catchers.

Moving up Scenic Drive, two more named

beaches lie along the five-mile stretch between Moonstone and the in-town shopping area. **Luffenholtz Beach, Baker Beach,** and **Indian Beach** are fan-shaped beaches that lie between eroding headlands. The best beaches are often the hardest to reach, and Indian Beach is a case in point. We never did figure out how to get down to it, but it makes quite a photo op from the road high above it. A giant, gumdrop-shaped sea stack parts incoming waves before they reach the beach. The walls of crashing water wrap around the rock from opposite sides and then meet at a perpendicular angle on the beach. We've never seen anything quite like it.

Luffenholtz Beach has a marked parking area on Scenic Drive, and a sign points to a beach-access trail. Unfortunately, the original path has been declared off-limits. A new trail has been carved into the bluffs a few hundred yards up the road—which means walking along one-lane, cliff-hugging Scenic Drive, with its hidden curves and vehicles that come hurrying around them. Be careful.

In town a natural harbor has been formed by **Trinidad Head,** a formidable seamount that has withstood the sea's pounding over countless millennia. An inviting calm-water beach occupies one edge of the harbor. There's a large parking lot, outlined by discarded boat tires, an old seafood restaurant of long-standing (the 1953-vintage Seascape), a bait shop, and a boat launch. The trailhead for paths leading up and around Trinidad Head lies at the far end of the lot.

Trails encircle the monolith, with dead-end spurs shooting off to vista points along the way. Stay on the main trail—named the Tsurai Trail—proceeding in a counterclockwise direction, and you can hike the whole thing in under an hour. Plenty of benches have been strategically placed along the way to allow walkers to savor the views. Even when the area is shrouded in fog, you can sit and listen to sea lions barking like foghorns in the distance. At the top of Trinidad Head, a concrete cross commemorates the explorers who landed here. There's also a giant Coast Guard satellite dish. At this point, the trip back down is an easy jaunt along a gravel road that meets smooth asphalt near the bottom.

On the ocean-facing side at the base of Trinidad Head is a beach on which we sat and ate an impromptu lunch of smoked salmon and albacore. We purchased it just up the road at **Katy's Smokehouse** (740 Edwards Street, 707/677-0151), which enjoys an unsurpassed reputation for smoked fish.

A trail leads from here to **Trinidad State Beach.** Alternatively, you can park closer, at the lot just above the beach, and hike down a well-graded trail. In either case no entrance fee is charged. Butting up against Trinidad Head at the south end and roaming north for a mile, it's a fairly lengthy strand for this tortuous part of the coast, especially when low tide allows beachgoers to walk from one cove beach to another. Watch the sea carefully, though, and keep track of tides. An unwary walker can easily get trapped in a cove or sea cave with no route out, as the tide can turn quickly. This is no joke. We walked to a couple of coves on wet sand. Five minutes later, the same cove beaches were a half foot under quickly rising water.

One of the most popular beaches in the area is **College Cove.** It's been known for years as a clothing-optional beach, especially at the south end. If nudity is indeed an option, no one was exercising it on the warm summer weekend that we ventured out. It's a gorgeous cove that's plenty wide at low tide, reachable from a gravel parking lot via trails leading into the woods. The trail at the south end leads to **College Cove South** (about 50 percent nude) and the trail at the north end leads to **College Cove North** (largely clothed). The trail to the latter descends 130 steps to the beach. The south trail eventually connects with Trinidad State Beach, passing through fern canyons and

Humboldt County

Sitka spruce forests that are cool and dark even at the height of summer.

At College Cove one can sunbathe, play volleyball, or just walk and wade along the water. Total immersion, however, is only for the young and hardy or the old and foolhardy, in our estimation. The tidal exchange here is fairly extreme, as a comparison between low tide and the uppermost watermark in the sand attests. Waves buffet the cliffs at their bases during stormy winter months. Let the hiker beware.

The prize gem of among all the jewels in the Trinidad vicinity is **Agate Beach,** in **Patrick's Point State Park.** The 640-acre park is worth exploring in its entirety, but Agate Beach is a treasure that ranks among California's most memorable. Like most Trinidad-area beaches, the cliffs drop so steeply to the beach that you must descend a long bank of stairs to get to it. The view from the top is worth savoring for a few minutes before taking the stairs down. Observe how the beach extends past the point where the cliffs give out, forming a sand bar that encloses Big Lagoon, just to the north. The lagoon is within **Big Lagoon County Park,** which offers a boat launch, picnic tables, and a tent/RV campground.

The hike from Agate Point to the end of Big Lagoon Spit is about three miles—and worth every footstep. Along this stretch of coastline, one can hunt for bits of agate and jade. The chances of striking it rich fall somewhere between slim and none, but the scenery is ample compensation. The cliffs overlooking Agate Beach are not completely vertical, which allows vegetation to grow on them. At the bottom a little creek empties onto the beach and seeps into the sand before reaching the ocean. In summer, breakers wash ashore, and the beach remains plenty wide throughout the tidal cycle.

Numerous sea stacks sit offshore from Patrick's Point, affording habitat to sea lions, whose barking fills the air day and night. Rock outcroppings found in the park's interior belong to an earlier generation of sea stacks, now high and dry due to geologic uplift. The largest stacks are Ceremonial Rock (287 feet) and Lookout Rock (250 feet). Trails lead to Mussel Rock, a stack that's barely connected to the mainland. Visitors can climb all over this unusual formation. Looking out to sea, observe the line of wave-formed ooze that follows the undulating shoreline.

Camping at Patrick's Point is some of the finest in any of California's coastal parks. The 124 sites are large and private, shaded and protected by spruce, fir, red alder, and hemlock. A popular addition to the park is Sumeg, a re-created Yurok village that offers some virtual reality to go along with its artifacts. A visit to Patrick's Point State Park should be mandatory if you venture up this way.

Bunking Down

Any number of rustic lodges and attractive bed-and-breakfasts line Patrick's Point Drive along the five-mile stretch between Trinidad and Patrick's Point State Park. We have a favorite in both categories.

The **Lost Whale Bed & Breakfast Inn** (3452 Patrick's Point Drive, 707/677-3425, $$$), only a half mile from Patrick's Point, is one of the few B&Bs that encourages families to stay. The inn was constructed in 1988, and since the owners were starting from scratch, they were able to build in extra reinforcement and soundproofing. Warm woods and comfortable furniture fill the common area downstairs.

Rooms at the back of the house have balconies and windows that look out over the ocean—as marvelous a view as you could hope to enjoy. Moms and dads have a bed of their own, while kiddies can ascend a ladder to a loft fitted with mattresses. Lee Miller, an innkeeper-cum-musician who escaped Los Angeles for the tranquillity of the North Coast, has built a stairway leading several hundred feet down to the beach. (If you're lucky, one of the Millers' cats will escort you to the beach.)

Map of Northern California—Page 463

Wine and snacks are served in the afternoon, and a full breakfast is placed on the table promptly at 8:30 A.M.

A fine old cottage court can be found at **Bishop Pine Lodge** (1481 Patrick's Point Drive, 707/677-3314, $$), where rustic cabins are spread on shaded grounds. Each unit has a full kitchen and a TV. A card informs you that the management will store your game and fish in the deep freeze. Moreover, "well-behaved pets" are welcome. The Bishop Pine Lodge is a restful, out-of-the-way spot charging reasonable rates. If longevity is any indication, this is the place to stay, as the Bishop Pine Lodge has been in business since 1927.

Coastal Cuisine

The **Larrupin' Cafe** (1658 Patrick's Point Drive, 707/677-0230, $$$) is hard to miss, and once you've eaten here, you'll take pains to return. Painted a bold mustard yellow and trimmed in red, this former dwelling retained its homey feeling when it made the transition to gourmet restaurant. The menu is heavy on items grilled on the mesquite broiler (filet mignon, fish kabobs, pork ribs, etc.). A few dishes from the oven (chicken in phyllo pastry, spanakopita) are thrown in for good measure. The grilled garlic plate makes a terrific appetizer, and you also can't go wrong with barbecued oysters or mussels steamed in white wine and tomatoes. A favorite entrée is the hot 'n' spicy snapper: a sizable serving of Pacific red snapper coated in ground pepper and grilled to a turn. Portions are generous, but leave room for dessert; the chocolate pecan pie in hot buttered rum sauce is worth all the hiking you'll have to do the next morning to work it off. Larrupin' Cafe is open for dinner six nights a week (closed Monday) from Memorial Day to Labor Day, and Thursday–Sunday the rest of the year.

Fresh seafood can be found at **Seascape Restaurant** (Trinidad Harbor, 707/677-3762, $$), beside the town's pier. It bustles with tourists and anglers, serving three meals daily. It's been here for going on half a century, so they must be doing something right.

For lunch fixings, we headed to **Katy's Smokehouse** (740 Edwards Street, 707/677-0151, $$$), another Trinidad landmark, which has been selling popular smoked fish for over 60 years, such as king salmon, salmon jerky, albacore tuna, Alaskan halibut, Pacific cod, and even scallops. The prices are steep for a takeout place ($21.99 per pound), but we snagged enough for 10 bucks or so to sate our appetites, having an ad hoc picnic near the lighthouse above Trinidad's tranquil harbor.

For More Information

Greater Trinidad Chamber of Commerce, P.O. Box 356, Trinidad, CA 95570, 707/441-9827, website: www.trinidadcalifchamber.org

Humboldt Lagoons State Park: Dry Lagoon and Stone Lagoon

You ask, What is a lagoon? We answer, A lagoon is a body of water produced from the combined action of wind and water. Ocean currents carry sand parallel to the coastline, and winds mold it into barriers that separate shallow nearshore coastal waters from the deep blue sea. Behind the barrier lies a marshy, landlocked wetland—to wit, a lagoon.

Humboldt Lagoons State Park, 13 miles north of Trinidad, offers camping and fishing opportunities galore at its dual lagoons: Dry and Stone, by name. You might inquire about them at the visitor center at the main south entrance, though it's open only 10 A.M.–2 P.M. The south end includes the spit and a marsh

Map of Humboldt County—Page 560

known as **Dry Lagoon,** with four picnic tables and six walk-in tent sites.

The more intriguing section of the park is **Stone Lagoon,** a short distance north off U.S. 101. The road down to it is a bumpy rollercoaster ride that makes a precipitous final dip. Picnic tables are nestled in thickets, and the parking lot is an unimproved gravel field. A former primitive camp area of 20 sites has been eliminated. The camping that can be done at Stone Lagoon these days is at six environmental sites that can be reached by boat only. This is an archeological resource area, and visitors are urged not to dig for or cart off artifacts. No problem—there's plenty of good fishing to keep everyone occupied. Incidentally, various points along U.S. 101 through the area offer wonderful overlooks of the lagoon and the sandy, straight-edged bar that divides it from the sea.

Redwood National Park

Approaching Orick from the south, U.S. 101 descends a hill and rounds a turn, at which point you'll see an amazing site: a centipede-like line of RVs parked by the side of the road just inside **Redwood National Park.** The area is known as **Freshwater Lagoon,** after the pristine blue lagoon east of the highway. The ground rules are simple. You may park your RV on the ocean side of the highway, no fewer than 30 feet west of its paved edge. You can stay up to 15 consecutive nights, and as many as 30 total nights in a calendar year. After a 15-day run, you must vacate the site for at least 24 hours before returning. No fee is charged, though a donation is requested.

RV vagabonds come here in droves, attracted by the broad, sandy beach on one side of the highway and the lagoon and green hills on the other. Not to mention the people-watching opportunities. Pulling out the folding chairs and staring at passing traffic seems to be a popular pastime. A loyal fraternity of like-minded RVers makes merry all along the road's shoulder as far as the eye can see. Only in America.

A visitors center for Redwood National Park is just above Freshwater Lagoon, before U.S. 101 takes a swing inland. (It's been relocated because coastal erosion claimed the old road in places.) The center is a cubist-style building fashioned from weathered wood, with a walkway leading out to the impressively large **Redwood Creek Beach.** Tell the staff what you have in mind—a short or long hike, viewing elk herds or redwood groves, camping in the backcountry or parking the RV—and they'll set you up with maps and advice. A stop here is a must if you're coming up from the south. Those headed down from the north will want to stop at park headquarters in Crescent City, where you'll receive the same sort of orientation. We found the staff at both visitor centers to be helpful and knowledgeable.

For More Information

Redwood National Park, 1111 2nd Street, Crescent City, CA 95531, 707/464-6101, ext. 5064, website: www.nps.gov/redw

Map of Northern California—Page 463

Humboldt County

Orick

The town of Orick falls outside Redwood National Park, encompassing a string of gas stations, cheap motels, and roadside stands selling "Burl Slabs" and "Redwood Creations." These include huge rearing bears, steel-eyed eagles, and grizzled sea captains, which local artisans have carved using chain saws. One stand posts a sign inviting you to "Come See What We Saw."

Beaches

For the truly adventurous, a turnoff onto Hufford Road carries you out to **Orick Fishing Access,** at which point you reenter Redwood National Park. The road quickly morphs into a bumpy one-lane marathon of curves, hemmed in on both sides by barbed-wire fences to hold back grazing cattle. At the end of the road is a gravel parking lot that looks out upon Redwood Creek's winding egress into the ocean. Anglers cast for salmon and steelhead in the diked waters here. They don't call Orick "Fisherman's Paradise" for nothing.

Bunking Down

You may come see, but you probably won't stay in Orick unless you've got a wild hair to bunk down at the "world famous" **Palm Motel and Cafe** (21130 U.S. 101, 707/488-3381, $), a humble but vaguely appealing roadside complex—motel, pool, restaurant, lounge—that's got character, not to mention an eye-catching mural.

For More Information

Orick Chamber of Commerce, P.O. Box 234, Orick, CA 95555, 707/488-2885, website: www.orick.net

Prairie Creek Redwoods State Park

One of the most beautiful beaches on the North Coast (and therefore, anywhere), **Gold Bluffs Beach** lies inside the boundaries of **Prairie Creek Redwoods State Park,** which itself is surrounded by Redwood National Park. In other words it is a beach within a state park within a national park.

To get to Gold Bluffs Beach, take Davison Road, a spur off U.S. 101 three miles north of Orick that passes through a portion of Redwood National Park. It's a winding little passageway—narrow, unpaved, and hazardous—and trailers are prohibited. After four miles of bumping, bouncing, and shouting "Watch out for that van!" you're there. Park the car, get out, and draw in a deep breath.

Now exhale, relax, and look around. Steep sandstone walls rise behind the beach. Forested bluffs overlook the beach. The ocean's thrashing kicks up a mist that bathes the beach in ghostly, low-lying sheets of white. Waves break and roll slowly across the shore, pushing a line of sea foam ahead of them. The salt-and-pepper sand is flecked with gold specks that gleam brightly in the overwash.

The beach is a vast, desertlike expanse virtually devoid of humanity, unchoked by seaweed or litter. It extends farther than the eye can see in either direction. This is an ideal spot for kicking off shoes and walking along the ocean's edge, ankle deep in the bracing sea water. (An exhibit in the parking lot warns beachcombers to keep an eye out for sleeper waves, so be careful.) If you continue driving north along Gold Bluffs Beach, you'll reach Fern Canyon in four miles. There are good camping, hiking, beachcombing, and picnicking opportunities all along this stretch of coastal road. **Gold Bluffs Beach Campground** is a 25-siter at ocean's edge. A larger campground (Elk Prairie, 75 sites) is inland, near park headquarters. A note to hikers: The Coastal Trail, which runs for roughly 30 miles from Orick to Crescent City, reaches a point on the north side of Prairie Creek Redwoods State Park, just above Butler Creek, that is passable only at low tide.

The northernmost beach within Prairie Creek Redwoods State Park is one of the most secluded on the North Coast. **Carruthers Cove Beach** can be reached by walking north along the Coastal Trail from Fern Canyon. (A beautiful, .8-mile loop trail circles this flat-floored, steep-sided canyon, which itself is a spectacle not to be missed.) Alternatively, Carruthers Cove can be accessed from the north via the Carruthers Cove Trail, which leads to the beach from the cliff-hugging Coastal Drive. It's a narrow, isolated beach, and it's unlikely you'll see anybody there—all the more reason to seek it out.

The state park is also home to a herd of about 30 Roosevelt elk. They can be seen grazing by the side of the road, and signs warn when you're in an "Elk Crossing Area." Tune in 1610 AM to receive information about where best to spot the creatures and to learn the dos and don'ts of elk-watching. We learned, for in-stance, that these critters have chased people at speeds of up to 50 miles per hour and that "elks will not tolerate dogs."

We have one complaint about this otherwise splendid park. Davison Road really needs to be paved. It bears a heavy volume of traffic, which kicks up an unholy cloud of dust. This dust storm coats all vegetation in the vicinity. It also blinds drivers, chokes the throat, and irritates the eyes and lungs. If you are driving through here, travel no faster than the posted speed of 15 mph. You won't kick up as much dust, nor will you imperil your fellow drivers by forcing them over the edge when you meet on a curve, as very nearly happened to us.

To get to Prairie Creek Redwoods State Park from Orick, take U.S. 101 north for five miles, then fork left onto Drury Scenic Parkway. Prairie Creek Visitor Center is one mile north. To get to Gold Bluffs Beach from Orick, take U.S. 101 three miles north to Davison Road. Turn left and continue four miles to the beach.

For More Information
Prairie Creek Redwoods State Park, Orick, CA 95555, 707/464-6101 ext. 5301, www.parks.ca.gov

Humboldt County

Map of Northern California—Page 463

© ROBERT HOLMES/CALTOUR

Chapter 15
Del Norte County Beaches

Del Norte County

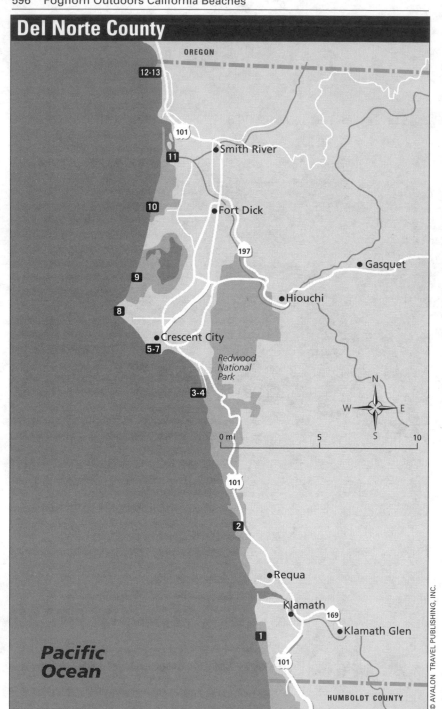

Del Norte County

Del Norte County Beaches

🔳 High Bluff Beach (Redwood National Park), page 601

Location: From Highway 1 at Klamath River, turn west onto Alder Camp Road. Follow it to Coastal Drive and turn right to High Bluff Picnic Area, where a trail leads to the beach.
Parking/fees: free parking lot
Hours: 24 hours
Facilities: picnic tables
Contact: Redwood National Park, 707/464-6101, ext. 5064

🔳 Wilson Creek Beach, page 604

Location: end of Wilson Creek Road, off U.S. 101 5.5 miles north of Klamath
Parking/fees: free parking lot. Camping fees are $13–16 per night, plus a $7.50 reservation fee.
Hours: sunrise–sunset
Facilities: restrooms and picnic tables
Contact: Del Norte Coast Redwoods State Park, 707/464-6101, ext. 5100

🔳 Enderts Beach (Redwood National Park), page 605

Location: end of Enderts Beach Road, off U.S. 101 south of Crescent City; trail leads to beach
Parking/fees: free parking lot; no fee for camping
Hours: 24 hours
Facilities: restrooms and picnic tables
Contact: Redwood National Park, 707/464-6101, ext. 5064

🔳 Crescent Beach (Redwood National Park), page 605

Location: along Enderts Beach Road, off U.S. 101 south of Crescent City
Parking/fees: free parking lot
Hours: 24 hours
Facilities: restrooms and picnic tables
Contact: Redwood National Park, 707/464-6101, ext. 5064

🔳 South Beach, page 608

Location: south of Anchor Way, off U.S. 101 at Crescent City Harbor
Parking/fees: free parking lot
Hours: 24 hours
Facilities: concession and restrooms (at Citizens Dock)
Contact: Crescent City Public Works, 707/464-9506

Del Norte County

Map of Del Norte County—Page 596

6 Beachfront Park, page 608

Location: along Howe Drive in Crescent City
Parking/fees: free street parking
Hours: 24 hours
Facilities: restrooms and picnic tables
Contact: Crescent City Public Works, 707/464-9506

7 Pebble Beach, page 608

Location: turnouts along Pebble Beach Drive in Crescent City
Parking/fees: free street and lot parking
Hours: 24 hours
Facilities: restrooms and picnic table
Contact: Del Norte County Parks and Beaches, 707/464-7237

8 Point St. George (a.k.a. Radio Beach), page 608

Location: From U.S. 101 in Crescent City, turn west on Washington Boulevard and follow it to Radio Road. Turn right and drive to Point St. George Public Access; trails lead to the beach.
Parking/fees: free parking lot
Hours: 24 hours
Facilities: none
Contact: Del Norte County Parks and Beaches, 707/464-7237

9 Tolowa Dunes State Park, page 610

Location: off Northcrest Drive, two miles north of Crescent City
Parking/fees: free parking lots. Camping is $6–7 for primitive sites, $8–12 for developed sites, and $16–18 for hookups.
Hours: sunrise–sunset
Facilities: restrooms and picnic tables
Contact: Redwood Coast Sector, North Coast Redwoods District, California State Parks, 707/464-6101, ext. 5112

10 Kellogg Beach Park, page 608

Location: Eight miles north of Crescent City on U.S. 101, turn west onto Kings Valley Road and follow "Coastal Access" signs to Kellogg Beach Park.
Parking/fees: free parking lot
Hours: sunrise–sunset
Facilities: none
Contact: Del Norte County Parks and Beaches, 707/464-7237

Del Norte County

Map of Northern California—Page 463

11 Smith River County Park, page 611

Location: south end of Smith River Road, in Smith River
Parking/fees: free parking lot
Hours: 24 hours
Facilities: none
Contact: Del Norte County Parks and Beaches, 707/464-7237

12 Clifford Kamph Memorial Park, page 611

Location: two miles south of the Oregon border, off U.S. 101
Parking/fees: free parking lot. Camping fee is $5 per night.
Hours: 24 hours
Facilities: restrooms and picnic tables
Contact: Del Norte County Parks and Beaches, 707/464-7237

13 Pelican State Beach, page 611

Location: a half mile south of the Oregon border off U.S. 101
Parking/fees: free roadside parking
Hours: sunrise–sunset
Facilities: none
Contact: Redwood Coast Sector, North Coast Redwoods District, California State Parks, 707/464-6101, ext. 5151

Del Norte County

Del Norte County

A s North Coast counties go, Del Norte owns a relatively small chunk of coastline. Compared to its neighbor, Humboldt County, it's but a sliver of sandy real estate. With less than 30,000 residents Del Norte isn't heavily populated, nor is it very prosperous, although the arrival of a maximum security prison north of Crescent City in 1989 has lightened welfare rolls in these parts. Yet while Del Norteans might not be rich in monetary terms, they've inherited a wealth of natural splendor.

From towering redwoods, preserved in the state and national parks that take up so much of the county, to pristine beaches that run for miles along its craggy coastline, Del Norte County offers no end of things to do in the outdoors. It's no secret that the county is an angler's paradise, boasting big rivers, such as the Klamath and the Smith, and numerous creeks that are ideal for landing steelhead and salmon.

The Del Norte coastline is less well known, since it is somewhat overshadowed by the redwoods, which rightly claim so much attention. But there are oceanside drives and trails that shouldn't be missed: the Coastal Trail, Enderts Beach Road, Requa Road, and Pebble Beach Drive. All follow the coastline, offering spectacular overlooks and beach access. The beaches themselves are alluring and underrated, from the indescribable isolation of High Bluff Beach (below Klamath) to the desolate dune fields of Kellogg Beach Park (above Crescent City).

Del Norte County

Map of Northern California—Page 463

High Bluff Beach

How about a little piece of Hawaii—in appearance, if not temperature—on the North Coast of California? Such is the look of magnificent **High Bluff Beach,** which lies below a cliff-hugging wonder known as Coastal Drive. To get to it from the south, disengage from U.S. 101 onto Drury Scenic Parkway and then turn onto Coastal Drive. From the north reach Coastal Drive via Alder Camp Road, a right turn off U.S. 101 just south of the Golden Bear Bridge over the Klamath River. Coastal Drive runs for eight miles, alternating paved and unpaved sections. The road is not in the best condition, but the scenery is so spectacular that it's worth the effort. This road used to be U.S. 101, before washouts and erosion necessitated its relocation east. Breathtaking glimpses of the ocean below are found around every turn.

High Bluff Picnic Area and the beach below are the overlooked gems of **Redwood National Park.** It is well worth pausing to ponder the vista from the picnic area, and hardier souls with a yen for wilderness beaches will want to hike down to the beach itself. To reach the beach visitors must walk a half mile along a trail that passes through cool forests before making a final descent in a series of switchbacks. A log ladder with a handrail of rope leads down to some planking that must be carefully negotiated. Then you're on muddy rocks, crawling and crab-walking until a final heave-ho lands you on the beach.

The sand is soft, light brown, and volcanic in origin. Waves overwash footprints at high tide, giving the area a virgin, unvisited appearance every 12 hours. On a sunny day this secluded cove resembles some sort of hidden tropical paradise, lacking only palm trees and balmy water to complete the scene. It's an illusion, but not such a far-fetched one if you're soaking up the sun's rays here on a warm, cloudless day (of which there are many June–September).

Klamath

One of the fundamental laws of physics, Heisenberg's Uncertainty Principle, applies to travel. A statement about the limited precision of scientific measurement, it says in essence, that one can specify either the position of a physical particle or its momentum at any given point in time, but not both. Therefore, because one of the variables is unknown, its value could be anything. With this equation the physicist is telling us that nothing is impossible. Or, put another way, anything is possible.

The same holds true on the road. For instance, while driving the desolate North Coast of California, one might think it unlikely to come upon a 49-foot-tall replica of Paul Bunyan standing in a clearing in the redwoods, with a 17-ton blue ox named Babe beside him. But it is no illusion. Paul and Babe are the gatekeepers for a tourist attraction called the Trees of Mystery (see sidebar).

Though hard to find, Klamath is a special place, one that a physicist, mapmaker, tourist, and travel writer could all find baffling. It's everywhere and nowhere, diffused over a seven-mile stretch on both sides of U.S. 101; along the inland valleys, canyons, and glens of the Klamath River; atop coastal bluffs and on the beaches below; squirreled away in the dark, spooky forests. There is no place that can be pointed to as the town center. It is difficult to say if the town is growing or dwindling, whether it is an actual town or just a scattering of RV parks, motels, restaurants, shops selling redwood gifts and knickknacks, salmon-jerky stands, and the Trees of Mystery. In the case of Klamath, both position and momentum are unclear.

Del Norte County

Trees of Mystery

Trees of Mystery celebrates the majesty of the coast redwoods and Sitka spruce that often grow to phantasmagoric shapes in this neck of the rain forest. Located 16 miles south of Crescent City and 360 miles north of San Francisco beside U.S. 101 in Klamath, Trees of Mystery is hard to miss, thanks to the gargantuan likenesses of Paul Bunyan and Babe the Blue Ox that hail passers-by. It's a worthwhile operation—educational, informative, and environmentally responsible, which is a winning combination in our book.

Before investigating the backcountry trails of Redwood National Park, take a crash course on the tall trees at Trees of Mystery, a private redwood forest offering the Trail of Mysterious Trees and the lately added Sky Trail. Redwoods are awesome to contemplate in any setting, but the stand at Trees of Mystery is especially impressive. Native Americans believed that the area was haunted with evil spirits, causing the trees to grow in crazy ways: twisting, turning, running horizontally, sprouting out of each other. It's really nothing more than good old biological Darwinism on overdrive, with the behemoth redwoods and spruces fighting for all the sunlight they can lay their limbs on, employing ingenious adaptive and reproductive techniques in the quiet struggle for survival. A highlight is the Cathedral Tree—nine redwoods growing in a perfect semicircle out of one root structure. As many as 40 weddings a year are held in the natural altar, and a crackly recording of Nelson Eddy crooning "Trees" plays continuously.

Trees of Mystery is run by a family of Klamath natives who exhibit a scholarly interest in and appreciation for Native American culture. Their on-site museum houses the largest private collection of Native American baskets, pots, ornaments, and apparel in the West. The main attraction is the Trail of Tall Tales, a half-mile walk that retells the myths and legends of Paul Bunyan and his brawny logging crew in wood. Kids, of course, will be in log heaven, but adults also will get something out of the 50 gigantic chain-saw sculptures and carvings, completed in a period of six months by a talented local artisan (now deceased) named Kenyon Kaiser. There is evidence of primitive genius in his work. His *Pooped Lumberman* is an American classic, kind of a Wild West version of Rodin's *The Thinker*.

The recently added Sky Trail takes you on a trip in a gondola to the tops of the trees. It climbs nearly 600 feet as it carries riders into the redwood canopy. This high-tech experience beats those "drive-through" redwood-tree attractions hands down. From its apex, you can see the ocean and an expanse of redwoods in all directions.

Trees of Mystery costs $15 for adults, $10 for seniors 60 and over, $8 for children 6–11, and nothing for kids 5 and under. It is open 8 A.M.–8 P.M. in the summer months and 9 A.M.–5 P.M. the rest of the year. For more information contact Trees of Mystery, 15500 U.S. 101 North, Klamath, CA 95548, 707/482-2251 or 800/638-3389, website: www.treesofmystery.net.

Del Norte County

Map of Northern California—Page 463

There's a good reason for this. The seemingly quiet, salmon-filled waters of the Klamath River conceal a terrible secret. Del Norte County is flood country, and a confluence of factors can turn the river into a raging monster. In 1964 the right—or terribly wrong—combination of factors occurred. A cold, wet winter blanketed the surrounding mountains with a dense pack of snow and ice. Then a fast-moving storm front passed through, inundating the area with rain. Finally, warm, high winds melted 10 feet of frozen precipitation in 24 hours, sending a 90-foot wall of water rushing down the canyon. With boulders and timber as battering rams, the flood wiped the unsuspecting town of Klamath off the map and out to sea.

Klamath was born in the mid-1800s during the fevered Gold Rush that swept California. It was a typical story of greed run amok in the wilderness. Mining camps sprang up along the Klamath River. The miners harassed and depleted the native Yurok population, while the riverbed became so silted with the detritus of their gold digging that the salmon stopped running. Klamath City was a thriving lumber port for most of this century, until the virgin forests were cleared. And then came the December 1964 flood, nature's angriest retort.

Before the flood Klamath was a highfalutin town, flush with prosperity when timber was king and the river was kind. In its heyday 20 bars lined its rough-and-ready Main Street. The flood left nothing standing but a small church and the massive golden bears that greeted visitors at the edge of town. The U.S. Army Corps of Engineers cleared an area to rebuild Klamath north of the river, at an elevation five feet above the river's highest recorded level. But the citizens of Klamath, most of them anyway, never returned. The new town site is now occupied only by a few mobile homes, and the original town is utterly abandoned. The foundations of old homes and businesses have been overgrown by weeds and reclaimed by nature. As for the bears, pairs of them guard each end of the rebuilt U.S. 101 bridge over the Klamath River.

If Klamath is more of a bear than a bull these days, it's still an inviting place for visitors with an appreciation of serene, unspoiled nature. Between fishing the Klamath River, camping and hiking in Redwood National Park, and combing isolated beaches, there is plenty to do in and around Klamath. The number-one item on the agenda is fishing. The Klamath is the second largest river in California and one of the best in the world for landing silver and chinook salmon, steelhead trout, and sturgeon, drawing anglers from far afield during their yearly runs. From the salmon's point of view, the angler-mania that the Klamath inspires is not all fair play. The mouth of the Klamath River used to be known as Suicide Row, because skiff-fishers would tie their boats together to form an impenetrable line against which the salmon, returning to spawn in their natal streams, didn't stand a chance. Dwindling salmon runs caused this practice to be outlawed.

An equally controversial method that yields similar results—catching so many fish that few survive to reproduce—has been the Native American practice of gill-netting. Anglers string monofilament nets across the river, trapping the returning salmon in a mesh that forces their gills together until they suffocate. Today, Yuroks alone employ gill-netting techniques for subsistence fishing in the Klamath, having won the right to do so in a controversial federal lawsuit in the mid-1980s.

Somehow, the fish continue to spawn in sufficient numbers to return year after year, though they are beleaguered by greedy outlaw anglers, Native American gill-netters, and various environmental affronts. Many anglers roll into Klamath with little more than a hook, line, and sinker. Three thousand RV and tent campsites are hidden around Klamath, and they fill up quickly when word gets out that the salmon and steelhead runs have begun in late fall and

Del Norte County

early winter. Nestled around bends in the river, out of sight of the highway, the RV parks metamorphose into busy fish camps overnight. Klamath celebrates the fishing frenzy with a Salmon Festival on the last Sunday in June.

There's more to be caught from the waters around Klamath than salmon, as any surf caster can tell you. Shore anglers pull in ling cod, black snapper, cabezon, flounder, perch, smelt, and sea trout. Dungeness crab and razor clams are also taken. Miles of sandy beaches and rocky shoreline beg to be fished or hiked. They can also be admired from vista points on the highway. In the words of a man who grew up here, "When the sun's shining, this is one of the most beautiful spots in the world." That is not just an idle boast from a prideful local; it is the honest truth, as anyone who's ever seen the sun set from the Klamath Overlook—a turnout off Requa Road, west of U.S. 101—can attest.

Beaches

The most accessible beach in the area is **Wilson Creek Beach,** which is one of those rare points where U.S. 101 flirts with the ocean's edge on the North Coast. Five miles north of Klamath, it is a wide, sandy beach in an area known as **False Klamath Cove.** Less than a mile away is **Lagoon Creek,** offering a freshwater lagoon, a blufftop trail, and picnic tables.

Bunking Down

Directly across the street from Trees of Mystery, where Paul Bunyan gives passersby the high-five, is a neatly kept motor court by the name of **Motel Trees** (15495 U.S. 101 South, 707/482-3152, $). Its 23 units are clean and comfortable, offering such diversions as cable TV and a tennis court on the grounds. You'll sleep like a Babe in this rustic setting, with the only possible disturbance being the odd, wandering bear who decides to leave his pawprints on the window.

The **Klamath Inn** (451 Requa Road, 707/482-1245, $), formerly the Requa Inn, is a 10-room, two-story white wonder that's up on a winding road leading to the gorgeous Klamath Overlook. The inn itself overlooks the Klamath River. An on-premises dining room continues the tradition of serving seafood and steaks.

In addition to cabin colonies dotting the roadsides, there are 1,200 campsites available within the town limits of Klamath alone. Many are along the Klamath River and primarily used by fishers, but there are also RV camps too numerous to list here. Check the Del Norte County website, www.delnorte.org, for a full listing.

Coastal Cuisine

At **Steelhead Lodge** (330 Terwer Riffle Road, 707/482-8145, $$), the cooks tend a barbecue pit, grilling salmon, Pacific snapper, ribs, and other charbroiled delights. The mountainous margaritas served here are guaranteed to chase away the gray skies, and the rustic lodge atmosphere will have you feeling fit and full of the outdoors. Several scenic miles up the Klamath River, with the river views becoming more photogenic en route, the Steelhead Lodge opens around the Fourth of July and shuts down for the winter.

The **Forest Cafe** (15499 U.S. 101 South, 707/482-5585, $), adjacent to Motel Trees and across from Trees of Mystery, has a rustic and woodsy exterior and mural-filled interior of nature scenes. The café tends toward surf and turf items for dinner and hearty breakfast platters. Hot blackberry cobbler is a specialty.

For More Information

Klamath Chamber of Commerce, P.O. Box 476, Klamath, CA 95548, 800/200-2335, website: www.klamathcc.org

Del Norte County

Crescent Beach and Enderts Beach

Surprises await the unsuspecting beach-lover in Redwood National Park. The northernmost section of the park, which touches Crescent City, includes two fine beaches in proximity. **Crescent Beach** is the more accessible of the two, with a beach-level parking lot right off Enderts Beach Road. Picnic tables are strewn about the flat, grassy areas behind the beachfront, which itself is wide and littered with drift logs and cobbles (especially along its landward edge).

For a real treat continue up Enderts Beach Road till it gives out in a parking lot that overlooks Crescent Beach. From here a 0.6-mile (one-way) trail leads to secluded **Enderts Beach,** the preferred location in terms of scenery, solitude, and beach quality. The beach and trail are part of the "Last Chance" section of the Coastal Trail. Informational signs along the path ask and answer tough questions (e.g., "Seal or Sea Lion?"). Approaching the beach, the trail gets steep, and you must slide down some volcanic rock slabs, on feet or fanny, before being deposited on the sand. It is a quarter-mile wilderness beach positioned between rock points. Little Nickel Creek runs into the ocean here, and shorebirds drink from it before returning to sentry duty along the water's edge. As many people come here with books in hand to read or meditate as show up in swimsuits to pursue the usual seaside preoccupations. It's truly a special place that's well worth the side trip.

Bunking Down

For those cycling along the coast, traveling on a shoestring budget, or simply out for new experiences, the **Redwood Hostel** (14480 U.S. 101, 707/482-8265, $) is in a turn-of-the-century ranch home, the DeMartin House. This 30-room hostel overlooks Wilson Creek from inside Redwood National Park. For $13 a night ($6.50 for children under 18 accompanied by a parent), you'll share dorm-style, bunk-bedded rooms with a host of fellow coastal wayfarers—foreign travelers, city escapees, and footloose free spirits. Reservations are accepted.

For More Information

Redwood National Park, 1111 Second Street, Crescent City, CA 95531, 707/464-6101, ext. 5064, website: www.nps.gov/redw

Del Norte Coast Redwoods State Park

Located 5.5 miles north of Klamath along U.S. 101, **Del Norte Coast Redwoods State Park** was one of the first parks in the California state system. It dates back to a deed of land made in 1926. Its 6,375 acres include eight miles of coastline. Mill Creek Campground is 2.5 miles east of U.S. 101. Closer to the ocean is **De Martin Beach Campground,** a primitive 10-siter overlooking Wilson Creek on the Coastal Trail. It's a half mile from the trailhead, on U.S. 101 at the north end of Wilson Creek Bridge.

At the bottom of a long hill lies **Wilson Creek Beach,** which extends for about a half a mile from the creek mouth south to an imposing point where a line of rocks runs out to sea with near-ruler straightness. Locals like to park here and fish or catch some rays. We even saw some people splashing around in the frigid water. Look, ma, no wetsuit! How do they do it?

For More Information

Del Norte Coast Redwoods State Park, c/o Redwoods Coast District, California State Parks, 1375 Elk Valley Road, Crescent City, CA 95531, 707/464-6101, ext. 5100, website: www.parks.ca.gov

Del Norte County

The Regal Redwoods

Redwood National Park is a 46-by-7-mile preserve for *Sequoia sempervirens* that was established in 1968 by an act of Congress and expanded 10 years later. Straddling both Humboldt and Del Norte Counties, it has been a boon to tourism and a blessing to the sacred trees, though chainsaw-crazed timber topplers in these economically beleaguered counties would not agree. Fully half of Del Norte County is state and federal parkland, forever off-limits to logging, and this has taken a painful toll on the ailing economy in this often overlooked corner of the state. Although the redwoods draw 600,000 visitors a year, the tourism numbers are still not enough to offset jobs lost in the timber industry. Meanwhile, Del Norte County gamely promotes itself as the "Redwood Gate to the Golden State."

October 2003 will marked the 35th anniversary of the park's founding. One of the loftiest stands in the park, the Lady Bird Johnson Grove, commemorates the first lady whose mission to "beautify America" is one of the better environmental memories of the 1960s. Unfortunately, a pathogen that had begun killing oak trees by the thousands in California in the late 1990s has also been found in the dying needles of coast redwoods. Known as "sudden oak death," and particularly lethal to tanoaks, the blight is caused by a deadly fungus. Scientists have not yet concluded whether the blight is killing redwoods or just injuring parts of the trees, but the very suggestion that California's redwoods are imperiled is cause for the highest levels of alarm.

Three state parks lie within the national park boundaries. **Prairie Creek Redwoods State Park** (in Humboldt County), **Jedediah Smith Redwoods State Park** (in Del Norte County), and **Del Norte Coast Redwoods State Park** (in Del Norte County) are fully developed, with campsites, hiking trails, information booths, ranger talks, and picnic tables. Considerable beach access is available along stretches of Redwood National Park, and at Prairie Creek Redwoods State Park and Del Norte Coast Redwoods State Park. Though it's a safe bet you won't want to dive into the frigid waters of the Pacific this far north, swimming in the creeks and rivers that run through these parks is a pleasantly bracing option in the summer months.

For more information contact Redwood National Park, 1111 Second Street, Crescent City, CA 95531, 707/464-6101, ext. 5064, website: www.nps.gov/redw. Park information centers are located in downtown Crescent City, at Second and K Streets; in Hiouchi, eight miles east of Crescent City, along Highway 199; and one mile south of Orick, along U.S. 101, in Humboldt County.

Del Norte County

Map of Northern California—Page 463

Crescent City

Road signs along a 10-mile stretch of U.S. 101 between Klamath and Crescent City read "Daylight Headlight Use." Yes, it's dark enough beneath the roadside canopy of redwoods to require the use of headlights in broad daylight. Crescent City—the last town of any size in California (population 4,600)—emerges on the other side of the tree-shrouded darkness.

This city has been defined by two events, one negative and one a mixed blessing. First, on March 28, 1964—only nine months before the calamitous Klamath flood—Crescent City was struck by a tidal wave that destroyed 29 city blocks. A violent Alaskan earthquake measuring 8.8 on the Richter scale sent a tidal surge down the Pacific coast, and it slapped Crescent City silly. It was a sad moment, almost the beginning of the end for a town that at one time bucked to become the capital of California. That was back in 1854, when the Gold Rush was burning up the north country.

The second defining event occurred in December 1989, when Pelican Bay State Prison opened its doors. This controversial prison houses California's most hardened felons—gang members, drug dealers, prison-guard assaulters, and cunning criminals in the Hannibal Lechter mold. The hardest of the hardened get thrown into the prison's Security Housing Unit, where they're confined to small, lightless cells for 22.5 hours each day. Already the prison has been the subject of a lawsuit charging excessive force and cruel and unusual punishment, though many would say this particular prison population requires such treatment in order to be controlled.

The prison was constructed eight miles north of Crescent City, and the arrival of 3,800 prison inmates has had a profound effect upon the town. The prison employs 1,200 and runs on an $86 million annual budget. Still more jobs have been created to serve all the new hires. Formerly, Del Norte County had the lowest per capita income among all of California's 58 counties. Thanks to Pelican Bay, Crescent City has rebounded from the sad-sack look it wore throughout the 1980s. Something good has come of all of the bad that's been exported up here. City officials are so pleased that they've approached the state about building another prison.

These days, Crescent City looks better than it did in the pre-prison era. There's a Kmart, Wal-Mart, and Safeway, and the shopping opportunities are the best between Eureka and the Oregon border (which really isn't saying all that much). Still, one wonders about the morality of Southern California, which imports what it needs (mainly water) from the north and exports what it doesn't want (mainly criminals) to the north. No wonder there is a movement gaining strength to split California into two, and possibly three, states.

Signs of this discontent could be read between the lines at the county fair, which comes to Crescent City the first week in August. It is not called the Del Norte County Fair, as it logically might be, but the Jefferson State Fair. The fair originates in Sacramento, which is in Jefferson County. A lot of folks in Northern California would like to see the founding of a 51st state: the state of Jefferson. Can you really blame them?

They may harbor some pretty scary felons at Pelican Bay, but the type of crime that goes on outside the prison walls, as reported in the local paper (the *Triplicate*), is the sort of small-town shenanigans that can bring a smile to your face. Amid reports of disorderly conduct (good ol' boys having too much to drink and revving their engines or throats), there are such entries as these:

• "A caller from the 600 block of Elk Valley Road reported someone had dumped a fish on her front lawn." (We would have fired up the grill and cooked dinner.)

Map of Del Norte County—Page 596

Del Norte County

- "A caller reported smelling something dead on Highway 199 at the second turnout on the left." (Dead skunk in the middle of the road?)
- "A caller reported her baby stolen. She soon remembered that she hired a babysitter." (Never mind.)
- "A caller reported loud music coming from the Seaview Motel." (We were not playing that Blink-182 tape too loud—honest!)

On our first pass through we noted that Crescent City was "more on the run than in the running." It pleases us to report that the town has made big strides during the 1990s. With so much scenic beauty and some of the best stream and surf fishing close at hand, it really deserves to be visited by more people. We certainly look forward to coming back.

Beaches

Crescent City has a bounty of beaches from the harbor north to Point St. George. Starting from the bottom, there's little **South Beach,** a triangle of sand formed by U.S. 101, the Crescent City Harbor, and the ocean. It's protected from the full force of the sea, and plenty of locals spread out on it.

Beachfront Park offers a serene, calmwater beach with a narrow strip of pebbly, dirty sand. People walk their dogs out here. The view across the harbor is pleasant. There's a pier and lighthouse at the end of B Street, where Howe Street gives out at Battery Point. Both Battery Point Vista and Brother Jonathan Point can be excellent spots for whale-watching December–February, when gray whales migrate from the Arctic to Baja, and March–May, when they return.

The beach makes a perpendicular turn, at which point the shoreline opens up into all sorts of fascinating shapes and formations. The **Pebble Beach Fishing Access** marks an interesting divide; the beach is rocky on one side, sandy on the other. Pebble Beach Drive runs along the ocean, giving out at Radio Road, which leads to Point St. George. From

Pebble Beach north to Point St. George is an amazing stretch of gorgeous, undulating shoreline. Sea lions can be heard barking on offshore rocks. Parking is available and plentiful along the beach, which was all but deserted when we visited on the prettiest summer Saturday of the year.

The land rises to a figurative crescendo at **Point St. George,** a public park that's jointly administered by the California State Wildlife Conservation Board and the Del Norte County Department of Parks and Recreation. The beach here is known to locals as **Radio Beach,** because of the old Coast Guard radio towers at the point. From the parking area a gravel road leads to the beach. You can also hike a dirt path out to the bluffs, savor the view, and then scramble down to the beach via gullied trails. It is a splendid, scenic coastline, especially on a clear, sunny day. The terraced bluffs are banded in shades of orange and light brown, and the coast runs in a broad arc for a good distance up to the next rocky point.

Kellogg Beach Park is the last in Crescent City's trove of beaches. It does not start off very encouragingly. Two signs point down the same road. One is a "coastal access" marker; the other shows the way to Pelican Bay State Prison. Fortunately, there is a lot of land out here and the routes to these destinations soon diverge. After a couple of turns, the houses thin out and give way to farmers' fields, which in turn give way to dune fields—broad, grassy expanses of them. The beach is wide and windswept, with driftwood scattered about the vast terrain. Winds blow the sand into rippled patterns, making footprints vanish quickly. We spied some RVs parked here, although camping is technically not allowed. It is not a well-developed park, just a mess of big, beautiful beach at the end of the road. Jeeps can continue riding along the beach after the road gives out. Fishing is about the most that can be done out here, unless you (like us) enjoy bundling up in sweatshirts and windbreakers

Del Norte County

and hiking along an empty beach that's buffeted by wind and waves.

Shore Things

• **Ecotourism:** Redwood National Park, Headquarters, 1111 Second Street, Crescent City, 707/464-6101; Ocean World, 304 U.S. 101 South, Crescent City, 707/464-4900
• **Lighthouse:** Battery Point Lighthouse, end of A Street, Crescent City, 707/464-3089
• **Marina:** Crescent City Harbor, 101 Citizens Dock Road, Crescent City, 707/464-6174
• **Rainy day attraction:** Trees of Mystery, Highway 1, Klamath, 800/638-3389
• **Surf shop:** Rhyn Noll Surfboards, 1220 Second Street, Crescent City, 707/465-4400
• **Vacation rentals:** Redwood Coast Vacation Rentals, Crescent City, 707/465-0150

Bunking Down

Some new arrivals have perked up the area, lodging-wise. The **Bayview Inn** (310 U.S. 101 South, 707/465-2050, $) is a trim and tidy three-story Cape Codder. Rooms at the height of summer go for $59–69, and the view of the bay is the best in Crescent City. The **Holiday Inn Express** (100 Walton Street, 707/464-3885, $) is another upgraded addition to the lodging scene, offering clean rooms and a free morning breakfast bar for around $75 a night in season. The **Best Western Northwoods Inn** (655 U.S. 101 South, 707/464-9771, $) has comfortable, modernized rooms and is across from Crescent City Harbor.

Out on U.S. 101 west of town, the **Pacific Motor Hotel** (440 U.S. 101 North, 707/464-4141, $) looks out on the county fairgrounds. It has clean, functional rooms, a separate spa/sauna building, and a liquor store in the lobby. The **Crescent Beach Motel** (1455 U.S. 101 South, 707/464-5436, $$) brags of being the only motel on the beach, and its location two miles south of town is another asset. Wooden decks look out over the shoreline and headlands that rise to the south. Then there's a real

architectural curiosity, the **Curly Redwood Lodge** (701 U.S. 101 South, 707/464-2137, $), which was constructed in its entirety from a single redwood tree that measured 18 feet in diameter and produced 57,000 board-feet of timber.

Finally, along the harbor sits **Shoreline Campground Accessway** (900 Sunset Circle, 707/464-2473, $), with 192 tent and RV campsites and a path that runs along the levee.

Coastal Cuisine

Crescent City still has a ways to go in terms of restaurants, but they are coming around, slowly but surely. The **Good Harvest Cafe** (700 Northcrest Drive, 707/465-6028, $) is a health-food emporium serving tasty sandwiches and brunch items in a real café/coffeehouse environment, with rattan chairs and newspapers strewn around for customers to linger over while they sip their French roast. On the sandwich front menu highlights include "Crescent City's Best Sandwich," a Dagwood-sized creation consisting of sautéed mushrooms, onions, garlic, melted Jack cheese, tomato, sprouts, olives, and sour cream served on a toasted whole-wheat English muffin. The Good Harvest Cafe has added some variety to the dining scene up here in redwood country.

The old reliable in town is the **Harbor View Grotto** (Citizens Dock Road and Starfish Way, 707/464-3815, $$), a rickety-looking green structure by the harbor. There's nothing fancy about this place, but the full house and lines out the door attest to its consistency and popularity. Seafood items are served either fried or poached. Calamari steak, with or without egg batter, is a good choice. But if you want a little bit of everything, ante up for the Grotto Fisherman's Platter, a heapin' helpin' of fish, oysters, scallops, and shrimp. The upstairs dining rooms have a bird's-eye view of the harbor; come at sunset for the best looks.

Acting on a hot tip from the gals at the Crescent City Information Center, we ate lunch at the **Chart Room** (130 Anchor Way, 707/464-

Del Norte County

5993, $). You'd likely overlook it if you didn't know to come here. The locals are certainly in the know, as the place was packed. The seafood preparations are simple, affordable, and delicious. We had the fried seafood combo—fish, shrimp, and scallops the size of hockey pucks— which was as fresh as it could be and nicely complemented by hand-cut French fries and homemade coleslaw. This is the kind of restaurant where working folks go, an informal community center where the conversation and the laughter slide down as easily as the home-cooked food. A sign by the clock over the register said it all: "This clock will never be stolen,

as the employees are watching it." Flags of many nations hang from the ceiling, with the Stars and Stripes by far the largest, naturally.

Night Moves

Crescent City now has its own microbrewery, **Jefferson State Brewery** (400 Front Street, 707/464-1139), a sign of progress in these parts.

For More Information

Crescent City/Del Norte County Chamber of Commerce, 1001 Front Street, Crescent City, CA 95531, 707/464-3174, website: www.del norte.org

Jedediah Smith Redwoods State Park

This park's namesake was a mountain man who led the first party of white explorers overland into California. Among other things, his travel journals of 1826–28 include the first description of coast redwoods. Nowadays he's remembered with a 10,000-acre park set in old-growth redwood forest along the Smith River. The park offers 30 miles of hiking trails, fishing and canoeing in the river, and a 108-site campground. **Jedediah Smith Redwoods State Park** is seven miles

east of Crescent City via Highway 199. It's not directly on the coast, but we felt it worth mentioning because of its sizable redwood forest and recreational opportunities.

For More Information

Jedidiah Smith Redwoods State Park, c/o Redwoods Coast District, California State Parks, 1375 Elk Valley Road, Crescent City, CA 95531, 707/464-6101, ext. 5100, website: www.parks.ca.gov

Tolowa Dunes State Park

In the extreme northwest corner of Del Norte County, two bodies of water—Lake Earl and Lake Tolowa—form the centerpiece of **Tolowa Dunes State Park** (formerly Lake Earl Wildlife Area). This 5,000-acre refuge includes a variety of terrain: wetlands, wooded ridges, meadows, dune fields, and river and sand beaches. Bird- and whale-watching are excellent. Twenty miles of trails fall within park boundaries, as do a horse camp and six-site walk-in campground (neither on the beach). Tolowa Dunes also has 7.5 miles of ocean frontage, including a broad, dune-covered strand that runs into Kellogg Beach.

To get to Lake Earl and Lake Tolowa, head north along Northcrest Drive from its junction with U.S. 101 in Crescent City. Northcrest turns into Lake Earl Drive, and the lakes lie five miles north of town. Beach access can be gained from either Sand Hill Road or Pala Road

For More Information

Tolowa Dunes State Park, c/o Redwoods Coast District, California State Parks, 1375 Elk Valley Road, Crescent City, CA 95531, 707/464-6101, ext. 5112, website: www.parks.ca.gov

Map of Northern California—Page 463

Del Norte County

Smith River

California runs out a few miles past the town of Smith River. There's not much here to eyeball: agricultural fields, sprinkler systems to tend them, last-chance-before-Oregon liquor stores. All that and RV parks, too. The town of Smith River lies off the highway at a point where U.S. 101 swings away from the coast. Smith River is the Easter-lily capital of the world. They grow more of them here than anywhere else—90 percent of the nation's commercial lily bulbs, they'll have you know.

It's a small town. When we asked a local what the population was, she replied, "Six hundred. That's including dogs and cats—and two emus." The town is built around the Smith River, one of the prime salmon- and steelhead-fishing rivers in the state. In 1990 the Smith River National Recreation Area, encompassing 300,000 acres, was established to protect the watershed of this Wild and Scenic River. Ample opportunities for recreation exist up-river and along the coast.

Yes, Smith River is the end of the line; four more miles and you slip out of California with little fanfare. After having traveled 1,500 miles of coastline inch-by-inch, we always expect some sort of grand reception—a marching band, a 21-gun salute, a token hunk of salmon jerky—when we finally reach the Holy Grail of the state line. But there's not even a sign saying "Goodbye to California" or "Welcome to Oregon." So it goes.

And so as the sun slowly sets in the West on another perfect California day, our pilgrimage up the coast finally comes to an end. We bid you good day, safe passage, and happy beaching.

Beaches

The beaches at California's northern end are interesting to ponder—that is, when you can get to them. **Clifford Kamph Memorial Park** sits beside the highway halfway between Smith River and the state line. The park borders someone's home; try to take a picture of the shoreline north to the Oregon border, as we did, and you might just interrupt a backyard cookout. The beach is wide, windswept, and wild. Tenters encamp in gullies behind dunes and anywhere they can find protection from the wind. An occupied RV near the parking lot serves as the campground host. Anglers cast for ling cod, rockfish, sand dabs, and cabezon.

California's bounty of beaches ends not with a bang but a whimper at **Pelican State Beach,** an undeveloped spot that's more notable for the symbolism of finality it embodies than for its particular qualities as a beach. Still, this is the last stretch of sand in California, sitting a mere half mile below the Oregon border and 21 miles north of Crescent City. Stop to take a snapshot, enjoy a sunset, or bow to Ra, but do something. This is it—California ends here!

Smith River (the actual river, not the town) is one of seven unhindered river deltas in California, thus earning Wild and Scenic River System distinction. A small, rocky beach sits along the northern tip of the river mouth, part of **Smith River County Park.** The fishing is reportedly excellent here, and elsewhere along this river, though swimming is not advised.

Bunking Down

If you're looking to park your RV, car, or carcass for the night, the spot to lay over in Smith River is the **Best Western Ship Ashore** (12370 U.S. 101, 707/487-3141, $). This riverside, ocean-view compound includes a 50-unit motel with hot tubs and an on-premises steak and seafood restaurant. There's also a sizable RV park and a museum and gift shop housed in a red, white, and blue ship that sits in the parking lot. Then there's the unpretentious **Pelican Beach Motel** (16855 U.S. 101 North, 707/487-7651, $), which sits at the intersection of U.S. 101 and the road that leads to Pelican State Beach.

Del Norte County

Coastal Cuisine

No slur on Smith River, but let's face it, "fine dining" is not what one expects up here. All of which makes the **Nautical Inn** (16850 U.S. 101, 707/487-5006, $$$) such a pleasant surprise. For years a local landmark known as the Knottical Inn (the former owners were Knotts), the current owners have corrected the spelling and spruced up the menu to include a fair selection of well-prepared seafood entrées and appetizers. Entrées include halibut Mediterranean, stuffed and baked with roasted garlic and sun-dried tomatoes; salmon with mandarin orange butter; scallops Provençal; sole in parchment spiced with lemon and rosemary; snapper Mazatlan; Cancun shrimp; and calamari with lemon aioli.

Night Moves

Hoist a tall, cool one at the **Captain's Lounge in the Best Western Ship Ashore Motel** (12370 U.S. 101, 707/487-3141). Here's to California! Cheers!

For More Information

Crescent City/Del Norte County Chamber of Commerce, 1001 Front Street, Crescent City, CA 95531, 707/464-3174, website: www.del norte.org

Del Norte County

Map of Northern California—Page 463

Resource Guide

Toll-Free Phone Numbers

Car Rental Agencies

Alamo Rent-a-Car 800/327-9633
Avis Rent-a-Car 800/831-2847
Budget Car Rental 800/527-0700
Dollar Rent-a-Car 800/800-4000
Enterprise
   Rent-a-Car 800/325-8007
Hertz Rent-a-Car 800/654-3131
National Car Rental 800/227-7368
Sears Car Rental 800/527-0770
Thrifty Car Rental 800/367-2277

Lodgings

Best Western 800/528-1234
Clarion Hotels 800/252-7466
Comfort Inn 800/228-5150
Courtyard
   by Marriott 800/321-2211
Days Inn 800/325-2525
Doubletree Inn 800/222-8733
Econo Lodge 800/553-2666
Embassy Suites 800/362-2779
Fairfield Inn
   by Marriott 800/228-2800
Four Seasons 800/332-3442
Friendship Inn 800/453-4511
Hampton Inns 800/426-7866

Hilton Hotels 800/445-8667
Holiday Inn 800/465-4329
Howard Johnson 800/446-4656
Hyatt Hotels 800/228-9000
Inns by the Sea 800/433-4732
La Quinta Inns 800/687-6667
Marriott Hotels 800/228-9290
Motel 6 . . . . 800/466-8356
Omni 800/843-6664
Quality Inn 800/228-5151
Radisson Hotels 800/333-3333
Ramada Inn 800/272-6232
Red Lion Inns 800/733-5166
Red Roof Inn 800/843-7663
Renaissance Hotels 800/468-3571
Residence Inn
   by Marriott 800/331-3131
Ritz-Carlton 800/241-3333
Rodeway Inn 800/228-2000
Sheraton Hotels 800/325-3535
Sleep Inn 800/753-3746
Super 8 Motels 800/800-8000
Travelodge 800/578-7878
Vagabond Inns 800/522-1555
Westin Hotels 800/228-3000
Wyndham Hotels 800/996-3426

General Information

For visitors information on California, contact the California Division of Tourism, 801 K Street, Suite 1600, Sacramento, CA 95814, 916/322-2881 or 800/862-2543. Ask for the latest edition of the *Official State Visitor's Guide*. The Division of Tourism is also online at www.gocalif.ca.gov.

For general information on California State Parks, contact the California Department of Parks and Recreation, P.O. Box 942896, Sacramento, CA 94926, 916/653-6995 or 800/777-0369. The Department of Parks and Recreation is also online at www.calparks.ca.gov.

For camping reservations in California State Parks, call ReserveAmerica at 800/444-7275 8 A.M.–5 P.M. Pacific time, seven days a week, or visit website www.reserveamerica.com. Camping reservations can be made anywhere from two days to six months prior to the desired date. A nonrefundable $7.50 reservation fee is added to the cost of the campsite. To cancel a confirmed reservation, call 800/695-2269.

For information on California fishing regulations, call 916/227-2244 or check the Department of Fish and Game's website at www.dfg.ca.gov.

Bare Facts: Clothing-Optional Beaches

Here is a listing of some of the better-known nude beaches in California:

- Black's Beach, San Diego, page 67
- Palos Verdes Peninsula (coves near Portuguese Bend), Los Angeles, page 184
- Nicholas Canyon County Beach, Malibu, page 228
- Pirate's Cove, Avila Beach, page 317
- Andrew Molera State Beach, Big Sur, page 358
- Garrapata State Park, Big Sur, page 360
- Four Mile Beach, Santa Cruz, page 429
- Red, White, and Blue Beach, Santa Cruz, page 430
- Bonny Doon Beach, Santa Cruz, page 430
- Pomponio State Beach, San Mateo County, page 443
- San Gregorio Private Beach, San Mateo County, page 444
- North Baker Beach, San Francisco, page 471
- Kirby Cove, Marin County, page 484
- Muir Beach, Marin County, page 485
- Red Rock Beach, Marin County, page 486
- Bolinas Beach, Bolinas, page 489
- Limantour Beach, Point Reyes Peninsula, page 492
- Gualala River, Gualala, page 535
- College Cove, Trinidad, page 589

Angling and Diving in California

Every ocean beach offers an opportunity for some type of fishing, be it casting from the surf, jetty, or pier. Anglers eager to obtain a copy of the latest California sportfishing regulations can drop by any bait-and-tackle shop or write to the California Department of Fish and Game, 1416 Ninth Street, P.O. Box 944209, Sacramento, CA 94244. Pay particular attention to chapter four of the regulations ("Ocean Fishing"), which lists marine ecological reserves, marine life refuges, and ocean waters with restricted fishing; prohibitions and restrictions are imposed on taking fish, mollusks, crustaceans, and other forms of marine life at these locales.

Anyone interested in information about diving on the California coast should pick up *California Diving News* at dive shops or order a subscription by writing to P.O. Box 11231, Torrance, CA 90510. It includes comprehensive listings of dive trips, events, and shops throughout California. To obtain an informative brochure about diving in California State Parks (whose holdings account for a quarter of the state's coastline), request a copy of *Dive In!* from California State Parks, Office of Marketing and Public Affairs, P.O. Box 942896, Sacramento, CA 94296.

Spout Spots: Whale-Watching on the Coast

Whales migrate south from late November to January, clinging to the coastline during their annual migration to warmer waters. Their migratory route carries them from plankton-rich polar feeding waters to their tropical or subtropical birthing grounds, where there is no food source. They survive the summer's deprivation by subsisting on energy supplies stored in the form of blubber. For their return trip north in the spring they retrace their route, but farther out to sea. Their transoceanic travels carry them 10,000 miles, the longest migration of any mammal. On a typical dive a whale will plunge 150 feet deep and 1,000 feet forward. The most visible kinds (from the California coast) are filter-feeding baleen-type whales, such as blue, humpback, and gray whales.

Here are some prime spots for whale-watching along the California coast:

- Point Loma, San Diego, page 40
- Torrey Pines State Beach, La Jolla, page 67
- San Clemente State Beach, San Clemente, page 111
- Point Fermin Park, San Pedro, page 181
- San Simeon State Beach, San Simeon, page 337
- Julia Pfeiffer Burns State Park, Big Sur, page 357
- Pillar Point, Princeton-by-the-Sea, page 450
- Montara State Beach, Pacifica, page 453
- Point Reyes, Marin County, page 490
- Bodega Head, Bodega Bay, page 512
- Mendocino Headlands State Park, Mendocino, page 545
- MacKerricher State Park, Fort Bragg, page 553
- Enderts Beach, Crescent City, page 605
- Brother Jonathan Point, Crescent City, page 608

Best California Beach Music

Top 5 Songs about California Beaches

1. "Surfin' USA," by the Beach Boys
2. "Surf City," by Jan and Dean
3. "Summer Means Fun," by the Fantastic Baggys
4. "I Live for the Sun," by the Sunrays
5. "Do It Again," by the Beach Boys

Top 5 Songs with "California" in the title

1. "California Dreamin'," by the Mamas and the Papas
2. "California Girls," by the Beach Boys
3. "Hotel California," by the Eagles
4. "California," by Joni Mitchell
5. "California Sun," by the Rivieras

Top 5 Surfing Instrumentals
1. "Wipeout," by the Surfaris
2. "Miserlou," by Dick Dale
3. "Pipeline," by the Chantays
4. "Penetration," by the Pyramids
5. "The Lonely Surfer," by Jack Nitzsche

Top 5 James Brown Songs (why not?)
1. "It's a New Day So Let a Man Come In and Do the Popcorn"
2. "Get Up I Feel Like Being a Sex Machine"
3. "Hot Pants (She Got to Use What She Got to Get What She Wants)"
4. "I Can't Stand Myself (When You Touch Me)"
5. "Give It Up or Turnit A Loose"

California Beach Climate

Here are the average high and low temperatures for several spots along the coast. The information has been sourced from National Weather Service data, National Oceanographic and Atmospheric Administration.

Location	Month	Daily High (°F)	Daily Low (°F)	Rainfall (inches)
Carmel	January	60	44	3.6
	February	62	45	3.0
	March	62	46	3.4
	April	64	46	1.6
	May	64	48	0.4
	June	67	50	0.2
	July	68	52	0.1
	August	70	53	0.1
	September	72	53	0.3
	October	70	51	0.9
	November	65	47	2.7
	December	60	43	3.0
	Yearly Average	**65**	**48**	**19.3**
Eureka	January	55	42	5.9
	February	56	43	4.7
	March	56	44	5.1
	April	57	45	2.8
	May	59	48	1.4
	June	61	51	0.6
	July	62	52	0.2
	August	63	53	0.4
	September	63	52	0.8
	October	61	49	2.3

Location	Month	Daily High (°F)	Daily Low (°F)	Rainfall (inches)
	November	58	45	5.9
	December	55	42	6.2
	Yearly Average	**59**	**47**	**36.3**
Fort Bragg	January	55	40	6.6
	February	57	41	5.9
	March	58	42	5.7
	April	60	43	2.7
	May	62	45	1.3
	June	64	48	0.3
	July	66	49	0.1
	August	66	50	0.4
	September	66	49	0.8
	October	64	47	2.5
	November	59	43	5.7
	December	55	40	6.7
	Yearly Average	**61**	**45**	**38.7**
Fort Ross	January	57	41	7.4
	February	58	42	5.6
	March	59	42	5.3
	April	61	42	2.3
	May	63	44	0.7
	June	65	46	0.4
	July	66	47	0.2
	August	67	48	0.3
	September	68	48	0.7
	October	66	46	2.3
	November	61	43	5.7
	December	57	40	6.2
	Yearly Average	**62**	**44**	**37.1**
Laguna Beach	January	66	42	2.5
	February	67	43	2.5
	March	67	45	2.5
	April	70	47	0.9
	May	70	52	0.2
	June	73	55	0.1
	July	76	59	0.1
	August	78	59	0.1
	September	78	58	0.3
	October	76	53	0.4
	November	71	46	1.6

Location	Month	Daily High (°F)	Daily Low (°F)	Rainfall (inches)
	December	66	41	1.9
	Yearly Average	**71**	**50**	**13.1**
Long Beach	January	70	45	2.7
	February	68	47	2.7
	March	68	50	2.2
	April	72	52	0.7
	May	74	57	0.2
	June	78	60	0
	July	83	64	0
	August	84	65	0.1
	September	83	63	0.3
	October	79	58	0.3
	November	73	50	1.5
	December	67	45	1.9
	Yearly Average	**75**	**55**	**12.6**
Newport Beach	January	69	47	2.4
	February	64	49	2.3
	March	63	51	2.2
	April	65	53	0.9
	May	66	57	0.2
	June	69	60	0.1
	July	72	63	0
	August	73	64	0.1
	September	73	63	0.3
	October	72	58	0.2
	November	68	52	1.4
	December	64	47	1.7
	Yearly Average	**68**	**55**	**11.8**
Oceanside	January	65	44	2.3
	February	65	45	2.1
	March	65	48	2.1
	April	66	50	0.9
	May	68	55	0.2
	June	70	58	0.1
	July	73	62	0
	August	75	63	0.1
	September	75	61	0.3
	October	73	56	0.4
	November	69	49	1.2

Resource Guide

Location	Month	Daily High (°F)	Daily Low (°F)	Rainfall (inches)
	December	65	44	1.7
	Yearly Average	**69**	**53**	**11.4**
Oxnard	January	66	45	3.2
	February	67	50	3.2
	March	67	47	2.8
	April	69	49	0.9
	May	69	53	0.1
	June	72	56	0
	July	74	58	0
	August	76	60	0.1
	September	75	58	0.4
	October	74	54	0.3
	November	71	49	1.9
	December	66	45	2.1
	Yearly Average	**71**	**52**	**15.0**
Pismo Beach	January	64	42	3.6
	February	65	44	3.2
	March	66	44	3.2
	April	69	45	1.2
	May	69	47	0.2
	June	71	50	0
	July	71	53	0
	August	72	53	0
	September	73	53	0.4
	October	73	50	0.7
	November	69	46	2.0
	December	64	42	2.8
	Yearly Average	**69**	**47**	**17.3**
Point Reyes National Seashore	January	57	38	5.3
	February	59	40	4.5
	March	59	41	3.5
	April	60	43	2.1
	May	61	45	0.6
	June	63	50	0.2
	July	64	51	0.1
	August	65	51	0.2
	September	67	51	0.4
	October	66	47	1.6
	November	63	41	3.0
	December	58	38	4.9
	Yearly Average	**62**	**45**	**26.4**

Location	Month	Daily High (°F)	Daily Low (°F)	Rainfall (inches)
Redwood	January	.55	.41	.10.1
National Park	February	.56	.42	.8.2
	March	.57	.43	.8.7
	April	.58	.43	.5.0
	May	.61	.46	.2.8
	June	.64	.50	.1.4
	July	.66	.51	.0.4
	August	.66	.52	.0.9
	September	.67	.50	.1.7
	October	.64	.47	.4.4
	November	.58	.44	.9.7
	December	.56	.40	.10.9
	Yearly Average	**.61**	**.46**	**.64.2**
San Diego	January	.65	.46	.2.0
	February	.66	.48	.1.8
	March	.66	.50	.2.2
	April	.68	.54	.0.8
	May	.69	.57	.0.2
	June	.71	.60	.0.1
	July	.75	.64	.0
	August	.77	.65	.0.1
	September	.77	.65	.0.2
	October	.77	.63	.0.4
	November	.74	.58	.1.4
	December	.66	.47	.1.7
	Yearly Average	**.71**	**.56**	**.10.9**
San Francisco	January	.57	.46	.4.2
	February	.61	.49	.3.3
	March	.62	.49	.3.2
	April	.63	.50	.1.3
	May	.64	.51	.0.3
	June	.66	.53	.0.2
	July	.67	.54	.0.0
	August	.68	.55	.0.1
	September	.70	.56	.0.3
	October	.70	.55	.1.1
	November	.64	.51	.3.2
	December	.57	.47	.3.2
	Yearly Average	**.64**	**.51**	**.20.4**
San Mateo	January	.59	.43	.5.1
	February	.60	.44	.4.1

Location	Month	Daily High (°F)	Daily Low (°F)	Rainfall (inches)
	March	60	44	4.2
	April	61	44	1.9
	May	61	47	0.5
	June	63	50	0.3
	July	64	51	0.1
	August	66	53	0.2
	September	67	51	0.4
	October	66	49	1.7
	November	63	46	3.7
	December	59	43	4.3
	Yearly Average	**62**	**47**	**26.5**
Santa Barbara	January	65	44	3.6
	February	65	45	3.9
	March	66	48	3.0
	April	69	50	1.0
	May	69	52	0.2
	June	72	55	0.1
	July	75	58	0
	August	77	59	0
	September	75	58	0.3
	October	74	54	0.3
	November	69	49	1.9
	December	65	44	2.6
	Yearly Average	**70**	**51**	**16.9**
Santa Cruz	January	61	39	5.7
	February	63	41	5.3
	March	65	43	4.7
	April	68	44	2.0
	May	71	47	0.4
	June	74	50	0.2
	July	75	52	0.2
	August	76	52	0.1
	September	76	51	0.4
	October	73	48	1.3
	November	66	43	4.2
	December	60	39	4.5
	Yearly Average	**69**	**46**	**29.0**

Location	Month	Daily High (°F)	Daily Low (°F)	Rainfall (inches)
Santa Monica	January	65	50	2.7
	February	64	51	2.9
	March	63	52	2.2
	April	64	54	0.6
	May	64	56	0.1
	June	67	59	0
	July	69	62	0
	August	71	63	0.1
	September	71	62	0.2
	October	71	59	0.3
	November	68	55	1.7
	December	65	50	2.0
	Yearly Average	**67**	**56**	**12.8**

Acknowledgments

How could we not have fun writing a book about California beaches? The coastline is unsurpassably beautiful, the natives are friendly, and the good times just roll on and on. We had a particularly enjoyable time working on this third edition of *Foghorn Outdoors California Beaches*. While the rest of the country was broiling, the coast of California was cool and comfortable: daytime highs in the low 60s, a clear azure sky, clean air, staggering scenery, breezes blowing. Often it reduced us to a reverential silence. In the more populous Southern California counties, on the other hand, we found ourselves whooping and hollering with the crowd.

Along the way we crossed paths with an endless number of people who shared information and helped us in various ways. A handful of them deserve singling out by name: Tim Scanlin, for insight into San Francisco; Allison Brown, for suggestions in La Jolla; and Tommy Chaltas, for the lowdown on Los Angeles. Many others provided us hospitality and friendship, most notably Jeff Stanford in Mendocino, Mark Carter in Eureka, and John Thompson in Klamath.

We're fortunate to have a publisher, Avalon Travel Publishing, who swings at any curve ball we throw them. It is rare to find a publisher that cares about every book it publishes—and not just the books but the authors as well. We'd especially like to thank our editor, Marisa Solís. Not the least of her virtues is patience. Once again, we pushed the deadline to the limit and beyond as we crammed as much as possible into this new edition. She bore with us through the painfully protracted process of revision and seemed genuinely appreciative of our hard work. And she had many valuable suggestions that have made it a better book. We're also lucky to have a wonderful friend, Anne Zeman, as our literary agent.

Hugs and kisses to our wives, Carol Hill Puterbaugh and Tracey O'Shaughnessy Bisbort, who have supported our endeavors and tolerated our wanderlust. As much as we love beachcombing, we're always glad to get home when we reach the end of the Pacific Coast Highway.

We'd like to dedicate this edition of our book to our children, Hayley Anne Puterbaugh and Paul James Bisbort, and all the other little daughters and sons of the beaches for whom a healthy coastline should be an inalienable birthright.

Beyond that, we'll keep it short and sweet by saying thanks, California. You're the greatest.

Index

Beach Hiking

Environmental Issues

Index

Museums

Nude Beaches

Surfing

Whale Watching

About the Authors

Parke Puterbaugh writes about beaches, travel, music, popular culture, and the environment. He is the author, coauthor, or editor of 10 books, including a guide to wetlands for the Environmental Protection Agency. A former senior editor and longtime contributor to *Rolling Stone,* his writings have also appeared in *USA Today, Outside, Men's Journal, Sound + Vision, Attaché, Us,* and many other magazines and newspapers. He is a curatorial consultant and exhibit copywriter for the Rock and Roll Hall of Fame and Museum in Cleveland. Puterbaugh holds bachelor's degrees in English and Sociology and a master's degree in Environmental Science from the University of North Carolina at Chapel Hill. He lives in Greensboro, North Carolina, with his wife Carol and daughter Hayley.

About the Authors

© ALAN BISBORT

Alan Bisbort is a writer, editor, and researcher. He has worked for the Library of Congress for the past quarter century and is coauthor of *The Nation's Library: The Library of Congress, Washington D.C.,* the authorized guidebook for visitors. His most recent published books include *Sunday Afternoon, Looking for the Car: The Aberrant Art of Barry Kite; The Works! The Art of Charles Bragg;* and *Famous Last Words.* His writings have appeared in the *Washington Post, New York Times, Hartford Advocate, American Way, American Politics Journal, Gadfly,* and *Connecticut* magazine. Bisbort holds a bachelor's degree in English from the University of North Carolina at Chapel Hill. He lives in Cheshire, Connecticut, with his wife Tracey and son P. J.

Former college roommates, Puterbaugh and Bisbort have collaborated on numerous books, including *Rhino's Psychedelic Trip,* a guide to the music and culture of the 1960s. They have researched and written three editions of *Foghorn Outdoors California Beaches* and two editions of *Foghorn Outdoors Florida Beaches,* all published by Avalon Travel Publishing. In these and other books, their verbiage on the subject of beaches approaches a million words. They have visited more beaches more often in the continental United States than anyone else. Puterbaugh and Bisbort truly are America's beach bums.

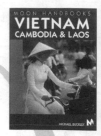

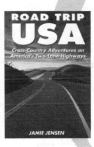